D1859501

THE THREE PRESIDENCIES OF INDIA

THE THREE PRESIDENCIES OF INDIA:

A HISTORY OF THE RISE AND PROGRESS OF THE BRITISH INDIAN POSSESSIONS,

From the Earliest Records to the Present Time

WITH AN ACCOUNT OF THEIR GOVERNMENT, RELIGION, MANNERS, CUSTOMS, EDUCATION, ETC. ETC.

BY

JOHN CAPPER, F.R.A.S.

LATE EDITOR OF THE CEYLON EXAMINER

Illustrated by Numerous Engravings, and Map by Wyld

GYAN

Published by

Gyan Publishing House
5, Ansari Road
Daryaganj, New Delhi-110002
Phone: 011-47034999, 9811692060
E-mail: books@gyanbooks.com

Distribution Network
gyanbooks.com
India, USA, Canada, UK, Australia, France

© Publisher

All rights reserved. No part of this work may be reproduced, stored, adapted, or transmitted in any form or by any means, electronic, mechanical, photocopying, micro-filming, recording or otherwise, or translated in any language, without the prior written permission of the copyright owner and the publisher.

ISBN : 978-81-212-4103-8 (PB)
First Published, 1853

2nd Impression 2020

Printed at: Gyan Press, Delhi.

The book is sold subject to the condition that it shall not, by way of trade or otherwise, be lent, resold, hired out, or otherwise circulated without the prior publisher's written consent.

The book at your disposal is the edition of an old book originally published long back. The Text quality of this book may not be at par as compared to our other books but many readers approached us to reprint this important book so that it could satiate their hunger. We request all the readers of this book to help us to improve its quality by providing the necessary text of those pages which are not properly visible. Your valuable support in this case will be highly appreciated and acknowledged and our future readers will be benefitted immensely.

THE

THREE PRESIDENCIES

OF

INDIA:

A HISTORY OF THE RISE AND PROGRESS OF THE BRITISH INDIAN POSSESSIONS,

From the Earliest Records to the Present Time.

WITH AN ACCOUNT OF THEIR GOVERNMENT, RELIGION, MANNERS, CUSTOMS, EDUCATION, ETC. ETC.

BY JOHN CAPPER, F.R.A.S.

LATE EDITOR OF THE CEYLON EXAMINER.

Illustrated by numerous Engravings, and a Map by Wyld.

LONDON:

INGRAM, COOKE, AND CO.

1853.

THE MARQUIS OF DALHOUSIE, K.T.

GOVERNOR-GENERAL OF INDIA.

PREFACE.

THE deep interest imparted to Indian affairs during the recent deliberations of the Senate, in the columns of the political journals, in reviews and pamphlets, and, indeed, wherever a vent for public feeling could be found, induces the Author to believe that no apology is needed for the publication of this volume.

Much has been already written on the subject of Indian affairs. No ordinary amount of ability has been brought to bear on most of the topics embraced in what is popularly termed "the Indian question." It was nevertheless felt that a work was still wanted which should place the public in possession not merely of such facts as bear upon the political phase of the subject, but also of a faithful picture, social and industrial, of the many races composing the people of British India.

A residence of many years in the East, a long connection with the Indian Press, and an acquaintance with civilians, merchants, and planters of the three Presidencies, have emboldened the Author to call Indian things by their right names. The vastness of the interests involved forbad their being handled less firmly.

The recent legislation upon the government of India is but the prelude to great and momentous changes, which cannot long be stayed; which must come—peaceably and lawfully, if we will—but they *must come*, as surely as the broad daylight of intelligence is penetrating the hearts and souls of a hundred millions of our fellow-creatures.

It is not by such means as the solemn farce enacting in the Committee-rooms of the House of Commons that this work will be aided. The dullest mind of the poorest Indian ryot must see through the transparency of that judicial mockery which pretends to give fair play to the plaintiff, by examining no other witnesses than the clients of the defendant. It is in India, and

India only, that the work must be done. It is there alone that a Committee of Inquiry can hope to hear the truth and the whole truth, regarding those matters which so deeply concern the future of British India,—matters which can be little more than glanced at in this volume. Petitions, newspapers, and pamphlets have gone far to prepare the ground, and much good seed has been sown; but the harvest-time has not yet arrived.

Happily for the cause, the day has gone past when an Indian speech was the dinner-bell of the House of Commons,—an Indian article the nightcap of newspaper readers. Englishmen have shaken off the antiquated belief that they are not interested in the welfare of the three Presidencies. The philosopher, the political-economist, the manufacturer, the merchant, the ship-owner, and, above all, the Christian, finds an ample field for sympathy and energy in that wonderful land, highly gifted by nature, yet prostrate in superstition and misery.

A country, the greater portion of which has been in our possession for three-quarters of a century; whose commerce has remained stationary during the last eight or nine years; whose inhabitants pay in taxes half as much as is collected in Great Britain and Ireland, and yet annually consume no more than one shilling's worth of British goods per head, or one-fourteenth part of the value taken by the inhabitants of Chili and La Plata; whose entire roads receive no greater outlay than is spent upon the streets and highways of one of our large towns; upon whose education the annual sum of three farthings per family is disbursed; where railroads, under the fostering care of the Court of Directors, have progressed at the rate of fifteen miles in fifteen years; within whose colleges, maintained by a Christian Government, the Holy Scriptures are a contraband thing,—the name of the Saviour a forbidden sound, heard but in stealthy whispers;—such a country as this cannot be an indifferent object to Englishmen in the nineteenth century. Nor is it. India has but to raise her voice, and she will be heard by a people to whom a cry for justice was never yet raised in vain.

Earls Court, Brompton,
August 1853.

CONTENTS.

PAGE
INTRODUCTORY SKETCH OF THE NATURAL HISTORY OF BRITISH INDIA . 1

PART I.—HISTORICAL.

Hindoo Period.

CHAPTER I.

The era of fable and the early Hindoo dynasties 37

CHAPTER II.

The Arab and Tartar invasions, and the final settlement of the Mahomedans in India 47

Mahomedan Period.

CHAPTER I.

Sultan Mahmoud and his successors of the Ghaznivide and Ghorian dynasties 54

CHAPTER II.

From the establishment of the kingdom of Delhi to its conquest by the Tartars 61

CHAPTER III.

From the reign of Baber to the deposing of Shah Jehan 67

CHAPTER IV.

PAGE

From the proclamation of Aurungzebe to the fall of the Tartar dynasty . . . 80

European Period.

CHAPTER I.

Early communication between the Eastern and Western World, with subsequent European progress, to the establishment of British supremacy in India 96

CHAPTER II.

From the permanent settlement of the British in India to the death of Hyder Ali 120

CHAPTER III.

From the accession of Tippoo Sahib as Sultan of Mysore, to his overthrow and death at the siege of Seringapatam 139

CHAPTER IV.

From the dismemberment of the Mysorean kingdom to the termination of the first Mahratta campaign 152

CHAPTER V.

From the renewal of hostilities to the termination of the second Mahratta war 165

CHAPTER VI.

The first Burmese war, and the cession of Assam and the Tenasserim provinces to the British government 189

CHAPTER VII.

From the administration of Lord William Bentinck to the annexation of Scinde and the pacification of Gwalior 207

CHAPTER VIII.

PAGE

The wars in the Punjab, and the annexation of the country of the Five Rivers to the British dominions 224

CHAPTER IX.

The second Burmese war, and the annexation of Pegu 238

PART II.—POLITICAL.

CHAPTER I.

The local governments of India from the Hindoo period to the present time, with a sketch of the covenanted and uncovenanted services . 251

CHAPTER II.

The fiscal systems of India, ancient and modern, and their effects on the industry of the people 272

PART III.—PHYSICAL.

CHAPTER I.

Hindoo art and science 291

CHAPTER II.

The manufactures of India 305

CHAPTER III.

Agriculture of the Hindoos, and the application of European skill and capital to the cultivation of Indian products 317

CHAPTER IV.

PAGE

The cotton industry of India,—its history, extent, and prospects . 337

CHAPTER V.

Roads, rivers, and railways 351

CHAPTER VI.

The commercial history of the three presidencies, with a sketch of the morality of Anglo-Indian commerce and banking in the nineteenth century 367

PART IV.—MORAL.

CHAPTER I.

Language and literature 395

CHAPTER II.

Religion and caste 400

CHAPTER III.

Manners and customs 412

CHAPTER IV.

Education and Christianity 430

CHAPTER V.

The administration of justice 448

CHAPTER VI.

The public of India, its constitution and its morality 465

LIST OF ILLUSTRATIONS.

PAGE

Marquis of Dalhousie, K.T., Governor-General of India . . . *Frontispiece.*
Vignette . . . *Title-page.*
Cashmere Goat . . . 30
Cobra Capella . . . 30
Himalayan Bustard . . . 31
Laughing Crow . . . 32
The Locust . . . 33
Bamboo Insect . . . 33
Leaf Insect . . . 33
The Rajah on his State Elephant . . . 48
Native Infantry . . . 160
Burmese General . . . 197
Troops going up the Country . . . 211
Storming of Ghuznee . . . 212
Camel-Battery . . . 226
Battle of Ferozepore . . . 228
Ancient Column . . . 292
Remains of Hindoo Architecture . . . 293
Cave Temple . . . 295
Arian Pillar . . . 297
Working Silversmith . . . 314
Native Goldsmith . . . 315
Diamond-Cutter . . . 316
Ryots irrigating Rice-Fields . . . 318
Cotton Plant . . . 338
Cotton Fibre . . . 339
Loaded Cotton-Hackery . . . 346
The Suggar, or Village Cart . . . 352
Indian Caravanserai and Travellers . . . 353
Camel-Courier . . . 357
An Indian Road . . . 359
An Escort of Treasure to Upper Provinces . . . 366
Madras Roads . . . 377
A Banian . . . 381

	PAGE
A Bengal Sircar	384
Rama	398
Brahma	401
Vishnu	402
Kurmawatara	403
Matsyavatara	404
A Fakeer	407
A Sudra Mendicant	410
A Hindoo Meal	414
A Water-Carrier	416
A Nautch or native Entertainment	417
A Riding Elephant	418
Indian Kite	419
Hindoo Funeral Pile	419
Hindoo leaving her sick Child on the Banks of the Ganges	422
A Thug	423
A Kidmutgar	424
A Bearer	424
A Mater	425
A Bheestie	425
A Peguan	426
Hindoo Washermen	427
Paradise Flycatcher	429
Burman Poonjie and Kioung	440
Lophophorus Impeyanus	447
A Peon	459
An Ekka	469
A Zemindar	479

THE

THREE PRESIDENCIES OF INDIA.

INTRODUCTORY SKETCH OF THE NATURAL HISTORY OF BRITISH INDIA.

THE various countries which now form the three Presidencies of India, together with those native states which are independent of, though in close alliance with, the East India Company, have been at various times known under several denominations. They have been comprehensively and indiscriminately spoken of as Hindostan, the East Indies, and the Indian Peninsula; they are now more correctly termed British India, which term, of course, excludes such independent states as have been alluded to.

Extending from Cape Comorin on the south to the Himalayan range on the north, and from the delta of the Berrampootra on the east to the Indus on the west, British India, exclusive of the recently annexed province of Pegu, may be said to include within its limits 1,200,000 square miles of territory. Of these, the Presidency of Bengal contains 306,012 square miles; Madras, 141,920; Bombay, 64,908; and Scinde and the Punjab about 160,000 square miles; the remainder being the extent of the allied states.

The coast-line of British India amounts to about 3200 miles. Of these 1800 miles are washed by the Indian Ocean, and 1400 miles by the Bay of Bengal.

The extreme length of India from north to south may be taken as 1800 miles; its greatest width, along the parallel of 25° N. latitude, is about 1500 miles.

Intersected by vast ranges of lofty mountains, the Indian peninsula presents a remarkably varied surface of table-land, delta, and valley; and extending as it does from 8° 4′ N. lat. to 34° N. lat., with tracts of country sometimes 2500 feet above the sea-level, it naturally comprises many varieties of climate and a great range of temperature.

Crossing the peninsula from east to west, between the twenty-third and twenty-fifth parallels of north latitude, we find the Vindya Mountains, a dividing range of a marked character, and the base of those various districts into which Hindostan has been divided.

These divisions are four in number: the Deccan, south of the Vindya Mountains; and to the north of the range, the Delta of the Ganges, Central India, and the Delta of the Indus. Some writers add a fifth division, by styling that part of the Deccan which is south of the river Kishna, Southern India.

The distinguishing feature of the Deccan consists of the lofty ranges of mountains which skirt it on every side; they are named the northern, southern, eastern, and western Ghauts.[1] The latter skirt the shores of the Indian Ocean and the Bay of Bengal at distances varying from one hundred to ten miles; those on the eastern coast being the most remote. Their altitude varies from 8000 feet downwards. On the southern extremity of the western ghauts are the Neilgherry Mountains stretching eastward, and famed throughout Southern India for their fine climate and fertile tracts of table-land. On this range have been established the sanitary stations of Ootacamund and Dimhutty, where Europeans enjoy the bracing temperature of alpine lands within a few days' journey of Madras.

At the northern extremity of the western range immediately opposite Bombay are the Mahabalipoora Mountains, rising to a height of 5036 feet, on which the sanitorium of Mahabeleshwur has been established for the benefit of that Presidency. The Aligherry Mountains are an offshoot of the southern ghauts.

In that portion of the Deccan known as Southern India are several independent states. The King of Travancore and the Rajah of Cochin are both allies of the Honourable East India Company, and offer every facility for the prosecution of commercial enterprise in their territories.

Deccan proper comprises all that portion of the peninsula which lies between the valley of the Nerbudda on the north, and the deep pass known as the Gap of Coimbatore, running from east to west at about 11° N. lat. The greater part by far of this tract consists of

[1] Ghaut, or ghât, is applied by the natives to the many openings or passes through these ranges; being derived from the Sanscrit *gati*, a way or path, but is used by Europeans to designate the mountains themselves.

elevated table-land of considerable fertility, skirted by long ranges of mountains or ghauts, which stretch coastward until they terminate in plains. This table-land is called by the natives Bala-ghaut, or the country above the ghauts, and varies in breadth from 150 to 400 miles. Its altitude ranges from 900 to 3000 feet.

A considerable portion of the Deccan proper is still ruled by native princes in alliance with the Company. The kingdom of Mysore on the south comprises an extent of 30,000 square miles. It is ruled by a Hindoo prince, and its capital is Seringapatam.

The territory of the Rajah of Hydrabad comprehends about 110,000 square miles, with a population of 10,000,000. It is situated in the north of the Bala-ghauts, and is chiefly noted for its diamond-mines at Golconda.

The Rajah of Berar rules over 3,000,000 subjects, with an extent of territory of about 65,000 square miles, situated to the eastward of Golconda.

The state of Satara comprises about 9000 square miles, with a population of 500,000. It is ruled by a Hindoo prince, and is situated on the western ghauts. To the south of this principality are the territories of the Rajah of Colapore; a small state, 3000 square miles in extent, under the sway of a Hindoo prince.

The British territories in the Deccan do not exceed 40,000 square miles, part of which are attached to the Presidency of Bombay, and a portion to that of Madras.

A considerable part of this table-land is highly fertile, and rich in natural productions; the ghauts, however, are for the most part barren, and it is only where their spurs form broken valleys that we find extensive forests of lofty timber stretching down to the plains below.

The belt of low country which extends round the Indian peninsula, between the ghauts and the sea-coast, is almost entirely in the possession of the British. It varies not less in its width than in its fertility and its population.

On the western side we find to the north the "Concan" extending from the Nerbudda to 15° N. lat. Thence southwards to 12° 3″ is the state of Canara, and from that point to Cape Comorin is the Malabar territory, although the whole extent of this western sea-board is often erroneously termed the Malabar coast. This long range of country is irregular in its surface; the first few miles from the sea being very flat and sandy, with no vegetation but topes of palms. Further inland the ground is broken into hillocks more or less covered with vegetation; and gradually elevating themselves, they become at last merged in the spurs of the ghauts, and crowned with dense jungle and heavy forests of teak and satin-wood.

Along this line of coast, in addition to Bombay, are the towns of Mangalore, Cananore, Tellichery, Calicut, Cochin, Aleppee, and Trevandrum, all of them trading ports, and during the north-east monsoon, from November to April, enjoying a considerable traffic with Bombay, Ceylon, the Persian Gulf, and lately with Europe. Goa is a Portuguese settlement in 15° 30′ N. lat., but without any trade worthy of mention.

At the southern extremity of the peninsula is Cape Comorin; and to the eastward of this, in the Gulf of Manaarlies, the small island of Remisseram, famed for its stupendous Hindoo temple, to which pilgrims annually flock in great numbers.

On the eastern coast-line we find Madras, the capital of the Presidency of that name, Negapatam, Vizagapatam, and Pondicherry and Tranquebar, the former a French, the latter a Danish settlement. This coast is much exposed to the fury of the south-west monsoon, during which period none of the native craft are able to venture out. The only harbour along the coast is that of Coringa, in which vessels of some size may find a safe refuge.

The Deccan is separated from Central India by the valleys of the Nerbudda and Tapty, according to some writers: others, with more propriety, make the Vindya Mountains the natural boundaries of these two territories. This range extends from 74° to 84° E. long., in a direction nearly due east, following the valley of the Nerbudda at a distance of a few miles. At no part do these mountains reach a greater elevation than 2200 feet above the sea-level, and frequently not more than 700 feet. They are crossed in several places by roads of indifferent character.

Central India assumes pretty nearly the shape of a triangle, having its base formed by the Vindya Mountains, and its apex to the southwards of Delhi. It consists for the most part of elevated table-land, freely interspersed with mountain-ridges and extensive plains, some of which latter are extremely fertile. Along the range which on the eastward divides this tract from the delta of the Ganges, are the coal-deposits which at the present time furnish large supplies to Calcutta.

Nearly the whole of Central India is governed by native princes, amongst whom are the Guicowar and Rajpoot chiefs. A considerable portion of the state of Malwa is under the rule of Maharajah Scindia; while other tracts are governed by numerous petty rajahs, amongst whom may be named the Mahratta princes of Holkar and Nagpore.

On the western side of this portion of India the British possess a considerable tract of the plain of Gujerat, which is annexed to the Bombay Presidency. On the eastern side we find adjoining the territories of the Rajpoot princes; and lying between the rivers Sone and Ganges, a region which has been annexed to the residency of Allahabad.

The next natural division is that of the Delta of the Ganges, which ranges from the mouths of that river to the base of the Himalayas, a distance in a straight line of about 300 miles, and varying in breadth from 150 to 180 miles. On the eastern side it is flanked by the Chittagong district and the valleys of Assam and Silhet, with the Tiperah hills; on its western side it stretches from Balasore in the Bay of Bengal, through Midnapore and Nagore, to Rajmahal, and thence by the river Coosie to the Himalayas.

A very considerable portion of this division is incapable of cultivation; on the southern side, between the mouths of the Ganges and the Berrampootra, is a low tract called the Sunderabunds, extending about seventy miles inland and fifty miles in width, covered with swamps and thick jungle, the resort of every variety of reptile and wild beast. The effect of the rising of the tides from the sea is such as to preclude any but the most scanty use of the soil, though recent attempts have been made with partial success to recover some portion of this sterile country. To the north of this tract, as far as 25° N. lat., and chiefly between the branches of the Ganges and the Berrampootra, the land is subject to an annual inundation during the early part of the south-west monsoon, when the country is covered by water to a great depth, some of the rivers rising as much as thirty feet above their ordinary level. This, although causing much inconvenience and loss to the inhabitants, proves a great fertiliser of the soil; and except in the immediate vicinity of the flooded rivers, the entire surface of these river valleys yield most abundant crops of grain on the retirement of the waters, which takes place during October.

Beyond the influence of these periodical floods, we find still a large range of rich fertile land, partly watered by many streams, and partly irrigated by artificial means: to the north of this, again, as far as the swamps at the base of the Himalayan range, are found numerous tracts of waste land covered with low jungle, reeds, and rank grass.

Stretching along the lower chain of the Himalayas is the Tarai, or the swamp, a rather extensive portion of peaty soil, through which innumerable springs burst, fed by the mountain-land above. The vast masses of vegetable matter swept down from the higher lands, and decaying on these swamps throughout the year, render them unfit for human habitation, and the scattered population suffer severely from fever in their attempts to earn a scanty living by felling timber for the supply of the low country.

The Plain of the Ganges comprehends within it the districts of Bengal, Behar, Tirhoot, Oude, Rohilcund, and Allahabad. It is the most populous and fertile portion of British India, containing about sixty millions of inhabitants, and, with the exception of the kingdom of Oude, is entirely under the dominion of the East India Company.

Calcutta is by far the largest and most wealthy city of this or any other part of India, containing at the present date about 600,000 inhabitants. The other principal commercial and political cities are Dacca, Benares, Allahabad, Mirzapore, Goruckpore, Cawnpore, Furruckabad, Agra, Delhi, Meerut, and many others, possessing populations varying from thirty to a hundred and twenty thousand souls.

Between the northern extremities of the Gangetic Plain and the Plain of the Indus is a flat sterile country termed the Doab, ruled over by a few Seikh chieftains in alliance with the British.

The Plain of the Indus is situated on the eastern flank of that river, and commences from the neighbourhood of Attock, extending southwards and westwards as far as the debouchure of the Indus into the sea. It comprehends the Punjab, Scinde, and other smaller states: a large portion of it south of the Punjab consists of desert, arid plains; and even in the more favourable positions, where the land is watered by the overflowing of the Indus and its branches, the soil can scarcely be termed fertile, yielding but indifferent crops of grass and grain.

The Punjab, or the country of the five rivers, forming the northern portion of the Plain of the Indus, extends from the base of the Himalayan range to the confluence of the Chenab with the Indus. It is the most populous part of this division of India, and contains several very extensive and densely peopled cities: its entire population is believed to be three millions. Its ancient capital, Umritsur, contains 100,000 inhabitants, and has long possessed a valuable trade with many parts of India. It is situated between the rivers Beas and Ravee. Lahore, the modern capital, possesses a population of 80,000. Mooltan, on the Chenab, contains 60,000 inhabitants, and possesses some valuable manufactures in silk and cotton.

This country contains some very fertile tracts, especially in its more northern part, where the supply of water is most abundant. Towards the south the land is generally less favoured, although there are still some rich valleys between the Ravee and the Beas, as also in the immediate vicinity of all the five rivers. These streams are, according to modern nomenclature, the Sutlej, the Beas, the Ravee, the Chenab, and the Jhelum, taking them from east to west: the names by which they were known to the early writers of the west were the Zaradus, the Hyphasis, the Hydrastes, the Acesines, and the Hydaspes. These rivers flow from the Himalayas in a south-westerly direction for about six hundred miles, when, after merging into the Chenab, their waters finally unite with those of the Indus at the northern point of the Desert of Scinde.

The Seikhs form the principal inhabitants of this country, and their chieftains proved themselves formidable enemies to the British during one of the most severely contested struggles that have occurred with any eastern power. The Punjab is now a province of the British empire in India, under a resident, whose seat is at Lahore.

To the southwards of the Punjab is Scinde, until recently a powerful state governed by Ameers, whose descent was from chiefs of Beloochistan, but now annexed to the Bombay Presidency. It is bounded on the north by Affghanistan and Mooltan, on the east by the state of Rajpootna, on the west by Beloochistan, and on the south by Cutch and the sea. By far the greater portion of Scinde consists of sandy desert known as the Thurr, and which extends over nearly the whole of the country east of the Indus. The desert is covered with long ridges of low undulating sand-hills, occasionally topped with a little jungle or rank grass. There are, however, scattered throughout this Thurr, many oases of considerable fertility, producing crops of grain and vegetables. Within twenty and thirty miles of the Indus the fertilising effects of its periodical floodings are felt, and there, as well as far on the western extremity of this province, the soil proves of a more generous nature. The total population of the country does not exceed a million souls. Its chief towns are Shikarpore, Sikkur, Hydrabad, Tatta, and Kurrachee. None of these cities possess more than 20,000 inhabitants: the last mentioned is situated on the west mouth of the Indus, has a good harbour, and carries on a considerable trade, which has much increased since being in British possession.

The Thurr or Desert is still ruled by petty chiefs, Rajpoot princes in alliance with the East India Company: these are the Rajahs of Jessulmere, Marwar, Bikanir, &c. In this part of Scinde there are several cities, having populations varying from 20,000 to 60,000 souls, and some of them carrying on a considerable traffic with the adjoining states.

We have still to notice a portion of the continental territories of the East India Company comprised within the limits of the Bengal Presidency. Of these the first is the district of Arracan, stretching from the north-eastern extremity of the bay of Bengal to the limits of the late Burmese province of Pegu. The features of the country, the habits of the people, and the natural productions, so nearly assimilate to those of the other fractions of the Burmese territories, that one general description may well serve for the entire tract.

The provinces of Tenasserim and Pegu, formerly sections of the Burmese empire, were annexed to the British-Indian empire, the former in 1826, the latter in 1853, and are now governed by a commissioner and the usual staff of European and native officials.

The Tenasserim provinces, as ceded to the East India Company, comprise an extent of country five hundred miles in length, and from forty to eighty in breadth, and reaching from the junction of the Salween and Thoongeen rivers on the north to the Pak Chan river on the south; on the west the sea forms the boundary; and on the east a chain of lofty mountains divides this tract of country from the kingdom of Siam. The seat of government here is Moulmein, situated at the confluence of these rivers, and no less admirably adapted for purposes of trade than as a healthy position for troops.

The country is divided into three provinces, those of Mergni, Tavoy, and Amherst, in which latter the capital is situated. The population, although still small compared with the extent of country, has greatly increased by emigration from the Burman and Peguan territories since our possession of these provinces, and amounts at the present moment to about 160,000 souls. These numbers are composed indifferently of Burmese, Arracanese, Peguers, Talamis, Karens, and Toungthoos, with an admixture of Siamese blood amongst them; whilst in the towns of Moulmein and Tavoy are to be found a sprinkling of Chinese, Jews, Moguls, Moors, Bengalese, &c. more or less occupied in trade.

Varied as are undoubtedly the geological features of India, the records we possess of them are not so full or satisfactory as might be wished; and many years may yet elapse before our geological knowledge of this vast and wonderful country shall be placed on a basis at once reliable and in strict accordance with the rules of a science which is as yet but in its infancy.

The superior strata of Southern India are chiefly formed by hypogene schists, penetrated and broken up by immense outbursts of plutonic and trappean rocks, constituting the great bulk of the Western Ghauts from about the 16th degree of latitude to Cape Comorin, and forming the base of the Eastern Ghauts from the parallel of the Vindyan heights to their deflection at Naggery in latitude 13° 20′. They are frequently capped in the Western Ghauts by laterite, and in the Eastern Ghauts by sandstone, limestone, and laterite. From Naggery to Cape Comorin they form, with few exceptions, the basis of the plains of the Carnatic, Arcot, Seringapatam, Salem, Travancore, Madras, and all the intermediate districts. Intimately associated with granite, they break with ranges of hills on the low lands of Salem, the valley of the Cavery, and north of it from the table-lands of Mysore, the Baramhall, Bellary district, part of Hydrabad, and southern Mahratta country. Towards the north-west from Nagpore by Bijapore to the western coast, the hypogene and plutonic rocks disappear, emerging only occasionally under one of the largest continuous sheets of trap in the world, which extends far into the table-land of Central India.

Gneiss is usually found lowest in the series, next to it mica and hornblende schist, actinolite, chlorite, talcose and argillaceous schist, and crystalline limestone. This rule of succession, however, is by no means unbroken, for each of the above rocks, crystalline limestone alone excepted, has been found resting immediately upon the granite. The strata are often violently contorted, though the disturbance is less than might have been expected from the amount of plutonic action that has been exercised. The slip, though very irregular, is usually towards the east in the Western, and towards the west in the Eastern Ghauts, the amount of the inclination varying from ten to ninety degrees. The most prevalent rocks are gneiss and hornblende schist; but to the gneiss the other rocks may be said to be subordinate. The composition of the gneiss, and of the other schistose rocks, varies considerably in different localities, but they are all highly ferriferous in their substance. Statuary marble is very rare, indeed so much so as almost to have escaped observation; clay slate is seldom met with, and blue roofing slate not often observed; but every other species of hypogene rock is constantly found.

Throughout the whole of the earlier-formed rocks fossiliferous silurian remains have been very rarely discovered; but there are many others in the several strata, to which at present the geologists have been unable to give a name, or to assign any certain position in the scale of sedimentary strata.

The sandstone and limestone beds have not been seen south of the Salem break, but north of that boundary they cover a considerable area, being chiefly confined, however, to the more elevated table-lands. This most extensive development is in the "Cuddapah Beds," where they cover an area of about 9000 square miles. They appear also between the Kistna and the Godavery, in the south Mahratta country, the Nizam's dominions, and elsewhere, preserving every where the same relative position, the same embedded pebbles and general lithologic appearance: the dip is mostly conformable to that of the subjacent rocks.

Geologists have found veins of coal associated with shale at Kotah, on one of the tributaries of the Godavery; and in the veins of the limestone at Nannoor, others have discovered myriads of what appear to be microscopic foraminifera.

The sandstones also afford traces of coal both bituminous and anthracitic, and are supposed to be identical with those that support the coal measures at Chirra Pungi, which abound in certain organic remains, with a few of the stems and leaves of plants among them. They have a certain degree of resemblance to the sandstones of the Devonian group, but they appear to be better classed with the ancient secondary or with the metamorphic rocks; but no positive conclusion can be come to with respect to them till the discovery of fossils. As compared with the other Indian rocks, they form, probably, the oldest of the fossiliferous beds. A peculiar interest attaches to the sandstone, in consequence of its being the matrix of the diamond; and one general fact is especially worthy of notice, that granitic or basaltic dykes are invariably found intruding into diamond areas.

Beds of shelly limestone have been discovered in the neighbourhood of Pondicherry, which have only recently attracted the notice of scientific men, although the very doorsteps of that place have long been formed of this interesting rock. These beds of limestone, in which the shells are singularly perfect, rise in gentle undulations at about nine miles from the sea, inland of Pondicherry, and run in a south-east-by-east direction to an extent which has not yet been definitely ascertained. The limestone of South Arcot belongs to nearly the same epoch, as do also the beds which occur in the vicinity of Trichinopoly, apparently resting immediately upon the plutonic and hypogene rocks. These beds have been considered with an unusual share of attention since Messrs. Kaye and Cunliffe forwarded to England their beautiful collection from all these localities; the Pondicherry beds yielding by far the greater proportion. The fossil fishes from these were found by Sir Grey Egerton and Professor Forbes to belong to the Squaloid family of Placoids, one Cycloid and one Ganoid alone excepted. These fossils are, in general, badly preserved, except the invertebrata, among which the Cephalopods, including twenty-eight Ammonites, are in a most beautiful condition. Professor Forbes assigns the Pondicherry fossils to the lower green sand or Neocomian beds, and those of Verdachellum and Trichinopoly, among which there are several species not found at Pondicherry, to the upper green sand; but Sir Grey Egerton, from an examination of the ichthiolites, places the Pondicherry beds somewhat higher, since they contain the genera Corax and Enchodus, which have not hitherto been found any where so low as the Neocomian range.

The tertiary beds were first discovered in the route from Hydrabad to Nagore, on the north bank of the Godavery, among the Nirmul Hills; and afterwards across the Warda to Hingan-Ghaut, where Mr. Malcolmson perceived beds of chert and limestone containing shells, which Mr. Lonsdale considered to be of fresh-water formation. The fossils were first found at Munoor, and between that village and Hurtnoor, which is near the top of the Muckelgundi Ghaut, and in different parts of the pass leading into the valley of Berar. Mr. Malcolmson describes the bed in which they were first observed to be a band of singular quartz rock, projecting about two feet from the surface, halfway up the escarpment of the principal mountain, ascending the steep pass leading up the south side of the Nirmul Hills, and which is composed of concentric nodular basalt imbedded in a soft greenish wacke. The fossils all belong to fresh-water genera, and to species which have not yet been discovered to be of recent origin. They are chiefly species of Physa, Cypris, Unio, Limnea, Melania, Paladina, and Chara, which have since been determined by Sowerby; the charæ occur in such abundance as to form entire rocky masses.

Other deposits of fresh-water shells occur between Beder and Hydrabad, and about five miles south of Puddpungalli, near Rajahmundry on the Godavery, the latter occurring in a limestone both resting upon and capped by trap. Here, however, Dr. Benza found *oysters* among the Limas and Melaniæ, so that the deposit must have been originally formed in a lake or estuary communicating with the sea.

One of the most extraordinary formations in India is that of the *laterite* rock, which, according to Francis Buchanan, is a peculiarity to be found only in the East Indies. It varies much in structure and composition, but generally speaking it presents a reddish-brown tubular and cellular clay more or less indurated, passing on the one hand into a hard, compact, jaspideous rock, and on the other into loosely aggregated sandstones or grits, as is the case near Calicut and Pondicherry; in other places, again, into red sectile clay and other soft substances. Sometimes it presents the appearance of a conglomerate containing fragments of quartz, the plutonic, hypogene, and sandstone rocks, and nodules of iron ore, derived from them all, imbedded in ferruginous clay. The geographical extent of this rock invests it with great importance; for it covers the western coast almost continuously, and nearly up to the very base of the ghauts, and from the south of Bombay to Cape Comorin. It is found also in detached beds along the Coromandel coast near Madras, Nellore, Rajahmundery, and Samulcotta, extending into Cuttack. It crowns the loftiest summits of the eastern and western ghauts, and some of the isolated peaks on the table-lands in the interior. It is found, indeed, in almost every part of the Deccan, always in an overlying position, and generally in large continuous beds; and there is reason to believe, from the marks of denudation, that it formerly covered much larger areas than it now occupies.

Of the sandstones which belong to the very *late tertiary*, or even very recent periods, there are beds on the eastern coast of the southern extremity of the peninsula which contain pelagic shells, which, as far as they have been examined, are of the species of fish inhabiting the adjacent sea; and it is this rock which stretches across the straits to Ceylon, constituting the remarkable barrier known by the name of Adam's Bridge, and which, in Captain Newbold's opinion, was elevated simultaneously with the laterite. Similar strata are met with in Tinnevelly, Ramnad, near Cape Comorin, and on the opposite coast of Ceylon.

True diluvium, it is said, is not to be found in Indian latitudes; but the remark is rather to be applied to the *erratic block* formation as it occurs in Northern Europe, Siberia, and North and South America. It is not found, Mr. Darwin says, in the equatorial regions of South America, though it is scattered over the southern portion of that continent. From these and other circumstances there is nothing like the true drift to be met with in Southern India. Northern India, however, shews transported blocks in sufficient abundance; but it is easy to trace them to a comparatively local source from their neighbourhood to the Himalayan Mountains, and there is none of that extensive diffusion of travelled masses which is accounted for in Europe by the constant phenomena of icebergs. There are, however, some beds of gravel and sand which occur in situations where their presence is not to be accounted for by the agency of transporting powers now existing; and at Condapetta, for instance, in the Cuddepah district, there is a bed of gravel which covers an area of several miles, principally composed of rounded fragments of trap, granite, and schistose rocks, which must have been transported from the distance of twenty or forty miles, intermingled with pebbles of quartz, jasper, and chert, and others from the adjacent sandstone and limestone. Other similar beds, enclosing fossils, and in one instance the bones of the mastodon, are met with at Parteal, Wakorry, and other places. Beds of dark-blue marine clay underlying the alluvium are found in many places along the Coromandel coast, sometimes extending two or three miles inland.

The only remaining sedimentary rock at present known is the curious soil called *regur* or *black cotton clay*, which covers at least one-third of the surface of Southern India. It is of a deep-bluish, or greenish, or dark-greyish black colour, and is remarkable for its absorbent powers and its extreme fertility, having yielded crop after crop, year by year, for more than 2000 years, without receiving any manure or other assistance from the hand of man. It principally occupies the elevated table-lands of the ceded districts of Hydrabad, Nagpore, and the Southern Mahratta country, thus including the whole plateau of the Deccan. It is not so common in Mysore, but is met with in continuous sheets of from six to twenty feet thick below the Salem break, covering the lower plain of Coimbatore, Madura, Salem, and Trichinopoly, to the vicinity of Cape Comorin.

There is yet another rock called *kunker*, which affords a remarkable instance of the compensating process of nature, by which the adaptation of the globe to the wants of man is every where kept up. India is but sparingly supplied with the sedimentary limestone of the sort which is fit for the kiln, and this deficiency is made up for by the substance which has just been specified, and which is found to contain upwards of seventy-two parts of carbonate of lime in its composition. The older kunker is usually of a light-brown, dirty, cream, reddish, or cineritious grey tint; and when compact, its substance resembles the older travertines of Rome and Auvergne. Kunker aggregates in horizontal overlying masses, usually intermingled with the soil without much appearance of stratification. It is broken up and used as a rough building-stone in the walls of tanks, huts, enclosures, &c. by the natives, and is universally employed to burn into lime. It is irregularly distributed in overlying patches over perhaps one-eighth of the area of the country, and no tract is entirely free from it except the summits of the Neilgherry hills. It is most abundant in districts penetrated and shattered by basaltic dykes, and where the metallic developments are the greatest; and is perhaps least met with in the localities where laterite caps hypogene or plutonic rocks: it is evidently of tufaceous origin.

There are some other aqueous deposits, chiefly local, which are mostly of very recent origin.

Granite and its congeneric rocks are abundantly developed throughout the hypogene area. The former shews itself under every variety of aspect. It starts up from the surface of the table-land in bold and sharply hewn peaks, or rises in dome-shaped bosses, or appears in profuse but distinct clusters and ranges, which affect no general line of elevation, but often radiate irregularly as from a centre. Some of the insulated peaks are exceedingly striking in outline and structure. The rock of Nundidrug for instance, which rises 1700 feet above the surface of the plain, looks almost as if it were formed of one entire mass of rock; and the rock of Sivagunga is still higher. The most remarkable of the insulated clusters and masses of granite on the table-land of the peninsula are those of Sivagunga, Severndroog, and Octradroog, some in Mysore, Gooty, Reidrooj, Adoni, and others in the central districts; but there are numerous masses almost equally remarkable scattered over all the southern part of the peninsula table-land, as well as in the maritime district of Coromandel.

The great part of the central table-land is also formed by it, and it there, over a very extended area, continually crops out in the more elevated and diversified districts.

Serpentine, greenstone, and green sandstone, with hornblende and schist, in smaller masses, are met with in every part of India.

The only formation that remains to be noticed is the immense diluvial deposit which has been carried down by the large and numerous rivers irrigating the whole of the country. In no part of the world is there a more fertile soil than that which encompasses these streams in Upper India; whilst along the lower portions of their course, and especially throughout thousands of square miles that lie stretching above, about, and beyond far into the interior from the embouchures of the Ganges, the Berrampootra, and the Indus, the most rich and exuberant scenery of Asia is to be met with.

The population of British India may be divided into aborigines and foreigners. Some writers have supposed, but evidently without sufficient foundation, that the Hindoos are not strictly the aborigines of this part of Asia. They are by far the most numerous of all the nations of Hindostan, and, with the various other aboriginal tribes, amount to about one hundred millions of the total population. The Hindoos are almost entirely in possession of the agricultural districts; whilst on the other hand we find the mountain-ranges and the elevated table-lands of the Deccan occupied by the Gonds, the Bhils, the Ramnois, and the Coulies, besides other insignificant tribes. All of these follow the chase and the rearing of cattle for a livelihood, and scarely cultivate sufficient ground to produce the most ordinary necessaries. Of these tribes, the Gonds are the least civilised, and the Ramnois the most advanced, as compared with the Hindoos.

Amongst the many grades of foreigners, both from Europe and other parts of Asia, who have at various periods helped to people Hindostan, we find the British race pre-eminent in intelligence and power, though not so in numbers. The total of the residents in India from the British Isles, including the military, is computed at 75,000 souls.

The Portuguese descendants are far more numerous, amounting to about 1,000,000. They are chiefly to be found along the western coasts and in the chief cities of India.

On the Malabar and Canara coasts we find Arabs in considerable numbers, together with Syrian Christians, or Parawas, and Jews, although not to any great extent.

Parsees, or Ghebirs, are to be met with chiefly at Bombay and other trading ports on that coast.

Throughout various parts of India the descendants of Affghan races are clearly to be traced to the extent of several millions; whilst in Scinde we find a strong blending of the blood of the Beloochees, the conquerors of that country, with the native races, as well as undoubtedly pure descendants of the Ameer tribes.

Extending through 23 degrees of latitude, we may expect to find in British India a great variety of climate, influenced, moreover, by the great irregularities of the surface of the country. We may thus meet a temperature of 28° on the Himalayan range or the Neilgherries; or if we turn to the Cutch country, find the thermometer during the dry months ranging as high as 106°.

The Indian seasons are, strictly speaking, two in number, and are called the monsoons, viz. the south-west and the north-east; and these are felt more or less throughout the entire length and breadth of Hindostan. But inasmuch as the north-east monsoon is again divided into the temperate and hot months, we may in truth say that there are three distinct seasons.

The south-west monsoon usually commences about the middle of May along the west coast, but later to the north and east. It is ushered in by violent gales of wind, thunder and lightning, and heavy falls of rain, which continue for six or eight weeks, at the end of which time the weather moderates and becomes close and oppressive, with heavy clouds and a dull calm atmosphere. The thermometer will now range at about 88° or 90°, until further heavy falls of rain take place, ushering in the north-east monsoon some time in October. The weather is now more pleasant, the long-continued rains having thoroughly cooled the land, and the thermometer will stand at about 80°. The cool portion of this monsoon extends from November to January; though to the north of Calcutta it lasts into February, and even March. The mornings and evenings are now remarkably pleasant and cool, not exceeding a temperature of 75°, and woollen clothing may at this season be worn with much comfort by Europeans.

During March, April, and the early part of May, the hot season prevails throughout India, though of course considerably modified by position and local circumstances. At this period the wind, especially upon the Coromandel or east coast, blows along-shore, and being extremely dry and hot, gives rise to much sickness, more particularly amongst European residents.

The winds, however, not less than the temperature, are greatly modified by localities, and thus we find that the south-west monsoon in some places really comes from the south-east; in like manner we meet with north-westerly breezes during the prevalence of the north-east monsoon. To the south of Bengal the winds are more strictly north and south; whilst in Assam and Behar they will be found nearly east and west.

The long and lofty ranges of mountains, the elevated table-lands, the gigantic rivers, the deep valleys of Hindostan, all exert a most sensible influence upon the direction and force of the prevailing winds.

Thus the south-west monsoon, which along the coasts of Malabar and Canara commences early in May, does not reach Delhi before the end of June, and the Punjab until early in July, where, as well as in the elevated lands of Cashmere, it makes its appearance with light fleecy clouds and gentle showers.

The seasons of Bengal are alternately hot, cold, and rainy. The pleasantest and coolest months are the latter part of February, March, and April; though April may sometimes be included with May and June as intensely hot, rendered still more oppressive by a scorching westerly wind, accompanied by small and almost invisible grains of sand. People are glad to remain under the shelter of their houses; the vegetable world seems at a stand-still, and nothing remains but barren tracts of soil, though the air of the distant mountains is fresh and delightful.

The rainy season commences in the upper provinces in April and May; in the plains not until June: it continues incessantly till the end of July. The rain tends greatly to cool the sultry atmosphere, although during the months of August and September the heat is still intense. The monsoon changes at this period. In October the cold begins to be felt, and increases throughout the three following months; it is frequently extreme in Bengal and Behar, where the atmosphere is moist and unhealthy, whilst on the mountains ice and snow are often to be met with.

Perhaps there is no part of Hindostan in which the oppressiveness of the climate, at certain periods, is so sensibly felt as at Calcutta and in its vicinity. Here, during the rainy season, when the monsoon comes across the Sunderabunds, and wafts with it a dense heated atmosphere deeply impregnated with vegeto-animal effluvia, the human frame suffers far more than with a much higher temperature and a pure dry air. The body feels hot and damp, as though immersed in a vapour-bath; a languor and listlessness creep over the frame; and so far from night bringing with it any relief, it appears but to aggravate the feeling of oppressiveness, and the restless sleeper rises in the morning wearied and unrefreshed, happy to resort to a chattie-bath of tepid water to relieve his over-loaded skin of some portion of the heavy coating of perspiration which clogs its pores.

The mean temperature of Calcutta is, in January 66°, April 86°, July 81°, October 79°, and November 74°. The annual average fall of rain is here about 60 inches; the greatest fall being in the months of May and June, when about 30 inches will be the quantity. No less than 16 inches have been known to fall in the space of twenty-four hours.

At Madras, from its contiguity to the ocean, the monsoon is not felt nearly so oppressively; neither are the cool months so pleasant as in Bengal. The minimum temperature is here 75°, and the maximum 91°, the mean being 84°.

Bombay approaches more nearly to the climate of the elder Presidency, both the heat and the rain being in excess at the change of the monsoon. In Cutch the temperature is as high as 110°, whilst in the elevated mountain tracts within two days' journey of Bombay the thermometer will stand at the freezing-point.

At the sanitarium on the Neilgherries, or the Blue Ghauts, may be found a climate very nearly approaching that of our own country, especially during the prevalence of the north-east monsoon. Without being so cold as Great Britain, it is far more equable; the maximum temperature being only 77°, whilst that of this country is 90°; the minimum point is 38° against 11° in England. The number of days on which heavy rain falls on these hills is 19 against 18 in this country;

whilst the fair days are 237 against 160. The fall of rain on the Neilgherries is 44 inches; in England it is 23.

At Saharamapore, in lat. 30° N., at an elevation of about 1000 feet, where government have a botanic garden, the mean temperature during the cold months of December and January is 55° and 52°. In May and June, when the hot dry winds prevail, the mean will be 85° and 90°; whilst in September and October the mean will not be more than 79° and 72°.

At this station, although the cool season is more agreeable and lasting, and the hot weather more endurable than in the southern districts of India, the climate and vegetation are nevertheless essentially tropical.

Fifty miles farther northwards, but at an elevation of 6000 feet upon the Mussoorri range of the Himalayas, is another botanic garden, where a climate more closely allied to that of central Europe is found. The thermometer there stands at 32° for several months in the night-time; and the means for December and January are 42° and 45°. The greatest heat is 80°, during the month of June; and the means of May and June are 66° and 67°.

Not the least favourite of the hill sanitaria is that of Dharjeeling, situated on the Sikkim Hills, near the Himalayas, on the north-east frontier of the Bengal Presidency: it is at an altitude of about 7000 feet above the sea-level, and distant from Calcutta about 350 miles. There are some excellent roads in its immediate vicinity, but travellers are compelled to travel to it from the capital by water and palanquin. The temperature at this station is pretty equal throughout the day, with clear dry cold in the winter season, and seldom, even in the hottest weather, approaching 70° of Fahrenheit. The average annual fall of rain is 130 inches, the wet season lasting from four to five months. The scenery around this settlement is of the most beautiful description, heightened as it is by the proximity of the snow-capped peaks of the Himalayas. This sanitarium has been found highly beneficial to invalids when resorted to in due season, though in all chronic cases it does not, of course, afford that relief which is to be found in a voyage to sea.

The forms of disease peculiar to the European residents in most parts of India, are congestive fever, intermittents, hepatic and other forms of disease, and rheumatism. Apoplexy is not unfrequent during the prevalence of the cold drying wind of the north-east monsoon; and occasionally, especially in Calcutta and Bombay, we meet with fatal cases of cholera.

A sojourn for a month or two on any of the elevated mountain-ranges will usually restore the invalid to health, provided he be not an old resident, or the disease has not assumed the chronic form, in which case there is little hope for him but in a return to the bracing climate and cheerful scenes of his native country.

Amongst the natives we find the prevailing diseases to be cholera, dysentery, fever, skin affections, leprosy, rheumatism, small-pox, elephantiasis, and beri-beri. The latter is a peculiar type of dropsy; and elephantiasis consists in a swelling of the legs and feet until they assume the shape and almost the size of those of the elephant. Neither of these complaints have ever been known amongst Europeans.

Cholera first made its appearance, in the form of endemic disease, in 1817, in the district of Nuddeah, and has since that time seldom been absent from all parts of India. Its advent took place immediately after a season of unusual storminess: falls of rain, heavy even for India, accompanied by terrific electrical discharges, ushered in this destroying agency. In regard to the influence of electrical matter upon the health of mankind, and their liability to attacks from this Asiatic scourge, an Indian medical authority[2] has remarked, that there is no reason to doubt but that either the absence of electricity from the human body, or some important change in its electrical state, arising perhaps from exposure to a negative electrical atmosphere, may be the cause of the dreadful and destructive epidemic which has recently ravaged the East, and that the vicissitudes of the seasons preceding this visitation may support this opinion. Should this be correct, we may readily account for the sudden attacks of the disease, the change in the temperature and sensibility of the body and in the fluids, and for the manner in which it has been limited to some districts, extending in turn to others, and sparing none.

Many of the above diseases, however, both of the European and native community, are the result rather of improper diet and living than the effect of climate, though this latter, of course, aggravates every disorder. With the European, the evil arises from a highly exciting dietary; with the Hindoo, a scanty supply of poor food, and wretched apparel at all seasons, are the sources of disease.

Foremost among the products of the soil in India may be mentioned saltpetre, or nitrate of potash, of which vast quantities are annually exported from Calcutta and Bombay. This useful saline product is found existing in caves, and also in the waters of stagnant marshes, frequently combined with the muriate and sulphate of soda.

[2] Mr. Ainslie in his work on the Diseases of India.

The existence of these salts is always indicated by the sterility of the adjoining land, which is incapable of cultivation.

Coal-deposits of considerable extent exist in the Bengal Presidency. The largest of these is in the Damoodah valley, stretching towards the Hooghly, not many miles from Calcutta, and according to recent investigations containing seams forty and fifty feet in thickness. These beds extend over a space of thirty miles, between the towns of Nagore and Bancoorah. The seams rest on metamorphic and crystalline rock of gneiss and mica schist, and at one point are covered by a ferruginous sand, an extension of the alluvium of the plains of the Ganges. A second set of beds is found in the valley of the river Sone, to the south of Mirzapore, in the Benares district, but not of similar extent or quality to the preceding.

This coal is of very fair quality, and the company working the mines are doing so at a fair profit. In heating power it has not the properties of English coal, but it is sufficiently good to be in constant use by the river steamers and such steam-engines as are employed in factories.

In gems India is exceedingly rich. The diamond-mines of Golconda have long been world-famed for the extreme beauty and great value of their yield. There are also valuable mines at Panna in Bundelcund, where the diamonds are found in a matrix of red iron-stone, gravel, and clay. The celebrated Koh-i-noor shewn in the Great Exhibition, no less than others of immense value in the possession of native princes, testify to the richness of India in precious stones. The ruby, the emerald, the sapphire, the turquoise, the opal, the amethyst, and indeed almost every known gem, are to be found in various parts of the many mountain-ranges and elevated table-lands of Hindostan, and often of great purity and beauty.

Although we are told in ancient records that the Ophir of the east yielded the gold of those remote days, there does not appear to be any trace of the precious metal in India proper. It is found in the Himalayas in small quantities. Iron is, however, found of good quality, especially in the Madras Presidency, where there is a company formed for the smelting and working the ore. The celebrated blades of Damascus bear testimony to the quality of Indian steel, and there is still some of equally fine quality produced.

In the province of Ajmeer there exist some lead-mines which yield at the present day a good quantity of ore; whilst in the hills near Nellore in the peninsula some very rich specimens of copper ore have been found, containing as much as 60 per cent of the pure metal.

The hilly country of Mewar appears always to have been known to contain an abundance of mineral riches, and it is not too much to believe that it was this very source of wealth which in former times enabled the Ranas of Odeypoor to oppose the Emperor of Delhi with such great and continued success. The most noted of the mines in this district were those of Jawar, which are believed to have yielded an annual revenue to the state of 22,000*l.*

The district of Jawar lies about twenty-five miles south of Oodeypoor, and is situated in an extensive valley, surrounded by hills overlooking a fertile but desolate plain, covered by the ruins of former prosperity. Many of these ruins consist of antique temples, erected on hills 160 feet high composed entirely of ashes, the very existence of which, under such circumstances, bears testimony to the remoteness of the period when the mines were worked.

At the present time no effort is made by the Rana to open up this source of wealth ; a feeling of jealousy and distrust appearing to exist in his mind as to the consequences of his doing so, though it seems that some very excellent specimens of zinc have been covertly obtained from that neighbourhood.

In the Tenasserim and Peguan provinces tin abounds; indeed the whole range of the hilly country forming the great dividing range between these and the Burmese and Siamese territories may be said to abound in mineral wealth. Nitre, alum, salt, mercury, lead impregnated with silver, copper in most of its varieties, the sulphurets, oxides, and sulphates of iron, besides rubies, sapphires, tourmalines, and jasper, are all found in greater or less abundance throughout that range of country. In the Tenasserim province coal is likewise found, though it does not appear that any steps have been taken to turn this natural product to account.

The forests of British India, if not so vast as those of America, are still of great value for domestic, commercial, and agricultural purposes: many of the woods grown in the Himalayan and Deccan forests, as well as those in central and north-western India, possess wonderful strength and durability, not unfrequently combined with much beauty. By far the greater portion of these are quite unknown in Europe, and not many of them are in general use even amongst the Europeans of the East. In some instances the remoteness of the places of growth from populous districts proves a great bar to their use, unless where water-conveyance, the cheapest of all modes of transport in oriental countries, is to be had.

To attempt an enumeration of even the principal woods of India would carry this portion of my work far beyond its limits. The extent of our present knowledge of Indian timber furnishes us with several thousands of specimens, of many of which we know little beyond the names. A large portion of them are fitted but for the most inferior description of work, many serving only for fuel or for garden-fences. On the other hand, there are a number of these woods which might well be imported into this country for furniture-work.

The ebony, sattin-wood, and calamander, are more or less known here for their hardness, beauty of grain, and susceptibility of high polish. There are also "blackwood," tamarind wood, cedar, sissoo, teak, and saul-wood. The two latter are in most general use throughout the coasts and southern and central parts of Hindostan, the first for ship-building, for which it is most admirably adapted; the last for house-building and general engineering purposes. Both of them grow to a vast size, often measuring nine or ten feet round the trunk. The teak is chiefly found on the Malabar coast, and in the northern division of the Madras Presidency, whilst the saul-timber is found growing in almost every latitude northward of Calcutta.

There are many other woods used for every variety of purpose, answering to our oak, elm, and ash, quite unknown except to native carpenters. Until very recently some of the finest forests in the Bombay Presidency were in great danger of utter destruction from the reckless manner in which the natives of those districts were accustomed to fell the finest trees for their most ordinary requirements, until at length the attention of the authorities was directed to the subject, and measures were adopted, not only to prevent this destructive wastefulness in future, but to ensure an extension of plantations of teak and other useful timber.

In the forests of Martaban, or British Burmah, on the east side of the Bay of Bengal, are extensive forests of teak and bamboos, attaining a great size; but the former wood is scarcely equal to that grown on the Malabar coast or in Ceylon. The license-fees for cutting this useful timber yield the Tenasserim government about 12,000*l.* per annum.

Perhaps in none of its vegetable products does India differ more sensibly from western countries than in its grasses. With its many varieties of soil and climate, its fertile valleys and richly clad table-lands, it nowhere possesses the constant and heavily-yielding pasturages of Europe. That there are many varieties of grasses, the large number of cattle, sheep, goats, &c. reared in many parts of India, not less than the numerous wild animals which inhabit its less frequented districts, bear ample testimony.

During the cool months and the rainy season there is little difficulty in finding pasture for cattle. The principal of the Indian grasses, and perhaps the most generally diffused, is the Doob-grass (*Synodon dactylon*), a creeping plant possessing much nourishing property in its long stems, no less than in its leaves. This endures the greatest elevation of temperature, as its roots penetrate far below the surface, and although during the dry monsoon giving no sign of life, it puts forth its tender leaves on the first approach of the rains.

A very nourishing grass, possessing a powerful aromatic odour, is met with on the elevated lands above the Ghauts of the south, as well as in the north-west provinces. So strong are its aroma and flavour, that the flesh, milk, and butter of the animals feeding upon it become in time sensibly affected both in taste and smell.

Upon the many slopes of the Himalayas there are found abundance of good nourishing pastures, admirably adapted to the requirements of cattle and sheep, and upon which many herds and flocks are reared when the dry season forces them from the plains below.

Throughout the flat countries, and spread over vast tracts of indifferent soil, we meet with grasses, or rather herbage, in sufficient abundance, but generally either coarse and poor, or rank and distasteful to animals. In swampy or sterile plains these reedy grasses often fail to tempt even the coarse-feeding buffalo and rhinoceros; and it is a common practice amongst all the Indian villagers, at the end of the dry season, to set fire to these tracts, on which the long withered herbage readily ignites, and after the first monsoon showers furnishes a rapid and abundant supply of young sweet blades.

In some parts of India, especially at the Presidencies, it is customary to cut grass for hay, as fodder for horses during the excessively dry months, but latterly artificial grasses have been introduced for this purpose. The Guinea-grass and Mauritius-grass are both admirably adapted for feeding cattle.

In plants yielding fibrous materials for cordage or cloth, India is peculiarly rich; and although many of these remain as yet but little known beyond the places of production, there can be no doubt but that the time will arrive when the attention of practical men will be given to them. Some few of these have already been successfully introduced into Europe, and become leading articles of commerce, as well as of considerable value to the manufacturers of this country.

Foremost among these latter may be instanced Jute, a species of *Corchorus*, growing very freely in the lowlands of Bengal. Twenty-five years ago this was scarcely known in England; yet so rapidly has it sprung into use for cordage, canvass, and purposes similar to those of flax, that for some time past the consumption of it has amounted to a thousand tons a month.

The China-grass is found abundantly throughout India; and now that an improved and economical process has been discovered for preparing the fibre for market, this too bids fair to become of great commercial value.

The fibre of the cocoa-nut, known as coir, is chiefly produced along the Malabar coast: it is of superior quality to that from Ceylon. Sunn, Indian hemp, Indian flax, and aloe-fibre, are also known as articles of export to Europe.

Besides these there are, however, a variety of others found in great abundance in most parts of Hindostan, and in much request among the natives, although very coarsely prepared. Of these may be instanced Toonda-coir (*Calotropis gigantea*), Umbarce (*Hybiscus canabinus*), Marool (*Sanseveira zeylanica*), pine-apple fibre, plantain-fibre, &c. &c.

The following table illustrating the breaking-point of some of the Indian fibres, as compared with English hemp, may not be without interest:

English hemp	*Cannabis sativa* . .	105 lbs.
Aloe	*Argave Americana* . .	110 „
Ejoo	*Saguerus Rumphii* . .	96 „
Coir	*Cocos nucifera* . . .	87 „
Indian hemp	*Cannabis sativa* . . .	74 „
Sunn	*Crotolaria juncea* . .	68 „
Broughi paat	*Corchorus olitorius* . .	68 „
Indian flax	*Linum usitatissimum* .	39 „

Flax has been long cultivated in India, particularly in the northern provinces, but solely on account of the seed, the linseed of commerce, which is shipped in large quantities to various parts of the world: the manufacture of linseed-oil is carried on to a small extent in Bengal; but in no case do we learn that any account is taken of the fibre of the plant, which, strange as it may appear, is lost in immense quantities, a portion only of it being employed for such purposes as thatching houses, feeding or littering cattle, &c.

Of far greater value, however, than any of the preceding is cotton. The species peculiar to the Indian continent in common with other parts of Asia, as distinguishable from the American and West Indian descriptions, is, according to Dr. Royle, the *Gossypium Indicum* or *herbaceum*; the *Gossypium arboreum*, peculiar to India alone, is unfitted for manufacturing purposes, and employed solely as a padding for cushions, pillows, &c., for which, from its silky softness, it is especially adapted. The former kind appears to have been produced in and exported from India since the most remote periods, and during the present century to have assumed a very important position amongst the articles shipped from each of the three Presidencies.

Great Britain at the present time takes on an average 90,000,000 lbs. annually. China consumes nearly as much; whilst the native manufacture for local use cannot be less than 600,000,000 lbs. yearly. This vast quantity will cease to cause astonishment, when we remember that the hundred million of inhabitants of India are accustomed to use cotton for all those purposes for which hemp, flax, wool, and hair are employed in European countries. Their finest, lightest dress for the hot months, as well as their warmer, well-padded garments for the rainy and cool weather, are alike wrought from cotton. The costly gossamer-web which adorns the rarest beauties of the harems, and the coarsest rags which envelope the emaciated form of the meanest outcast, are produced from the same fibres. The richest trappings and hangings which grace the state canopy of the nabob, and the rope which terminates the existence of the vilest criminal, owe their common origin to the cotton plant of India.

Extensively as it is employed in manufactures in the East and West, it is nevertheless deficient in those qualities which have secured to the cottons of North and South America the favour of the merchants and manufacturers of Europe, viz. length of fibre or staple, and cleanliness. The former is dependent on cultivation, the latter on the after preparation.

In commerce Indian cotton is known under the name of Surats, Tinnevelly, Bengal, Broach, &c., according to the locality of its growth or place of shipment. Dr. Royle[3] gives three distinct varieties of cotton, all indigenous to Hindostan. The common description is found scattered more or less throughout India, reared either as a triennial or annual. It reaches the height of five or six feet in warm, moist climates; the seeds are five in number, clothed with a short greyish down. In the peninsula there are two distinct species of this sort, known amongst the natives as *Oopum* and *Nadum*. The first thrives only on the richest black soil, and is an annual, producing a fine staple; the latter is a triennial plant, and grows on the poorer red soil, yielding small crops of inferior quality.

Next to these we have the Dacca cotton, as a distinct variety of the *Gossypium Indicum*. It differs from the previous in the plant being more erect, with fewer branches, and tinged with a reddish hue, whilst the cotton is finer, softer, and longer. This variety is reared

[3] The Culture of Cotton in India, p.139.

more or less extensively throughout Bengal, especially in the Dacca district, where it is employed in the manufacture of the exquisitely fine muslin cloths known over a great part of the world as Dacca muslins, and whose delicacy of texture so long defied the imitation of the art-manufacturers of the West.

A third variety is the Berar cotton, grown in the Berar country, in the northern provinces of the Madras Presidency, and in Surat and Broach. This plant attains a greater size than the preceding, bears for a longer period, and produces a fibre of a finer quality than the former. It appears to thrive best on a light black soil of vegetable composition.

Amongst commercial men the term *Surat* includes the produce of Surat, Berar, and Broach, with occasionally some from Dacca; it comes mostly from Bombay. The Madras cottons are those shipped from Tinnevelly, Coimbatore, and other parts of that Presidency, whilst the Bengals take in the Bundelcund, Nagpore, and the far northern provinces.

Examined under a microscope the staple of these sorts appears to range from seventeen-twentieths to one and one-tenth of an inch in length; the staple of the celebrated Sea-Island cotton being usually an inch and a half in length.

The soil in which all these Indian varieties thrive may be classed under two distinct heads, the black and the red cotton soil. The former, as its name indicates, is of a black or deep brown colour, of a clayey nature, blended with the red *kunker* of the country (a calcareous iron-stone), forming in the rains a heavy tenacious mass, and drying into solid lumps in the hot months. An analysis of this gives 74 per cent of silex, 12 of carbonate of lime, 7¾ protoxide of iron, 3 of alumina, 2 of vegetable matter, and ⅓ salts, with a trace of magnesia.

The red soil of India has been found in some localities better suited to the growth of cotton than the black earth. It is a rather coarse yellowish-red soil, commingled with particles of kunker, silex, felspar, and aluminous earth. It mainly differs in composition from the preceding in the iron existing in the state of peroxide or red oxide, whilst the carbonate of lime is found present in greater abundance.[4]

Analyses of the best cotton-soils of America prove that they differ from those of India chiefly in the large portions of peaty matter contained in them; and there appears to be little doubt but that this fact,

[4] Royle's Culture of Cotton, p. 162.

and the peculiarity of the climate of the American sea-board, sufficiently account for the great superiority of the cottons of that country over those of any other part of the world.

The medicinal plants, and the various substances yielded by them, are far from unimportant in an enumeration of the natural products of British India. There is little doubt, however, that at present the medical world are very imperfectly acquainted with the greater portion of the remedies employed, often with very marked success, by the native practitioners. Many of these remedies are probably of small value; but there are, on the other hand, a number of them which already have proved valuable auxiliaries to the pharmacopœia. Senna, rhubarb, and castor oil, are the leading medicinal exports. In the gum and resin series, also an important branch of trade to Europe and America, we find the gums arabic, olibanum, ammoniacum, assafœtida, benjamin, gamboge, mastic, and shellac.

In dyes our eastern possessions are equally rich. Prominent amongst these is indigo, one of the most valuable dyeing substances known to us. Lac-dye, used for dyeing a fine scarlet, safflower, turmeric, madder, chaya-root, and annotto, are all freely exported to Europe and elsewhere, as well as some barks for tanning purposes. There are, however, many other dyes in use among the natives, which, although unknown to Europeans, might be found of some value.

Caoutchouc, or india-rubber, has long been an article of export to this country. Kattemandoo is a vegetable substance partaking somewhat of the joint natures of india-rubber and gutta-percha; it has only recently been brought to England, and will at no distant date form a valuable item of export.

Of starches India boasts of several kinds. Some of its arrowroot is pronounced by competent judges to be equal to the best Bermuda. The Cassava starch, sago, and sago-meal, are also amongst the useful products of the south of India.

If the seeds and seed-oils to be found in India are not as important as many other of its products, they are nevertheless most useful as articles of commerce. Linseed and rapeseed are shipped in considerable quantities, as well as their oils, and the oil from the ground-nut and cocoa-nut. The two latter are chiefly produced on the east and west coasts of the peninsula. Sesamum-seed is likewise brought to Europe for crushing; and the seed of the cotton plant is not only extensively employed in feeding cattle, but a very useful burning oil is extracted from it. Besides the above, the natives produce a great variety of other oils for burning, cooking, or anointing, unknown out of

India. Of these may be enumerated cadju-apple oil, poonga oil, oil of kossumba, poppy oil, poonseed oil, simboolie oil, karrunj oil, and many others.

There are also several varieties of vegetable butters and tallows expressed from seeds and plants, and employed in cooking or in lamps.

The spices for which Hindostan is known are cinnamon of second-rate quality, from the northern parts of Bengal; cassia, from the Malabar coast, where also are grown ginger, pepper, and cloves; cardamums are found generally in the peninsula, as are red and green capsicums.

Tobacco, although grown to considerable extent in various parts of India, is nevertheless of very inferior quality; that from Trichinopoly and Madras being coarse and acrid. The best is probably to be found growing on the banks of the Mahamuddy and the Godavery.

The great staple of India, rice, is produced in every variety of soil, at every altitude and in every latitude. To name a tithe of these would prove a tedious and useless task, for they vary with every district in which they grow. The finest of these, which is the Bengal table rice, is inferior to the Carolina kind, whilst the great bulk of them would be unmarketable in Europe, from their poverty of body and the slovenly manner in which they are prepared. The Arracan rice is a greyish opaque grain, used in England only for manufacturing starch. Copious irrigation is required for all these varieties; the Himalayan and other hill rices alone requiring no such aid, their elevation, at times as much as 6000 feet, securing them from the great heat to which the other varieties are exposed.

Maize is freely cultivated, but very far from equal to the American variety. A number of millets and other fine grains are also reared in districts where irrigation for rice-culture is not obtainable, or where the ryots are too poor to obtain rice-seed, which, indeed, is the case in many of the more remote districts. The grains most commonly employed for food in place of rice are called Jowár, Bájra, and Rági.

In some of the northern provinces wheat is cultivated for local consumption; whilst, on the other hand, in the south, whole districts subsist upon roots and inferior vegetables, with small portions of rice or some kind of pulse.

In few natural products is India more prolific than in its fruits. The pine-apple, mango, mangosteen, jambo, tamarind, &c., are amongst the best known, besides an infinite variety of smaller fruits partaken by the natives, either dried or in their curries. To the north, and in the hill-districts, peaches, grapes, figs, &c., are both abundant and of good quality. In the south and central parts of Hindostan the fruits and vegetables in general use amongst the people are melons, gourds, cucumbers, water-melons, plantains, guavas, jugubes, custard-apples, and figs. In some of the hill-districts the wild raspberry and a species of gooseberry are found in great abundance and of good quality.

Those who would study the Flora of Hindostan and the Himalayas will do well to consult the able and interesting works of Roxburgh, Wight, Wallich, &c., on this subject. It will suffice to mention in this place, that India, both in its plains and its lofty table-lands, possesses some of the choicest flowers in the world, many of them very little known to Europeans, and possessing perfumes far more powerful than any in more temperate climates. The oleander, the Persian rose, the gloriosa superba, the passion-flower, and many other exquisite plants of great beauty and fragrance, are found wild in the jungles. The lotus, the water-lily, and other similar plants, add beauty to every sheet of water; whilst far up on the Neilgherries and the Himalayas we find the rhododendron attaining a size and beauty unknown in the West. The Indian ferns are also remarkable for their great size and exquisite structure.

In few countries are wild animals met with in greater abundance or of more varied types than in British India.

The elephant has from the earliest period been highly esteemed for his great utility to man, when caught and broken into harness or to carry loads upon his back. These animals exist wild in great numbers through many parts of India, and whilst in that state commit great injury to crops on the ground. When tamed, they are the most useful of animals except the horse, and prove invaluable to an army for the transport of its heavy baggage.

The camel is scarcely less valuable; for, though inferior in strength to the elephant, it is far swifter. For mountain work it is even more useful; and the camel-batteries and camel-expresses, so frequently employed in our last wars in the north-west, prove the great value of this animal.

In the forests are to be found rhinoceroses, buffaloes, bears, lions, wolves, foxes, antelopes, deer, wild boars, &c. The smaller jungles and low underwood are the haunts of tigers, jackals, leopards, and panthers; whilst monkeys and apes abound on every side. The jackal, although occasionally a troublesome frequenter of poultry-houses, is nevertheless of great service in removing carrion from the crowded streets of all large towns and cities, which he does during the night-time.

The wild goat of Nepaul, although frequenting the highest peaks of the mountain-ranges, is nevertheless capable of being domesticated in the warm plains of the low country. It is remarkably well-shaped, with light graceful limbs and fine expressive head. Its colour is slaty grey, mixed with rusty brown and black.

CASHMERE GOAT.

In the same country is to be found a small red deer, the flesh of which is highly esteemed.

Perhaps the most highly prized of any animal in the East is the goat of Cashmere, with the long silky hair of which are worked the world-famed Cashmere shawls. They thrive best on the grassy slopes of the Cashmere hills, but are also reared with success in Lahore and still further to the south.

COBRA CAPELLA.

The boa, the rattlesnake, the cobra capella, the tic-polonga, and many other varieties of snakes, are in great abundance. Porcupines, armadilloes, ichneumons, guanas, and lizards exist in vast numbers.

The birds of India are scarcely less beautiful than numerous. Perhaps the choicest of them all are those of the Himalayan pheasant tribe, birds distinguished for their very graceful and rich plumage. The Himalayan bustard is another bird remarkable for its form and varied colour. Peacocks, eagles, falcons, vultures, kites, cranes, wild geese, wild fowl, snipes, bustards, parrots, and parroquets, the latter in every conceivable variety, abound in all parts at various seasons.

HIMALAYAN BUSTARD.

Crows, and a bird called the adjutant, are to be seen in all large towns in thousands, and prove very serviceable in removing offal of every description from the streets: they are the best, and indeed the only scavengers known in India, and no one ever attempts to kill these birds.

The laughing crow is met with in great numbers in the vicinity of the forests of Hurdwar and Sireenagur, feeding on the wild fruits of the jungle. These birds are usually seen in flocks of fifty or a hundred, making a noise resembling loud laughter. The plumage of the back

LAUGHING CROW.

wings and side is olive-brown; on the tail the brown is that of amber. The head is ornamented with a crest of rounded feathers. A black line passes from the beak across the eyes to the ear-covers, and excepting this the whole of the head is white, as are also the throat and breast.[5]

Amongst the insects, the locust is of common occurrence, frequently visiting particular districts in such clouds as to darken the air. The natives fry these creatures in oil, and eat them with considerable relish. The leaf-insect, which in shape and colour bears so close a resemblance to a number of leaves as to render it impossible to detect them on

[5] Gould's Birds of Hindostan, plate xviii.

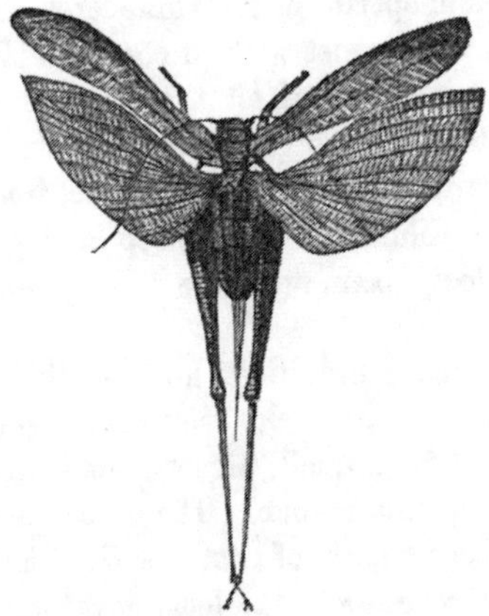

THE LOCUST.

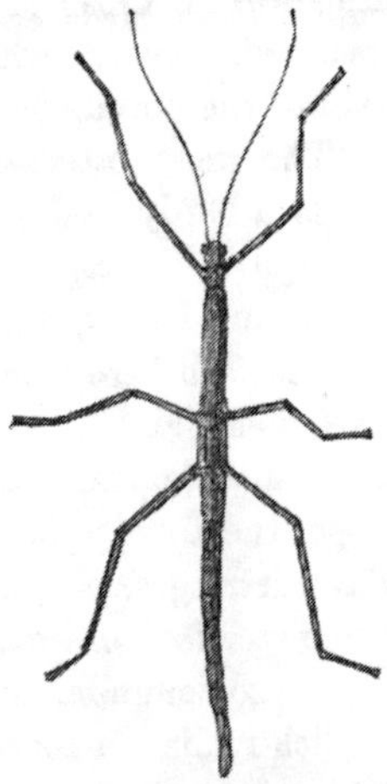

BAMBOO INSECT.

plants; the stick-insect, which in like manner wears all the appearance of a heap of dried sticks; and the bamboo-insect, shaped precisely as a small piece of bamboo, are all perfectly harmless; whilst the myriads of centipedes, scorpions, ants, musquitoes, and other creatures, prove extremely obnoxious to Europeans, more especially to new-comers.

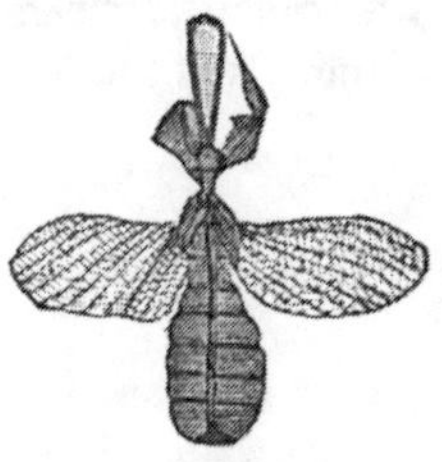

LEAF INSECT.

The rivers and bays of India abound with various descriptions of fish, some of which have been long known to and much esteemed by Europeans. A far greater number, however, although said to be excellent eating by the natives, have never been met with on an English table. The objection to many of these latter consists in the great number of small bones contained in them; in spite, however, of this, the natives use them in a variety of ways, either as curries or stews.

Amongst those known to Europeans are the mango-fish, a great favourite in Calcutta during the mango season, the Indian mullet, the sable-fish, the whiting, a species of perch of great size, the kowall, the rowball, the inkle-fish, the nattoo, the mountain mullet, a species of sole, several kinds of herring, the white and black pomfret, and a very excellent salmon. Most of them are salt-water fish.

The animals of the Tenasserim and Peguan provinces differ in few particulars from those of Hindostan proper. Elephants, tigers, bears, and panthers abound; whilst several species of the rhinoceros, the hare, the rabbit, the porcupine, are also to be met with in considerable numbers. The most interesting and valuable of all the animals of this region is a hardy and swift-footed pony, highly esteemed throughout all parts of India, especially for mountain journeys, where, from their being so sure-footed, they are invaluable. The sheep and goat are rarely met with here; but buffaloes, oxen, and several varieties of the deer are plentiful.

In ornithological specimens these provinces are peculiarly rich; amongst them may be instanced a peacock of surpassing beauty, besides partridges, pheasants, wild fowl, quail, pigeons, and an abundance of water-fowl of great delicacy and flavour. The edible-nest swallows are also common, and furnish a supply of nests for the China market, which realises a considerable revenue to the local government.

There is nothing to remark in the fishes of Pegu, similar as they are in every respect to those of the Bay of Bengal. The only exceptions which claim our notice are the climbing-perch, which makes its way inland to some distance, and a barbel of extraordinary beauty, whose scales, when fresh from the water, glisten in the sunshine like diamonds of the first quality.

PART I.

HISTORICAL.

THE HINDOO PERIOD.

CHAPTER I.

THE ERA OF FABLE AND THE EARLY HINDOO DYNASTIES.

THE early history of India, like that of many other countries, presents little else than a confused series of mythological tales, full of absurd recitals and chronological inconsistencies. To place any credit in the writings of the first Hindoo chroniclers, would be to carry the history of their country to a date long anterior to the creation of the world. The exploits of Rama, one of their favourite heroes, are stated by them to have taken place a million of years since; whilst one of their records claims an antiquity of double that extent. The labours of such oriental scholars as Colebrooke, Jones, Wilson, Prinsep, &c. have done little more for Hindoo history than point out the utter worthlessness of its earliest records. The most that can be made of that period is a tolerably accurate guess as to the probable dates of such events as need not be put down as altogether fabulous. From the time of Alexander's invasion of India we are enabled to arrive at something more like certainty with regard to Indian events and Hindoo sovereigns; but until Hindostan became known to and finally conquered by the Mahometan race, there was at best a most uncertain and irregular chain of records, from which the modern compiler of history can glean but vague and unreliable details.

Of late years the labours of Mr. Prinsep have brought to light the means of deciphering many ancient inscriptions upon columns and on the walls of rock-cut temples, which had hitherto defied the investigations of the learned. These prove to have been in the Pali dialect, and when read by the aid of Mr. Prinsep's key, were found to throw considerable light upon some portion of Hindoo history, and eventually to enable the discoverer to fix something like a date of certainty to the reigns of monarchs which had previously been but ill defined.

Of the great antiquity of the Hindoos there can be no doubt. Whilst Joseph was ruling under Pharaoh in Egypt, there were Hindoo princes who possessed considerable territories, and could bring large armies into the field. The "Ramayana," an Indian epic, although undoubtedly replete with fables and exaggerations, cannot but be regarded as shadowing forth, however falsely coloured, certain events and exploits which possessed reality in themselves.

The first mention made of this nation gives as their residence a tract of country between the rivers Sersooty and Caggar, distant from Delhi about one hundred miles north-west. It then bore the name of Bramhaverta, as being the haunt of gods; and although it was but about sixty-five miles long by forty broad, it was the scene of the adventures of the first princes, and the residence of the most famous sages.[1] At no very distant date from the first records, the Hindoos appear to have extended their territory, which then seems to have included the districts of Oude, Agra, Allahabad, Lahore, and Delhi. The city of Oud, or as it was then termed, Ayodha, appears to have been the capital of the kingdom. There were born, as emanations from Brahma, two princes, whose descendants were known as the solar and lunar races. Of these upwards of sixty appear to have lived; but the accounts of their exploits are so fabulous, that no use can be made of them, and we must therefore pass on to Rama, whose deeds, as already mentioned, were chronicled in the "Ramayana."

In this oriental epic we find the most extravagant recitals and supernatural occurrences detailed with the minuteness of facts. The hero is Rama, a king of Oude, who having resolved on a life of penance for a certain period, retired to a secluded forest with his wife Sita, a woman of surpassing beauty and extraordinary accomplishments. During their residence in this solitary spot, Ravana, the king of Ceylon and ruler over a race of demons, chanced to see the beautiful queen, and became so enamoured of her that he carried her away to his capital, Lanka.

Rama, roused to activity by this loss, called to his aid Hanuman, the pretended monarch of a race of supernatural monkeys; and these warriors, with their united followers, are made to march through the Deccan, cross the Pamben Passage by a miraculous bridge, and encountering the wicked but mighty Ravana near his city, totally defeated him and his warrior-demons. Sita was of course released; but the tale

[1] Wilson's preface to Vishnu Purana, p. 67.

ends gloomily, for Rama, having accidentally killed his brother Lachmen, threw himself in his grief into a river, and was re-united to the divinity.

Whatever fable and romance there may be in this great Hindoo poem, it is more than probable that Rama did carry his arms to the south, and with some degree of success; the Ceylon invasion, however, would appear to belong to a more recent period than that named in the "Ramayana." Nothing can be stated of the long line of solar princes who succeeded Rama; and there is good ground for believing that during that after period the seat of government was transferred from Oud to Canouj.

The contents of the "Maha-Barat," which is the second great Indian epic, read far more like history than those of the "Ramayana." It relates to the great war which arose out of the claims of two rival branches of the then reigning family for the district of Hastinapoora, supposed to be a country to the north-east of Delhi, on the Ganges. Into this quarrel most of the neighbouring princes of India seem to have been drawn, and the war appears to have raged with great fury for a long period, carrying with it the partial ruin of some of the most flourishing districts of Hindostan. The victors of the Pandu branch suffered so severely in this violent contest, that for one or two generations they did not recover their former position.

The probable period in which this famous war occurred may be some time in the fourteenth century before the Christian era. Of the race of Pandu kings who filled the throne from this period, we find nothing on record beyond a mere list of their names; and even here the loosely compiled annals of those remote times differ as to whether there were twenty-nine or sixty-four of them.

Dismissing from our minds all that portion of the "Maha-Barat" which deals in marvellous occurrences and extraordinary exploits, we may still glean from its pages much matter of a more solid and reliable tone. There are scattered through it a great number of useful facts bearing upon the position of the several kingdoms and independent states, their social condition, power and influence, which greatly redeem the general character of this Iliad of the East. From it we may learn that there were at least six distinct kingdoms in this part of India. Greek writers speak of as many as one hundred and eighteen; but they probably intended to have written tribes, and not independent states.

Besides the kingdom of Hastinapoora, we find one very powerful monarchy mentioned—the sovereignty of Magada. The king of this country at the period of the great war was Sahadeva; and from that time until A.D. 436, we find a long line of kings chronicled in one unbroken succession. It was in this state that Sakya or Gotama Buddha, the founder of the Buddhist religion, was born, somewhere about B.C. 550, during the reign of Ajata Satru, the thirty-fifth sovereign from Sahadeva. It is the ancient language of this country, Magadi or Pali, which has ever since been employed in the sacred writings of this widely spread religion.

Following this race of monarchs, we find that the fourteenth of the line was murdered by Chandragupta, who was of the Sudras, a low caste. It has been successfully shewn by Sir W. Jones and Mr. Prinsep, that this king is the Sandracottus, or Sandracoptus, of the Greek historians, whom they represent as having concluded a treaty with Seleucus, one of Alexander's successors, about the year 310 B.C.

The third king after Chandragupta, named Asoca, appears to have been the first who really had any claim to the title previously bestowed on many others, that of lord paramount or emperor of India. The mastery obtained by the indefatigable Prinsep over the old Pali inscriptions scattered throughout so many remote parts of India, has amongst other points satisfactorily established this one regarding the rule of Asoca, that his dominion extended from far northward of Delhi, even southward to Taprobane or Ceylon, and embraced a wide extent of country east and west. It appears from the same inscription that his government partook of a highly civilised nature, more advanced than might have been expected; for many of those ancient writings appear to be edicts for the establishment of hospitals and dispensaries in distant parts of his empire, and also for the sinking wells and planting shady trees along the public highways for the benefit of travellers.[2]

The Magada kingdom appears to have gradually lost its ascendency, until, in the fifth century of our era, we find it brought under subjection to the kings of Canouj, and its territories no longer recognised as a separate state.

The kingdom of Bengal, although at various periods attaining to a considerable degree of power, if we may judge from inscriptions on copper and stone, cannot be awarded the supremacy in India which has been claimed for it by several Hindoo writers. We can lay our hands upon very little reliable data as to the actual position of this state, though the lists of four distinct dynasties are preserved to this day, and may be tolerably correct. The last of the Hindoo dynasties,

[2] Elphinstone's India, vol. i. p. 393.

whose names ended in Sena, was subverted by the Mahometan invaders about A.D. 1203.

Gujerat appears to have had an independent existence at an early date, though we are without any reliable particulars. In the middle of the second century of our era, it seems beyond a doubt that a government existed at Balibi, under a Rajpoot race of rulers. In A.D. 524 these princes were expelled by an incursion of Indo-Bactrians from the north, but again held the reins of power in A.D. 531.

In the eighth century the Balibi rulers appear to have been succeeded by the Chauras, another tribe of Rajpoots, who eventually removed their capital to Anhalwara, now Patan, and in after years attained to considerable power amongst the native states. This race became extinct in A.D. 931, when the Rajpoot tribe of Salonka succeeded it, and remained on the throne until early in the thirteenth century, when they in their turn were followed by a dynasty who ruled until the conquest of the country by the Mahometans in A.D. 1297.[3]

Of the kingdom of Canouj, our information is far from perfect, though such as has reached us, aided by the deciphering of various inscriptions, leads to the belief that this was not only one of the most ancient, but equalled any other state in its extent and importance. The splendid ruins of the capital of Canouj, to be seen at the present day on the banks of the Ganges, attest the wealth and magnificence of this people in their palmy days.

This state bore in remote times the name of Panchala. It extended from the Banar and Chambol in Ajmir eastwards as far as Nepal, which it included. The princes of Canouj appear at various times to have carried their arms into the states of Bengal and Orissa on the east, and as far northward as the Indus. Little is known of them except what we gather from the Rajpoot writings and traditions, that the original race was subverted by a Hindoo dynasty, who subsequently succumbed before a Rajpoot tribe, who continued to govern Canouj until its final conquest in A.D. 1193 by the Mahometans.

Cashmere may undoubtedly claim equal antiquity with any of the preceding, though it may well be questioned if the dates assumed by the local histories be correct. According to the Cashmerian annals, that country was an independent state 2600 years B.C. There is a very imperfect list of the monarchs of Cashmere, with a most meagre summary of events. After the succession of five distinct dynasties, the government was seized upon by Mahmoud, of Ghazni, in A.D. 1015.

3 Briggs' Ferishta.

Scinde appears, beyond a doubt, to have been a distinct kingdom at the period of the "Maha-Barat," though when Alexander invaded India it was evidently divided into some petty states, all, however, independent. Early in the seventh century it was again united under one government. During the early part of the next century it was invaded by the Arab tribes, but subsequently retaken by the Rajpoot tribe of Samera, A.D. 750, and eventually fell before the rulers of the Ghorian dynasty in A.D. 1015.

The earliest mention made of the kingdom of Malwa appears to be about fifty years previous to the death of Buddha. This state must at one period have been in a highly flourishing condition, and to one of its rulers, Vicramaditya, is attributed almost universal sway over India. Certainly he extended his possessions far beyond the ordinary limits of the country, through the centre and west of India. We have little more than a long list of princely names in the "Ayeni Akberi" in connection with this state, though one of its early rulers, Rajah Bhoja, would appear, by traditional records, to have acquired a more than common reputation. It lost its independence about the year 1231 of our era, when the Mahometan arms swept over the whole of India.

Of the remaining states or principalities we can say little more than that they comprised Gour, Mithili, Benares, Mewar, Jesselmere, and Jeipoor; the three last of which still continue to exist as independent states.

Leaving Hindostan, and its fragmentary histories, we turn southwards, and find that the Deccan, if it be less involved in obscurity, is at the same time of far more modern date, and even less interesting in its details.

There seems to be little doubt but that at one period this part of India was peopled by others than Hindoos. The aborigines are said to have been foresters and mountaineers, leading a wild and lawless life. But this must have been at a very remote period, for there is abundance of proof that an advanced state of civilisation prevailed previous to the time of the Greek notices of India.

Through this tract there are not less than five dialects spoken: the Tamil, the Telugu, the Mahratta, the Canarese, and the Urya. The Tamil tongue prevails over the whole district to the south of Madras, on both sides of the peninsula.

Of all these southern states, that of Pandya is the most ancient, together with the neighbouring kingdom of Chola. They were both founded by men of low origin; and although for some generations they made frequent and destructive wars upon each other, there seems to have been at a later period a long and cordial understanding between them. Pandya extended not farther than the present districts of Tinnevelly and Madura, its capital being the town of the latter name.

The kingdom of Chola extended over a wider range of country than the preceding,—from Madura to Nandidroog, and at one time over a portion of Carnata. The twelfth century, however, saw this state much humbled, and losing some part of its independence, until a Mahratta chief being called in to aid the reigning rajah in some troubles, deposed him and assumed the sovereign power, thus founding the family of Tanjore. The capital of this state was generally Conjeveram, west of Madras.

The state of Chera, which we find mentioned by Ptolemy, comprehended Travancore, Coimbatore, part of Malabar, with some portion of Carnata. It does not appear to have risen to any consequence, and in the tenth century was over-run by the troops of the neighbouring kings, and partitioned amongst them.

Kerala included within its original boundaries Canara and Malabar; but about the commencement of our era these two districts appear to have become separated; the former remained independent until far into the twelfth century, when it became a tributary of one of the neighbouring states. The Malabar country seems to have been broken up into a number of petty states, one of which was that of the Zamorins, whose capital was Calicut, and where they were found by Vasco di Gama in the fifteenth century.[4]

The kingdom of Orissa, although during a long period in a highly flourishing condition, has left little to tell its history beyond the most absurd recitals of native writers up to A.D. 473, when a more intelligible narrative takes up the thread of events. We hear of it in the "Maha Barat," and afterwards in connection with the names of Salivahana and Vicramaditya, who appear to have occupied the country. From A.D. 473 to A.D. 1131, the government was administered by rajahs of the Kesari race, under whom many petty wars were entered upon, until a prince of the house of Ganga Vansa seized upon the throne, whose successors were afterwards supplanted by a Rajpoot family of the race of the sun. This dynasty was, about the middle of the sixteenth century, expelled by a Telinga chief, and thirty years later Akber annexed the country to the empire.[5]

Powerful as the Mahrattas became in more modern times, and ex-

[4] Elphinstone's India, vol. i. p. 415. [5] Asiatic Researches, vol. xv.

tensively though their language be spoken, we find far less of them in historical records than of any other race or country. Indeed, until the Mahometan writers mentioned them, there was nothing to mark their existence beyond some inscriptions which allude to their capital, Tagara, as a place of considerable commercial importance, though its site has been long since lost. This place is also mentioned by Arrian as a great emporium of the Deccan country, though with a very vague allusion to its position.

A race of kings of Rajpoot descent ruled over Maharashtra, as this country was called until the twelfth century, when a family of Yadus supplanted them.[6] Towards the end of the following century a Mahometan invasion took place, and after the reigning rajah had for some length of time been tributary to the Emperor of Delhi, the government was finally subverted by that power about A.D. 1317. How this people at a later period rose to great military power, and proved one of the most formidable opponents to and chief destroyers of the Tartar empire, will be seen in succeeding chapters.

It may be sufficient to notice the Chalukya rajahs of Rajpoot descent as having ruled over a tract of country bordering on Carnata and Maharashtra. Another line of these chiefs governed Calinga, extending from Orissa to Dravira. Their rule appears to have lasted from the tenth to the twelfth centuries, at which latter period it yielded to the supremacy of the kings of Andra, and subsequently to the rajahs of Cattac.[7]

The Andra kings reigned over a tract of country to the north-east of Hydrabad early in the Christian era. We possess little information concerning them, though it is certain that towards the end of the thirteenth century they had risen to some importance and power, and had extended their limits on the south. In A.D. 1332 the country was overrun by an imperial army, afterwards by the kings of Orissa, and finally became annexed to the kingdom of Golconda.

Before closing this sketch of the early history of Hindostan and the Deccan, it may be well to glance at the view taken of India by the Greek writers shortly after that country became opened to the western nations.

Alexander himself evidently did no more than touch upon the very outskirts of India. Having checked the advance of his army on the banks of the Hyphasis, when the eastern world had but just been glanced at, he bent his steps towards the south-west, and passed on-

[6] Wilson's Preface to the Mackenzie Papers.
[7] Elphinstone's India, vol. i. p. 417.

wards between the desert and the Indus, leaving some few garrisons behind him, and one or two kings and chiefs allied to his government.

A perusal of the writings of Ptolemy, Arrian, Aristobulus, and others of the early historians, cannot fail to impress us with a favourable opinion of their general accuracy, if we consider how limited the extent of their knowledge must have been, and under what disadvantages they must have written. We shall find that they represent the position and habits of the people, the state and form of internal government, the religion and literature of the Hindoos, precisely as we have in later days found them to be; and so far from expressing surprise at any erroneous statements they may have advanced, we should rather wonder that their mistakes have been so few.

Of the division of society into distinct castes, the Greeks were perfectly aware, though they have added to the number of classes through some misconception. They appear to have been much struck with the absence of slavery in India; for the servile state of the Sudra caste would hardly have attracted the notice of men accustomed to the domestic slavery of Greece and Rome.

The subdivision of Hindostan into a great number of kingdoms and petty states and principalities did not escape the attention of the Greeks, who, however, greatly overstated their number, calculating them at upwards of one hundred.

The forces which the Indian kings were capable of bringing into the field in those days were doubtless overcharged, but their composition and arrangement are truly enough described.

Their account of the revenues of the country, and the sources whence derived, quite agree with our own knowledge of those matters. In the minute descriptions given of the assessment of lands and crops, of the irrigation and culture of the soil, of the duties of the various functionaries of the revenue department, of the natural products of the earth, of the articles forming the commerce of the country, —on all these points they relate that which might equally be written at the present time.

We find the public festivals and royal shows[8] of the Hindoos described as they are known to have taken place in much more recent times. And not less precise and accurate are the early writers in their account of the dress, the domestic manners, and social habits of the various classes[9] composing an Indian community. In speaking of the personal appearance of the Hindoos, both Arrian and Strabo notice the difference between the inhabitants of the north and the south country.

[8] Strabo, lib. xv. p. 493.

[9] Arrian's Indica, cap. xvi.

The southern Indians they describe as swarthy, tall, and handsome, not unlike Ethiopians in some respects; whilst the denizens of the northern latitudes are said to be much fairer, and not unlike the Egyptians.

The weapons employed by the Indian soldiers were, excepting fire-arms, precisely such as are in use at the present day. The valour of the Hindoos is always highly spoken of, and they are described as being far more formidable enemies than any the Greeks had previously encountered in the East.

That the country was in the days of Alexander in a highly flourishing condition there can be but little doubt, even if we make some allowance for exaggeration. There were said to have been 1500 cities, thickly peopled, between two of the rivers of the Punjab; and one city is described as being 8 miles long, and 1½ mile broad, surrounded by ditches and ramparts, with 64 gates and 570 towers.

CHAPTER II.

THE ARAB AND TARTAR INVASIONS, AND THE FINAL SETTLEMENT OF THE MAHOMMEDANS IN INDIA.

A.D. 664-1022.

THE earliest appearance of the Arab armies of the west on the confines of the Indian territories was in the year 664, during an expedition of this people into the Afghan country, when, having penetrated as far as Cabul,[1] and made its ruler a tributary prince, a portion of their army under Mohalib, a celebrated Moslem commander, pushed on as far as Mooltan, sacked the city and carried away numerous prisoners. Although the Arabs made several fresh inroads into the Afghan territories, at subsequent dates, it does not appear that the country eastward of that land possessed any attraction for them, since no further mention is made of any inroads by this people across the northern waters of the Indus.

We hear, however, of numerous incursions by Arabs into the Scinde country as early as the reign of the Calif Omar; but these would appear to have been chiefly of a piratical character, with no other aim than plunder. The seizure of one of these marauders' vessels, at a subsequent date, in one of the sea-ports of Scinde, led to the invasion of the country by a numerous army under Mohammed Casim, the younger son of Hejaj, the governor of Basra. This juvenile warrior met with the most complete success, capturing the fortified city of Dewal,[2] overthrowing the son of the Rajah of Scinde, and spreading terror and carnage as far as the capital itself. Here the Rajah Daher interposed with a powerful army of fifty thousand men, and a numerous troop of elephants. Small as was the force of the Arab general, he had no alternative but to fight; and availing himself of a strong position, he waited within it for the attack of the Hindoos. The great advantage possessed by the troops of Scinde proved of little avail; for at an early period of

1 Briggs' Ferishta, vol. i. p. 4.
2 Believed to have been on the site of the modern Kurrachee.

THE RAJAH ON HIS STATE ELEPHANT.

the engagement, the rajah's elephant having been wounded by a fire-ball, rushed from the field of battle, smarting with pain, and plunged into the water of the neighbouring river. This untoward circumstance struck dismay into the Hindoo soldiers, who, dispirited at the absence of their royal master, began to give way; and although the rajah soon re-appeared, mounted on his war-charger, the fortune of the day had been already decided. Finding all his efforts unavailing, Daher determined not to survive the disgrace of a defeat, and rushing with a chosen few amongst the thickest of the Arab horse, fell covered with wounds.

It was in vain that his widow, with more than woman's courage and all a woman's hope, endeavoured to rally his broken forces. She, however, placed the chief city, Brahmanabad, in a posture of defence, holding it against the victors for some time; and when at last all hope had fled, the women and children of her adherents perished in a huge funeral pile; and the small Rajpoot garrison, flinging wide the gates, rushed out, and met their deaths upon the Arab weapons. Such as remained within the walls were slaughtered without mercy, and the younger members of their families carried away into captivity.[3]

Casim, it appears, met with but little opposition from this time, and found sufficient leisure to settle the administrative affairs of the newly conquered territory, which he arranged on a just and politic foundation, appointing many of the old Hindoo governors who had held office under the late rajah to similar posts, on the plea that they were best qualified to maintain the established institutions of the country.

Having arranged much of the internal affairs of the country, Casim directed his attention farther eastward; and, bent upon the acquisition of fresh territory, commenced a march towards the celebrated city of Canouj, on the Ganges. He had marched as far as Oudipur, when an unlooked-for catastrophe cut short at once his plan of conquest and his career. Amongst the captives carried away from Scinde were the two daughters of Rajah Darhe; these, on account of their high lineage and great beauty, were destined for the harem of the Commander of the Faithful. Arrived at the court of the Calif, they were presented in due form to the sovereign, who had been curious to witness the charms of the elder of them, who was indeed surpassingly beautiful. On being conducted to his presence, she burst into a flood of tears, and exclaimed that, having been dishonoured by Casim in her own country, she felt that she was not worthy to appear before the commander of the faithful. The calif, incensed at this outrage, which thus became an insult to himself, and smitten moreover by her beauty, ordered that the offending general should be sewed up in a raw hide and dispatched in that state to Damascus. This order was of course carried into effect; and the body of the late conqueror of Scinde having arrived at the palace, it was laid before the princess, who, unable to contain her delight at the sight of it, declared to the astonished calif that Casim was indeed innocent of the charge imputed to him, but that he had brought ruin and death upon her family, and she was now avenged.[4]

From this time the Arab arms appear to have made no progress. All ideas of further conquest seem to have died with Casim, whose authority was handed over to less ambitious commanders. The rule of the Musselmen in Scinde continued until about A.D. *750*, when the Rajpoots uniting their forces with the Hindoos made a desperate effort

[3] *Briggs' Ferishta, vol. iv. p. 409.*

[4] Ayeen Akberry, vol. ii. *Briggs' Ferishta, vol. iv.*

to expel the foreigners from their country, in which, after some severe struggles, they eventually succeeded.

The declension of the Arab sway may be said to have commenced at this time; certainly the empire of the califs at no later period extended over so large an extent of country. The death of the famed Haroun-al-Raschid was not long afterwards followed by the secession of Khorassan and Transoxana. By degrees other provinces fell away from the califate; and at no distant date the commanders of the faithful were reduced to puppets in the hands of their Turkish guards, and the dissolution of their empire was sealed.[5]

Amongst the many petty dynasties of mixed Turkish and Mogul descent, which now swept over the northern provinces of the Arab possessions, were the Samanis, a family of Bokhara descent, who, having firmly established themselves in Khorassan, ruled over that country for upwards of a century. It was during their sway that the first member of the house of Ghazni, afterwards the founders of the Mahometan empire in India, assumed an importance which his descendants turned to good account. Alptegin, the founder of this new dynasty, was a Turkish slave in the service of Abdulmelek, fifth prince of the house of Samani, and in that capacity performed the most menial offices. Finding that this slave possessed not only great personal courage, but many natural good qualities, his royal master, as was then a frequent practice, promoted him to some important posts, and eventually made him governor of Khorassan.

Alptegin held this command until the death of his patron, when, having given offence to his successor, he was forced to seek safety in flight; accompanied by a faithful band of adherents, he took refuge amongst the hill tribes around Ghazni, in the very heart of the mountains of Soliman, where he bid defiance to his enemies, and secured himself in the sovereignty of that part of the country. The hill tribes of the vicinity were nothing loath to receive amongst them one who was both able and willing to enlist their swords in his service, and provide them with pay; and such as did not directly submit to his sway remained in friendly relation with him. During a period of fourteen years he appears to have maintained his position in the Ghaznivide country, supported by a numerous and well-appointed army, chiefly made up of Mameluk horsemen and Afghan freebooters.

His death, which occurred in the year 976, placed on his mountain-throne one who like himself had been a slave. Sibektegin had served Alptegin with fidelity from the day that he had purchased him from a

[5] Price, vol. iv., quoted by Elphinstone, vol. i. p. 521.

merchant travelling eastward from Turkistan, his native country; and having proved his faithfulness and ability, he promoted him to the highest office next to himself. Whether he was named by the dying ruler as his successor, wanting heirs, does not appear certain, but the accession of Sibektegin to his master's power, under the circumstances, was the most natural occurrence. He is said, likewise, to have married a daughter of his late chief, and thus to have strengthened his hold on the popular feeling of the hill tribes of Ghazni.[6]

Events were now about to occur which speedily called forth the activity and courage of the new ruler. The Hindoo rajahs of the country east of the Indus viewed with considerable apprehension the establishment of this Mahometan power so contiguous to their own country; and aware of the passion for aggrandisement manifested on every fitting occasion by this race, prepared to adopt aggressive measures, with a view of ridding their neighbourhood of such a dangerous rival. Acting on these feelings, Jeipal, rajah of Lahore, prepared a large army, marched across the Indus, and approached the hilly regions of Ghazni, when he was encountered by Sibektegin. A fierce storm of wind, rain, and thunder so damped the energy of the Hindoo troops, unaccustomed to the severe cold of these climates, that Jeipal found himself under the necessity of coming to terms with his adversary, and agreed, as the price of peace and safety, to pay fifty elephants and a large sum of money. The elephants were surrendered on the spot, and the two armies separated, the Hindoos retracing their steps to their own country.

Once safely within his own territories, Jeipal forgot his former danger and fears, and refused to complete his engagement by withholding the money-payments agreed upon. The Tartar chief was not likely to submit to this insult, and placing himself at the head of a numerous force of Turki and Afghan horse, marched rapidly towards the Indus. Jeipal was prepared for the coming storm; he strengthened himself with the powerful assistance of the rajahs of Delhi, Ajmir, Calingar, and Canouj, and soon found himself at the

[6] "A story is told of Sibektegin while yet a private soldier, which proves the humanity of the historian, if not of the hero. One day, in hunting, he succeeded in riding down a fawn; but when he was carrying off his prize in triumph, he observed the dam following his horse, and shewing such evident marks of distress, that he was touched with compassion, and at last released his captive, pleasing himself with the gratitude of the mother, which often turned back to gaze at him as she went off to the forest with her fawn. That night the Prophet appeared to him in a dream, told him that God had given him a kingdom as a reward for his humanity, and enjoined him not to forget his feelings of mercy when he came to the exercise of power."—*Elphinstone*, vol. i. p. 526.

head of a hundred thousand cavalry and a vast number of foot-soldiers. Sibektegin did not muster a fourth part of this number; but nothing daunted by the numerical strength of his adversaries, he relied on the superior strength and discipline of his chosen horsemen.

Events proved the soundness of his judgment. The enormous masses of Hindoo troops were unequal to the shock of his Mameluk and Afghan charges, and once having succeeded in breaking their lines, he found little difficulty in completing their disorder and final overthrow. Jeipal's huge army fled in the utmost disorder, and were closely pursued by Sibektegin as far as the Indus, up to which point he at once established his authority, and left a governor with a numerous body of horse in command of the country about Peshawur.

How far Sibektegin might have pushed his conquests cannot be known, since he was required in another quarter to aid his neighbours and former masters, the Samanis, in repelling attacks from some turbulent chiefs of Bokhara. These refractory tribes were with difficulty reduced to submission; and the ruler of Bokhara, to reward the services of Sibektegin and his son Mahmoud, conferred on the latter the government of Khorassan, and recognised the father in all his present possessions as far as the Indus. Matters having been thus settled in the west, Sibektegin prepared to return to his government, but on his way thither was seized with illness and died.

No sooner did Mahmoud find himself firmly established on the throne, and invested with the new title of sultan, than his restless and ambitious spirit, long nurtured by the military exploits and bold daring of his father, sought for some field on which to establish a new and dazzling reputation.

It is scarcely matter for surprise, that the world-wide reputation of India for wealth should have led the young sultan of a semi-barbarous nation to turn his eyes in that direction. Added to this, it may fairly be presumed that Mahmoud was not altogether unmindful of the glory he would acquire by extending the Moslem faith on the wreck of Hindoo idolatry.

In the year of the Christian era 1001, Mahmoud crossed the Indus with an army whose chief strength lay in its horse, for even at that period the Afghan cavalry were nearly always irresistible in open warfare. Defeating the rajah of Lahore at Peshawur, and carrying off a vast quantity of treasure, the sultan returned to Ghazni for a season.

Three other expeditions into the Indian territories followed at various intervals, in the last of which the conqueror secured treasure and precious stones, to an amount previously unheard of, from the sacred shrine in the fortress of Nargacot at the foot of the Himalayas. To celebrate this achievement, Mahmoud gave a triumphal feast, which lasted many days, during which the rich spoils of the war were exposed to public gaze upon tables of pure gold, amidst the sound of martial music.

Victories but served to stimulate this warrior-king to fresh achievements; and the glory and treasures which would have proved to many inducements to after-repose, only whetted the royal blade of the Ghaznivide sultan for new and mightier strokes of conquest. The Nargacot exploit was followed after a year or two by the reduction of the Ghor country, the capture of Mooltan, an expedition to Tareesa near the Jumna, and two attacks upon the Cashmerian provinces.

In the year 1017 Mahmoud took the boldest step eastward that had been made by any foreigner within the Indus. The victories he had already acquired, seemingly with so much ease, over the Hindoo rajahs on the north-west frontiers, emboldened him to attempt something on a more enlarged scale. Accordingly, we find him assembling an army of 100,000 horse and 20,000 foot at Peshawur, with which he crossed the river, and taking his course due east as far as the Jumna, he turned southwards, and arrived at the gates of Canouj before the rajah had received notice of his approach. After destroying many temples and razing a number of fortresses, Mahmoud returned once more to Ghazni laden with the wealth of India.

It was in the year 1022 that the first permanent settlement of the Moslems east of the Indus took place, by the annexation of the Punjab to the kingdom of Ghazni; and from this event may be dated the rise of the Mahometan power in India. Hitherto all the conquests of Mahmoud had been but of a transitory nature. Renown and plunder appeared to be the leading objects of his expeditions; but in this year, during a march to relieve his ally, the rajah of Canouj, Mahmoud was refused a passage for his troops through the territories of the Lahore rajah. This ill-judged step called down upon the offending Hindoo the vengeance of the Moslem conqueror, who did not quit the country until he had annexed it to his own dominions, and by that act laid the foundation of the Ghaznivide dynasty in India.

THE MAHOMETAN PERIOD.

CHAPTER I.

SULTAN MAHMOUD AND HIS SUCCESSORS OF THE GHAZNIVIDE AND GHORIAN DYNASTIES.

A.D. 1022-1206.

THE reduction of the Lahore territories thus brought the Mahometan conqueror within the limits of India; and having by this stroke made himself permanently master of the whole country as far as the Sutlege, re-inforced his army of occupation, and strengthened the various garrisons in these districts, he felt himself at liberty to undertake further conquests.

Two years later we find him entering upon his twelfth and last expedition in India; but this time not so much on political as on religious grounds. The temple of Somnát, situated at the extreme southern boundary of Gujerat, was famed for its sanctity in the eyes of all good Hindoos. Mahmoud determined to evince the ardour of his zeal for the Prophet, by destroying this high place of heathen worship; and it may not be incorrect if we surmise that the reputed wealth of the Indian shrine had some influence in drawing upon it the warlike notice of the Sultan of Ghazni.

Crossing the desert which separates Scinde from Mooltan, a distance of 350 miles, in perfect safety, the invading army found itself in Ajmir. Meeting with no resistance, the sultan pushed on towards the object of his journey, and soon arrived before Somnát. The Hindoo defenders of their faith in vain offered a gallant resistance; Mahmoud carried all before him, and became master of the gorgeous temple and its vast treasures.

Returning to his capital, the victor appeared for a time disposed to remain in quiet; but fresh opportunities offered themselves, and once more tempted him to take the field. His last exploit was the crowning one of his reign: the conquest of Persia seemed to leave him the most potent prince in the East; and certainly there was no power near to disturb his security. But amidst all this glory the conqueror was cut off; and almost before his victorious army had had time to gather repose from their last exploits, ere their Persian laurels had lost their first bloom, their leader and sultan was taken from amongst them—the founder of the Afghan dynasty in India was no more.

Mahmoud, if not the greatest sovereign the world ever saw—as maintained by most Mahometan writers—was assuredly the most famous of his age. Uniting in his person many brilliant and estimable qualities, he possessed but few of the failings so peculiar to the time in which he lived. To the character of a great general he added that of a liberal encourager of literature and the arts; and although he was not wanting in religious zeal, and lost no opportunity of humbling the power of Hindoo idolatry, he cannot be charged with any acts of cruelty against his heathen adversaries; and it is said that he never took the life of a Hindoo save in battle or during the storming of a fortress. This, it must be remembered, is the character of a prince who lived in an age when imprisonment and murder were ordinary steps in a royal career.

Perhaps his greatest failing, and one which grew with his years, was that of avarice. His Indian conquests helped to fill his treasury to an extent unknown in any previous or future reign. It is reported, that upon his hearing of the great wealth of some contemporary monarch, who had managed to amass as much as seven measures of jewels, he exclaimed with great fervour, "Praise be to God, who has given me a hundred measures."[1]

His love of riches was, however, blended with a spirit of liberality in certain directions. Besides founding a university in his capital, with a museum and library attached, Mahmoud set apart a large yearly sum, amounting to fully 10,000*l.* a year of our money,[2] for the maintenance of a body of professors and students, as well as pensions to learned men. Amongst the literary characters who were attracted to his court by this patronage, was the poet Ferdousi, who composed an epic poem of 60,000 couplets, celebrating the exploits of the Persians previous to the Mahometan conquests, a work which occupied his energies during a period of thirty years, and which has been

[1] Elphinstone, vol. i. p. 572.

[2] Briggs' Ferishta, vol. i. p. 60.

deservedly admired by Europeans not less than by Orientals for its many surpassing beauties. Mahmoud, however, for some cause not quite clear, disappointed the poet in his promised recompense for this noble production; and it is said that Ferdousi died of a broken heart.

Mahmoud was not often wanting in his public duties; and it is related of him, that on one occasion a woman went to him to complain of the death of her son, who had lost his life from robbers in a remote part of some newly-acquired territories. The sultan observed that it was impossible that he could enforce the laws in such a distant corner of his kingdom; the woman replied—"Why, then, do you take countries which you cannot govern, and for the protection of which you must answer in the day of judgment?" Mahmoud felt the justice of the reproof, and at once gave instructions to afford better protection to his distant subjects.[3]

Mohammed, who had been nominated by his deceased father as his successor to the throne of Ghazni, in preference to his brother Masaud, did not reign many weeks. The more warlike and popular character of the latter gained for him the suffrages of the people and the army, who proclaimed him sultan so soon as he made his appearance at the capital from the province of Ispahan.

The military qualities of the new sovereign were very shortly in requisition; for whilst a rebellion broke out in Lahore, the Seljuks, a warlike and powerful tribe of Tartars on the north of the Oxus, threatened his dominions with an invasion on the west. The troubles in his eastern possessions being quelled, Masaud marched against his new enemies, who had in the mean time (A.D. 1034) defeated and killed one of his ablest generals. A campaign of two years on the western frontiers of his dominions ended in a decisive battle near Mero, in which the Seljuks (A.D. 1039) were left complete masters of the field.

The sultan retreated with the shattered remains of his army to Ghazni, where finding disunion and discontent amongst his people and army taking a formidable shape, he determined to retreat beyond the Indus, and seek to recruit his shattered fortunes in his Indian territories. On his way to Lahore discontent took the form of mutiny, which ended in his deposition, and the restoration to power of his brother Mohammed. The immediate result of this was the death of Masaud, by command of Ahmed son of Mohammed, after a turbulent reign of ten years.

The rule of Mohammed was not, however, destined to a long con-

[3] Elphinstone, vol. i. p. 571.

tinuance. The deceased sultan's son, Módúd, took immediate steps to avenge his father's death. Marching from the western frontiers with a small body of troops, he made his way through Ghazni to Lahore; and meeting Mohammed and his son at Fattehabad, he attacked and completely routed their army, making themselves and families prisoners, and eventually put them to death to secure to himself the undisturbed possession of the throne.

The whole attention of the new sultan was for a time directed to the west, where the movements of the Seljuk invaders were becoming daily more alarming. Either from the circumstance of Módúd having espoused a daughter of one of the Seljuk chiefs, or from more important matters engrossing their attention elsewhere, they appear not to have offered any real opposition to his regaining possession of Ghazni, which he did in the year following his accession to power.

Disturbances now occurred in the east (A.D. 1042), caused no doubt by the absence of the new sultan from his Indian territories. The rajah of Delhi made this the occasion of recovering all the cities captured by Masaud on the east of the Sutlege; and elated with his first successes, the Hindoo prince pushed his forces to the very gates of Nargacot, to recover which holy shrine vast crowds of Indian volunteers flocked to his standard. The religious zeal of the Hindoos bore down all opposition, and despite the strong military position of this temple-fortress, the shrine fell once more into the hands of its votaries.

Stimulated still further by this new success, and assured by the absence of the sultan, the rajah called around him the whole Hindoo population of the Punjab, and proceeded at once to deliver the country from the Ghaznivide yoke.

Lahore was shortly after (A.D. 1044) invested by the Indian army, and the garrison, receiving no succour or supplies during a siege of seven months, began to be reduced to great extremities. They must soon have yielded before fatigue and famine, but determined to make a last desperate effort, they sallied so vigorously upon the besiegers as completely to disperse them and raise the siege.

The remainder of Módúd's reign was occupied in keeping within bounds the turbulence of his subjects, the disaffection of his Indian possessions, and the restlessness of his Seljuk neighbours. In the midst of these conflicting occupations Módúd expired after a reign of nine years (A.D. 1049).

The throne was now occupied by the late sultan's brother, Abul Hasan, who, however, after a short rule of two years, gave way to his uncle, Abul Rashid.

This prince was not more fortunate than his predecessor; for before the second year of his reign he was besieged in Ghazni by a revolted chief, captured, and put to death with all his family. The successful rebel enjoyed the fruits of his treason but a month, at the end of which time he was assassinated; and the army sought for some member of the rightful family to occupy the vacant throne.

The choice at length fell upon a young prince, Farokhsád, who had passed many years in prison through the jealousy of previous outlaws. His reign, although it lasted but six years, may be called a prosperous one compared to those preceding it. He managed to curb the restless, aggressive spirit of the Seljuk tribes, and at the same time to preserve order and quiet within his own dominions, but at last fell by the hand of an assassin.

His successor was his brother Ibrahim, a prince of widely different tastes and temperament from all who had gone before him. His desire was peace; and having conciliated his troublesome neighbours, the Seljuks, he devoted himself steadily to the internal affairs of his kingdom. Religion, the administration of justice, and the encouragement of learned men, appear to have engrossed the chief of his time; and the only mention we find of him, in any of the historical records, as engaged in a military undertaking, was upon some expedition to the Sutlege, on which occasion he captured several cities from the Hindoos. Little as there is to record of this monarch of a political nature, his reign nevertheless lasted for the unusual period of forty-one years, and terminated as peacefully as it had commenced.

The next in succession was Masaud II. (A.D. 1089), who enjoyed a peaceable reign of twenty-five years, during which period the greater portion of his attention was devoted to legislating and improving the condition of his country. Some expeditions into Hindostan were undertaken by his generals, but with no great or lasting results.

Arslan, the elder son of the deceased sultan, commenced his reign with violence, and ended it in his own blood. Having imprisoned his brothers, their uncle, the Seljuk sultan, marched against him with a formidable army, defeated him, and placed one of his brothers, Behrám, on the throne. Arslan was pursued from the battlefield and slain.

The new sultan (A.D. 1118) appears to have inherited the love for literature which had distinguished so many of his predecessors. Learned men, poets and philosophers, were welcomed at his court, and treated with the greatest consideration. The peaceful and prosperous state in which he found the kingdom greatly favoured this, and for a period of nearly thirty years allowed him ample opportunity to gratify his tastes. The peaceful tenour of his long reign was unfortunately broken through an act which could scarcely have been expected from a monarch of such elevated tastes.

Having had a difference with his son-in-law, Kutb-u-din Sur, prince of Ghor, he contrived first to get him into his power, and then to kill him. The brother of the murdered prince lost no time in avenging him, and marching upon Ghazni with a numerous army, drove out the treacherous Behrám. The defeated monarch, however, found means and opportunity to fall upon the invader and completely routed his troops, making himself prisoner, and eventually putting him to a cruel death.

Retribution for this double crime was at hand. Ala-u-din, another brother of Kutb-u-din, entered the Ghaznivite territories at the head of a small but determined body of troops; and although in the first instance fortune did not appear to favour him, he finally succeeded in compelling Behrám to fly for safety to his Indian territories, where he shortly afterwards died from exhaustion and grief.

His son, Khosru, who had shared his prosperity, had now (A.D. 1152) to participate in his reverses. The discomfited army of Ghazni, finding itself deprived of its leader, followed the son with more than ordinary devotion, and succeeded in fighting a way to Lahore, where the new monarch found his Indian subjects ready to receive him with open arms. It does not appear that the reign of Khosru was marked by any political events of consequence. His tastes led him to consult the prudent policy of peace, and to rest contented with the Indian limits of his ancestral possessions; nor do we find that he suffered any molestation from the new dynasty ruling at Ghazni.

At his death (A.D. 1160) he was succeeded by Khosru Malik, who, after a most tranquil reign of twenty-seven years, was attacked by the Ghor kings, and eventually defeated and slain. The kingdom of Lahore from this date became a portion of the Ghaznivite territory in the hands of the new line of princes.

Gheias-u-din, the Ghorian sultan of Ghazni and Lahore, aided by the military talents of his brother, Shahib, had not long been settled in his new conquest before he began to turn his attention eastward, and, like many of his predecessors, to attempt new conquests on the Indian side of the Sutlege. The rajah of Delhi was the first Hindoo potentate attacked; but so well was he supported by his followers, that the fierce and warlike forces led against them from the north failed in their efforts; and despite the terrible charges of Afghan horse, the troops of

Delhi were left masters of the battle-field; Shahib, who commanded the invading forces, escaping with great difficulty and badly wounded.

Two years later (A.D. 1193) Shahib, burning with a desire to wipe out the stain upon his military reputation left by his former defeat, again marched an army of Turks and Afghans across the frontiers, and encountered Pritwi, the Delhi rajah, whom he found assembled with a powerful array from many Indian states to oppose his further progress. Upon this occasion the Afghan cavalry decided the result of the day, for having drawn the Hindoo troops from their line of battle, Shahib suddenly wheeled round a body of chosen horse, 12,000 strong, and charging the vast mass of troops whilst in broken columns, succeeded in utterly routing them.[4] The rajah was made prisoner, and ultimately put to death whilst in confinement.

This victory was followed by other conquests. The rajah of Canouj was defeated in a pitched battle, and his territories were at once annexed to the dominions of the victor. Gwalior, in Bundelcund, as well as several strong positions in Rohilcund, were next taken possession of; and in the following year the Ghaznivite warrior extended his arms still farther, subduing the fine provinces of Oude, Behar, and Bengal.

The death of Gheias-u-din, which took place after a reign of forty-five years, placed his brother, Shahib-u-din, on the throne. India, however, saw no further exploits of this successful warrior. He was engaged in a war with the sultan of Kharism, which terminated to his disadvantage, and led to the defection of some portion of his western possessions. A second expedition against that country was on the point of being undertaken, when Shahib fell by the hands of assassins after a short reign of four years. Few soldiers had been more successful or enterprising than the conqueror of the central provinces of Hindostan; even the brilliant achievements of Mahmoud were unimportant in extent compared to those of the Ghorian sultan, who had extended the Afghan rule as far as the extreme limits of the Ganges.

Upon the death of Shahib (A.D. 1206), his nephew, Mahmoud Ghori, was proclaimed sovereign; but he continued to rule over no more than Ghor, and so far abandoned claim to any further territory as to send the insignia of royalty to the viceroy of India, Kutb-u-din, then resident at Delhi. Thus India became an independent power; and in the person of the new monarch commenced the line of kings of Delhi.

[4] Ferishta, vol. i. pp. 173-177.

CHAPTER II.

FROM THE ESTABLISHMENT OF THE KINGDOM OF DELHI TO ITS CONQUEST BY THE TARTARS.

A.D. 1206-1526.

KUTB-U-DIN was the first of a line known as the slave-kings of Delhi, from the fact of their having been originally Turki slaves. The present monarch had been raised to his high rank through the favour of Shahib, who greatly admired his many good and shining qualities. He seems to have been a prudent and just monarch, and to have attached his subjects to his person by the wisdom and gentleness of his rule, which, however, lasted for but four years as king, though he had governed the state of Delhi as viceroy for fully twenty years. His son Aram was a weak prince, and was set aside shortly after his accession for Altamsh, son-in-law of Kutb-u-din, who, like his predecessor, had been raised from slavery to high favour.

Altamsh was not deficient in military talent and personal courage, and found ample occupation during his reign for both qualities. The Mahometan power was never so thoroughly established in any portion of India proper, but some rajah or dependent sovereign found occasion for attempting an assertion of their territorial rights. In this way Behar, Malwa, and Gwalior called down upon them the chastisement of Altamsh. It was during this reign that the celebrated Ghenghis Khan poured his Mogul myriads from the north over a great part of Asia, and at one time threatened the Indian monarchy with an invasion.

The death of Altamsh at Delhi brought his son, Rukn-u-din, to the throne, whence his indolence, indifference, and dissipation shortly drove him in favour of his sister Rezia.

The sultana (A.D. 1236) was a woman of more than ordinary attainments, and seems to have administered the affairs of the kingdom with wisdom and industry. Her talents, however, failed to secure her in the possession of the throne. Jealousies crept in, a party rebelled against her authority, and finally, after a severe engagement, her troops were defeated, and Rezia made captive and slain in cold blood.

During the two short reigns of Behrám and Masaud which followed, the most prominent event was the invasion of India at different points by armies of Moguls, one of which penetrated as far as Bengal. They were, however, driven back with considerable loss.

Nasir-u-din Mahmoud (A.D. 1246) was the grandson of Altamsh. Of studious disposition, he committed the charge of government and of all military operations to his vizier, formerly a Turki slave of his grandfather, and a man of great ability. Through his energy several revolts in the remote Hindoo states were suppressed, and the inroads of the Moguls on the western frontier effectually checked.

Upon the death of Nasir (A.D. 1266), his vizier, Gheias-u-din Bulbun, stepped quietly to the throne, where he maintained himself by a line of rigorous cruelty to all suspected of being inimical to his interest. His reign, which lasted for a period of twenty years, was marked by insurrections and invasions, all of which he overcame with the same success which had marked his career whilst vizier.

With his successor, Kai-Kobad, ended the race of the slave-kings. This monarch ruled but for a brief period; and at his death the choice of the people fell upon Jelal-u-din, in whose person commenced the house of Khilji. His reign, as also that of his nephew and successor, Allah-u-din, was a constant succession of plots, intrigues, and murders.

At this period a third Mongolian invasion of India took place, more formidable than either of the previous. Thanks, however, to the bravery and experience of his general, Zaffer Khan, the sultan was victorious, though his success cost him the life of his heroic commander, who fell covered with wounds. This victory induced Allah-u-din to turn his arms to the peninsula of India, where he defeated several of the hitherto independent rajahs, and compelled them to pay him tribute. Jealous of the influence and number of the Moguls in his army, the sultan ordered them to be dismissed his service without pay, and afterwards to be exterminated to the number of fifteen thousand.

The death of Allah (A.D. 1316) was said to have been hastened by poison administered by his favourite general, Mallek Kaffir, who thereupon caused the late king's youngest son, an infant, to be proclaimed. This meeting with the disapproval of the nobles and army of Delhi, they placed Mubarik, the eldest son of Allah, on the throne, slew Mallek, and so far restored tranquillity. The new sovereign, although he began his reign with no less an exploit than the conquest of the Malabar country, quickly abandoned himself to dissipation, and left all authority in the hands of a low Hindoo, one Mallek Khosru, who shortly afterwards found an opportunity to murder his master, together with every member of his family.

This treason drew upon him the speedy vengeance of the nobles, who, with the rajah of the Deccan, dispersed his adherents, and terminated his power with his life. The race of Khilji ended with Mubarik, and with his successor commenced the rule of the house of Toghlak.

There being no member of the royal family left (A.D. 1321), the choice of the nobles and of the army was naturally directed towards those chiefs who ranked highest amongst them. Their selection was Gheias-u-din Toghlak, governor of the Punjab, a man of high reputation in military and civil affairs, and who proved himself not unworthy of the popular choice. He shewed both activity and wisdom during his short reign. The threatened invasion of the Moguls on the north-western frontiers was effectually checked by a line of defences thrown up along the Afghan boundary, whilst on the south he busied himself by subduing a further portion of the Deccan, and arranging matters in Bengal and Tirhoot, as well as annexing the territories of the rajah of Dacca to his dominions.

Returning from this last expedition, he was killed by the fall of a bungalow erected expressly to receive him by his eldest son, not without strong suspicion of premeditation against the latter, who, as a consequence of this occurrence, mounted the throne.

Mohammed Toghlak was proclaimed sultan (A.D. 1325) amidst a great shew of ostentatious liberality to all about him. He was a prince of great ability, and possessed more than ordinary acquirements; and few monarchs evinced a greater desire to patronise men of learning and distinction than did the new sovereign. His accomplishments, however, did not counterbalance his terrible crimes; and, if possible, his talents served but to add to the violence of his outrageous actions.

An army of Moguls, which found means to enter the Punjab, was bought off by a large sum of money. The subjugation of the remainder of the Deccan was completed, and general good order was restored throughout the most remote provinces of his vast dominions.

From this time Mohammed seems to have abandoned himself to a most extraordinary and violent line of conduct, quite at variance with the previous reputation he had earned. An invasion of Persia with a gigantic army,—the conquest of China,—were both productive of disastrous consequences to himself and his people. And added to these freaks were his excessive fiscal imposts, his tampering with the currency, and terrible cruelty to the inhabitants of many districts.

These excesses produced open rebellion (A.D. 1338) in many quarters; and during the next thirteen years we read of a succession of revolts, which seem to have kept the sovereign constantly employed. Many of these outbreaks were quelled for a time; but in several instances the disaffected provinces defied the power of the tyrant, and maintained their independence. Amongst these were Bengal, the Carnatic, and the Malabar territories.

Mohammed is reported to have died of a surfeit of fish at Tatta, whilst on his way to quell one of the numerous revolts of that unsettled period, leaving no family behind him.

Firuz Toghlak, the late king's nephew (A.D. 1351), was raised to the throne in the absence of any direct heirs. His reign, though not distinguished by any great military exploits, was yet one of prosperity, and attended with the happiest results to his people. He reversed all the fiscal and monetary decrees of his uncle, and busied himself more in the execution of works of public utility and improving the resources of his dominions, than in seeking to add to their extent.

In the eighty-seventh year of his age, Firuz, from bodily infirmity, resigned nearly all his power into the hands of his vizier, who soon began to use his authority against the claims of the heir-apparent. He failed, however, in his plots; for the son persuaded Firuz to banish his minister and invest him with supreme authority. His dissolute conduct soon disgusted the nobles; and eventually he was compelled to fly to the mountains for safety, and the old king once more resumed the reins of government.

Upon his death a scene of disorder, struggles, and bloodshed followed. Two grandsons reigned after him in succession, each for but a few months; Nasir Toghlak, the banished son of Firuz, returned and resumed the government during three years; after which his son, Humayun, assumed the sceptre, but lived only forty-five days.

Mahmoud Toghlak, the younger brother of the preceding, was a minor when he ascended the throne (A.D. 1394). This circumstance, added to the previous distracted state of the kingdom, induced the governors of Gujerat, Malwa, and Juanpoor, to assert and maintain their independence; and it was soon evident that the new sovereign, so far from being able to turn his attention to them, would find occupation nearer home, where civil troubles awaited him.

In the midst of these commotions (A.D. 1398) a fresh calamity descended upon the country, which at once threatened the speedy dissolution of the empire. Tamerlane, having overrun Persia, Georgia, and Mesopotamia, with portions of Russia and Siberia, at the head of vast hordes of Tartars, turned his attention to India, and sent forward his grandson, Pir Mohammed, to prepare the way for the main body of the invaders.

The Tartar general swept the Punjab with his fierce troops, and after carrying fire and slaughter through the entire province, took possession of the fortified city of Mooltan. Tamerlane meanwhile had effected a passage across the dangerous defiles of the mountain-ranges to the north of Afghanistan, marched for the Indus, which he crossed at Attok, and thence made for Samana, massacring the inhabitants of every town through which he passed.

Reinforced by a junction with the army of his grandson, Tamerlane marched towards Delhi, where he found the Sultan Mahmoud prepared to receive him with a large force, aided by many auxiliaries and a numerous body of elephants. The invaders proved superior to the Indians both in numbers and valour; and although the sultan did his best to defend his kingdom, the Hindoo army was defeated with immense slaughter. Mahmoud sought refuge in Gujerat, whilst his broken forces took shelter within the walls of Delhi, where they made terms with the Tartar chief, and submitted to his authority as Emperor of India, which he was then proclaimed.

The capitulation of the city did not save it from the plunder and violence of the Tartar troops, who, meeting with some resistance in their excesses, fell upon the inhabitants, and a general massacre ensued: "some streets were rendered impassable by heaps of dead; and the gates being forced, the whole Mogul army gained admittance, and a scene of the utmost horror ensued."[5]

Tamerlane quitted Delhi when there seemed nothing further to be gained by remaining; and carrying with him an immense booty and a vast retinue of slaves of all ranks, he marched through Meerut and up the banks of the Ganges as far as Hurdwar, thence across Lahore to the Ghazni country by the route he had followed on entering India.

The Tartar monarch may be said to have found Hindostan a garden—he left it a desert, A.D. 1399. Famine and pestilence were the gifts he showered on the inhabitants, whom he deemed not worthy of slavery in a distant land. Acquisition of territory seemed to be no part of his plan. A fame such as in those days of bloodshed was deemed worthy of a despot, he certainly achieved, but with no advantage to himself beyond the amount of treasure he managed to carry with him on his way to meet other foes.

After various struggles and some bloodshed in Delhi for the mastery, Mahmoud at length came forward and re-asserted his claim to the throne. He lived a few years after this; and was succeeded by Doulat Khan Lodi, who, after a rule of one year, gave way to the governor of the Punjab, Khizir Khan; and thus ended the Toghlak dynasty of the Afghan race of kings.

[5] Ferishta, vol. i.

Khizir Khan affected to rule in the name and under the authority of Tamerlane, and by this artifice gave a stability to his government which it could not otherwise have possessed. His reign of seven years was followed by that of his son Syed Mobarik, a just and prudent ruler, who was, however, during thirteen years, continually embroiled in disturbances.

Seyd Mohammed, his grandson, was placed on the throne upon the assassination of Syed Mobarik. He ruled for a brief period, and was succeeded by his son, Seyd Allah-u-din, who, after reigning for seven years in great weakness, abdicated, and made way for the fifth or Lodi dynasty.

Behlol Lodi, governor of the Punjab, was descended from an Afghan family of high character, whose power and influence had caused the jealousy and persecution of the late dynasty. The outbreak which drove Seyd Allah from his throne called Behlol to Delhi; and although meeting at first with some resistance, he soon established himself on a firm footing, and reigned peacefully and successfully for a period of twenty-eight years.

His son and successor Secander Lodi maintained himself in his father's possessions with vigour and firmness, managing the internal affairs of the kingdom with great leniency and prudence. He was, however, a bigot, and persecuted the Brahmins with great cruelty. The territories of Behar were re-annexed to Delhi by Secander, who was not deficient in military talent. He died at Agra in A.D. 1516.

Ibrahim Lodi, his son, possessed all his father's intolerance, without any of his good qualities. By a course of cruelty and oppression he alienated the affections of his people from his family, and at length drove his nobles to open rebellion. These called to their aid one who was only too glad to avail himself of the opportunity of re-conquering the old acquisitions of Tamerlane. Baber, a descendant of the last-named emperor, and who then reigned supreme in Ghazni, accepted the invitation of the governor of Lahore, and passed the Indus at the head of a small but well-appointed army. After some encounters in the upper provinces, Baber advanced towards Delhi, where Ibrahim met him with a large body of troops far superior in number to his own. The superior tactics of the Tartar chief, and the valour of his well-disciplined troops, gave them the advantage over the huge but unwieldy mass of Hindoo soldiers. The last of the Afghan race of monarchs fell on the battle-field, leaving Baber in possession of the country, with no obstacle between himself and the empire.

CHAPTER III.

FROM THE REIGN OF BABER TO THE DEPOSING OF SHAH JEHAN.

A.D. 1526-1658.

DESCENDED in a direct line by his father's side from Timur, the first Tartar scourge of India, Zehir-ed-din, or, as he is more generally styled, Baber the tiger, claimed equal consanguinity by the maternal line with another great warrior, Ghenghis Khan, the Mogul conqueror. It is from this latter circumstance, doubtless, that nearly all writers have erroneously applied the term "Mogul empire" to the rule of this Tartar dynasty.

Contrary to the general expectations of his followers, Baber determined upon exercising the title by which he was now known, and as Emperor of India to remain at Delhi, strengthen his position, and even add to his already extensive territories. This resolve, although disapproved of in the first instance by the chiefs of his army, soon found favour in their eyes when they began to taste the pleasures of an Indian life, and became accustomed to the soft enervation of a southern climate.

The various governors and subordinate rajahs, who had assumed something of independence during the recent disturbances, were not disposed quietly to submit themselves to the rule of the newly-made emperor, and several of them set him openly at defiance. To chastise these became his first duty; a task, however, more arduous and dangerous than he had at first contemplated. The Afghan chiefs and the Hindoo and Seikh soldiery fought with determined obstinacy, and disputed every battle with desperate valour. On more than one occasion Baber, who did not spare himself, was in imminent danger of falling into the hands of the enemy; and it was not until the end of the fourth year of these hard-fought struggles that he brought the various provinces once more under the dominion of Delhi.

The emperor was not destined to outlive these successes long. A life of strange vicissitude and great bodily hardship had made inroads upon his constitution, not to be shaken off. He was sensible that his end was drawing near, and accordingly prepared for it by many judicious arrangements relative to the future government of the country, which he bequeathed to his son Humayun, and finally expired at the end of the year 1530, having reigned over India five years.

Humayun ascended the throne with the most brilliant prospects. The empire appeared to be firmly established; the revenues were in a flourishing condition, and he himself a prince well calculated to secure the goodwill of all those about him. Of an amiable disposition, with a great taste for literature, and a considerable share of military reputation, he gave promise of swaying the destinies of the Indian people to their happiness and his own glory. But his character proved far from suited to the spirit of the age in which he lived, and which could adapt itself to none but an iron rule.

An excursion against Gujerat was followed by one into the Afghan territories, where, although victorious, he nearly fell a victim to treachery, and only succeeded in escaping with his life. Hearing of his reverses, his brothers and some chiefs rebelled against him; and after one or two attempts to recover his authority, he was eventually compelled to seek safety in the kingdom of Persia, where he was received with great kindness, and even promised assistance, by the monarch of that country.

By the aid of this new ally, Humayun was at length enabled to punish his rebellious relations, and retake a portion, though a small one, of his former dominions; and after an absence of nearly sixteen years re-entered Delhi in triumph. His restoration, however, was not long enjoyed by him; for missing his footway whilst walking on a terrace of his palace, he fell to the ground below, and suffered such severe injuries as caused his death a few days afterwards.

Before proceeding to narrate the events which distinguished the career of Akbar, the successor of the preceding monarch, it may be well to place before the reader a brief account of the other Indian states, partly independent and partly owning the supremacy of the emperors of Delhi, inasmuch as most of these will figure in the pages which chronicle the deeds of the new monarch.

The empire of Delhi had reached its utmost limits in the reign of Mohammed Toghlak; but upon the death of that monarch many provinces of the kingdom threw off their allegiance, and with but few exceptions maintained their independence until the reign of Akbar. Of these the most important were, perhaps, the kingdoms of the Deccan, viz. Deccan proper, from the ruins of which sprang the kingdoms of Bijapoor, Ahmednegar, Golconda, and Berar. The kingdom of Gujerat, founded in A.D. 1396, continued independent until A.D. 1561, when it was conquered by Akbar. It comprehended pretty nearly the tract of country at present known as the Gujerat country. The Malwa kingdom lasted from A.D. 1401 until 1512; whilst that of Candeish continued intact from A.D. 1399 to 1599. Besides the preceding were the Rajpoot states of Scinde, Bundelcund, Gwalior, Oodipoor, Marwar, Jesalmeer, Jeipoor, and some petty hill tribes in the western deserts.

The kingdom of Bengal remained independent from A.D. 1338 to 1573, governed by Hindoos, whilst Mooltan and a part of the Punjab were governed partly by Afghan families and partly by descendants of Tamerlane.

At the time of his accession to the throne Akbar was little more than thirteen years of age. His youth and inexperience were fortunately fully compensated by the wisdom and vigour of his vizier Behram Khan, his father's general and prime adviser. This able commander lost no time in putting down the insurrections which broke out in various parts of the empire at this time, as was usual upon the death of an Indian monarch; and by carrying the young emperor, nothing loath, with him, he helped to complete the military education which had been commenced in his father's reign.

The first who brought upon him the chastisement of Akbar was Hemu, a Hindoo prince who had assumed the title of Emperor of Delhi. This usurper had collected a powerful body of troops favourable to his claims and inimical to the Mahometan rule, and by their religious zeal was enabled to make a good stand against the Tartar army. A great battle was fought at Paniput, in which the Hindoo prince bore a conspicuous part; but despite the number and valour of his devoted followers, victory, which for some time appeared doubtful, at length declared in favour of the Mahometan forces, and Hemu was taken prisoner after being badly wounded in his howdah. It is related that the captive was brought to Akbar in his tent, where his minister, Behram, desired him to give the first blow to the Hindoo, as a signal for his death. The brave young emperor refused to strike his wounded prisoner, upon which the vizier, enraged at his unlooked-for generosity, struck off the head of the captive with his own hand.

This victory was followed by the complete submission of the provinces of Delhi and Agra, and shortly afterwards by the pacification of the Punjab. The young emperor had, however, to deal with another and more dangerous opponent in the person of his prime minister and general, Behram Khan. This able but violent man, raised by his undoubted ability and past services to the highest offices and greatest authority, began to give evidence of a cruel and jealous spirit, in the many deaths which he caused amongst those about the court, who might in any degree oppose his authority or wishes. He soon became not only hated and feared by the nobles of Akbar's court, but an object of distrust and aversion to the monarch himself, who at length formally deposed him and sent him on a pilgrimage to Mecca; on the road thither he was assassinated by a relative of one of his former victims.

At this period (A.D. 1560) the dominions of the emperor included only the Punjab, Delhi, Agra, Lucknow, Ajmeer, and Gwalior. A general spirit of insubordination ruled through most of these provinces, which was no doubt ministered to by the belief that Akbar's extreme youth rendered opposition to his authority an easy matter. The emperor soon shewed a determination not only to restrain and punish these refractory spirits, but also to recover all those portions of the empire which had fallen from it during the past century, and so make India but one country under one common head.

Malwa was the first province annexed by Akbar, though not without some hard fighting and a good deal of subsequent insubordination on the part of the generals and governors put in command, against whom the young emperor was compelled to proceed in person. Other revolts in various parts of the kingdom followed, which occupied the attention of the monarch for seven years, at the end of which period he had either slain or conciliated all his unruly chiefs and opponents.

The Rajpoot princes were the next who drew against them the arms of Delhi. The strong fort of Chitur, in Oodipoor, was besieged, and after a gallant resistance captured with all its treasures; the rana was never taken, and the country managed to hold out against Akbar through his entire reign.

Gujerat was next (A.D. 1572) subdued by Akbar in person, and annexed to the empire; after which Bengal was attacked by one of the imperial generals and finally subdued, though not without some hard-fought battles. Here, too, Akbar had to contend with rebellious chiefs, who appear to have given him more trouble than the original possessors of the country. By means of great firmness, and judiciously blending with it a degree of moderation and clemency, Akbar finally succeeded in quieting all this portion of his dominions,[1] and firmly establishing his power throughout the whole of central India.

His attention was next turned to Cashmere, a country situated on

[1] Stewart's History of Bengal.

the Himalayas, above the reach of the temperature of Hindostan, and gifted with fertility and a salubrious climate. The dissensions of the reigning dynasty, a race of Mahometan adventurers, opened a tempting door to the ambitious spirit of Akbar, who forthwith sent an army, which, forcing the mountain passes leading to that country, soon compelled the king and his chiefs to accept the terms offered them, namely, complete subjection to Akbar's sovereignty. From this period Cashmere seems to have been the summer residence of the emperors of Delhi so long as that monarchy lasted.

A war with the Afghans of the north-eastern provinces of Cabul did not interfere with the quiet government of Hindostan, the whole of which was now under the rule of Delhi as far as the Nerbudda, excepting only a few of the Rajpoot territories.

The Deccan became the scene of Akbar's further conquests in the year 1596; and after two years spent by his generals in that country, he himself marched to the scene of operations before Ahmednegar. The war in the peninsula was terminated by the defeat of the reigning princes and the annexation of a considerable part of that state to the emperor's dominions.

Leaving the prosecution of further objects (A.D. 1601) in the hands of his minister, Abul Fazl, Akbar quitted the Deccan and proceeded to Agra. This was rendered necessary by the rebellious conduct of his eldest son, Selim, who, instigated by bad advisers, and under the influence of opium and wine, had seized upon Allahabad and declared himself king of Oude and Behar. This rupture was, however, healed shortly afterwards: Selim was declared heir to the throne, admitted at court, and permitted to wear royal ornaments.

The many years spent by Akbar in warlike operations, the daring and reckless manner in which he had ever exposed himself to the dangers and privations of the field and the camp, had not failed to work their effect upon his constitution; despite his abstemious habits, he appears to have laboured under severe and frequent ailments during the latter years of his reign, and in the month of September 1605 his illness assumed so alarming a form as to leave little doubt what would be the result.[2]

A combination was attempted on the part of some of the nobles to set up Selim's son, Khusru, as successor, but it broke down; and Selim, who at first had absented himself from his father, remained by his side during the last days of his mortal illness, and received from his hands the royal scymetar.

[2] *Price's Memoirs of Jehan-Ghir*, p. 70.

Akbar died after a reign of forty-nine years, passed amidst almost continued warfare, leaving his kingdom on a firmer basis than it had been at any previous period. Possessed of all the military genius so necessary in those times, Akbar was endowed with many excellent qualities not often combined with royalty in the East. A lover of science and literature, a most rigorous dispenser of justice, a practised financier, a thorough master of all business details, the late emperor found time amidst all his wars to pursue the peaceful studies of a philosopher. Tolerant in the extreme to all religious sects, Akbar frequently held discourses with Brahmins and Christians upon their creeds, and would permit no persecution for difference of opinion. His intimacy with the learned Abul Fazl and his brother Feizi contributed doubtless to his moderation; and to the same cause may be ascribed his own free-thinking ideas, which, whilst they rendered him a very good sovereign, made him a very indifferent Mahometan.

The revenue of the empire was placed upon a sound footing; many splendid works of military and ornamental character were undertaken, and the whole of his own royal establishment, although on a vast and magnificent scale, was reduced to the most systematic order.[3] In short, no part of his government appeared too insignificant in his eyes to deserve its own share of regular attention.

No opposition was offered to the succession of Selim, who was saluted by the title of Jehan-Ghir, or "Conqueror of the World." But before the end of the first year of his reign, it became apparent that the peace of the empire was to be disturbed by Jehan-Ghir's own son Khosru, who, raising levies, marched northwards and seized on the city of Lahore. His father followed him at the head of a chosen body of troops, and, in an engagement which followed, totally defeated the rebel army, making many prisoners, amongst whom was the author of the treason, Khosru, who was loaded with chains and kept a close prisoner for a year.

About this time (A.D. 1611) the emperor married the widow of a late governor of Bengal, who became so famed for her unrivalled beauty and brilliant accomplishments as to receive the title of *Noor-mahal*, or "Light of the Harem." This favourite obtained complete ascendency over the emperor's mind, but exercised it with great wisdom, influenced, it is believed, by the sage councils of her father, a man of high repute. The emperor resigned to Noor-mahal the direction of his imperial household, and by her aid it was managed not only with magnificent pomp, but with a great regard to economy and order.

[3] Ayeen Akberry.

The monarch alludes most feelingly to the good influence of his sultana and her family in his autobiography, and ascribes much of his prosperity to their wise councils and devoted services.

Some disturbances in Bengal were soon quelled, as was also a difference with the Rana of Oodipoor, who was forced to submit to the authority of the emperor. Jehan-Ghir's attempts upon the Deccan were less fortunate, and after an obstinate resistance his army was forced to quit that country with heavy losses.

At the conclusion of these operations (A.D. 1615), an ambassador from the British Court, Sir T. Roe, reached Ajmeer, to form a treaty of amity with the emperor, or, as he was then termed by European writers, "the Great Mogul." Sir Thomas remained in the country three years; and in the account of his embassy, written by himself, he has left a very ample description of the Delhi court, and the state of the country at that time.

From this it appears that, however rigorous in his outward bearing, the emperor indulged in free living when in private, and even in the company of the English ambassador. Jehan-Ghir gave every encouragement to Europeans, and permitted the free exercise of their religion. It is said also that he wore figures of Christ and the Virgin at the head of his rosary, and that two of his nephews embraced Christianity with his full consent.[4]

The prodigious wealth of the emperor may be judged from the circumstance related in his memoirs of his presenting the bride of one of his sons on the evening of her marriage with a pearl necklace valued at sixty thousand pounds, and a ruby worth twenty-five thousand pounds, with a yearly maintenance of thirty thousand pounds.[5]

The great and unbounded influence of Noor-mahal over the emperor raised up many enemies to her authority, and amongst others Korrun, or, as he was afterwards styled, Shah Jehan, the monarch's third son. Fearing her power as adverse to his claims, and possibly having advices of some intrigues against him at court, the prince threw aside all disguise, and boldly raised the standard of rebellion by laying siege to Agra. Here he was defeated with considerable loss, and compelled to seek his safety in flight; but nothing daunted by his first failure, he continued to maintain his struggle for several years with varied fortune.

An incident at this time had well-nigh changed the whole course of events, but for the device and boldness of the famed Noor-mahal. Mohabet Khan, governor of the Punjab, having incurred the displeasure

[4] Sir T. Roe.

[5] Memoirs of Jehan-Ghir.

or jealousy of that favourite, was ordered to repair to the presence of the emperor, then encamped on the Hydaspes, to meet certain charges against him. He set out at the head of a few thousand chosen horse, and perceiving that his ruin was intended, resolved to strike a blow that should frustrate the plans of his enemies. Being encamped at no great distance from the royal quarters, he made a forced march at daybreak, when the bulk of the imperial army had crossed the river, and finding little opposition, rushed to the emperor's tent and at once made him prisoner.

Noor-mahal was not likely to remain an idle witness of her husband's captivity; and although Mohabet evidently intended the seizure to serve to secure his own safety, she at once made an attempt at his rescue by open force. This was frustrated by the vigilance of Mohabet; but an after effort carefully planned and executed met with better success, and the monarch once more found himself safe among his own troops.

A reconciliation with Mohabet then took place, and he was put at the head of an army to march against Shah Jehan, who still continued in open revolt in the south. Instead of attacking that prince, the old general came to terms with him, and their forces united in the Deccan against their mutual enemy Noor-mahal.[6]

Meanwhile (A.D. 1627) Jehan-Ghir had proceeded to Cashmere to enjoy the bracing air of that mountain country, and whilst there was seized with an attack of asthma, from which he had been previously a sufferer, and which at once assumed an alarming character. His physicians ordered an immediate removal to a warmer climate, and as a last hope he was conveyed towards Lahore, but expired before he had been many days on the road, in the sixtieth year of his age and the twenty-second of his reign.

Noor-mahal in vain attempted to assert the claims of her favourite, Sheriar, to the throne. No sooner did Shah Jehan receive tidings of the emperor's death than he marched with all speed to Agra accompanied by Mohabet, and there caused himself to be proclaimed. Sheriar was defeated and slain; Noor-mahal retired into private life with a yearly allowance of a quarter of a million sterling; and the new sovereign found himself in quiet possession of the throne.

The emperor soon gave evidence of his love for splendour and magnificent buildings by the costly and beautiful public works he began to erect, and the festivals he held on the anniversary of his accession, which were marked by a profusion unknown even in those days of

[6] Gladwin's Memoirs of Jehan-Ghir.

oriental luxury. This first annual celebration is said to have cost him nearly two millions sterling.

Amidst all this enjoyment, troubles were in preparation in more than one part of his vast empire. Cabul was invaded by a strong party of Uzbecs, who, however, were soon driven back with heavy loss. In the Deccan a formidable opponent sprung up in the person of Khan Jehan Lodi, an Afghan general, who had distinguished himself under Jehan-Ghir, but who proved an unruly and troublesome adherent. He allied himself with the King of Ahmednagar, and prepared to invade the Deccan territories of the emperor, who at once took the field with a powerful armament.

Khan Jehan, unable to cope with the superior force brought against him, retired to the most inaccessible districts of the country, and for a long time evaded the pursuit of the imperialists, but was at length compelled to fly to Bijapoor, where he hoped to receive assistance. Disappointed in this expectation, he endeavoured to reach the northern frontiers, but was cut off in Bundelcund.

The Deccan was still unsubdued; and although the war was prosecuted with unabated vigour for several years, and Ahmednagar and the Nizam's territories were soon overrun, Bijapoor offered a bold and determined resistance, and it was not until A.D. 1636 that terms were finally settled with the king of that country, who agreed to pay an annual tribute to the emperor. In the following year Shah Jehan returned to his capital; not, however, to quiet enjoyment, for other occupations awaited him.

Candahar being made over to him by the governor of that country, Shah Jehan seized the opportunity of dissensions among the chiefs of Balkh to invade that country with an army chiefly composed of Rajpoots, under the command of Prince Morad, his second son. Success attended most of these operations; but the inclemency of the seasons and the want of supplies caused more distress than the arms of their enemies, and eventually led to the evacuation of the country, after a lavish expenditure of life and money.

Candahar, the possession of which was disputed by the Afghan and Persian forces, was invaded in three successive years; twice Aurungzebe, the younger of the princes, and lastly by Dara, the eldest brother, but each time with ill fortune.

During the interval of peace which followed these enterprises, Shah Jehan found the means of completing the entire survey of his vast dominions, preparatory to re-assessing the lands for revenue purposes; this task, it is said, had occupied his attention for a period of twenty years.[7]

Other less tranquil occupations awaited the monarch in the south. The Deccan, which had never been effectually settled, gave unmistakable signs of approaching disturbances. A difference between the king of Golconda and his vizier formed a pretext for the interference of the emperor, who dispatched Aurungzebe against the king; and the young prince, partly by artifice, partly by force, managed to seize on Hydrabad, and finally to dictate most severe terms to his opponent, the chief feature of which was the payment of a million sterling in cash into the emperor's treasury.

It was about this period that a race of men but little known, and only casually mentioned by one of the Mahometan historians, began to attract some small degree of attention in their immediate neighbourhood, and by degrees so to strengthen their position in the Deccan, that at a later period they rose to sufficient importance, not only to affect the destinies of the Mahometan rulers of India, but at one time to cause serious uneasiness to the British government of that country.

The existence of the Mahrattas was noticed by Ferishta as early as A.D. 1485;[8] but until the period at which we are now arriving, they had not been recognised as a distinct people. We have no certain data as regards their origin, which they themselves boasted was from the Rajpoots, and which may possibly have been the case with one or two of their chief families. But there was nothing in common between these two races. Whilst the Mahrattas were in person small and sinewy, and in their character crafty, persevering, and enduring, the Rajpoots were of a noble and commanding figure, proud but open in nature, indolent but brave.

They had located themselves in a tract of mountain country situated above the high lands of the western ghauts of the Deccan, in the immediate vicinity of the states of Golconda, and forming the most inaccessible portion of the Bijapoor territories. Their chiefs had by degrees established themselves in the confidence of the local government; and many of them were appointed to offices of trust in the villages and districts; many held inferior commands in the Bijapoor army; whilst others were entrusted with the custody of hill forts and revenue stations.

Sevaji, the founder of the Mahratta dynasty in the Deccan, was born

[7] Duff's History of the Mahrattas, p. 126.

[8] Elphinstone's India, vol. ii. p. 457.

A.D. 1627; and at the period of which we are now treating was, although scarcely eighteen years of age, admitted by his father, Shahji Boola, to the joint management of his jagir, or collectorate, at Poona. Whilst in the exercise of these duties, he found ample opportunities of gratifying his love of a wandering romantic life; and it is even said he not unfrequently took a part in the depredations of the lawless tribes who frequented the hilly country in the vicinity. Certain it is that he found means to win over the attachment of large parties of the Mahratta soldiers, who were doubtless struck by the bold daring of their young chief, and only too ready to connect themselves with any enterprise calculated to lead to their enrichment and independence, however desperate it might appear.

Having collected around him a party of his most trusty followers, he contrived by dint of stratagem to obtain possession of one or two hill forts, and eventually to seize on the revenues of his father's jagir. This success emboldened Sevaji so far as to lead him to open revolt against the authority of the king of Bijapoor. The whole of the hill forts of the ghauts, and next the northern Concan, fell into his hands; and the treasure of which he became possessed by these exploits enabled him to augment his forces and place them on a footing of respectability.

Matters were in this state with the young Mahratta chief when Aurungzebe invaded Golconda; and Sevaji, profiting by the opportunity thus afforded him by the prospect of a tedious war, ventured to enter the imperial territories; and attacking the town of Juner when unprepared for defence, obtained possession of it, and carried off considerable booty.[9] This daring act was subsequently overlooked, if not forgiven by Aurungzebe, who was just then called away by his father's illness to take part in proceedings of a more important nature than the chastisement of a lawless freebooter; and Sevaji thus found himself at liberty to carry out his plans of aggrandisement at the expense of the Bijapoor sovereign.

In the year following the Golconda affair (A.D. 1657) an expedition against Bijapoor, although successful, was brought to a sudden termination in consequence of the dangerous illness of the emperor at Agra. The eldest prince and heir to the throne, Dara Shako, was with his father, and had long wielded the powers of the crown; but so soon as intelligence of the sovereign's danger reached the younger sons, Morad and Aurungzebe, they instantly made common cause, and set out together for the capital at the head of 35,000 horse. Dara opposed

[9] Elphinstone's India, vol. ii. p. 466.

them with an army greatly superior in numbers, but not so in discipline and valour. In the battle which followed, one day's march from Agra, all the princes distinguished themselves in a manner worthy of a nobler cause. Dara was, however, defeated, and fled in the direction of Delhi with 2000 followers. The immediate consequences of this decisive engagement were the imprisonment of Morad in the strong fort of Gwalior, the confinement of Shah Jehan to his palace at Agra, and the proclamation of Aurungzebe as emperor. The deposed monarch lived for fully seven years after this event in indifferent health, and possibly not loath to be saved the labours of government, though he would doubtless have preferred that his eldest and favourite son Dara should have held the reins of power.

Thus ended the rule of Shah Jehan, a prince who had reigned thirty years, the greater part of which was spent in wars and various military expeditions. Whatever fault is to be found with him before he came to the throne, his after conduct merits unqualified praise as regards his duty to his subjects, and his liberality accompanied by wise economy. The revenues of his kingdom must have been enormous; for with all his profuse expenditure in gorgeous spectacles and public works, not less than his many costly wars, he managed to accumulate in his treasury a sum in coin amounting to twenty-four millions sterling, besides a vast heap of jewels and gold ornaments and vessels. His famous peacock-throne is said to have cost six millions and a half sterling, and was one blazing mass of diamonds, rubies, emeralds, and sapphires, representing the plumage of a peacock in its natural colours.

The city of Delhi was rebuilt by him in a style of surpassing splendour and of great extent. But the most celebrated work of this monarch was unquestionably the Taj Mahal, a magnificent mausoleum of white marble and mosaic work at Agra, the delicacy and richness of which has ever drawn forth the admiration of all beholders.[10] The beautiful mosaic work so profusely and elaborately scattered over this sepulchre is believed to have been the work of Italian artists.

Judged by the standard of Asiatic sovereigns in his days, Shah Jehan must be awarded a high rank amongst the rulers of the East, whether we regard him in his military or civil capacity. Both European travellers and Oriental historians agree in one general commendation of his character as a warrior, a ruler, and a lawgiver. At no time had the Tartar empire in India been more frequently and seriously threatened by external enemies, and yet it would be difficult to point

[10] Taj Mahal is a corruption of Mumtaj Mahal, the name of Shah Jehan's queen, whose sepulchre it forms. *Elphinstone's India.*

to a period when those dominions were more consolidated, more secure within themselves, or when the revenues were more thriving, or the laws more promptly and equitably administered. It is no small praise to tell of this monarch, that although the magnificence of his public festivals, the splendour of his daily court, and the lavish outlay he incurred in vast public undertakings, were such as had scarcely had a parallel in the reigns of any of his race, they were followed by no harsh or unusual exactions from his subjects, who were, on the whole, more lightly burdened than any of their ancestors.

CHAPTER IV.

FROM THE PROCLAMATION OF AURUNGZEBE TO THE FALL OF THE TARTAR DYNASTY.

A.D. 1659-1765.

ON his assumption of the imperial dignity, Aurungzebe took the title of Alamghir, by which he is still known amongst Asiatics, although his former name continued to be used by Europeans.

The new emperor did not find himself in quiet possession of his father's throne. Dara his elder brother, although a fugitive in Lahore, had still many adherents amongst the Hindoo chiefs and Rajpoots, the more so as it was known that he was favoured by his father. Another adversary came forward in the person of Soliman, Dara's son, who, aided by Rajah Jei Sing and Dilir Khan, marched to meet Aurungzebe at the head of a strong force. Treachery, however, overcame the young prince, and he soon afterwards found himself a prisoner in the hands of a petty chief.

The emperor's pursuit of Dara, who now moved towards Scinde, was diverted by news of the advance of another of the royal brothers, Shuja, who, as governor of Bengal, had found means to raise a considerable force of cavalry and artillery, and was then marching towards Allahabad to dispute his brother's supremacy. The two armies met at no great distance from this city; and after lying close to each other for some days, a decisive engagement followed, in which Shuja was defeated with the total loss of his army.

It was in vain that the unsuccessful prince endeavoured to retrieve his fortunes by further struggles in his own province. The imperial army under Prince Sultan drove him from post to post, until at length, being hard pressed at Dacca, he fled with a few followers to the rajah of Arracan, in whose territories he appears afterwards to have lost his life.[1]

The after career of Dara and his family was one of successive de-

[1] Elphinstone's India, vol. ii. p. 449.

feats, desertions by adherents, and flights from province to province, ending in his capture and ultimate death at Delhi. It was during these reverses that the traveller Bernier encountered the fugitive prince and his family near Ahmedabad, and spent some days with them, as related by himself in his published travels.

Not long after this occurrence, Aurungzebe, under various pretences, contrived to despatch his brother Morad and his son, as also the two sons of Dara, all of whom had been imprisoned by him in fortresses in Gwalior.

Freed from all claimants to his usurped throne, the monarch looked around him for the means of employing his large army and the energies of his vizier Meer Jumla, who might, if remaining idle, be tempted to projects inimical to the peace of the empire.

The rich country of Assam offered a tempting bait to his ambition; and thither the old general was despatched at the head of an army whose strength defied all opposition. In a few months the country was overrun, and the capital in the hands of the invading army; and it appeared to the mind of Aurungzebe that it would require but his instructions to enable his victorious troops to march forward and obtain possession of the Celestial Empire.

Before these ambitious plans could be attempted the winter season began. The troops, cut off from all supplies by the artifices of the natives, and exposed to the rigours of an unusually severe monsoon, began to suffer from want of food and proper shelter. Unaccustomed to such rigorous weather as they found themselves exposed to in an enemy's country, many fell victims to disease; and finally the army, which had defied the utmost efforts of powerful antagonists, was driven back to its own territories by the attacks of the elements. The commander, Meer Jumla, died before reaching Dacca, a victim to the rigorous season and the unceasing hardships he had endured for many months.

About this period Aurungzebe was attacked with an illness of such a severe character as at one time to place his life in great jeopardy. This was the signal for many intrigues amongst his chief adherents, some of whom looked to Shah Jehan, the deposed monarch, who still lingered out his days in regal confinement; others brought forward the claims of Akber, third son of Aurungzebe, who was already a great favourite amongst the army.[2] But the emperor, having notice of these designs, ordered steps to be taken which effectually prevented them

[2] Bernier.

from being carried into execution. He soon afterwards rallied, and sought repose and renovated health in the cool valleys of Cashmere.

Whilst absent on the northern frontiers of his dominions, events were occurring in the Deccan which were destined at no remote period to afford full occupation for his activity and talents. Sevaji, the Mahratta chief, from some cause not explained, had thought fit to break the alliance he had formed with the emperor, and commenced a series of attacks upon the forts in the vicinity of Aurangabad, besides ravaging the towns in the plains. This drew upon him the chastisement of the imperial viceroy of the Deccan, who, notwithstanding the daring opposition and unflinching valour of the Mahratta troops, contrived to drive them back to their own fortresses.

A successful raid into Surat, when that town was completely sacked by the troops of Sevaji, and shortly afterwards the assumption by that chief of the title of rajah, and the act of coining money bearing his own effigy, were the means of bringing against this troublesome vassal a greatly increased force of imperialists under the command of Rajah Jei Sing. Sevaji, shut up in his hill-forts and closely besieged by the royal army, found himself compelled to make submission to the emperor, abandon the greater part of his fortified posts, and hold the remainder under the authority of that monarch.

For a time the Mahratta chief served in the Delhi army against his old opponents of Bijapoor, and earned high commendation from Aurungzebe; but subsequently, on Sevaji presenting himself at the court of the emperor by invitation, his reception was so cold and even humiliating, that he determined on breaking with his superior; and having found means to elude the close surveillance kept over him at Delhi, effected his escape to his own territories by means of careful disguises.

In this year (A.D. 1666) died Shah Jehan, after an imprisonment of seven years in the citadel-palace of Agra, during which time he appears to have remained master of his own acts within the limits prescribed to him.

Fortune seemed to smile on the emperor in all his undertakings up to this period. Little Thibet on the north, and Chittagong on the east, were added to his dominions, and neighbouring potentates courted his friendship and alliance.

The Deccan, however, continued to baffle the efforts of every commander sent against it, and Sevaji, once more among his old followers, proved as formidable a foe as he had before been useful as an ally. He did not rely on his arms alone, but succeeded so far with presents to the imperial general, as in the end to prevail on the emperor to grant him peace on most favourable terms.

Bijapoor and Golconda, both wearied of protracted struggles, were too glad to purchase a respite at the hands of the Mahratta by a large payment of money; and Sevaji, left thus in quiet possession of his territories and hill-forts, turned his sole attention to strengthening his position and regulating the internal affairs of his little kingdom.

This tranquillity proved but a temporary lull, and two years after the conclusion of the late hostilities, Aurungzebe broke the treaty by an open attempt to seize the person of Sevaji. This led to the recovery by the Mahrattas of many important posts from the emperor, and also their overrunning the states of Surat and Candeish.

Although the imperial army far outnumbered that of the Mahratta chief, the want of unanimity amongst them, the daring attacks of Sevaji, and the vacillating conduct and continued jealousy of Aurungzebe in regard to his various generals, contributed to procrastinate the war in the Deccan until his attention was called to another quarter.

A war had been carried on for some time with one or two of the Afghan tribes under the direction of a son of the celebrated Meer Jumla. The success which at first attended the imperial arms was finally converted into severe defeats; and just at this time, A.D. 1672, the emperor determined to attend personally to the prosecution of the war.

His presence in the north appeared to serve his cause but little, and after several campaigns of more than doubtful results, he returned to Delhi, having come to some sort of arrangement with the refractory tribes.

The attachment of his Hindoo subjects was severely tried after his return from the north-west provinces by a variety of edicts and regulations of an extremely harsh and oppressive character.

Amongst other orders, he determined that none but Mahometans should be employed in any office of trust under the government. Various taxes were increased that bore especially on the cultivators of the soil; and the most obnoxious of all imposts, the jezzia, or poll-tax on infidels, was re-instituted, much to the dissatisfaction of all classes save the Mahometans.

These and some personal disputes led the Rajpoots of western Rajpootana to combine against the authority of the emperor, and we accordingly find a considerable army sent against them. Peace was temporarily made, but finally broken, and a still larger force detached against the Rajpoots. Fire and sword were carried through their territories, and their families made prisoners, but in vain. The brave

Rajpoots defended their hill-fortresses with unflinching obstinacy, and being afterwards joined by Prince Akbar with a strong body of his adherents, they hazarded a meeting with the royal army in the plains. Treachery, however, was employed against them, and finding themselves exposed by this means to far superior numbers, they fled from the field; Akbar and the Rajpoot Rana sought refuge in the Deccan with the Mahrattas. Other Rajpoot chiefs, however, remained to dispute the possession of their territories with the imperial troops, and though they did not succeed in driving them out, they so continually harassed and cut them up as to keep them in a constant state of alarm.

Once more the emperor turned his arms towards the Deccan, and a variety of encounters took place, most usually to the advantage of the Mahrattas. Sevaji had just at this time made an incursion on the southern states of the peninsula, and had succeeded in annexing a considerable part of the Mysore Jagir to his territories. Continued invasions of the imperialists called him again to the north, and he was engaged in repelling their attacks when a sudden illness carried him off in the fifty-third year of his age (A.D. 1680).

Sambaji succeeded to his father's authority, but to none of his good qualities, and almost the first days of his rule were disgraced by acts of wanton cruelty to some members of his family.

The conduct of the new chief towards his subjects was not less impolitic than it was cruel to his relations. New taxes were levied, the revenues of the country were squandered, his father's chief advisers were neglected, and most of his troops were left greatly in arrears of pay.

These grounds of complaint, added to the appearance of the fugitive Akbar in the Mahratta territories, induced some of the most disaffected to make overtures to that prince to give the sanction of his name to the pretensions of a half-brother of Sambaji, one Rajah Ram. The plot was, however, discovered and frustrated, and Sambaji, to find employment for his people, led them against the Abyssinians of Jingera, and engaged soon afterwards in hostilities with the Portuguese, who had settled on the same coast.

A more formidable enemy, however, now (A.D. 1683) made his appearance in the person of the emperor, who, having settled his affairs with the Rajpoots, found leisure to turn his attention once more to the Deccan.

The two following years did little to bring matters to a settlement, though causing great suffering and loss on both sides. Sambaji ravaged part of Gujerat whilst the imperial forces were engaged in the south;

and although he found himself unable to cope with the large force brought against himself and his allies, he contrived, by a continued succession of sorties from his mountain fortresses, to cut off the supplies and embarrass the movements of the invading army.

These efforts did not prevent the imperial forces from laying close siege to the capital of Bijapoor, which eventually capitulated, and being dismantled, was never afterwards capable of affording shelter to troops. The subjugation of the kingdom of Golconda followed; and shortly afterwards the rajah of the Mahrattas fell into the power of the emperor, and was beheaded in prison.

The country was, however, as far from being subdued as ever. Sambaji's brother assumed the command of the Mahratta forces, who, following the practice of previous campaigns, harassed the enemy in every possible way without exposing themselves to any serious danger. Larger armies were brought into the field, and endeavoured by attacking the foe on various sides to distract their attention and weaken their resistance. But the nature of the country was against these vast bodies of troops, whose supplies had to be collected from a great distance and at a heavy expense. It was in vain that Aurungzebe with untiring perseverance took the field himself, and personally superintended the siege of some of the most important strongholds of the Mahrattas. It seemed a fruitless task to capture fort after fort and city after city, whilst the enemy lurked as bold and as unsubdued as ever amongst their hills and thickets.

More than ten years were thus spent by the emperor, at the end of which time his prospects appeared less hopeful than when he commenced. The heavy drain upon his resources caused by this most costly warfare, and the defalcation of some portions of his territorial revenues, gave him much uneasiness, and before long embarrassed his movements. His troops began to clamour for their arrears of pay, which it was not in his power to give them; angry expostulation and many defections were the consequence; and to crown all, a very severe fall of rain flooded his encampments, and caused the loss of much of his stores and baggage, and of some thousands of his troops.

Hard pressed on all sides and in all ways, the emperor would now have gladly listened to any terms for an accommodation of matters; but the Mahrattas, conscious of the growing weakness of their opponents, were so unreasonable in their expectations, that Aurungzebe felt himself compelled to break off all negotiations. Finding it impossible any longer to maintain his large force in such a country and under so many serious disadvantages, and himself being worn out by fatigue and annoyed by financial embarrassments, he at length ordered a retreat to Ahmednagar, and considered himself fortunate in arriving safely within that city with the loss of a considerable portion of his once proud and invincible army.[3]

It soon became evident that the days of Aurungzebe were numbered. He seems, indeed, to have felt a strong persuasion that his end was not remote, from the day he entered this his last earthly resting-place; and his letters, many of which are still extant, serve to shew the state of his body and mind.

Ever suspicious of all about him, his jealousy seemed increased as the prospect of his death drew near, and his utmost efforts were employed to foil any possible plotting on the part of his sons. In his last moments he dictated several letters to these princes, whom he had studiously kept at a distance from him, which, whilst they contain much useful admonition and advice for the future, shew not less his own remorse for the past.[4] He drew up a will a short time previous to his death, in which he expressed a wish that his sons should divide the empire amongst them; the eldest, Moazzim, taking the northern, and Azim the southern districts; whilst the youngest, Cambakhsh, was to have the kingdoms of Golconda and Bijapoor. This appears to have been his last act. He soon afterwards expired, amidst many pangs of remorse and great terror of the future, in the fiftieth year of his reign and the eighty-ninth of his life.

Thus departed one of the greatest and least happy of the Tartar monarchs who had ruled in the East. Possessing bodily and mental faculties inferior to none of his predecessors, and superior to most of them, he was yet singularly unfortunate in his own personal career, not less than in his rule over his many subjects and his undertakings against foreign or tributary states. The hollow hypocrisy of his nature, and his narrow-minded policy, did far more to estrange the hearts of his friends and a great portion of his subjects than any acts of open cruelty or decided oppression.[5]

It was during the reign of this monarch that the British East India Company's servants, by the determination with which on several occasions they attacked and defeated the Portuguese and other enemies of the empire, first laid the foundation of their political power, which at no very distant date was destined to spread, and at length overshadow the Tartar dynasty.

[3] Duff's History of the Mahrattas, vol. i. p. 409.

[4] Elphinstone's India, vol. ii. p. 549.

[5] Ibid. vol. ii. p. 552.

Confined within the limits of the old native towns of Calcutta, Madras, and Surat, with the island of Bombay, the English traders acting for the East India Company had scarcely attracted the attention of any eastern government. The embassies which had been at various times despatched from Britain to the Court of Delhi had been received with marks of favour bordering upon patronage, and there appeared no jealousy on the part of any of the sovereigns with regard to the unostentatious establishments of these European factors.

British influence in the East had far more to fear from the power and jealousy of the Dutch, who had not long succeeded in wresting from the Portuguese a great part of their possessions and trade in the eastern seas, and who seemed determined, if possible, to close the commerce of India against their British competitors. Nor were these the only obstacles to the progress and prosperity of the company. Internal mismanagement, and incompetency and tyranny on the part of one or two of the governors of their settlements, tended to prostrate the energies of those who served them faithfully, and at one time jeopardised the very existence of the association.

The rash conduct of Sir John Child, governor of Bombay, brought against that small settlement the arms of Aurungzebe, who would unquestionably have reduced the place, but for the timely death of the incompetent commander, upon which the emperor agreed to a treaty on very moderate terms.

At the period of which we are now detailing the events (A.D. 1707), a new chartered company was established in London for the purpose of trading to the East, and before long the two had merged in one body, much to the advantage of both. The Court of Directors became better constituted as a governing body, their powers were more clearly defined, and new vigour and life seemed infused into all branches of their service, which before long bore fruitful results in the operations carried on with the distant settlements.

But to return to the affairs of the empire. The injunctions of Aurungzebe regarding the succession were altogether unheeded by his sons. Whilst Moazzim was proclaimed emperor of all India at Cabul, under the title of Bahadur Shah, his brother Azim took the same step at Agra, whither he returned so soon as he received tidings of his father's death. Both of these made preparations to assert their claims to the throne by force of arms. A battle was the consequence, in which Azim and his two sons fell, leaving Bahadur Shah in possession of the field and the crown.

Prince Cambakhsh, the youngest of the two brothers, being indisposed to admit the claims of the new emperor, was attacked near Hyderabad, his army utterly routed, and himself mortally wounded. This event left Bahadur without a rival, and he at once gave his attention to the troubles of the Deccan, where the succession to the command of the Mahrattas was being disputed by the nephew and the guardians of the infant son of the late rajah. These disputes were shortly afterwards arranged, as were also the imperial differences with the Rajpoots, who now gladly accepted the overtures of the sovereign.

Bahadur Shah was well disposed to conclude these matters, as the Seikhs were giving his governors in the north more occupation than they could well undertake; and he accordingly marched to the Punjab, resolved to put down the rebellious outbreak with a strong and determined hand. He was not long in forcing these rude warriors within their own territories, and eventually succeeded in capturing their strongest forts, and scattering their forces with considerable loss.

Returning to Lahore after this undertaking, Bahadur Shah died after a short illness, in the seventy-first year of his age, having reigned five years.

No sooner had the emperor breathed his last, than his four sons strove for the mastery. Battles were fought, negotiations were set on foot, and every artifice and effort employed to strengthen the cause of the various claimants; but in the end Jehandar Shah, the eldest, succeeded in defeating his brothers, and for the time securing possession of the throne.

The contemptible character of this monarch (A.D. 1712) soon estranged the affections of the nobility and the people from him; and there is every reason to believe that open revolt would have been the result, but for an event which at that moment took place. This was the appearance of a rival candidate for the crown, in the person of Farokhsir, the emperor's nephew, who assembled an army at Allahabad, repelled one or two detachments sent against him, and finally routed the troops of Jehandar near Agra so completely, that the monarch was forced to fly to Delhi in disguise. He was there seized by his late vizier, and delivered up to Farokhsir, who, in putting the fallen sovereign to death, meted the same end to his traitorous minister.

The empire had gained but little by the change of sovereigns. Farokhsir was not less contemptible than his predecessor, though with the additional vices of cruelty and jealousy. He intrigued to secure the death of Hosen Ali, one of his most able and active supporters, whom he had found himself compelled against his will to make commander-in-chief of his forces. The plot failed, and the intended victim of his master's jealousy proceeded on his expedition against the Mahrattas in the Deccan.

The reputation of this general suffered in the campaigns which ensued. The Mahrattas followed up their old tactics with so much perseverance, as in the end to baffle the utmost endeavours of Hosen Ali to bring them to a decisive engagement, and he was eventually glad to compromise matters by several concessions, which, however, Farokhsir refused to ratify.

This led to a misunderstanding between the monarch and his general, and subsequently to a difference with the vizier, the brother of the latter. Farokhsir, with all the desire, but none of the determination needed to rid himself of these powerful and able men, began to plot against them, though in such an unskilful and undecided manner as served but to expose his own imbecility and fears, and at the same time thoroughly to disgust and alienate those who would have seconded his views.[6]

The immediate result of these weak and futile attempts on the part of the emperor was the march of Hosen Ali to the capital at the head of an army devoted to his service. After some treating with the weak-minded sovereign, and a rising of the inhabitants of the city against Hosen's followers, the brothers formally took possession of the citadel, seized the person of the emperor, and quietly put him to death after an inglorious reign of six years.

Upon the deposition of Farokhsir, two young princes of the royal family were successively elevated to the throne, each of them living but a few months. Subsequently the vizier and his brother raised to the imperial dignity another prince named Roushu Akhter, who was declared emperor under the title of Mohammed Shah.

From the commencement of this reign (A.D. 1719) there were not wanting unmistakeable signs of the approaching decline and fall of the Tartar dynasty in India. The overbearing conduct of the vizier and his brother, coupled with the disgust created by the knowledge of the means by which Farokhsir had met his death, tended to estrange the minds of the people from the ruling powers, who, besides, gave evidence of their own weakness by continued disagreements.[7]

Insurrections took place at Allahabad, and other large cities, as well as in the southern division of the Punjab, which occupied the imperial forces for some time.

It was during the rule of this monarch that an embassy was despatched from Calcutta to the court at Delhi, by the company's servants,

[6] Elphinstone's India, vol. ii. p. 581. [7] Ibid. vol. ii. p. 584.

with the view of obtaining some further grants of territory and greater privileges than they then enjoyed. The emperor received the British officials with some show of favour; but through the secret influence of his vizier, who was also governor of Bengal, and extremely jealous of the European settlers, matters appeared for some time likely to result far from satisfactorily to the embassy. Fortunately for the English, the emperor was seized with a dangerous illness, which baffled the skill of the royal physicians, and in the hour of need recourse was had to the aid of the medical officer attached to the embassy, who succeeded in restoring his imperial patient to health in a short period. This led to a concession of all the demands of the British, who returned to Calcutta well satisfied with the results of their journey to Delhi.

Amongst other turbulent proceedings which agitated the empire, was the conduct of Asof Jah, governor of Malwa, who, under various pretences, managed to raise a considerable body of troops, at the head of which he marched towards the Deccan, and encountering detachments of the royal army, routed them, and established himself, by the cooperation of the Mahrattas, in possession of a large tract of that country.

To oppose this formidable chief, Hosen Ali marched towards the south, taking care that the emperor accompanied him, in order to prevent plots during his absence. Mohammed, disgusted with the state of servitude in which he lived under the rule of the brothers, and eager to be rid of them, fell into a plan for the assassination of Hosen, which took place not far from the royal tent. This led to the revolt of Abdallah, the vizier, who was, however, soon afterwards defeated and made prisoner, surviving his reverses but a short time.

These occurrences were followed by the appointment of Asof Jah to the viziership. This austere and ambitious man, however willing he may have been to aid in the government of the empire, was soon disgusted with the frivolous life of Mohammed and the little regard paid to himself. At the end of the first year of his tenure of office he threw up the viziership and withdrew to the Deccan, where it at once became apparent that his design was to render himself independent of the imperial authority.

Establishing himself at Hydrabad (A.D. 1723), Asof took immediate steps to secure the possession of the states around him, and at the same time to turn the Mahratta power to his own advantage by directing against the empire the arms of that restless people. Saho was at this time the dominant rajah of the tribe; whilst another claimant, Samba, held himself prepared for any opportunity which might offer of asserting his rights, real or pretended. By playing one of these against the other, Asof contrived to strengthen his own hands, and at last induced Saho to agree to a treaty, by which he undertook to invade the imperial territories.

At this period (A.D. 1731) we first hear mentioned the names of Holkar and Sindia, afterwards so famous in eastern history. The ancestors of these noted chiefs were, at the time of which we are now treating, the former a shepherd on the Nira, south of Poonah, the latter, though of a good family near Sattara, in such reduced circumstances as to be serving as the domestic of a Mahratta general.

The events of the succeeding half dozen years (A.D. 1737) may be comprised in a few sentences, no occurrences being of sufficient importance to deserve separate notice. On all sides the Mahrattas continued to make encroachments, adding to their territories as occasion offered, seldom with any real opposition, never with any that was effectual. The empire was yearly becoming weaker, and required but some sudden or violent shock to cause its total dismemberment.

Meanwhile the possessions and influence of the European settlers throughout India had been gradually extending. The French had appeared on the scene, and their naval force, under the command of the brave Labourdonnais, acted so effectually against the fleet of the British, as for a time to cripple most seriously the operations of the latter. Peace being restored between the two nations, they still continued their operations against various native states on one pretext or the other. The governor of Madras took up the cause of a deposed rajah of Tanjore, and marched a body of troops into those territories to assert his rights, without, however, carrying out any real or permanent object. It was during these operations that the since renowned Clive, then a young lieutenant, took the field for the first time, and in his earliest action gave evidence of that cool valour and sound judgment which before long earned for him a world-wide reputation.

The troubles of the Deccan (A.D. 1739) and the frivolities of his own court had so occupied the attention of the emperor that no heed had been given to the movement of the ambitious monarch of Persia, Nadir Shah, who having left his kingdom at the head of a brave and well-disciplined army, conquered a great part of the Afghan territories, and was already turning his attention to India, where he well knew a sure victory and rich booty awaited him. He did not wait long for the pretext necessary to give a shadow of justification for crossing the Indus, which he did at the close of the year 1738. Mohammed Shah, oroused by this intelligence, collected a force but ill calculated to oppose the veteran army of the invader, though aided by the questionable presence of the Nizam of the Deccan. Early in the following year a battle was fought at Carnal, which resulted in the defeat of the imperial army and the submission of Mohammed Shah. The emperor was treated with great consideration, and permitted to reside unguarded in his own quarters. The two monarchs afterwards proceeded in company to Delhi, where they resided under the same roof.[8]

The stay of the Persian monarch at the Indian capital, though brief, was marked by rapacity and bloodshed. A tumult having arisen in the city, the pretext was afforded the Persian troops of an indiscriminate massacre of the inhabitants, which lasted for a whole day, the loss of life during which time has been variously estimated at from 30,000 to 150,000.

This was followed by a general plunder of the city, from the royal treasury down to the most humble dwelling, when an incredible amount of coin and jewelry of various sorts appears to have been brought together and appropriated by the Persian king as payment for the cost of this most unwelcome visit.

The value of the gold and silver coin thus carried away is said to have been nine millions sterling,[9] whilst the gold and silver plate and jewels amounted to quite as much more. Besides a great number of the finest horses, elephants, and camels, Nadir Shah carried with him several hundreds of the most skilful artisans and workers in the precious metals.

Nadir Shah at length took his departure from the capital of India, after a sojourn of fifty-three days, the memory of which outlived the perpetrators of the atrocities committed therein. Before quitting Delhi, the king of Persia seated Mohammed upon his throne, and with his own hands placed the diadem upon the brow of the re-instated emperor, at the same time enjoining the strictest obedience to him from the nobles and chiefs assembled about them to witness and partake in the ceremony.

Freed from the dreaded presence of these powerful invaders, the emperor had full opportunity to observe and deplore, without the power of remedying, the misery which threatened him. With scarcely the shadow of an army, an exhausted treasury, a devastated country, cities in ruins, and surrounded by many and designing enemies, the prospect for the future was indeed dispiriting.

The nabobship of the Carnatic being at this time (A.D. 1740) the subject of contention between two rival candidates, the aid of the Mahratta army was called in by one, which very shortly settled the

[8] Elphinstone's India, vol. ii. p. 627.

[9] Scott, vol. ii. p. 212.

question for the moment, and resulted in the imprisonment of the defeated candidate. This interference was looked upon with a jealous eye by Asof, or, as he was then more generally styled, the Nizam al Moolk, who finally used his influence to bestow the rank of nabob of the Carnatic upon one of his own connection. The French commandant of Pondicherry, anxious to obtain a footing with some of the native chiefs, used his interest and some money to obtain the liberation of Chanda Sahib, the deposed nabob, who no sooner found himself at liberty than he commenced raising troops and sacking such towns and forts as he found unprotected.

From this date to the year 1748 the troubles in the state of Arcot continued to occupy the attention of the nizam, who died at that period, at the great age of one hundred years. This event, as was almost always the case in eastern governments, led to contentions in the family as to his successor, in which both the English and French took an interest, according as their own advantage might be best served.

From the time of the departure of Nadir Shah from Delhi but few events had occurred within the then prostrate empire. The sole exception to this quiescent state of things were the rise of the Rohillas, an Afghan tribe inhabiting a mountain tract near Oude, and an invasion of India by an Afghan chief, Ahmed Shah Durani. The former was put down by the emperor in person; the latter was repelled by the imperial forces at Sirhind under Prince Ahmed, though not without a severe contest.

Immediately after this battle, the prince was called off to Delhi, by intelligence of his father's dangerous illness, which ended fatally a month later. Mohammed Shah had reigned twenty-nine years. There was no opposition raised to the succession of his son, who was accordingly proclaimed emperor under the title of Ahmed Shah.

One of the new monarch's earliest efforts was directed against the Rohillas, who still continued to be troublesome neighbours. The vizier, Safder Jang, was sent against them, but was repulsed; and finally, driven to extremity, was forced to the humiliating expedient of seeking the aid of the two Mahratta chiefs, Holkar and Sindia. With the aid of these useful auxiliaries, the vizier obtained a decisive advantage over the Rohillas, and succeeded in driving them from their strongholds to the foot of the Himalayas, when they were glad to sue for peace on any terms.[10]

A more formidable enemy appeared next in the person of the Afghan king, who once more marched into the Punjab, seized upon

[10] Elphinstone's India, vol. ii. p. 660.

Lahore and other principal cities, and finished by demanding that the emperor should regularly cede to him the possession of the entire country. Too weak to refuse, and fearing another invasion of India, Ahmed Shah at once consented to the terms proposed, and was only too glad to buy off on such terms an enemy of this formidable character.

Dissensions at the court followed closely upon these external troubles. The assassination of a favourite eunuch of the emperor by his vizier led to an open rupture, and eventually to the expulsion of the offending minister. His successor, however, proved not more acceptable to the monarch, who commenced plotting against his life; and upon the discovery of these intrigues open war was declared between the emperor and his subject. The latter proved victorious; and obtaining possession of the monarch's person, he caused his eyes to be put out, and a young prince of the same family to be proclaimed in his stead as Alamghir II.

The new emperor evinced (A.D. 1754) as little cordiality towards the vizier, Ghazi-udin, who had placed him on the throne, as had his predecessor. It was evident that the minister intended to rule with an iron hand, whilst his royal master should look on and sanction his acts. The rigorous severity of his government soon caused an open mutiny, which had nearly cost him his life. Nor was this the sole result of his conduct. Having treacherously seized on Lahore and other cities in the Punjab, contrary to the treaty lately entered into with Ahmed Shah of Afghanistan, that king again crossed the Indus, marched to Delhi, and meeting this time with no opposition, took possession of the capital, and abandoned it to slaughter and plunder.

Having no intention of retaining possession of Delhi, the Afghan king contented himself with securing such treasures as had escaped Nadir Shah, and then retreated across the Indus; having meanwhile left a Rohilla chief in command of the capital, as a check upon the tyrannical power of Ghazi-udin over the emperor. The ambitious minister once more had recourse to his old friends the Mahrattas, to second his efforts at supremacy. By the aid of that power, he eventually succeeded in wresting the Punjab from the hands of the Afghan monarch, took forcible possession of Delhi, and having made the unfortunate and helpless Alamghir prisoner, put him to death.

Shah Alum, the heir to the throne, owed his safety at this moment to his absence from the capital. Ahmed Shah Durani of Afghanistan was not long in taking revenge for the occupation of the Punjab. He prepared a formidable body of troops for a further invasion of the empire, crossed the Indus at a time when armies seldom take the field, and marching southwards, encountered the Mahratta forces in the plains of Paniput, near the Jumna, under Sedasheo Bhao. The forces of the latter comprised about 100,000 cavalry and 15,000 infantry, many of whom were sepoys, besides a large park of artillery and a liberal supply of rockets. The Durani brought against this army about 50,000 horse, composed of Persians and Afghans, with 30,000 infantry, partly of Rohillas and partly Indian soldiers, but ill trained.[11]

After facing each other for some time, during which the Mahrattas suffered much from want of supplies, an engagement took place, when, after a terrible slaughter on both sides, the Durani's army was victorious. The survivors of the Mahrattas fled from the field, but were so hotly pursued that but very few of them escaped to tell the tale of their disasters. The power of this people was so effectually broken by this battle, in which most of their chiefs fell, that many years elapsed before they were in a position to exercise any influence in Indian affairs.

The invading army having thus effectually broken up the last remnants of the empire, retired beyond the Indus, and appeared no more on the eastern side of that river.

The history of the Tartar dynasty may now be said to have closed, as the remaining events which occurred in the various provinces and states of India comprising that once powerful empire belong so entirely to the history of the British power in the East, as to render it necessary to link them together. The fugitive Shah Alum subsequently obtained possession of the capital of his ancestors; but being without the power to retain it, he fell into the hands of a Rohilla chief, who deprived him of sight, and afterwards gave him into the power of Sindia, one of the Mahratta chiefs, who retained him in close confinement at Delhi until that city was taken by the British forces in 1803. Shah Alum and his son, Akbar Shah, both died pensioners on the bounty of the East India Company; and with the last of these princes ended the race of the Tartar monarchs of India.

[11] Duff's History of the Mahrattas, vol. ii. p. 152.

THE EUROPEAN PERIOD.

CHAPTER I.

EARLY COMMUNICATION BETWEEN THE EASTERN AND WESTERN WORLD, WITH SUBSEQUENT EUROPEAN PROGRESS, TO THE ESTABLISHMENT OF BRITISH SUPREMACY IN INDIA.

THE earliest records which we possess of commercial intercourse between the inhabitants of India and those of countries to the west of Arabia relate to the Jewish kingdom (B.C. 1014). History informs us that Solomon drew large and frequent supplies of spices and cotton goods from the southern and eastern parts of Asia, and even in his time the Phœnicians were said to have been long in possession of the bulk of the Indian trade, which was chiefly carried on by way of the Red Sea and the Persian Gulf. An overland communication appears to have existed through Persia and Arabia; but with this double intercourse, the western nations remained in deepest ignorance of the country and the people that lay towards the rising sun.

All that Europe knew of India prior to the expedition of the Macedonian monarch was through its gold, its pearls, its spices, and its rich cloths. But the length of time occupied in the voyage, the circuitous route by which these goods were conveyed, and the many hands through which they passed, rendered it highly improbable that any but the most wild and fanciful pictures of the East ever reached those who consumed the products brought from those distant lands.

It was reserved for Alexander the Great (B.C. 331) to achieve, amongst other things, the opening of this hidden region, although he himself visited but its confines on the west. Unlike the progress of those northern conquerors who came after him, carrying fire and sword and scattering death and ruin about their footsteps, the Macedonian carried with him the softening influence of civilisation. Of the knowledge of

India, which flowed westward consequent upon the invasion of Alexander, we have already treated at the conclusion of our first historical section.

The early death of the conqueror destroyed any plans he may have formed for opening up a trade with, or settling an empire in Hindostan; and for nearly three centuries the commerce between the eastern and western worlds was conducted by the Egyptian and Arab merchants, by way of the Red Sea, the Nile, and the Mediterranean; the ports being then Berenice, Coptos, and Alexandria.

There were, however, two other routes by which a small portion of the traffic with the East was carried on. One of these lay through Persia and the upper part of Arabia to the Syrian cities; a desert and difficult route, but one of great antiquity. The only halting-place on this dreary road was the famed city of Tadmor, or Palmyra, so called from the abundance of palm-trees which flourished around its walls. This regal city owed its prosperity to the commerce which passed through it, and which, in the course of time, raised the state to a degree of importance and power that exposed it to the jealousy of imperial Rome. A war ensued, in which its brave and noble-minded queen, Zenobia, was captured, her city destroyed, and with it the overland traffic of the desert, which had existed since the days of Abraham.

The second route was by way of the Indus upwards, across the rocky passes of the Hindoo Cush, and so on to the river Oseus and the Caspian Sea, whence the merchandise was conveyed by other land and water conveyance to the cities of the north and north-west. Even in the present day we find this a route of some importance, serving as the means of carrying on a trade between India, Persia, and Russia, which is of more real value to the latter country than is perhaps generally known in Europe. The richest silks, the finest muslins, the most costly shawls, the rarest drugs and spices, are bought up by Russian dealers and transported by this tedious route to the cities of the great Czar.

With the Palmyra route the carrying-trade of Egypt with the East suffered equally from the ravages and conquests of the Roman emperors, though not so permanently. We read that during the reign of the Emperor Claudius, one of the kings of Ceylon, then famed for its spices and pearls, despatched an ambassador to the Roman court, loaded with many costly gifts. At a later period still the Chinese were visited by an emissary from the great ruler of the western world.

With the decline of the Roman empire the trade with India rallied, and gathered something of its olden strength. The two events, however, which most sensibly contributed to the re-opening of this commerce, were the removal of the seat of imperial government from Rome to Constantinople, and at a later period the invasions of the Saracens.

Not less enterprising than brave, the Saracenic conquerors of the East were active in forming commercial depôts, and opening a trade wherever nature favoured their designs. By them the city of Bussorah was built on a spot peculiarly adapted for navigation, and before long the Euphrates and the Tigris swarmed with the mercantile marine of this new and energetic race. The genius, however, of the Saracens was not such as to fit them to become civilisers and traders. They possessed too much of the military fire of conquerors to sit down and open out the many commercial advantages which lay before them: it sufficed them to have shewn the path.

The Turkish rulers of Syria, who followed upon the ruins of the Saracenic dynasty, cared as little for the great prize of eastern commerce as had their predecessors, and were content that Constantinople should be the centre of the traffic which they allowed quietly to pass into the hands of the Genoese.

This was but a moiety of the eastern trade. The Arabs, as hardy and venturesome at sea as on land, had resuscitated the traffic through Egypt; and by dint of many explorations along the coasts, they boldly sailed from the ports on the Red Sea, through the Straits of Babelmandel, and stretching eastwards, reached in due time the coasts of Malabar. It is believed that we owe the introduction of the mariner's compass from the East into Europe to these enterprising navigators. This portion of the commerce of India passed into the hands of the Venetians in Egypt, and rapidly raised their republic to an importance and power which has seldom been equalled by any other modern state of similar extent.

Such was the position of oriental commerce, when an event occurred which led to mighty results, and changed the whole course of affairs, Christopher Columbus, in searching for the East, found a new world in the West; and at no great distance of time, Bartholomew Diaz (A.D. 1486) stumbled upon a road to the East round the "Cape of Storms," so called by him in token of the disastrous weather he there experienced.

The Portuguese monarch, in whose service Diaz had sailed, was naturally elated at the importance of this discovery; for it was easy to see, that by means of this new passage to India the trade carried on by the Italians, at a great hazard and cost, would rapidly fall into the hands of their western neighbours.

Maritime affairs were in those days (A.D. 1498) carried on in a very different fashion to the business of present times; and, anxious as the court of Lisbon was to profit by the fortunate discovery, it was not until eleven years afterwards that a large and well-appointed fleet sailed for India under the command of Vasco de Gama. The Cape of Good Hope, as it was now re-christened, was safely doubled; and at the end of the tenth month from their departure, the ships composing this first Portuguese fleet of India anchored in the roads of Calicut on the Malabar coast. A valuable cargo of the precious things of the East recompensed the enterprising navigators for all their toils and dangers; and the king of Portugal had the proud satisfaction of witnessing the spoils of Indian commerce piled at his feet; whilst the merchants of Italy and Egypt looked on in undisguised alarm. It was soon demonstrated that the monopoly of the eastern seas was at an end. It was in vain that Venetian merchants leagued with Egyptian Mamelukes to fit out a powerful squadron, and endeavour to annihilate the fleets of the Portuguese. The latter proved more than a match for their assailants, and remained masters of the Indian waters. Soon after this the power of the Venetian state became crippled, and at last annihilated, so that the merchants of that country ceased to hold any influence amongst other powers. Egypt too passed into new hands; and although the Turkish successors of the Mameluke rulers would gladly have weakened the power of the Portuguese, they lacked the skill and enterprise to do any mischief in that direction.

The merchants of Lisbon had, however, other opponents to encounter—opponents possessing both daring and skill. The Moorish traders—half merchants, half buccaneers—had to this period held possession of the Indian seas without opposition; and long habitude had impressed them with the feeling that in them rested the sole right to navigate and traffic on the waters of the East. It was not to be expected that these people would quietly see any interlopers trenching on their vested interests; nor was it long before the subjects of King Emmanuel found this to their cost.

The Portuguese monarch was not ignorant of the opposition which his attempt to open a trade with the natives of India would meet with from the Moors. Every care was taken to render the armaments which followed the first expedition as strong and efficient as was possible. A fleet of thirteen sail of all sizes, well manned, and carrying out upwards of a thousand soldiers, was despatched from Lisbon, for the purpose of extending the commercial operations already so favourably commenced by Vasco de Gama, but under command of another officer, one Pedro Alvarez de Cabral. This commander had orders to open commercial negotiations with the Zamorin of Calicut, with the view of obtaining permission to form a settlement for trading purposes within his territories.

It was during this voyage to India that Cabral accidentally discovered the Brazils, having been driven near the South American coast by stress of weather. Arrived at Calicut, the Portuguese commander found little difficulty in persuading the prince of the country to accede to such proposals as he made. A treaty of commerce was entered into, and the new-comers very shortly found themselves established within the boundary of the city.

The Moors, from their long intercourse with the natives of India, had naturally great influence with the Zamorin, who may have looked upon the Portuguese with eyes not more favourable than the former. They contrived in a very short time to work upon the fears and jealousy of this prince to such an extent, as to induce him, with their co-operation, to attack the European factory, and kill the whole of the residents therein.

Cabral was not slow to avenge this cruel treachery. Bringing his entire force to bear upon the city, he found little difficulty in burning or sinking the greater part of the Moorish vessels at anchor under its walls, and reducing the place to a heap of ruins. The Zamorin, upon this, was glad to purchase safety at the expense of several new concessions to the victors; and a treaty far more favourable to the latter was concluded upon the spot.

This decisive blow at the power of the ruler of Calicut was shortly afterwards productive of the best results to the Portuguese. Impressed with the courage and success of the new-comers, many of the petty sovereigns of the adjacent states sought their friendship, entered into amicable treaties with Cabral on behalf of his sovereign, and allowed factories to be established at various points where the localities presented favourable opportunities for opening a trading intercourse with the interior of the country.

Having so far established the supremacy of the Portuguese flag upon the Malabar coast, Cabral prepared to return to Europe with a fleet freighted with the rare and costly products of the East, and not a little experience of oriental affairs, at that time shrouded in the greatest mystery.

Arrived at Lisbon, this successful commander was received with the utmost favour and distinction by his royal master, upon whom the precious freightage of the ships, and the boundless prospect for the future, made no slight impression. The wealth of India brought thus, as it were, to the very threshold of Europe, was well calculated to arouse the energies of a nation, at that period deeply imbued with a chivalric spirit of enterprise and discovery. The rich display of spices, silks, precious stones, and gums, were but types of the boundless mines of wealth to be opened in that far-off land of rich promise. The envied power and riches of the merchant-princes of Venice might now be their own destiny. The East lay, as it were, prostrate at their feet; and it required but an outstretched hand to seize the willing prize.

The king, Emmanuel, was not tardy in turning the information brought by Cabral, as well as the enthusiasm created in the minds of the people, to full account. A fleet of twenty sail, all good ships and royally found, was immediately equipped, and the command of the armament given to Vasco de Gama, who, from his former experiences, was well fitted for this distinction. The monarch had no reason to regret the selection he had made. De Gama rapidly placed matters on a sounder and more thriving footing than they had hitherto been, by cultivating the friendly acquaintance of all those native princes who appeared willing and able to further his views. With the Zamorin of Calicut he was less careful to keep up an intercourse, being thoroughly convinced of the duplicity of his character, and of his prejudice against Europeans. This slighting of his importance led the prince to take aggressive steps: he despatched his fleet to attack the ships of De Gama; but although they were far superior in number, it was in vain to contend against the superior skill and courage of the Portuguese; and the result was, that the Zamorin was compelled to see his adversaries successful in all their undertakings.

Shortly afterwards the Portuguese commander, having fulfilled his mission in the East, took his departure for Europe, leaving a small fleet, and sufficient forces to protect their factories, under the direction of one Loche. This officer, however, proved unequal to the task; and instead of guarding the trading settlements and the territories of such native princes as had favoured his countrymen, and thus excited the enmity of the powerful ruler of Calicut, he proceeded in various directions in quest of adventure and riches. The immediate result of this conduct was the attack and capture of Cochin, a friendly state, by the Zamorin. The return of the fleet to the Malabar coast, the death of the unqualified commander, and the final appointment of Albuquerque to the post of captain-general of the Portuguese forces in India, were the means of restoring matters to their original footing. The king of Cochin, with the aid of his European allies, defeated the numerous troops of the Zamorin, and recovered from that chief possession of his city.

It was fortunate for the Portuguese that they possessed such an able commander as Albuquerque; for all that valour, judgment, and decision could effect, was needed to preserve their power and influence among the native states. The promulgation of a papal bull, couched in the arrogant and dictatorial tone peculiar to those insolent documents, and assigning to the king of Portugal the possession and sovereignty of the whole of India, so far from serving the cause of the interlopers, tended to jeopardise their very existence in that part of the globe. It was found an exceedingly difficult task to persuade the benighted denizens of the eastern world, that any Christian dignitary, however exalted his earthly station might be, possessed any right to bestow their territories, their possessions, and themselves upon any band of adventurers who chose to set up a claim to such lavish gifts.

The attempts made under cloak of this Catholic document brought down upon the heads of the Portuguese the enmity and hostility of every race they came in contact with; and before long they found themselves in the unpleasant predicament of carrying on their barter at the cannon's mouth. Their factors were compelled to go about armed to the teeth; every bale of goods was bought at the cost of blood; each entry in their books was made under the protection of drawn swords.

The indomitable energy and perseverance, no less than the prudence and foresight of Albuquerque saved the Portuguese from the imminent danger which at this period (A.D. 1511) threatened their possessions in the East. A series of bold enterprises, crowned in every case with undoubted success, served to reinstate their name and reputation upon the old footing; and before two years had passed, this excellent commander had the satisfaction of beholding the neighbouring rajahs and princes eager to ally themselves and open trading treaties with him. Goa was taken possession of, and strongly fortified. The island of Malacca was conquered and garrisoned; and, in short, at every point along the eastern and western coasts of the Indian peninsula, where there appeared an opportunity for commercial intercourse, there Alberquerque planted the flag of his sovereign and built a factory. Not content with his conquests in India, the Portuguese commander opened communications with China, and freighted several ships for that remote country.

By a series of wise and liberal enactments, he gave such encouragement to trade and navigation, that soon his ports were crowded with vessels of merchants from every eastern state, anxious to transact business where they could do so in the greatest security and to the most advantage.

Having thus fairly established the Portuguese empire in India, Albuquerque might have extended his influence still farther, had he not been cut off by death in the height of his successes, after a brilliant rule of five years. His loss was felt not less keenly by the natives of India than by his countrymen; far and wide the influence of his name had been felt for good, and wherever it was known, regret, deep and universal, was expressed for the death of one so good and talented.

His successor, Soarez, was opposed to him in nature and reputation; and in proportion as his conduct departed from that steady and unflinching course pursued by Albuquerque, so did the prosperity of the Portuguese settlements suffer in their transactions with the native dealers. Self-interest was the dominant feeling with the new commander; and as his example was not long in being followed by those under his authority, it became a struggle amongst the whole body of military to enrich themselves as rapidly as possible, without regard to the public service, or the means used to attain their ends. Corruption and oppression ruled rampant at all the stations; justice was forgotten amidst the general scramble for wealth; and it soon became evident, that before very long the position of Portuguese affairs in India would be in no better condition than they were previous to the government of Albuquerque.

Fortunately for their reputation, the authorities at Lisbon gathered tidings of the existing state of things in the East, and recalled Soarez whilst there was still something to be saved; although the successor appointed, Sequera, did nothing to retrieve the confusion into which matters had fallen. The power of the Portuguese was at that period at an extremely low ebb; and there is little doubt but that, had the native princes made any combined and well-directed attack upon them, they could hardly have helped proving completely successful. As it was, however, the old-established reputation of the Portuguese arms served to keep them safe at that time from any plots.

At length a change was wrought in the councils of the court at Lisbon by the decease of King Emmanuel. The veteran Vasco de Gama, under the title of Count di Vidigueyra, was appointed to the sole command, as captain-general of the Indian empire, and sailed once more for the scene of his former exploits at the head of a well-appointed civil and military staff. Unfortunately the old commander lived but three months after his arrival in India; yet in that brief space of time he managed, by dint of activity and boldness, to correct many of the abuses existing, and to put down the swarms of pirates and robbers who infested both sea and land, equally with the numerous peculators in high places.

His death was followed by a long series of disgraceful struggles amongst the Portuguese leaders for the supreme command; and when at length a superior officer was sent out from Lisbon to assume the chief authority, it was not without difficulty that he asserted his office, and dispatched one of the principal misdoers under arrest to Europe.

The good offices of Nunio were needed to endeavour to place Portuguese affairs upon a better footing. Yet it seemed a hopeless task, so widened had been the breach between the Europeans and the various rajahs. To add to his difficulties, he involved himself in a war with the emperor of Delhi, taking up the cause of the sultan of Gujerat. Subsequently, the emperor having been worsted, the sultan and his allies came to an open rupture, and war was declared, which led to a protracted struggle between the two powers, and gave occasion to the emperor to avenge his defeat by sending reinforcements to aid his countrymen against the Europeans. The valour and discipline of the Portuguese troops proved in the end too much for the hordes of rude soldiers brought against them; and thus the danger was averted, and at the same time the singular bravery and skill displayed by the garrisons of the factories so influenced the feelings of the many petty rulers in the vicinity, that those who had before been ready to declare against the Portuguese, and waited for the moment to do so, now professed the most devoted attachment to them, and sought their friendship by every means.

Stephen de Gama, the son of the veteran of that name, although in every way qualified for the important post, was not permitted to hold the reins of government in the East long enough to effect any beneficial improvements; whilst the notorious conduct of his successor, De Souza, went far, by cruelty, oppression, and religious persecutions, to ruin the Portuguese character and influence in that part of the world. So infamous was the conduct of this sanguinary and haughty man, that the sultan of Gujerat once more declared war upon the oppressors of India; and with the assistance of numerous reinforcements from the court of Delhi, he laid close siege to a fortified town, and pressed it so severely, that it must have fallen into his hands but for the timely arrival from Lisbon of De Souza's successor, De Castro, a man of very different stamp, who relieved the garrison of the besieged city, defeated the besieging army with great slaughter, and finally carried the war so vigorously and successfully into the heart of the enemy's country, as to induce the sovereigns of the Deccan and Gujerat gladly to sue for peace on terms proposed by himself.

The successful general followed up these exploits by a course of wise and conciliatory measures, calculated to remove the evil impression left by his several predecessors. In this he finally succeeded: enemies were made friendly; peaceful trade took the place of warfare and persecution; religious toleration was the order of the day; and before a year had elapsed, prosperity once more smiled upon the Portuguese settlements. Their ports were crowded with shipping; their factories teemed with produce and merchandise; and on all sides were heard the busy sounds of industry. At no period of their Indian history could it be said that the Portuguese had attained any greater degree of prosperity than they enjoyed under the wise administration of De Castro.

The establishment of Jesuit institutions in the East by the monk Francis Xavier must not be omitted, as it forms an important epoch in the history of those colonies, and at no distant date exerted a sensible influence upon the course of events. Of limited capacity in ecclesiastical matters, he compensated for religious deficiencies by energy and untiring zeal; and not particularly exacting in the degree of sincerity of his followers, contrived, in an incredibly short space of time, to convert vast numbers of heathens to a nominal Christianity. The new faith, in his skilful and enterprising hands, assumed a degree of elasticity and pliability which moulded it to the temperament of any of the Hindoo or Moslem races; and as Xavier looked more to the number than the faith of his disciples, he was met on all sides with open arms.

To the zeal of a religious apostle he added the enterprise of a politician, and carefully played into the hands of the civil government; not making himself a party to any of the corrupt malpractices of those times, but rather setting himself in opposition to the misdoers. At the death of De Castro, however, the old leaven of corruption, which had during his rule lain dormant amongst the civil and military servants of the Indo-Portuguese government, shewed itself in undisguised colours. It was in vain that the Jesuit exerted his strongest influence to avert the evil effects of this state of things; equally useless was it to represent the misconduct of the officials to the court at Lisbon. The evil-doers had powerful friends at home; and at that distance, with the then tardy and uncertain means of communication between remote parts of the globe, it was not to be wondered at that justice was long ere it found a response in the royal mind which then ruled the destinies of Portugal.

During the rule of the various governors who followed De Castro, little occurred worthy of record, save events which shock humanity, and cause us to blush for the deeds committed under the cloak of *religion.* Jesuitism had, unfortunately for India, brought in its train the institution of that infernal machine of evil passions and fanatical bigotry, the Inquisition, the architype of Roman Catholicism. This devilish engine was set to work at Goa, and made to do the bidding of priestly intolerance and lay enmities; and when, by the death of Don Sebastian, the crown of Portugal fell into the hands of Philip of Spain, the work of wickedness received a stimulus that wrought it up to the highest pitch of cruelty.

The enormity of the crimes perpetrated within those fearful walls, the terror which the name of a priest of Christ inspired in the breast of every Christian and heathen dweller in those devoted colonies, spread a sad and heavy gloom over the land that but a few short years previously had revelled in the sunshine of happy, peaceful industry. The records of these terrible times are far too sad to be long dwelt upon. It is enough to know that such things were, and leave the dark veil unlifted.

As evil has ever been known to work out good, so these persecutions and religious slaughters led in the end to favourable results. A cry for vengeance arose from the priestly shambles of the Inquisition. It went forth over that devoted land from shore to shore, and found an echo in many a heart,—sympathy in many a home. Insurrections, revolts, massacres, and burnings were to be met with far and near. Armed with another Papal bull, the Portuguese *Christians* deluged the country with blood; but in vain. Even the native converts joined the standard of the Hindoo and the Moslem, whose practice, if not their creed, was more merciful and tolerant than that of the civilised crusaders from the western world.

And now another people appeared on the bloody stage; a race of persevering, industrious merchants, who, by their cautious and humane policy, founded an empire in the East more durable, because more merciful, more kindly, than that of the intolerant Portuguese.

The Dutch (A.D. 1509) having gathered some information respecting the trade and possessions of the Portuguese in India, and lured by the prospect of a share of those costly spoils, fitted out a fleet of merchantmen under the direction of an East India Company, and despatched it laden with goods and merchandise for barter, and well armed. The advent of this first armament from Holland was the dawn of salvation to India; and from that time may be dated the decline and ruin of the Indo-Portuguese empire.

It was in vain that the governor of Goa, alarmed by the appearance of these formidable rivals on the eastern waters, endeavoured to excite the natives of India against the Dutch. He soon found that so far from the new-comers being regarded with fear or jealousy, they were looked upon with favourable eyes by the princes who ruled upon the Malabar and Coromandel coasts, and that these people began to count upon the assistance of the Hollanders, as a foil to the oppressions of the Portuguese. Equally in vain was it to endeavour to repel the intruders by force of arms; they would gladly have found a pretext for a quarrel, but the wary policy of the Dutch disappointed them in this, and the latter were, moreover, too well armed to be easily taken by surprise.

Following closely in the steps of these came the English, seeking their share of the wealth of these fabled regions. The fame of the Indian name, the marvellous tales told of the wonders and boundless riches of the land of the sun, had made their way across British waters, and found ready listeners amongst the merchants of London. Previous to this period the English had received the uncertain and ill-assorted shipments of Indian goods through the Venetians, who, enjoying a monopoly at that period, had imposed such terms on their traffic as seemed best to them. Subsequent negotiations with the sultan of Turkey had enabled the British to trade to greater advantage by sending their ships direct to the ports of that country, and purchasing such eastern goods as they required direct from those merchants, who imported them by the way of Persia. The opportunity, however, which was now presented, of being able to share in the lucrative commerce of India by a more direct and profitable means, was too tempting to be thrown away; and incited by the news of the entire success of the Hollanders in obtaining a large share of the spice-trade of the East, at that time the most valuable traffic, and furthermore emboldened by the reports of several English travellers and adventurers who had visited various parts of India, and forwarded home copious results of their observations, it was at length determined upon to follow the example of the Dutch, and form an English East India Company.

It was in the year 1600 that a number of London merchants formed themselves into an association for trading purposes, with a capital of 369,891*l.*; and applying to the sovereign (Queen Elizabeth) for a charter, they were finally incorporated under the designation of "The Governor and Company of Merchants of London trading to the East Indies." The charter of incorporation thus obtained named the first twenty-four directors, and the chairman, Thomas Smythe; but the power of nominating their successors was vested in the subscribers to the stock of the company, which was by shares of 50*l.* each. The following are the terms in which the powers of this new company were defined: "To traffic and use the trade of merchandise by sea, in and by such ways and passages already discovered, or hereafter to be discovered, as they should esteem and take to be fittest, unto and from the East Indies, unto the countries and ports of Asia and Africa, and unto and from all the islands, ports, havens, cities, creeks, rivers, and places of Asia, Africa, and America, or any of them, beyond the Cape of Good Hope to the Straits of Magellan, where any trade or traffic may be used; to or from every of them, in such order, manner, form, liberty, and condition, as they themselves should from time to time determine."

Amongst other stipulations inserted in this original document was a proviso, by the cautious Elizabeth, to the effect that if within the time allotted to the corporation by the charter it should in any way appear to her majesty that the privileges and immunities of the company worked detrimentally to the welfare of the trading or other portions of the community, then, by giving two years' notice, it would be lawful for the crown to cancel the entire deed of incorporation. On the other hand, if the course of events went to shew that the company carried on their operations in a right and public-spirited manner, then her majesty agreed to renew the said charter, and at the same time strengthen the powers and privileges of the company in many ways, as might appear unto her and her advisers most conducive to the general good.

The first English fleet which was dispatched to India (A.D. 1601) consisted of five ships, under the command of Captain Lancaster. These anchored in the roads of Achen in June of the following year; and one of the first acts of the commodore was to form a commercial treaty with the prince of the country. Having bartered some of the merchandise for such articles as the place furnished, Lancaster made sail for Java, to complete the homeward lading with spices, gums, silks, saltpetre, &c.; and finally, after arranging another treaty with the king of Bantam, he returned home well freighted with a valuable cargo.

This and similar successful voyages (A.D. 1605) by the fleets of the English company did not fail to arouse the jealousy of not only the

Portuguese but the Dutch, who had by this time established many factories and settlements along the Indian coasts, and upon some of the islands of the Eastern seas. Malacca was taken possession of by them; and from that point they made several efforts to open a trading communication with other countries to the eastward. Although cordially detesting each other, the merchants of these two nations at once agreed upon a mutual course of action as regarded the new interlopers upon the Indian seas. They united to thwart and damage, by every means in their power, the traffic of the English; and at length this secret opposition was flung aside, and exchanged for a more open hostility. Fleets were sent out to cut off the British merchantmen, by both the Portuguese and Dutch; and so determined was the opposition, that it was eventually deemed necessary for the English East India Company to despatch much larger ships well armed with heavy cannon. The result of this decision was, that when next the Portuguese fleet made an attack upon the English vessels, which they did in the neighbourhood of Surat, they experienced a terrible defeat, amounting almost to annihilation. A second engagement led to precisely similar results; and it then became evident to the native princes and sovereigns of India, no less than to the Portuguese and Dutch, that on the seas no power that could be brought to bear upon them was sufficient to master the English, and that in *their* hands must remain the dominion of the Indian waters.

The like desire which had in years past animated the petty and superior rulers of those countries to court a friendly alliance with the Portuguese, was now (A.D. 1632) manifested by them towards the British, whom they considered as perfectly invincible.

Advantage was taken of the favourable impression thus created, by despatching embassies from the British settlements to several of the native potentates, especially to the emperor of Delhi, by whom Sir Thomas Roe was most warmly received. By these means permission was gained for the formation of several new and important settlements, with factories for purposes of trade; so that, indirectly, the very opposition of the Portuguese had proved the means of the advancement of their new rivals.

The rule of the Portuguese in India was now rapidly on the decline; the Dutch were sensibly on the ascendant in many places where the former had ruled paramount; and it became evident that in future the struggle, if there should continue to be any, would be between the Dutch and the English. Negotiations were entered upon in Europe with a view to prevent any further acts of hostility between the subjects of two powers at amity with each other; but with little effect. The Dutch East India Company relied so confidently upon the strength of their position in the various trading countries of India, that they regarded any amicable arrangements as weak concessions on their part, and accordingly threw every obstacle in the way of an arrangement. The weakness and vanity of James I., and the troubles during the greater part of the reign of Charles, favoured the desired procrastination of the Dutch merchants, and left the English company to their own resources.

The active mind and energetic character of Cromwell (A.D. 1654) viewed matters in a far different light, and he at once perceived the importance of fully protecting our eastern commerce; and having in the war which he waged with Holland completely beaten that people where they had believed themselves the most powerful, he felt himself in a position to dictate his own terms in reference to Indian matters; accordingly, in April 1654, a formal treaty was concluded, in which the rights and privileges of the British East India Company were fully and honourably maintained.

From the weak and profligate Charles II. (A.D. 1669) little was to be expected; and the only advantage the British company derived during his reign was the cession to them of the island of Bombay, which had formed part of the dowry the monarch had received from Portugal on the occasion of his marriage with a princess of that country.

During the reign of James II. the Company might have strengthened their position with the utmost ease; for that prince, whatever were his other faults, did not possess that of inattention to the commercial interests of his subjects. He readily conceded them all the privileges they sought, and was prepared to forward their views in any manner that might have been desirable; but with all these advantages, the company suffered much from the incapacity or dishonesty of their own servants; and so great was this evil in the case of the governor of Bombay, Sir John Child, that the emperor of Delhi deemed it necessary to proceed to open hostility with the English, and was only prevented from sacking that town by the timely death of the unpopular governor.

The early part of the reign of William and Mary saw little improvement in the management of the affairs of the Company, or in their prospects in the East. The outcry against the misdirection of these affairs became loud and general; and it was only by heavy and frequent bribes in influential quarters that the directors contrived to maintain their position. At length a new East India Association was formed, which, after some years of bitter animosity, became fused in the old one (A.D. 1708); and eventually the two obtained a new charter, which, amongst other concessions, granted to the Company the privilege of holding courts of session and appeal, as also a mayor's court, at each of the three Presidencies, then created, of Madras, Bombay, and Calcutta.

By slow but sure steps (A.D. 1715) the servants of the Company advanced their superiors' interests; and it was so far a fortunate circumstance for them that, upon the decease of the then Emperor of Delhi, Aurungzebe, many dissensions and cabals took place, which enabled them to work out their own particular views. Another embassy was undertaken from Calcutta to the court of Delhi; and although many difficulties and delays intervened, the objects of the mission were eventually gained, much to the annoyance of the Viceroy of Bengal, who cordially hated the English, and who would gladly have denied them the possession of a foot of land within the imperial territories.

The commerce between France and India attained about this time such an importance as to excite the envy of the English; and when at length there was a declaration of war between the two countries, a fleet was equipped for the purpose of capturing Pondicherry. This expedition failed through the incapacity of the English commander, and the valour and skill of the French Admiral Labourdonnais, who, in his turn, attacked and reduced Madras, A.D. 1747. A second naval expedition against Pondicherry was attended with as little success as the first; and Boscawen, the English admiral, was forced to a humiliating retreat. These, and the failure of an expedition against Tanjore, served for a time to dim the lustre of the British arms in the East. Major Lawrence undertook a second expedition against Tanjore in aid of the dethroned rajah; and on this occasion the English, though with little permanent advantage, came off victorious. These operations were shared in by one who was afterwards destined to play an important part in Indian warfare. The name of Clive is inseparable from the history of British influence in the East, and ranks second to none other in its world-wide fame. At this time Clive was a young lieutenant in one of the regiments engaged upon this occasion, and his abilities and sound judgment were at once perceived by Major Lawrence, who did not fail to turn them to account.

The peace of the Indian peninsula was at this period greatly disturbed by repeated disputes between the nabobs of the Carnatic and the Nizam al Mulk, viceroy of the Deccan. The treachery, the cruelties, the bloodshed which arose out of this struggle are scarcely to be paralleled in any country out of the East. At length, after a long series of crimes and treacheries, the nabobship of the Carnatic was assumed by Chanda Sahib, formerly the minister of that state. The death of Nizam al Mulk followed soon after; and disputes arising between his son and grandson, Nazir Jing and Murzafa Jing, respecting the succession, Chanda Sahib, noted not less for his cowardice than for his ambition, formed an alliance with the latter; they were soon joined by the French, and for a time victory declared in their favour; but so elated were they with their success, that instead of ensuring at once the power that now lay so easily within their grasp, they repaired to Arcot and Pondicherry, where they spent their time in pompous display; and thus afforded time to their enemies, who, being joined by Mohammed Ali, governor of Trichinopoly, and a detachment of English troops under Major Lawrence, came upon them unawares, and gained an easy victory. Murzafa Jing was flung into prison, whilst Chanda Sahib escaped with difficulty to Pondicherry.

Nazir Jing was shortly after shot in an engagement with the French, who captured the important fortress of Gingee. Murzafa was now released, and raised to the dignity of Viceroy of the Deccan; he did not, however, long enjoy his power, but was murdered by a party of the Patan troops; and Salabat Jing, son of Nizam al Mulk, was nominated by the French to succeed him.

The military energies of the English, which had suffered severely since the departure of Major Lawrence from India, were now retrieved by Clive, who requested and gained permission to attack Arcot, in order to divert the attention of Chanda Sahib, who was then engaged in the siege of Trichinopoly. Arrived at Arcot, Clive, in spite of the most inclement weather, at once made himself master of the town and citadel. But more memorable by far than the capture of the place was the defence made by this young officer when besieged. With but 200 Europeans and 300 sepoys, Clive withstood the attacks of fully 9000 of the nabob's troops, and 150 French soldiers. Breaches were made in the walls; but so bravely and effectively were they defended by the little band within, that the nabob's army finally fell back from the struggle; and, in spite of overwhelming numbers, retreated precipitately, after a siege of nearly two months. Not content with this, Clive, on being reinforced by a small detachment from Madras, pursued the retreating foe, and scattered the retiring host with terrible slaughter.

This siege terminated hostilities for a brief period; but before Clive had been many weeks at Madras, the French again took the field and threatened Arcot, though without effect. More serious work was before the English commanders. The siege of Trichinopoly had to be raised; and this was performed by Lawrence and Clive in conjunction with the forces of the rajahs of Mysore and Tanjore. The French troops, although greatly strengthened by those of Chanda Sahib, were unequal to the contest. D'Auteuil, a French general, coming to the relief of M. Law, was made prisoner; and eventually the latter was forced to capitulate, whilst the unfortunate Chanda Sahib, falling into the hands of the rajah of Tanjore, was sacrificed to the hatred of his enemies. This obstacle being removed, Mohammed Ali was declared nabob of the Carnatic.

Although in many respects the fortune of the French in the Indian peninsula appeared more than desperate, there were other circumstances which favoured them. M. Bussy possessed great influence at the court of the viceroy of the Deccan. He had risen to importance in the estimation of Salabat Jing, by the advice and assistance he had rendered him, not only in his promotion to the vice-royalty, but in the subsequent government of that country. The friendly aid of the French general was eventually rewarded by the gift of the governorship of the tract of country known as the Northern Circars,—a large, populous, and thriving district, and in many ways calculated to strengthen the influence of the French in the peninsula.

The raising of the siege of Trichinopoly, narrated above, was followed by a series of incessant attacks and petty warfare between the troops on either side, with but little advantage resulting to either party; whilst the expenses of the French and English companies' establishments were necessarily much augmented by the constant hostilities carried on. A few years of this heavy drain upon their resources induced both to consider that the policy of their respective commanders was not the one best calculated to further their substantial interests.

The governments of the two countries being then at peace, it appeared a monstrous anomaly that their subjects in India should continue to wage war upon each other with so little pretext; and in the end, the consideration of this state of things led to an understanding between the French and English East India companies. It was arranged that M. Dupleix, the French governor-general, should be recalled, and that various concessions should be made on either side, though mostly in favour of the British. To render the cause of the French still more unsatisfactory, M. Bussy about this time gave offence to his friend and patron the viceroy, who removed him from his government, flung off the friendship of the French people, and sought the acquaintance and friendly aid of their opponents, the British.

Clive, who had visited England to recruit his health during recent events, reached India once more in June 1756, and assumed the command of Madras. At this time events were occurring in the northern presidency which shortly called forth the activity and enterprise of the young commander.

Suraj-al-Dowlah, who had succeeded his uncle, Alverdi Khan, as viceroy of Bengal, was a cruel and rapacious tyrant. Not content with possessing himself of all the treasures which his relation had accumulated during a series of years, he determined to seize on the English factory and property at Calcutta; which, from the extensive commerce carried on, he imagined must be of great value.

He marched suddenly upon Calcutta with a large force; and, despite the gallant resistance of the little band who garrisoned the British factory, he took possession of the place and gave up the town to pillage. Such of the English residents as were able, sought shelter in the few ships at anchor in the river; but one hundred and forty-six fell into the hands of the tyrant, who ordered them to be confined until the following morning. The unfortunate prisoners were forced into a miserable, badly-ventilated cell, known as the "black-hole," and kept there during one of the most sultry nights of an oppressive season. In vain the wretched men supplicated for air and water; immense sums were offered to their guards for a change of prison. The soldiers outside could or would do nothing, and seemed to enjoy their sufferings, which, as night drew on, became intense. It was in vain they tried to force the door. Madness came on many; numbers fell fainting on the ground, and were at once trampled to death. Others fought for a place near the small hole which served as a window, and died in the madness of the struggle.

When the door of this horrible prison was flung open in the morning, a shocking sight presented itself. Of the hundred and forty-six who on the previous evening were forced within its walls, but twenty-three remained alive, and those so ghastly, so exhausted, as to look like spectres.

This tragedy brought speedy retribution upon the head of Suraj. Clive took the command of such forces as could be spared from Madras, and making his way rapidly to Calcutta, found small difficulty in possessing himself of that town. This was followed up by the capture of Hooghly, further up the river; and eventually, by the decision and rapidity of his movements, Clive compelled the viceroy to sue for peace.

It became evident, however, that Suraj did not intend to remain long on friendly terms with the English; for, upon their marching to besiege Chandenagore, a French settlement, the viceroy thwarted them by every means in his power.

Clive determined that the nabob should be deposed, as a treacherous and dangerous enemy; and this resolve was strengthened and aided by events which at that time occurred in Bengal.

Mir Jaffier, who had married the sister of Alverdi Khan, plotted against Suraj; and having secured the co-operation of the English, found no difficulty in inducing Clive to take the field. On the 22d June, 1757, the British commander took up his position in the Grove of Plassy. Clive's forces amounted to about three thousand men, one-third of whom were Europeans; those of the subahdar consisted of fifty thousand foot and eighteen thousand horse; but, notwithstanding this disparity of numbers, the battle terminated in favour of the English, and Suraj fled from the field. Finding himself without a friend on whom to rely, he sought to escape in disguise, but being recognised by an enemy, he was delivered up and placed in the custody of the son of Mir Jaffier, who ordered him to be assassinated.

Mir Jaffier being called upon to defray the expenses that had been incurred, it was discovered that the late subahdar's treasures were inadequate to meet the demand; after some tedious negotiations, it was agreed that one-half of the money should be paid immediately, and the remainder in three equal payments in three years.

About this time Major Coote was sent to expel the French from Behar; in which enterprise he succeeded, and an amicable arrangement was entered into with the governor of the province.

Whilst the above events occurred in the north, affairs were not less complicated in the south. War was again raging between France and England, and a fleet was daily expected with reinforcements for the French in Pondicherry. Captain Calliaud, the governor of Trichinopoly, was ordered by the Council of Madras to reduce Madura and Tinevelly, which he at once undertook; he was, however, soon recalled to Trichinopoly, which had been besieged by the French during his absence. He contrived by forced marches to effect a junction with his garrison; and the French, disheartened by his successful daring, marched back to Pondicherry on the following day. The enemy having been reinforced by troops from Europe under the command of the Count Lally, that general laid siege to Fort St. David, and finally captured it on June 1st, 1758. Bussy had meanwhile established the French arms in the Deccan. Having forced the Nizam and his Omrahs to submit to his terms, he proceeded to the Northern Circars for the purpose of collecting the revenues of these provinces. Lally, determined, if possible, to strike a blow that should at once overthrow the supremacy of the British in India, and supply his exhausted treasury with means, ordered Bussy to join him with the whole of his forces. The harsh conduct of the French general towards all classes had rendered him most unpopular in his camp and in the native states, so that when he laid siege to Tanjore, he found but little cordiality or co-operation. His attempts against this city were rendered fruitless by the arrival of an English fleet in the vicinity, and relief afforded to the garrison by the governor of Trichinopoly; the result was the retreat of Lally to Carical.

The siege of Madras ended with no better success to the French arms. Lally retreated from the trenches; and shortly afterwards, in an engagement with the English under Coote, before Wandewash, suffered a complete defeat; Bussy being captured with most of the artillery and baggage. Coote steadily pursued his victorious career; Arcot, Timery, Devi-Cotah, Trincomalee, Pennacoil, Alamparva, Carical, Valdore, Cillambaram, and Cuddalore, all surrendered to the British troops.

Meanwhile, at Moorshedabad, Clive received intelligence of the engagement between the English and French fleets on the Coromandel coast, and the investment of Fort St. David, upon which he hastened to Calcutta, critical affairs requiring his presence. On his arrival he found instructions from England constituting a council of ten, and appointing four governors to manage the affairs of India. Clive's name was omitted; but the administration invited him to accept the office of president, by which they anticipated fresh instructions, that were forwarded upon the intelligence of the battle of Plassy reaching England.

Mir Jaffier, his son Meeran, and Nuncomar, a Hindoo, having combined to destroy Dooloob Ram, the Dewan of the Viceroy, Clive was obliged to protect him in Calcutta. Active measures on behalf of the injured minister were prevented by the misfortunes of the English in the Carnatic, Fort St. David being taken, and Madras threatened with a siege. He resolved not to send troops to Madras, but entered upon a diversion favourable to that presidency, and of infinite service to Bengal.

Rajah Anunderaz, dissatisfied with the conditions on which Bussy had invested him with power, on the departure of this officer attacked and captured the French settlement of Vizigapatam, and made an offer to the Madras government to surrender his capture, provided a body of troops were furnished him to aid in subjugating the Circars. The executive of Madras being apprehensive of Lally's progress, declined a distant enterprise; and the rajah addressed himself to Clive, who, in opposition to the entire council, concluded a treaty with Anunderaz, and despatched Colonel Forde with a large force to aid him.

Forde's operations were retarded both by want of money and supplies; but being joined by the rajah, he advanced against the French under M. Conflans, who with superior force held a strong position at Rajamundri. Forde ordered an immediate attack; and although deserted by Anunderaz, defeated the French, captured their camp, and drove them from Rajamundri. The rajah's penuriousness prevented Forde from taking immediate advantage of his success; and when the English, after a vexatious delay, began to advance, M. Conflans retired into the fort of Masulipatam. Forde upon reaching it summoned the garrison to surrender, but was treated with ridicule, the defenders being more numerous than the besiegers, with an army of observation in the field; while Salabat Jing was on his march to support them with the army of the Deccan, and a reinforcement expected from Pondicherry. Though his troops were in a mutiny for their pay, and his ammunition short, Forde commenced a siege on the 25th of March, and maintained it vigorously until the 6th of April, 1759, when his engineers reported but two days' ammunition in store; at the same time intelligence reached him that the army of observation was effecting a junction with the advancing forces of the Deccan; whereon he resolved to storm the fort. As hot a fire as possible was ordered during the day, and the troops to be under arms at ten at night. Forde divided his little army into three divisions, and at midnight led them under the walls. The assailants gained the palisades of the ditch without discovery, when a heavy fire was opened on them; but they advanced determinedly until the ramparts were possessed, when separating to the right and left, they stormed with success bastion after bastion; surprised, terrified, and panic-struck, the firing coming from every direction, the French force surrendered at discretion as morning broke upon the scene.

The effect of this gallant achievement was great and immediate. Salabat Jing entered into a treaty with Forde, ceding Masulipatam to the English, and consenting to banish the French from his dominions for ever. The Pondicherry reinforcement arrived too late to be of any service, and returned after enduring great privations.

Bengal was threatened at this time with a fresh danger. Alumgir II., dissatisfied with Mir Jaffier, invested his son with the government of Bengal, Behar, and Orissa, and the prince collected an army to assume his rights. Ramnarain, the ruler of Berar, joining Mir Jaffier and the English, closed the gates of Patna upon the prince, who besieged the place; upon which Clive hastened to its assistance: but before his arrival, the prince's allies had quarrelled with one another, reducing him to so much distress, that he wrote to Clive requesting money for his subsistence, and promising to withdraw from the province. The terms were acceded to, and the danger removed. Mir Jaffier was so grateful for his deliverance, that he made Clive a chief Omrah of the empire, and bestowed upon him a jaghire or estate round Calcutta worth thirty thousand pounds a year.

Clive, upon returning to Calcutta, was joined by Forde in time for another emergency. Though peace existed between England and Holland, the Dutch, jealous of the English progress in Bengal, fitted out a fleet at Batavia to counterpoise the English in that province, consisting of seven ships manned by 700 Europeans and 800 Malays. Entering the Hooghly, they landed their forces a few miles from Calcutta, to march to their settlement at Chinsura. Forde was ordered to intercept their progress, which he did with so much success that fourteen only reached their destination, the remainder being either slain or captured. The seven Dutch ships surrendered to the company's vessels; and the Dutch, in order to avoid being totally expelled from Bengal, were compelled to pay the expenses of the war.

In the Madras Presidency the tide of fortune flowed still in favour of the British. The French had retreated to Pondicherry, where, in May 1760, they found themselves completely hemmed in by the English. After sustaining a siege of eight months, the fort and town capitulated, upon which their remaining settlements fell an easy prey to the victors.

From this date the destiny of the French in India was sealed. Bussy had been killed some time previously in an engagement. Lally returned to Europe, and on his arrival in France was put on his trial for treason by the French parliament. Defence was in vain; he was condemned, and put to death by the hands of the common hangman. With him expired the French East India Company; and though some few isolated attempts were afterwards made to resuscitate that body, they never again took any part in Indian affairs.

The disappearance of the French, the impotency of the Dutch, and the subjugation or disunion of the native powers, promised to secure to the English undisturbed possession of India. Clive, having placed matters on a firm basis, took the opportunity of this political calm once more to visit his native country, full of honours and years, leaving the British power both feared and respected throughout those vast dominions.[1]

[1] The authorities consulted in this and the following chapters of the historical section have been Mill's *History*, Aubir's *Rise and Progress of the British Empire in the East*, and files of the *Bombay Times*, *Calcutta Englishman*, and *Friend of India*.

CHAPTER II.

FROM THE PERMANENT SETTLEMENT OF THE BRITISH IN INDIA TO THE DEATH OF HYDER ALI.

THE departure of Clive for England left the command of the army to Colonel Calliaud, who, though not wanting in energy and ability, had neither the prestige nor the military genius of Clive.

The emperor's son again made an attempt upon the power of Mir Jaffier, and thus kept Calliaud and his forces on the alert. Before long, however, another revolution took place at Delhi. The emperor was murdered, and his son invested with the dangerous title, under the name of Shah Alum.

The supremacy which orientals ever attach to the royal name, added to the direct influence of his vizier, the nabob of Oude, soon added large and seasonable reinforcements to his army, so that he found himself in a formidable position for warlike operations, and accordingly marched with his large army upon Patna.

Arrived before that important town, Ramnarain, in opposition to his counsellors, attacked him, but was signally defeated, and the detachment of English stationed there were cut to pieces. Calliaud immediately advanced to save Patna, and upon coming up with the imperialists, attacked them and gained a complete victory. The emperor having been reinforced by M. Law and his body of French troops, subsequently stormed Patna a second time, and was repulsed with great difficulty. A third assault was anticipated, but fortunately a strong reinforcement reached Patna under Captain Knox, who, upon finding how affairs stood, without allowing his troop time for refreshment, ordered an attack upon the imperial camp during the hour of the afternoon's repose, when he surprised and drove his enemies from their position, to which they never returned.

This gallant affair was speedily followed by the advance of the Naib of Poorania with 12,000 men and 30 pieces of cannon upon Patna.

Knox, whose forces amounted only to 200 Europeans, one battalion of sepoys, 300 irregular horse, and 5 pieces of ordnance, determined to cross the river and encounter the Naib, in which he was supported by a friendly rajah with 300 men. His intent was a night surprise of the enemy's camp; but through a mistake of his guide this was frustrated. In the morning, the Naib's army advanced and literally surrounded Knox, who, however, defeated him in every quarter, drove him from the field, and followed him with destruction until incapacitated by fatigue, when Calliaud took the retreating Naib off his hand, and pursued him vigorously for several days.

Upon Clive's departure for England the Court of Directors appointed Mr. Vansittart to the head of the executive,—a proceeding alike injurious to the government and offensive to the remainder of the council; it having been the usage to nominate the senior member of the council for the appointment, such a deviation, even in favour of a talented individual, would necessarily engender much unfriendly feeling, but in the case of Vansittart, whose only statesmanlike recommendation was a grave demeanour, it was highly offensive, and produced very violent dissensions in the Calcutta council, which often terminated most disgracefully. Vansittart found the treasury empty, the troops at Patna in mutiny for pay, Mir Jaffier's allowance to his auxiliaries in arrear, with little prospect of his paying either that or his large balance to the Company.

Instead of advising with his council, he arranged his plans with a secret committee, and determined to depose Mir Jaffier, and substitute in his stead his son-in-law Mir Casim, for which purpose he proceeded with some troops to Moorshedabad. Mir Jaffier naturally opposed this unjust arrangement as long as a probable chance of success remained, when, scorning an empty title, he retired to Calcutta on a pension.

Mir Casim's elevation was for a stipulated payment, the English undertaking to supply him with troops for the collection of his revenues. These payments, with the expenses of subduing some rebellious chiefs aided by the Mahrattas, exhausted his finances, which he determined to recruit by plundering Ramnarain the Hindoo governor of Berar; and to forward his views, charged the governor, who had been a faithful ally of the English, with various offences, which Mr. Vansittart, in defiance of the caution afforded him both by Major Carnac and Colonel Coote, listened to. The result is easily foreseen: Ramnarain was seized by Mir Casim, plundered, and eventually put to death with great barbarity.

Vansittart's government daily diminished in popularity; and all confidence in the English was destroyed when the natives learnt the sacrifice of Ramnarain, who had so steadily supported the English interest; while it was generally promulgated among the Europeans that the partiality to Mir Casim was the effect of corruption. Vansittart's principal supporters in the council were at this period recalled in consequence of their having presumed to censure the proceedings of the Court of Directors, which left him in a minority; and Ellis, the most determined of his opponents, was appointed resident at Patna: he treated Mir Casim without the least deference, seized his officers for interfering with the transit of goods, and forcibly took possession of a quantity of nitre which had been purchased for the viceroy's use. In these acts Ellis was supported by the entire of the Company's servants. The seizure of his officers induced Mir Casim to abolish all transit-duties in his dominions; but it will hardly be credited at this time that peculation was then so rife in the council of Calcutta, that this abolition of duties was declared an act of hostility against the India Company, and threats of war were made unless the edict was cancelled; a proposition which Mir Casim took no heed of, and both parties prepared to solve the dispute by force.

The viceroy, knowing that Mr. Ellis, the resident at Patna, intended seizing that city, stopped some boats laden with muskets for the troops, and it was with considerable difficulty that Messrs. Amyatt and Hay, who had been instructed to remonstrate with him, could obtain his sanction to allow the boats to pass. He eventually granted Amyatt permission to return to Calcutta, holding Hay as a hostage. Upon learning Amyatt's departure, Ellis intemperately took the city by a night attack. Mir Casim, enraged at this outrage, despatched a body to overtake and bring back Mr. Amyatt, who resisted, and was, with several attendants, slain. This seizure of Patna did not long remain unpunished; the troops dispersed in search of plunder, and the governor, who retreated but a few miles, receiving a reinforcement from Mongheer, returned, and again possessed himself of the city, when the English surrendered and were sent prisoners to Mongheer.

Upon intelligence of these events reaching Calcutta, the council determined that no proposals should be received from Mir Casim, and that Mir Jaffier should again be invested with the power he had been deprived of; and, on the 2d of July, 1763, the English army opened the campaign. The first engagement was with the van of the viceroy's army, near Moorshedabad, which terminated unfavourably to him, when the Indian troops retreated upon Gheriah, where Mir Casim joined them with all his forces. He was again attacked on the 2d of August, and totally routed after four hours' hard fighting, losing all his cannon, baggage, and one hundred and fifty boats laden with provisions.

After this last engagement he retreated with his forces to Oodiva, where, among the hills, he entrenched his army with so much judgment, that his adversaries were kept at bay for a month; but, on the 5th of September, a sudden and successful assault was made, which compelled Mir Casim to fall back upon Mongheer, then his capital; which place, with its garrison of two thousand men, shortly surrendered to the English arms. Increased rage and cruelty attended each defeat of the viceroy: at Gheriah he executed the unfortunate Ramnarain and several nobles; at Oodiva, two of the Sets of Moorshedabad; while at Mongheer the whole of his European prisoners were slaughtered at his command, with the single exception of a Dr. Fullerton, whose professional services and skill proved his safeguard.

On the 6th of November Patna fell by storm, when Mir Casim, considering his position irretrievable, fled to Oude, and requested the protection of its nabob, which was granted; for some time the English remained upon the confines of Oude, anticipating that the nabob would surrender Mir Casim; but in this they were disappointed, the nabob feeling somewhat confident in his position, owing to the insubordination which at the time prevailed in the English forces. This mutinous spirit prompted Sumroo, one of Mir Casim's chiefs, to attack the English near Patna, when he was repulsed with dreadful slaughter. Unfortunately the illness of Carnac procrastinated the war until the arrival of Major Hector Monro with a detachment from Bombay.

The mutinous spirit that existed in the army under Carnac prevailed more strongly upon Monro assuming the command; an entire battalion of sepoys, with arms and accoutrements deserted to the enemy, but were overtaken and brought back; twenty-four of the principal offenders were sentenced to be blown from the mouths of cannon, and the whole army ordered to witness the execution of the sentence. Four of the unfortunate men having been executed, the officers of the sepoys waited on the major, and stated that their men would not permit any more to be sacrificed. A command to load the field-pieces with grape, and for the Europeans to form in line, with the guns at proper intervals, was Monro's reply; at the same time he ordered the sepoy officers to return and command their men to ground their arms; and declared that if a single man stirred from his position, he would order his guns to be immediately opened upon them: this firmness intimidated the mutineers, and the execution was completed.

Monro's spirit effected a great improvement in the army; after which he marched against the nabob of Oude, and destroyed his forces near Buxar; the Emperor Shah Alum upon this sought the friendship of the English, and concluded a peace, which gave the latter supreme power in Bengal. Mir Casim fled to the Rohillas, the nabob of Oude being no longer able to afford him shelter.

The finances at Calcutta at this period were in a wretched state; and Mir Jaffier being totally unable to liquidate the Company's claims, independent of those demanded from him by private individuals for losses both real and imaginary, sunk under his embarrassments in January 1765.

The council invested the second son of Mir Jaffier with the vice-royalty, and installed Rez-Khan, his prime minister, which was by no means agreeable to the new ruler; nor were these arbitrary proceedings supported by Vansittart, who, upon their adoption, resigned, and was succeeded by Mr. Spencer.

The company's servants in India had hitherto been little controlled by the proprietary at home; but the latter, alarmed at the recommencement of hostilities in India, with a mutinous army and exhausted treasury, petitioned the Directors that Clive, who had been created a peer, should be appointed to the head of affairs, he being the only man who could extricate them from their difficulties. This was far from palatable to the directory, Clive having, previous to leaving India, treated their authority with contempt, and sued them for the rental of his jaghire. But, after a warm discussion among the directors, his appointment was carried by thirteen against eleven votes. Upon this he demanded, and was invested with, the authority of commander-in-chief, president and governor of Bengal, and, with a committee of four nominated by the directory, empowered to act without consulting or being subject to the control of the council.

The capture of Pondicherry raised Mohammed Ali, who was the creature of the English, to the sovereignty of the Carnatic; and the nabob soon felt that it was for their, not his own pleasure and profit he reigned. In a short time, however, the administration of the revenues of the Carnatic was determined upon. The nabob, although unwilling, could offer no opposition, and was therefore compelled to submit.

The custom of receiving, or rather extorting presents, and the abuse of private trade, which had become great evils, were two things Clive immediately investigated, believing them fraught with danger to the Company, and pernicious to its servants. As a remedy for the first, he compelled both the civil and military servants of the company to sign a declaration that they would not accept presents from the native princes under any pretext whatever. With the abuses in trade he found it more difficult to grapple; feeling that some sort of emolument was due to the Company's servants, their salaries being miserable and inadequate, he created a monopoly in salt, betel-nut, and tobacco, for the benefit of the superior servants, the profits to be apportioned to their respective grades. Though no statesman would now be found to defend such a proceeding, he acted upon the principle, that the Company was a monopoly, and that the servants were merely adopting the practices of their masters.

The nabob of Oude having placed himself at the mercy of the English, submitted to the terms of their dictation, by which he retained his dominions, excepting Korah and Allahabad. These were transferred to the emperor; who, in consideration, promised not to interfere with his vassal, Bulwant Sing, rajah of Benares, for having joined with and rendered the English good service during the war. Understanding well the abuses, under the name of free trade, that the company's officers had perpetrated in Bengal, Orissa, and Behar, the emperor refused to negotiate upon the subject, and trade was not mentioned in the treaty; but he was compelled to forego all arrears of revenue due from the Bengal province, and to cede to the Company the dewanee, or right of collecting the revenue in Bengal, Behar, and Orissa, on condition of receiving twenty-six lacs of rupees annually.

To cover the heavy expenses which service in the field necessitates in India, the Company made an extra allowance to their officers, termed batta; and upon the army marching to aid Mir Jaffier, he promised the officers double batta. But when the revenues of Bengal reverted to the Company, this was a charge that could be ill supported. Clive determined to remedy the evil, and issued an order to the effect that double batta should cease on the 1st of January, 1766, excepting in some few instances.

Hereupon the officers determined, unless the double batta was restored, to resign their commissions simultaneously upon a certain day. Clive having good information of what was proceeding, sent expresses to Calcutta and Madras for fresh officers, and arrested the principal conspirators. Many of the leaders, among others General Sir R. Fletcher, were tried and dismissed the service. Fletcher, however, through family interest, was reinstated, and subsequently appointed to the command of the forces at Madras. Clive would doubtless have more severely punished the promoters of this conspiracy, but it was considered uncertain at this period whether the Company had the power to enforce capital punishment upon Europeans.

Clive's health at length failing him, he resigned his command, and returned to England in the end of January 1767, leaving affairs in the hands of the select committee, at the head of which was Mr. Verelst.

The most extravagant expectations took possession of the proprietors of India stock, in consequence of Clive's acquisitions. Overlooking the vast outlay involved by his conquest, and the incidental expenses of upholding them, they outvoted the directory, and declared the dividends should be increased to twelve and a half per cent. This could not be effected without borrowing at an enormous interest; and the interposition of the ministry and parliament was solicited, which, much to the chagrin of both parties, canvassed the policy of allowing a trading company to exercise imperial power over a great and extending dominion. During the peaceful administrations of Mr. Verelst and Mr. Cartier, the revenues scarcely defrayed the expenses of government; notwithstanding which the delusion as to the riches of India continued to prevail, although it was at the time well known that an expedition to depose the Ghoorka, and reinstate the rajah of Nepaul, who had been dethroned by him, was abandoned in consequence of the want of funds, all the resources at control being required to arrest the impending dangers which threatened Madras.

The control of the Carnatic, obtained by the capture of Pondicherry, involved the English in all the political intrigues of the Deccan; and in their endeavour to obtain quiet possession of the Circars, they had to encounter the most hazardous war they had yet experienced in India.

Salabat Jing, subahdar of the Deccan, had not miscalculated when he reckoned that the departure of the French under Bussy would jeopardise his safety: he was assassinated by the confederates of his brother, Nizam Ali, who determined to maintain his vice-royalty in the Deccan, and to re-establish his authority over the Carnatic. He invaded and laid desolate the country; but made a precipitate retreat upon the advance of the English. When the Emperor Shah Alum ceded the Northern Circars to the English, the Deccan was esteemed a part of the vice-royalty; but this Nizam Ali would not admit, and resisted all attempts to take possession of it, until the English stipulated to pay him an annual tribute, and to assist him when necessary with troops; an undertaking which soon brought them into collision with Hyder Ali, the governor of Mysore.

While the French and English were fighting in the Carnatic, Hyder had risen from a subordinate rank to the command of the army of Mysore; and by subjugating the Nairs of Malabar, and taking possession of several small tracts of land in Southern India, established a principality for himself. According to their treaty with the nizam, the English joined him in invading Hyder Ali's territory, when our faithless auxiliary made peace with Hyder, and turned his arms against the English, whom he intended betraying to Hyder; but Colonel Smith discovering his treachery, retreated to Trincomalee, having previously engaged the combined forces of these native princes. The nizam, finding in several subsequent actions that the English were invariably victorious, became alarmed, broke his treaty with Hyder, and again addressed the Presidency of Madras, who, elated with the prospect of territorial aggrandisement, and presuming Mysore to be easily subjugated, bestowed its sovereignty upon Mohammed Ali; at the same time Colonel Smith, an experienced officer, was superseded in the command of the forces by the appointment of Colonel Wood, who was wholly destitute of knowledge in Indian warfare. This Hyder soon discovered, and defeated Wood, capturing the whole of his baggage. Subsequently, feigning to retreat, Hyder drew him from Madras; then, by forced marches, his son Tippoo, at the head of 6000 horse, appeared suddenly at the suburbs of the English capital. All was terror and confusion, amidst which Hyder was enabled to dictate terms of peace, which were agreed to.

Shah Alum, impatient of restoration to the throne of Delhi, unavailingly urged the English to yield their promised assistance. His prayer being disregarded, he formed an alliance with the Mahrattas; and by their aid easily reached his capital, rewarding his auxiliaries with the plunder of the country of the Rohillas. The emperor joined them in an attack upon Zabita Khan, whom, having deprived of the government of Delhi, he regarded with suspicion. Unable to withstand the imperialists and the Mahrattas combined, he was, after a spirited defence, defeated; and his country, then in a most flourishing condition, was, despite the emperor's wishes, laid waste by the Mahrattas. The remainder of the Rohilla chiefs being alarmed, sought their old enemy, the subahdar of Oude, engaging to pay him thirty lacs of rupees upon his driving the common enemy from their country. At this period the Mahrattas quarrelled with the emperor, and returned to Delhi, making him virtually a prisoner, and extorted from him the districts of Korah and Allahabad, after which they repaired to the Ganges, which they prepared to cross. The subahdar of Oude, though urgently pressed, never afforded any assistance to the Rohillas; yet, when the Mahrattas retreated, he demanded the payment of the thirty lacs as stipulated.

The subahdar and Warren Hastings, who had now succeeded Cartier as governor-general, met at Benares in September 1773, and signed a treaty, by which the emperor of Delhi and the Rohillas were sold to the subahdar. When Shah Alum joined the Mahrattas, the English held his conduct a justification for stopping the Bengal tribute. Hastings now went further. The districts of Korah and Allahabad he sold to the subahdar for fifty lacs of rupees; and for an additional forty lacs, and the expenses of the troops employed, he agreed to assist in the extermination of the innocent and peaceable Rohillas. Upon the subahdar demanding assistance, Colonel Champion, with a brigade, was despatched to join in the invasion, which ended in the total defeat of the Rohillas, and the fall of their general, Hafiz Rahmet Khan. The atrocities of this victory are almost unequalled; but the terms of the treaty were fulfilled, and the conquered country, excepting a small tract, was assigned to the ruler of Oude.

The three commissioners from England, who had been despatched to enforce the new constitution which parliament had framed, arrived on the 19th of October, 1774; they, with Hastings and Barwell, were to form the executive. The first subject discussed was the Rohilla war, which the three newly-arrived councillors censured with undisguised severity. They likewise complained that the correspondence of Mr. Middleton, the political agent at Oude, was withheld. They then voted the agent's recall, the withdrawal from the subahdar of the forces, and immediate payment for their services. Suja-ed-Dowla dying at this time, the council insisted that his son and successor should be held to his engagements, deliver the country of the zemindar of Benares to the Company, and augment the pay of the European brigade. Hastings ineffectually opposed these measures, the councillors being supported by the home authority.

Although in other parts the Company had largely increased their territory, but little augmentation appeared in Western India. Bassein and Salsette, commanding the Bombay harbour, were Portuguese settlements until 1750. A dispute among the Mahrattas respecting the succession to the post of Peishwa, presented a favourable opportunity for the interference of the Bombay authorities, who supported the claims of the Ragonat Ras, and stipulated that Bassein and Salsette should be ceded for this assistance. These terms were agreed to, and the English garrisoned both places. An army was now sent to place Poonah, the Mahratta capital, in Ragonat's possession; but orders arrived from the supreme council of Calcutta disapproving the Bombay policy, and commanding the abandonment of Ragonat. Upon which the English restored Bassein, with some territory in Gujerat, but retained Salsette and its tributary islands. Shortly after this mandate from Calcutta, despatches from the Court of Directors arrived, highly approving the policy of the Bombay Presidency, which naturally tended to increase the existing confusion and jealousy.

At this period the integrity of Warren Hastings was seriously impeached; charges of peculation and corruption, which he vainly endeavoured to suppress, were brought against him. The most important charge was that made by the Rajah Nuncomar, who proved that his son Goordass and Munny Begum had paid for certain offices they held. The council, upon this evidence, ordered Hastings to refund the money; but he refused to acknowledge their authority, and returned no reply to their order.

Nuncomar was, with others, indicted for conspiracy; but the attempt failed. He was afterwards, however, indicted for perjury at the instance of an obscure native, and tried before the Supreme Court by a jury of Englishmen, when he was convicted and hanged. Perjury was not capital by any existing law; and there now remains no doubt that the law was most shamefully perverted, in order to get rid of a person objectionable to certain official parties.

The death of one of the members of the council gave Hastings a majority; but he had authorised a Mr. Maclean to convey to the Court of Directors his resignation, which was accepted, and Mr. Wheeler named his successor. General Clavering, being senior member of the council, was empowered to officiate until Mr. Wheeler's arrival. Hastings, upon reconsideration, refused to carry out his resignation, disavowing Mr. Maclean's proceedings, and insisted upon being recognised as governor, threatening an appeal to arms. Eventually, however, the matter was referred to the courts of law, which pronounced for Hastings, who immediately proceeded to reverse all the former acts of council, a step highly disapproved by the Court of Directors; but to that Hastings paid no attention.

The Supreme Council having, by their interference, involved the authorities of Poonah and the Bengal government, it was proposed, in order to conciliate the Mahrattas, to give up Rajonat. Hastings, however, who recently censured the Bombay policy, now warmly advocated it, and ordered six battalions of sepoys, one company of artillery, and a corps of cavalry, under the command of Colonel Leslie, to act in concert with the Bombay army, entrusted to Colonel Egerton, for the purpose of restoring Rajonat as Peishwa.

The results of these expeditions were disgraceful to a degree.

Egerton was worsted by the Mahrattas, retreated, and eventually entered into a most humiliating treaty for the safety of his forces. Leslie's hesitation and negotiations carried on with different chiefs led to the suspicion of dishonourable motives; and the council finding their orders disregarded, deprived him of his command, and appointed Colonel Goddard in his stead, who advanced into the interior of the Mahratta country, hoping to join the Bengal army, when he learned the disgraceful treaty of Egerton, and refusing to acknowledge it, led his army to Surat, where Rajonat, having escaped from Poonah, joined him.

Goddard, having command of the army, took the field in January 1780, and shortly possessed himself of Dubhoy and Ahmedabad. The Mahrattas, by simulated overtures for peace and prolonged discussions, tried to overreach his diplomacy; but their efforts were futile, for on the morning of April the 3d he surprised both Scindiah and Holkar in their camp, routing their forces without loss on his side.

Sir Eyre Coote, who, by Clavering's death, was appointed a member of the Supreme Council, arrived in Bengal as a treaty was concluded with Rana, a Hindoo prince, whose territory was on the Jumna, between Oude and Scindiah's country. This prince was shortly after invaded by the Mahrattas, whom he could not resist. But a small force, under Captain Popham, was sent to the Rana, and expelled the Mahrattas from Gohud, driving them into their own country. This victory was succeeded by the capture of the fort of Gwalior, believed by the native princes to be impregnable. It was garrisoned by a thousand picked soldiers; nevertheless Popham, on the 3d of August, carried it by escalade, and by this act struck so much terror into the Mahratta ranks that they deserted the surrounding country.

This war occasioned fresh quarrels between Hastings and Francis, who mutually accused each other of falsehood and fraud. Their differences resulted in a duel, in which Francis was wounded; and it being evident that they could no longer act together, Francis returned to England.

The position of the Company in the Carnatic was becoming somewhat critical; the imbecility of the nabob compelling the Madras government to employ British forces to protect the country, they accordingly insisted that he should defray their expenses. The inadequacy of his revenue compelled him to borrow at exorbitant interest; and his embarrassments increased in proportion to the exactions of the lenders. At this period, July 1770, Admiral Sir John Lindsay reached Madras, armed with authority from the home government; and, acting in direct opposition to the Court of Directors and Madras executive, recognised the nabob as an independent sovereign, and openly espoused his cause.

By virtue of the stipulation entered into between Hyder and the English in 1769, to afford mutual support, he applied for assistance in an insurrection against the peishwa, but was refused. Again, in 1770, when the Mahrattas invaded Mysore, he demanded effectual support, offering three lacs of rupees to defray the expenses. Circumstances determined the English to avoid compliance until compelled; they therefore evaded his demands, while the nabob, being stimulated by the Mahrattas, was anxious to form an alliance with them. The nabob's views were supported by Lindsay, and opposed by the council; which ended in the recall of Lindsay, and the promotion in his stead of Sir Robert Harland, who also supported the alliance between the nabob and the Mahrattas, but met with decided opposition at Madras. A peace was eventually concluded between the Mahrattas and Hyder, unfavourable to the latter, who accordingly vented his anger against the English for their desertion of him.

Little as the authorities were inclined to favour the alliance of the nabob with the Mahrattas, they were not disinclined to support him against the rajah of Tanjore, who having attacked the polygars, or chiefs, of the Marawar districts, was ordered to desist by the nabob from offering violence to his vassals. The rajah was obdurate; when an army, under General Smith at Trichinopoly, was ordered to combine with the Carnatic forces, commanded by Omrah-al-Omrah, the nabob's son, and advance on Tanjore, the capital. This they invested, and made every preparation for an attack, having effected a breach; but at the last moment, to the indignation of the English authorities, Omrah-al-Omrah informed Smith that he had concluded a treaty with the rajah, and hostilities had ceased. Well knowing this arrangement could not be permanent, the English left their forces in the nabob's service, and retained the frontier town of Tanjore.

The nabob instantly demanded English assistance to subdue the very polygars upon whose behalf he had declared war with the rajah of Tanjore; and the government without demur joined in the expedition, which ended in the defeat of the Marawars. When this petty war was concluded, the nabob, upon the pretext that the late treaty had not been maintained, determined to attack Tanjore again; which he did on the 20th of August, 1773, and captured it on the 16th of the following December, taking the rajah and his family prisoners.

The Court of Directors highly disapproved of this step, and sent out

Lord Pigot, with orders to restore him, which he effected despite all opposition; but was eventually arrested and placed in confinement by the majority of the council, and after eight months died in imprisonment.

The government of Madras, on Pigot's death, was administered by Sir Thomas Rumbold, Mr. Whitehill, and Sir Hector Munro. Rumbold's first measure was to adopt new arrangements in the collection of the revenues of the Northern Circars, which, it was asserted, was for the corrupt gain of himself and his supporters; this would appear to have been verified, as large sums were brought into Madras which never reached the treasury.

It was agreed, in 1776, with the Nizam, that his brother, Salabat Jing, should retain the Circar of Guntur for life, or so long as the subahdar remained in friendship with the Company. But when it was found that Salabat Jing had enlisted a French force, a negotiation was set on foot, by which, for an annual sum, he ceded Guntur to the Company, and engaged to dismiss the French on receiving an English force, under General Harper, to protect his country. The French passed from Salabat Jing into his brother the Nizam's service, who was jealous of this alliance with the English, and indignant at the refusal of the Madras council to pay the stipulated tribute for the possession of the Northern Circars. The Supreme Council at Calcutta remonstrated against the impolicy of the Madras proceedings, to which Rumbold replied in no measured terms; and in order further to shew his defiance, granted a lease of Guntur to the nabob of Arcot for ten years. At length the Court of Directors, aroused to a sense of the true state of affairs, dismissed Rumbold and one of his advisers from their service, and two others from their seats in the council; severely reprimanding Sir Hector Munro, the commander of the forces, for his share in the late proceedings.

Rumbold had, however, been guilty of faults of omission as well as of commission, some of which subsequently proved sources of great calamity. Hyder, who had really great cause of complaint against the Madras government, formed an alliance with the French; and the governor of Pondicherry furnished him with arms, ammunition, and stores of every description from the French settlement of Mahe on the Malabar coast. Rumbold was informed of this, but took no notice; and while he treated Hyder with contempt, allowed the military establishment at Madras to fall into miserable inefficiency.

Intelligence being received at Bengal, in July 1778, that war had broken out between England and France, it was determined to capture the French settlements in India. Chandernagore, Carical, and Masulipatam surrendered at once. Pondicherry capitulated after a vigorous defence, the garrison marching out with the honours of war. The defences and fortifications were then destroyed. The small fort and settlement of Mahe was the sole spot left to the French in India; this place Hyder had previously threatened in the event of its being invaded to revenge upon the Carnatic; but despite this, and the defeats the British forces had formerly sustained in the Mahratta country, the government of Madras persevered, and Mahe was taken on the 19th of March, 1779, by Colonel Braithwaite, who, when ordered to join General Goddard at Surat the following November, destroyed the fort. Before Braithwaite had commenced his march for Surat, the chief of Tellicherry sough this assistance to avert the hostility of Hyder, who was offended in consequence of the former harbouring a Nair chief who had displeased the ruler of Mysore; whereupon Braithwaite moved his forces towards Tellicherry.

The political atmosphere had for some time been getting more and more disturbed; and at length, in November 1799, the Nabob of the Carnatic gave the Madras executive warning that Hyder, the Nizam, and the Mahrattas had united in a determination to expel the English from India. The only heed taken was in the following June, when Col. Baillie, who then commanded the forces protecting Salabat Jing, was ordered to cross the Kistna in the event of disturbances in the Carnatic. On the 21st of July Hyder crossed the frontier with an army of 100,000 men, and upwards of 100 pieces of artillery, well manned; he was counselled by M. Lally, the commander of the French force, a gentleman skilled in his profession, and of high integrity. The English forces comprised 6000 infantry, and 100 cavalry, to which the Nabob's irregular horse and a few pieces of cannon were additions; while the people were disaffected at the miserable and divided government of the Company and the Nabob.

To add to existing perplexities, Munro was reluctant to command, and wished Lord Macleod, who had just arrived, to assume the management; but Macleod declined risking his reputation in executing Munro's plans, doubting their judiciousness. At length Munro, after ordering Baillie to join him at Conjeveram, marched from St. Thomas's Mount, persisting in encumbering himself with heavy artillery, although he had no fortifications to attack, and it was difficult to find cattle to carry his provisions.

Arcot was besieged by Hyder, and Munro felt anxious for a junction with Baillie's force, in order to relieve the place; but on the 31st of August he learnt that Baillie was stopped by the swelling of a river a few miles north of Trepossore, and the same day that Hyder was moving on Conjeveram, having left Arcot. At Perambaucam, fifteen miles from the main army, Baillie was attacked by Tippoo Saib, Hyder's son, with a very superior force, which was repulsed by the English; but Baillie was so weakened, that, instead of advancing, he urgently requested Munro to push on with the main body to relieve him. Munro, however, sent a detachment under Colonel Fletcher to join Baillie, who, believing further reinforcements would arrive, left his position on the 9th of September, and, despite the vicinity of Tippoo's forces, continued his march during the night. In the morning intelligence was brought into camp that Hyder with all his strength was advancing upon him. What courage and discipline could do, Baillie's gallant band accomplished; and with the slightest assistance from Munro, Hyder would have been defeated. As it was, left to himself, and losing two of his tumbrils by an explosion, Baillie found his forces reduced to 400 men, and at length exhibited a flag of truce. No sooner had they laid down their arms, quarter having been promised upon immediate surrender, than Hyder's troops rushed upon them, and would have murdered the whole, had not M. Lally and the French officers boldly and generously interfered, by which the lives of 200 men were saved. This disaster compelled Munro to retreat upon Madras, which he reached on the 13th of September.

The council now began to regret the corrupt practices and indifference it had previously exhibited; while its thorough destitution of supplies and military appliances had no tendency to diminish the uneasiness of the authorities. But the Governor-General, acting up to the exigencies of the occasion, proposed that fifteen lacs of rupees and a large detachment of European infantry and artillery should be sent to Madras; that Sir Eyre Coote should command the army, and alone expend the money transmitted; and that the governor of Fort St. George should be suspended.

These orders were reluctantly obeyed by the Madras Council. On the 7th of November Sir Eyre Coote took his seat in the Madras Council, and produced the decree deposing the governor, which was supported by the majority. Arcot having been captured, Coote proceeded to protect Vellore and Wandewash, both being closely besieged and gallantly defended. Wandewash was abandoned upon the English approaching, who could not pursue their advantage. The arrival of a French fleet compelled them to march on Pondicherry, where the French inhabitants, hoping to recover their former position in India, had enlisted troops and collected stores. Coote speedily disarmed the inhabitants, removed the stores, destroyed the boats, and marched on Cuddalore, then threatened by Hyder, whom he endeavoured to draw into an action; failing in which, he moved his army on to Trichinopoly, and on his way unsuccessfully attacked the fortified pagoda of Chillingbram: his failure encouraged Hyder to risk a battle, which terminated, after six hours' desperate fighting, in the complete defeat of the Mysore army.

Coote, being now joined by a body of sepoys from Bengal, marched upon the enemy, who were strongly posted; when Hyder's army nearly suffered a total rout, which he had tact enough to declare a drawn battle, and marched towards Vellore; Coote followed, and once more defeated him, having surprised him in his camp. Hyder's cavalry were nearly all sacrificed in his anxiety to save his guns. After this engagement, Coote returned to Madras, having lost nearly one-third of his forces in his severe engagements with Hyder.

England and Holland being now at war, Lord Macartney, who had just arrived at Madras as governor, resolved on attacking the Dutch settlements in India, and commenced with Pulicat and Sadras, both of which places surrendered on the first summons. He then determined to attack Negapatam; but here Coote's jealousy developed itself; he would neither march himself nor spare any of his troops; upon which Lord Macartney collected the remainder of the forces in the Presidency, and gave the command to Munro, who displayed great energy and ability, and compelled the governor in less than three weeks to surrender. From thence a detachment was sent which took possession of Trincomalee in Ceylon.

The capture of Negapatam had no tendency to allay Coote's feelings; and Lord Macartney experienced great difficulty in maintaining a semblance of good feeling while negotiating with the nabob. But the intelligence of the loss of Chittore, and the consequent exposure of Vellore, effected more than either remonstrance or supplication. Coote took the field, though so ill that he was obliged to be carried in a palanquin, and would not return until an apoplectic fit compelled him to quit the camp.

The Madras detachment occupied Tellicherry after the capture of Mahe, closely besieged by the Nairs,.but was relieved by Major Abingdon, who arrived with a force from Bombay. The fortress was shortly afterwards invested by a general of Hyder's, and Major Abingdon applied to Bombay for assistance, upon which he was ordered to evacuate the fort; but upon a second application was supplied with a considerable force. Abingdon now resolved to act on the offensive. In the night of the 7th of January, 1782, he made a vigorous sally and attacked the enemy's camp, throwing it into such disorder that they fled in every direction, leaving their wounded leader a prisoner in the hands of the British. After destroying the enemy's works and improving the fortifications of Tellicherry, he marched against and captured Calicut, garrisoning it with English troops.

During the preceding events a secret expedition was planned and fitted out in England for offensive operations against the Cape of Good Hope and in the Indian seas. The designs and destination of this armament were discovered by M. de Suffrein, the French commander, who followed the English with his squadron to the Cape de Verd islands, where, in Praya Bay, he attacked them, but was beaten off. The English, nevertheless, required so much refitting, Suffrein having made the Cape previous to them, that he strengthened and improved its fortifications so as to render the contemplated attack abortive.

Commodore Johnstone, who commanded the English squadron, having captured a number of Dutch East-Indiamen in Saldanha Bay, returned home with his prizes, leaving a portion of his armament to proceed to India with the troops on board. At this period General Meadows and Colonel Fullarton, with the strength of the army, sailed in search of Admiral Hughes on the Coromandel coast, while the remainder, under Colonel Mackenzie, sailed for Bombay. The latter learnt upon his arrival that Madras was in danger; he accordingly joined Abingdon at Calicut, and entering Hyder's territory, was successful in creating a diversion.

M. de Suffrein, having reinforced his fleet at the Isle of France, made for the Coromandel coast; from whence, after an indecisive action with Admiral Hughes, he retreated, and landed an army of 3000 men under M. Bussy at Porto Novo.

These auxiliaries Tippoo hastened to join, he having just destroyed Colonel Braithwaite's force at Tanjore. Braithwaite, whose little band consisted of 100 Europeans, 1500 sepoys, and 300 cavalry, was encamped near the banks of the Coleroon in fancied security. But Tippoo, with 10,000 cavalry, the like amount of infantry, 400 Europeans, and 20 pieces of cannon, surrounded him when least expected. For twenty-six hours Braithwaite fought and repulsed Tippoo; but when M. Lally, with his Europeans, advanced, the sepoys were disheartened, fell into confusion, and victory declared against the English commander, who was made prisoner with the whole of his force.

With the French reinforcement, Tippoo's designs became more

enlarged; and on the 3d of April, Cuddalore, an excellent military and maritime station for the French, surrendered to him. Had the king's officers deigned to receive orders and advice from the Company's servants, this loss would have been prevented; and upon several other occasions the like cause was seriously prejudicial to the public service.

Disputes with the civil authorities, and absence of proper supplies, kept Coote in cantonments until the 17th of April. His first object was the protection of Parmacoil; but reaching Caranjoly, he learned its surrender. He then attempted to surprise Arnes, Hyder's principal depôt; but Tippoo removed the treasure while Hyder engaged the English with a distant cannonade, and Coote fell back upon Madras.

During his preparations to join the French fleet, and in retaking Negapatam, Hyder amused Coote by pretending to negotiate. And it most fortunately happened, that as Suffrein was making for that place, Sir Edward Hughes fell in with and brought him to action. The engagement was most severe, and victory was declaring against the French, when a sudden shift of wind enabled Suffrein to bear off for Cuddalore, where he quickly repaired his vessels, and again put to sea.

When the news of this action reached Madras, Lord Macartney pressed Sir E. Hughes, as both Negapatam and Trincomalee were threatened, to put to sea and protect them; but disinclination to receive orders from a Company's servant made the admiral obstinate, and he put to sea when more convenient to himself, on the 20th of August, three weeks after Suffrein had sailed from Cuddalore. The result may be anticipated. Trincomalee had surrendered three days before his arrival. Eager to avenge this loss, he immediately engaged the French fleet with an inferior force, and obtained a victory, but did not know how to profit by it. He disabled one of the French ships, and two others were so crippled that it took them ten days to get into harbour; but Hughes made no attempt to capture them, and returned to Madras.

The monsoon coming on, Hughes determined to leave the coast of Coromandel and seek shelter in Bombay, notwithstanding Negapatam was attacked, and Bickerton on his way to join him with five sail of the line. Four days after Hughes's departure Bickerton was in the Madras roads, when, ascertaining the admiral's movements, he followed him to Bombay. Sir Eyre Coote at the same time resigned the command of the army to General Stuart, a man as obstinate as himself, but of far inferior ability. Within a short period of his resignation, Coote was again attacked with illness, under which he sank in a few days.

The governments of Bengal and Bombay having declared war against the Mahrattas, Goddard besieged Bassein, and sent Colonel Hartley to secure for the British the revenues of the Concan, and cover the besieging army. Hartley drove the Mahrattas from the Concan, taking a position near the Bhore ghaut, thence he retreated on Doogaur before a host of the enemy. On the 10th and 11th of December, an army of 20,000 Mahrattas attacked him; the result proved a complete victory for the British, the Mahratta general being among the slain.

Bassein having surrendered, Goddard advanced on Poonah, whence he soon returned, the Mahrattas following him and ravaging the country as he descended the ghauts. On the Bengal side, Popham had been superseded by Colonel Carnac, whose position was so critical, that he resolved, as a last resource, to attack Scindiah's camp by night. The stratagem succeeded perfectly; the enemy fled in every direction, most of their guns, elephants, and a quantity of ammunition, being left to the conquerors. Colonel Muir, who was Carnac's senior, then took the command; shortly after which Scindiah, whose resources were exhausted, entered into negotiation with him, and a treaty was concluded at Salbye on the 17th of May, 1782.

Reinforcements having been supplied to Colonel Mackenzie at Calicut, he opened the campaign in September, and took several forts; but the capture of Palagatcherry was essential to perfect his success. This was, however, impossible without artillery, which he had been compelled to leave behind, wanting draught cattle; upon which Colonel Macleod, who had been dispatched by Coote to take the command, retired to a camp a few miles distant, until his battering-train should arrive. Through the negligence of the officer who conducted the retreat, the baggage, stores, and ammunition were placed in the rear. This did not escape the enemy, who, when the main body had passed a narrow defile, made a sudden attack, and carried off the provision and greater portion of the ammunition. The sea-coast was now the only retreat the English could make. Tippoo hastened after and overtook them with 20,000 men; but as they retreated they fought until Panrani was occupied by them. Here they with difficulty maintained their ground, and were anticipating a second attack, when Tippoo's army was seen in full retreat, and in a few hours not one of his forces remained. The death of Hyder had reached Tippoo secretly, and caused the sudden movement, leaving the English force at full liberty.

CHAPTER III.

FROM THE ACCESSION OF TIPPOO SAIB AS SULTÁN OF MYSORE TO HIS OVERTHROW AND DEATH AT THE SIEGE OF SERINGAPATAM.

A.D. 1782-1799.

THE enemy in vain endeavoured to keep secret the death of the old monarch Lord Macartney was not long in ascertaining the nature of the intelligence which had so promptly withdrawn Tippoo from the field; and fully aware of the confusion which invariably arises in all native states on an occurrence of this kind, wished to profit by the opportunity thus presented to him, and urged General Stuart to attack the Mysorean army, which he rightly judged would be easily overthrown in the absence of their leader. Stuart, however, either did not credit the report of Hyder's death, or disliking to expose himself and his troops at a time of year not usually one of action in that country, delayed operations until the season had changed; and it was consequently February in 1783 before he was in motion. Stuart having thus lost this opportunity, withdrew the garrisons from Wandewash and Caranjoly, and blew up both forts; then marching to Vallore, he heard that Tippoo was retreating from the Carnatic, and had ordered the evacuation of Arcot.

The necessity of establishing his hereditary authority, and repelling a formidable invasion of the Sikhs, obliged Tippoo to visit the western side of India. The English army, after his sudden departure, divided; the sepoys marching by land to Tellicherry, while the Europeans proceed by sea to Merjee, where they were joined by General Matthews with a considerable army, who passed the ghauts, took Bidnore and Ananpore, and compelled Mangalore to capitulate.

The treasure found at these places Matthews refused to apply in payment of the arrears due to the army, which Colonel Macleod, Colonel Mackenzie, and Major Shaw quitted, to complain to the authorities at Bombay, who superseded Matthews, and appointed Macleod in his stead. Returning by sea, these officers fell in with a Mahratta fleet; and, ignorant of the treaty recently made, an engagement ensued, in which Macleod was wounded and made prisoner, Mackenzie mortally wounded, and Shaw killed.

The army of Matthews being most injudiciously dispersed in small detachments, gave Tippoo an opportunity for concentrating his forces; suddenly attacking Bidnore, he forced it to capitulate after a gallant resistance. Matthews, who commanded the garrison, previous to surrendering, distributed the treasures in his possession among his soldiers, which Tippoo held to be a breach of the terms of capitulation, and made it a pretext for the imprisonment of Matthews, who was subsequently assassinated; his companions in arms were likewise subjected to long and rigorous confinement. After this action Tippoo invested Mangalore, a sea-port to which he attached great importance.

The Madras army being inactive, Suffrein landed Bussy with a reinforcement at Cuddalore; during which time Lord Macartney in vain remonstrated with General Stuart against the impolicy of allowing the French to occupy a post so important. After several weeks, Stuart marched, but with so much reluctance, that he put his men over three miles a day only. In the meantime the fleet, which had been augmented, returned to Madras, and was sent to assist in the recapture of Cuddalore. By the time Stuart arrived at Cuddalore the French had erected several fortified points, which he attacked with partial success, but made no attempt to improve his victory.

Affairs at sea were managed still worse. The English and French fleets engaged off Cuddalore. Suffrein was thoroughly defeated, but remained to repair, while the victorious admiral sailed for Madras, which afforded Suffrein the opportunity of landing men from his fleet to reinforce Bussy, who attacked the English, but unsuccessfully. Bussy, undaunted, prepared for another attack, when intelligence arrived that peace was established between France and England. A cessation of hostilities was agreed upon, and Tippoo was invited by Bussy to join in the treaty; the French soldiers in his service being at the same time recalled. The same messenger that brought intelligence of peace brought orders for General Stuart to appear before the governor and council of Madras, a summons he reluctantly obeyed: it was resolved he should be dismissed the Company's service. To this sentence he refused to submit, and was supported by Sir John Burgoyne; but Lord Macartney arrested Stuart, and sent him in a few days to England.

These errors and disgraces were retrieved by Colonel Fullarton, who commanded in the southern districts. In the height of a victorious career, Stuart stopped and ordered him to join at Cuddalore; while marching, he learnt of the armistice and also of Tippoo's demonstration against Mangalore, and without further orders he pushed on to Seringapatam. In his way he captured Palagatcherry and Coimbatore; but received orders, on the 28th of November, to cease all offensive operations, and evacuate the places he had captured.

Fullarton well knew Tippoo's treacherous nature, and delayed executing the orders he had received; which foresight was amply verified by his receiving directions, on the 26th of the ensuing January, to renew the war. Tippoo would not listen to peace until the reduction of Mangalore, which he had besieged upwards of twelve months. A force was sent to relieve the place under Macleod, who, instead of doing so, negotiated with Tippoo to be allowed to supply the garrison with provisions: the result of these delays was, that Campbell was obliged to capitulate, marching to Tellicherry with all the honours of war.

A treaty of peace, embracing a mutual restitution of all captured places, was signed on March 11, 1784, and ratified by the Supreme Council at Calcutta during Hastings's absence, who wished subsequently to introduce modifications, which Lord Macartney honourably rejected.

From the uncertain way in which the act of parliament was drawn up which created the Supreme Court, consisting of one chief and three puisne judges, a conflict ensued between it and the council, virtually involving the Company's right to the provinces acquired. The civil jurisdiction of the Supreme Court compassed all claims of the Company against British subjects, and of British subjects against the natives, presuming the parties disputing acquiesced in appealing to its decision. In criminal cases it extended to all British subjects and servants of the Company; but the act did not define what constituted a British subject, and the judges classed, not only all the subjects of the Company, but even subjects of the native princes over whom the Company exercised any influence, as coming within its jurisdiction. The effects of this interpretation were not long before they manifested themselves. Writs were issued against the Zemindars by individuals for ordinary debts, upon which the defendants were ordered to appear at Calcutta; if they neglected, they were arrested, or if upon their arrival they were unable to procure bail, they were carried off to prison, where they remained pending the litigation of the suit. It had been the usage in

India, in collecting the revenue, to exercise summary jurisdiction in cases of disputed payments, which power was vested in the provincial councils called Dewannee Adaulut, with which the Supreme Court soon interfered; and when any summary process was enforced, the defendant was encouraged to take out a writ of habeas corpus in the Supreme Court, when the judges took bail for the appearance of the parties, and liberated them. More than this, the Company had reserved to the nabob of Bengal the administration of all civil cases. The Supreme Court, however, did not heed this reservation, and disputed its enforcement. Whereupon Mr. Hastings instituted a new court, the Sudder Dewannee Adaulut, and placed Sir Elijah Impey at the head of it. The office and emoluments being held during the pleasure of the governor and council, it was presumed that Impey would no longer support the pretensions of the Supreme Court against the Dewannee Adaulut, and would effect a reconciliation between the antagonistic courts. But the House of Commons censured these proceedings; and Impey was recalled to answer several criminal charges.

Hastings made some important alterations in the finance department. A revenue-board was formed at the Presidency to superintend the collection and lease the revenues to the Zemindars. He then made a tour of the upper provinces; and, as the government was pressed in its finances, determined to obtain assistance from the rajah of Benares and the nabob of Oude.

The rajah of Benares, Cheyt Sing, paid a tribute upon receiving protection of the Company; and an addition was demanded, which the rajah paid, stipulating that after the year it was not to be re-demanded. It was, however, again demanded, and remonstrated against; when an army was sent to enforce it, with 2000*l.* besides for the payment of the troops employed. The same proceeding was repeated the third year, with an additional fine of 10,000*l.*, although the rajah's agent had presented the governor-general with two lacs of rupees. Hastings, having determined on his line of proceeding, upon reaching Benares refused Cheyt Sing an audience, and had him arrested as a defaulter; when the population broke into the palace, and cut down the larger portion of sepoys and their officers having custody of the rajah. The latter, in the confusion, escaped to the opposite bank of the river. Hastings, who was comparatively wanting both in men and money, escaped to Chunar. Cheyt Sing, when all his offers of submission had been rejected, raised a few troops, who, after encountering a severe defeat from the British troops, disbanded themselves; and the unfortunate rajah fled to Bundelcund, leaving his wife and treasure in the Bejygur fort, which was soon taken, and Cheyt Sing formally deposed. A grandson of the late rajah, Bulwant Sing, being declared the ruler of Benares, the tribute was raised to forty lacs, and the administration of the laws was placed under the control of the Company.

Hastings next directed his attention to the nabob of Oude, whose tribute was in arrear 1,400,000*l.*, the payment of which he intended to enforce. Previous, however, to any hostile display, he appointed a fresh resident, named Middleton, at Lucknow, in direct opposition to the wishes of the directory. Hastings instructed this official to proceed in his demands, although knowing the nabob's revenues had been eaten up in the support of the English forces he had been compelled to maintain. Middleton, however, was to look to another quarter for the deficiency. At this period there were resident at Lucknow, in possession of large revenues, two native princesses, or begums, the mothers of the late and present nabobs, to whom Suja-ad-Dowla had bequeathed the larger portion of his treasure. These princesses, it was suggested by the nabob, were far richer than they should be, and were fair objects of plunder, under the plea that they had endeavoured to excite rebellion in favour of Cheyt Sing. They were accordingly stripped of their revenues forthwith, through the instrumentality of the nabob, who, having invested their palaces, crowned his proceedings by putting the chief and confidential attendants in irons, and threatening to keep them without food until the treasures of the princesses were yielded up. By means of this violence half-a-million was extorted, which sum failed to procure the release of the unfortunate captives for some months; indeed, not until it was manifest that the begums would surrender nothing further, were their attendants liberated. Hastings' share in these proceedings was rewarded by a present of 100,000*l.* from the nabob, which he asked the Company's permission to accept, as a reward for his services.

The sums of money thus obtained—whatever may be thought of their source—were undoubtedly the means of saving the Carnatic, and probably of preserving our empire in the East. The sinews of war thus fortunately supplied, enabled the campaign in the Carnatic to be pushed on with renewed vigour, and finally ended in the complete overthrow of all our enemies in that quarter,—a consummation that no doubt soothed the great man's mind during after annoyances and persecutions.

Having thus consolidated the British power in India, and having during the two years of peace which followed the wars in the Carnatic, placed the revenues and general administration of the country in a sounder and more efficient state, the Governor-General tendered his resignation, and in the early part of 1785 embarked for England. Seldom, if ever, has any man quitted the shores of India so universally admired and beloved as did Warren Hastings. Military men, civilians, and natives, all united by one common consent in regretting the departure of the man who, after a thirty years' residence and a fourteen years' rule, had endeared himself to all sections of the community.

The East India Company having received formal intimation that their charter would expire in three years from the 25th of March 1780, great interest was excited regarding the principle of its renewal. The political events and charges of peculation and oppression laid against the Company's servants in no wise favourably influenced either the public or parliamentary feeling; while Lord North, the minister, held it as the law of the constitution, that acquired territory belonged solely to the crown. This was spiritedly opposed by the Company; and Lord North, whose administration was extinct in 1782, promised an extension of the charter, with this one further condition, that all despatches received by the directors from their servants in India should be open to the inspection of the minister.

The Marquis of Rockingham, a known antagonist to the East India Board, succeeded North; but his death shortly afterwards placed the Earl of Shelburne, since the Marquis of Lansdowne, at the head of affairs. Fox, who was greatly hurt at being passed over, left the cabinet, and joined North in the opposition which defeated the Shelburne administration; and, to the annoyance of George III., brought about the celebrated Coalition Ministry. Fox soon introduced a bill for the better government of India, which proposed vesting the patronage of the directory and proprietary in seven commissioners appointed by the legislature; and also proposed measures for affording a more creditable local government to India. Calumny and interest represented his efforts as a means of personal aggrandisement, the seven commissioners being represented as ready instruments in his hands for ruling India. The House of Commons, whose select committees had made valuable reports upon India, were uninfluenced, and passed the bill by large majorities. Its fate was different in the House of Lords; for there the king, acting most unconstitutionally, authorised Lord Temple to state that he should personally regard every man as his enemy who supported the bill; which was consequently thrown out by a majority of eight, the numbers on division being eighty-seven against seventy-nine.

Shortly after, Pitt, as prime minister, introduced and carried his India bill, and established the Board of Control, composed of six privy councillors chosen by the king; whose powers, as their title implies, authorise them to check and control the most important functions of the Company.

Upon the departure of Hastings, the senior member of Council, Mr. Macpherson undertook the government, which he conducted with great ability, and much to the satisfaction of the directors.

After some delay in the nomination of a successor to Hastings, the Court of Directors appointed Lord Cornwallis to the vacant office; and that nobleman arrived in Calcutta and assumed the reins of government in September 1786, taking at the same time the command of the forces in India.

Promising as were the appearances of the political horizon at this juncture, the new governor-general soon found it as difficult to maintain peace as had his predecessor. The first symptom of approaching troubles was by an act of Tippoo, sultan of Mysore, who on some pretence invaded the dominions of the rajah of Travancore, an ally of the English, and succeeded in introducing a portion of his army within the intrenched lines of the rajah's fortifications. The resolute daring of a small body of Nairs, however, turned the fortune of the day; and Tippoo had the mortification of beholding his numerous troops flying before a mere handful of Hindoo warriors. The sultan himself had some difficulty in escaping with his life, so hotly was he pursued by the resolute band of Nairs.

Tippoo endeavoured to persuade Lord Cornwallis that it was an unauthorised attack of his troops; his lordship, knowing his adversary's character, negotiated treaties with the Nizam and the Mahrattas at Poonah, to control the restlessness of Tippoo, who meanwhile renewed his assault upon the lines of Travancore, which he carried on the 7th of May, 1790, razed them, and desolated the country. This attack was met by the advance of General Meadows with the Madras army on Coimbatore, and thence to the interior of the Mysore country; while General Abercrombie with the Bombay army descended by the Malabar coast on Tippoo's territory. The campaign was terminated in Tippoo's favour, Meadows having ineffectually endeavoured to draw him into a general engagement, which he dexterously avoided, and captured several depôts well supplied with stores and provisions.

The necessary arrangements having been completed, Cornwallis personally opened the second campaign, and reached the pass of Mooglee before his enemy could offer any resistance. On the 5th of March,

1791, the English arrived before Bangalore. Colonel Floyd on the next morning, with a strong detachment, unexpectedly fell in with Tippoo's army, and rashly ordered an immediate attack; which would probably have been successful, had not a severe wound prevented him from directing the operations. The retreat was covered by Major Gowdie, who with a few guns effectually checked the pursuit. Cornwallis, on the night of the 21st of March, though the Sultan and his army were in sight of the town, attacked and captured Bangalore, when a terrible slaughter ensued, upwards of 1000 of the besieged falling during the storming. The possession of Bangalore did not produce the advantages anticipated; there were scarcely any provisions, stores, or draught cattle; and the Nizam's contingent was worthless. But the governor-general, undaunted, advanced upon Seringapatam, having previously ordered an invasion of Mysore on the Malabar side by the Bombay army. Tippoo was defeated; but the want of supplies and increasing sickness compelled Cornwallis to retreat, with the loss of his battering train and stores. The Mahrattas joined his lordship a few days after this loss, well supplied with draught cattle and provisions; but the season was too advanced for active operations, and the army retreated to Bangalore.

The third campaign having been well prepared for, was opened with spirit, detachments securing the hill-forts which protected the passes into the Mysore country. Amongst the captures was the celebrated Savendroog, which, from its natural position and artificial advantages, appeared impregnable, but was taken by storm on the 21st of December; and Octadroog, a fortress almost as strong, fell a few days later.

A detachment under the command of Captain Little, sent to aid the Mahrattas, obtained great advantages over the enemy; his allies, however, instead of assisting, proved an incumbrance. With 700 men he attacked a strongly-fortified camp of the Mysorean army, consisting of 10,000 men, whom he routed, capturing their guns and stores. After this fell the fortress of Lemoga, opening a portion of Tippoo's territory till then free from the ravages of the war. The Mahrattas, instead of advancing to support General Abercrombie, who reached the top of the ghauts on the Malabar side, made a miserable attempt on Prednore, for the sake of plunder, thus interfering with the plan of the campaign, and causing the fall of Coimbatore before the Mysore army. The capitulation being flagrantly violated, Lord Cornwallis refused to listen to Tippoo's solicitations for peace.

On the 5th of February, 1792, reinforcements from Hyderabad having arrived, the governor-general advanced to lay siege to Seringapatam. On the 6th, in the evening, the troops having been dismissed from parade, were ordered to fall in again with their arms and ammunition. By eight all was completed for a surprise on Tippoo's fortified camp, the army advancing in three columns. Tippoo's army, which consisted of 50,000 infantry and 6000 cavalry, under his own command, were routed; and their assailants, after storming several batteries, obtained a defensible position before the dawn of morning. At daybreak hostilities were more fiercely renewed, the fortress opening a destructive fire on the redoubts captured by the English, and vigorous attempts were made to recover their lost positions; but Tippoo's soldiery were beaten in every direction, and the battle terminated on the evening of the 7th: 535 men were killed and wounded upon the English side; but the adverse army suffered to the extent of upwards of 4000. General Abercrombie joined Lord Cornwallis nine days after with an augmentation of 2000 Europeans and 4000 native troops.

On the 24th Tippoo yielded to his fate, and most reluctantly signed a treaty, by which he bound himself to give up one-half of his territories to his conquerors, pay three crores and two lacs of rupees as the expenses of the war, and to surrender two of his sons as hostages for the performance of these stipulations.

Tippoo evinced great disinclination to complete his promises, notwithstanding his sons were in the English camp. The independence of the rajah of Coorg was most objectionable to him; and it was not until he found preparations were being made for a renewed attack, that he submitted on the 19th of March, when his hostages delivered in the definitive treaty. Upon the conclusion of this treaty, Lord Cornwallis took possession of all the French settlements in India, the revolution in France having brought on a war with England and that country.

The charter of the East India Company met with but little opposition or discussion when renewed in 1793. At this period Sir John Shore, a civil servant of the Company, was appointed successor to Lord Cornwallis; whose financial and judicial measures, especially the Permanent Settlement, had proved far from advantageous to those whom he really intended to benefit; hence Shaw's appointment, who was well acquainted with the financial administration of India.

The treaty between the English, the Mahrattas, and the Nizam did not provide for the possibility of disagreement among the contracting parties, which soon afterwards occurred. The Mahrattas were desirous of grasping the spoils of the Nizam, and at the same time apprehensive of the increasing power of the English. Their chief Scindia openly expressed his dissatisfaction, and at the same time made no hesitation in asserting that Tippoo should be strengthened as a necessary opposing power to the English. His death shortly afterwards prevented this formidable combination from taking place; upon which the Nizam, believing the court of Poonah to be in a state of confusion, hastily invaded the Mahratta territory, but was encountered by a body of troops near Kurdla, where an action took place, from which the Nizam and his officers fled, leaving his army to suffer a total rout. The Nizam sheltered himself in the fort of Kurdla for two days; at the end of which time he submitted to his enemies' conditions. The Company refused upon this occasion to allow the British in the Nizam's service to join him; and upon his return he dismissed them, and appointed a French officer to discipline his troops. This gave the English great uneasiness; and not less so from the fact of the attempt of some French officers to escape from Madras, and the desertion of several sepoys from the Madras to the French service.

Sir John Shore, desirous of effecting a reconciliation with Tippoo, immediately the terms of the treaty were fulfilled, delivered up his sons with due honours. But the sultan, as revengeful as proud, declined to meet Shore's advances, treating the officer who accompanied his sons with great coolness, and refusing a second interview with him.

The extravagance and incapacity of the nabob had produced lamentable effects in Oude, to which a disputed accession upon his death added considerably; his brother claiming the throne, asserting the nabob's reputed children to be the offspring of others. The governor-general, until visiting Lucknow, favoured the pretension of young Vizir Ali; but whilst there he obtained such information, that he confirmed the claims of Sadat Ali, the late nabob's brother, who was proclaimed on the 21st of January, 1798.

In the Carnatic, affairs were not more promising than those of Oude. Lord Hobart, governor of Madras, endeavoured to prevail upon the nabob to renounce his authority; but the governor-general refusing to allow any intimidation, all his endeavours on this point failed. But if unsuccessful with the nabob, Lord Hobart proved otherwise with the Dutch; for immediately on receiving the news of the outbreak of war between England and Holland, he took possession of Ceylon, Malacca, Banda, and Amboyna, all Dutch settlements, with scarcely a struggle. Shortly after, he was superseded by Lord Clive as governor of Madras; and Sir John Shore being elevated to the peerage as Lord Teignmouth, sailed for England, having resigned the governor-generalship.

The affairs of India were now placed under the control of Lord Mornington, who assumed the office of governor-general on the 17th of May, 1798. Shortly after his arrival he received the copy of a proclamation, issued by the French governor of the Mauritius, certifying that Tippoo Sultan had sent two officers to propose an offensive and defensive alliance with the French; and soliciting soldiers to drive the English out of Southern India. The document also requested the citizens to enlist, for which Tippoo would pay handsomely. This was at first considered a forgery; but upon its proving genuine, no alternative appeared to be left, and accordingly war was declared against Tippoo.

General Harris, the governor of Madras, could not respond with promptitude to the orders of Lord Mornington, owing to the embarrassed state of the finances of his presidency, as well as to the opposition offered to the war by several of the leading men of the government. Little activity prevailed, therefore, until the arrival of Lord Clive. At this critical period fortune favoured the English in a direction in which they had very little reason to look for it. The French soldiery, whom the Nizam had engaged when he dismissed the English troops, were disbanded, and in such a state of insubordination and dissatisfaction, that their officers gladly entered the English lines for protection; the place of these rebellious troops being again occupied by the British battalions formerly in the Nizam's service.

In November a remonstrance was forwarded by the governor-general to the sultan; and he immediately afterwards proceeded to Madras, where all arrangements were completed for the campaign. Generals Harris and Stuart commanded the armies of the Carnatic and Bombay; and the latter was ordered to join Harris as he advanced on Seringapatam. On the 6th of March General Harris had invaded Tippoo's country, taking a few hill-forts. The Nizam's troops were at this time commanded by the Hon. Col. Arthur Wellesley, subsequently Duke of Wellington, just entering upon his military career. Tippoo gave out reports that the Bombay army was the first contemplated object of his attack; but meanwhile he marched 200 miles in an opposite direction to intercept Col. Montressor at Sedasser, who had three battalions of sepoys under him. Accident frustrated his intentions; for on the evening of the 5th of March the rajah of Coorg, who had been entertaining Montressor and his English officers, conducted them to the heights of Sedasser for the purpose of viewing the Mysore country; when to their astonishment, in the plain below, they discerned Tippoo's encampment. Montressor took every precaution time and place would allow for defence, and sustained Tippoo's attack the next morning most gallantly. In the afternoon General Stuart arrived and relieved him from his perilous position. Tippoo having exhausted himself in the effort to prevent the junction, his troops became disheartened and fled in every direction, throwing down their muskets, swords, and turbans, and indeed every thing that impeded their flight.

Tippoo neglected several favourable opportunities for attacking the army of the Carnatic; but at length changed his plans, and determined upon engaging at Mallavely. The plan of attack was, for three hundred picked men, under the command of Tippoo's counsellor, Poorniah, to charge and break the right wing of the English; upon which Tippoo was to pour his entire cavalry upon the weakened part, and cut through the army, and thus by dividing, destroy it. But Poorniah's detachment was discovered in time; and the Scotch brigade ordered to receive the attack were strictly enjoined to withhold their fire until the enemy were close upon them. Scarcely had they formed when the three hundred men rushed from the jungle; steadily obeying their orders, the Scotch, with national coolness, waited the word to fire, which Harris timed so judiciously, as to lay forty men and horses on the ground at the first discharge. Harris then advanced his right wing; but Tippoo's soldiers, discouraged by the failure of the first onset, retreated rapidly; of which advantage could not be taken, owing to the want of means for transporting the artillery and stores.

The left wing, under Wellesley, was even more successful. Tippoo's troops, thrown into confusion by the close and steady fire he maintained, were charged at an opportune moment with great slaughter and the loss of six of their standards. The comparative losses in this battle were, on the English side, sixty-six men killed, wounded, and missing; while Tippoo suffered to the extent of two thousand.

Harris now prepared to cross the Cavary, near Soosilly, if practicable, and attack Seringapatam on the west side, in order to facilitate the junction of the Bombay army, and obtain the requisite supply of grain expected through the western passes. This movement, unexpected by Tippoo, filled him with alarm. On the 5th of April the English army were before Seringapatam. In the evening Colonels Shaw and Wellesley were ordered to attack a watercourse and tope, or clump of trees, forming an outpost of the enemy; through some confusion, owing to the darkness of the night, Wellesley was unsuccessful, barely escaping with life; and by some mischance was too late the next morning to take the command for a renewed assault upon the post, which was then carried in twenty minutes.

The siege steadily advanced, several breaches having been made, until the day of assault, the 4th of May. At one o'clock in the day, the usual Indian hour of repose, Syed Goffhar, Tippoo's best general, sent word to the sultan that an attack was about to be made; but Tippoo's faith in astrological predictions overweighing the general's warning, he refused to listen to the message; and while Syed was deliberating upon the answer, he was killed by a cannon-shot. At half-past one General Baird stepped from the trenches, sword in hand, and gave the orders to advance. In seven minutes the English colours were planted and floating at the summit of the breach. The storming divisions, as they ascended, wheeled to the right and left, fighting along the northern and southern ramparts, every inch of which was bravely defended by the Mysoreans. Thousands fell; and the slaughter terminated only when the two storming parties met on the eastern rampart. Tippoo's palace alone remained to be captured, the surrender of which was withheld in consequence of the uncertainty of its master's fate. He had fallen in the thickest and hottest of the fight, shot in three places by musket-balls. It was late in the evening before Tippoo's body was discovered; and on the ensuing day it was placed in the tomb of Hyder Ali, the highest military honours being paid to the deceased sultan. Tippoo's family were immediately taken under the protection of the English, and treated with every respect due to their exalted station.

Thus fell one of the most cruel and implacable enemies the British had ever encountered in India. His love of war appeared to have its origin in the misery and ruin it carried in its train. An enemy to the human race, he seemed to take especial pleasure in exercising his ferocity upon such English prisoners as fell into his power. Death by the sword was considered a fortunate termination to their existence, even when safety had been guaranteed by capitulation; and many were the cold-blooded atrocities revealed when his death unloosed the tongues of his oppressed people.

His name signifies a tiger; and so attached was Tippoo to these savage animals, types of his own ferocious character, that he kept numbers of them about his palace, and often made them his executioners. One of his favourite toys is still to be seen, though sadly disarranged, in the East India Company's museum in Leadenhall-street. It consists of the figure of a tiger in the act of tearing a European to pieces; on turning a handle some mechanism in the inside moves the jaws and limbs of the animal, and at the same time emits sounds intended to represent the growls of the tiger mingled with the groans of the dying man.

CHAPTER IV.

FROM THE DISMEMBERMENT OF THE MYSOREAN KINGDOM TO THE TERMINATION OF THE FIRST MAHRATTA CAMPAIGN.

A.D. 1799-1806.

THE death of the tyrant Tippoo was followed by the occupation of the numerous strongholds of the Mysorean country, which at once fell into the possession of the British commander.

Colonel Wellesley was appointed governor of Mysore, and assumed charge of Seringapatam, much to the annoyance of General Baird, who, as his senior in years and service, had calculated on the post. How far the relationship of the young commander to the governor-general may have exercised an influence in this arrangement is little to the purpose, since it afforded Wellesley an opportunity for displaying those administrative and military talents which were at a future period destined so greatly to distinguish him. He succeeded most completely in restoring order and security throughout his government, and earned for himself at once the approval of his superiors and the respect and attachment of the natives of the country.

The governor-general, in the distribution of the late sultan's territory, determined that his family should be no participators in it; he nevertheless apportioned them an extremely liberal annuity, with a residence in the fort of Vellore. That part of Mysore approximating to the former capital was created a principality for the Hindoo rajahs who had been deposed by Hyder Ali. The Nizam had several rich districts, whilst the English kept Seringapatam and the mountain-passes and forts. A small portion was set apart for the Mahrattas as allies, although their forces had not joined during the war.

Lord Mornington being now comparatively unfettered, directed an expedition against the Isle of France, which had for years been the rendezvous of several buccaneering vessels, the captains of which had openly carried on attacks upon British commerce. The island being deemed also a very favourable point for assembling an enemy's fleet, its tenure was held to be indispensable. Colonel Wellesley was accordingly commanded to prepare an armament for the capture of the place; and Admiral Rainier, who commanded in the Indian Ocean, was ordered to Trincomalee to co-operate in the attack. This order the admiral refused to execute, or join in such an expedition without instructions from home. Whatever the admiral's motives, the results were most disastrous; for these privateers continued during our subsequent wars to levy tribute upon the commerce of the Indian seas with impunity.

Being foiled in this, the governor-general projected an attack on Batavia with the forces at Ceylon; but orders from home directed him to send a body of troops into Egypt to expel the French; and thus, for a time, the attack upon the Dutch settlement was delayed. The troops at Ceylon were accordingly dispatched to Bombay, and joined by some native infantry in readiness for foreign service. The combined body was commanded by Baird, and sent by the Red Sea to Egypt; but the French had capitulated before its arrival, and it therefore took no share in the honours of the campaign.

The Nizam being unable to protect himself without the British contingent in his service, and the governor-general apprehensive that the Mahrattas would invade his country, arrangements were entered into between them, that certain districts should be assigned to the English for the maintenance of his auxiliaries. This was rendered necessary by the inconsistencies and jealousy of the Nizam's court, some portions of whom endeavoured to persuade him to dismiss these forces and rely upon his own enlistments. The acquisition of new territory was in opposition to the act under which the Company held their authority; but the prudence of the policy pursued prevented any objection to this infringement. Indeed, the court of Hyderabad presented such a scene of corruption, imbecility, and profligacy, that, had the Nizam surrendered all his power and dominion, little opposition would have been offered, even by the greatest opponents to the East India Company.

During and indeed for some time previous to the war with Tippoo, Shah Zeman, the Afghan sovereign, had threatened an invasion of India, which enterprise Tippoo urged him to undertake, persuading him that the attempt would be joined by all the Mahomedans in India. Tippoo's advice so well reconciled itself to Shah Zeman's wishes, that he invaded the Punjab in 1795; but a rebellion at home compelled him, in less than a fortnight, to recross the Indus. His second attempt was in January 1797, when he advanced to Lahore, and, by mediation, made a successful impression upon the Sikhs and their chieftains. These people were originally a quiet, inoffensive sect, having a mixed creed of Mahomedan and Hindoo tenets, but had become a warlike and independent people, owing to the cruel persecutions inflicted upon them by the emperors of Delhi. The efforts of Shah Zeman to conciliate the Sikhs were, however, opposed by the Mahomedan priests following his army, and the licentiousness of the army itself, which he could not suppress; despite these, however, he continued to hold the Punjab, and prepared for an attack upon Delhi. The occupation of Lahore by the Afghans produced a sensation throughout India. The weakness of the Mahrattas, and the incapacity of the nabob's government, predisposed the populace to revolt; and the Rohilla chiefs, ready to avenge the harshness suffered at the hands of Warren Hastings, were soon in arms. It required but the farther advance of Shah Zeman to have matured these elements of discord, which would probably have gone far to have annihilated the power of the British in India.

His brother, Prince Mohammed, having headed a rebellion, Shah Zeman was again compelled to return, in the summer of 1797, threatening another and early invasion. He returned to Lahore in the ensuing year; but the Persians attacking his dominions, he was forced to quit India, in order to protect his own territory. This presenting an extremely favourable opportunity, the governor-general sent an embassy to the shah of Persia, and negotiated an offensive and defensive alliance, which, however, was of little use, for Shah Zeman, in 1801, was dethroned and imprisoned by his brother.

The affairs of Oude, under Lord Teignmouth's arrangement, had proved most unsatisfactory. The nabob being irregular in the payment of his subsidies, his army harassed the people much more effectually than it could protect them against an enemy; whilst his civil government was a mass of corruption. These circumstances induced the Marquis of Wellesley, formerly Lord Mornington, to correct the abuses existing in Oude; to which he was also prompted by the irruption of Shah Zeman, the effect of whose occupation of Lahore was not lost sight of.

Another circumstance determined a prompt line of action. Vizir Ali, after his deposition, was permitted by Sir John Shore to reside at Benares; but this place being considered too close to his former sovereignty, it was determined to remove him to Calcutta: to this he objected. On the 14th of January, 1799, he called on, and complained in very indiscreet language to the resident, Mr. Cherry; while the latter was remonstrating with him, the vizir started from the ground and struck him with his sword, upon which his companions rushed on and murdered the unfortunate gentleman. Four other Englishmen were similarly butchered; but a fifth so effectually defended himself, that assistance arrived, upon which Ali and his fellow-assassins fled from the spot. Vizir Ali immediately collected a body of adventurers, who speedily deserted him upon some slight reverses. He then sought the protection of a Rajpoot chieftain, who surrendered him to the British.

Colonel Scott was now despatched to the nabob of Oude, with instructions authorising him to demand the immediate dismissal of the nabob's native troops, and their replacement by a British army, retaining such as were acquainted with the mode of collecting the taxes. The nabob delayed as long as possible, when he declared his desire to resign the sovereignty; which the governor-general hesitated upon, unless made in favour of the Company. It soon became apparent that delay was his object; upon which Wellesley adopted measures that forced compliance; and, upon the nabob asserting his inability to defray the expenses of the English troops, the transfer of the civil and military government of his country was demanded, his court and family being provided for by the Company; while he was also informed that so much territory as would afford a revenue to defray the subsidy agreed upon with Lord Teignmouth must be yielded absolutely to the English.

Every delay that his ingenuity could devise he adopted, until he heard that troops were actually advancing upon him, when he reluctantly consented. Wellesley proceeded with the same promptitude with which he had commenced. On the day the treaty was signed, he issued a commission for the provisional government of the country, nominating the Hon. Mr. Henry Wellesley the head of the commission.

These proceedings were unpalatable to the Court of Directors, and Wellesley's policy it was rumoured was to secure family appointments; that of Mr. H. Wellesley was particularly censured, as he did not belong to the class of Company's servants to which, by act of parliament, such appointments were confined. The Board of Directors thereupon ordered his immediate removal; but the Board of Control refused to sanction it, remarking that the appointment was temporary, and hence not within the restrictions. Pending these dissensions, Mr. Wellesley concluded a treaty with the nabob of Furruckabad, having similar stipulations to those of Oude; but Rajah Rajwunt Sing refusing to acknowledge the treaty, his two fortresses Pridgeghur and Sansu were besieged and captured. There were also some refractory Zemindars, who had gained by the misrule in the Doab, whom it was necessary to coerce; which being accomplished, and having thus established tranquillity, Mr. Wellesley voluntarily resigned his commission.

The East India government, never wasting opportunities nor wanting pretexts, now discovered that Surat was shamefully misgoverned. This, and the non-payment of the tribute, formed a good justification for annexing it to the Company's territories; which plea was further strengthened by the constant difficulties arising out of the right of succession. The nabob of Surat, like many other vassals of the Delhi empire, when strong enough, became virtually independent, and rendered his succession hereditary. But disputes having arisen respecting the inheritance, the British interfered and exercised their authority. A subsequent dispute upon the same subject, in 1789, afforded a further opportunity for the Company, and the nabob was treated similarly to the ruler of Oude, being compelled to surrender the civil and military government of his dominions to the English, receiving in lieu a pension, and with it protection. But the chout, or tribute, he had agreed to pay to the Mahrattas was not so easily settled. The Guicowar prince declared his readiness to relinquish his portion of the tribute to the Company, but the Peishwa was not so yielding.

In Tanjore like circumstances produced similar results. The late rajah, Zuljajee, on his death-bed, had appointed his adopted son Sarbojee his successor; but the English government decreed in favour of Zuljajee's brother, Amar Sing. Sarbojee was compelled to fly to Madras in consequence of Amar's tyranny, and was subsequently declared rajah on the condition that he would cede the civil and military government of his kingdom to the English.

The position of the nabob of Arcot had caused great inconveniences between his government and that of Madras. His revenues were nearly all absorbed or mortgaged, and consequently fell into arrears. After the capture of Seringapatam records of treacherous correspondence were discovered amongst the sultan's papers, involving the late nabob Wallajah, as well as the present, Omdah-al-Omrah, with Tippoo. Omdah died while preparations were being made for taking possession of the civil and military administration of the Carnatic. He was succeeded by his reputed son, Ali Hassein, with whom Lord Clive personally negotiated, and received his assent to the proposed terms, which he, however, subsequently rejected; upon which his lordship deposed him, and gave the throne to his cousin, Azim-ed-Dowlah. Ali remonstrated, and expressed his willingness to abide by Clive's previous decision; both alike were disregarded, and death soon after terminating his career, as well as that of the rajah of Tanjore, the governments of the latter country and of the Carnatic were established without further difficulty.

Lord Wellesley was equally desirous of maintaining the same relations with the Mahrattas, their troops being little better than banditti, living rather on plunder than pay, while the maintenance of such forces hourly jeopardised the peace of India. On the other hand, an auxiliary disciplined army would protect the native princes from their continual apprehensions of insurrection, and restrain their habits of rapine and extortion. Negotiations were commenced with the Peishwa, who was legally the Mahratta sovereign, though only in name, for both Holkar and Scindia, who held their feudatories by military tenure, rejected his supremacy; the latter indeed so controlled the Peishwa Bajee Rao, that Lord Wellesley imagined he would readily accept the offer of British troops to rid himself of this insolent chief. Fortune seemed to favour the governor-general's intentions. Holkar's family, who had for nearly a century been acknowledged in the northern states, having established their virtual independence, and an extent of country scarcely inferior to that of the Peishwa, were at discord upon the right of succession, which afforded Scindia an excuse for interfering, who declared Cashee Rao sovereign, and put Mulhar Rao, his brother, to death, retaining a posthumous son of the latter for the fidelity of his uncle. Jesswunt Rao, an illegitimate son of the late Holkar, escaped from Scindia, and shortly appeared at the head of a body of adventurers; but was defeated near Indore, on the 14th of October, 1801, losing his artillery and baggage.

In the ensuing year he again appeared with a better-disciplined and more numerous army, and marched against the united forces of the Peishwa and Scindia near Poonah. After a severe engagement, Scindia's cavalry gave way, and a decisive victory was obtained by Holkar. The Peishwa left his palace with an intention of taking part in the engagement, but being alarmed, he retreated to wait the result; upon ascertaining it, he fled to the fort of Senginh, previously sending to Colonel Close, the British resident, the outlines of a treaty, binding himself to maintain six battalions of sepoys, and yield twenty-five lacs of rupees of his revenue for their maintenance. The day following his victory Holkar requested an interview with the resident. Colonel Close at once proceeded to his tent, where he found him suffering from a spear-wound in the body, and a sabre-cut on the head. He expressed great anxiety for the mediation of the resident, with a view of arranging matters with the Peishwa and Scindia. Holkar's propositions had no effect upon the Peishwa's fear, who fled in an English ship to Bassein.

The Guicowar having previously declared his readiness to yield his share of the chout levied on Surat, further to secure the British alliance, yielded the Chourassy district. His death, in September 1800, produced great disturbances; for his son was perfectly imbecile, and unfit to control the intrigues of the court of Baroda. These intrigues speedily brought on a war between the late prime minister Nowje Apajee and an illegitimate brother of the deceased Guicowar; but the English siding with the minister, and furnishing troops, victory declared in his favour. Nowjee being unfettered, pursued his economica reforms by dismissing the Arab mercenaries; but this body refused to disband, demanding enormous arrears; afterwards mutinying, they seized Baroda and imprisoned the Guicowar. The English immediately invested Baroda, which surrendered in ten days. Contrary to capitulation, many of the mutineers joined the rebel Kanhojee; but were pursued, and ultimately, with the latter, driven from Gujerat.

Bajee Rao's flight to Bassein, Holkar treated as an abdication, and with other Mahratta chiefs proclaimed Amrut Rao Peishwa; upon which the most violent excesses commenced: the ministers of the late prince were tortured to reveal his treasures, and every presumed wealthy person in Poonah was seized, and terrified into the delivery of his property. When these atrocities began, Colonel Close proceeded to Bassein, and concluded a treaty with Bajee Rao, by which the Peishwa agreed to accept an English force, providing for its subsistence, to exclude from his territories Europeans of whatsoever country hostile to the English, to relinquish his claims on Surat, and submit all points between him and the Guicowar to the arbitration of the English.

This treaty was no sooner executed than Bajee Rao began intriguing with Scindia and Raghajee Bhouslay, rajah of Berar, to frustrate the execution of it, in which these chiefs willingly assisted, as its operation would have overthrown the influence they possessed in the Mahratta states. The governor-general promptly restored the Peishwa, and Amrut Rao, subsequent to his deposition having deserved it, was awarded a liberal pension and a residence at Benares.

The governor-general, after restoring Bajee Rao, endeavoured to obtain the acknowledgment of the Bassein treaty by the Mahratta chieftains; Raghajee Bhouslay, however, offered every opposition, and endeavoured to unite Scindia and Holkar to defeat the English policy, which end they fancied might be attained by procrastination. But General

Wellesley, who was invested with the joint powers of political agent and commander of the army of the Deccan, felt little inclined to submit to evasions, and without circumlocution insisted that the troops of Raghajee should retire to Boxar, and Scindia's to Hindostan. This proposition admitted of no escape, and greatly disconcerted the Mahratta princes; being thus forced to determine at once, they refused, which was of course regarded as a declaration of war.

Scindia had a numerous army in the northern Mahrattas, disciplined and officered by several French officers, against whom General Lake was directed to act, while General Wellesley and Colonel Stephenson commanded in the Deccan. Wellesley's first operation was against the reputed impregnable fort of Ahmednuggar, which withstood his attack but four days. He then pursued the Mahrattas, who avoided an engagement; but being determined to bring them to a decisive action, on the 21st of September, 1803, he marched in one direction, ordering Stephenson to take another, so that their forces might again unite on the 24th, when he fancied the Mahrattas would, from his apparently small army, be drawn into action. But, on the 23d, intelligence reached him that the Mahrattas, fifty thousand strong, with a hundred pieces of artillery, were encamped close at hand; he at once decided to attack them, without waiting for Stephenson's re-inforcement, although his force was only four thousand five hundred men strong. This engagement was the celebrated battle of Assaye, and began with a terrible discharge of canister, grape, and round shot from the Mahrattas, which told with fearful effect upon the English ranks, which were entirely destitute of artillery; nevertheless, the English troops undauntedly advanced, when a body of Mahratta horse charged the 74th. A counter-charge of the 19th Light Dragoons and 4th Madras horse was ordered, and executed with such irresistible effect, that the enemy's advanced line fell back upon the rear, and the British and native infantry rushing upon them with impetuosity, drove both into the Juah. As the enemy attempted to re-form on the opposite side of the river, the British cavalry again dashed amongst them, and completely sealed the fate of the Mahrattas, ninety-eight pieces of cannon being captured. The loss was severe on the British side, one-third of the troops being wounded or killed. Stephenson did not join until the evening of the 24th, when he pursued the fugitives, but unsuccessfully; he, however, reduced the city of Burhampore and the fort of Asseeghur, while a portion of the Gujerat forces took Baroach and other fortresses.

During these proceedings, General Lake, who held powers in Hindoostan similar to those of Wellesley in the Deccan, advanced from Cawnpore against Scindia's northern army, under M. Perron. The

NATIVE INFANTRY.

campaign opened with the storming and capture of Alijurh; but, as a set-off, Shekoabad was surprised by some Mahratta cavalry, commanded by a French officer, and the garrison compelled to capitulate, the detachment Lake sent to their relief arriving too late.

Information reaching M. Perron that Scindia intended superseding him, he addressed a letter to General Lake, requesting permission to pass, with his family, property, and officers of his suite, through the Company's territories to Lucknow, which was immediately conceded by the governor-general.

After capturing Alijurh, Lake advanced upon Delhi, where his advanced guard suddenly encountered a destructive cannonade, M. Louis Bourquin, next in command to Perron, having cleverly ambuscaded his guns in long grass. The Mahratta position was too strong to draw them from it. Lake therefore commanded the cavalry to retire, which the enemy mistook for a retreat, and rushed after them. The cavalry retired in close order, until it reached the advancing column, when opening from the centre, the British infantry passed to the front. The battalions advanced under a destructive fire from the enemy's guns until within a hundred yards, when they fired a volley, and charged with the bayonet. Scindia's infantry abandoned their guns and fled. The English broke into open columns of companies, and the cavalry charging through them, the slaughter was dreadful. After this victory Delhi was taken immediate possession of, and Shah Alum delivered from Mahratta captivity.

Lake then marched against Agra, which was a prey to the greatest anarchy. Before the war the garrison was commanded by English officers, who were confined upon the outbreak of hostilities, by their own men. Seven battalions of Scindia's infantry encamped upon the glacis; but the garrison were afraid to admit them lest they should plunder the treasury, which they wished to keep for themselves. These battalions were defeated by Lake with the loss of twenty-six guns; after which the garrison liberated their officers and capitulated, being allowed to retire with their private property.

The forces sent by Scindia from the Deccan, reinforced by the remnants of Bourquin's army, were General Lake's next pursuit: he came up with them on the 1st of November at sunrise, and fancying they were in retreat, sent his cavalry to turn them. But the Mahrattas occupied a strong position, with seventy-five pieces of cannon chained together, to resist cavalry, in their front. The cavalry were forced back, and the infantry and guns came forward. In the attack Scindia's cavalry proved most cowardly; but the battalions disciplined by the French fought with desperate determination; refusing to surrender, they died with their weapons in their hands. This battle of Laswarree destroyed Scindia's power in Northern India; at the same time Kuttack and Bundelcund were subdued.

The rapidity with which the enemy moved in the Deccan harassed Wellesley much; but at length, on the 20th of November, he routed them at Argoam, and there captured Gawelgush, which led to proposals for peace. The rajah of Berar was the first to capitulate, yielding a large amount of territory to the English and their allies, and all claims against the Nizam; agreeing also that no European should be admitted into his dominions unless permitted by the British; accredited ministers were to reside at the respective courts, the rajah receiving a resident at Nagpore. Scindia succumbed to similar terms, but was compelled to sacrifice much more territory and power than his ally.

Pending these hostilities, Holkar at Malwa was plundering friend and foe, incredulous of the British achievements. When too late, he determined to make an effort for the independence of the Mahrattas, and sent to Scindia, pressing him to break the recently-signed treaty, which fact the latter immediately made known to the British. Lake believing Holkar amicably disposed, invited him to send officers to negotiate a treaty. Upon their arrival, their terms were found so preposterous they were forthwith dismissed; and the governor-general being made acquainted with their demands, ordered Generals Wellesley and Lake to march upon Holkar's territories, Scindia professing the greatest willingness to co-operate.

Colonel Monson was sent to act in concert with Colonel Murray, and attack Holkar's territory on the Gujerat side. Monson advanced with spirit, but retreated upon hearing that Holkar with a large force was marching against him. It was an injudicious movement, and deplorably conducted, while a want of confidence existed between the colonel and his army: the officers and men desired an engagement, Monson sought shelter under a fortress. The forts on the line of his retreat pronounced against the English; and the troops, weary and starving, broke through all discipline, and fled in parties to Agra. This panic increased both Holkar's reputation and his army.

Lake took the field to reclaim these misfortunes; but failing to bring the Mahrattas to an engagement, wasted his time at Mutha, which afforded Holkar the opportunity of attempting the surprise of Delhi and securing the emperor, which he nearly accomplished. Lake then marched to relieve the capital; but Holkar five days before had joined the rajah of Bhurtpore, who had broken his treaty with the English. General Frazer then undertook the pursuit, and came up with the enemy's infantry near Deeg fortress on the 13th of November, and drove them from their first line of guns, but fell mortally wounded at the second, when Colonel Monson assumed the command and captured eighty-seven pieces of cannon; amongst them were fourteen he had lost in his retreat. Four days later, at Furruckabad, Lake routed Holkar, slaughtering three thousand of his men. Deeg was then invested, and stormed in ten days. The power of Holkar now seemed destroyed, his territory reduced, his forts and capital possessed by the English. Bhurtpore alone remained to shelter him. This place of refuge Lake attacked on January 2d, 1805, and then, as on subsequent occasions, with great valour, though but little engineering skill. The siege being converted into a blockade, the rajah sued for peace, which was accorded him on favourable terms, renewed hostilities being anticipated with Scindia, who had advanced towards Bhurtpore, when Holkar joined him, and was still hovering about the neighbourhood and harassing our outposts.

The policy of Lord Wellesley had been that of stripping the native princes of military, and leaving them civil power only; which gave the East India Company entire control over the foreign relations of these rulers. By the treaties with the Peishwa and the Nizam, the governor-general not only protected the frontiers of both, but secured tranquillity in the southern parts of the peninsula. This prevented Scindia from levying tribute on the more feeble states, while Holkar moved about at the head of a mere rabble. Necessarily such important results occasioned vast expenditure; but the diminished cost of governing and the growing revenues of the conquered states promised an ample return.

From July of this year (1805), when Lord Cornwallis succeeded the Marquis of Wellesley as governor-general, hostilities continued between the troops of Scindia and Holkar and those of General Lake. Driven from the Bhurtpore territories, the Mahratta chieftains fled towards the north-west frontier, where they appear to have expected some countenance.

Lake having conferred with the governor-general, pushed on towards the Sutlej in pursuit of his troublesome opponents, satisfied that the only prospect of continued peace in that quarter lay in the utter overthrow of their power. Undismayed by the perils and trials of a long and harassing journey through countries then but little known, the British commander halted not until, having crossed the boundary-line of Alexander's conquests, he encamped his troops on the banks of the Hyphasis (the Beas), where, upwards of two thousand years before, the veterans of the Macedonian conqueror had pitched their tents. The snow-capped peaks of the Himalayas, the green hills and valleys of the country of the five rivers, the noble stream whose waters fell into the Indus at some distance below,—all these were before their eyes, whilst, at the distance of a few miles, and within his reach, lay Holkar, the object of this long and toilsome march.

To have dashed at him, and thus have finished the struggle, would have been the policy of Lake; but a controlling power was at hand. Sir George Barlow had succeeded as acting governor-general, in the room of Cornwallis, who died but a few months after his arrival in the country; and the policy of this civilian was to purchase peace and security at all hazards, at all cost. With the instructions which at this juncture reached him, Lake, however unwilling, had no alternative but to consent to a peace, the preliminaries of which were arranged in December, and the treaty was finally ratified in the month of January 1806.

By the terms of this agreement the British reinstated Holkar in all his possessions, broke off their alliance with the rajah of Jeypoor and other Hindoo chiefs to the westward of the Jumna, and finally marched back to Delhi. The peace policy of Sir George Barlow, however it may have served a present purpose, did not satisfy those who, like Lord Lake, viewed matters in India with reference to the future as well as the present; and no one who was really competent to form an opinion believed for a moment that this disgraceful treaty would be observed one moment beyond the time which it might serve the purpose of the Mahratta chieftains; and so it indeed proved, as the following chapter will demonstrate.

CHAPTER V.

FROM THE RENEWAL OF HOSTILITIES TO THE TERMINATION OF THE SECOND MAHRATTA WAR.

A.D. 1806-1822.

THE new policy of the supreme government was not long in producing its fruits, as might have been anticipated; and first we find matters in the Deccan promising a crisis.

Mir Allum, the prime minister of the Nizam, had, by his attachment to the English, lost the confidence and regard of his master; and intrigues were at this time discovered at Hyderabad for his removal and the disruption of the alliance with the British. This conspiracy calling for decisive steps, orders were forwarded to the resident and commander of the troops, by means of which it was frustrated.

It was at this period that the Court of Directors, in order to mortify Lord Wellesley, urged the governor-general to modify the treaty of Bassein; which proceeding Sir George Barlow, with more than ordinary courage and determination, opposed most strenuously, and declined carrying out.

Upon the restoration of the Mahratta chief Holkar, he intimated that, from pure necessity, he must at once disband so many as twenty-thousand of his cavalry; whereupon, large arrears being due to them, a mutiny ensued, which was only quieted by placing Holkar's nephew in their hands as a hostage. Having thus the heir to the throne in their possession, the troops once more mutinied, but were subdued and their arrears paid; while the innocent object of their revolt was sacrificed by his uncle. Shortly after Holkar became insane, and so remained until his death on the 20th of October, 1811.

On his thus becoming incapacitated, the regency was divided between Toolzee Rye, one of his concubines, and Ameer Khan, who administered for Mulhar Rao Holkar, about four years old, the son of Jeswunt Rao. This imbecile government swayed between two parties, the Mahrattas and the Patans, whose respective ascendency was the signal for the renewal of the most sanguinary atrocities.

Lord Minto was appointed governor-general, and arrived in India in July 1807. He was a statesman of ability, hated precedents, and judged invariably for himself. He soon found that Wellesley had adopted a firm, but right policy, the very reverse of Cornwallis and Barlow, whose imbecility was near proving most fatal to British ascendency in India. There existed in the Deccan at this period a body of freebooters called Pindarries, who hired themselves indiscriminately to the best paymaster. Upon the defeat of the Mahrattas, these people, left to their own resources, wandered through the country, and pillaged every place that was too weak to oppose them. Subsequent to the last treaty, they were confined in their ravages to Malwa, Rajpootana, and Berar; a few ventured into the dominions of the Peishwa and Nizam, but so long as they left the inhabitants at peace they were not molested.

The policy of non-interference adopted by Sir G. Barlow had not only exposed the Rajpoot states to great danger, but thrown the Sikh chieftains into considerable consternation; they were apprehensive that this apparent withdrawal of British assistance might lead to their subjugation by Runjeet Singh, whose recently-established throne in the Punjab hourly increased in strength. The abandonment of the rajah of Jeypore, and the employment by Scindia of Rao Ghatkia as minister, who had previously planned the attack on the British residency, at length induced the Directory to express their dissatisfaction with Barlow's policy; at the same time they wished to avoid a further extension of political supremacy.

The Nizam's court had been an exception to Barlow's tactics, he having been compelled to support the minister Sheer Alum; upon whose death an arrangement was effected between the Nizam and the governor-general to divide the office, appointing the Nizam's favourite, Moneer-al-Mulk, minister, while Chand-u-lal, a supporter of the British, performed the duties of deewan. The Brahmins of the Carnatic, the sect of Chand-u-lal, are frequently men of good education, with enlarged commercial knowledge, while the Mahomedan Omrahs, to which Moneer-al-Mulk belonged, are the very reverse. Chand-u-lal at once discerned the difficulties and danger of his position, and that his tenure of office rested upon the supremacy of the British at Hyderabad; he therefore exerted himself to establish the Marquis of Wellesley's military reform, and organised an army commanded by English officers. In return for which he was supported by British influence against his enemies, and allowed to administer the government without interference. The result of this was, that the Nizam fell into a state of melancholy despondency, while the deewan and his relatives flourished at the expense of British reputation; and Lord Minto found that, without overstepping his instructions, a remedy was almost hopeless; matters were therefore allowed to remain as they stood during his administration.

Upon Bajee Rao being reinstated by the treaty of Bassein, he did not hesitate to declare that revenge was his motive for allying himself with the English: he was of a most profligate character, choosing his favourites and ministers from those who gratified his lusts or his cruelties; and through their agency maintained a correspondence with those who were most opposed to the English. General Wellesley well knew the character of Bajee Rao, and urged a speedy settlement of the relations between the Peishwa and southern chiefs, who, though nominally subjects, obeyed the Peishwa only when he was strong enough to enforce obedience. The terms of settlement proposed by the resident at Poonah for adjusting these differences were, the oblivion of past injuries, the abandonment of all money claims, the guarantee of the lands granted for supporting a certain number of soldiers for the Peishwa, attendance with the whole of their forces when required, and of a third portion under command of a relation at all times. Upon adhering to these stipulations, the British guaranteed the personal safety of the chiefs and their relations. Upon which Lord Minto sent to Madras, Mysore, and the Deccan to have an adequate force to compel the submission of any refractory chief.

At first neither the Peishwa nor the Jaghiredars, or chieftains, were willing to submit to English dictation; but the presence of a powerful force quieted dissatisfaction, and the feudatories accompanied the Peishwa to Poonah; and under the mediation of the resident, came to an arrangement, which greatly increased the Peishwa's power and resources.

Upon the insanity of Jeswunt Rao incapacitating him from exercising authority, Ameer Khan declared himself regent; and quitting Indore, headed a body of Pindarries, and began plundering the people. His next act was to threaten Berar, under the pretence that the rajah owed Holkar large sums of money. Upon this Lord Minto at once abandoned the old policy of non-interference; and tendering the rajah British protection, Ameer Khan was subsequently driven into his own dominions with heavy loss.

Early in the year 1808 it was rumoured that Napoleon was again endeavouring to establish French influence in India; and, moreover, that his ambassadors in Persia had been received with great marks of distinction by Futteh Ali Shah, the reigning monarch, who had concluded with them a treaty most inimical to British interests. When this intelligence reached London and Calcutta, missions were sent from each to the court of Persia; but without any privity or concert. Lord Minto despatched Captain Malcolm; but his advance on Teheran was stopped by the king of Persia, who at the same time insisted that he should negotiate with his son, the Viceroy of Shiran. To this Malcolm refused to accede, as unbecoming the dignity of the country he represented; and, after embodying his sentiments in a memorial to the court, he sailed for Calcutta. The ambassador from the British court, Sir Harford Jones, was a most incompetent person, who seemed only anxious to shew his independence of the Calcutta council. At the time of which we are writing, it was the custom with England to subsidise all her allies; in other words, to pay them for protecting themselves; and a treaty was signed in 1809, by which Great Britain bound herself to pay a yearly sum of 100,000*l.*, while the king of Persia was at war with Russia; and in addition supply 16,000 stand of arms and twenty field-pieces, together with artillerymen and officers to instruct the Persians; for which Persia agreed to oppose any attempt of the French to invade the Company's Indian territory.

A similar impression respecting French influence originated a mission to the court of Cabul, governed at that time by Shuja-al-Mulk. An alliance was concluded with this potentate, who was, however, shortly after driven from the throne, and pensioned by the British.

It has been before remarked that the Marquis of Wellesley's judicious plans for the occupation of the French and Dutch possessions in the Indian seas were frustrated by Admiral Rainer. For several years the weakness of the French fleet precluded them from doing more than annoy; but in the winter of 1808, a number of French frigates sailed from various ports in France and Holland, and reaching the Indian seas in the ensuing spring, committed great injury upon our commerce. Still more serious results being apprehended, Lord Minto announced his intention of reducing the islands which sheltered them, and depriving our adversaries of any port of refuge. The reduction of Bourbon and the Mauritius was effected with but little difficulty; but Java was considered an affair of considerable importance. The command was given to Sir Samuel Auchmuty, under whom the governor-general served as a volunteer. On the 4th of August, 1811, the whole of the troops were disembarked in twenty-four hours without an accident, and marched against the Dutch at Cornellis, who were protected by a series of batteries mounting 300 guns. On the 26th orders for assault were issued, which terminated in the storm of the Dutch camp, and surrender of 5000 prisoners of war. But Jansen, the Dutch governor, refused to submit; and it was not until garrison after garrison capitulated, that he surrendered the island on the 16th of September.

The principle of non-interference prevented Lord Minto from checking the tyranny of the nabob of Oude towards his subjects; but he secured the allegiance of Travancore and Bundelcund, and restored tranquillity, to which they had long been strangers. The same absurd policy prevented him from chastising the Pindarries, who, having increased in audacity, at length plundered Mirzapore, committing, as usual, all sorts of excesses. The apprehension of a Mahratta war, which Lord Minto knew would be displeasing to the Directory, deterred him from punishing these lawless freebooters.

The tranquillity of our Indian possessions was now disturbed by the Ghoorkas, a warlike race on the north-eastern frontier, who, taking advantage of the disputes and distress of their neighbours, extended their sway through the entire province of Nepaul, and thence to the plains inhabited by the dependent rajahs, committing great excesses at Gurruckpore and Sarun. These were at first regarded as individual and unpremeditated acts; but at length their frequency compelled Lord Minto to address the Ghoorka rajah in determined language, demanding redress and threatening retaliation. But his lordship's recall threw the duty of curbing these marauders upon his successor. We might here, if space allowed, allude to the vast benefits both the home and Indian community had enjoyed through the sagacity, discretion, and even temper of this really great man, whose doctrines, in the words of Sir John Malcolm, were "to conciliate and carry his superiors along with him; but not from the apprehension of responsibility; for wherever the exigency of the case required a departure from this general rule, he was prompt and decided."

The arrival of the Marquis of Hastings as governor-general took place on October 13th, 1813. His appointment was hailed with great satisfaction: having proved himself an able diplomatist and brave soldier on many occasions, he was justly esteemed the most suited to the exigencies of the times; more particularly so, as it was now well known that neutral policy was rapidly declining in favour at home, and that determined measures were to be taken to repress the insolence and violence of treacherous allies and open enemies.

In the following December the rajah of Nepaul sent a reply to

Lord Minto's despatch. It was couched in servile and evasive terms, and led to the appointment of commissioners on both sides to discuss the various points at issue. After repeated interviews, the English commissioners reported that it was useless longer to protract their powers, it being evident that the Nepaulese, who were adepts in dissimulation, negotiated merely to gain time; upon which the governor-general dismissed the Ghoorka commissioners, with instructions to their rajah to confine himself to his own territory, if he wished to avoid punishment. At the same time the chief was ordered to restore certain lands belonging to the British government which he had seized; and that in the event of his not complying, troops would at once occupy them. This notice being disregarded, the magistrate at Gurruckpore, Sir Roger Martin, took possession of Turall, and the villages near Sarun were also occupied without resistance. The rainy season now setting in, the charge of these places was left to native officers, and the troops withdrawn; upon which the Nepaulese, who had been watching their opportunity, attacked the civil officers and police, who were completely defenceless; and after murdering the superior officer, they killed eighteen, and wounded six, of the police establishment. This outrage was committed in the presence of the Nepaulese commander-in-chief, who offered neither restraint to the assassins nor assistance to the victims. Immediate representations were made to the rajah, who, instead of offering reparation, justified the outrages which his troops had committed; upon which the Marquis of Hastings prepared for war, the means of defraying which, had it not been for the nabob of Oude, who lent the governor-general large sums at lower rates of interest than the market prices, must have been found by the home government, the Bengal treasury being completely empty.

The Pindarries, like the Ghoorkas, it was known, were only waiting the opportunity to renew their predatory excursions; and the Marquis of Hastings forcibly represented to the home executive the urgency of its sanction to a series of determined proceedings, to avoid the impending danger. With the view of strengthening the British power, the governor-general had commenced a defensive treaty with the rajah of Berar, who, however, after a protracted correspondence, declined acceding to it; and, breaking through the existing treaty of 1814, joined Scindia in the attempt to subjugate the nabob of Bhopaul, who had long maintained himself against the Hindoo princes.

The friendship invariably shewn by the nabob, particularly in the Mahratta war, induced us to join him, as well as Govina Rao, the prince of Sagur, in offensive and defensive treaties, by which means were furnished for watching the Mahratta princes, Runjeet Sing and Ameer Khan, leader of the Pindarries. Scindia, who pretended that the rajah of Bhopaul was one of his vassals, became greatly enraged at this alliance, and threatened retaliation; upon which a body of troops was marched on Bundelcund, while another force, under the Nizam, advanced to Elichipore, the capital of Berar; and the governor-general then gave his undivided attention to the coming war in Nepaul.

The frontier of Nepaul consists of mountain ridges, extending 600 miles from east to west; and it was determined to penetrate it by four armies marching simultaneously. General Ochterlony, with 6000 sepoys, was ordered from Loodiana through the hill-passes overlooking the Sutlej; General Gillespie, from the Doab to the west of the Jumna, and so on to Nahir; General Wood, through Bootwal to Palpa; and General Morley, with the main body, was ordered to force the Gunduck passes and march direct on Katmandu, the Ghoorka capital.

General Gillespie crossed the frontier on the 22d of October, 1814, and captured Dera without opposition; while Balbhadur Sing, to whom the defence of the town had been entrusted, retreated to a steep and well-fortified hill called Nalapanee. Gillespie, who miscalculated the strength of the position, determined to carry it by assault, but had scarcely reached the wall when he was killed by a musket-ball, and his troops fled to their lines, leaving many comrades behind. Colonel Mowbray, with the remainder, retreated on Dera until he obtained a train of heavy artillery; then advancing, after two days' firing, he effected a breach, when an assault was attempted; but the Ghoorkas drove back the storming party with great loss. This so disheartened the sepoys that they would not renew the attack; and Mowbray compelled the garrison to surrender by bombardment, after it had been reduced from 600 to 70 inhabitants.

General Martindell, Gillespie's successor, having joined the camp, marched against Nahir, which the Ghoorkas evacuated, retiring to Jythuck, a fortress built on a ridge 4000 feet above the adjacent plain. The general, having reconnoitered, resolved to turn it on both flanks, concealing his intentions by an attack in front; but, most unfortunately, the grenadiers leading the southern column, underrating their adversaries, rashly attacked a stockade well flanked with rocks, and were received with a heavy and well-directed fire from all sides, and driven back upon the sepoys, who had not formed into line so as to support them. The Ghoorkas, perceiving their advantage, dashed forward, driving the British before them to the confines of their camp; after which, General Martindell retreated to Nahir.

General Ochterlony, with the army of the Sutlej, was as conspicuous for caution as Martindell for rashness. He was opposed by Ameerah Sing, the most experienced and courageous of the Ghoorka leaders, whose generalship was well and successfully tested. By a series of manœuvres the general obtained possession of post after post, until the entire country between Plassea and Belarpore submitted to him.

General Wood, on the other hand, was most unfortunate; while passing through the Sal forest, his troops came upon an unexpected and well-appointed stockade, which opened a fearfully destructive fire; but Colonel Hardyman, of the 17th Royal regiment, turned both flanks of the Ghoorkas, and was rapidly securing the victory, when the general, disheartened by the surprise, to the astonishment and indignation of the entire force, sounded a retreat. This was a type of Wood's campaign, timidity and injudiciousness invariably betraying the incapacity of the commander.

The fourth army, under General Morley, was quite as discreditably commanded as that under Wood. Dividing his forces, he posted three large detachments twenty miles distant from each other; and was panic-struck when two of them were cut off by the enemy. Upon learning this, he suddenly left the camp, and fled to Calcutta. His successor, General George Wood, was a cautious but timid man; and the consequence was, that the remainder of the campaign was passed in disgraceful idleness.

The effect of this disastrous campaign naturally induced a feeling of confidence amongst the enemies of the British in India. In the Peishwa and Scindia there was a marked alteration; while Runjeet and Ameer Khan shewed they were ready, and only wanted the opportunity to act. But the Marquis of Hastings was nothing daunted; and having ascertained that Kumaoon, in the north of Nepaul, was destitute of troops, he determined, as he could not spare any of his army, to send an irregular force; for which purpose he appointed Lieut.-Colonel Gardiner and Captain Hearsay, formerly in the Mahratta service, to enlist a force among the Patans of Rohilcund.

A considerable number of men were thus collected and divided between Gardiner and Hearsay. The latter blockaded Koolulgurt; and while in this position, the enemy advanced to relieve the place, and forced him into an engagement, in which he was wounded, captured, and sent to Almora by his conqueror, Hasta-Dal. Gardiner, understanding well the mode of Patan warfare, submitted to their ways, but proceeded nevertheless with skill and caution, and advanced to Almora shortly after Hearsay's defeat, where he was joined by Colonel Nicholls with a small train of artillery and 2000 regular infantry. Hasta-Dal attempted to relieve Almora, but was defeated, and fell in the skirmish; which so disheartened the Ghoorkas that they surrendered the place, and with it the prisoner Hearsay.

Notwithstanding repeated orders from Calcutta, General Martindell remained comparatively inactive; and when he did move, he had neither plan nor object in view. He wasted the season before Jythuck: now trying an active siege, but wanting courage to push it boldly; then a blockade, without cutting off the enemy's communications. His only success was in wasting men and money, and destroying British reputation in India.

General Ochterlony, however, prepared to follow up his advantages, while the Ghoorkas retired before him to a formidable position, consisting of a mountain-ridge of elevated peaks, all but two of which were stockaded, and further protected by the redoubts of Maloun and Seringhar. The two unprotected peaks Ochterlony seized, being confident their attempted recovery would bring on a decisive battle. And so it proved. The Ghoorkas attacked the British with desperation for two hours, when they were driven back, with the loss of their commander and one-third of their force. Ameera Sing would have continued to resist, but was deserted by the other chiefs; eventually he procured safety for himself and followers by surrendering to the British the country west of Kalee, as well as the fortress of Jythuck.

Proposals having been made for peace, the English insisted on stipulations to which the Nepaulese refused to accede; and Ochterlony was ordered to take command of the main army. In February 1816 he penetrated into the forests which protect the frontier of Nepaul, and soon reached the fortifications guarding the chief pass through the hills. A brief inspection satisfied him of the inutility of attempting to capture the stockades by assault, and that he must adopt other plans. Upon further inspection of the locality he discovered a narrow water-course, which was forthwith entered by a column of troops, headed by Ochterlony. After imminent danger and privation, the summit was attained, and the enemy abandoned their intrenchments as useless. The Ghoorkas now brought their whole force to bear upon a post occupied by the English at Makwanpore, but were completely defeated; and Colonels Kelly and O'Halloran having obtained another victory, the rajah of Nepaul solicited peace upon the terms he had recently rejected. During this war the Ghoorkas, nominally subjects of the Celestial empire, had applied in that quarter for assistance; upon which the Chinese assembled an army, but procrastinated marching until the war had terminated. Upon learning, however, the origin of the war, they pronounced the Ghoorkas well-deserving punishment, and unhesitatingly left them to their fate. The governor-general was not inclined to act with oppressiveness, nor encumber himself with useless possessions; he therefore limited the Ghoorkas to Nepaul proper, without disturbing their ancient dominions.

Our reverses at the commencement of the war gave rise to fresh Mahratta intrigues. Scindia, who headed the confederacy, had established a permanent camp, protected by the fort of Gwalior, which had become a flourishing town in a few years, the increase of which contributed largely to his pride, as proof of his growing power. He not only intrigued with the Peishwa at Poonah, and Holkar at Indore, but entered into alliance with the rajah of Berar, and obtained promised assistance, upon emergency, from Runjeet Sing and the Rajpoot rajahs, and even sought to win the rajah of Mysore. This combination during the Nepaulese war, had it been brought into operation, would assuredly have seriously affected the British authority; but the mutual jealousy of the Mahrattas, and knowledge of each other's treachery, combined with suspicion of their allies, required too much time to organise with effect such a confederacy, during which peace was concluded with the Ghoorkas, and the British concentrated their attention upon central India.

During this period of uncertainty and anxiety, the residents at Poonah and Nagpore were Messrs. Elphinstone and Jenkins, diplomatists of unrivalled ability, possessed of enlarged experience, great decision, and intimately acquainted with the relations between the native states. The position of the resident at Poonah was one of much difficulty, arising out of the treaty of alliance signed between the Peishwa and the British. The Marquis of Wellesley at the time knew that necessity only had induced the Peishwa to contract the alliance, and foresaw that jealousy would rankle in the native prince's mind, and a period arrive when he would display his hostility. This view was a correct one: the state of the Peishwa's affairs being now much improved, and the various Mahratta states tendering him their support, he became desirous of cancelling his engagement with the British. He was likewise much dissatisfied with various decisions of the English governors in their capacities of arbitrators between himself and his vassals, conceiving that interest, not right, had been the foundation of them. Another great source of annoyance was compelling him to renounce his supremacy over Kolapore and Sawant Waree, on the coast of the Northern Concan; these states fitted out small piratical vessels, and had been the scourge of the western seas for years. In 1812 Lord Minto obliged them to succumb to his power, taking possession of their principal ports, and preventing their maritime depredations, the loss of which was the ground of offence to the Peishwa. It is almost unnecessary to remark, that, like most Asiatic princes, Bajee Rao was equally ambitious and timid, fond of intriguing, and swayed by alternate desires and fears. Mr. Elphinstone, by combining discretion with decision, held him in restraint, until his inclinations being inflamed by a profligate minister, he dashed on through criminality and treachery to his eventual destruction.

Upon the death of the rajah of Nagpore, in 1816, his son, Pursajee Bhonslah, who was blind, paralysed, and idiotic, succeeded him, when two factions divided the court; the resident secretly supported Appa Sahib, the next heir, securing him to the British interest. This was a blow to the Mahratta confederacy; for though Appa proved treacherous, his timely withdrawal from that union was considered of the greatest importance to the British.

The most depraved minister of the Peishwa was Trimbuckjee Danglia, who commenced life as a runner, then became a spy, and after passing through a variety of degrading offices became the Peishwa's favourite, with the command of the artillery and rank of prime minister. These steps were rewards for pandering to his master's licentiousness and innumerable daring crimes. Trimbuckjee shared in the Mahratta hatred to Europeans, whose presence he believed prevented the Peishwa's supremacy; it was therefore a studied policy with him to join any attempt to expel or reduce the British power; he accordingly instigated Bajee Rao to renew his claims upon the Nizam and Guicowar, seizing the estates of the principal landholders, whose revenues enriched his treasury. By this audacious step he collected five millions sterling previous to the commencement of hostilities.

The claims against the Nizam and Guicowar Mr. Elphinstone knew were pretences urged for the purpose of keeping open the communications between the courts of Poonah, Baroda, and Hyderabad. He therefore strove for an arrangement; but was thwarted by the Peishwa and his minister. The Guicowar was also anxious for a settlement between the Peishwa and himself; he accordingly sent a representative to Poonah, with power to conclude a treaty, who, after wasting twelve months, resolved to return and leave the arbitration to the

British government. This would have foiled the plans of the Peishwa and Trimbuckjee, who accordingly made every exertion to conciliate the envoy's favour and arrest his return. Gungadhar Shastre, a Brahmin of repute, the Guicowar's representative, was excessively vain, and readily duped by the professed respect Trimbuckjee paid to his abilities, to whom he proposed resigning his office, that the Peishwa might secure more able services. Mr. Elphinstone having guaranteed the Shastre's safety, finding negotiations dormant, proposed his return; to his surprise the envoy refused, when it transpired that a marriage was negotiating between the Shastre's son and Bajee Rao's sister-in-law. The Guicowar refusing to cede some territory, the marriage was broken off. The refusal of the Shastre to permit his wife to visit the palace proved another offence in the Peishwa's eyes.

These differences soon produced a quarrel between the Peishwa and the Shastre. Trimbuckjee therefore determined, as he was too deeply committed to extricate himself, to alter his policy, and resolved upon assassination. The Shastre being invited to accompany Bajee Rao on a pilgrimage to the temple of Binderpore, Mr. Elphinstone proceeded with them as far as Nafik, where he was induced to remain while his companions went forward. The night after their arrival, the Shastre, instigated by Trimbuckjee, joined the Peishwa in some ceremonies of much sanctity, receiving in return the warmest assurances of friendship and esteem. Immediately, however, on quitting the temple, the unfortunate Shastre was almost hewn to pieces by hired assassins. The murder of an envoy, whose safety the British had guaranteed, excited universal indignation; and the sanctity of the spot, and the character of the victim, afforded additional ground of condemnation. The strict inquiry Mr. Elphinstone enforced fixed the guilt upon the Peishwa and his minister. Hereupon Bajee Rao was informed that he might attribute the culpability to the actual perpetrators, but that his crafty and guilty minister must be surrendered to the British authorities. The Peishwa hesitating, a British force was quickly assembled at Poonah; upon which he delivered Trimbuckjee to the resident, having obtained a promise that his life would be spared. Accordingly the minister was confined in the Tannah fort, on Salsette island, where he admitted his participation in the murder, in obedience to the Peishwa's instructions.

Tannah being entirely garrisoned by Europeans, Trimbuckjee was enabled, by some native servants, to correspond with his friends; a horsekeeper, who passed his place of confinement daily, being his chief agent. This man carelessly sung, in the peculiar Mahratta recitative style, his information, while the sentries, ignorant of the language, were incompetent to detect the plot, even had they had any suspicion. All being ready, Trimbuckjee made an excuse for quitting his rooms, dressed himself as a servant, reached an embrasure, and lowered himself into the ditch by a rope which one of his accomplices had secured to a gun. He had friends ready outside; and long ere his flight was discovered he was safe from pursuit. The Peishwa disclaimed acquaintance with Trimbuckjee's escape; but Mr. Elphinstone ascertained that he not only supplied him with money to raise troops, but had given him an audience. A remarkable display of duplicity ensued. Trimbuckjee disciplined large numbers of Mahrattas and Pindarries, whose existence the Peishwa denied; and when his falsehood became transparent, he repudiated their actions and threatened them as insurgents. Eventually he placed a price on Trimbuckjee's head, and forfeited the estates of his principal coadjutors.

It is here necessary, before entering upon the results of the events just recorded, to review other portions of the Indian possessions. The reputation gained by the British from the issue of the Nepaulese war was augmented in the ensuing year by the capture of Hatrass, a fort belonging to a tributary of the Company named Diaram, who, relying upon its position and reputed impregnability, became contumacious, and determined the authorities upon his chastisement. The military depôt at Cawnpore furnished a large train of artillery, which in a few hours effected a breach in the walls, and the principal magazine exploding, finished the demolition of this invulnerable fort, unaccompanied with loss to the besiegers. The affair effected a sensible impression upon the refractory chiefs in Hindostan Proper.

The Pindarries, however, increased in numbers and daring proportionately with the success of the British arms; upon the destruction of Hatrass, a large body entered and desolated a portion of the Madras territory; and in the following season, despite our exertions, ravaged the Deccan. The governor-general, convinced that eventually these audacious proceedings would be noticed and ordered to be suppressed by the authorities at home, merely acted on the defensive, waiting events, and watching the growing treachery of the Mahrattas, at the same time making every preparation for a war, which he saw was inevitable.

This course received the sanction of the home executive, who became at last convinced that Cornwallis and Barlow had erred in their policy of non-interference; and upon the renewal of the charter in 1813 orders were despatched to place Jeypore under British protection when opportunity favoured. Upon the termination of the Nepaulese war, the capital of Jeypore being threatened by Ameer Khan and the Pindarries, overtures of an alliance with the prince were made; but these advances were received with indifference, owing, it subsequently appeared, to a supposition entertained by the Jeypore prince that Ameer Khan would abandon his plans, under the impression that British protection could be secured at pleasure; upon which the governor-general abandoned any further negotiations until he adopted the line of action he had in view.

The Peishwa, though professing the most perfect amity towards the English, was known by the resident to be in league with Trimbuckjee, and fostering a rebellion nominally against his own dominions. He was manifestly preparing for war;—his treasures were removed from Poonah, his forts repaired and garrisoned, and he levied troops from all quarters. Upon this the governor in council declared that Bajee Rao had broken his treaty with the English, and should be forced to render satisfaction for his past, together with security for his future conduct. His principal forts being at the time in the hands of the British, he had no choice between war or concession; he reluctantly adopted the latter alternative, and a treaty was signed on the 18th of June, 1817, in which he abandoned his pretensions to be considered as the head of the Mahratta chiefs, giving up a quantity of territory and the fortress of Ahmednaggar to the British.

As a sequence to the foregoing treaty, a supplementary one was executed in the following November with the Guicowar, in which the claims of the Peishwa upon him were commuted by the payment of four lacs of rupees annually; the British receiving, as their share of the agreement, the city of Ahmedabad, the capital of Gujerat, a place of considerable political and commercial importance.

The Marquis of Hastings, being now comparatively unfettered, proceeded to execute his plans against the Pindarries. He resolved on pushing forward unexpectedly several corps to occupy certain positions, so that the enemy were prevented from concentrating their forces. The success of this plan he considered rested upon secrecy and celerity. The first effort of his policy which greatly influenced the succeeding war was directed against Scindia, to whom both the Pindarries and Mahrattas looked for support. Two corps, one under the governor-general, the other under Major-General Dorkin, so effectually isolated him that he was forced either to fight or treat. The latter, placed as he was, he knew was his only alternative, though repugnant to his sentiments; and thus early in the war the promoter and supporter of opposition to our rule was detached from his associates.

The treaty was to the effect that Scindia should use his best exertions to annihilate the Pindarries, and furnish a contingent to act with the British, under the direction of a British officer; for the complete efficiency of which, as well as the pay of the troops, he was to resign for three years his claim against the Company; that the sums paid as pensions to his family and ministers should be appropriated to the payment of the cavalry he was to furnish; and it was further agreed that the rest of his army should occupy posts assigned by the English, who alone could order their removal. A further stipulation admitted the British to garrison the forts of Asseerghur and Hindia during the war, as pledges for his fidelity; and the eighth article dispossessed him of the absolute control of the Rajpoot states.

This treaty, so adverse to Scindia's inclinations, was opposed in its execution by every sort of pretext: his contingent was with difficulty obtained, and Asseerghur not delivered up, the governor, it was stated, refusing to comply with his instructions. The British eventually besieged and captured the fort, when a letter was discovered from Scindia directing the governor to comply with any and every command of the Peishwa. This letter Scindia endeavoured to palliate upon the plea of the long-established friendship between their families, an extenuation Lord Hastings admitted; but as a penalty for so gross a violation, he demanded the absolute cession of Asseerghur, which in our keeping placed an effectual check upon the freebooters and robbers who had hovered about it, while under the Mahratta government it being a sure refuge for them.

The main attack against the Pindarries was now arranged. Situated as they were in Malwa and the valley of the Nerbudda, the armies of Bengal, Gujerat, and the Deccan moved simultaneously towards them. The army of the Deccan, numbering fifty-three thousand men, under Sir Thomas Hislop, formed the centre, being supported by the Bengal army, twenty-four thousand strong, on one side, and the Gujerat army, nearly as formidable, upon the other; while the entire force of the enemy scarcely numbered thirty thousand, and from the jealousy of their chiefs, Cheetor, Kurrur Khan, and Nasil Mahomed, were destitute of all unity of action. Favourable as circumstances thus appeared, events at Poonah entirely altered the campaign, and brought us into a war with the Peishwa.

An impression prevailing that the treaty which Bajee Rao had signed at Poonah was intended to be infringed, the resident declined attending him when he paid his next annual visit of devotion to the temple of Pundesore. This was done with a view to restore the confidence between the British government and the Peishwa, while he, under pretence of meeting this concession, dismissed a body of his cavalry; but it was ascertained that each officer had seven months' pay in advance, with orders to be vigilant and ready, and when summoned, to bring as many volunteers as possible.

Instead of returning to Poonah, the Peishwa proceeded to Maholy, near Satara, a place invested with great sanctity by the Hindoos: while there, he was waited on by Sir John Malcolm, political agent to the governor-general, who had been visiting and instructing the different residents respecting the proceedings against the Pindarries. Sir John, usually held to be an able diplomatist, was completely duped by the professions of the Peishwa, and returned to Poonah, satisfied that by encouraging his desire to augment his forces, and treating him with confidence, the British would find an able ally. The resident, Mr. Elphinstone, differed entirely from Sir John's views, but was overruled, and the hill-forts, which were held for the performance of the treaty, were delivered up to the Peishwa, while General Smith's force, placed so as to intimidate Poonah, was marched to the frontiers of Candeish, leaving scarcely any protection for the residency. The Peishwa returned to Poonah in September, after having matured his plans against the English at Maholy. The Mahratta chiefs, however, before uniting with him, doubting his resolution, compelled him to swear that he would be guided by the advice of Bappoo Gokla, a general who had their entire confidence.

The Peishwa did not neglect Malcolm's absurd recommendation to recruit his army; upon that point his exertions were unceasing, neither did he omit storing and repairing his forts, or manning his fleet. Trimbukjee Danglia likewise contributed his assistance by engaging the Bhuls, Ramoosies, and various predatory tribes; while constant despatches passed to Nagpore and the encampments of Scindia, Holkar, and Ameer Khan. The assassination of the resident and disaffection of the troops were personally undertaken by the Peishwa.

The fidelity of the sepoys had never been suspected; but the reports from every quarter, together with the largeness of the offered bribes, and a still more important fact, that several of their families were in the Peishwa's power, and suffering from his vindictiveness, at length created some apprehension. But to the honour of these gallant men, neither domestic considerations, nor the rewards held out, had any influence on them. All attempts were ineffectual; some indignantly spurned the offers, while others appeared to accept them, for the purpose of learning the nature of the intrigues, and then divulged them to their officers. If there was this principle of honour exhibited on our side; on the Peishwa's, it would not be doing justice to a brave soldier if we omitted stating that Bappoo Gokla would not for a moment listen to or sanction the assassination of Mr. Elphinstone; on the contrary, he immediately sent word to the resident to apprise him of his danger. That gentleman, knowing that a European regiment was marching to support him, and aware of the indecision of Bajee Rao, entertained hopes that his courage might fail at the last moment.

The forces in cantonments being badly posted, Mr. Elphinstone moved them to Khirkee village, which had been pointed out by General Smith, in the event of a rupture. This withdrawal the Mahrattas attributed to fear, and the abandoned cantonments were immediately plundered. Parties of horse at the same time advanced on the British lines, while the language of the Peishwa's ministers became most offensive and insulting. On the 3d of November, Mr. Elphinstone deeming longer delay inimical to our interest, ordered the light battalion and a body of auxiliary horse to march on Poonah, when the Peishwa resolved at once to commence hostilities.

The only portion of the Mahratta army visible was the infantry assembling on the tops of the surrounding heights. Ascending one of these, it was perceived that a mass of cavalry covered nearly the whole of the plain below, towards the city; while endless bodies were pouring in from every quarter. Mr. Elphinstone, discovering the attempt the infantry were making to cut him off from the camp, retired with his family to Kirkhee, exposed to the Mahratta fire from the opposite side of the river; at the same time ordering Lieut.-Colonel Burr to attack the Peishwa's forces, and Major Ford to support him with the irregulars. The Mahrattas, surprised at this movement from troops they had fancied disheartened, hesitated; Gokla, however, encouraged his men to advance, using praises, taunts, and implorations, as best suited his purpose; but the Peishwa, after the troops had advanced, sent word to Gokla not to fire the first gun. The general, seeing the messenger, and guessing his errand, instantly opened a nine-gun battery, detaching a corps of rocket-camels to the right, and advancing his cavalry upon both flanks, nearly surrounded the British; but the rapidity of the cavalry movement left the infantry in the rear, with the exception of a battalion under a Portuguese named De Pinto, who had taken a shorter route, and concealed his men amongst the low jungle. De Pinto formed with great steadiness, but was suddenly charged by the English sepoys, who, in their impetuosity, became detached from the rest of the troops. Gokla, to take advantage of this, led forward six thousand cavalry, but was perceived by Colonel Burr, who instantly stopped the pursuit of De Pinto's routed force, and ordered the sepoys to reserve their fire. In front of the British left, and unknown to either party was a deep swamp, into which the Mahratta horse dashed with such impetuosity that those behind rode over their sinking companions in front. The sepoys poured their reserved fire into them with terrible effect; whilst the few who reached the sepoys' bayonets were despatched with ease. A company of Europeans now advancing in support, the Mahrattas fled in a body, leaving the English victors over a body ten times their number, with the loss of but eighty-three in killed and wounded.

Upon the declaration of hostilities, Bajee Rao gave vent to his sanguinary and vindictive disposition. The residency was plundered and burnt; the families of the soldiery that fell into his hands beaten, robbed, and many mutilated; the crops destroyed, trees torn up, and even the graves violated. An engineer officer, surveying, was killed. Two brothers named Vaughan, one a captain in the Madras army, were captured whilst travelling near Poonah, and hanged; but Gokla terminated these atrocities, Mr. Elphinstone representing to him that a severe retaliation would follow the continuance of such acts.

The communications from Poonah having ceased, General Smith, suspecting something amiss, prepared to return, and was followed and harassed by parties of the Mahratta light horse. On the 13th of November the two detachments effected a junction, marched towards the camp of Bajee Rao, who, after a sharp engagement, fled to Sattara, leaving his capital to the mercy of the English. Possession was at once taken of it, and further reinforcements having arrived, General Smith started in pursuit of the Peishwa.

At Nagpore very similar occurrences had taken place. Notwithstanding that Appah Sahib was chiefly indebted to the English for his elevation, he soon exhibited his ingratitude, by entering into secret correspondence with the Peishwa. This, although a violation of his treaty, the English government did not notice, the resident considering it would be impolitic to betray any suspicion respecting the rajah's integrity, his communications being frank and unreserved. Mr. Jenkins did not, however, trust to demeanour only; the increase of the Nagpore army, and the growing correspondence with the court of Poonah, spoke more plainly than the rajah's professions. But it was hoped that Bajee Rao's defeat would have had its influence upon the rajah; still the worst was prepared for, and instant reinforcements demanded. In a short time suspicions were confirmed, news being brought of an intended attack upon the residency and cantonments, which the movements of the rajah's army tended to confirm, and defensive measures were at once taken. Colonel Scott with his brigade forthwith occupied the residency and neighbouring heights. The British force, about 1500 strong, were here attacked, on the night of the 26th of November, by an army numbering 18,000 men, and again on the following day, when, after many hours' severe fighting, the enemy were repulsed with great loss.

The defeat of his army, added to the appearance of reinforcements, destroyed the hopes of Appah Sahib, who sought to make his peace with the British, declaring the late attack had been made without his cognisance. He was ordered to draw off his troops from the vicinity before any reply would be made, with which he instantly complied, but still continued to vacillate in his conduct. General Doveton having now arrived with his army in support of the resident, the following terms were offered the rajah: viz. to deliver up his ordnance and military stores, disband his Arab mercenaries at once, and his own troops afterwards; that the British should occupy Nagpore, and himself reside at the residency as a hostage. He was still left with the nominal sovereignty and functions, against the wish of the governor-general, who acceded to the representations of Mr. Jenkins; and the latter, after many evasions, and a further struggle with the Arab troops, brought the rajah to accede to the British terms.

The Marquis of Hastings ordered the embodiment in a treaty of the provisional engagements with Appah Sahib; but before final instructions reached Nagpore a fresh revolution had burst forth. The cession of the forts of Berar was refused by the governors. This, it was suspected, and soon confirmed, was at the instigation of the rajah; while correspondence between the rajah, his troops, and former ministers, clearly demonstrating renewed hostility, was detected. The murder likewise of his predecessor was clearly brought home to him. These offences, great as they were, would not have induced Mr. Jenkins to have adopted extraordinary measures; but information of the rajah's intended escape reaching him, he ordered a detachment to occupy the palace and capture the rajah, who was placed in confinement at the residency until ordered to be sent, strongly escorted, into Hindostan. But while on his way to Benares, appointed as his residence, by pretending illness and bribing his guards, he escaped. The officer in charge visited the rajah at the usual hour at night, found him apparently asleep in bed, the attendants requesting him not to disturb their master, repose being essential to his enfeebled condition; this was acceded to, and a hasty glance failing to detect a pillow as a substitute for the invalid, the officer departed, Appah Sahib at the time being miles away. His escort, it subsequently appeared, were his own soldiery, whom he had been allowed to select, the authorities not wishing, upon his leaving his kingdom, to irritate his feelings by a denial. Appah fled to the Mahedo hills, and thence to Asseerghur, where he joined Cheeto, the leader of the Pindarries.

General Smith, who pursued the flying Peishwa, had a harassing chase through the ghauts; and getting too far to the north, Bajee Rao returned and threatened to retake Poonah. Upon which Colonel Burr ordered to his assistance the Seram detachment, which marched under the command of Captain Staunton. It consisted of one battalion of native infantry, three hundred irregular horse, and two six-pounders manned by twenty-four Europeans. A night-march brought them to the hills overlooking Konjaum, where Captain Staunton suddenly found himself confronting the Peishwa's army twenty-five thousand strong.

An engagement ensued, which, incredible as it may appear, terminated in favour of the British; men and officers gallantly supporting the reputation of the English. The feats of daring performed this day were never excelled in Indian warfare; while, on the side of the enemy, acts of barbarity which were intended to intimidate produced a contrary effect, and added to the desperate valour displayed on the part of the English. The Peishwa, his general Lokla, and Trimbuckjee Danglia witnessed the engagement with dismay, and when night came on made a rapid retreat. The Peishwa was pursued; but, as usual, without success.

Sattara was then attacked by General Smith, and capitulated; after which a proclamation was issued deposing the Peishwa; and, with the exception of a small portion retained for the rajah of Sattara, his territories were declared forfeited to the Company. Regulations were also issued for equitably adjusting the rental and taxation of the country.

Bajee Rao, who had retreated to Sholapore, being joined by a body of horse, moved westward. General Smith, discovering the enemy's tactics, pursued with cavalry and horse-artillery, and came upon the Mahrattas suddenly. In the engagement which ensued, Gokla was cut down by a dragoon, and the Mahrattas fled, leaving their baggage and several elephants, and their captive hostage the rajah of Sattara. Bajee Rao now moved on Nagpore; but finding the dissimulation of the rajah of that country had been punished, he returned to the northern confines.

The Marquis of Hastings having resolved upon the extermination of the Pindarries, Sir John Malcolm and Colonel Adams, acting with General Marshall, drove them from their strongholds; upon which Wasil Mohammed and Kharrum Khan united their forces and proceeded to Gwalior, whither they were invited by Scindia. Cheeto took to the north-west, trusting to Holkar for support.

These movements being known, the governor-general sent a strong force to cut off the enemy before reaching Gwalior, bringing one division close on Scindia's camp. The Pindarries failing in their object of entering Gwalior, took flight into Mewar. One body, however, ravaged the Deccan and entered the Carnatic, where they were destroyed or dispersed before the ensuing February; and Cheeto, pursued by Malcolm, sought refuge in Holkar's encampment.

On the 21st of December the English sighted the enemy's entrenchments. Holkar's army was strongly posted near Mahedpore, the river Supra covering his left, and a deep ravine protecting his right flank, with a strong display of artillery in front, amounting to seventy guns, well manned by the Patans. The British, while fording the Supra, suffered severely from the enemy's guns; and each regiment, in order to escape the slaughter, was ordered, after taking its position on the other side of the river, to lie on the ground. At length, the whole having crossed, the signal was given, when they advanced rapidly to the charge, carrying all before them. Holkar's lines were broken, his guns captured, and a complete though bloody victory was obtained. A large amount of military stores was left on the field by the enemy, in addition to the whole of their artillery.

After this engagement the British forces marched to Mundinore, where envoys met them, deputed by young Holkar to treat for peace, which was granted more favourably for him than he might have anticipated. The victory over Holkar rendered Scindia perfectly submissive: he could not, however, control his feudatories, one of whom sheltered Cheeto and his Pindarries; this was immediately noticed, and General Brown sent to resent his contumacious behaviour. A more efficient man for the service could not have been selected; he acted with such promptitude, that Juswunt Rao's camp was surprised, his town stormed, all his guns captured, and another prince substituted for him over the district he governed.

Cheeto now fled with his Pindarries to the north-west districts; and the pursuit was then handed over to the Gujerat division, by whose efforts he was at length surprised, and his army dispersed by a small detachment from the fort of Hindia. Escaping with a few followers, he sought protection from the nabob of Bhopal, who, however, rejected his overtures. Thus situated, he was compelled to join Appah Sahib, also a fugitive, but who was unable to afford him an effectual shelter; and having left this, his last hope, he wandered friendless through the fastnesses, and finally fell by an attack from a tiger. The Pindarries were now prostrated; destitute of leaders and homes, their position had become desperate, and eventually such as remained of them settled down to agricultural pursuits.

On his return to Madras, Sir Thomas Hislop proceeded to possess himself of the various forts yielded by Scindia and Holkar. Matters proceeded peaceably until the advanced guard approached the fort of Talnier, when a fire was opened from the walls. This unprovoked assault, and rupture of the treaty by which Talnier was ceded to the English, occasioned much surprise. General Hislop not being desirous of having recourse to severe measures, sent a message to the governor, informing him of the stipulations, and that in the event of any further opposition, he would be treated as a rebel. Instead of this message producing the effect intended, the reply was of a hostile character; upon which a six-pounder and two howitzers were ordered at once to play on the gateway of the fort. The enemy briskly replied, and opened a spirited fire upon the besieging force. The British guns were found too small to do much damage to the walls; and it was at length decided to carry the gate by assault. A storming party was ordered to advance; upon which a flag of truce was exhibited on the walls, and the commander shortly after appeared, and declared his readiness to surrender the fort according to the stipulations acceded to, time being allowed to make the requisite preparations. To this the British general replied, that the surrender must be immediate and unconditional, and directed his reply to be made known to the adverse troops. Great reluctance being shewn to convey this message, the storming party were led on, passing through the dilapidated walls, and advanced to the last gate without opposition. On arriving there, a small gate was opened, through which Major Gordon, with a few supporters, entered; a short conference ensued, the enemy closing round Gordon, who was thus completely entrapped, and with his party barbarously murdered.

This treachery being made known, the English soldiery attacked the place with desperation, to avenge their murdered comrades. The pioneers soon forced an entrance; and the besieged, to the number of 150, were destroyed: some few hid themselves in haystacks; but being discovered, the stacks were fired, and the fugitives, in attempting to escape from the flames, were shot like dogs by the infuriated soldiers.

Two Arab boys and an old woman, who had secreted themselves in a well, were the only survivors of this fearful assault. The Killidan and Arab commander of the fort, Sir Thomas Hislop hung as rebels. Their execution was strongly remonstrated against by several of the officers, both of them at the period of Gordon's murder being prisoners in the keeping of the British. Hislop's line of action proved correct, and ensured the peaceful surrender of the other fortresses. The keys of Chandore Galna and Unktunky were sent into the British camp, and immediately occupied. All that was now wanting to terminate the war was the capture of Bajee Rao and Appah Sahib.

The Peishwa moved about with a daily decreasing army, and at last was surprised and defeated by Col. Adams, who crowned his victory by the capture of Chandah fort. Bajee Rao now made proposals to Mr. Elphinstone; but as they implied the possession of authority, he was informed that nothing short of unconditional submission would be listened to. Deeply mortified, he retreated with about 8000 men to a strong hill-post, whence he sent agents to Sir John Malcolm, the nearest of his adversaries, to treat for a surrender. Malcolm, coveting the honour of being considered the terminator of the war, entered into negotiations at once; the terms of which were his surrender to Sir John, the abdication of his throne, and the passing the remainder of his life within the British territory, the Company allowing him 80,000*l.* a year, and the retention of his private treasures. These concessions were reluctantly confirmed by the governor-general, who considered them greatly disproportioned to the condition of the Peishwa; and he condemned Malcolm in strong terms for his injudiciousness. Trimbuckjee Danglia did not long remain free after his master's surrender; and being captured, was confined a prisoner for life.

Appah Sahib was for some time blockaded among the hills; but at length made his escape to Asseerghur, which was then invested by General Doveton, supported by Malcolm with the Malwa contingent, a strong force of artillery.

Asseerghur, after an obstinate defence, surrendered on the 9th of April, 1819; but Appah Sahib had fled previously to its capture, and was not to be heard of. Fort after fort was now surrendered, and the governor-general commenced his plans for managing the captured territory. The possessors of property were treated with every consideration, and the law little changed in its enforcement; but an increased vigilance was needed in the criminal courts to suppress the organised bodies of murderers and robbers that infested the country. By these means a great change in the condition of the natives was effected, which, on the whole, gave much satisfaction. At Barcilly in Rohilcund, however, some resistance was made. A tax was there levied to defray the cost of the police; unpopular in itself, it was rendered still more so by its mode of collection. The head of the police, a man hated for his audacity and severity, was appointed by the magistrate to collect the tax. In consequence of the offensiveness of the tax, several meetings were held, and a petition against it presented by the mufti to the magistrate. The petition was unnoticed; and popular discontent was aggravated by a female being wounded by the police while distraining for the tax.

These occurrences led to a collision with the people, which was attended with bloodshed, and left behind it a strong feeling of discontent.

With the fall of Asseerghur ended the Mahratta war, famous alike for the many engagements which had taken place, and the difficulties presented by the nature of the country in which they occurred. The loss of the British in killed, wounded, and invalided was considerable; and amongst other enemies which our troops had to encounter during this harassing campaign, not the least was the cholera, which made its first appearance in the south of Bengal during the rainy season of 1817. Thence it made its way westward to the English camp, where it committed great havoc, especially among the troops of the governor-general in Bundelkund, where about a tenth of the entire number were carried off. Europeans and natives were alike attacked, though not with equally fatal effects, the more poorly clad and fed suffering the most. Since that time the disease has scarcely ever been absent from some part of the Indian territories.

Early in 1822 the Marquis of Hastings, having resigned the high office he had filled during nine years, returned to England, leaving India, as several of his predecessors had done, in an apparent state of tranquillity. A review of his active administration will shew that it had been attended with the most striking and brilliant events. The aggressions of the Mahrattas and Pindarries had been put an end to, and the power of those daring and restless people completely broken; whilst Scindia alone remained of all the disturbers of the public peace, almost powerless, and no longer feared as a dangerous adversary. The Company's name and reputation had been extended by the addition of large territories; and on all sides the revenues and trade had increased, and the people appeared to be contented and prospering.

CHAPTER VI.

THE FIRST BURMESE WAR, AND THE CESSION OF ASSAM AND THE TENASSERIM PROVINCES TO THE BRITISH GOVERNMENT.

A.D. 1822-1827.

If the Marquis of Hastings had the honour of terminating successfully one of the many important struggles in which the British forces had been engaged with native powers, he enjoyed the credit of having bequeathed to his successor a war as tedious and harassing, if not as brilliant, as any in which that government had ever been involved. Before proceeding to detail the events of the first Burmese war, it will be necessary, in order to preserve this historical narrative in its integrity, to advert in the first place to the nomination of Earl Amherst as governor-general mainly through ministerial influence; which was successfully urged against the superior claims of Lord William Bentinck, who had previously distinguished himself as governor of Madras.

The temporary administration of Mr. Adams, pending the arrival of this latter nobleman, was rendered notorious by the exercise of a power which had hitherto not been used, though vested in the supreme government. To the censorship of the press of India was added the discretion of banishing any refractory or troublesome editor from the Company's territories. This despotic control was exercised by Mr. Adams against the editor of the *Calcutta Journal*, who, upon publishing some stringent remarks upon the acts of the executive, received notice to quit the country within a few days. This tyrannical proceeding, involving as it did the ruin of an individual, called forth some severe strictures in England, but was nevertheless supported and approved by the home government.

It was at this period also that the negotiations among the European powers, relative to the various Dutch settlements in the East, captured during the war, were brought to a final issue by the British authorities ceding to Holland the islands of Sumatra and Bencoolen, the former retaining possession of Malacca and Singapore. This last, under the auspices of Sir Stamford Raffles, was destined to rise to an importance as a commercial settlement unknown to any other of our eastern possessions; and at the present time may be considered the heart of the Indian seas.

Another event occurred, during the short administration of Mr. Adams, most disastrous to many of the European community of India. The commercial firm of Palmer and Company had for a series of years, and with the private cognisance of the Marquis of Hastings, contracted for loans of money to the Nizam of the Deccan, amounting in the aggregate to 700,000*l.*; and, as security for the repayment of the balances, they had received a lien on the revenues of the Nizam. Such transactions were contrary to the laws of the Company, which reserved to itself alone the right of entering upon monetary transactions with native powers. Some difficulties having arisen between the contracting parties, the entire affair came under the notice of the supreme government; whereupon the acting governor-general declared Palmer and Company had throughout acted illegally, and could not recover from the Nizam. The effect of this was to cause the immediate insolvency of this wealthy firm, to the serious injury of great numbers of the service, who had employed them as their bankers.

Whilst the British had been engaged in the extension of their territories on the west and north-west of India, the Burmese had been scarcely less actively employed in the enlargement of their dominions on the east. In this way the frontiers of the two powers approached each other, until the occupation of Assam, Arracan, and Cachar, finally rendered them near neighbours. On the part of the Company there was little to hope for by any aggression in the direction of Burmah; whilst, on the other hand, the *éclat* of successes over the inhabitants of the subjugated provinces led the advisers of the golden-footed sovereign of Ava to indulge in dreams of further and more noble acquisition to the westward.

Matters might have remained undisturbed for a long period but for an occurrence which took place on the confines of the south-east territories. In order to render this affair intelligible, it will be first necessary to refer to events which had occurred on our Burman frontier during the previous thirty years.

It was in 1798 that as many as 30,000 of the Mugs, a race inhabiting a part of Arracan, fled from the oppression of their Burmese masters, and sought refuge within the British district of Chittagong. An asylum was not refused them, and they settled down in villages and towns to various pursuits. Many attempts were subsequently made by the Burmese authorities to persuade the resident at Chittagong to deliver up the fugitives; but without avail. An embassy was afterwards despatched by the court of Ava to Calcutta, but without inducing any change in the policy of the supreme government. In 1802, and again in 1809, embassies were sent to the governor-general by the Burmese sovereign, having the same subject for object, always with apparent friendly results, but still leaving the matter rankling in the mind of the latter potentate. In 1818 it appeared probable that a rupture would ere long take place between the two powers. The governor-general, however, had no desire for a war which held out such small prospect of gain or renown, and assumed a conciliatory tone in all negotiations. This demeanour was not unnaturally construed into weakness by the barbarian monarch; and his tone and demands became more assuming as that of the other evinced a more friendly disposition. On the arrival of Lord Amherst in India, a lull in Burmese agitation had taken place; and it might have been imagined by ordinary spectators that the threatening storm would pass over. Suddenly, however, it burst upon the British territories in a night-attack by the Burmese troops upon the island of Shahporee, at the entrance of the Tek Nauf, or arm of the sea dividing Chittagong from Arracan. It had been usual to keep a small guard on duty to protect the island from any marauders; but an attack from the Burmese not having been anticipated, the small force was overcome, and the island formally occupied by the Burmese. The governor of Arracan, when called upon to explain this invasion, impudently announced the annexation of it by his government; and that, moreover, unless the acknowledged right of the Burmese to the island was admitted, the sovereign of Burmah would invade the British territories. This violent act was shortly followed by the imprisonment of the commander and several of the crew of the Company's cruiser *Sophia*. Other open acts of hostility were committed; and finally large bodies of troops from Assam and Munnipore crossed the frontiers, and, plundering the villages, established themselves within a few miles of Sylhet by means of their usual defences, bamboo stockades. From this position they were driven with considerable loss, as also from several other stockaded posts on the eastern frontier, though not always without loss on the side of the British. These operations occurred during January and February of the year 1824; and when a more imposing force under the command of Colonel Innes was preparing to march against the invaders, intelligence was received of a numerous army of the Burmese having penetrated our territories on the Arracan side, led on by Maha Bandoola, the favourite general of the sovereign of Ava, who, it was stated, was so confident of success, that he carried with him golden fetters, in which the governor-general was to be led captive to the presence of his royal master.

Hostilities being no longer doubtful, Lord Amherst proclaimed war in due form, by issuing a manifesto declaring the Burmese public enemies, stating the various causes of complaint against them, and interdicting all British subjects, European and native, from holding intercourse with them. This proclamation also stated, that the "deliberate silence of the court of Ava, as well as the combination and extent of the operations undertaken by its officers, leave it no longer doubtful that the acts and declarations of the subordinate authorities are fully sanctioned by their sovereign. The governor-general in council therefore, for the safety of the subjects and security of our districts, already seriously alarmed and injured by the approach of the Burmese armies, has felt himself imperatively called on to anticipate the threatened invasion. The national honour no less obviously requires that atonement should be had for wrongs so wantonly inflicted and so insolently maintained, and the national interests equally demand that we should seek, by an appeal to arms, that security against future aggression which the arrogance and grasping spirit of the Burmese government have denied to friendly remonstrance and expostulation."

The ignorance of the authorities upon the geography and resources of the Burmese territories caused some hesitation in adopting a plan of action. It was intended at one time to march on Ava through Arracan, a subsidiary force moving simultaneously from Cachar; but on inquiry this plan was abandoned, the unhealthiness of Arracan being considered insurmountable. It was then resolved that Madras and Bengal should provide an army which should capture Rangoon, the principal Burmese sea-port at the mouth of the river Irrawaddy. The seizure of this place, it was believed, would intimidate the king, and induce him to sue for peace; if otherwise, it was resolved to establish a depôt of ammunition and military stores at Rangoon, to seize the boats and ascend the river to the capital, a distance of six hundred miles. Port Cornwallis, a harbour in the Andaman Islands was the place of rendezvous to which the Bengal division was conveyed in April, to be followed in May by the Madras force. The united forces were commanded by Sir Archibald Campbell, who had served with great distinction in the Spanish campaigns, but knew little either of Indian wars or discipline. Commodore Grant commanded the naval part of the expedition, consisting of the *Liffy*, *Larne*, *Sophia*, *Slaney*, with several cruisers, and a small steam-vessel.

The 10th of May found the squadron anchored within the bar of the Irrawaddy, to the great consternation of the Burmese authorities; and as the night advanced watch-fires were lighted in every direction along the shores. The British resolved at once to make for Rangoon, trusting, by the great consternation evinced, that the place would surrender, and afford at once cattle, boats, and boatmen, all of which the expedition was destitute of. Accordingly, arrangements having been speedily made, the fleet sailed up the river on the ensuing morning. At noon the *Liffy* anchored in front of the king's battery at Rangoon, the remainder of the vessels taking position in her rear. These arrangements were effected without the slightest interruption, the enemy appearing completely intimidated. The Burmese authorities, however, at length succeeded in persuading their mercenaries to open a cannonade upon the ships, to which the *Liffy* replied, quickly driving the troops from their guns, and leaving the town deserted by both soldiers and inhabitants.

The complete evacuation of Rangoon was at first viewed with suspicion, it being apprehended that it was intended as a ruse. It soon, however, transpired that upon the arrival of the British becoming known, the governor, aware of the defenceless nature of the place, had ordered the inhabitants to be driven into the thick jungle of the interior, drafting the males into the army, and retaining their wives and children as hostages for their fidelity. This appears to have been a customary practice with the Burman government. The position of the victors was now one of considerable anxiety; for, destitute of supplies, and without the means of travelling either by land or water, it was evident that during the approaching monsoon the hovels of Rangoon were to be their quarters, with an uncertain supply of provisions, and but a remote prospect of reinforcements from Calcutta.

It was known previous to the capture of Rangoon, that there were a few British and American residents in the town, whose absence afforded considerable anxiety to the captors. It subsequently appeared that they were seized and confined, and after repeated examinations by the governor were condemned to death. In this condition the prisoners remained several hours, when a 32-pound shot from the *Liffy* struck the place in which the chiefs were assembled, upon which they hurried off with their prisoners some miles into the interior. An advanced guard of the British fortunately followed in their track, and so alarmed the

Burmese escort that they fled in great haste, leaving their prisoners behind them, who were thus liberated.

The possession of the Golden Dagon Pagoda, about two miles and a half from Rangoon, was Sir A. Campbell's first care. The approach to it on the southern face was through a row of mango, cocoa-nut, and other beautiful trees leading from the town, and shading a good road, at each side of which were monasteries of great antiquity, and richly carved with curious images and ornaments; whilst here and there appeared huge images of griffins and other hideous monsters, guarding the entrance to different pagodas; at the end of this road rose abruptly the eminence on which stood the golden Dagon.

The removal of the inhabitants from Rangoon was but the prelude to the desolation of the country, in the hope that famine would drive the British from the place. This would, doubtless, have been good policy, had humanity accompanied the perpetration; but the evils that it was intended to inflict upon the invaders fell with tenfold severity upon the poor inhabitants, who were as little cared for as though they neither belonged to the country nor were worthy of a moment's consideration to those who directed the war.

The Burmese, who formed a cordon round the British, resolved, while they harassed them, to avoid an engagement. They were concealed in their impenetrable forests, and carried their measures into effect without the slighest chance of observation, whilst with their adversaries all was doubt and uncertainty. Their scouts came in without intelligence, and the natives previously removed from the vicinity, all means of communication were destroyed. The English commander had been induced to suppose that the occupation of Rangoon would instantly have produced its effect upon the court of Ava, and that the demands of the governor-general would have been immediately complied with; but the present aspect of affairs led him to doubt the accuracy of these conclusions. Even the rising of the inhabitants of Pegu against the yoke of the Burmese, which he was informed might be safely relied upon, had not been manifested by the slightest movement.

The court of Ava had been both expecting and preparing for war, but not in the quarter in which it appeared. After the insolent message sent to Chittagong, respecting the retention of the island of Shaporee, preparations upon an extensive scale were made for invading Chittagong from Arracan; and reports were circulated that, in the event of the British refusing to give up all claims to the island, an army of thirty thousand men would invade Bengal, and march directly upon

Calcutta. Upon the arrival of the British at Pegu active preparations were made to expel them. Every town and village contributed its quota of armed men to its respective chief, and the Irrawaddy was covered with boats conveying troops to the main army assembled at Hengawaddy. At the end of May, strengthened in numbers, they approached the British, and began stockading themselves in the jungle, to which Sir A. Campbell offered no opposition, trusting for an opportunity to impress a lesson upon the court of Ava. A stockade having been thrown up at a short distance from our pickets, the general headed a reconnoitring party, it being reported the governor of Shudauny was there stationed with a large force to harass the English, and prevent the inhabitants from quitting the jungle. The stockades being incomplete, were abandoned as the troops advanced, who found unfinished works in every direction, demonstrating that this movement had not been anticipated by the enemy.

A sudden tempest falling as the British passed from the jungle into the adjoining rice-fields, compelled them to advance on the villages without their field-pieces. As the huts were approached, it was discovered that they were protected by two stockades of considerable strength, well mounted, and guarded by troops, who uttered loud shouts of defiance. The rain which had prevented the guns from being brought forward, had also rendered the muskets of the British comparatively useless; and as they could not return the enemy's fire, which was well maintained, no time was lost in attacking them. Three companies rushed gallantly forward under the command of General Campbell, and forced their way through the stockade, killing or driving out the Burmese, who refused to give or take quarter.

The irrepressible valour of the English, which thus foiled the dogged determination of the Burmese, impressed the latter with a respect for the courage of their adversaries they had not before felt; and anxious, moreover, to gain time, they endeavoured to practise upon the patience of their invaders by strong professions of friendship and desire for peace; but Sir A. Campbell was not so easily duped, and did not for one moment delay his preparations for attacking Kemmendine, a war-station up the river, which the enemy were daily strengthening. On the 9th of June it was announced that two officers of rank from the enemy were solicitous to confer with the general. Permission was given, and two war-boats appeared, from whence the deputies landed, and were escorted to the house of the British commissioners. Assuming an easy familiarity, it was soon discovered they were either unwilling or not authorised to treat, and that their object was simply to delay affairs; and upon their requesting a suspension of hostilities for a few days, it was at once refused. At 2 o'clock on the following morning the British advanced on Kemmendine by a road parallel to the river, and at no great distance from it. The advancing column was soon checked by a formidable stockade, flanked on three sides by the jungle, and fourteen feet high in front, protected by cross-bars and palisades driven diagonally into the earth. Two eighteen-pounders having reached the spot, and opened a fire upon the defences, a gap was soon made, and an assault at once ordered. In a few minutes the British found themselves in complete possession of the position, after a loss of 200 men on the part of the enemy. At the rear of the fort the gilt umbrella, sword, and spear of the Burmese commander were found, the umbrella much shattered by a shower of grape; and the body of the chief was found a few yards farther in the jungle. He had apparently received his death-wound where the emblems of command were dropped, and had probably been carried off by his attendants, until their own safety rendered it expedient to leave their burden behind them. The chief was said to be recognised as the elder deputy of the day before, whose pacific tone had so much amused the English commissioner.

The Kemmendine stockade was reached the same day at 5 P.M., and was found by General Campbell to be much more formidable than he had anticipated. He therefore postponed his attack until the ensuing day. As morning broke, the mortar batteries were opened, and told with such effect, that the attacking columns were marched forward, and the position captured without resistance; the Burmese having retreated to avoid the destruction our shells were making in their crowded stockade. This victory, although it had the effect of striking terror into the enemy's soldiers, had little influence upon the court of Ava, which continued to authorise the military chiefs to lay the country waste, in order effectually to render the British dependant for their resources upon India.

About the end of the following June it was known that Sykia Woongee, a minister of state, had received the imperial order to drive the British into the sea. To enforce this command, a large body of the enemy emerged from the jungle early in July, and advancing in a parallel line to our front, attacked the British position near Rangoon, where a regiment of sepoys being advanced and supported by two guns, the Burmese commander ordered a retreat; when the news of this action reached Ava, he was dismissed with disgrace, and the second minister of state, Soomba Wongee, appointed to the command of the army in his stead.

The new commander occupied a very strong post at Kummeroot with his force, about five miles from the Dagon pagoda, and had likewise fortified a commanding point of the river above Kemmendine, where he not only prevented the navigation of the river, but constructed fire-rafts to destroy the British vessels of war. Both positions General Campbell attacked simultaneously, leading the column against the river position in person, whilst he left the advance on Kummeroot to General M'Bean.

BURMESE GENERAL.

Campbell found his undertaking really formidable; the stockades on both sides of the river being not only admirably posted and strongly constructed, but well found with guns and men. A naval force under Captain Marryat, consisting of a brig and three cruisers, were ordered to clear the obstructions on the river. These soon silenced the Burmese artillery; and a breach having been effected, the storming party crossed the river and carried the stockade with little loss. General M'Bean, approaching Kummeroot, found himself completely surrounded by well-constructed stockades, garrisoned by large bodies of troops, who watched his advance with great contempt. Destitute of guns, he determined on an immediate assault upon their principal stronghold, consisting of three stockades, one within the other; the last was Soomba Wongee's head-quarters. The Burmese general was taking his forenoon meal when the report of the British advance was made to him; but satisfied with his position and the valour of his troops, he merely commanded his officers to their post, with orders to "drive the audacious strangers away."

He was not allowed to finish his repast in quiet; the rapidly-approaching volleys of musketry announced the forcing of his outer line. Hastening to the scene of conflict, he found his men crowded together in the centre stockade, upon which the British fire was pouring with terrible effect. Panic-stricken and confined, all attempts of their leader to get them into order were unavailing. At length Soomba Wongee fell, and the Burmese troops fled, leaving 800 dead in the stockades; while the jungle and neighbouring villages were filled with the wounded and the dying.

Although General Campbell had captured ten stockades, covered by thirty guns, and well garrisoned, he was unable to take advantage of the panic his successes had created by marching upon the capital. He determined, therefore, to act against the maritime province of Tenasserim. The principal places offered little opposition; several excellent harbours were secured; and what was all-important, a salubrious country discovered for our troops, whom the pestilential air of Rangoon had seriously affected.

The king of Ava, surprised at the audacity of an insignificant number of men, and unable to understand their success, despatched his two brothers to superintend the war. These were accompanied by numbers of astrologers, who were to foretell the periods most favourable for success. They were likewise attended by a body of warriors termed the "invulnerables." The distinguishing features of this ludicrous and pantomimic force consisted in the short cut of their hair, and peculiar method of tatooing, the figures of elephants, lions, and tigers being elaborately and somewhat abundantly displayed all over their persons. Gold, silver, and precious stones were also inserted in their arms, introduced under the skin when young. They are considered by their countrymen to be invulnerable; and to judge from the absurd exposure of their persons to the fire of an enemy, they are either impressed with the same opinion, or find it necessary to shew a marked contempt for danger, in support of their pretensions.

The English commander had ascertained that the princes were warned by the astrologers to wait for the first lucky moon, and as this was not very near, he determined not to lie idle, and forthwith attacked several posts which had prevented provisions being brought to Rangoon. One of these, Syriam, a fort originally erected by the Portuguese, had been recently repaired and strongly stockaded. Against this place a strong party in boats was sent, and it was captured, notwithstanding the advantages in favour of the besieged; the Burmese retreated to the pagoda, leaving eight guns and a quantity of ammunition behind them. From the fort the English advanced to the pagoda, which was also carried without loss.

The astrologers, it was ascertained, had at length discovered the favoured time for attacking the British, viz. at midnight on the 30th of August. Sir A. Campbell, having made his preparations, was in readiness to receive them. The invulnerables boldly rushed up the road leading to the great pagoda, uttering threats and imprecations against the impious strangers who defiled the place with their presence. The English remained perfectly quiet until the multitude approached the gateway, when the guns were opened with discharges of grape, whilst the musketry poured in rapid volleys among them. The invulnerables, astonished at the carnage, fled to the jungle, leaving the dead and dying in every direction.

This success General Campbell determined to improve by driving the enemy from all their posts near Rangoon. Major Evans was accordingly dispatched with three hundred men to ascend the Lyne river, and Colonel Smith with the light division on the road to Pegu. Colonel Smith having cleared several stockades, learnt that a large body of the enemy, with cavalry, elephants, and guns, were in a fortified pagoda at Kytloo. As his men were all sepoys, he sent to General Campbell for a European reinforcement. His request was refused, with what appeared to Colonel Smith an imputation on his motives. Conceiving that his courage was doubted, he resolved to hazard an attack, which proved unsuccessful; and, after severe loss in killed and wounded, he was compelled to order a retreat, the gallantry of the officers being unsupported by their men, who were alarmed at the superior physical strength of the Burmese.

The Burmese had in the meantime commenced preparations in Arracan for invading Bengal. Maha Bandoola, their commander, with a powerful force, marched on Ramoo, and attacked a small body of

British stationed there. These, after a gallant resistance, were overwhelmed and nearly all destroyed or captured. The intelligence of this catastrophe reaching the commanding officer, who was marching to their relief, he made for Chittagong, considering that would be the next place upon which the enemy's power would be directed. The Burmese, however, never attempted to turn their advantage to account; and before Bandoola entered upon fresh aggressions, he was recalled to defend his country. This affair produced most painful impressions throughout Bengal. The peasantry fled from the invisible Burmese, as they were called; and the native merchants of Calcutta were dissuaded with difficulty from removing their families and property from that city. These alarms were fostered by the Peishwa and other Mahratta princes at Benares, as was subsequently ascertained.

By the end of the rainy season the British in Rangoon had formed far more favourable opinions of their position. Great improvements were visible in the health of the troops, and hopes of an early advance were entertained. Five hundred Mugh boatmen from Chittagong were brought in and employed in preparing boats for the river service; a reinforcement also had arrived, consisting of two British regiments, some native infantry, a squadron of cavalry, and a troop of horse-artillery. Added to these, transports with draught-cattle began to arrive; all of which tended to impart fresh spirit to the men, who were busily preparing for their advance when the approach of Maha Bandoola and his force was announced. He was the best general in the Burmese service, and commanded the largest army they had ever sent into the field.

The enemy's approach was learnt by means of an intercepted letter from Bandoola to the ex-governor of Martaban, stating that he had left Prome at the head of an army well disciplined and supplied, either to capture or drive the English from Rangoon.

On the 30th of November the Burmese assembled in the forest in front of the Shoe-dagon Pagoda. Their lines, extending from above Kemmendine in a semicircular direction to the village of Puzendown, were easily traced by the smoke from their watch-fires. As night set in, the hum of voices from this multitude ceased, and in its place was heard the sound of heavy columns marching to the very edge of the jungle which formed our barrier. The greatest alertness was displayed by the British, a furious assault on the pagoda being momentarily expected; but day broke without their expectations being realised. Scarcely had the day dawned when hostilities commenced with a heavy fire of musketry at Kemmendine, the reduction of that place being preliminary to any general attack. The firing was long and animated; and from the commanding situation at the great pagoda, though nearly two miles from the scene of action, the troops posted there could distinctly hear the yells and shouts of the infuriated assailants, occasionally returned by the hearty cheer of the British seamen, as they poured in their heavy broadsides upon the resolute and persevering masses.

In the afternoon several Burmese divisions were discerned marching towards the Dallas river; and later in the day dense bodies issued from the forest, about a mile from the east front of the pagoda, taking position on the river at Puzendown, already strongly occupied by cavalry and infantry. These formed the left wing of the Burmese army. The centre was posted in the forest, and defied all conjecture as to its strength or position. In a few hours the British were completely surrounded, with the narrow channel of the Rangoon river alone unoccupied in their rear. The line of circumvallation taken up by the enemy extended a considerable distance, and being divided by the river, weakened Maha Bandoola's means of assailing us on any particular point; but the celerity, order, and regularity with which the different corps took up their stations reflected much credit on the Burmese general.

In the afternoon a sortie was made to ascertain the disposition of the Burmese; and as they were entirely unprepared for this movement, they were forced from their earth-mounds, or coverings, which they had rapidly thrown up, with severe loss, leaving a great quantity of arms and tools in the trenches. But in the evening the Burmese returned to these works, and began fresh excavations. Soon after sunset the enemy's activity was again evinced by a fierce attack on Kemmendine, the country being simultaneously illumined by the flames of their tremendous fire-rafts, set adrift in the river to destroy our shipping at Rangoon. These rafts the sailors secured and towed ashore, where they were consumed, whilst the attack on Kemmendine by land was also repelled.

For three or four days Sir A. Campbell allowed the enemy to advance their outposts until within fifty yards of his lines, when ascertaining that they had brought all their ammunition and stores from the jungle into their entrenchments, he resolved on a decisive attack. Two bodies under Majors Sale and Walker were ordered to advance, while a number of armed boats under Captain Chads proceeded to Puzendown Creek, and opened a fire upon the enemy's intrenchments. Walker's column was stoutly opposed; but advancing, it drove the Burmese from their trenches at the bayonet's point, though with the loss of its leader. Sale's column met with less resistance, forcing the centre with ease, and then uniting with Walker's troops, it ended in driving the enemy from all parts into the jungle, leaving the earth strewed with the dead and wounded. The whole of their guns, tools, and other stores were at the same time captured.

Still undaunted, Bandoola persevered in his attempts, his troops labouring to make good their approaches to the great pagoda. On the morning of the 7th four attacking columns from the British lines once more forced their entrenchments, and again the Burmese were compelled to retreat into the forest in their rear. In the evening a detachment from Rangoon attacked the position at Dalla, which had enabled the enemy to keep Kemmendine in a state of siege. The attempt was successful; and the Burmese were driven from their line of circumvallation, with the loss of the remainder of their guns, ammunition, and stores.

These reverses caused hundreds of Bandoola's troops to desert, while he was personally fearful that his tyrannical sovereign would wreak his vengeance upon him for his losses. He therefore determined to maintain his position if possible. Four miles in the rear he had an army of reserve busied in stockading and strengthening a position near the village of Kokien, where considerable reinforcements were ordered to join him; and finding he could still face the enemy with twenty-five thousand men, he resolved to risk another action should the English again attack him. With the view of assisting his operations, he bribed several of the inhabitants to set fire to Rangoon in various places, hoping that in the confusion some favourable opportunity might present itself to advance his schemes. The fire was, however, soon extinguished, and on the 15th the English advanced to the attack of Kokien at three different positions. As long as our troops were advancing, the enemy maintained a heavy fire; but no sooner had the advanced column penetrated the works than the enemy fled in every direction, and the entrenchments were carried with little loss to the assailants, but great sacrifice to their adversaries. It was estimated that from the 1st to the 15th of December, six thousand Burmese were slain, while the total on our side killed and wounded did not amount to six hundred, officers and men.

Notwithstanding the repeated defeats of Bandoola, it was evident that the war would be indefinitely protracted unless the interior of the country was penetrated. Accordingly, Sir A. Campbell resolved to march on Prome, while General Cotton proceeded thither with another division in boats; Sale being ordered, at the same time, to reduce Bassein. The march was commenced on the 11th of February, 1825; and on the evening of the 25th of the ensuing month, Sir A. Campbell reached a village from which Bandoola's position at Donoobew was visible. The general continued to advance, without much opposition, until the 25th, and halted within cannon-shot of the enemy's stockades. On the morning of the 27th the flotilla was seen in full sail, and, after an unsuccessful attack by the Burmese, captured or reduced every thing opposed to it.

Bandoola having been killed by a shell, the troops refused to obey any other commander, and deserted Donoobew, which was immediately occupied by the besiegers, who forthwith prepared to march on Prome, which, in its turn, was abandoned as the British advanced. The court of Ava defeated, but not disheartened, once more tried to organise a fresh army, and raised levies from every part of the kingdom. This heterogeneous force was commanded on the right division by Sudda Woon;—the prime minister, Kee Woongee, commanded the centre; while the left wing, under Maha Nemiow, followed a route about ten miles from the centre. On the 10th of November Maha Nemiow occupied Wattygoon, sixteen miles from Prome, whither Colonel M'Dowal was sent to dispossess them; but the Burmese, learning his advance, marched to meet him. In the engagement which followed M'Dowal was shot, which so dispirited his sepoys, as to cause them to retreat. The Burmese, elated with this trifling advantage, resolved to retake Prome. The English having completed their arrangements, on the first of December, two columns, respectively headed by Generals Sir A. Campbell and Cotton, marched against Nemiow. The engagement that followed was obstinately contested by the enemy, and terminated in the death of the Burmese general, and the total annihilation of his army. Napaadu was next assaulted, and was carried at the bayonet's point, with great slaughter amongst its defenders.

On the 5th of December the remaining division of the Burmese army under Sudda Woon was attacked and defeated, the troops flying in consternation to the woods for protection. General Campbell, with the view of ending the war, began his march on the enemy's capital early in December. After the capture of several stockades, and some slight skirmishes, Patanagoh was reached, when offers of negotiation were renewed, and a meeting to agree upon the terms of a treaty was appointed for the first of January, 1826. It was, however, discovered that the Burmese were dissimulating; and consequently, upon the armistice expiring, notice was given that hostilities would be renewed on the 18th. It was now evident that the Burmese cause was hopeless,—all exertions upon the part of the officers were useless; the soldiers, too dispirited to offer any defence, were driven from their entrenchments, leaving the whole of their artillery and stores. Prince Memiaboo and his defeated army retreated as quickly as possible, closely pressed by the British.

On the 25th the army was again on its march through a country desolated by fury and fanaticism. On the 31st two Burmese of rank arrived, with full authority for negotiating a treaty, and General Campbell refusing to waive one point of his former demands, was assured they would be yielded; but no entreaty prevailed on him to arrest the progress of his army; he, however, agreed not to pass Pagham Mew for twelve days.

Notwithstanding the assurances of these envoys, Campbell, as he proceeded onwards, ascertained that hostilities were to be renewed. The king, instigated by a warrior of low origin, believed his boast, that with thirty thousand men he could annihilate the rebellious strangers. A fresh levy was accordingly made, and the force honoured with the title of "Retrievers of the king's glory." The British army, weakened by the absence of two brigades, did not muster two thousand men; nevertheless Campbell determinedly pushed on to Pagham Mew. Clearing the jungle, he debouched on the Burmese army sixteen thousand strong; regardless of their position and numbers, the British dashed into their centre, which was speedily overthrown, and the wings with great difficulty reached the second line of redoubts under the walls of Pagham Mew. No time was allowed for rallying; the English troops rushed into the Burmese entrenchments and within the city, and thus secured the victory. This was the most sanguinary defeat the Burmese had yet experienced. Severe as had been their former engagements, this was still more so; but thirteen hundred men, with their boastful leader, returned to Ava out of all that numerous host.

The army was still kept marching until it arrived at Gandaboo, forty-five miles from the capital, when the Burmese monarch, completely humbled and disheartened, sent envoys to conclude peace upon any terms, which were at length arranged, and the treaty signed and sealed at Gandaboo on the 24th. By this act the king of Ava renounced his claim to the sovereignty over Assam, Cachar, and Jylna; declared Munzipore an independent kingdom; acknowledged the mountains of Arracan as the boundary between his territory and the Company's, and yielded the whole of Tenasserim to the British. He further agreed to pay, in four payments, a crore of rupees, not to punish any of his subjects who had assisted us during the war, to include the king of Siam in the amnesty, and to grant to British vessels visiting his ports the same privileges enjoyed by his own ships. The English, on their part, undertook to fall back on Rangoon at once, to leave the country entirely upon the payment of the second instalment of the crore of rupees, and to return all prisoners with as little delay as possible.

On the 5th of March Sir A. Campbell gave the order for returning to Rangoon, which he reached without any casualties. The whole of the troops did not, however, return by this route; a body of sepoys, conducted by native guides, were directed to cross the country to Arracan, where they arrived without much trouble. Ava was thus proved to be accessible, upon any future occasion, by land as well as by water.

During our operations against the Burmese in 1825, the attention of the Bengal executive was called to affairs at Bhurtpore, where Durgoon Sal, immediately upon the rajah's death, usurped the throne rightfully belonging to Bulwunt Sing, a minor, whose interests we had promised to protect; upon which the guardians of the prince fled with him to Calcutta, and prayed the assistance of the governor-general. Lord Lake's failure at Bhurtpore had created a strong party there inimical to the British; and it had been wished for some time, upon political grounds, to destroy this influence. A favourable opportunity for so doing now presented itself, and it was determined to destroy the hallucination that Bhurtpore was impregnable. Lord Combermere happening to arrive in India at this juncture, assumed the command of the army; and on the 10th of December, at the head of twenty thousand men, supported by a hundred pieces of artillery, appeared before the walls. Unwilling that the females and children should encounter the horrors of such an assault as must ensue, he addressed a letter to Durgoon Sal, on the 21st, urging him to send them out of the fort, and offering safe conduct to them, and further gave twenty-four hours for the execution of his humane desires; he afterwards further extended the time twelve hours, though without any result.

On the 23d besieging operations commenced, the north-east angle being selected as the *point d'appui*, the British at the same time possessing themselves of Kuddum Kundee, a village, and completing their first parallel eight hundred yards from the fort. The remainder of the month was employed in constructing and repairing batteries and making preparations for the general assault, a heavy and destructive fire being sustained by the town during the whole time. At length, on the 3d of January, 1826, the artillery began to breach the curtains. The tough mud-walls were, however, much more effective than masonry; and, as the batteries produced but little effect, recourse was had to mining.

On the 16th two mines were driven, and sprung successfully (previous mines had proved ineffective, or were rendered abortive by the besieged); and an excellent breach in the walls being reported, the 18th was fixed on for the assault. Early in the morning, the troops forming the storming-party reached the advanced trenches without being discovered; while General Nicholls and General Reynells, at the head of their brigades, were respectively to mount the left and right breaches, the explosion of the mine being the signal for attack. The explosion took place at eight o'clock in the morning, carrying away the entire salient angle and a great portion of the stone cavalier in the rear. The troops immediately advanced with great order and determination; and shortly, notwithstanding the fury of the besieged, carried the breaches, and in two hours the whole rampart environing the town and the gates of the citadel were in the hands of the besiegers: very shortly afterwards the citadel itself was captured. General Hugh, who had been specially appointed to prevent the enemy's escape, so judiciously disposed his men that Durgoon Sal, his wife, and two sons, were, with a strong body of horse, made prisoners in their attempt to force a passage through the 8th Light Cavalry.

It was estimated that not less than four thousand of the besieged fell in this assault, and scarcely a man escaped through Hugh's cordon of cavalry. The whole of the military stores and ammunition being captured, the political and military power of Bhurtpore was annihilated, and the fortifications demolished, by Lord Combermere's order, on the 6th of February. All the remaining fortresses belonging to the rajah surrendered, and the rajah himself was reinstated; after which Lord Combermere broke up the camp, and returned to Calcutta on the 20th of February.

This gallant assault merited, and received, the thanks of Parliament and the East India Company; and what was still more gratifying, the prize-money which the king presented to the Company was ordered by the Court of Directors to be distributed among the troops.

In 1827, the whole of British India being in a state of tranquillity, Lord Amherst proceeded to the upper provinces, and visited Delhi, expressly to arrange the relations of the British government with the nominal king of that country; his negotiations were ended by setting aside the shadow of sovereignty which had nominally attached to the last descendant of the Mogul. At the end of March Lord Amherst embarked for England in his Majesty's ship *Herald*, leaving the Hon. Mr. Bayley to administer the government of India pending the arrival of his successor.

CHAPTER VII.

FROM THE ADMINISTRATION OF LORD WILLIAM BENTINCK TO THE ANNEXATION OF SCINDE AND THE PACIFICATION OF GWALIOR.

A.D. 1828-1844.

THE administration of Lord William Bentinck, who succeeded Earl Amherst, was, unlike that of any of his predecessors, marked by no warlike demonstrations. The inroads of hordes of hill-tribes, the punishment and dethronement of the petty rajah of Coorg, and some other arrangements with various tributary powers, were not sufficient to disturb the general tranquillity which now pervaded India, and which it was his lordship's fortune to turn to profitable account. The state of the services received the governor-general's earnest attention, and many reforms were introduced into their various branches, which, however unpalatable to the members, were calculated greatly to improve their efficiency. Many concessions were also made to the natives of India; not the least valuable of which was an enactment freeing seceders from the Hindoo or Mahomedan faith within the Bengal Presidency from the penalties which had, under the old native laws, attached to such an act, viz. the forfeiture of their personal and family property.

Educational and other public institutions received his lordship's warmest support; and to this day the name of Bentinck is gratefully remembered by the inhabitants of British India. Two projects of national importance were at this time undertaken; of one of which the ultimate benefits can scarcely be over-estimated—the opening of communications between British India and the countries west of the Indus as far as the Caspian Sea, and the establishment of an overland steam communication between England and India.

The former of these projects had for its objects the extension of British commerce, and the ascertaining the feasibility of a Russian invasion from that quarter. This important and dangerous task was confided to

Lieutenant, afterwards Sir Alexander Burnes, who gathered and published some valuable information respecting the political condition, the commercial relations, and the geographical features of the countries lying between the Indus and the Caspian Sea. No commercial advantages have as yet sprung from his labours, with the exception of the complete navigation of the Indus by steamers; whilst, as regards political occurrences, the only result has been the disastrous Afghan campaign, which may truly be traced to this exploration.

Of far greater magnitude and solid advantage to Indo-British commerce was the rapid and safe communication, first commenced during Lord W. Bentinck's administration, between India and this country by way of the Red Sea, Egypt, and the Mediterranean. To Lieutenant Waghorn belongs all the merit of having conceived and thoroughly carried out this scheme in the teeth of all the constituted authorities of India, at home and abroad. Thanks to the enlightened man who at this time ruled India, Waghorn's efforts were rightly estimated, and in the end completely carried out, to the lasting advantage of every interest connected with our possessions in the East.

The navigation of the Ganges by steam-vessels was during this peaceful administration set on foot with the most complete success; and has since, under a completer system, afforded great facilities to the internal traffic of the Bengal presidency.

In the year 1833, the discussions in parliament on the renewal of the East India Company's charter led to some great and important changes in the functions of this powerful body. The principal of these changes may be placed under the following heads: The Company retained its political rights, and, in conjunction with the Board of Control, gave its entire attention to the government of India. It ceased to be a commercial body, gave up its monopoly of the Chinese trade, and abandoned that of India; the trade to both countries was declared to be free to every British subject. British subjects were permitted to settle in any part of the Indian territories. The shareholders were guaranteed a fixed dividend upon their capital of 6,000,000*l.*; and a sinking-fund was set aside for the purpose of redeeming the Company's stock at the end of fifty years, if deemed necessary. With these leading provisoes, the charter was renewed for a further term of twenty years, expiring in the year 1853.

Lord William Bentinck resigned the administration of Indian affairs early in 1835, owing to the failure of his health; and in the month of March set sail for England, regretted by the native and a large portion of the European community.

The advent of Lord Auckland as governor-general of India was destined to prove a momentous epoch in the Anglo-Indian annals. On this appointment being made known, the public were somewhat at a loss to guess what peculiar quality of his lordship had formed the justification of the act. None knew what his administrative ability might amount to; and all who took the trouble to form any opinion on the subject, were unanimous that the name of Auckland could by no human possibility become distinguished in connexion with the government of the vast territories over which it was decided that he should hold an almost uncontrolled sway. But these cavillers were mistaken; they knew not their man. Before these sceptics in the achievements of an Auckland were three years older, they had the strongest possible reasons for according to his lordship a distinction and a notoriety as world-wide, and as indelible, as any achieved by a Clive or a Wellington. It was Lord Auckland's destiny to place the British arms in a position they had never previously occupied on the continent of India; to carve out for the British forces a career as disastrous as its origin was unjustifiable and unworthy; to peril our position in the East; to sacrifice an army of brave men; and finally, to clothe half the nation in mourning, and to overwhelm the other half with shame and indignation.

On the arrival of this amicably-disposed nobleman in Calcutta, he found India rife with rumours of Russian diplomacy and Russian intrigue. Every political occurrence of the day was set down to autocratic influence; every foreign traveller in moustaches was believed to be a diplomate or officer of engineers from St. Petersburgh; and every Arab or Beloochee trader who crossed the western frontier was transformed by these political genii of the Company's service into a Russian spy.

Shah Soojah, the imbecile ruler of Afghanistan, had been expelled that country, in the ordinary eastern style, to make room for one far better able to rule such a turbulent people as were his subjects; and the deposed chief appeared well satisfied to find himself with his head on his shoulders, eating the Company's "salt" within the walls of the British fortress of Loodianah, one of the north-western frontier stations.

The Punjab or "Country of the Five Rivers," which formed the barrier between our extreme frontiers and the turbulent Afghans, was at that time under the sway of Runjeet Singh, a chief whose valour and indomitable energy and activity had won for him the title of the "Lion of the Punjab." Between this chief and the Afghan rulers a constant succession of hostilities took place with varying results, though most frequently in favour of the "Lion."[1]

The mission of Captain, afterwards Sir Alexander Burnes to Cabul in 1837, although apparently successful at the time, bore no fruit; and it soon became evident that the ruler of that country, with many promises on his lips, cared as little for our friendship and our commerce as for our hostility.[2]

Another party of diplomatists, military and civil, was dispatched to Lahore, the capital of the Punjab, with the view of forming a treaty with Runjeet Singh. So far as the signatures to a parchment were concerned, every thing was attained that had been hoped for; and the governor-general, who was already planning, at the instigation of others, the chastisement of Dost Mohammed, the restoration of the imbecile Shah Soojah, and the defeat of the so-much-dreaded Russian influence in that quarter, flattered himself that Lahore would prove a safe and accessible road by which to reach the walls of Cabool.

In October 1838 war with the Dost was proclaimed from the cool retirement of Simla; and so determined were the abettors of this ill-advised scheme, that before the close of the year the Bengal and Bombay armies were at the appointed rendezvous, Shikapore in Scinde. These forces amounted to 15,000 men, with a reserve of 4000 at Ferozepore, and a native contingent provided by Shah Soojah, but paid by us, amounting to 6000.

Our troops encountered disasters from the outset. The cholera, want of a sufficient means of transport, jealousy and heart-burnings amongst the commanders, and lastly, the trying season during the greater part of the march, all contributed to impart a prestige of no cheering character to the commencement of the campaign.

Sir John Keane, appointed to the command-in-chief of the army of the Indus, was seconded by officers as brave and energetic as any in the service. Among them were Major-General Nott, Sir W. Cotton, Brigadier Sale, and Colonel Dennie. The arrangements for the supply of the commissariat were, however, of the worst possible kind; and added to this was the enormous number of camp-followers, amounting

[1] The Sikh ruler appears to have been keenly alive to the process of absorption of native states by the English, although he felt it to be his policy to remain on friendly terms with so powerful a neighbour. It is related of him that in a conversation with a Company's officer, he pointed to a large map of India before him, on which the British territories were defined by a narrow red band, and exclaimed, "When Runjeet dies, Company's red line swallow up all Punjab country."

[2] Alexander Burnes' Travels in Afghanistan, &c.

to nearly 100,000; these had to be provided for amidst strange and unfriendly countries, upon a march of extraordinary length and of great physical difficulties.[3] It was not surprising, therefore, that these

TROOPS GOING UP THE COUNTRY.

circumstances, added to the want of unanimity in action amongst the divisions of the army, should have placed the invaders in a difficult and perilous position.

On the 6th of March the Bengal column, under Sir John Keane and Sir Willoughby Cotton, reached the foot of the mountains of Western Afghanistan, scarcely on the threshold of their journey; yet even then their provisions ran short, and the allowance of the troops was reduced to one half. The dangerous and difficult passage of the

Buist's Outline of the Operations of the British Troops in Scinde and Afghanistan.

Bolan Pass, seventy miles in length, was effected after much suffering; and when the troops reached Quettah on the 4th of April, so reduced were they in all their supplies, that the camp-followers were under the necessity of feeding on roots, skins of beasts, &c.

Thence to Candahar the sufferings of the soldiers and followers were very great; and when they reached that city on the 4th of May, the latter dwindled down to 20,000. The expectation that supplies would be there obtained was doomed to disappointment. The army found itself as badly fed as ever; and, in order not to exhaust completely the miserable means of the commissariat, a move onward towards Ghuznee was at once decided upon, although the distance was fully 230 miles, and the army wanted most of the requisites for a long journey.

On the 21st of July the British troops encamped under the walls of Ghuznee, which were found to be far stronger than had been anticipated. Hesitation would have been ruinous; and the choice lay between making a dash at this stronghold, and a timely retreat to the starting point. Fortunately for the besiegers, it was discovered that one of the gates of the town had not been built up with masonry, and accordingly this was blown in with gunpowder during the night, the breach thus effected being at once taken advantage of by a storming party, seconded by all the troops available for an assault of the kind. The town was quickly captured; and, in spite of some desperate resistance from the Afghan garrison, the citadel fell within a few hours. The loss of the British in killed and wounded was but trifling; that of the besieged amounted to 1000 slain, and 3000 wounded and captured.

The fall of this stronghold of the Afghans was fortunate in many respects; for it not only afforded the troops much that was needed, but struck terror into the hearts of the enemy, and at once opened the road to Cabool. The army was not allowed a long halt; Colonel Wade, who was moving onwards from Peshawur, fought his way through the Kyber Pass and seized Jellalabad, driving before him Akbar Khan, the second son of the Dost, and capturing a large supply of arms, ammunition, and horses. On the 30th of July the main body of the army, with Sir John Keane, Shah Soojah, and Mr. MacNaghten, marched towards the capital; from which, as they approached, Dost Mohammed fled with a chosen body of horsemen, making his way to the west, beyond the reach of regular troops.

Deserted by their ruler and every chieftain of any consequence, the inhabitants of Cabool had little choice left them but to open their gates to the advancing columns of the British, who entered the Afghan capital, with Shah Soojah at their head, in all the pomp and circumstance of vic-

BATTLE OF FEROZEPORE.

tory. There were none to oppose the placing the English nominee on the throne; and this was accordingly done; though it does not appear to have occurred to any of the actors how they were to manage to keep him there without the presence of an overwhelming military force.

Thus far the game had proceeded smoothly enough; despite the privations of the troops, every thing had succumbed to them; and if the miserable arrangements of a most defective commissariat had not involved the army in utter confusion, it was owing rather to good fortune than to any other contingency.

The commander-in-chief hastened from the scene of his hollow exploits; and scarcely resting at the seat of government, took his way home, to shew himself to the British public as the conqueror of Afghanistan, receiving, as the fruit of his splendid achievement, a title and a pension; the greatest exploit of the entire campaign having been the blowing open of a wooden door with a few bags of gunpowder.

The bulk of the troops followed their retreating commander; a small force being left behind in various positions, scarcely any of which were tenable against an enemy. Sir Alexander Burnes and Sir William MacNaghten were left at Cabool in a political capacity, with a garrison under the command of Major-general Elphinstone and General Sale, badly housed, and still worse provided with a commissariat. So miserably, indeed, was this department conducted, that it was frequently only by dint of hard bribing, that any provisions could be procured from the neighbouring country.

Matters remained tranquil through the first winter; which, in that country, proved a most severe season for our troops, both European and native. The spring ushered in a foretaste of what was in store for the British. Dost Mohammed was known to be at no great distance from Cabool, raising the people, and inciting them to vengeance on the unbelieving invaders of their country. Akbar Khan, his "fighting" son, was every where leading large bodies of Afghan troops against our outposts; cutting off supplies, and harassing the troops in every possible manner.

In the summer of this year (1840) some sharp encounters with the enemy took place, much to his discomfiture; the rude courage and brute energy of his wild troops being quite unable to cope with the disciplined bravery of English regiments. After many desperate engagements, Dost Mohammed surrendered himself a prisoner to the British envoy, Sir W. MacNaghten; and was, before the end of the year, sent beyond the frontier. A pension of 30,000*l.* a year was allowed him, and a residence for himself and his numerous family allotted at Mussoorie, on the north-western frontier, where he quietly remained awaiting the course of events.

They were not very long in casting their shadows on the foreground. Akbar Khan had been no party to his father's submission; and so far from contemplating a similar course, omitted no opportunity of falling upon any British force which came in his way. Month after month witnessed the same system of desultory warfare; always to our damage, and seldom to that of the enemy, who were completely masters of this art of campaigning.

Beyond this system of petty and vexatious warfare, and the evidently-growing dislike of the people to our influence and presence in the country, there was little to disturb the course of events at Cabool. At the same time there were not wanting those who could see below the surface of things, and who prophesied the approaching storm. Hints, warnings, and advice were alike thrown away upon the British envoy, who appeared to discredit all that did not coincide with his own previously-formed opinions.[4]

This strange infatuation clung to him up to the last moment; and when the 2d of November, 1841, ushered in a general rising of the people of Cabool, he was still unpersuaded of any real danger, and expressed a belief that "it would all blow over." It did blow over; but it swept with it the existence of the whole English force. From that fatal morning the record of events in Afghanistan is a sad and terrible recital, uncheered by but one single bright and stirring deed—the gallant and apparently hopeless defence of Jellalabad by its small and ill-provided garrison.

The massacre of Burnes, and every officer, woman, and child found with him in the city, was followed by the seizure of the commissariat, and the gathering of numerous bodies of Afghans within and about the walls. The energy and faculties of both officers and men seemed to have been completely paralysed by the suddenness, rather than the greatness of the danger; and in this manner many valuable days were suffered to pass, adding to the confidence and numbers of the enemy; and in proportion dispiriting our own troops. Resistance did not form a part of the tactics adopted by this most unfortunate body of men, who preferred trusting to negotiations with men who were proverbial for their utter faithlessness, rather than to their own energy.

Towards the end of November Akbar Khan arrived in Cabool with a chosen body of horse; and from that day matters drew rapidly to a crisis. Conferences were held between the chief and the British envoy,

[4] The Military Operations at Cabool, &c., by Lieutenant Vincent Eyre.

which resulted in an arrangement that the British should immediately evacuate Afghanistan, being guaranteed a safe passage to India and supplies of provisions. Dost Mohammed was to be permitted to return to his country, Shah Soojah to retire within British territories, and perpetual friendship to be firmly established between the two powers.

The troops began to prepare for their humiliating march on the 14th December; on the 23d, as the remainder of the forces joined the main body, Sir W. MacNaghten was invited to a final conference with the Afghan chief, and during a short interview was killed by a pistol-shot, as some have declared, fired by the hand of Akbar Khan.

The retreat of the English forces, amounting to 4500 men and some 12,000 of camp-followers, took place, as arranged, on the 6th of January; but no sooner had they cleared the walls of Cabool than parties of Afghans harassed their rear and picked off the stragglers day and night. The horrors of that humiliating retreat were heightened by the severity of the season and the difficulties of the country. First the wounded, and then the ladies and children, were given up to the Afghans as the only hope of saving them; finally, abandoning all further hope, the soldiers and camp-followers gave themselves to despair, and either lay down to die in the snow, or fell in the rear, and were despatched by Afghan bullets. From straggling shots the work of death proceeded until it became wholesale slaughter; and before many days had elapsed, of all that host of twenty-six thousand souls but one Englishman, Dr. Brydon, and a few sepoys and followers, escaped with the terrible tidings to Jellalabad, where the gallant Sale held his position with the courage and determination of a hero.

Meanwhile Candahar was held by General Nott and a strong body of troops; Ghuznee was kept possession of by Colonel Palmer and a mere handful of sepoys; whilst Shah Soojah contrived to make good his position in Cabool itself, despite the presence of Akbar Khan and the treachery or feebleness of nearly every Afghan chieftain.

Determined, if possible, to obtain possession of the fortress of Jellalabad, Akbar Khan invested it with an army strong in numbers, but deficient in every requisite for conducting a siege. With the old crumbling walls of the fort tottering at every discharge of cannon, with wide gaps in their defences, which any other enemy would have known how to avail himself of, Sale and his gallant little party not only bid the besiegers bold defiance, but sallied out for forage, and did no small mischief in the Afghan camp.

Whilst the above was transpiring, and when the English captives, ladies, officers, and children, were dragging on a miserable existence in Afghan dungeons, General Pollock was making his way with a relief across the Punjab; and at the same moment, the instigators of all these disasters were issuing instructions for the withdrawal of our troops from Cabool, leaving the prisoners of course to their fate.

The winter of 1841 brought no hope for the pent-up garrisons or the captives in Afghanistan. The troops of Akbar continued to press hard upon every fort in the possession of the English; and though Jellalabad and Candahar held out gallantly, Palmer was compelled to evacuate Ghuznee, when, as was usually the case, nearly every man, woman, and child of the garrison was butchered as they marched out under the capitulation. Palmer was reserved for torture and imprisonment, with one or two of his officers.

At length brighter days dawned upon the army of the Indus. The nervous and imbecile Auckland was replaced by Lord Ellenborough, a man of other mettle, who, though pestered by the fears and phantasies of the incompetent Council of Calcutta, acted on the impulsive feeling of doing that which alone could retrieve our tarnished reputation, and rescued the British captives by the means alone consistent with our national honour. The word was given, and heard but to be joyfully obeyed. No second bidding was needed. Pollock continued to move forward with his troops to the relief of the gallant band in Jellalabad. The Afghans, under Akbar Khan, opposed the passage of the Kyber Pass in vain; driven from every point by the bayonet, the enemy fled before the British troops, and from the moment of emerging from that dangerous mountain-gorge the British forces met with no further resistance. The army of the Khan had melted away like snow before the noonday sun.

On the 16th April the troops of Pollock and Sale met under the tottering walls of Jellalabad, with what delight to all parties may be readily imagined. But all felt that the time was too precious to be wasted in mere rejoicings or congratulations. Both generals knew well the critical position of the remainder of our pent-up forces, the revengeful, impetuous temper of Akbar, and the imminent danger of the prisoners, among whom were the wife and daughter of Sale; and they felt that if any decisive blow was to be struck, it must be achieved at once, with the *éclat* of Pollock's recent victories still fresh in the minds of the enemy and their own troops. Had their own impulses only been consulted, Cabool would have been in their hands within a week; but unfortunately a reference was yet to be made to the Supreme Government!

It was thus the middle of August before a combined movement was made by the three generals, Nott, Pollock, and Sale, from Candahar and Jellalabad. The former moved out with seven thousand troops; and defeating one of the Afghan chiefs, who attempted to intercept his march, razed the walls and fortifications of Ghuznee, the scene of so much treachery and disaster to our countrymen. On the other side, the combined forces of Pollock and Sale did not proceed without force; but in every case in which opposition was offered victory declared for them. Indeed every sword that was drawn, every shot that was fired, told in honour of the British, and served but to render the cause of the Afghans more desperate.

The final struggle for the mastery took place at the Khoord Cabool Pass, a most difficult and commanding position, where the enemy mustered in considerable numbers; but to oppose in vain. Nothing could now restrain our troops, who seemed eager for the fray, and driving the foe before them from every defile and mountain-path, sealed the fate of that short and glorious campaign.

On the 15th of September, the forces of Pollock and Sale arrived at Cabool, where they found, as expected, that numerous changes had taken place. Revolutions and savage conflicts had succeeded each other with rapidity. The chiefs had been divided among themselves in the support of the two rulers, and eventually the assassination of Shah Soojah had to a degree paved the way to something bearing the semblance of amity. No sooner did the news of the junction of the British forces at Jellalabad reach the ears of Akbar than he prepared for flight, making arrangements at the same time for carrying his numerous prisoners with him into the wilds of Toorkhistan. On the notification of the advance of the generals towards the capital, the Afghan chief put his plans into execution; and whilst he hurried off his own treasures and family towards the north-west, and himself hastened to watch the steps of the British, the English captives, to the number of one hundred and twenty-two, were despatched, in charge of an Afghan khan, towards Bameean, where they were detained for upwards of a week, awaiting further instructions from Akbar. The orders of the latter had been to kill all the sick, wounded, or feeble, so as to prevent any delay in their march; but although the khan shewed little regard for his charge, he hesitated to carry into execution these barbarous instructions.[5]

Fortunately for the prisoners, this chief was easily swayed by interest; avarice was his ruling passion; and the officers in his custody were not long in ascertaining that a bribe sufficiently liberal would induce their jailor to open the doors of their prison-house. The result of their negotiations was, that 2000*l.* were to be paid down to the

[5] Journal of Imprisonment in Afghanistan: Lieutenant V. Eyre.

khan and a pension settled on him; for which he was to fling off allegiance to Akbar, and maintain the party in the fort against all enemies until relief could be obtained. The position of independence taken up by the old khan and his followers and British companions soon drew around them some of the neighbouring chiefs, who doubtless were aware of the present aspect of affairs at Cabool, and were able to make a shrewd guess at the probable course of events. These people guaranteed support and aid to the English party; and at length, when news was brought the latter of the successes of Pollock and the dispersion of Akbar's forces, they moved boldly and rejoicingly from their prison-fort, and turned their steps in the direction of Cabool. Their party was, however, but a small one; and they were not without apprehensions lest Akbar might still be hovering about to intercept any relief sent to them, the more so as some report reached them that a strong body of Afghan horse was following in their steps to hurry them off to the banks of the Oxus.

On the first evening of their bivouacking, they received decided intelligence of the complete successes of the various bodies of British troops, and of the dispersion of the Afghans and their chief Akbar. The glad intelligence was confirmed during that night by the arrival in their little camp of a native trooper, bearing a letter from Sir Richard Shakespeare, informing them of his near approach to their assistance with a strong body of Kussilbash horse. Before daylight the little party set forward on their way to meet their deliverers with beating hearts; and at noon, whilst resting under the shade of a ruined fort, they were gladdened by the approach of Sir Richard and his cavalry, mustering six hundred.

Fears were, however, still entertained that an attempt at rescue might be made by the desperate Akbar, especially as a dangerous pass had to be traversed on their road to the capital. Accordingly, a messenger was despatched to General Pollock, requesting instant reinforcement; whilst on their part every available means were used to push on their way, with but little rest or desire for halting. On the 20th they encountered an officer who had ridden on in advance of the approaching relief; and from him they gathered the joyful intelligence that General Sale's brigade was but a mile or two in the rear.

The happiness of this day may be imagined. The long-lost wife and daughter were restored in safety to the man who had so gallantly maintained the honour of his country within the little fort of Jellalabad; and many a missing one was met that day by friends or anxious relatives.[6] It was indeed a joyful meeting, and gladly did the whole party set forward to retrace their steps to the camp outside the city of Cabool. This they reached by sunset on the 21st, the British artillery rending the air with the glad echoes of their thundering welcome.

The remainder of this eventful history may be soon told. By a proclamation issued at Simla, the governor-general declared, that having retrieved the disasters of the past, and taught the Afghans a lesson not likely to be soon forgotten, the British army should now evacuate that country and retire to Ferozepore. After a short period employed in interring the thousands of skeletons of our slaughtered countrymen that literally strewed the scenes of the massacres of Cabool; and after effectually demolishing the citadel, the walls, the Bala Hissur, and every building of any strength in the capital, the army of the Indus set out on its homeward march upon the 12th of October.

At Ferozepore the troops were received by the governor-general and his staff, and many and hearty were the congratulations given and received upon this happy termination to a sad and fatal campaign.[7] Rejoicings and festivities wound up that which had been begun in rashness and infatuation, and consummated in disgrace, bloodshed, and imprisonment. Heavy as was the retribution that descended on the actors in the Afghan tragedy, the remembrance of our errors and our disasters will live long and sadly in the recollection of this generation.

For a time it appeared as though peace was firmly established on the Indian continent; but to those who could see below the surface of things, the tranquillity was but a deceptive lull, a calm ushering in the tempest that was soon to burst forth in another quarter.

The treacherous conduct of the Ameers of Scinde during our Afghan campaign was not mended on the return of the army from that country, the Ameers judging that we should not have retired so soon unless we had met with further reverses. Our evacuation of Afghanistan was looked upon by them as a virtual defeat; and it soon became pretty evident that their feelings towards us were not improved, nor their disposition more friendly, in consequence of that impression. Grave doubts have been since entertained by many with regard to the propriety and justice of our operations in the Scinde country; but there appears to be no question, that whilst the rulers of that territory entertained the hostile feelings to us which they did, no security could for a moment exist for the tranquillity of the state, and that sooner or later the events which were then brought about must of necessity have occurred.

[6] Journal of Imprisonment in Afghanistan: Eyre. [7] Lady Sale's Journal.

Cautions, warnings, and every friendly means were employed towards the Ameers, to induce an amicable disposition, or at any rate a peaceful line of conduct; but all these means seem to have been employed in vain; and when it was evident that but one course must be adopted, Lord Ellenborough was not slow to order its execution.

The Ameers had during the entire winter season of 1842 been busily engaged in gathering their forces and taking up a menacing position; whilst the veteran Sir Charles Napier strengthened his own attitude, and made every disposition for acting so soon as the proper moment should arrive. That moment occurred in the early part of February. The British residency at Hyderabad was attacked with great fury by a large and desperate body of the Ameers' troops; and it was not without difficulty that the English officials were enabled to make good their retreat and join their friends within the camp at a short distance from the city.

Sir Charles, with his small but well-disciplined band of 2100 of all arms, moved across the Indus and approached the enemy's position, which was a remarkably strong one, near the village of Meeanee. Their forces amounted to fully 30,000 infantry and 5000 horse, with a train of 15 guns well served on the European system. A stronger position than that occupied by their main body could scarcely be conceived. A natural ravine of considerable depth protected them in front, whilst their flanks were well sheltered by extensive forests and broken ground. Formidable as their entrenchment appeared, the British general did not for a moment hesitate about the attack, but on the morning of the 17th of February gave the signal for the assault.

Moving rapidly forward from their open position on the plain, the English and sepoy regiments advanced gallantly towards the thickly guarded ravine, behind which bristled myriads of glittering weapons. Cheering each other on, regardless of the storm which swept their ranks from the Scinde artillery, they plunged into the dangerous ravine, and rushing up the opposite bank, which they strewed with their dead and wounded, made for the top of the embankment, where the enemy stood matchlock in hand to receive them. The gallant 22d, an Irish regiment, led the way; and quick as thought were on the summit of the entrenchment, behind which they found awaiting them with a glittering forest of steel and a barrier of bucklers, vast masses of Beloochee swordsmen, whose numbers and savage shouts must have struck dismay into the hearts of any but such as were opposed to them. Shout for shout was given, cheer for cheer, and lowering the queen of weapons—the bayoneted musket—the little handful of heroes rushed upon the vast force opposed to them.

The conflict was long and bloody. Valour could but do its utmost; and the sweeping discharges from the thickly, well-planted Scinde artillery on their flank told fearfully upon the courageous band who strove against this mighty host. For every score of Beloochees who fell before the British bayonet an English soldier was swept away by the murderous discharge of grape; and although each gap was gallantly filled up from the rear, their numbers went on thinning hour after hour, whilst the multitude opposed to them seemed to be as numerous as ever, so little was the havoc amidst their ranks perceptible.[8]

Victory seemed about to declare against the small band of assailants: the greater part of their officers were killed or disabled; and the sepoys, without a leader, more than once made a retrograde movement. At this critical juncture a charge was ordered to be made on the enemy's right by the small body of horse under Colonel Pattle, which had the effect of at once deciding the fate of the day. The British cavalry did their duty nobly; and the Beloochees, finding themselves in danger on their flank, began to move slowly but defiantly from the field. Resistance was no longer thought of; and the British guns in their turn swept all before them, whilst cavalry and infantry carried on the work of destruction until nature became exhausted, and they could do no more.

On the following day Sir Charles summoned the Ameers, who had remained safely within the fortifications of Hyderabad, to surrender their persons and their authority into his hands without delay, in default of which he threatened to storm the city. The mandate was obeyed by the entrance within his camp of six of these chiefs, who proceeded to lay at the feet of the British general their swords and insignia of royalty. "Their misfortunes," said Sir Charles in his dispatches, "were of their own creating; but as they were great, I gave them back their swords;" and doubtless he knew full well the utter uselessness of those weapons to men who looked on from their fortified walls whilst the brave but mercenary troops of Beloochistan were fighting their battle. One other action, that of Dubba, and the power of the Ameers was for ever annihilated; and when one or two turbulent bands of marauders had been swept from the country, the British flag waved supreme to the borders of Beloochistan.

The immediate consequence of these decisive victories was the annexation of Scinde to the territories of the Company. In a pro-

[7] Major-General W. F. P. Napier's *Conquest of Scinde*.

clamation dated on the 5th of March, 1843, from Agra, the governor-general announced that the conquered territories had become part of our eastern dominions. On the 15th of the same month Major-General Sir Charles Napier was appointed governor of this province; and a declaration was made relative to the manumission of all slaves within the boundaries of Scinde, the free passage of the Indus to the commerce of the world, and the abolition of all transit-duties.

Scarcely had this proclamation been made generally known, when troubles, though of far less magnitude, awaited the government in another direction, and nearer home. The independent Mahratta state of Gwalior had been for a long period the scene of great confusion and strife, giving ample employment to the British resident at its court, under whose protection the reigning family held their authority. The decease of the last rajah, and the consequent regency of his widow during the minority of his successor, opened the door to endless intrigues and difficulties. Ministers of pacific views, and favourable to the English policy, were rudely set aside by the widow for others of questionable character, and holding opinions directly opposite. Plots, conspiracies, and insurrections split the country from one end to the other; until, determined that such an unquiet and dangerous neighbour could not be permitted, the governor-general ordered a force to enter the maharajah's territories, in order to assert his just authority, and give security to his person and power.

This army was conducted by Sir Hugh Gough, accompanied by Lord Ellenborough, and moved from Agra in the early part of December; whilst a second division, under Major-General Grey, advanced from Bundelkund. The first and main division crossed the Kohuree river on the 29th December, and took up a position not far from the village of Maharajpoor, where the Mahratta army lay strongly encamped, mustering fully eighteen thousand men, a strong body of cavalry, and a hundred guns. The British troops amounted to fourteen thousand men, with forty pieces of artillery.

The attack was commenced by Major-General Littler's column charging full upon the enemy's front. The advancing regiments were received with a furious and deadly cannonade, which sensibly thinned their ranks, whilst the Mahratta troops gave them a warm reception from their matchlocks. Nothing, however, could stem the torrent that swept up to the mouths of the enemy's cannon, bayoneting their gunners and driving all before them. Flinging away their matchlocks, the Mahrattas fled to the village, where, sword in hand, they made a desperate stand, but in vain. The small but dashing brigade of cavalry, under General Valiant, charged Maharajpoor in the rear, cut up the flanks of the enemy, and effectually sealed the fate of the now defeated and flying Mahratta force.

The loss of the enemy in this hard-fought battle was believed to have been from three to four thousand in killed and wounded, besides all their cannon and stores. The victory, however, was not purchased without cost on the side of the British. Upwards of one hundred killed, of whom seven were officers, and nearly seven hundred in the hospitals, told of the severity of the conflict.[9]

Whilst the roar of the hundred and forty opposing guns at Maharajpoor sent forth their deadly echoes, and almost within sound of them, another struggle was maintained, equally decisive, though less fatal. General Grey's column, moving towards the capital from Bundelkund, encountered a strong Mahratta force at Punniar, but twelve miles distant from their destination. The action was sharp but brief. The enemy stood no more than the first charge of the British infantry, and fled to the heights, whence they were driven at the point of the bayonet, and finally scattered through the country.

The two armies united beneath the walls of Gwalior, where, having no alternative, the Durbar immediately made every submission to the terms imposed by the British. It was stipulated that Gwalior should in future be protected by a British subsidiary force, paid from the revenues of the country; that an English officer and garrison should hold possession of the fort of Gwalior; and that the state should pay all the expenses of the war.

Thus ended the brief but glorious military career of Lord Ellenborough, who, during the short tenure of his office, had accomplished more than any other man for the pacification of India; and when, through intrigues and jealousies, he was shortly afterwards recalled by the Court of Directors, his departure was deeply regretted by all who wished well to good government and the security of our Eastern possessions.

9 Sir Hugh Gough's dispatch.

CHAPTER VIII.

THE WARS IN THE PUNJAB, AND THE ANNEXATION OF THE COUNTRY OF THE FIVE RIVERS TO THE BRITISH DOMINIONS.

A.D. 1844-1849.

On the arrival of Sir Henry Hardinge in India as governor-general, in the summer of 1844, he found the vast territories under the British rule in the most profound peace. This able and indefatigable man had ample leisure to make himself master of very many details of government, which he was not slow to discover needed much reform. He did his best to bring about a better and more friendly feeling between the services; he furthered the claims of the native army to many privileges; he promoted a stricter discipline amongst the troops generally; he aided in the organisation of railway companies in India; and, in short, did all that lay in his power, during so short a period, to promote the welfare of many sections of the community.

But the course of Indian events was not long destined for this pacification. One more storm of war and bloodshed was gathering in the north; another fierce struggle was about to overwhelm a vast tract of fruitful and populous country in its calamities and its sufferings; and Sir Henry, peacefully as he may have been disposed, could not avoid the career that was awaiting him.

The decease of Runjeet Sing, the Lion of Lahore, in 1839, had paved the way to an infinity of intrigues, plots, and counterplots at and around the capital of the Punjab. The death of the "Lion," soon followed by that of the grandson, not without suspicion of design; the struggles for the viziership; the intrigues of the ranee, or queen-mother; and the subsequent assassinations of rival chiefs which took place at Cabool, bore testimony to the absence of any controlling power in the state. Indeed, the only parties who appeared to be endowed with any faculty for directing the course of events were two French officers, promoted to the rank of generals by Runjeet Singh, and who had brought the army of the Punjab into a state of high efficiency, more especially its ordnance department.

The young maharajah, Dhulup Sing, a child of four years, and his mother, although nominally at the head of affairs, were really in the hands of the Sikh soldiery; these, clamouring for their arrears of pay, and anxious for some occupation which might bring with it a chance of spoil, sought to be led against their English neighbours, whom they considered their enemies. How far this feeling may have been fostered by the French officers, who, it was known, always possessed great influence amongst them, it is not easy to judge. This hostile passion was kept up, until at length the ranee became a party, unwillingly, to a demonstration in the direction of the Sutlej. Ghoolab Singh, brother to the late vizier of the "Lion," was pressed in vain, first, to accept the dangerous office of vizier; secondly, to join the war-party against the British. It would have been equally dangerous to have openly opposed the movement; Ghoolab therefore contented himself with taking no part in the preparations, and under various pretences absenting himself from the scene of military activity. When at last the war had actually begun, and he could no longer avoid acting in some way, he prudently declined any command in the army, preferring to remain at the head of his own immediate followers, ready for any special service that might present itself.[1]

The preparations which were now being made at Lahore for the passage of the Sutlej could not be kept a secret; and long before the public had any idea of what was going on, the governor-general had expeditiously but quietly concentrated thirty-two thousand men and sixty-eight guns in and about Ferozepore, Loodianah, and Umballa. In the early part of December, the intelligence forwarded to head-quarters respecting the warlike preparations in the Punjab were of such a definite and unmistakable character, that Sir H. Hardinge at once made his way to the camp at Umballa, though without at that time having any belief in the intention of the Sikh army to invade the British territories in considerable numbers. From Umballa the governor-general proceeded onwards to Loodianah, inspecting the various cantonments, and generally making himself acquainted with the actual position of affairs.

On the 7th and 8th of December, intelligence was received by the governor-general from Lahore, of such a nature as at once to induce him to issue instructions to the commander-in-chief to move up the

[1] Macgregor's History of the Sikhs.

whole of his force from Umballa, Meerut, and other minor posts. On the 9th, a portion of the Sikh army had approached to within a few miles of Ferozepore; whilst further advance along the river-line shewed that the most active preparations were being carried on for hostile purposes. By the 12th of December the whole of the Umballa and reserve forces were in full march towards the appointed rendezvous; and at the same time orders were issued to Brigadier Wheeler, at Loodianah, to be prepared to move up with his force of five thousand men

CAMEL BATTERY.

and twelve guns at a moment's notice. During this day more precise information was received as to the Sikh movements; and on the following morning intelligence was brought in that the enemy had crossed the Sutlej, and were concentrating in great force on the left bank of the river.[2]

Affairs having arrived at this point, the governor-general issued a proclamation, setting forth the unprovoked nature of the Sikh invasion, declaring the territories on the left of the Sutlej annexed to the British possessions, and calling upon all friendly and well-disposed natives to aid in the restoration of peace, and at the same time cautioning all evil-doers as to the consequences of their acts.

Brigadier Wheeler was immediately ordered up with his force of

[2] Despatch from Sir H. Hardinge to Secret Committee.

four thousand five hundred men and twenty-one guns to cover Bussean, where a large depôt of stores for the army had been collected; and by the afternoon of the 14th he was in position before that place. Two days later, the main column from Umballa, under the commander-in-chief, arrived at the same spot. At that moment, the Sikhs were completing the passage of the Sutlej with their heavy artillery and trains; and on the 17th their main body, consisting of twenty-five thousand regulars and eighty-eight guns, under the command of Lal Singh, moved into position at the village of Forozshah; whilst another force of twenty-three thousand men and sixty-seven guns encamped opposite Ferozepore. The Sikhs commenced throwing up earth-works around their camps, and preparing for a vigorous contest. The governor-general and commander-in-chief pushed on with their main column towards Ferozepore; and at mid-day halted at the village of Moodkee, where they snatched some hasty rest and a little refreshment, after a long and harassing march.

The repose of the troops was soon broken by intelligence that at no greater distance than three miles a large body of the enemy were encamped, chiefly cavalry, with twenty-two guns. The troops were immediately called to arms, placed in position, and moved forward to meet the enemy.

The cavalry, under Brigadiers White, Gough, and Mactier, were advanced rapidly to the front, and occupying the open plain gave good cover to the infantry whilst forming. The horse-artillery speedily followed, flanking the cavalry. In a short time the Sikh artillery, which was well secured behind a quantity of low jungle, opened a brisk and rather telling fire upon the advancing columns, which was replied to with great spirit by the British horse-artillery and the light field-batteries, which had by this time moved up. These directed such a steady and judicious fire, that the enemy were for a time shaken, and, seizing the opportune moment, the commander-in-chief ordered a cavalry charge upon the left flank of the Sikhs, whilst a similar one was directed upon their right.

Both of these succeeded to admiration; the charges of the British horse sweeping every thing before them, up to the very guns, and nothing but the irregularity of the ground and the dense cover of the jungle saved the enemy from far heavier loss.

In the meantime, the infantry was moved on to the charge, covered by the vigorous fire of the horse-artillery, brought close to the low jungle in front of their lines. Sir H. Smith, Sir John M'Caskill, and General Gilbert led on the troops in echellon of lines, and pouring in upon their close ranks a murderous fire, soon taught the enemy the efficacy of the British musket. From position to position the Sikhs were driven; and so often as they stood, the bayonet was resorted to with fatal and unerring effect.

The day was thus won from the enemy; and making the best of their way from the field, with the loss of great numbers of their troops and seventeen of their guns, they sought shelter within their camp at Ferozshah. The slaughter was only stayed by the weariness of the troops and the spreading darkness, for the last two hours of the conflict had been carried on by a dim and uncertain light. When the British moved back to their camp at Moodkee it was midnight.

The loss on the side of the British was severe for the duration of the struggle, the chief execution having been from the Sikh artillery. The number of killed was sixteen officers and two hundred men; that of the wounded, forty-eight officers and six hundred men; and this was out of a force of twelve thousand rank and file. Amongst those who fell at this time, deeply regretted, was General Sir Robert Sale, the hero of Jellalabad, who fell with his left thigh shattered by grape-shot.

This victory was at once followed up by preparations for further efforts; for it was well known that the enemy would not long remain inactive under their late severe discomfiture. Some heavy artillery was brought up from the rear, escorted by several fresh regiments. Sir John Littler was ordered up from Ferozepore with all his available force, in order to effect a junction with the main body, and, in concert with them, to attack the Sikh entrenched lines.

Accordingly Sir John moved off with one-half of his force, amounting to five thousand five hundred, together with twenty-one guns, leaving the remainder in Ferozepore, to maintain that post, and watch the movements of Tej Singh and his army encamped against it. This was early on the 21st: by eleven o'clock on that day the main body had advanced from Moodkee and taken up a position opposite the intrenched camp of the Sikh army, which contained a total force of thirty-five thousand soldiers and eighty-eight guns, whilst that of the British comprised less than eighteen thousand rank and file and sixty-five guns.

The Sikh lines were about a mile in length and half a mile in breadth, strongly placed, and ready to receive an enemy from whatever quarter it might advance. The ground in front of the army was flat, and interspersed with low jungle. The three divisions of the British army having been placed in line, the artillery was stationed in the centre, with the exception of three troops of horse-artillery, placed on each

STORMING OF GHUZNEE.

flank, and in support. The reserve, under Sir Harry Smith, with the cavalry, formed the second line.

The engagement was commenced by the British artillery advancing and pouring in rapid and well-directed charges upon the Sikh lines until within three hundred yards, when the guns were unlimbered, and a further heavy and continuous discharge kept up, until the word was given for the infantry to charge and seize the Sikh guns, which continued to be served with murderous effect. This heavy and bloody task was performed with matchless courage and rapidity, and the enemy's artillery in the centre was for the time silenced. On the left, Littler's brigade had done wonders; but the storm of grape and shot which fell amidst them caused them to stagger, and make a retrograde movement, which was, however, supported by a portion of the reserve under Sir Harry Smith. The centre and right divisions, under Generals Wallace and Gilbert, were successful at every point; and the battle seemed to be won, when unfortunately night fell so suddenly as not only to prevent the decisive blow being struck, but to cause not a little confusion and danger from the extreme proximity of friends and foes.

In this critical position the main body of the troops were withdrawn to a few hundred yards from the Sikh camp, where they rested during the remainder of the night under arms. About midnight, however, some of the Sikh guns which had not been taken possession of were brought to bear upon the British column as they lay on the ground, doing considerable execution. The governor-general mounted his horse, and calling on the 80th Regiment and a portion of the 1st Bengal Europeans, led them against the annoying guns, which were carried at a charge, and spiked.

That night was one of intense anxiety to the commanders: their loss had been most severe; they were within a few hundred yards of an enemy still formidable, with a heavy reserve under Tej Singh, no doubt on its way up from Ferozepore; whilst Littler's and Sir H. Smith's divisions had been compelled to retire from the left, and nothing was known as to their position.

The spirit of the troops was, however, admirable; and weary and harassed as they were by long marching and hard fighting, all seemed animated with but one spirit,—a determination to finish the work so gloriously begun, and drive the enemy beyond the Sutlej. At early dawn this portion of the army was put under arms, deployed into line, and led on at once against the Sikh entrenchments, without waiting for the other divisions. A few volleys, a round or two of grape, and the bayonet did the rest most effectually. The troops having secured the whole of the seventy-six guns opposed to them, now wheeled rapidly round, swept past the village of Ferozshah, and in this way cleared the entire length of the enemy's works, who retired upon their reserve, which at that moment appeared in sight.

The remaining divisions of the army now effected a junction with the centre and right; and thus reinforced, ill provided as they were with ammunition, the British commanders would have had no hesitation in advancing against their new enemy, had there been any disposition shewn to await an attack. But such was not the intention of the Sikh generals: disheartened and alarmed, the discomfited troops of Ferozshah communicated to their comrades the panic which they themselves felt, and at once moving off with a few flourishes of their remaining artillery, made for the banks of the Sutlej, which river they quickly left behind them.

To follow up this decisive victory, as inclination would have prompted, was rendered impossible by the want of cavalry and ammunition, nearly the whole of the latter having been exhausted during the recent engagements; and the commander-in-chief was therefore fain to content himself with seeing the enemy fairly across the river, and await reinforcements from the rear.

That day and several following were fully occupied with the care of the wounded, numbering upwards of seventeen hundred. Ferozepore was converted into a hospital, until the sick could be conveyed to a place of greater security; and during the time of their sojourn there, the governor-general was most unremitting in his personal inspection of their comforts. The British loss in killed was heavy: 694 were found dead in the field; and of the wounded 595 died in the hospital, or were disabled from further service.

The same cause which had compelled Sir Hugh Gough to allow Tej Singh to recross the Sutlej unmolested, prevented him from marching on Lahore, and finishing the war under its walls. Nearly two months were spent in waiting for the arrival of a battering train, and reinforcements of both infantry and cavalry; during which period the Sikhs, recovering from the first shock of their disaster at Ferozepore, commenced preparations for the defence of their territories on an extensive scale, and with considerable skill. Throwing a bridge of boats across the Sutlej, the enemy took up a position of much strength on its left bank, and at once commenced forming entrenchments of great extent and solidity, under the superintendence of a French officer of engineers. At the same time a strong body of Sikhs, numbering about 15,000 men and fifty-six guns, crossed the river in the immediate neighbourhood of Loodianah, and took up a position at the village of Aliwal.

As soon as the commander-in-chief was strengthened by the fresh troops ordered up, he despatched Sir H. Smith with a force of 7,000 men and 24 guns to relieve Loodianah, threatened as it was by the advance of the enemy in its vicinity. The object was speedily and most completely effected. Sir Harry, although harassed in his march by many rear and flank attacks, during some of which he lost much of his baggage, pushed on with determination for the main body of the enemy, which he knew was not far distant.

On the 27th of January the British troops found themselves opposed to the Sikh forces under Runjoor Singh, now reinforced by 4000 more regular troops and twelve field-pieces. On the morning of the 28th, Sir Harry Smith, having with him by that time nearly 10,000 men, advanced to the attack with his entire line, warmly received by the enemy's artillery. After a brief cannonade and a cavalry charge the infantry moved up in gallant style; and though opposed with a well-served artillery force, swept all before them. The village of Aliwal, the enemy's chief position, was carried at the point of the bayonet; the British cannon cut up the heavy masses of Sikh troops; and Her Majesty's 16th Lancers, by their brilliant charges, completed the triumph of the day by capturing every gun opposed to them, and driving the foe, with terrible slaughter, across the river.

The total discomfiture of this body of the enemy left the British at liberty to direct their full attention to the works carrying on by the Sikhs at Sobraon, which were rapidly assuming an importance that promised to render them truly formidable. But the much-needed heavy artillery had not yet reached the camp; and without it operations against the enemy's works would have been deemed most injudicious. On the 8th of February Sir Harry Smith joined the main army with his forces; and on the following day the long-expected heavy guns reached the camp. Not a moment was lost after the receipt of this much-needed arm of war. On the morning of the 10th, long before daybreak, the troops moved out of camp, and marched to the position assigned them, opposite the enemy's works. The British troops numbered somewhat above 16,000 rank and file, with 99 guns; the Sikh force consisted of 34,000 men within the entrenchments, and 20,000 of reserved troops, with seventy pieces of artillery.

The enemy's position was a most formidable one, and had cost them much labour during several months. It was, indeed, considered by them as perfectly impregnable to any force that could be brought against it; and when it is considered how strong was the army posted within those massive fortifications, behind three lines of trenches, and how ably their artillery was served, the victory of the small British force which carried those vaunted works must be allowed to have been no ordinary achievement.

From six until past eight o'clock the artillery maintained an incessant roar of destruction, aided by that fatal weapon the rocket. At nine the command was issued for the troops to move forward to the attack; and supported on either flank by troops of horse artillery, the infantry advanced to test the vaunted strength of the Sikh fortifications. They were received by a tremendous fire from cannon, muskets, and camel-guns; and so murderous was the discharge from the entrenchments, and so completely exposed were the advancing troops, that it appeared impossible that any body of men could stand such havoc. If there was any halting or indecision under this fearful fire, it was but momentary; the charge was renewed, and in a few more short minutes the advanced troops of the column were within the fatal works. Other divisions of the army met with an equally desperate resistance on either wing, and in more than one place the attacking column was forced back several times, again and again returning to the charge with undaunted valour. At length line after line was entered at the bayonet's point; and to make victory still more decisive, a gallant charge of cavalry under Major-general Thackwell followed up the blow, silenced the Sikh guns, and drove the retreating mass over their bridge of boats and into the river. Great was the slaughter of the flying foe by the light field-pieces of the British; hundreds were cut to pieces by our horse-artillery in crossing the Sutlej, and many more drowned in the confusion.

The fruits of this victory were 67 guns, 200 camel-swivels, and a great number of standards. But these trophies were purchased at a cost of 320 killed and 2063 wounded, including many valuable officers, amongst others, the veteran Sir Robert Dick.

This decisive battle was at once followed up by a movement on Lahore; and although endeavours were made by Ghoolab Singh to divert the governor-general from his resolution, the troops proceeded on their way, and encamped beneath the city walls. There a treaty was drawn up and formally executed, by which the whole expense of the war, amounting to a million and a half sterling, was undertaken to be paid by the Lahore government. The guns taken by us were to be retained, and all those which had ever been pointed against us were to be delivered up; whilst the Sikh troops and their leaders were to receive instant dismissal. Subsequently it was arranged that a strong garrison was to be left in Lahore by the British, for the protection of the inhabitants and the security of the Maharajah's authority; and in accordance with this, Sir John Littler was left there with 10,000 men.

Thus terminated the first Punjab war, having occupied but sixty days, and beheld the complete dispersion of the Sikh forces. Upwards of 200 pieces of their best artillery had fallen into our hands; and of 100,000 fighting men, not 30,000 remained together. The cost of the war had been defrayed by the vanquished; and on the whole the campaign appeared to have been not only the most decisive but the most important in its results of any that the British forces in India had been engaged in.

At the close of 1848 the Earl of Dalhousie assumed the supreme government of India. On his arrival he found the most apparently profound tranquillity reigning; and there seemed for the time every probability of his rule being one of an entirely pacific nature. But, as with his predecessor, it soon became evident that he was destined to heighten the reputation of the British arms, and to extend our triumphs and our possessions.

The first indication of trouble came from Mooltan, the capital of a petty state situated between the Indus and the Sutlej. Moolraj, its governor, first shewed signs of unfriendly feeling towards us, and eventually assumed a hostile attitude by the assassination of the British assistant political resident, Mr. Vans Agnew, and Lieutenant Anderson of the Bombay army. This treachery brought forward Lieutenant Edwardes and a party of Sikh horse, who, being reinforced by Colonel Cortlande's troops and some pieces of light artillery, and further aided by the auxiliary forces of the khan of Bhawulpore, attacked and defeated Moolraj on two several occasions with considerable slaughter.

The chief then fell back upon Mooltan, to which the troops under Cortlande and Edwardes would have at once laid siege had they been provided with the necessary guns; they were compelled, therefore, to sit before it and keep up a simple blockade until the 18th of August, when they were opportunely reinforced by General Whish with two regiments of native infantry, one of horse, and a troop of horse-artillery. Other forces reached at nearly the same time from Ferozepore with that which was most needed, a battering-train of considerable weight, and further horse-artillery and light horse. With these various reinforcements the besieging army amounted to 28,000 men, of whom about 6000 were British, and the operations were accordingly pushed forward with vigour. Early in September several successful attacks were made on the enemy's outworks, and one or two sallies of the garrison repulsed with considerable loss to them; but the aspect of affairs was suddenly changed by a large party of the Sikh allies under Shere Singh going over to the enemy. This compelled the British to abandon their operations, and retire to a strong position at a short distance from Mooltan.

The defection of the Sikhs had been doubtless brought about by the intelligence that Chutter Singh had collected a body of insurgents in the Hazerah district, and made an attempt upon the fort of Attock. Foiled in this, the chief pushed rapidly forward to Peshawur, where, the British force being greatly reduced in numbers, the resident, Major Lawrence, and his lady were compelled to fly to Kohat and put themselves under the protection of the khan of that place. They were, however, given up to Chutter Singh, together with Lieutenant Borrie.

Another Sikh war now became inevitable. The forces under Chutter Singh and Shere Singh united; other chiefs flocked to their standards, and they were not long in mustering an army of 30,000 troops eager for plunder or any prospect of employment as preferable to a state of peace. The enemy now took up a position at Ramnugger, near Wuzeerabad, having the Chenab flowing in their front, and strongly flanked by artillery.

Reinforcements having reached the British army at Ferozepore, the commander-in-chief, Lord Gough, moved forward to Saharun on the 21st of November, and prepared at once for action. At two o'clock on the following morning the troops moved forwards in the most perfect silence and with as much order as though on parade. Arrived at Ramnugger, the troops were placed in position, whilst our horse-artillery pushed on in advance towards the enemy's lines, which were then distinctly visible, and commenced a sharp fire upon them. This seemed to make but little impression; and the heavy guns of the Sikhs beginning to return the cannonade, it became apparent that these two branches of the armies were most unequally matched.

The enemy, determined to act vigorously and on the offensive, pushed across the river a strong body of their best cavalry under the fire of their heavy batteries. These were immediately charged by the 5th Light Cavalry and the 14th Dragoons, and driven back to the entrenchments, though not without heavy loss being sustained by these two regiments, especially in officers. Amongst others who fell from the heavy cannonade the troops were exposed to were General Cureton, Colonel Havelock, and Captain Fitzgerald.

At length, after sustaining a furious fire from the British guns, and giving way to the infantry charges in several places, Shere Singh thought it prudent to abandon his camp and works, and rapidly withdrew towards the Jhelum in tolerably good order.

Preparations were now made by Lord Gough to follow up this victory by advancing in the direction of Lahore, and driving the enemy before him. Whilst this was being carried into execution, events of a stirring nature were enacting before Mooltan, which was once more standing a siege from the British under General Whish; and fresh troops having arrived from the south, the siege was carried on with the utmost vigour, as Moolraj soon found to his cost. The cannonade kept up by the Bombay artillery was incessant and destructive. Wall after wall crumbled before the fury of the battering-train. The suburbs were taken, the powder-magazine in the fort blown up, breaches in the fortifications effected, and at last, in spite of desperate sorties and counter-works, the town was stormed, and the British colours planted on its walls on the 2d of January.

The citadel still held out, and the courageous Moolraj appeared bent on no surrender so long as a wall was left standing. By the 21st the huge works of the fortress were undermined and several practicable breaches opened in them, so that orders were given for the troops to be in readiness for storming the citadel at daybreak. The chieftain, however, saved them any further trouble by appearing at the gate of his fort as the troops were forming for the attack; and proceeding straight to the general's tent, he there handed up his sword.

The fort having been garrisoned, the army moved off to join the camp of the governor-general; and, to prevent any accident, Moolraj was conducted with them. This junction was effected too late for the Mooltan troops to share in the dangers of the battle of Chillianwallah, to which we must now return.

The preparations for marching on Lahore having been completed, the commander-in-chief proceeded, in the early part of January, towards the Chenab, where, as expected, he found the Sikhs strongly entrenched. On the 10th Lord Gough moved his troops forward, with the view, in the first instance, of at once attacking the enemy. This resolve, however, appears from some cause to have been abandoned; and the evening was allowed to draw on without any further demonstration being made on the side of the British. The Sikhs had, however, evidently made every preparation, and were bent upon an engagement. Throwing some flying artillery towards our centre, they brought out a few of our heavy guns, which at once silenced the others, but were in their turn responded to by a tremendous cannonade of heavy guns from a quarter much nearer than had been anticipated. Under cover of some low but dense jungle, the Sikhs had planted their artillery in a commanding and safe position; and the advantage of the ground was fully proved by the terrible havoc their guns committed in the ranks of the British army.

To charge in the face of a murderous storm of grape and shell was the only alternative known to British troops; and, as had been the result at Ferozshah and other places, the bayonet and the spur wrested from the enemy their ruinous and fatal guns, and earned a dear-bought victory. This furious engagement lasted until after nightfall; and on the morrow, when the troops were mustered and their loss ascertained, it was found that the killed amounted to 26 officers and 731 men; whilst in wounded the numbers were 66 officers and 1446 men.

Great as was the loss on the English side, the carnage amongst the Sikhs must have been far more terrible. Nevertheless, they did not yet think of submission, but, being joined by a strong body of Afghan horse, prepared with undaunted determination to renew the struggle for supremacy.

Reinforced during the early part of February by the Mooltan troops, Lord Gough made every disposition for striking another and, if possible, a more decisive blow at the Sikh power in the Punjab. It was evident that nothing short of utter and complete overthrow, a perfect annihilation of their military power, could by any possibility restore tranquillity to that country or give security to the neighbouring states for the future; and on this impression the commander-in-chief at once prepared to act.

The Sikh army had again strongly entrenched themselves in a most favourable position, within a few miles of the town of Goojerat. Hither Lord Gough marched his recruited forces, and on the 21st of February commenced a furious and most effective cannonade on the enemy's lines. Shere Sing was this time at the head of 60,000 men and 59 guns of heavy calibre; but nothing could withstand the deadly fire of the British artillery-men. For three hours this arm of the force did its work; and by the end of that time it was quite apparent that the Sikh troops were not only thinned, but making a retrograde movement. The whole force of the British infantry and cavalry were then let loose upon the enemy, and, relieving the heavy guns from further service, the bayonet, lance, and sword accomplished the remainder of the bloody task.

A more complete and effectual overthrow had never been given to the enemy;[3] that they felt it to be so was manifested by the surrender shortly afterwards of Chutter Singh, Shere Singh, and the other Sikh leaders who had escaped our bullets. The Afghans fled across the Indus; the Sikh forces were disbanded; and the Punjab was declared annexed to the British territories in India.

Moolraj was placed upon his trial for the murder of Mr. Vans Agnew and Lieutenant Anderson, found guilty, and had his sentence of death commuted to imprisonment for life.

[3] Punjab Blue Book: Despatch of Lord Gough.

CHAPTER IX.

THE SECOND BURMESE WAR AND THE ANNEXATION OF PEGU.

A.D. 1850-1853.

THE year 1850 was ushered in by a peace as profound as any hitherto witnessed during the British rule in India, and with every promise of its proving complete and lasting. During the decade of wars and insurrections which had just terminated, nearly all the most determined opponents of the British power in the East had been compelled to sue for peace, or had beheld their power irretrievably lost, and their countries permanently annexed to the territories of Great Britain.

Looking, therefore, at the state of India in the last year of the first half of the nineteenth century, it appeared difficult to imagine that any political event could occur to disturb the tranquillity of our vast empire in the East. But this security had not been obtained without considerable cost. Glory and conquest have their price, as well as other and more vulgar things. The Afghan retribution, the "Lion's skin," the Punjab trophies, the gates of Somnooth,—these, and a few other items on the scroll of fame, had cost the government, in round figures, twenty millions sterling. By their means, the public debt of India had been swollen from 32,000,000*l*. to 46,000,000*l*., the difference of the twenty millions having come out of the current revenues of the state.[1]

Little occurred during this and the following year to disturb the deep calm which fell like a shade over the realms owning our sway in India. In the shape of aggression, indeed, there was literally nothing to record, save the harassing predatory inroads of the Affredees and some others of the hill-tribes on our north-western frontier, in the vicinity of Peshawur. These marauders had for ages been a source of annoyance to the Sikhs, and appeared equally disposed to find occupation

[1] Calcutta Review for 1851.

for our troops. One raid followed another in quick succession; and although Sir Colin Campbell and his detachment inflicted severe chastisement upon them, it seemed to be in vain; until at length, worn out and beaten at all points, these marauding freebooters agreed, on certain terms, to cease from further depredations upon the border villages or wayside travellers.

The year 1851 will long be memorable in Indian annals, as having witnessed the commencement of railways and electric telegraphs in two of the three presidencies. At Calcutta and Bombay the first sections of the East Indian and Great Indian Peninsular railways were put in train; whilst an electric telegraph was begun between the former city and Diamond harbour, and is now in active operation,—the first of a series of wires which will eventually connect the City of Palaces with the various seats of government throughout that presidency.

Not the least notable occurrence of this year was the passing an act which effected for all India what Lord William Bentinck had done for Bengal alone, by abolishing all pains and penalties attaching, under the old Hindoo and Mahomedan laws, to any seceders from those faiths to Christianity, and who had hitherto, by such secession, forfeited all rights to family or other property.

Towards the latter part of the year the political horizon was dimmed by a small cloud in the direction of Burmah, arising out of sundry acts of cruelty and oppression to British subjects. These acts it was deemed by the authorities impossible to overlook; and an expedition was accordingly despatched in November from Calcutta, under Commodore Lambert, to demand reparation for the past, and a guarantee for the future.

Early in January (1852), it appeared as though the sovereign of Ava was disposed to come to a friendly understanding with the governor-general; but before long it was too evident that this appearance of amity was but a pretext in order to gain time. A new viceroy arrived at Rangoon, and commenced active preparations, by no means of a pacific nature. It was in vain that Commodore Lambert endeavoured to obtain an interview with this functionary; at first his letters were treated coolly, but eventually with contempt; and it became evident that, in order to bring the Burmese to terms, forcible means would have to be resorted to.

Matters being in this state, the commodore directed all British residents in Rangoon who valued their lives to seek refuge on board the fleet. This order was at once obeyed, though a number of Europeans and natives were detained on shore and thrown into prison. On the morrow the fleet moved down the river, the steamers towing out some of the smaller ships. An insolent message from the viceroy, threatening to fire on our ships if they passed his forts, was disregarded; but as one of the steamers proceeded past the town with a Burmese man-of-war in tow as a prize, the garrison commenced firing upon her, which was at once so warmly returned by the guns of her Majesty's ship *Fox*, as to cause the immediate abandonment of the Burmese forts.

Upon this open rupture, Commodore Lambert, being anxious for more positive instructions from the governor-general, left for Calcutta in a steamer, first declaring the ports of Burmah in a state of blockade. Although not quite satisfied, it is said, with one act—the seizure of the Burmese ship-of-war—the governor-general ratified all that had been done at Rangoon, and at once resolved upon pursuing the most energetic and prompt measures for the adjustment of these differences. Orders were despatched to Bombay and Madras for the immediate preparation for use of all the steamers available, with contingencies of such troops as could be spared; whilst active measures were at once taken at Calcutta for despatching, by steamers and transports, a powerful body of European and native troops, as well as a strong accompaniment of artillery.

The result was, that, by the 24th of February, six steamers left Bombay for Madras, where they embarked the troops destined for the Burmese campaign, under the command of General Godwin, viz. two European and four native regiments, with four corps of artillerymen, chiefly Europeans. These left Madras on the 29th of March; whilst at Calcutta the armament had been equally hastened. The last of the force despatched there left the Hoogly on the 25th March; the total having been similar to the Madras force—two European and four native regiments, with their accompaniments of artillery, in four steamers and four transports. These amounted in the aggregate to about eight thousand men.

The 1st of April being the latest day fixed by the governor-general for the ultimatum of the Burmese sovereign, a steamer was despatched to Rangoon on that morning to ascertain if any reply had been received from Ava. In place of a letter, the British envoy received a shower of shot from the stockades lining the river, and was thus compelled to return.

Admiral Austin, in H.M. steamer *Rattler*, having now joined from Singapore, and the Bengal squadron arriving at the same moment, it was resolved to attack Martaban, the first Burmese town, without waiting for the arrival of the Madras force: this was accomplished with little difficulty on the 5th. The Madras troops reached on the 7th, and within three days from that date the united force proceeded up the river, and commenced operations by a bombardment of the strong stockades, which were found well mounted with guns, and defended by 25,000 Burmese troops. During that and the four following days the troops were occupied in reducing the numerous outworks and fortified pagodas which studded the environs and heights. This was not accomplished without the loss of 17 killed and 132 wounded, besides the loss of two officers by *coup de soleil.* The force of the British in Burmah at that time consisted of two ships of war, 16 steamers, and 14 transports, with 2700 European and 3000 native troops, and about 1800 marines and sailors, making a total of 8000 men.

One of the first fruits of the capture of Rangoon was the quieting of the alarm of the natives, who perhaps, naturally for them, expected that our troops would retaliate the cruelties of the Burmese authorities on all British subjects who had fallen into their hands. Once assured of our friendly disposition, the inhabitants flocked back to the city in thousands, whilst the people of the neighbouring province of Pegu, at no time well disposed to their Burman conquerors, declared they were ready to place themselves under our protection. This becoming known to the native authorities, led to the exercise of great cruelties towards the unfortunate inhabitants, who were given up to the robbery and violence of the Burmese soldiers.

It had been the opinion of the British commander in the first instance, that our troops would be compelled to remain inactive during the whole of the rainy season, extending from May to October inclusive; but circumstances overruled this. It became evident early in May that the Burmese were mustering very strongly at Bassein, a town of some importance about sixty miles up one of the branches of the Irrawaddy, and bordering on the British territory of Arracan, which there was no doubt they intended to invade. General Godwin resolved, under these circumstances, to drive the enemy from that quarter, and place a garrison in the town.

On the morning of the 17th, a detachment, consisting of 400 European, and 300 native infantry, with 100 sappers and miners, and some artillery-men, aided by a party of marines, were sent off in four steamers. These descended the main river to the sea by the evening, and next morning began to round the smaller branch of the Irrawaddy, on which Bassein is situated. A number of large stockades were passed, which, however, offered no resistance, and the fleet arrived off the town without interruption by the afternoon. Here it was evident the enemy mustered pretty strongly, entrenched behind some mud forts defended by stockades, and within a large pagoda. Their numbers were estimated at 7000 men.

No opposition being still offered, the troops were at once landed; but on a detachment under Captain Salter moving towards one of the stockades, they were greeted with a sharp volley of musketry, which did some mischief. The men were at once led against the defences, which were stoutly defended by artillery, the Burmese gunners being bayoneted at their posts; first, the pagoda, and lastly, the mud fort, was carried with a loss to the enemy of about 800 men, and on our side of a few officers and men wounded. The town, being deserted by the Burmese troops, was taken possession of, and a garrison of 500 men left in it.

On the 26th the Burmese made a sudden and desperate attempt to retake Martaban with a force of about 1200 men, but were so warmly received by our troops, that they were glad to retire, having suffered considerable loss, which on our side amounted to but one killed and thirteen wounded.

Although the weather was by no means favourable, the general dispatched a small force on the 3d of June, in a steamer, to capture Pegu, the former capital of the kingdom of that name, and now in possession of the Burmese. The expedition consisted of 100 Europeans, and an equal number of sepoys, with 30 sappers and miners. These arrived off the town early on the following day, landed, and at the first charge drove the enemy before them; who, flying in great numbers from their pagoda and stockades, left the town in the hands of the British, who were hailed by the citizens as their deliverers; but having accomplished this much, the expedition returned, leaving Pegu unoccupied. During the remainder of June the troops remained inactive, but, despite the unfavourable weather, in a good state of health. General Godwin availed himself of this cessation of hostilities to dispatch a steamer to Calcutta, with a request for an additional force of Europeans and natives, with a detachment of light cavalry, a field-battery, and some horse-artillery. These were at once prepared for sea, and dispatched from Madras and Calcutta with all celerity. Meanwhile the governor-general visited the seat of war, in order to examine the true posture of affairs, and consult with the commander of the forces as to future operations.

On the 9th of July a force was dispatched against Prome, which, after meeting with some slight resistance from river-defences, came upon the rear of the Burmese general's army. After exchanging a few volleys, the enemy fled in all directions, leaving twenty-eight guns, the general's state-barge, and a quantity of standards and camp-equipage behind them. Prome was at once entered by the British without further resistance, but, owing to the insufficiency of the force, not retained in our possession. Consequently, as soon as our troops returned to Rangoon, the Burmese again took possession of the place, and commenced putting it in a state of defence. What General Godwin's motive may have been for such an empty display of conquest, it is difficult to tell, but the proceeding gave rise, as well it might, to considerable surprise and dissatisfaction amongst the troops.

August was opened in general inactivity, although the weather was by no means so unfavourable as usual at this season, and there was nothing to prevent our troops from at once proceeding by water to Ava, the capital of the empire, had the lethargy of the commander of the forces permitted such a movement.

The expected reinforcements having reached head-quarters, the force available amounted in the month of September to nearly 20,000 men, in the highest state of efficiency, and quite large enough to have at once swept all before them to the very gates of the emperor's palace. But this did not appear to be the view taken of the matter by General Godwin, who now made preparation for once more attacking Prome. In the middle of this month two regiments, a field-battery, with a detachment of sappers and miners, left Rangoon, followed within a few days by the general and a party of artillerymen. They ascended the river without opposition until the 9th of October, when, as they approached the stockaded defences of the city, they were fired upon from many sides. The enemy's gunnery was not of first-rate quality, and in less than two hours was entirely silenced, the ground being completely cleared of the opposing force by the shells thrown from the steamers. The troops were landed towards the evening, and advancing at once upon a pagoda and the few remaining defences, carried every thing before them at the point of the bayonet. Night fell before the town could be reached, and it was therefore not until the next morning that Prome was occupied for the second time by our troops.

A large body of Burmese troops, amounting to upwards of 6000 men, were known to be posted within a few miles of the town, strongly entrenched behind stockades, and out of reach of our steamers, the artillery practice from which appears to have impressed them with a proper sense of our superiority in that arm of war. To have dislodged them with the force at his command would have been a matter of comparative ease; but so thought not General Godwin; who, fearful probably of terminating the war too quickly, determined to await the arrival of further troops before attempting any forward movement. He did not wait long, however; but within a day or two left for Rangoon in search of the troops considered to be requisite for further operations. This reinforcement was despatched towards the latter part of the month. By this time the Irrawaddy, which had been previously deep enough throughout for our largest steamers, sank so suddenly, and, as it appears, so unexpectedly, that several of the flotilla were left aground in the middle of the stream, with every prospect of having to remain there until the next rains should float them.

With a view to assist the intended advance upon Ava, the Calcutta authorities dispatched 250 elephants overland to Prome, by way of the Arracan province, and the Aeng Pass, leading from those territories into the Burman dominions. It being reported that the enemy were stockading the pass, a force was sent forward from Arracan to clear the way, and keep open the road to the south-east.

Notwithstanding that a second force was despatched to Prome, nothing further was accomplished in that quarter, save the occupancy of a few villages in the immediate vicinity, for the protection of the inhabitants against the Burmese troops. The general's attention was now devoted to making another of his famous second-hand conquests. He resolved that, inasmuch as the town of Pegu had been, like Prome, captured only to be abandoned, it should, like the latter city, be once more stormed. Acting upon this resolve, a force of 1100 rank and file, with 30 artillerymen, 60 sappers, and two 24-pounders, started for Pegu in four steamers, under the command of General Godwin himself, on the 18th of November.

On the evening of the 20th they arrived off the town, which it was now evident had been strengthened since its last capture. Numerous stockades were to be seen filled with troops, who made a show of stout resistance. During the night our troops effected a landing without molestation; and at an early hour next morning made an advance on the principal stockade, one party charging it in front, whilst a second effected a diversion on the flank. Its defenders contented themselves with one smart volley, after which it never appears to have occurred to them to reload; but flying from the rear of their defences, they mounted a troop of elephants and ponies, that were evidently ready for the purpose, and left us in undisturbed possession of the place.

This time the general decided upon placing a garrison in the town, with a party of sappers and the two 24-pounders; and having arranged the completion of this almost bloodless expedition, he retraced his steps with the steamers and the greater part of the troops to Rangoon, which place he reached on the 23d. In three days the general was once more on the move upwards to Prome with another reinforcement of native troops, a field-battery, and some irregular horse; though with what object in view does not appear.

The Burmese, despite their many overwhelming defeats, were not disposed to leave us in quiet possession of our conquests. On the 8th of December the commissariat boats off Pegu were fired into; whilst at the same minute a body of 8000 troops atacked the town and its outworks, which were gallantly defended by the little garrison. Intelligence of these events being received at Rangoon, a reinforcement of 200 men were sent off towards Pegu; but meeting there with a powerful enemy at an advantageous position on the river, they were compelled to retire and fall back upon Rangoon. On this a force of 1400 men, the greater part consisting of cavalry, was started by land and water, which pushed on through every opposition, driving before them a large body of Burmese horse. In the neighbourhood of Pegu, the enemy, to the number of 8000, were encountered; and, as usual, completely overthrown at the first onset, leaving many of their force on the field. In this expedition the Sikh irregular horse behaved in the most admirable manner, shewing that a change of masters had in no way lessened their courage.

The various operations detailed in the preceding pages, led to that which might have been anticipated—the annexation of the conquered portion of the Burmese empire. By a proclamation bearing date December 28th, 1852, the governor-general declared the province of Pegu annexed to the British territories; and called upon all the inhabitants to submit themselves to the authority and protection of the government. He moreover intimated that no further conquests were intended; but that, in the event of the king of Ava refusing to hold friendly intercourse with the British government, or seeking to disturb their quiet possession of Pegu, further hostilities would necessarily ensue, which could have no other result than the total subversion of the Burman empire, and the exile of the king and his family. The effect of this proclamation was to bring about a revolution at the capital, headed by the emperor's brother, who appears to have been backed by a large peace-party holding friendly opinions in regard to the English. The sovereign was at once deposed and made prisoner, and the brother placed on the throne in his stead. In consequence of this altered state of things, an embassy was despatched from Rangoon, backed by a steamer and a strong armed party.

Meanwhile our troops had not been idle. The stockaded defences of the Aeng pass, by means of which the Burmese had hoped to cut off communication between Arracan and Pegu, were carried by a small detachment of troops, without the loss of a single man; although the pass was of a most formidable nature, and considered impregnable. The enemy still continued hovering about our stations in force, watching for a favourable opportunity of annoying us, and plundering the villages; during the whole of January various detachments were employed in scouring the country, and chastising these bands of marauders. At the date of our last advices, extending to the middle of May 1853, the whole of the Burmese troops appear to have retired upon Ava, in consequence of the recent revolution in state affairs; an embassy had been dispatched by the new emperor to meet and confer with our representative, which at first promised to terminate in a friendly manner; but the Burmese soon intimated that no portion of their territories would be allowed to remain in our hands without a further struggle, which now appears inevitable.

From our knowledge of the antecedents of this people, and of the policy of their rulers, it is scarcely possible to calculate upon any lasting peace between the two powers. The final result will, no doubt, be the subversion of the Burman dynasty, and the annexation of that empire to our already enormous possessions in the East.

Before closing the present chapter, and with it the historical section of this volume, it may be well to notice the few events of the past year within the remaining portion of the three Presidencies. Throughout India, with the exception of the north-western frontier, the most profound peace has reigned. The only disturbance which broke this complete tranquillity was the periodical incursion of some of the hill-tribes, especially of the Momunds. Their forays were mainly directed against the inhabitants of the villages in their vicinity, where they frequently committed great destruction of life and property.

These marauders occupied the forces under Sir Colin Campbell from early in January, at various periods, until quite the end of the year, often falling upon our troops when not expected, and inflicting considerable loss. These freebooters mustered very strong in light horse, and by the rapidity of their movements and their intimate knowledge of every mile of the country, bade defiance to such of our troops as were brought against them.

In Scinde, the occurrence of the year was the deposition of Ali Morad from his princedom. The plots and falsehoods of this designing intriguer having been completely brought home to him, and it being made clear how nefariously he had deprived both his brothers and the British government of large tracts of territory, no time was lost in stripping him of his ill-gotten honours and estates, and reducing him to the rank of a simple chief.

An attempt was made during 1852 to establish an annual fair at Kurrachee, for the supply of the great commercial marts above the Indus with European goods, and the disposal of their produce in return; but, as far as the first endeavour has gone, no success appears to have attended it, however praiseworthy its object. The supplies of merchandise and produce were considerable, but without leading to any extended dealings.

In February 1853 the first fifteen miles of Indian railroad were opened with some ceremony, between Bombay and Tamrah, and this small line has continued in active operation since that time.

PART II.

POLITICAL.

CHAPTER I.

THE LOCAL GOVERNMENTS OF INDIA FROM THE HINDOO PERIOD TO THE PRESENT TIME, WITH A SKETCH OF THE COVENANTED AND UNCOVENANTED SERVICES.

BEFORE attempting to describe the present constitution and functions of the local governments of British India, with their effects upon the industry of the people over whom their rule is established, it is necessary that the reader should peruse a sketch of the form of government prevailing in the early times of Hindoo supremacy, with a few notices of the modifications the system underwent during the Afghan and Mahomedan rule in India. This is the more essential, because by so doing I shall render this picture of British India more complete, and at the same time provide the means of rightly estimating the value and effects of the changes introduced in the government and taxation of the country by the legislature of Great Britain. We can but judge of men and things by contrast, and it is only by looking back to what has been done during times long since past in this vast but half-known country, that a right appreciation can be formed of the shortcomings of the present, and the hopefulness of the future of our Indian empire.

In the time of which the first records are handed down to us through the code of Menu, it appears that the government of Hindostan was founded on the relative positions of the four classes of society existing at that period.

It was vested in an absolute monarch, whose authority arose out of the necessity, and partook of the character of the extremely simple state in which the people of India lived in that remote age. He was apparently controlled by no human power, but yet was so limited in his dominance by the moral influence of the code, and the necessities of the people over whom he was placed, that they were to a very great extent defended from any acts of tyranny on his part. For any breach of his high trust he was threatened with punishment in one part of the code, and is spoken of as subject to fine in another; but no means were provided for enforcing any of the penalties to which he might be liable; and neither the councils who were to assist him, nor the military chiefs who were to execute his behests, possessed any constitutional power which did not emanate from his will. The superintendence of a divine intelligence was felt and acknowledged, and the superstitious effect of the Brahminical priesthood pervaded the realm to the regulation of the subjects and of their king.

He appointed seven ministers, or councillors, who were generally of the military class, and who had above them all one distinguished Brahmin, in whom he was to repose his full confidence.[1] Another officer was also appointed, who was called an "ambassador," though his functions were rather those of a minister of foreign affairs than representative at foreign courts. All these officers were to be of noble birth; and the ambassador especially was selected for his great abilities, penetration, and sagacity, and he was required to be honest, dexterous in business, to make himself acquainted with other countries, and the circumstances of the times.

The king's duties were those of every executive monarch, the defence of his own country, and the chastisement of its foreign foes. It was his duty to attend to the advice of his Brahmins, from whom he was to derive his notions of justice, policy, and theology, and who thus acquired almost the entire control of the state. He was also expected to possess a knowledge of agriculture, commerce, and some general acquaintance with the mechanical arts, in which the people at large were generally engaged.

Not only were the duties of the monarch prescribed, but advice was given to him in the code, which coming from such a source had all the authority of law. The capital was to be fixed in a fertile part of the country, but in a place difficult of access, and incapable of supporting the armies of an invader. These two injunctions may seem to imply conditions which it was frequently impossible to fulfil; but it is remarkable how exactly they have to a great extent been carried out; for, owing to the peculiar nature of the country, and the judgment with which the several sites have been chosen, few places are stronger in their natural defences than most of the great cities of India. The

[1] Elphinstone's India, vol. i. p. 38.

monarch was to keep his garrison always well-provisioned, and in the centre of the fortress his own palace was to be placed, "well-finished and brilliant, surrounded by water and trees," in order that it might be equally accessible on all sides, and also of course more easy of defence.

His queen was to be chosen for her birth and beauty, and he was to appoint a domestic priest. The habits which the code directed the monarch to observe were all calculated to endue him with bodily health, and to enable him to exercise his faculties when in their clearest and most efficient state. He was to rise in the last watch of the night, and after sacrifices to hold a court in the public hall, dismissing his subjects with kind looks and words.

The precautions which contrast with this pleasing picture of fealty to the sovereign, and of parental care on his part for his dependents, were necessitated by the peculiarities of the Asiatic character. His food was only served by trustworthy persons, and was always accompanied, when placed before him, with antidotes to poison. He was usually armed when he received his emissaries, and even his female attendants were commonly searched, lest they should bear upon them concealed weapons; and whether at home or abroad he had constantly to be on his guard against the plots and attempts of his enemies.

The army was regulated by a commander-in-chief, but the actual infliction of punishment was committed to the officers of justice. The treasury was regulated by the monarch himself, and under his supervision the declaration of war or the arrangements for peace were committed to the ambassador, who was in all these affairs the king's supreme representative. Great power was thus necessarily intrusted to this important and often essential officer.

Foreign policy and war, as might naturally be expected, were the subjects of many of the rules of government in the code of Menu; and these rules are particularly interesting as affording numerous proofs in their construction of the division of India at a very early period into a number of unequal but independent states, disclosing besides the signs of a people who were already civilised and of gentle character. It would be foreign to my object to trace whence this civilisation arose; but it may not be impertinent to remark, that it must have arisen from a people far advanced in the codification of their laws. In Menu it was provided that the king should always care for the safety of his subjects by a vigilance that was unceasing, and a sufficient state of preparation to meet all emergencies; and this he was to do so far as in him lay without guile. The arts enjoined to be employed against enemies were four: firstly—making presents, shewing friendship, and allaying hostility; secondly—sowing divisions amongst his opponents, which was not quite consistent with the previous rule, and the observance of which was the great cause of all the after-misfortunes of India; thirdly—negotiations, in which the inhabitants of that clime were always adepts; and lastly—the force of arms, in which to a certain extent they were equal to their enemies. With a sagacity worthy of all praise they were recommended to prefer the last two courses.

The king was prompted to regard his nearest neighbours and their allies as hostile; the powers beyond those as possibly amicable; and all by whose enmity they could not be immediately reached as neutral, and only to be propitiated or subdued as circumstances might require. A natural result of a policy like this was an injunction that in ordinary cases a resort was to be made to the protection of a more powerful, if not a neighbouring prince, notwithstanding that this protection involved the necessity of unqualified submission to the power that had rendered the necessary assistance.

Great importance was attached to the use of spies, both in negotiations and in warfare, and minute instructions were given concerning the sort of persons who were to be engaged in that employment; nor has the principle died out with the lapse of ages. They were to be artful active youths, degraded anchorites, distressed husbandmen, decayed merchants, and fictitious penitents.

The rules of war were simple, and having been drawn from the usages and maxims of the Brahminical priesthood, were little suited to the carrying on of conflicts in a widely extended country, and where large numbers of men were employed. The plans of their campaigns resembled rather that adopted in the contests between the Grecian republics and the early tribes of Italy, before Rome had attained to the state and empire which she afterwards wielded with so much effect upon the destinies of the world.

In order that the march of a hostile force might be as detrimental as possible to the inhabitants of the invaded district, each sovereign was directed to advance when the vernal or autumnal crop was upon the ground; for it must not be forgotten that there are always two crops in the year in the most fertile districts of India; and to shew how much "fenced" cities were relied upon, it is stated in the code that one hundred bowmen in a fort were equal to the ten thousand enemies who might besiege it. The army was composed of both cavalry and infantry, the great weapon of both arms of the force being the bow, aided by the sword and shield for close quarters. Elephants were much employed then, as they have been ever since in every stage of warfare; and the chariots, such as were used in Arabia and Egypt, formed no unimportant part of the forces.

That the science of war was not altogether in its infancy was shewn in the fact, that precise directions were given for the order of march and the arrangement of the troops for battle; but above all, the king was enjoined to recruit his forces from the upper parts of Hindostan, where the best men are still invariably found for warlike purposes. Prize-property belonged of right to him that took it; but if of great extent, and not consequently captured separately, it was divided among the troops who either actually made or assisted in the assault.

The laws to be observed in war were humane in the extreme, and the settlement of a conquered country was conducted on equally liberal principles. Immediate safety was secured to all by proclamation; the religion and the laws of the country were to be especially respected; and as soon as it could be ascertained that the conquered people were to be trusted, a prince of the old royal house was to be placed on the throne, and to hold his kingdom only as a fief of, and doing allegiance to, the conqueror.

It is strange that, with all this minutiæ of expression with respect to the orderly government of a conquered state, not a word was said with respect to the pay of the military by whom it was achieved. In all probability the members of an Indian army were secured by a donation out of the revenues of the state, or by an assignment of lands for their use and support. This assertion would appear to be founded on the fact that the civil officers are all, almost without exception, provided for by the assignment of lands.

These assignments were made in the first place for specific sums, generally equal to the necessity of the case, and amply sufficient for the services which were to be performed; but it was natural to simplify the arrangements by transferring the onus of the collection from the simple officer charged with that duty to the chief in the state where the military body was employed.

According to the plan adopted by the Mahrattas, the number and description of troops to be maintained by each chief was prescribed; the pay of each division carefully calculated, allowances to the several officers specified, and a certain sum allotted for the personal expenses and remuneration of the chief himself; the terms of service and the mode of mustering, and all the other arrangements, being carefully laid down in the directions.

Some portion of the territory was then selected, of which the share set aside for the government should be sufficient, after all the other demands had been satisfied; and the whole territory yielding that amount, and all above it that he could obtain, was then turned over to the military chief, to make the best he could of it, for himself, his family, or his successors.[2]

As time progressed, the art of war among the Hindoos became much more complicated; and when the Mahomedan invasions from Ghuzni began, they had become acquainted with systematic plans, carried on through several campaigns, instead of the mere forays by which they were previously distinguished. The introduction of regular battalions entirely changed the face of war; and the people of India began to shew a skill in the choice of ground, an activity in the employment of light troops, and a judgment in securing their own supplies and cutting off those of the enemy, which has seldom been surpassed by any other people.

The longer duration of the campaigns rendered their military life more marked than it had been; and some of the Mahratta chiefs lived so entirely in the camp, that they had, apparently, no other capital. From this circumstance, the number of individuals assembled were out of all proportion to the fighting men; and when they moved, they formed a disorderly crowd spread over the country, from ten to twelve miles in length, and from two to three in breadth, besides the parties scattered from the line of march in search of forage or plunder.

The main body was very unequally composed. In some places it constituted a compact force, but was in others thin and dispersed, consisting of elephants and camels, horse and foot, carts, palankeens, and bullock-carriages, loaded oxen, porters, women, children, droves of cattle, goats, sheep, and asses, all mingled together in the utmost conceivable disorder, and all enveloped in a thick cloud of dust, which, from its height, was easily discernible from a distance of several miles.

When there were regular infantry, they marched in a compact body, the guns forming long lines, and occasioning frequent obstructions from the badness of the roads or the breaking down of the carriages. Many of the troops, however, straggled among the baggage. The usual signs of assemblage were two tall standards, accompanied by kettle-drums representing a following body, which ought to comprise from five hundred to five thousand men, but which seldom consisted of more than from five to fifty; the other horsemen riding singly or in troops, each with his spear poised upon his shoulder, as suited his pleasure, and the

[2] Elphinstone's India, vol. i.

whole array generally so loose that any one might have ridden at full trot from the rear to the front without causing any particular discomposure of the general mass. Yet, with all this disorder, they were not unprepared on the line of march; and it would be difficult, even in our wars, to find an instance of the baggage of a native army cut off, unless when fairly run down by a succession of hard marches.

When the troops reached their ground, a better arrangement occurred than might have been expected. Conspicuous flags were planted, marking the places allotted to the several chiefs, and every man knew therefore the part of the encampment to which he belonged. The tents were mostly white, but often striped with red, blue, and green, consisting sometimes wholly of these colours. The bazaars were ranged in long and regular streets, comprising shops of all descriptions, as in a city, while the guns and disciplined infantry also occupied regular lines, the other forces being distributed without any visible arrangement.

The common tents were low, and of black woollen cloth, sometimes being merely a blanket thrown over the heads of three spears stuck in the ground. Those of the chiefs, some of them especially, were extremely rich, formed of canvass screens, divided into courts, reception and sleeping rooms, which were quilted and adorned with most splendid damask or other hangings.

The armies were generally fed by large bodies of Banjaras, a tribe whose business it was to carry grain, bring it from distant countries, and sell it to the wholesale dealers, while smaller dealers went to the neighbouring villages and bought from the inhabitants; and though the government never interfered, the native camps were almost always well supplied, though the villagers around were generally rendered destitute by their visit.

The most important feature of an Indian battle in the present day consists in their cannonade, for in the management of large guns they are very skilful, and our troops have frequently suffered very severely in consequence. But their most characteristic mode of fighting, besides skirmishing, which is a favourite kind of warfare with them, consists in a grand charge of cavalry, which soon brings the battle to a crisis.

Nothing can be more magnificent than such a scene. The sea of horsemen, clad in all the panoply of war, advancing slowly at first, brandishing their spears and other weapons in the light of an Indian sun, shaking their banners, and then thundering along the ground apparently in an impenetrable phalanx against the opposing force. Their mode is generally to charge in front, and then, by a sudden diversion of a part of their force, attack the flanks at the same time; and the manœuvre has frequently called forth the admiration of European antagonists, and is certainly performed with surprising skill by a comparatively undisciplined body of men. These charges, however, though grand in aspect, almost always prove ineffectual against regularly trained soldiers.

Frequently there is a body of irregular cavalry attached to an Indian army, who are picked men, well mounted and appointed, of high courage and spirit, and who receive extra pay. The best infantry are men from the banks of the Jumna and the Ganges, besides Arabs and Scindians, especially the former, who are superior to most of the other inhabitants of Asia in discipline, fidelity, and courage.

The internal administration of the country was conducted by a series of civil dependents, consisting of lords of single townships or villages, very much answering to our superintendents of hundreds under the Saxon wittengemote, lords of ten towns, lords of a hundred, and lords of a thousand towns. These were all appointed by the king, and each of these lords had to make a regular periodical report of all the offences committed, and of all the disturbances created, to his immediate superiors.[3]

Each lord of one town was entitled to the provisions and other impositions which pertained to the crown; the lord of ten towns was entitled to take for his emolument the produce of two ploughs of land; the lord of a hundred towns enjoyed the whole of the land attached to a village; and the lord of a thousand, that which was attached as public property to a large town or city; for the Indian officials had what was equivalent to our city demesnes.

All officers of this rank were subject to the supervision of state superintendents, who held their authority directly from the sovereign or the state. One of these had to make his residence where complaints might be made or whence orders might be issued; the object being to check abuses, to which, as was very naïvely said in the code, officials were very prone.

With regard to its military government, every state under the ancient regime was partitioned into divisions, in each of which there was a commanding officer, approved for his skill or fidelity, and most probably for both; but the limits did not at all times, as might naturally be supposed, correspond correctly with the bounds of the civil jurisdiction.

Under the Mahomedan rulers of India the form of government underwent a considerable modification. Whilst in the village communities and rural districts much of the ancient Hindoo municipal admi-

[3] Elphinstone's India, vol. i. book ii. ch. xi.

nistration was still maintained, in other and more important districts, as well as in all the large towns and cities, the government assumed a more monarchical form, and became far more centralised.[4]

The country under this new regime was divided into provinces, the affairs of which were administered by governors holding their appointments direct from the emperor; and these again were, in some instances, as in the Deccan and Bengal, under the superior control of governors-general or viceroys. The governors had under them agents or kardahs, for the smaller divisions of the province. The supervision of the police and the collection of the revenue appears to have been under one management, except in the cities, where the police was maintained in a more distinct and independent form.

To the Mahomedans is to be traced the origin of the class known as zemindars, though in those days they were not precisely such as are to be found at present. They were not then landowners, though the term does signify a "holder of land," but were merely placed over a district or pergunnah, in conjunction with the kardah, with the same functions as those of the headmen of villages, whilst the village accountant was again duplicated in the districts by officers termed canoongoes, without detriment, however, to those ancient Hindoo officials who still continued to exercise their proper functions within their own limits.

The real value of any particular form of local government can be best estimated by its effects upon the social condition of the people under it; and judging of the Mahomedan administration by this standard, we are bound to admit that it was not ill suited to the wants of the country. Whatever of despotism there may have been, whatever individual cases of suffering, there is no doubt that the lives and property of the people at large were well cared for. Watchhouses were placed along the main lines of road, and properly guarded by patroles; whilst in the rural districts the inhabitants of each village were held accountable for any crime or offence against the laws committed within their limits. Harsh as this may appear in modern days, it nevertheless worked exceedingly well under the early rulers of Hindostan.

With the preceding sketch of the Mahomedan form of government before him, the reader will be prepared for an account of the local government of India as it at present exists.

The supreme government of India is vested in a governor-general, who is aided by a council, composed of the commander-in-chief, three civil servants of not less than ten years' standing, and one unofficial member, usually a barrister. The governor-general is also governor of

[4] Modern India, by George Campbell, p. 75.

the presidency of Bengal, with a deputy-governor to act in his absence, and a lieutenant-governor for the north-west provinces, whose station is at Agra. There is no Bengal council; but at each of the other presidencies the governor is assisted by the commander-in-chief and two ordinary civil councillors, as in the case of the supreme council at Bengal.

The government of India is centralised to a vicious degree. The subordinate governments of Bombay and Madras can make no law, nor expend any sum beyond 1000*l.*, without reference to the supreme government at Calcutta, which must also be furnished with copies of all their proceedings. The patronage of each presidency is exercised by the head of that government, which has also the direction of the military operations of the presidency.

The administration of the Bengal government in itself, and irrespective of the supreme functions of the governor-general, is by far the heaviest; extending over a much larger tract of country, including not only the vast densely-peopled provinces of Bengal, Behar, and Orissa, and the Assam and Arracan countries, but likewise the Tenasserim, and recently the Peguan province. The governor of Bengal does not interfere with the administration of the north-western government any further than with that of the other presidencies; and looking to the wide difference which exists between the mechanism of these respective governments, that of Bengal being on the modern Anglo-Mahomedan plan, whilst that of Agra is almost purely on the old Hindoo system, there can be little doubt of the wisdom which has to this extent separated the workings of these two portions of this great presidency.

The Bombay government, though small, is not an unimportant one, having many petty states in connexion with it, as well as some political relations along the African and Arabian coasts, together with the charge of the Indian navy.

The Presidency of Madras is of considerable extent, comprising the whole of the east and south of the peninsula; yet the duties of its government may be said to be limited, as they are by no means numerous or complex. The European community here is far less than in either of the other presidencies.

The administration of the Punjab and of the Sikh states bordering on the Sutlej is vested, not in the government of the north-west provinces, but in that of the supreme government at Calcutta, and distinct from the administration of Bengal Proper.

Each of the three presidencies, as well as the sub-presidency of Agra, is divided into districts for purposes of revenue and judicial administration. Under the government of Bengal there are fifty such districts, comprising an area of about 225,000 square miles, and a population of 41,000,000; the amount of land-tax derived from this territory being in round numbers 1,500,000*l.*

The Punjab and other provinces under the supreme government alone contain thirty districts, an area of 100,000 square miles, and a population of 10,000,000, with a land-tax yielding to the amount of 1,800,000*l.*

The north-west provinces, or government of Agra, with thirty-five districts, embrace an extent of 85,000 square miles, a population of 23,800,000, producing in land-tax 4,100,000*l.*

Madras is divided into twenty-one districts, contains an area of 144,000 square miles, with a population of 16,000,000, and yields for its land-revenue 3,400,000*l.*

Bombay, with its seventeen districts, comprises 120,000 square miles, 10,000,000 inhabitants, and yields in its land-tax 2,290,000*l.*[5]

The machinery by means of which the governments of the various presidencies are carried on does not differ in any sensible degree, with the exception of the north-western provinces and the Punjab, where the subordinate functions are almost all performed by the old village municipalities as existing since the time of the Hindoo sovereigns, and which are found to work remarkably well both as regards revenue and judicial matters.

Immediately under the authority of government, the revenue of each presidency is managed by a board similar in a great degree to our own Board of Customs. This, however, is not the case in Bombay. There are also military boards for the supervision of public works and buildings, and councils of education. These are the controlling powers. The real executive of the country consists of a great number of civil and military servants administering the affairs of each presidency by means of the district divisions already alluded to. At the head of each of these districts is a collector of revenue, who is also a magistrate; he is assisted by a deputy and an assistant-deputy, both of the privileged covenanted service, and by two or three uncovenanted assistants, either European or native: these latter are supposed to be entrusted with all work of too much minutiæ or of too little importance to occupy the time of the covenanted servants, but who in reality perform by far the greater portion of the revenue work. Indeed, it is stated that ninety per cent of the real work of the country is performed by the uncovenanted servants of the Company.

[5] Modern India, by George Campbell, pp. 230-1.

Attached to each collectorate and deputy-collectorate are numerous native establishments, poorly paid, and with no hope of rising by integrity and energy. The working establishment of the collector is kept perfectly distinct from his magisterial department, and is often distantly situated. In Bengal Proper these offices are seldom combined in one person; whilst in what are termed the non-regulation provinces, such, for instance, as the Punjab, one official will be judge, magistrate, and collector.

A civil judge is in fact a superintendent of the administration of justice, the original cases being tried by his many native assistant-judges, the moonsiffs; whilst as criminal or sessions judge he tries, every month, all such cases as have been committed by the magistrate, or sits in appeal on the summary judicial decisions of that functionary.[6]

The above constitute the machinery by means of which the government of British India is carried on. And here it may be worth while to state the emoluments drawn by the covenanted civil servants of the Company, *i.e.* of those who come out through the narrow portals of the India House and Haileybury College. In the Bengal and Madras branches of this service we find 43 offices with emoluments ranging between 10,000*l.* and 4800*l.* a year; 156 ranging from 3900*l.* to 1900*l.* a year; 157 between 1800 and 1200*l.* a year; and 128 where the salaries vary from 1000*l.* to 600*l.* a year. Such being the rate of remuneration given to the elect of Leadenhall Street, it will be instructive to compare it with the emoluments of those who confessedly carry on, in the name of the European covenanted servants, by far the larger portion of the actual work of the country, the uncovenanted servants. These officials, numbering about 3000, are remunerated in the following proportion: 20 at from 960*l.* to 720*l.* per annum; 137 from 720*l.* to 480*l.*; 325 between 480*l.* and 360*l.*; 1173 between 240*l.* and 120*l.*; and 1147 between 120*l.* and 24*l.*

The totality of the Indian appointments rest in the hands of the Directors of the East India Company;[7] and seeing that they amount in number to upwards of eight hundred, all of which are certain of entitling their incumbents to from 1000*l.* to 2000*l.* a-year, with the probability of attaining the higher emoluments of from 2000*l.* to 10,000*l.* per annum, the avidity with which a seat in the direction is sought, in spite of the humiliation and toil which it for a long period entails on the candidates, may be readily understood. Nominated between the ages of seventeen and twenty-one, the candidate is expected to pass a classical examination previous to admission at the Company's College

[6] Modern India, p. 250.

[7] Appendix A.

at Haileybury: this is so slight that very few indeed require training for the occasion. At Haileybury the embryo civilian is located for two years, during which time he is supposed to be qualifying for the discharge of his future Indian duties by the study of Sanscrit, a language as likely to assist him in his after career as would be the dialect of the Ojibbeway Indians. To this very practical course is added a knowledge of the Persian alphabet. But the Sanscrit is the one thing needful, the alpha and omega of the Haileybury professors. At the public examination which takes place before the students receive their diplomas enabling them to be drafted off to the scene of their future Sanscrit exploits, there is a great show of orientalism, a strange jargon of unknown tongues utterly bewildering to the listeners; there is a total absence of any acquaintance with the ordinary affairs of the world, or the business of every-day life; and, amidst all the glitter and sound of oriental alphabets, nineteen out of twenty students are declared to have highly distinguished themselves, while the remaining one is stated to have passed with great credit.

The fitting sequel to this imposing exhibition is a carefully studied, carefully delivered oration by the deputy chairman to the highly distinguished candidates for eastern celebrity. He dwells upon their happy prospects; upon the vast and magnificent career to which they are destined; upon the magnitude of the British power, the glory of the British name; upon the high charge which will be placed in their hands, and bids them go forth to aid in ruling over a hundred millions of fellow creatures; he declares his conviction of the great utility of the Sanscrit language in developing the resources of that promising country; of the service the Persian alphabet will render them in ameliorating the condition of the Indian ryots; of the enormous advantage which an acquaintance with Paley will prove to them in the collection of the land-revenues; of the aid which the Greek authors will give them on the benches of the civil and criminal courts of India. Thus qualified and thus exhorted, the half-fledged civilian finds his way out to one of the presidencies, well stocked with Sanscrit, natural philosophy, and conceit.[8]

Arrived at Calcutta or Bombay, as the case may be, the "writer," for so he is termed until placed in some department, is supposed to be occupied for a year or two in perfecting himself in those studies in which he has already so "highly distinguished" himself. Armed with

[8] "All those who are at all idle, who are not inclined to serve two masters, stick to the Oriental languages, and despise the European sciences, because the one secures their appointment and their pay, the other only tends to make them efficient, which is quite another matter."—*Modern India*, p. 265.

the qualifications and credentials of Haileybury, the "writer" naturally feels somewhat hurt at the idea of another course of study within the College of Fort William, and accordingly passes the two or three years considered necessary for his sojourn there in spending in gaiety about thrice the amount of pay allotted him,—400*l.* a-year, or equal to the salary of two native judges of long service. As another examination is required, a few months spelling and reading over Persian or Urdu books by the aid of native pundits generally enables the young civilian to pass; when he is at once drafted off as magistrate, or assistant collector, or both, to some remote district, the language of which will be perfectly unintelligible to him.[9]

Once away from the Presidency College, all goes on swimmingly with the young civilian: he will be attached to the collectorate, or made assistant magistrate, and in either case rapidly falls into the ordinary routine of signing his name to reports, making out abstracts of documents, spelling over the native returns, or doing the preliminary drudgery of the magistrate's office. This latter functionary will be sure of promotion in less than three years, upon which the assistant is moved up as a matter of course to his seat, where, with a smattering of the dialect of the district, a slight acquaintance with the people, and a still slighter knowledge of their manners and habits, he contrives to get through the work which is allotted to him with not more blundering than did his late superior when first discharging the same duties. Two or three years in that office, and if he be not placed in some better-paid magistracy, he will be sure to be made a deputy-collector, for which, of course, his magisterial training will have peculiarly fitted him. His next step will necessarily be to the collectorate; and by the time he has become tolerably efficient in that department, he is once more moved up, and by way of a little change created a judge in civil

[9] The late principal of the Calcutta College was a colonel in the Company's service, who endeavoured, but vainly, to enforce greater attention on the part of the students. On one occasion he detected one of these distinguished youths in the act of copying the Persian exercise of a fellow-student, to save himself the trouble of rendering it. On being remonstrated with, the embryo collector fired with indignation, and told the Colonel that he had acted in a most ungentlemanly manner in looking over his shoulder. The Colonel reported this language; but it was passed over by the "proper authorities." Determined, if possible, to compel some amount of study, the principal, previous to an examination, gave each young gentleman an exercise to be rendered into Persian or Urdu, and had them locked up in separate rooms until the page was completed. The weather was sultry, and they prayed the indulgence of syces, or native grooms, to pull the punkahs to cool them; the request was granted, and it was so contrived that each student was waited on by his pundit, or teacher, in the garb of a groom. This accomplished, they changed places; the young civilian pulled the punkah, whilst the sham syce finished off a first-rate page of Persian.

and criminal matters, unless indeed he has evinced a more than ordinary ability and energy, when he will be considered far too good for the bench, and must remain in the collectorate, the rigid collection of the taxes being considered of much more importance than the proper administration of justice.

The duties of a collector, however multifarious they may appear, and however large his district, are not in reality of an alarmingly burdensome nature. He is, in fact, but a general supervisor, expected to be moving about a good deal, and which, during many months in the year, is indeed his most agreeable occupation. Many of the collectorates are as extensive as any two of our English counties; and over a great part of this wide range he has a little army of functionaries, who need an occasional visit from him, if only to assure himself that they are within their proper divisions.

The morning levee of a civilian, previous to mounting his horse for field work, is often a numerous and motley assemblage. Natives of almost every rank press round the great man's path, each anxious to prefer some prayer, or exchange a friendly greeting with the "Burra Sahib." Not unfrequently a good deal of business of a slight nature will be transacted at this moment between the collector and his many native petitioners and clients; and the Hindoo, ever alive to his own interest, reckons, and not untruly, that "master" is more likely to be in an amiable mood when just risen from rest, than at the end of a long and wearisome ride, or after the discharge of a string of vexatious petty duties.

From the office of collector, upon 2800*l.* a year, the civilian may look upwards to some of the better things to be met with at the Boards of Revenue, or in the Secretariat Department, worth 4000*l.* to 5000*l.* per annum, which in due time, should he not be promoted to the bench, he will, by the regular course of seniority, be certain to attain.

After a service of ten years, the East Indian civilian can claim a furlough of three years to Europe, on 500*l.* a year; but if he avails himself of this, his post is filled up, and on his return he must take his chance and wait his time for another appointment. He may, however, obtain leave to the Cape, Australia, and some other places, on one-third of his pay, and without resigning his office. At the end of twenty-two years' service he may retire on 1000*l.* a year, having in the meanwhile subscribed at the rate of four per cent to the annuity fund, and a further certain per centage towards the widow and orphan fund.

The uncovenanted service consists of the employés of government, nominated on the spot, for the purpose of filling certain subordinate posts, not worth the notice of the regular service, or requiring qualifications to which they cannot pretend. These consist indiscriminately of Europeans, Indo-British, and natives, and number amongst them 1805; but there appears to be no means of ascertaining the relative proportion of each class. These perform by far the greater part of the work of the country, and may not inaptly be termed the "boots" of the service, embracing a wide range of appointments, from the judicial office of principal suddur-ameen on 800*l.* a year, down to a patrol of the customs department on 50*l.* No especial length of service is required of them; but when a man becomes quite worn out, not before, he receives one-half or one-third of his salary as pension, according to the period during which he may have served.

The lower grades of officials are composed entirely of natives, generally the poorest and most unprincipled, who look to the peculation and bribery of such places as sure means of fortune. When it is remembered that the pay of some of these sub-officials does not amount to more than a few shillings a month, and that every means of adding to their emolument is considered as a legitimate consequence of their position, we can scarcely wonder that extortion and oppression are the universal rules amongst them. Men can be pointed out at the present day in Calcutta who have risen from the most menial posts in police-offices, places of ten shillings a month, to high station and wealth as banians or native money-lenders; and who have but too frequently a dozen or two of their former European masters in their books as their debtors. Once in the power of these men, and a magistrate or civil judge can no longer pretend to independent action. The relative position of the needy magistrate and the wealthy banian is notorious among the common people; and a native having a suit before the former has but to rank himself by bribes as a client of the latter, to insure the complete success of his case.

Such is a picture of the constitution of the present civil service of India, and its offshoot, the "uncovenanted." From the lips of all but civilians is gathered one unanimous verdict upon the civil service of India—that its exclusiveness should be swept away, and that it be made the *public* service of British India; that in place of the appointments to these eight hundred valuable posts being left in the hands of twenty-four elderly gentlemen, to be dispensed to relations and personal friends, they should be made available to the entire community of the parent country and of India, by being left open to public competition as prizes for the most talented youth of the day.

The efficiency of the judicial branch of the service will be examined hereafter. That the revenue-branch is not far in advance of it, there is just ground to believe, except that all those civilians who possess any degree of ability are carefully retained for revenue purposes; and therefore there are in this department some creditable exceptions to the all-but-universal barrenness. The most able advocate of the service[10] cannot defend the general low tone of ability and acquirements amongst his confreres; and even their own masters, the Bengal authorities, in recently published documents, declare that their servants of the collectorate are grossly inefficient; for they are told that "it is unreasonable to expect a collector to be competent to review a settlement, if he does not know what a settlement is, or how it is to be made!" And further, "it cannot be right that the officer who has to review all the settlements made in his district, to administer every ward's estate, and to manage every estate that comes under his own immediate superintendence, should have no personal acquaintance with any part of his district out of sight of his own house; should never have any direct or intimate relations with ryot or talookdar, *or any practical knowledge of the rates, tenures, and common agricultural customs of his district.*"[11]

It is clear that, notwithstanding the Sanscrit of Haileybury and the Persian of Fort William, the exotics of the Company's service are but ill adapted for the tasks allotted them. They are not more vigorous or healthy than the productions of any other forcing-house. Whatever may be the difference of opinion as to the mode of remedying this state of things, there can be no question as to the existence of the evil. Neither can it be denied, that whatever may be the future mode of distributing the patronage of the service in England, a fair share should be left for the native talent of India. That the necessary talent is to be found sufficiently abundant, there is most ample testi-

[10] Mr. George Campbell, B.C.S., in his Modern India.

[11] "The bulk of both services are below the average of educated men at home; and it is not difficult to understand why they should be. * * * * They settle down in some civil or military station, as the case may be, where temptations to idleness are always greater than inducements to exertion; their acquaintance is exceedingly limited; and they are throughout life absolutely without the stimulants that rouse ability in great communities; if they live, they rise, and in this conviction they remain in a state of mediocrity and contentment. It is worse with the soldier than with the civilian, because he comes out at an earlier age, and, as a rule, with an inferior education. It is not an uncommon thing to find officers in this country who cannot write a common letter with ordinary propriety, who cannot spell as well as a boy of twelve might be expected to do; who have the most confused idea of the use of capital letters, and of punctuation none at all. We have lately smiled when perusing some questions in history, ancient and modern, the classics, &c. &c. prepared for our embryo heroes. and wished that they had been replaced by moderate tests in reading, writing, and arithmetic."—*Indian Charter*, 1851.

mony; talent, too, combined with the most perfect integrity. India must not be judged by the vile offscourings of native society gathered about the courts of justice, as sheristadars, amlahs, &c., the merest jackals of the law. The large number of native gentlemen who ably and honestly fill judicial and magisterial subordinate situations—subordinate in emolument, though the very reverse in duties—testify to the abundance of native talent.

In the Bengal presidency the number of offices with more than 30*l.* a month, held by natives, does not exceed one hundred and five, and this amongst a population of forty millions. At the same time, the British foreigners in the same presidency monopolise amongst them three hundred and twenty-seven offices, the salaries of which vary from 600*l.* to 10,000*l.* a year!

There was, it is true, a great parade of doing justice to the natives in the charter of 1833, wherein it was especially enacted, that no disability from holding office in any subject of the crown, by reason of birth, religion, descent, or colour should any longer continue. No doubt the friends of India believed at the time that a most important concession was made in that very liberal clause. But the Court of Directors, in becoming parties to the enactment, did so in much the same spirit as that in which Pecksniff, when parting from his pupil, bade him "be jovial and kill the fatted calf." The Pecksniffian clause, like the permission of the sham architect, has proved a "polite compliment" rather than a "substantial hospitality:" the practice of excluding natives from all important and really remunerative offices remaining as universal in 1853 as it was in 1833.

It is monstrous to say that the natives of India are unfitted to carry on the work of the state. They do carry it on, and have done so for many years in the name of their English superiors, who get all the credit and nearly all the pay, leaving them the poor satisfaction of beholding their light exalted in another's candlestick. It has been truly observed by a most competent authority in Indian matters,[12] that it is absurd to suppose the native should be less able to do well when working on his own responsibility and for his own credit, than when he works on the responsibility and for the credit of his European superior.

Our Mahomedan predecessors may have been less enlightened in their theories of government than ourselves; but they were at any rate more just, and shewed more wisdom in their practice than we can boast of. They found it, as they believed it to be, best to employ the

[12] Lord Metcalf.

native talent of the country in the administration of affairs. There was no exclusive foreign service, no privileged exotic class, no hot-house civilians in those barbarous days. They were content to use the indigenous talent of the country, blended with a few Mahomedan governors of provinces; and hence it was, that although they could afford to pay all liberally, there were no enormous civil lists; consequently we find that although the emperors of Delhi possessed not nearly the territory in the hands of the East India Company, and collected less revenue by a third than is raised at the present time, and were moreover always engaged in costly wars, they nevertheless found ample means for carrying out gigantic works of public utility, lived in a state of the most gorgeous orientalism, and yet contrived, notwithstanding all this, to accumulate many millions sterling in their treasuries. Well may it be said that our government of India is a "costly sham,"—a gilded mockery. It is time it was made a stern reality, a substantial good to a hundred millions of our fellow-subjects, dark-skinned though they be.

The relations subsisting between the East Indian government and the many native states comprised within the limits of the British territories require some notice in this chapter, not only from their connection with our rule in the East, but as testifying to the state of governmental morality in these distant possessions.

Within the red-line which marks the extent of the Company's dominions are many native states, varying as much in extent and condition as in their form of government. Amongst them may be found regions under the rule of Hindoos, Mahomedans, Mahrattas, and Rajpoots. Together they comprise an area of about 700,000 square miles, with a population of 52,000,000, and yielding revenues amounting in the aggregate to nearly 13,000,000*l.* sterling. With the single exception of the small northern state of Nepaul, the whole of these are directly subject to our political power, and dependent upon us for their military protection. They maintain amongst them a large number of irregular troops, understood to be at our disposal on any emergency, and on no account to be employed beyond their own territories, unless with our express sanction. Besides these they maintain about 30,000 well-disciplined troops, commanded by British officers, also at our disposal, but ordinarily left for their own requirements.

The British government have guaranteed them full protection against all external enemies; for which a consideration has been stipulated for, either in the shape of territory annexed, as in the cases of the Nizam, the king of Oude, &c., or by annual tributes, which latter amount to upwards of half a million sterling. This may appear a small sum for their protection; but the territories relinquished by them in addition were of far greater value, and the support of the native contingents must also form an important item during the year. Valuable, however, as were the countries ceded under these arrangements, they appear to have resulted in absolute loss instead of gain; and whereas under their own native governments they yielded considerable sums to the local treasuries, now that they are ruled by the Honourable Company they are absolutely barren and unproductive as far as any revenue is concerned; a poor return, the reader may imagine, for the great honour conferred upon them of British Company's collectors, judges, and magistrates, and above all British Company's law!

I cannot, I must confess, agree with those advocates of universal Indian annexation, who persist in attributing all our failures in these cases to stopping short of the complete subjugation of every independent state. Their advice is precisely that of the great quack vegetarian, when told by a patient that his pills were inefficacious, although his instructions had been most rigidly observed. The vendor of pills declared that the sick man could not have taken enough of them; to which the other replied, that he had swallowed the largest dose prescribed in any case, viz. a whole boxful. "But," asked the impudent quack, "did you swallow the box also?" The patient was staggered, and declared that such a proceeding had not occurred to him. "Ah!" rejoined the bold vegetarian, "I thought not. Go home and try the box." Even thus our Indian quacks would have the state try the native "box," regardless of the consequences.

The loss of revenue, however, is not the only disadvantage we labour under in regard to our intimate connection with the native states. There is the loss of reputation to be taken into account; a loss which although not as yet apparent in this country, has long been matter of notoriety in India, and cannot any longer be hidden even here.[13] It will reflect everlasting disgrace upon the British name that the most solemn engagements, the most formal treaties with many native princes, some of whom had long proved themselves our staunch and unfailing allies, should have been utterly disregarded and cast aside to suit the political or pecuniary purpose of the day; that reputation should have been weighed in the balance against rupees, and made to kick the beam; that the good faith of a Christian country should have been thought as nothing when placed against a few hundred miles of Indian territory!

[13] While these pages are going through the press, a very interesting and truthful pamphlet has made its appearance, which the reader will do well to peruse: *Indian Wrongs without a Remedy* (Saunders and Stanford, Charing Cross).

By those who are anxious to defend the existing state of things, a great parade has been made of the sums paid annually as pensions to the ex-rajahs and nabobs; but all mention is carefully avoided of the obligations of the East India Company to make not only those payments, but others which have been shamefully put aside. Not a word is said of the immense tracts of country made over to the government, for which those pensions were a consideration; nor is any thing said of the large extent of private landed property belonging to those ex-rulers, which, contrary to all plighted engagements, have been confiscated by the Honourable Company, and for which act of spoliation there is no redress! Even worse than this, some of the stipulated pensions, after being paid regularly to the ex-princes and their families for a score of years, have been cut down to the merest pittance; so that these descendants of the former rulers of India find themselves in danger of coming to beggary and starvation.

The case of the kingdom of Oude is a peculiar one, but not less revolting to all right-minded men. In that country a native force is kept up nominally as a contingent for our use when required, which it is never likely to be, and which is commanded by British officers. The government of Oude, unlike that of other native states of the present day, is in the hands of a weak and dissolute prince, who confides all power to the hands of his minister, a man of an avaricious and cruel disposition. The people of Oude are so ground down by the arbitrary taxation of this vizier's minions, that it rarely happens that some province is not in open revolt against the farmers of the revenue. It is not at all an uncommon thing for these creatures of iniquity to declare to the minister that the people of a certain province refuse to pay their share of taxation, when they have already received and squandered it. A force is accordingly sent into the unfortunate district to compel payment, and the people, naturally enough averse to pay a second time, oppose force by force. In this manner we see British officers heading the Oude contingent, and leading on the troops to seize cattle, tools, household property, &c. in satisfaction of claims long since settled. Many of our countrymen are quite aware of the real state of things, and are naturally disgusted at having to act the part of sheriffs' officers to an Indian despot. But protests are in vain; and the Indian government, when it might well disclaim all participation in such transactions, rigidly acts up to the letter of its Oude treaty, although disregarding more honourable engagements.

CHAPTER II.

THE FISCAL SYSTEMS OF INDIA, ANCIENT AND MODERN, AND THEIR EFFECTS ON THE INDUSTRY OF THE PEOPLE.

HAVING shewn the nature of the ancient political institutions of India as compared with those existing at the present time, it will be not less necessary to the right estimation of the modern fiscal system of the three presidencies, that an account of it be prefaced by an outline of the mode in which the Hindoo and Mahomedan rulers of India raised their revenues.

Commencing with the earliest records bequeathed to us,—the code of Menu,—it will be seen that the public revenue of the state was in those remote ages derived from a comparatively small number of sources. By far the largest portion arose from a share of the agricultural produce of the country; next to this came certain taxes on commerce, a trifling impost levied on persons engaged in business, —small traders and shopkeepers; and lastly, twelve days' service from every mechanic during each year.

On grain, from one-twelfth to one-sixth was levied, according to the soil, the labour, and the expense involved in its cultivation; but this also might be raised in times of emergency to one-fourth, and must have been, in all ordinary seasons, the main dependence of the state. On the clear annual increase of trees, honey, perfumes, and the other natural productions of the country, not excepting manufactures, one-sixth was levied.

But the king had another means of obtaining revenue. He was entitled to one-fifth on the profits of all sales. Estates for which there were no ostensible heirs were dealt with as escheats to the crown; and so was all property which remained for three years unclaimed after a proclamation of its vacancy. The sovereign was also entitled to half of the precious minerals contained in the earth within the bounds of his dominion.

It has been supposed that, in addition to the rights thus exercised by the king, he possessed an absolute right in the soil of the country, since in one of the articles of Menu it is directed that where an occupier neglects to sow his land, he shall be directly responsible for the consequences to the king. It is, however, pretty clearly stated elsewhere in the code, "that land was the property of him who cut away the wood;" that is, of him by whom it was cleared and tilled. Yet it is strange that, although so many occasions must have called for it, little, indeed no mention is made of the property of individuals in land. It is true that there is something said of the boundaries of different properties; and in one place an argument is illustrated by supposing seed belonging to one man being sown in land which was the property of another. Gifts of land are spoken of elsewhere, as if it were in the power of individuals to confer them; and the division of inheritances, and the rules about mortgages, in describing the wealth of individuals, and for disposing of the property of banished men, are clearly laid down.

As time advanced, the form of Hindoo municipal government was modified, but never altered in principle.

Throughout all the convulsions of India, the townships still remained entire. In those days the district thus named was a compact piece of land; for the size of which, as in English parishes, there was no prescribed rule. The lands were divided into portions, the boundaries of which were as carefully marked as those of the township; and the names, qualities, extent, and proprietors were all minutely entered in the records of the community. Each township conducted its own internal affairs, had its regular coterie of municipal officers, levied the revenues due to the state from its members, was collectively responsible for the full amount, managed its own police; and though entirely subject, as a portion of the state, to the general government, was, in almost every respect, an organised commonwealth, complete within itself. This independence, with its concomitant privileges, though often violated by the government, was never denied.

A township, in its simplest form, was under the direction of an officer called the headman, considered to be the representative of the king, and formerly removable at pleasure; but the office finally became hereditary, and the headman in reality became the representative of the people; for although he had an annual allowance from the government, the greater part of his income was derived from fees paid by the villagers. He was held personally responsible for their state engagements, and was often thrown into prison in cases of resistance and failure of revenue from the township. He was the principal authority in all disputes; decided every point of public interest; consulted freely with the villagers, whenever the general welfare required it; let such lands as had no fixed occupants; and, in short, was the head and chief of the municipal government.

The headman had associated with him two other officers, called respectively the watchman and the accountant. The latter kept the village records, containing a full description of the nature of the lands of the village, with the names of the former and present owners, the rent, and other terms of occupancy. He also kept the accounts of the villagers both with the government and between themselves. The watchman was the guardian of the boundaries, both public and private, watched the crops; was the public guide and messenger, and, next to the headman, the chief officer of police; was bound to find out the possessor of any stolen property within the township, or to trace him till he had passed the boundary, when the responsibility was transferred to the next neighbour.

The money-changer may also be considered as an assistant to the headman, as he was the assayer of all the money, and also the silversmith of the village.

This was the usual mode of village government, where there was no intervention between the actual occupier of the soil and the prince; but in some parts of India in the present day, especially in the north, and the extreme south, there is in each village a community which constitutes the township by itself, and which has the other inhabitants for its tenants. The persons constituting this community are generally regarded as the absolute proprietors of the soil, and are acknowledged to possess a heritable and transferable interest in the land wherever they exist. Such villages are sometimes governed by one head; but more generally each branch of the family composing the community, or each family, if there be more than one, has its own head, who manages its internal affairs, and unites with the heads of the other divisions to conduct the general business of the village.

Where there were village landholders, they formed the first class of inhabitants; but there were four other classes of inferior degree. They were termed respectively permanent tenants, temporary tenants, labourers, and shopkeepers, who took up their abode in a village for the advantage of a market.

The rights of the landholders pertained to them *collectively*,—and though they had more or less a partition amongst them, there was never any thing like an entire separation of the property. Their rights varied in different parts of the country; and where their tenure was most perfect, they held their lands subject to a *fixed* produce-payment to the government.

In all villages there were two descriptions of tenants who rented the lands of the village landholders, where there were such proprietors; and of the government, where there were none. These tenants were commonly called *ryots*, and were divided into two classes—the temporary and the permanent. The permanent ryots were those who cultivated the lands where they resided, retained them during their lives, and transmitted them to their children at their death. They have often been confounded with the village landholders; but the distinction is sufficiently marked where any proprietary fee exists, for in that no tenant ever participates. The temporary tenant cultivated the land of a village to which he did not otherwise belong, holding by an annual lease, written or understood, the best description of land being occupied by the resident tenant; an inferior kind, for which there was little competition, fell to him; and for that reason, and on account of his other disadvantages, he held his land at a lower rate than the permanent tenant.

There was, however, another description of tenant who ought to be mentioned, though he held a very different position to the others. This grade consisted of men whose caste or condition in life prevented their engaging in manual labour; or their women from taking part in any employment that required them to appear before men. In consideration of these disadvantages, these tenants were allowed to hold land at a favourable rate, so as to enable them to avail themselves of their skill and capital by means of hired labourers.

In Canara, Malabar, and Travancore, the land is held in absolute property by single individuals, subject to a fixed payment to the state. The zemindars, or great lords of the soil, derive their property from direct grants by the king, who also frequently alienates lands for religious objects, or as rewards for military services.

In later periods during the rule of the Tartar conquerors of Hindostan, innovations of various kinds crept in, pressing more or less upon the industry of the people. These innovations, however, in no way affected the forms of assessment, or the machinery for the collection of the taxes; these were, doubtless, found to do their work too well to be interfered with. It was in the augmentation rather than the mode of levying the local taxation that the cultivators felt the hardship of the new order of things.

This increase was made not so much by openly raising the king's proportion of the crop, as by means of various taxes and cesses, some falling directly on the land, and others directly or indirectly affecting the cultivator. Taxes on ploughs, cattle, &c. constituted the first kind; and those on music at certain ceremonies, or marriages with widows, &c., and new taxes on consumption, constituted the other.

Practically there was no regular limit to these demands but the ability of those on whom they fell to satisfy them, and consequently the villagers used every possible endeavour to conceal their incomes. For this purpose they resorted to all kinds of devices, understating the amount of their crops, and abstracting a part without the knowledge of the collector. Very often they concealed the stated quantity of the land under cultivation, and falsified their records, so as to render detection all but impossible. By these means, not less than by the connivance of such revenue-officers as were open to bribes, the actual revenues of the crown were at best an uncertainty, and a continual source of heart-burnings between the governing and the governed.

This unsatisfactory state of things was understood, and to a great extent remedied, by some of the Tartar rulers of India. Akbar Khan, the great reformer of taxation, probed deeply into the then wide-spreading disease which threatened to eat into the vital prosperity of the country. From the published memoirs of his talented prime minister, Abul Fazl, we gather, that for a period of more than twenty years the exertions of this sovereign were directed to a complete examination into, and revision of, the taxation of land.

The result of this laborious and minute investigation was the compilation of a series of tables shewing the collection per *beegah* (a measure of land) on twenty articles of the spring, and thirty of the autumn crops, in the years 1560 to 1578 inclusive, in the vice-royalties of Agra, Oude, Allahabad, Delhi, Malwa, Moultan, and Lahore. From these an assessment was formed, not on the land but on the crops produced by it, shewing rates, which, taken in reference to the surface of the land under culture, gave averages of from 1*s.* 7*d.* for linseed to 14*s.* 2½*d.* for sugar-cane.

The settlement of these taxes on the above tables was for a period of ten years, when a re-assessment would take place. But, independently of these reforms in the fiscal administration of the country, Akbar appears to have kept up the integrity of native institutions of police, courts of justice, &c.; and, whilst he gave security to life and property, was not less attentive to the moral and social wants of his subjects, providing them liberally with the means of education, with good roads, bridges, and artificial means of irrigation, at all times of the utmost importance to the well-being of an Indian agricultural country.

If, then, as has been argued, though not proved, the Tartar rulers of India wrung as much from the inhabitants as has been taken by their English successors, the advocates of the former may at least maintain, what cannot be advanced by the latter, that they gave full value for what they took; that they administered a full measure of justice to high and low; that the agriculturist had most ample means of irrigation; that the trader could convey his goods many hundreds of miles along roads at all times safe and in good repair; and that, whatever fault may be found with this system, the bulk of the people lived in those times in comparative affluence and security. That all this must have been so, we need seek for no further proofs than are to be found among the remains of the magnificent public works of those days,—the noble aqueducts, the vast tanks, the interminable roads planted on either side with shady trees, the many wells and rest-houses for travellers, the splendid palatial dwellings of the rich still abounding throughout the country, the mouldering ruins of once-busy cities, the desolate market-places, and the jungle-grown towns and villages. The moss-grown marble terraces, the stagnant water-courses, the owl-inhabited mansions and temples, the solitary pillar and arch, the tiger-swamps that engulf whole cities of the dead,—all these bear silent testimony to the once-happy working of that system which we of the civilised West—of Christian England, have rooted out from the land, to replace with a miserable mockery, a governmental fraud of such enormous magnitude, of such wicked viciousness, that future generations, without ample testimony to the contrary, may well discredit the possibility of its existence, even in the very worst days of the worst types of bureaucratic imbecility and red-tapeism.

The subversion of the ancient order of things was not the work of a short period; it was not the earlier administrations which undertook this crusade against existing institutions.

As in religious matters, the British rulers of India have swept away heathenism and its morality, and replaced it by infidelity and no morality,—as in the administration of justice, they have rooted out the old simple codes and effective establishments, and substituted for them a legal patchwork administered by functionaries of whom nearly all who are not incompetent are corrupt; so in the more important part of their fiscal system, they have overturned the labours of many ages, scorning the lessons of dear-bought experience, and, except in the countries on the north-west, have supplanted the righteous taxation of Hindoo rulers by the most impracticable and the most ruinous systems which it ever fell to the lot of politico-economical quacks to hazard.

Before discussing the present amount of and mode of levying the land-tax of India, I will place before the reader a general statement of the revenues of the three Presidencies, from which he will at once perceive that the tax above alluded to forms by far the largest item of the whole income of the government. The following table presents a comprehensive view of the entire taxation of British India as it exists at the present time, the amount being stated in pounds sterling for convenience sake, taken at 2*s.* the rupee.

Source of revenue.	Gross revenue.	Nett revenue.	Cost of collecting per cent.	Per centage on total revenue.
	£	£		
Land revenue	15,178,676	13,551,752	10½	58½
Excise and moturpha . . .	1,088,254			
Opium	4,562,586	3,358,684	26½	14½
Salt	3,189,214	2,703,752	15	11¾
Customs	946,561	816,074	13⅓	3¼
Stamps, fees, and fines . .	593,982	590,169	4	2½
Tobacco	115,000	88,448	23	⅓
Post-office, mint, and other sources	[1]1,979,041	1,979,041	[2]	8⅔
£	27,753,314	23,067,920		

It is thus seen how large an item is formed by three of the leading taxes of India, viz. on land, opium, and salt, whence, indeed, are derived about eighty-five per cent of the entire revenues.[3] Deducting the sum received from native states in payment of military protection afforded them, we have a round sum of twenty-two millions sterling as forming the revenues of India at the present moment. By reference to the tables in the Appendix,[4] it will be seen in what proportion this is derived from the several divisions of the country, and in what marked contrast the charge of each presidency stands as against their income.

So much has been said and written about the taxation of British

[1] Of this sum, 566,694*l.* are receipts from native states towards the support of British troops for their protection.

[2] Cost of collection charged against general revenues, and said to be equal to the gross amount collected; actual nett revenue from these would therefore be *nil.*

[3] Campbell's Modern India, p. 427.

[4] Appendix B.

India, that it will be well, before proceeding any further, to examine the bearing which the above amount must have upon the actual resources of the people. The taxation of a country may be vicious in two very different shapes,—either by its excessive amount, or, being moderate, by the mode in which it is levied.

The bulk of the people of India, unfortunately, suffer from both these evils. Taking the gross revenue of the country, and deducting from that sum the amount of the opium-tax as really paid by foreigners, and the sums received from native princes for military protection, we have a total amount of 22,000,000*l.* levied upon the inhabitants of the three Presidencies. The population of British India at the present time is, in round numbers, one hundred millions.[5] These figures will therefore give an average of nearly 4*s.* 5*d.* a-head; not a large sum in itself, but when compared with the earnings of the great mass of people, a heavy and oppressive load.

In Great Britain the taxation gives, as nearly as possible, 33*s.* per head of the population, about seven times that of our Indian fellow-subjects. But the paying powers of the two nations widely differ. Fifteen shillings a week is a fair average, in the present day, for the earnings of the English labouring classes; accordingly, they appear to be taxed to the extent of thirteen days' labour in the year. To estimate the actual earnings of the great mass of Hindoos, wages in the cities and towns must not be taken as a criterion; for whilst in England the townspeople are the greater tax-payers, in India 70 per cent of the taxation falls upon the mass of the people not dwelling in towns. Some reliable official documents on this subject,[6] fortunately, leave no doubt upon the matter. These statistical returns shew, that in a rural district (that of Cawnpore) fairly representing the average of the agricultural part of the country, the greater portion of the cultivators realise but 5*l.* per annum; from this, one-fourth, at the lowest calculation, must be taken for government land-tax, and one-fourth as rent to the proprietor, leaving 2*l.* 10*s.* to defray cost of seed, tools, &c., and support the *ryot and his family* during the year. With the calculation of four persons to a family, and without any deduction for seed, tools, &c., we have something over twelve shillings per annum to support each individual! These are not extreme cases, but actually represent, I regret to say, the present condition of a very large portion of the agricultural population of British India. Striking an average between these figures and the wages of natives in the

[5] See Blue Book, 1852, p. 339.

[6] Quoted in Calcutta Review, vol. xvi. p. 87-8.

towns, a greater sum than 1*l.* 10*s.* a year, or one penny a day, cannot be taken as the general average earnings in India. It appears, therefore, that whilst the Englishman contributes sixteen days' labour in each year to the maintenance of institutions which provide him with the utmost security to life and property, the Indian ryot contributes an equivalent to the labour of fifty-three days for the support of institutions which, so far as they tend to afford him any security from oppression, or in any way to ameliorate his social condition, might as well be swept from the face of the earth, deep into the Indian Ocean.

If that unhappy land suffers from the amount of her taxation, the mode in which that revenue is raised presses with still greater severity upon her industry. The taxes which will now be examined are those on land and salt. The opium-tax is felt but little by the natives of India, and that only within certain districts, where the evil arises more from the temptations to smuggle, and the consequent vexatious nature of the government supervision.

In the early part of this chapter I have endeavoured to shew the nature of the tenure under which land was held in India and was assessed to the sovereign, as also the system which prevailed under the Mahomedan rulers of India. The former is still working to perfection, not only in the many native states of Hindostan, but in our own north-west provinces and the Punjab, where the Company did not feel it safe to overturn the existing order of things, as they had done in earlier acquired territories. In those districts, we are assured by a writer well qualified to give an opinion, that the old native system works admirably.[7] The people are thriving, the tax is easily collected, and there are no complaints.

It may be said that experience has taught the Indian executive wisdom, and they are giving the newly-acquired territories the benefit of it. An impartial mind might be inclined to think that it would be as well if some of the older provinces reaped a share of the advantage, especially as it has been purchased at their expense.

It will neither interest the reader nor serve any good purpose to dwell upon the many patchwork experiments, the numberless fiscal tinkerings, which the unhappy land was made to undergo from the time of the first British occupancy of India until the famous "permanent settlement" of Lord Cornwallis in 1793, a year fatal to the peace and welfare of millions of industrious cultivators.

His lordship was one of those amiable men who contribute largely

7 Campbell's Modern India, chap. viii.

to the stock of "good intentions" which are said to pave the way of a certain region; and truly his "intentions" have paved the way to beggary and death for myriads of Hindoo ryots.[8] In his endeavour to fix the land-revenues of Bengal upon a firm and profitable footing, Lord Cornwallis perpetrated one of the greatest wrongs, committed one of the most enormous blunders, that is to be found on record. He propounded a scheme by which the proprietary right in the whole soil of Bengal was to be vested in the zemindars or hereditary *superintendents* of land, not for one year, or ten years, but for ever. They had been the farmers of the land-tax for years past; they stood in that capacity between government and the village proprietors and cultivators; but to suppose that therefore they possessed any claim to the land yielding that tax, was a monstrosity reserved for the conception of this very amiable nobleman. The scheme, hollow and unrighteous as it was, seemed to promise such security to the revenue by creating this large class of landed aristocracy by a mere stroke of the pen, that the authorities at home were deceived into compliance, and the fiat went forth by which twenty millions of small landholders were dispossessed of their rights, and handed over, bound hand and foot, to the tender mercies of a set of exacting rack-renters.

The injustice of this gigantic robbery, great though it seems, was not by any means the whole of the cruelty. Wrong upon wrong was committed; fraud upon fraud. It was ordered that the amount of the assessment should be made in conformity with the average yield of former years; but it was in reality laid at such a rate as would suffice to meet the pressing wants of the government, and that rate was above fifty to sixty per cent of the produce of the soil! More than this; although the regulations of 1793 expressly determined the rate to be paid by the newly-created Cornwallis-aristocracy as above stated, not one word was said as to the amount *they might levy on the ryots.* What that amount has been, there is unfortunately but too little doubt.* The only limit to the exaction seems to have been the utter inability of the wretched people to pay any more. Lord Brougham, in speaking of this celebrated settlement, said that it wrung from the ryot eighteen shillings out of every twenty. His assertion was laughed at as a figure of speech; but unfortunately he spoke literally within the mark. Mr. Colebrook, well acquainted with the resources of the country, states[9]

8 "The 'permanent settlement' has produced more distress and beggary, and a greater change in the landed property of Bengal, than has happened in the same space of time in any age or country by the mere effect of internal regulations."—*Fifth Report of Finance Committee of Bengal.*

* Appendix C.

that a cultivator paying half his produce in tax is worse off than a hired labourer in the same field at three pence a day. The condition, therefore, of those from whom eighty and ninety per cent are wrung may be readily imagined.

The zemindars did not fail to use the new power given to them to the utmost stretch. Summary process was allowed them against the ryots, and this begat such misery, strife, and litigation, that the law-courts were literally overwhelmed with land-cases. In a single season there was in one district, that of Burdwan, thirty thousand suits of zemindars against ryots ![10] It is true the government regulations stipulate that the former shall not exact from the latter more than the local rate; but the difficulty is to determine what *is* the local rate, though that point is always settled against the poorer suitor, to his utter ruin.

Under this zemindari system the oppression of the ryots is aggravated by the custom of sub-letting the land-tax to various grades of middlemen, who, interposing between the zemindar of the district and the cultivator, adding their own shares of profit to that of the great man, and having no sort of interest in the matter beyond extorting as much as possible in a given time, press upon the means of the wretched tiller of the soil, until his case is so hopeless, that, worn out by years of toil and oppression, he flies from the scenes of his misery, and if he has not heart enough left to turn docoit (gang-robber), in all probability dies of starvation in the jungle.[11]

Ever in poverty, the ryot is compelled to seek aid from the mahajun or money-lender. This man will usually be one of the sub-renters of the land-tax; and availing himself of that position, demands whatever rate of interest he pleases, and which often amounts to one per cent per week—fifty-two per cent per annum. More than this, the accounts of these advances are kept only by the lender, who, aware of the utter ignorance of the ryots, falsifies his books without the least fear of detection. Thus at the end of the year, however favourable the season may have been, whatever the amount of crop, the mahajun, uniting his

9 Remarks on the Husbandry of Bengal.

10 Calcutta Review, vol. vi. p. 318.

11 That I am not dealing in fiction may be ascertained by reference to the evidence on this subject given before the Parliamentary Committee in 1830 by Mr. H. C. Christian, of the Board of Revenue of Lower Bengal; Mr. F. Fortescue, Commissioner for Civil Affairs at Delhi, and others equally beyond suspicion of overstating the case against the government system. The following evidence given on that occasion by Mr. Mill, the *Company's* historian, is worth noting. "They (the zemindars) take from them (the ryots) all they can get: in short, they exact whatever they please. They (the ryots) have no defence whatever but that of removal; they must decline to pay what is exacted and quit the land."

claim as money-lender to that as Talukdar or sub-renter, makes it appear, with the aid of fifty per cent interest, false entries, and increased rent, that the *whole* belongs to him. Should the ryot appear in sufficiently good health to toil on for another season, he may obtain from the mahajun further advances for seed, tools, and his own miserable existence, which is barely supported on pulse, roots, and wild herbs, with occasionally a little salt, taxed five hundred per cent by the government, and another five hundred per cent by dealers' profits and cost of transport!

To the above must be added the iniquitous practice of extorting *abwabs*, or presents, from the villagers upon every possible occasion.[12] These abwabs are of long standing; and although the enactment of 1793 expressly declares them to be illegal, and punishable by fine, they exist to this day in pristine vigour. Every feast, festival, or visit received by the talukdar or zemindar is made the pretext for robbery. The herdsman furnishes a goat, the milkman milk and ghee, the oil-maker supplies oil, and so on through the community. Nor is it only the renters who thus extort; every one of their subordinates, from the naib, or accountant, who helps to falsify the books, down to the paiks, or collecting and distraining peons, exact their own share of abwab; and so long as the ryot possesses any thing worth drawing from him, so long is he a subject for oppression and wrong; when the hydraulic pressure ceases to squeeze another drop from him, he is only then cast off as a useless object.

To seek protection in the local courts of *justice*, the poor wretch knows from sad experience is worse than useless. There the renter is all-powerful with the amlahs of the courts, and there *he* is powerless. He toils on, dispirited and hopeless, feeling certain that before long he shall be worn out, and then flung aside to make room for a younger and stouter ryot. There are doubtless exceptions to this sad state of things under some humane zemindars, but they are few indeed and far between. The rule is misery and starvation—the exception, a bare subsistence. The whole of this wretchedness may not arise immediately from the permanent settlement of 1793, but it has its origin in it. What that has left undone, the inefficiency of our local executive and the corruption of the courts have consummated, until trade has died away, agriculture become a desperate and hopeless struggle, and the

12 Mr. Piddington, a civilian, in his replies to the queries of the Board of Revenue says, in reference to these extortions, "I fear to be discredited when I state, that from twenty to forty per cent on the actual jummabundi (legal rent) is yearly extorted from the poor ryot."

native community merged into two classes—a monied aristocracy, and a beggarly race of peasants, who, though nominally free-born British subjects, are more degraded and less cared for than the slaves of Cuba or the serfs of Russia. Yet these are the men through whose ill-requited labours the Indian government derive fifteen millions sterling of their annual income, about two-thirds of their entire revenue.

In strong contrast to the permanent or zemindari settlement of Bengal is the ryotwari system of Madras, which, though differing from the former so essentially in its machinery, has proved scarcely less fatal to the industry of a once thriving, happy country. I cannot do better than describe the nature of this system of assessment, as originated by Sir T. Munro in 1812, in the words of a civilian well acquainted with the workings of the various settlements:[13]

"The assessment is rather fieldwar than ryotwar. The government deals directly, not only with each ryot, but with each field. Instead of assessing each village, it assesses each plot of ground. A field is not, in India, a large piece of land fenced and hedged, but a minute portion, suited to the minute tenantry, divided from the rest by a little gathering together of the earth about six inches high. Fencing is not common; and in a dry flat plain containing thousands of such fields side by side, it may be supposed that boundaries are only permanent when the fields belong to different owners on the spot, with different interests. Moreover, instead of assessing at a fixed sum for a series of years, there is fixed on each *field* a maximum rent to be paid for good seasons and good crops; and it is undertaken, not as an incidental indulgence, but as an essential part of the system," that this rent shall be annually reduced when necessary. "To effect then the commutation of the share of grain into money-rates, all the land was surveyed according to the native mode of measurement . . . . . there were no maps."

Such is the mechanism of this system, and upon this the collector has to base his preliminary or standard settlement. After this first survey another and final inspection has to be made:

"When the crops are nearly ripe, the collector goes out into the district to look at them and make his annual settlement. The village accountant makes out a statement shewing the cultivation of each ryot, his crops and circumstances, the number of his cattle, sheep, and children . . . . . At this time all who think they should not pay full rent apply for reduction. All these cases are settled, and *then only*

[13] Mr. G. Campbell, in his Modern India.

does the collector make up his annual settlement, grant formal leases, and take formal engagements for the crop, which by this time is *past*, and generally *paid for*. The settlement is not made up till *after* the crop is ripe, in fact, generally does not reach the collector's office till *after* most of the money has already got there, and after making all the remissions and reductions of the season from the standard assessment."

The suffering and poverty entailed by this ryotwari system of assession are admitted by every one at all acquainted with the existing state of things in the Madras presidency. It has been well known to the home authorities for many years past, yet no attempt has been made at reformation, although it is found most difficult to get ryots to cultivate land under it, and that the cultivation is only kept up by forcing, by government advances, &c.

The evils of this state of things are only equalled by the absurdity of supposing that any collector is really able to deal separately and efficiently with 150,000 tenants, as is often the case, "not one of whom has a lease, but each pays *according as he cultivates and gets a crop, and with reference to his cattle, sheep, and children*, and each of whom gets a reduction if he can make out a sufficiently good case. What a cry of agricultural distress and large families there would be in England or any other country under such a system! Would any farmer ever admit that his farm had yielded any thing, that his cattle had produced, or that his wife had not produced? If the collector were one of the prophets, and remained in the same district to the age of Methuselah, he would not be fit for the duty; and as he is but an ordinary man and a foreigner, and continually changed, it would be strange if the native subordinates did not do as they liked, and having the power, did not abuse it. Accordingly, it is generally agreed that the abuses of the whole system, and especially that of remission, is something frightful; and that the opportunities of extortion, peculation, chicanery, and intrigue of all kinds, are unbounded."[14]

The above, it must be remembered, is the testimony of a member of the Honourable Company's service, and given but the other day. What the results of that "peculation, extortion, chicanery," &c., are likely to be, the reader may imagine from what he has read of the effects of the Bengal settlement.[15]

[14] Modern India, chap. viii. p. 361.

[15] "In many instances the earnings of a ryot are not sufficient for his family; and his wife and sons are obliged to betake themselves to some pursuit, and assist him with all they can get. He lives generally upon coarse rice and *dholl* (pulse); vegetables and fish would be luxuries. His dress consists of a bit of rag and a slender

The system pursued in the Bombay presidency, although based on the ryotwari, has been so modified, contrary to the wishes of the home authorities, as to be comparatively a harmless affair. Its chief evil, indeed, is one that more nearly concerns the government—that of the enormous cost of collection of the tax. This tax, within the division I am now referring to, produced in 1849-50 a gross sum of 2,290,969*l.*; against which were placed allowances to district and village officers, *mosques, temples*, &c., 982,684*l.*, and a further charge for collecting of 280,000*l.*, in all 1,262,684*l.*; considerably more than 100 per cent on the net revenue from this source!

I will now briefly touch upon the salt-tax, than which no more impolitic or unjust impost could well be devised. The climate, not less than the vegetable nature of the food of the population, renders the free use of this article one of imperative necessity, if due regard be had to health. Yet we find a tax laid on it amounting to five shillings the *maund* of 82 lbs., being nearly four hundred per cent on its prime cost in Calcutta, and which, with all the profits of the wholesale and retail dealers, the cost of transport up-country, and the further profits of the country licensed dealers, who, of course, require a profit on the duty as well as the original cost of the salt, brings the selling price to the consumer to something like a thousand per cent on the original value. This is on an article, it must be remembered, which the poor ryot needs more of than the wealthy dwellers in towns, who can obtain other condiments with their food, and who require far less, owing to the difference in their dietary.

The enhanced price is, however, not the only evil inflicted on the poorer consumers. Every dealer through whose hands the article passes mixes with it a portion of sand, to add to its weight. The first or wholesale vendor in Calcutta will blend ten per cent of its weight of sand; the agent who buys from him for transmission up the country adds another ten per cent; the up-country dealer follows his example; and by the time it reaches the ryot through the bazaar vendor, the salt will be nearly half impurity, dark in colour, and flavourless to a degree.

chudder (sheet); his bed is composed of a coarse mat and a pillow; his habitation a thatched roof; and his property a plough, two bullocks, one or two *lotahs* (brass pots), and some *bijdhan*. He toils 'from morn to noon, from noon to dewy eve;' and, despite this, he is a haggard, poverty-smitten, wretched creature. This is no exaggeration; even in ordinary seasons, and under ordinary circumstances, the ryots may often be seen fasting for days and nights for want of food. The inability of the ryot to better his degraded condition, in which he has been placed by the causes we have named, is increased by his mental debasement. Unprotected, harassed, and oppressed, he has been precluded from the genial rays of intellectuality. His mind is veiled in a thick gloom of ignorance."—*Indian Petition presented by the Earl of Albemarle.*

So systematic is this fraud, that should any more scrupulous dealer dare to sell a clean, wholesome article, the whole trade will league against him, and by means of the bribed aid of the native police, soon effect his ruin.

The only defence for this tax is, that it yields an amount of revenue that cannot be spared; precisely the reason given, for centuries past, by all upholders of vicious taxation in every part of the world. Of a truth, it can hardly be spared, when we look at the costly establishment of the Honourable Company. This tax, which in the early days of our sway in India produced but 100,000*l*., is now made to yield nearly three millions and a quarter sterling. Whilst such wickednesses as the Afghan campaigns are permitted; whilst commanders-in-chief are allowed to pocket half a million sterling in a few years, for civil duties never performed nor expected to be performed; whilst the salaries of Indian officials obtain, on a scale of regal extravagance, out of all proportion even in a highly civilised and prosperous country; whilst the mockery of the home government is continued at its present cost,—it is of course impossible to forego the proceeds of a tax, however iniquitous, however fatal to the industry of the country.

To attempt an enumeration of the privations endured, of the oppression, the extortion, and the robbery practised by the subordinates engaged in the salt department of the government, would carry me far beyond my limits in this volume. Enough has been said as to the use made by those who, clothed in a little brief authority, have it in their power to tyrannise over the poor of the land. It may afford a tolerable idea of the extent of these iniquities, to mention, as a known fact, that natives frequently pay largely to their *European superiors* for the most trivial appointments in this branch of the service. Places with a salary attached of thirty-five rupees a month have been thus disposed of for five hundred rupees, paid monthly to the European; the probability being that the native clears another five hundred of net profit!

All this is humiliating to know. It is humbling to the honest pride of an Englishman, to feel that we, who have so long pictured ourselves as the apostles of freedom, as a pattern of national integrity amongst the kingdoms of the earth, should have been for ages, even up to the present moment, abettors of all these crying iniquities.

PART III.

PHYSICAL.

CHAPTER I.

HINDOO ART AND SCIENCE.

ALTHOUGH the nations of the West have far outstripped the Asiatics in art and science, no less than in other branches of human skill and ingenuity, the craftsman of the East can point to ages long past, when as yet the people of European countries were unknown, even by name—when the Christian religion had not been proclaimed to the nations of the earth—as to a period when his country shone as a bright luminary amidst the darkness around; when intellect and skilled labour had their home in his fertile and beautiful land; when all that was intelligent, and rare, and excellent, was to be found within the limits of Hindostan.

Every wreck that we meet with pertaining to this wonderful country tells the same tale of departed greatness and excellence. Perhaps with few things is the modern student of history more struck than with the architectural remains of the Hindoo period.

The great antiquity of the works of extruction or excavation, which are to-day met with in many parts of India, bears testimony to the fact of superior skill having been employed upon them. If we find few objects of construction remaining to attest the position of this science in the early days of Hindooism, a ready reason may be found in the numberless successive invasions of the land which took place, and during which havoc and ruin were but too frequently the accompaniments, prompted by bigotry and religious fanaticism. The stupendous rock-cut temples of Ellora, Ajunta, and Elephanta, have, from the peculiarity of their structure, defied these agents of destruction; and, in the case of the two latter at any rate, are witnesses to the skill and industry of the Hindoo craftsmen in an age when what we term civilisation was as yet unborn.

Although we possess a multitude of pictures and plans illustrative of the architectural remains of Hindostan, the subject does not appear to have engaged the attention of any professional man on the spot: I am therefore under the necessity of dwelling on this topic in a brief and general manner, wanting any connected detail of the styles practised throughout India in the various periods during which architecture may be said to have flourished in that country.

There is, however, one exception to this general neglect of the study of Eastern architecture: an enterprising officer of the Indian army has shewn, by a connected series of drawings, that in Cashmere a style prevailed as regular and severe in its details as those of Greece and Rome. It may therefore reasonably be conjectured that similar results will attend like inquiry in other parts of India, and that at no distant date we may be in possession of a perfect system of Indian architecture as practised in the early part of our era.

ANCIENT COLUMN.

From the limited data we possess of the raised edifices of Hindostan, the Indian architects would appear to have indulged in the most fanciful and grotesque vagaries, agreeing neither with taste nor propriety. The Hindoo columns, for instance, are met with of all shapes and all dimensions. Sometimes we find them tall, slender, and thickly placed;[1] again they are found ponderous and massive, with the lowest fourth of their height square; the next kind is eight-sided, the third sixteen-sided, and the upper part round. In many instances we meet with columns having a double capital with a low flat base; and others, again, forming perhaps a portion of the same temple, with shafts of only one fourth of their height, the remaining three-fourths being all base and capital.[2]

As many as twelve distinct kinds of mouldings appear in these temples, some few of which bear a close resemblance to our own, but they are mostly quite original in their character. The Hindoo style, so far as it is known, is believed to bear an affinity to that of the Egyptian;

[1] Elphinstone, vol. i. p. 303.

[2] Journal of Asiatic Society of Bengal, vol. xvii. part ii. p. 242.

and in the hugeness, the massiveness of some of the works still extant, a degree of resemblance may perhaps be traced; but in most other respects the two would seem to be widely different. In many of the Hindoo buildings there is a great profusion of ornamental work about the panels, door-posts, and other parts, not inelegantly formed, and frequently blended with a considerable degree of taste.

REMAINS OF HINDOO ARCHITECTURE.

In many cases the walls are covered with representations of the wars of the gods, and groups illustrative of ancient legends. But the temples of Hindostan are all deficient in boldness and grandeur, and frequently wanting in their due proportions of height and breadth. Such faults are not, however, observable in the caves and subterraneous structures, which are remarkable for their regularity, not less than their sublime vastness. These gigantic excavations are very numerous throughout India; the mountains of Cashmere are said to contain twelve thousand of them. The caves of Ellora are of Buddhistical origin, and are not supposed to be very ancient indeed; they are known to have been executed as late as the eighth or ninth century of the Christian era.

The prodigious extent of most of these rock-cut temples astonishes the spectator not less than the elaborate finish of their complicated details delights him. The ingenuity and skill, equally with the labour of the architects, must have been called into active demonstration in the excavation of these extraordinary places. Perhaps there are none more celebrated and truly magnificent in their solemn vastness than the caves of Ajunta.

They are situated in a wild and picturesque part of the peninsula, excavated from a portion of the huge ghauts, which, to the south of the valley of the Taptee, rise some hundreds of feet, and support the great table-land of the Deccan. The entrance to the caves is through one of the many narrow and winding ravines which exist in various parts of these ghauts. They are twenty-seven in number, and vary as much in their size as in their form and degree of ornament. A few of them are vaulted without cells; but by far the greater number are monastic in construction, having cells and flat roofs. In one or two of these caves there exist no ornaments whatever beyond a reeded course over each of the cells; whilst in shape they are square, and about thirty-six feet each way.

In others pillars are found; and here they have been used standing on the cills for the purpose of dividing the windows into three lengths. On the walls are sculptured various figures of lions, antelopes, and boys in attitudes of prayer, executed in the very best style of the ancient Hindoos. It would appear that in more than one instance the walls have been stuccoed and painted; but of these works of art little now remains, not more than sufficient to determine their nature.

The largest of these cave-temples had at one time as many as twenty-nine pillars surrounding the nave; they are simple octagons, without either capital or base; and have been at one time elaborately decorated.

The aisles in this cave are of stone; whilst the nave had evidently been ornamented with wood, which has now disappeared, with the exception of some of the pins and battens which served to fasten it to the rock; as also the fastenings of the ribs, which, having been sunk to some depth in the solid rock, still remain. The whole of the walls appear to have been covered with ornamental stucco-work; and on some of the pillars, as well as in the panels of the roof of the aisles, a few of the paintings still remain in tolerable preservation. There are also the remains of several inscriptions; but, with the exception of one on the exterior of the cave, high above the entrance, they are too imperfect to be of service. The external inscription alluded to is of some length, and in the Lath character; from which it may be inferred that these excavations were the work of the first or second century before our era.

There are others of these temple-caves of later date, richly ornamented, and in some instances in tolerably good preservation. The walls are covered with human figures, many of which are fully armed, and illuminated with scrolls and wreaths of flowers; whilst the pillars are gracefully and artistically formed. Some of these groupings are executed with a high degree of art, bearing in mind the age in which they must have been executed; they certainly leave the works of Europe of the same period far behind in perspective, grouping, and general details. The human figure is especially well executed. The character of all these caves is Buddhistical, the figure of that deity being found in several of them.

CAVE TEMPLE.

There are still many noble remains of the palatial residences of the Hindoo and Tartar chiefs of India, some of them in good preservation. They are remarkable for their solidity rather than style; the roofs are terraced, the floors built one above another, frequently to an immense height. The state-rooms of these residences are on the upper floors, and open on one side; the stairs being narrow and steep, and dug out from the depth of the wall.

The tanks are very extensive, some of them stretching for several miles and of enormous strength; temples are frequently built round their edges, and shrines on the steps leading to them. Some of these useful public works more closely resemble lakes than artificial reservoirs, and frequently serve to fertilise an entire district. The value of these stupendous works can scarcely be over-estimated in a country so subject to droughts as Hindostan. The Hindoo and Mahomedan rulers of the country were well aware of their great importance, and spared no pains to keep them in good order. It was left for their English successors to neglect these and the equally valuable works of roads and bridges. The wells are both deep and broad; galleries run round the walls, and broad stone steps are carried beneath these down to the water's edge. Such of their bridges as remain are composed of stone posts, held together by beams of masonry, some of which are surmounted by small Gothic arches.

The order of architecture prevailing in Cashmere, and which has been denominated the "Arian order,"[3] exhibits undoubted traces of Grecian art, and is distinguished alike for its graceful outline, its massive boldness, and the happy propriety of its decorations. Amongst the peculiarities of this order are its lofty roofs, its trefoiled doors, surmounted by pyramidal pediments, and its wide intercolumniations.

The temples of Cashmere are of three kinds: the oblong, the square, and the octagonal; which are again subdivided into the closed and the open, the latter having doors on four sides; the former but one entrance. In their proportions the architects appear to have made the height of a temple equal to twice its breadth; and this has been but in few cases departed from. Their basements are divided into two kinds, the massive and the light, according to the character of their mouldings. The walls of the Cashmerian temples are made of huge blocks of gray limestone, secured together by iron clamps; their dimensions vary

[3] So called from the Greek architectural term *Araiostyle* applied to the intercolumniation of four diameters, and which is one of the distinguishing features of the architecture of Cashmere.

considerably, the older ones being shorter than those of more recent origin.

The roofs of these Cashmerian temples are of pyramidal shape, sometimes broken into two equal portions, divided by a broad moulding, and occasionally into three or four such divisions. The height of the portico varies in different localities; sometimes it reaches only to one-third of the height of the roof; in others it extends to the top of the roof.

The pillars in the Cashmerian temples are of two kinds, round and square; and, unlike the many varieties of Hindoo pillars, are always divided into the three distinct parts of base, shaft, and capital. The square pillars are only employed in corner positions; whilst the round pillars are used throughout the colonnades, and in porches. These are always fluted with from sixteen to twenty-four flutes; the numbers increasing with the diameter of the column. The shafts were usually three or four diameters in height. The capital seems to have been nearly always equal in its height to the upper diameter of the column. The heights and breadths of the bases do not appear to have been formed by any fixed rule. The distances between the columns were nearly always equal to two-thirds of the total height of the pillars.[4]

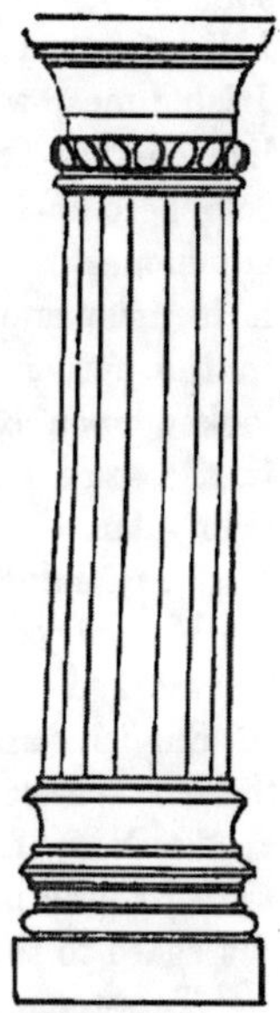

ARIAN PILLAR.

The Hindoo paintings are generally accurate; but they seldom evince much attention to light and shade. Some of their walls are ornamented by mythological representations, as already stated; others by battles, figures of human beings, and animals, sometimes accompanied by an awkward attempt at a landscape. They have also pictures and illustrated manuscripts; but with the figures of these they were not very happy. The portraits executed by the Mussulmans are far superior to those of the Hindoos.

In the manipulation and laying on of their colours they were very successful; so much so, that at the present time many of the paintings to be found in the rock-cut temples appear as fresh and brilliant as though but the work of a few years since; whereas many of them must have existed for little less than 2000 years. In the paintings

[4] Journal of Asiatic Society of Bengal, vol. xvii. part ii. pp. 241-327.

alluded to, especially in those of Ajunta, there has been far more attention bestowed on the grouping than is usually met with in Hindoo works of art; and at the same time a nearer approach to modern notions of perspective.

The Hindoo music consists of eighty-four modes, each of which possesses a different expression, capable of exciting emotions and feelings of various kinds.[5] These modes derive their names from the seasons and hours, to which they are supposed to bear reference in some way. Some of the airs are remarkable for their sweet and melodious sounds; some bear a striking resemblance to the Scotch and Irish tunes; whilst others are characterised by a native wildness peculiar only to this nation. For the due appreciation of their songs, a solo, accompanied by the vicca or Indian lyre, should be heard. The commonest music is performed with the fingers on drums or fiddles; it is noisy and discordant, particularly when the native singers unite in the uproar. It is said that the ordinary Hindoo musicians are looked upon by those of their countrymen who are versed in the art, in the same light as the street ballad-singer of this country is by a prima donna of the Italian Opera.

The fondness of the natives of India, especially the inhabitants of the Malabar and Coromandel coasts, for this monotonous music is not less marked than their indifference to the most finished performance of an English band. A native who passes heedlessly a house in which the most perfect instrumentation may be heard, will pause enraptured at the door of a mud-hut wherein a party of women and children are seated round a huge tom-tom, or drum, beating it vehemently in utter disregard to the rules of harmony.

Tom-toms and small wheezy pipes are the invariable attendants at all Buddhistical festivities, during which a score of these discordant instruments will not unfrequently do duty night and day.

On the antiquity of the Hindoo medical system, oriental scholars are not agreed. The impression is, however, strong amongst those who have examined the question in all its bearings, that the Hindoos are in no ways indebted to the Greek writers for any portion of their medical knowledge; but rather that the latter may have derived some of their earlier data from an Eastern source.

The *Ayur Veda*, which is the most ancient of the Hindoo works on medicine, is said to have been the production of Brahma himself; whilst

[5] Asiatic Researches, vol. iii. pp. 55-87.

the works of Susruta and Charaka abound in details which furnish abundance of evidence as to the knowledge attained in India in those days. Anatomy formed an essential part of the Hindoo practice; and it does not appear that any prejudice existed in regard to their using the dead for the advantage of the living.

According to the Hindoo practice of medicine, life consists of a combination of the soul, the mind, the five senses, and the three qualities of goodness, passion, and meekness.[6] The soul is believed to be the animating principle of the body, and a shadow or emanation from God the Eternal. The vital principle is supposed to be situated in the centre of the chest, and to be the result of a mixture of the pure fluid; in the same manner as the bee sucks the juice from different flowers, and produces honey.[7] The vital parts of the body are one hundred and seven; and their medical writers were, moreover, well acquainted with the serious consequences attending a wound on the great toe, in the palm of the hand, or in the groin.

The Hindoo system divides the life of man into twelve distinct phases, each having its own peculiar characteristic, until that of decrepitude, in which the body resembles an old house, requiring many props in the rainy season. Death is believed to be the separation of the soul from the body, and is supposed to occur in one hundred and one ways, of which one only is natural. The body after death is by them likened to a house without a tenant, and is burnt, in order that it may be purified to join the mass of the elements of which the earth is composed.

Hindoo practitioners declare that diseases owe their origin to three causes: to sins committed in a former existence, and in this list they wisely place all those which defy their skill; to derangements of the humours, the only diseases which yield to their art; and lastly, to a combination of the two, which also are of the incurable class.

The materia medica of the Hindoos embraces not only a vast number of drugs and vegetable simples abounding in their country, but a variety of chemical compounds, as well as acids and some of the oxides, with the uses of which they appear to have been conversant from an early period. Their pharmacy, although embracing many matters of value, and in some parts much in accordance with European practice, is nevertheless so overcrowded with innumerable substances as to bewilder and perplex the student. They employed in their pharmacy prepara-

[6] Wise's Hindoo System of Medicine.

[7] Calcutta Review, vol. viii. art. Hindoo Medicine.

tions of mercury, gold, zinc, iron, and arsenic to a degree that could scarcely have been expected from people who blended so much of the fabulous and the absurd in their practice. In their measures of time they commenced with fifteen winks of the eye; and their apothecaries might begin with four of the particles of dust which are seen floating in the sun's rays as they enter a dark room. The rules laid down for the administering of medicinal doses are minute to tediousness; and among other things it is expressly stated that the patient must not make faces when taking medicine, as by doing so he would be like Brahma and Shiva, and therefore commit a great sin.

However deficient we find the present race of Hindoo practitioners in the science of surgery, there is no doubt but that their ancestors possessed a skill in the performance of delicate and dangerous operations scarcely to have been expected in those days. The treatises still extant on these subjects are good proof of the state of their surgery, which, however, was evidently, as in other branches of the art, mixed up with much puerility and childish superstition. Certain times were to be selected for the performance of operations; devils were to be driven away from the wound by burning certain sweet-scented flowers; the patient and operator must be placed in certain relative positions, and other observances equally frivolous and absurd.

In the writings of Charaka, one of the oldest medical authors of Hindostan, we find the number three availed of to a great extent in the medical system. Thus it is stated that there are three general causes of diseases; three sorts of medicine—one that cleanses internally, one that purifies externally, and another that includes the aid of surgical skill; three objects of inquiry in this world—the means of preserving health, the means of acquiring wealth, and the securing of happiness in a future existence; there are also three means of preserving life—"proper food, sleep, and the proper government of the senses and passions." The following instructions in the case of a patient suffering from some incurable disease, and which is therefore considered as the result of sins committed in a former state, will hardly be coincided in by European science. "If a disease be incurable," says the code, "let the patient advance in a straight path towards the invisible north-eastern point, feeding on air and water, until his mortal frame totally decay, and his soul becomes linked with the Supreme Being."[8]

Small-pox and measles appear to have been familiar to the Hindoo

[8] Manu, chap. vi.

practitioner in ages far remote; as, indeed, there is no doubt that it is to the East we are indebted for at any rate the former of these complaints. Inoculation seems to have been practised amongst them, but with limited success. The whole string of nervous diseases, rheumatic affections, leprosy, and epilepsy were all well known to, and written upon, by Hindoo physicians of an early date, as was also insanity.

We find, in their medical treatises, mention made of sixty-five diseases of the mouth, twenty diseases of the ear, thirty-one of the nose, eleven qualities of headache, besides an infinity of disorders of the throat. Mention is likewise made of consumption, as though it were not only of frequent occurrence, but oftentimes fatal in its result.

The study of poisons and their antidotes formed by no means an insignificant portion of medical study among the Hindoo practitioners of all ages; a fact, considering the oriental fashion of getting rid of an enemy by this means, is not to be wondered at. There was also the study of animal poisons; the dissertations upon the bites of snakes, poisonous insects, &c. are numerous, and at the same time in accordance with the practice of experienced surgeons of the present day. Hydrophobia was also known, and prescribed for in a variety of forms.[9]

That the science of astronomy was understood by the Hindoos at an early period there is strong evidence; though it is not so easy to determine at what precise time that knowledge first obtained amongst them. It is clear, however, that although the ability to calculate eclipses was possessed by the Hindoo astronomers at a distant epoch, their acquaintance with celestial bodies has made little if any progress during several centuries.

The astronomical works of the Hindoos are of two kinds, scientific treatises and tables. Of the latter, four are in existence; the most complete, and, it is believed, the most ancient of which is known to European astronomers as the Tirvalore Tables. The chief astronomical work of India, the Surya Siddhanta, upon which all their tables appear to have been founded, was for some time believed to have been of very extraordinary antiquity. Doubts were subsequently thrown upon the validity of this claim; and more recent inquirers have shewn, with some degree of plausibility, that this work can scarcely boast of any higher antiquity than about the tenth or eleventh century of the Christian era.

The astronomical system of the East, as contained in the above

9 Wise's Commentary on the Hindoo System of Medicine.

work, differs in very few particulars from that of Ptolemy. Their notions of the heavenly orbs appear to be, that the earth is placed in the centre of the celestial system, with the moon, the sun, and the planets revolving around it. The Siddhanta accounts for the irregularities in the motion of the sun and moon, by a theory that those bodies move in epicycles, whose centres revolve in circles; shewing an utter ignorance of the eccentricity of the earth's and moon's orbits. The main scope and object of Hindoo astronomy is, after all, the calculations of eclipses; which is admitted to be accomplished by their rules with a rare degree of accuracy. The process by which these results are arrived at is remarkably ingenious, but at the same time exceedingly tedious; and there are few, if any, of the native professors of the present day who are able to explain the theory of the system, however apt they may be in working out its details.

It is not a little remarkable that the Hindoos divide the Zodiac, and name those divisions, almost precisely as is done in our system; a fact which induces the belief that this, and the divisions of the Arabs, from which ours was derived, must at some very remote period have had one common origin. Their signs are twelve in number, and are termed:

Mesha, the Ram.
Vrisha, the Bull.
Mit'hunna, the Pair.
Carcota, the Crab.
Sinha, the Lion.
Canya, the Virgin.

Tula, the Balance.
Vrischica, the Scorpion.
Dhanus, the Bow.
Macara, the Sea-monster.
Cumbha, the Ewer.
Mina, the Fish.

In like manner they connect the seven planets with the days of the week, and name those days in reference to the planets precisely as is done by us.

Thus we find them to have the planets as follows: *Addila*, the sun; *Toma*, the moon; *Brahaspati*, Jupiter; *Mangala*, Mars; *Bonta*, Mercury; *Soucra*, Venus; *Sanni*, Saturn. Their week begins on Friday, and the days are thus named:

1. *Soncravaram*, or day of Venus . . . . Friday.
2. *Sanivaram*, ,, Saturn . . . . Saturday.
3. *Additavaram*, ,, the Sun . . . . Sunday.
4. *Somavaram*, ,, the Moon . . . Monday.
5. *Mangalavaram*, ,, Mars . . . . . . Tuesday.
6. *Bontavaram*, ,, Mercury . . . Wednesday.
7. *Brahaspativaram*, ,, Jupiter . . . . Thursday.

It appears that the Hindoo astronomers were well aware that the intersection of the equator and ecliptic is not always in the same point, leading to the difference called the precession of the equinoxes. This difference they reckoned at fifty-four seconds in a year, being precisely four seconds too much.

To find the latitude of a place, the Hindoos observe the length of the shadow of a perpendicular gnomon when the sun is in the equator, and compute the angle which their instrument makes with the line drawn from its top to the extremity of the shadow. The longitude is found by observations of lunar eclipses calculated from the meridian of Lanca, which passes through Ongein, in the Mahratta country.

The progress of the Hindoos in other branches of science may be considered as remarkable. Great geometrical skill was shewn by their demonstration of the various properties of triangles, especially of that one which expresses the area in the terms of the three sides, and which remained unknown for a long period in Europe, as shewn by their knowledge of the proportion of the radius to the circumference of the circle.

Beyond their own country the writers of Indian geography in the earlier ages appear to have been completely at fault, and the boldest of modern speculators have been unable to rescue any thing like sound information from the best of their books.

Few even of the neighbouring towns are mentioned; but they seem to have known something of the Greeks, their knowledge having, most probably, been obtained after the expedition of Alexander the Great. To the Greeks they applied the name of *Yarvan;* but this term was afterwards applied to all the conquering people who came from the north-west; and there is some reason to suppose that they knew the Scythians under the name of Sacæ. But it was within India that they became acquainted with both these nations, and they appear to have been totally ignorant of the regions whence the strangers came.

The first indication of any knowledge among the Hindoos of the inhabitants of the outer world, appears in a writer of the seventh or eighth century, who states that the barbaric tongues are called the Parasica, Yavana, Raumaen, and Barbara; the three first being supposed to mean the Persian, Greek, and Latin, and the last those of a number of nations whose languages they could not characterise.

China they certainly knew, for we have the travels of a native of that country in India in the fourth century; and the king of Magada is attested by Chinese authors to have sent embassies to China in the second and following centuries of the Christian era. There is a people spoken of in Menu as those of China; but they are alluded to as existing among the tribes who lived to the north-west of India, and most probably were the enterprising community who took possession of the extensive country to which they afterwards gave their name. The term is evidently of Indian origin, though the name of *Chin* was not adopted until long after Menu's time.

The Hindoos, however, were never a navigating people, and from their ignorance of Egypt, and of the inhabitants of those countries in which enterprise had its seat, they seem to have been content with a meagre knowledge of the districts which they themselves inhabited.

CHAPTER II.

THE MANUFACTURES OF INDIA.

A NOTICE of the industry of the Hindoos would be manifestly imperfect without some account of their progress in the manufacture of textile and other fabrics, especially since, in at any rate one of these arts, that of cotton-weaving, they had arrived at a high state of perfection long prior to any extensive manufacture of the article in Europe. If it be also considered, in reference to this branch of industry, that the natives of India, whilst they so far, and for so long, excelled the skilled craftsmen of the West in the production of exquisitely fine muslins, richly worked and highly ornamented, possessed a raw material confessedly of great inferiority to the cotton imported into England from all other parts of the world, we cannot fail to award them a considerable meed of praise. It required the science of a century, the combined efforts of a Watt and an Arkwright, to compete successfully with the simple handicraft of the Indian village-weaver; whilst in some of the finer goods, it is still questionable whether the British capitalist can equal the patient productions of the simple Hindoo.

The actual date of the birth of cotton-weaving in India cannot be arrived at, though there is little doubt of its high antiquity. The cotton plant being indigenous to the country, we have every right to presume that the uses and value of this admirable production of nature would not have been long hidden from the early Hindoos, especially as the art of weaving flax and cotton was well understood by the Assyrians, Egyptians, and other nations of antiquity.

We learn that Joseph was arrayed by Pharaoh in fine linen; and indeed the knowledge of the Egyptians in this respect may be traced on the monumental remains of that country. Layard, in his Assyrian labours, has, amongst other things, demonstrated the degree of perfection to which weaving was brought in the days of Ninevite greatness; and we know, moreover, that the Jews, in the first years of their existence as a nation, employed cloths of various fabrics both linen and cotton, which undoubtedly came from the East.

The earliest records which we possess bearing upon the people and produce of India, inform us of the existence in those remote days of woven cloths of great excellence. One of the oldest Greek authors,[1] in speaking of the land of the Hindoos, says: "The wild trees of that country bear fleeces as their fruit, surpassing those of sheep in beauty and excellence; and the Indians use cloth made from those trees."

Amongst the goods which appear to have been brought to Europe from the Indian seas, in the days when Arab traders were the only medium of intercourse between the eastern and western worlds, we find mentioned cloths of silk and cotton of various colours and devices.[2] It does not appear, however, that there existed any great demand for cottons, the consumption of the Roman people, who were then the customers for all luxuries, being chiefly confined to cloths of silk and wool.

During the early trade of Europeans with India by the long sea route, the calicoes and fine muslins of that country came first into general notice; and from that date until the production of machine-made fabrics in England, they continued to rise in public estimation. It was deemed a great thing with our Lancashire manufacturers, when, by the aid of mechanical and artistic skill, combined with the potent agency of steam, they found themselves able to produce an article which was considered equal to that which the unlettered Hindoo had manipulated in his little mud hut on the remote banks of the Ganges, and which had been produced of like excellence by their ancestors, when the "father of history" penned his observations upon their country.

That the Hindoos paid considerable attention to the details of this manufacture, in the most remote ages, there remains sufficient proof on record. In the Indian work of highest antiquity, the *Rig Veda*,[3] believed to have been written fifteen centuries previous to our era, occurs the following passage: "Cares consume me, Satakralu, although thy worshipper, as a rat gnaws a weaver's threads:"—the temptation to the rat was evidently the starch employed by the spinner to impart tenacity to the thread; nor can there be any doubt that cotton was the thread alluded to.[4]

Again, in *Menu*, we find it directed as follows: "Let the weaver who has received ten palas of cotton-thread, give them back increased of eleven by the rice-water (starch), and the like used in weaving; he who does otherwise shall pay a fine of twelve panas."[5]

[1] Herodotus. [2] Arrian's Periplus. [3] Hymn cv. v. 8.
[4] Royle's Culture of Cotton in India, p. 118. [5] Menu, book viii. p. 397.

The cotton fabrics of India formed a considerable item in the exports from the East to this country during the early days of British Indian commerce; the delicacy of their fabric, the elegance of their design, and the brilliancy of their colours, rendered them as attractive to the better classes of consumers in England, as are, in the present day, the shawls of Cashmere or the silks of Lyons. So much superior indeed were the productions of the Indian spinning-wheel and hand-loom, to those turned out by the manufacturers of Lancashire in the middle of the last century, that not only were Indian calicoes and Indian prints preferred to the home-made articles, but the Manchester and Blackburn weavers actually imported Indian yarns in large quantities for employment in their factories.

It was about the year 1771-2 that the Blackburn weavers, taking advantage of the recent discoveries and improvements of Arkwright, Hargreaves, and others, found themselves in a position to produce plain cotton goods, which, if they did not quite equal the fabrics of the East, at any rate found their way very rapidly into general consumption in Europe.

The invention of the mule-jenny, in 1779, was the commencement of a new era in the history of the cotton manufacture of Great Britain; and when, six years later, Arkwright's machines were thrown open to the public, a revolution was effected in the production of all kinds of yarns; England found herself able, not only to supply all her own wants with cotton goods of every variety of quality, but also to carry the produce of her looms ten thousand miles across the seas, and placing them at the doors of the Indian consumer, undersell the goods made by his own hands from cotton grown in his own garden.

Nor is it only in the heavier goods that we in the West are able to beat out of their own markets the weavers of the East. There have long been masters in their craft who can and do produce fabrics more exquisitely delicate and light in texture than those beautiful muslins of Dacca, so long and justly celebrated with a world-wide fame; and although in some particulars these latter fabrics still claim a certain degree of superiority, and although many of the Hindoos prefer their own woven goods to those of Manchester and Glasgow, the cotton manufacture of British India, in spite of its supply of the raw material growing often close to its door, in spite of labour absurdly cheap, may truly be said to have ceased in favour of the far-off industry of Lancashire and Scotland.

The actual result of this revolution of half a century has been that, in place of our importing cotton goods and yarns from the East to the yearly value of about 800,000*l.*, we are able, in the present day, to ship to the various ports of India cotton fabrics to the value of upwards of three millions sterling. The decay of this branch of our Indian imports has been steady and certain. In 1827-8, Bengal shipped but to the value of 275,000*l.*; in 1837-8, not more than 69,000*l.*; and at the present moment our supplies from the East are limited to about five thousand bales from Madras, solely for re-shipment to our western colonies, and various parts of northern and western Africa.

Calicoes and muslins, both plain and printed, formed a staple of the Portuguese and Dutch trade with India.[6] As early as 1628 these goods were taken by the English merchant to the value of 50,000*l.* Fifty years later they amounted to 160,000*l.* annually, and began to supplant the French goods in the English markets.

Early in the eighteenth century, the British legislature, anxious to foster the home manufacture of cotton goods, prohibited the wearing of Indian muslins and calicoes; but in vain; the latter were so far superior to any that were produced in Europe, that they continued in general use until the discoveries of the spinning-jenny, the power-loom, and the steam-engine flung the competition of the East far into the shade, and created a new era in the industry of mankind.

From the year 1771 to 1793, the annual imports into Great Britain of India piece-goods were, on the average, 1,250,000*l.* From that period until 1806 they appear to have increased to something over 2,000,000*l.*, but afterwards declined to the old figures, and eventually ceased altogether; to be supplanted, in the place of their manufacture, by the produce of the steam-engine.

The French were, previous to the war of the Revolution, large consumers of both calicoes, prints, and muslins, frequently taking as much as their English neighbours. The Dutch purchased these goods to the yearly value of about 100,000*l.*[7] To America, Denmark, Portugal, and Germany, there were also exports of India cottons of about 700,000*l.* annually; and to these may be added as much more for the various ports to the eastward of the Bay of Bengal.

Dacca was the seat of manufacture of the muslins known by that name, and spoken of by the ancients as "woven webs of air." The most delicately worked and highly ornamented scarfs and dresses are wrought at Delhi, Benares, and Ahmedabad. Fine goods were also

[6] Amongst the numerous articles found in the vessels captured by the English in 1592, were "book calicoes, calico lawns, broad white calicoes, fine starched calicoes, and brown broad calicoes; also canopies and diaper towels, quilts and calico carpets, like those from Turkey."—Milburn's *Oriental Commerce*, p. 230.

[7] Milburn's Oriental Commerce.

produced at Allahabad, Hurripaul, and Santipore; whilst the more substantial and useful fabrics were wrought chiefly as Patna, Luckipore, Lucknow, Balasore, and other places in the Bengal presidency, as well as at Pondicherry and Cuddallore, in the presidency of Madras, and in Surat.

Few textile articles require such delicate manipulation as lace; and in this the Hindoo women highly excel, so much so, that their beautiful goods have been considered equal to any of Brussels or Valenciennes.

Highly as the silks of India were at one period esteemed in Europe, whether for dresses, for hangings, or coverings for furniture, they are now scarcely, if at all, used in this country, with the exception of handkerchiefs, known as Corahs and Bandannas. The beauty of design and richness of colouring which have from the earliest time distinguished the shawls of the East, appear at no time to have found a place in the getting up of the ordinary silken goods manufactured in India. On the contrary, the decay of this branch of trade with Europe takes its origin altogether in the absence of all taste and propriety of colouring in such goods as were for a long time tolerated in England, but which, with the growth of a more suitable manufacture at home, went rapidly out of the market.

The Bengal silk handkerchiefs, however, being either quite plain, and therefore capable of receiving dyes and patterns, or containing simply a few spots or cheques, continue to find favour, and up to the present time form a considerable item of our eastern import trade. These goods are almost exclusively from Bengal; and although there are some shipments to countries and states to the eastward, by far the bulk of the exports find their way to this country.

There is, besides the above, a manufacture of cloths composed of silk and cotton, exclusively for the use of Asiatics, either as garments or head-dresses, and, in addition to large quantities of this description of goods used by the inhabitants of the cities and large towns of India, shipments take place to the Persian and Arabian ports, the coasts of Coromandel and Pegu, and some of the eastern islands, to the yearly value of thirty or forty thousand pounds sterling.

Although in so many branches of textile manufacture England has outstripped her oriental teacher, we still find amongst the workmen of the East a degree of taste in the adjustment of their designs, an amount of skill applied to the getting-up of the fabric, and the blending of patterns and colours so aptly combined, as to leave nothing to be desired, but rather to shew that what we are now arriving at in art-design by the aid of scientific teachings, has been practised amongst that ancient race during the last thousand years. The correct principle which science has laid down in the schools of the West, that the patterns and colours of woven goods should diversify plain surfaces without disturbing the impression of flatness, has evidently been known to them from the earliest times. Nor is it in this alone that the workmen of the East excel: they are equally celebrated for the rich and varied beauty of their patterns, and the strict appropriateness of these to the colours employed.

Foremost amongst the woven fabrics of India are the world-famed shawls of Cashmere, the finest of which, in spite of many imitations in this country, are still produced in the "Vale of Cashmere," whence continues to come the supply of the most valuable wool employed in the manufacture. The Cashmere goat thrives nowhere so well as amidst the grassy ravines and shady clefts of the Cashmerian hills; and from the neck and under part of the body of the animal is taken the fine, flossy, silk-like hair, which is worked up into these beautiful shawls with an exquisite taste and skill which all the mechanical ingenuity of Europe has never been able to imitate with more than partial success.

Mention may be found of these shawls in the *Mahabharat* and other ancient works of the East. The people of the countries adjacent to Cashmere are there spoken of as bringing skins and cloths of wool embroidered with gold as tribute to the sovereign.

From the *Ayeen Akberry*,[8] written in the sixteenth century, we gather that the Emperor Akbar encouraged the manufacture of these shawls by every means in his power, even designing some himself, and introducing a greater and richer variety of colours in their patterns. The same work informs us of the extension of this manufacture to the state of Lahore, where it is said there were then a thousand manufactories employed on them.[9] A mixture of wool and silk for turbans is also spoken of; and some space is occupied with an enumeration of the various qualities of shawls and turbans, and the mode of classifying them for value.

Since the above period, the many troubles and political changes in the position of the country have materially affected this branch of industry; and we accordingly find that from 30,000 looms, which was at one time the number at work in Lahore, there were, some years since, but 16,000. Doubtless the more settled state of the country,

[8] Vol. ii. p. 140.

[9] Vol. i. p. 105.

and the increasing demand for the article in various parts of the world, will now help to revive this manufacture. In all eastern countries the shawl is ever considered the most essential and graceful part of ornamental dress; and even in Europe, with our many beautiful imitations, the true Cashmere shawl is still sought and paid for at enormous prices. Even in India it is by no means unusual for a rajah to pay ten thousand rupees (1000*l.*) for one of the finest of these productions; and which, in all probability, will have cost the labour of a whole family for a life-time.

The annual value of these shawls imported into Great Britain does not exceed six or seven thousand pounds, and forms no sort of criterion as to the yearly produce of the Cashmerian looms, since by far the most valuable are taken by native kings and rajahs, and large quantities are also dispatched to Russia, Turkey, Greece, America, and continental Europe. Previous to the imitation of these goods at Paisley, the imports had amounted to as much as 16,000*l.* annually.

In embroidered shawls, scarfs, handkerchiefs, &c., in silk, cotton, and mixed fabrics, India stands pre-eminent. Here also, as in the make of Cashmere shawls, the Hindoos, by their skilful and delicate manipulation, are able to produce fabrics of such exquisite fineness, as to defy the more scientific labours of European nations. Their scarfs of brocaded gold and silver, laid upon red, white, and green grounds, and worked in and interspersed with beetle's wings, and other ornaments, are at once the wonder and admiration of the world.

The Indian carpets most commonly met with are of cotton, in blue, red, and white; and although durable, possessing no other good quality. Some few made of cotton and silk for great potentates are extremely beautiful.

Another manufacture carried on in India is that of rope and bagging, chiefly from the fibre of jute (*Corchoris capsularis*), the trade in which has of late years grown to considerable magnitude.

The common gunny-bag of Bengal is a miserable article; so thin, weak, and open, that it is generally used double. In past ages the inhabitants were doubtless content to employ for this purpose the supple bark of various kinds of trees, as may be still observed in use in some remote districts; the transition from the use of this primitive description of package, to that of a rudely-manufactured article, such as the ordinary gunny-bag, could not have been a work of great time or difficulty; but there appears to have been no attempt at improvement in the working of these fabrics, until, as in most other cases, European intelligence and energy came to the task; and we find at the present moment an admirable sacking made in the neighbourhood of Calcutta, equal in durability and appearance to those of Dundee.

Not only is the manufacture of this article carried on with great imperfection, but in the first preparation of the fibre the utmost carelessness and want of attention or system is observable. From this cause the raw material often comes to market in very inferior condition both for appearance and strength. A very useful kind of common rope is also made from the coarser parts of the fibre; though in no way equal to the Coir rope manufactured from the fibres of the cocoa-nut husk.

This latter branch of industry is confined to the Malabar coast, along which for some hundreds of miles the cocoa-nut palm flourishes in great abundance. The process by which the fibre is removed from the outer shell is very primitive; and like that observable in the preparation of jute, open to much objection. The husks or skins are laid in deep pits, and covered with water frequently of great impurity, which, of course, imparts some of its quality to the fibre. They are often left in the water until quite offensive; when removed, they are beaten roughly until the covering of the husk separates from the fibre, which is then slightly washed and dried, and afterwards twisted by hand into yarn for a great variety of purposes, from ships' cables to sewing-thread.

The coir rope and yarn of the Malabar coast are greatly esteemed in all parts of the East, not less than in this country; and a considerable trade is carried on from the vicinity of Cochin and Cannonnore to nearly all parts of the Eastern seas, as well as to Great Britain and America.

The importance of the fibrous materials of India may be partly estimated by a glance at the annual value of the exports from Calcutta to all parts of the world, of the raw material, and of the cloth and bagging made from jute.

In 1848-9 the value of the jute shipped in its natural state was 69,000*l.*; and in the following year it amounted to 89,000*l.* The shipments of bagging and cloth manufactured from this article amounted in the former year to 140,000*l.*, and in 1849-50 to 277,000*l.*, chiefly to North America and the eastern ports and settlements. This, however, can be but a fraction of the bagging manufacture of India; for not only are these packages employed universally throughout that vast country for the local transport of grain and other dry goods, but the whole of the shipments of sugar, cotton, rice, saltpetre, seeds, &c. &c., are made in bags or wrappers of gunny cloth; and looking to the great extent of the internal and external traffic of the three Presidencies in every direction, the consumption of this article must be one of enormous magnitude.

In scarcely any part of the world, England excepted, does iron ore abound to such an extent as in Central and Northern India. In the peninsula also it is met with in considerable quantities; and of such fine quality has it been proved to consist, that a company with English capital has, in the Madras Presidency, supplied the public of India with this useful metal for a number of years past.

Experiments made with the iron ores of India shew them to be far more productive in metal, and much more valuable, than those of Britain. Indeed, the pure ore obtained from them equals in value that of Sweden and Russia. Thirty to thirty-three per cent is the amount of metal obtained from the Welsh iron-stone; the generality of Indian iron-ore contains from thirty to fifty per cent of metal; and in the northern Himalayan district of Kumaon as much as sixty-five per cent is proved to exist in the ordinary iron-stone of the locality.

The native process of smelting ore is most primitive and wasteful. A miserable little forge of sticks and clay, with an inflated skin for bellows, worked by a boy, or perhaps a woman, is the only provision for this work. Charcoal is invariably employed, which, of course, goes far to give quality to the metal produced; yet even in this great unnecessary waste of timber occurs. With the rude implements, the imperfect process, and the want of ordinary care and attention on the part of the native smelter, it is but seldom, indeed, that this rich ore, which is known to contain sixty-five per cent of metallic iron, is made to yield more than *nine* per cent.

It will be interesting to compare the yield of the rich ore of the Himalayan districts with that of the Welsh iron-stone, as the result will most forcibly demonstrate the vast benefits arising from enterprise and scientific skill in this branch of industry.

To produce a ton of metallic iron in Kumaon from the rough ore of that district, containing sixty-five per cent, would require one ton, fourteen hundredweight of ore, at two shillings the ton = 3*s*. 4*d*., with one ton and six hundredweight of charcoal, costing 14*s*. 8*d*.—total cost 18*s*. per ton, without labour, which is there three pence per diem. To obtain a ton of this metal, inferior in quality to the above, would require, at thirty-three per cent, three tons of clay iron-stone, costing at 8*s*., 1*l*. 4*s*.; with three tons of coals, at 3*s*. 6*d*. = 10*s*. 6*d*.; total cost, 1*l*. 14*s*. 6*d*. without labour, which, in Wales, is at the rate of three shillings per diem.

In working up the pure ore into malleable metal, the difference is still more marked. Thus we find that the Hindoo, by his rude process and unskilful manipulation, obtains from one hundred tons of his rich ore thirty-five tons of crude metal, and of bar-iron 8 tons 16 cwts. The iron smelter of Wales, on the other hand, with the same quantity of iron-stone, containing little more than half the material of the Indian stone, contrives to extract from it every ounce of metal; in other words, thirty-three tons of metal, which he works into 26 tons 10 cwts. of bar iron.

Without a knowledge of these facts, it would appear incredible that, whilst the north-western provinces of British India possess, at their very door, an exhaustless mine of iron wealth of almost unequalled quality, with labour of the cheapest, and an abundance of water and excellent fuel, they should still look to England for their general supplies of this metal, which, despite the cost of labour, twelve times that of India, the long sea-voyage and the inland transit of a thousand miles, can compete with the native article in the bazaars of Delhi, Lahore, and Cashmere.

It will cease to be matter for surprise, having the above in view, that the quantity of iron used throughout India is most insignificant

WORKING SILVERSMITH.

when compared with the population, and the employment of this necessary metal by other nations. The quantity of imported iron into India averages 18,838 tons annually, which does not give more than six ounces and a half for each inhabitant. Assuming that an equal quantity of native metal is used, we have still but *thirteen ounces* per head per annum, whilst in England it is known that the yearly consumption amounts to an average of 112 lbs. for each individual.[9] The dearness of the metal, added to the abundance of fibrous materials throughout all parts of India, will fully account for the natives employing coarse yarns in place of nails whenever it is possible to do so, whether in boat-building, or the erection of huts, or the construction of bridges, or other large works.

The same manual dexterity which has ever distinguished the unlettered Hindoo in the production of fine textile fabrics, has enabled him with equal success to produce some of the most exquisite specimens of gold and silver work. The rose-chains of Trichinopoly may be cited

NATIVE GOLDSMITH.

as illustrative of their delicate workmanship in the precious metals; whilst the inlaid work of gold and silver upon iron and steel, as practised at Benares and others of the cities of Hindostan, shew their skill and taste in this more useful branch of industry.

[9] Asiatic Review, December 1852.

Scarcely equal to their other productions are the works of the Indian jewellers: the setting of precious stones forms an exception to the general good taste and high finish of Eastern artificers. There is invariably a heaviness and total absence of propriety in the jewelled ornaments of India, which, despite the rare beauty of the gems and the richness and profusion of the ornamental work lavished upon them, cannot fail to strike an European eye as singularly in contrast with their other mechanical productions, whether of the loom, the forge, or the crucible.

DIAMOND-CUTTER.

The taste and skill of the Hindoos are in few things more apparent than in the graceful pottery-work to be met with in Bengal; of these there were some beautiful specimens in the Indian department of the Great Exhibition, both painted and gilt. Equal in every respect to these were the carved marble works and productions in pietra dura, in the shape of vases, garden-seats, &c., some of which rivalled the most finished performances of the Italian artists, and elicited general admiration.

CHAPTER III.

AGRICULTURE OF THE HINDOOS, AND THE APPLICATION OF EUROPEAN SKILL AND CAPITAL TO THE CULTIVATION OF INDIAN PRODUCTS.

THERE is little doubt that in their agriculture, as in many other matters of daily life, the Hindoo pursues identically the same system as was followed by his ancestors at the commencement of the Christian era. The soil of his native country is in the most densely peopled districts so highly fertile, and the climate and seasons so favourable to the fullest development of every function of nature, that man is scarcely called upon to do more than scatter the seed and gather the harvest. A bountiful Providence does for him in that genial clime what the utmost efforts of skill and energy alone can accomplish in more temperate lands.

The agricultural implements of the natives of India are simple to rudeness. Their ploughs are usually of a light and fragile description, only calculated, and indeed only required, to make a slight entrance into the friable soil. These are of hard wood, and drawn by one or at most two bullocks or buffaloes. A heavier iron-shod plough is occasionally employed on ground that is rather stiff, or which has perhaps become weedy or less fruitful, and therefore requires somewhat deeper ploughing. Their harrows consist of a mere board pierced with rough pegs, or more frequently of the bough of a tree, on which one or two children will be seated to give it the necessary pressure. These, and a hoe and mattock, comprise the entire stock of farming implements of the Hindoos.

Generous as the Indian soil usually is, and favourable as are the seasons, there are times and places when the husbandman is called on to exercise some degree of skill and industry. In the plains and valleys rain is frequently absent for many weeks, and without some artificial means of supplying the soil with moisture, no crops could be taken off the ground at those periods. In the chapter on "Roads and Rivers" will be found an account of the great public works of irrigation in India. What is there described as accomplished on a large scale by the local governments, is throughout many parts of the country performed by the villagers themselves. For miles the patient Hindoo will carry his tiny stream of water along the brow of mountains, round

RYOTS IRRIGATING RICE-FIELDS.

steep declivities, and across yawning gulfs or deep valleys, his primitive aqueducts being formed of stones, clay, and hollow bamboos. Sometimes, in order to bring the supply of water to the necessary height, a bucket-wheel is employed, worked by oxen.

It is but seldom that manure is employed, nor indeed is it often needed, although some few plants, such as the sugar-cane and tobacco, require such stimulus to bring them to maturity. An agricultural district in the East bears but small resemblance to such a tract in England. No hedges mark the boundary of every field or the possessions of each cultivator; no stacks of corn greet the eye; no well-filled barns stud the country. A row of stones, or a small ridge of earth, defines the extent of the ryot's possessions; while rice, cotton, fine grain, and tobacco, may be seen growing in close proximity, as though the seed had been scattered over the land by the merest caprice.

Harvest-time is a season of anxiety to the Indian cultivator; for there are many destructive foes ready at this time to prey upon his little field. His sugar-canes may be swept away in one night by the ravages of the elephant, the wild boar, or the porcupine; his tobacco may be uprooted or trampled down by herds of wild swine; and his grain may be devoured in the ear, in open day, by flights of birds, which are every where most numerous and harassing. To guard against all these calamities, the ryot is compelled at the critical season to mount guard over his little tract of produce, which he usually does perched up in a sort of jungle-stage, open on all sides but covered at the top, whence he is able to watch the whole extent of his field, and by dint of cries and sundry artificial sounds he is enabled to scare away all unwelcome intruders.

The harvest being secured, the grain is trodden out by the feet of buffaloes, and the little that may remain, if indeed it be any, is carefully stored in deep pits lined with straw; but in too many cases all that the ryot retains possession of will be just sufficient for seed for his little tract of land at the next sowing time.

With such a soil, and at the same time with so few inducements to exercise any agricultural ingenuity, the Hindoo raises most of his vegetable productions in a very imperfect and inferior condition. Indifferently grown, often taken from the ground before reaching maturity, imperfectly cured, badly housed, and taken to market in a slovenly and dirty condition, the agricultural productions of Hindostan are all highly susceptible of improvement. That this is so, there cannot be a greater proof than in the vast changes effected in some articles which have been taken in hand by Europeans. Wherever their skill and capital have been brought to bear, we find a perfect revolution effected in the quality and value of the productions grown or manipulated; and, although in the article of cotton not nearly so much has been accomplished as in other produce, an improvement is still visible in that valuable staple.

Within the province of Bengal, as well as in the Madras districts, the principal cultivation is that of rice. In most other districts this vegetable is comparatively rare. There is a great variety of the grain, differing widely in colour, shape, and weight; but the ordinary description grown does not extend beyond three or four varieties. The first sowing takes place between the end of March and the latter part of May; and as it matures and ripens within a period of about ninety days, it follows that the harvest takes place between the end of July and the middle of September. This crop is taken from sloping ground not subject to inundation, and is by far the safest, though not by any means the most abundant.

Another sowing takes place on low alluvial tracts between the middle of May and the end of June, and requiring five months to reach maturity, will be cut between November and January. This is usually the most profitable harvest, although, from the position of the land, liable at certain times to be seriously damaged by inundations; when, indeed, it is not an unusual thing for entire fields to be swept into the rivers.

With some cultivators a practice prevails of *planting out* their rice from nurseries reared near their dwellings. In this case the corn is removed when about eight or nine inches high, carried carefully to its destination, which will be some spot that was, perhaps, not available at the proper sowing time; and there the young stalks will be planted in rows, and pressed down about the roots with an inclination towards the direction whence the prevailing wind blows. These plants are said to thrive remarkably if properly placed, and to attain maturity in an incredibly short space of time. Sometimes a heavy flood will unexpectedly sweep away his first planting, in which case the ryot, nothing disheartened, sets to work, and repeats the task, knowing well that if it thrives it will amply repay him for his labour by its heavy crops.

After the rice-harvest the ground will be sown with some of the innumerable grains met with in India; in some cases with barley, in others with gram, a kind of pea admirably suited for the food of horses.

With indigo, sugar, tea, coffee, and opium, the success of the English cultivators has been most complete. The article of silk, although not coming under the head of agricultural products, is still so intimately dependent upon the culture of the mulberry, that it may well be classed with the above, and will therefore find a place with them in this chapter.

In the history of the indigo trade of India, we meet with a most instructive lesson upon the great advantages arising to a country from the application of skilled labour and scientific knowledge to an ordinary and indigenous product. In no other case has the energy and skill of the European been applied with such marked results as in that of indigo. From being an article greatly inferior in quality to that produced by other countries, and leaving a considerable annual loss upon its manufacture, we see it in the present day forming one of the most valuable, if not the most valuable of Indian products, bidding defiance to the utmost efforts of the manufacturers of other countries in quality and price.

Indigo is indigenous to India, as indeed its former name of *Indico* would shew. It was known to, and in constant use amongst the Greeks and Romans; and is mentioned especially by Arrian in his *Periplus* as imported by way of Egypt from the country in the vicinity of the Indus. The Venetians, the Portuguese, the Dutch, and subsequently the English imported indigo amongst other articles of the dye and dry-saltery trade. Early in the seventeenth century we find this article becoming one of increasing consumption among the dyers; so much so indeed as to interfere seriously with the trade in woad. So jealous were the authorities of that age of any commercial innovation, of any encroachment upon vested rights, that, in the year 1654, the use of this article, which was called "the Devil's dye," was strictly forbidden within the Austrian dominions, by imperial proclamation. Not content with this extremely conservative measure, the good people of Nuremberg compelled the dyers of their city to take oath each year, that they would employ no indigo in their work.[1]

Despite imperial edicts and Nurembergers' oaths, this Devil's dye continued to find favour generally throughout Europe; and indifferent as was the article produced in those days, the trade became one of considerable value until the close of the seventeenth century, when they were driven from the European markets by the active competition of the West Indian planters and the colonists of America. Subsequently, however, when the States declared their independence, and the culture of the West Indian plant was neglected for other articles, the Company resumed their dealings in it, and by giving all the encouragement in their power not only to native but to European planters, they succeeded, after a number of years, in establishing the manufacture of indigo on such a firm footing, that the Bengal article now ranks the highest in public estimation, having fairly driven all competition from the field. It is highly problematical, however, if the manufacture of indigo in British India would have arrived at its present state of prosperity but for the spirit evinced by the Directors of the East India Company, who, in the teeth of losing markets, continued to make extensive purchases of the article from the European

[1] Bancroft's Permanent Colours, p. 166.

planters, shipping their investments to a certain loss, until, after a series of years, the agriculture of the plant, and the chemistry of the manufacture, became so thoroughly investigated, and received so many improvements, as to place the trade beyond the necessity for any further fostering.[2]

The first, or London East India Company, carried on a very profitable trade in this dye for upwards of a century; purchasing it from the native makers at about a shilling the pound, and selling it at five times that price. Between the years 1664 and 1694 their imports of the article into Great Britain did not exceed 60,000 lbs. annually.

In those days the seat of the native manufacture of indigo of the finest quality was at Agra. Lahore contributed a good article, as did the Golconda country. The inferior sorts came from Surat, Berampoor, Indore, Oude, and Bengal. At the present time the finest indigo is manufactured in the Bengal presidency, where it has been found that both soil and season are highly favourable to the culture and development of the plant. A considerable quantity, about 4000 chests, is produced in and about the vicinity of Madras, some of which is of superior quality.

Towards the close of the last century, say in 1786, the shipments of indigo to Great Britain amounted to 245,000 lbs. Shortly after that period the attention and capital of English cultivators were turned towards the article, as already related; and we find the results of this enterprise in the statement of exports to all parts of the world, but mainly to this country: this gives the quantity for 1795 as 2,644,710 lbs.; for 1799, at 4,571,420 lbs.; for 1810, at 5,520,874 lbs.; and for 1848-9, at 9,920,000 lbs., of which three-fourths were to Great Britain.

The dye known in commerce as indigo is obtainable from several varieties of the plant, though that of the finest quality is made from the *Indigofera tinctoria*. It grows to a height of three or four feet, with a hard and woody stem of a grey colour about the root, green in the middle and reddish in hue towards the top. It is divided into a variety of knotty stalks, with small sprigs terminating with about eight pairs of leaves each, of an oval shape, thick, and of a deep green on the under-side. The flowers make their appearance on the extremity of the branches, of a rich reddish colour, but devoid of any smell.

It is in these leaves that the colouring-matter forming the dye is found; and it is obtained by macerating, beating, and washing them,

[2] Boyle's Productive Resources of India, p. 101.

and afterwards passing the highly-coloured liquor into boilers, where it is subjected to a certain degree of evaporation, and eventually run off into moulds, pressed free from moisture, and dried ready for the market.

It is estimated that there are at the present time not fewer than three thousand Europeans engaged in the indigo manufacture in different parts of Bengal and Behar. The finest quality of dye is produced by factories in the Jessore and Kishnagur districts. An ordinary plantation comprises 4000 acres of land, which may yield on an average 1000 maunds of 82 lbs. each. The annual outlay for labour, seed, &c., on this one branch of industry is seldom less than a million and a half sterling, of which fully nineteen-twentieths are expended by Europeans. The cultivation is generally one of hazard, as the fields are always liable to be swept of their produce during any heavy or sudden fall of rain, when, as it happened in 1852, one-third of the entire crops will be lost. Should this not occur, the plant often suffers from long drought. With a few good seasons, favourable soil, a thorough knowledge of the business, and a certain degree of industry, an indigo-planter may reckon on realising an independence in less than a dozen years. This is, of course, supposing him to have started with ample means.

The life of an indigo-planter, however successful it may be, is by no means one of pleasure. He has many drawbacks to his good fortune, even if he chance to miss the fatality attendant upon floods and droughts. From the first onset of indigo-planting, European settlers in India were regarded with the utmost jealousy, and were only permitted to reside in Bengal by an act of courtesy on the part of the government; and even in the present day, although all restrictions to free residence have long since been withdrawn, and the Company derive great advantages from the employment of so much European capital in the country, the planter is still looked upon as an interloper by the civil service, and treated as such.

It is matter of notoriety that in any suit instituted between an indigo-planter and a native before any of the local officials, judgment is invariably given in favour of the latter. So far is this feeling carried, that a judge has been known to tell the planter that "he had no right to come there;" and such would appear to be the impression on the minds of these dispensers of *justice*. On one occasion, when an indigo-factor ventured to expostulate with the judge in open court, the brutal dignitary ordered his peons to gag him; and the order was actually carried into execution by a brace of the native police pinioning the Englishman, whilst others of their fraternity forced a huge wooden gag into his mouth. This occurred within the last three years, and at no greater distance from Calcutta than a few hundred miles.

The unfair position in which the indigo-planter of Bengal has been thus placed, added to the jealousy with which he has ever been regarded by the zemindars of the country, who feel in him the presence of a dangerous rival for the labour of the ryots, have between them given birth to what is known in India as the "lattial" system; in other words, "club law."

In a country where there exist no hedges, nor other artificial divisions to mark the boundaries of various properties, disputes in regard to fields and crops must frequently occur. In all these cases the zemindars urged on the villagers to acts of aggression and trespass; and at length they went so far as to assemble in large bodies, and, armed with sticks, or "lattials," drove off the planter's people as the indigo was ready for the knife, and seized the produce. The Englishman was not likely to stand quietly by and submit to this injustice. To take the matter into court, supposing him to be within fifty miles of a magistrate, he well knew would be unavailing, worse than useless; he therefore profited by the lesson taught him by the zemindars, and met force by force. Henceforward the "lattial" warfare became a general practice, and, as may be imagined, usually resulting in favour of the planter. Once feeling the necessity for this feudal mode of protection, the English factors spared no pains or cost to perfect themselves in this mode of warfare; and where the zemindar mustered his tens, the planter brought forth his scores. A rupee a head is the usual fee for lattials, who are always to be hired in any number, and who are quite indifferent for whom they fight, so long as the rupee is forthcoming.

This system is, of course, never acknowledged by any concerned; and as regards the "blood-money" for the "lattials," the amount is invariably placed in the planter's monthly account under the head of "cases in court." These affrays do not perhaps occur quite so frequently as of old, nor are they so sanguinary. In the good old days, it was not unusual for half a dozen lives to be sacrificed in such encounters, to say nothing of a hospital full of wounded; and planters are still alive who can relate strange escapes from waylaying parties, or from amidst the flames of a burning bungalow.[3]

Few if any articles of East-Indian produce have formed the basis of such reckless speculation in the commercial world, both in Calcutta

[3] Calcutta Review, vol. vii.

and London, as this one dye. Having almost the entire supply of the manufacturing world dependent upon this article, it follows that any unlooked-for or sudden falling off in the supply of the plant must be sensibly felt; and with a commodity so valuable, the room left for profit in any emergency of this sort is necessarily ample. For many years past speculative men on both sides the world have been in the frequent habit of turning these periodical disturbances in the supply to account; sometimes to their enormous advantage, but as often only to bring ruin on themselves and many others around them. The tone of Indo-British commercial morality we have attempted to illustrate in a separate chapter; and it may suffice in this place to mention, that where natural causes for a rise in the indigo-market did not occur sufficiently frequent for the gambling propensities of some of the Calcutta merchants and bankers, aids were put in requisition, in the shape of false reports of inundations and short crops, or by what is technically termed "working the market," which is simply making speculative purchases of the article, and by these means running up the price sufficiently high to leave a large profit on the transaction; and having done that, selling out by degrees at the ruling rate. It not unfrequently happens that these speculators burn their fingers; and when that is the case, it is fortunate if they have not gambled with the funds of other parties, entrusted to their care, or obtained possession of by some process peculiar to the Calcutta commercial world.

Coeval with the use of other vegetable products for domestic purposes in India appears to have been the employment of the juice of the sugar-cane; though it would not seem that the ancients possessed any knowledge of the process by which this saccharine matter is converted into a crystallised substance. Every mention made of it, from the various passages in Scripture down to the commencement of the Christian era, is simply that of a "sweet cane," or of a "fine kind of honey found in an Indian reed." Nearchus, the admiral of Alexander the Great, was the first who made known the existence of the sugar-cane, in the western world; and from his time we find frequent allusion to this vegetable product, by Theophrastus, Varro, Dioscorides, and others. Herodotus alludes to "honey made by the hands of men;" but enters into no details. Lucan speaks of the sweet juice expressed from reeds, which the people of India were fond of drinking, and which Pliny calls "saccharine." Still later, Arrian, in his *Periplus of the Red Sea*, alludes to the honey from reeds called sacchar, as an article of trade between the Indian ports and the countries of the Red Sea.

The sugar-cane was found growing in the meadows about Tripoli in

Syria; and mention is made by a writer of that day of eleven camels loaded with sugar being taken by the Crusaders. Marco Polo, who travelled in the East in the year 1250, found abundance of sugar produced in the province of Bengal; and from the almost universal growth of the cane in that presidency at the first occupation of the country by the British, there is good reason for believing that its culture had rapidly extended at a very early period. From the earliest European intercourse with India, sugar in a great variety of forms was met with in daily use. No Hindoo lives without it, either as sugar, in its natural state, or in cakes called "jaggery."

Upon the first possession of Calcutta by the Company there was a flourishing export trade in sugar to the Indian coasts, some of the Eastern islands, and a few ports in Arabia and Persia, to the extent of about 1500 tons; whilst the local consumption of the article was enormous.

The quality of this sugar was, however, very inferior; and about the year 1776 some attempts were made to introduce into India the Jamaica mode of growing the cane, and manufacturing the sugar; but at that time these efforts were not attended with any success. The culture of the cane was nevertheless greatly extended; and by the year 1792, when the British duties on tea were reduced, and a consequent increased demand for sugar arose, not only in England but in many parts of Europe, so as greatly to enhance its price, the Company made large shipments of the article home; although all endeavours to get it rated for duty on the same scale as that from the West Indies failed. The price realised in the English market for the Company's sugars was at this time 88*s.* 6*d.*; but it rose gradually until it reached 156*s.* per hundred-weight: a figure which, in spite of discriminating duties and high freights, left to the importers a clear profit of eighty or ninety per cent.

The first agitation against the slave-trade and slave-grown produce helped to bring East-India sugars into more favourable notice; and the result of this growing demand, met by increasing culture in Bengal, was, that from 100 or 200 tons shipped home in 1790, the imports into London from Bengal in 1805 and 1807 amounted to 5000 tons.[4]

[4] The following were the exports of Bengal sugar to Great Britain between the years 1803 and 1810:

Years.	Cwts.	Value.	Years.	Cwts.	Value.
1803	27,608	£56,789	1807	105,755	199,873
1804	78,619	208,060	1808	48,499	88,016
1805	102,732	295,814	1809	33,617	68,750
1806	67,455	150,250	1810	43,236	101,040

From this time forward the sugar-trade with British India steadily increased: the throwing open of the Indian ports to private ships; the final cessation of the Company's trade; the reduction of the imperial duties on sugar the produce of the British possessions in the East; the failure of the West India plantations, aided by the growing demand for sugars of all kinds,—were all causes that had a sensible influence in bringing this branch of commerce to a degree of importance, which fifty years since could not have been anticipated by the most sanguine.

In 1844 the imports of Bengal and Madras sugars into the port of London alone amounted to 31,000 tons; in 1846 to 44,000 tons; and in 1851 to 43,000 tons; of which 30,000 were from Bengal, and 13,000 from Madras.

The great importance to which the tea-trade of China has attained, and the almost universal employment of the article amongst European nations, as well as the prominent part it plays in yielding large revenues to the government of the various countries consuming it, have for a long period attracted to tea more than an ordinary degree of attention. During the last thirty years much valuable information regarding the natural history and culture of the plant has been placed before the world; and it has been made evident that it is not nearly so delicate or so limited in its geographical distribution as has been generally supposed.[5] It has been shewn that it thrives equally well in the vicinity of Canton, and the milder climate of Nankin, as in the northern latitudes of Pekin and Japan; embracing, therefore, a distribution over twenty degrees of latitude.

The knowledge of this fact led to an inquiry in India, so long since as 1827, as to the practicability of introducing the culture of the tea-plant into the northern regions of that vast country; and the result was an opinion of the Company's botanist, Dr. Royle, that it might be successfully grown in the north-western portion of the Himalaya districts. He pointed out some localities particularly suited to the experiment in the district of Kumaon, a portion of the province of Delhi, and situated between the 29th and 30th degrees of north latitude, to the north-west of Nepaul. This opinion was afterwards backed by the investigations of others, who agreed in the belief that there was no impediment to the successful introduction of the tea-culture in the Himalayan regions beyond the difficulty of obtaining a supply of plants, and some details relative to the Chinese mode of cultivation and curing of the article.

In 1834 Lord William Bentinck formed a committee, with the view of adopting measures for attempting this cultivation in India; and the

[5] Royle's Productive Resources of India, p. 258.

first step taken was the dispatch of agents to the tea-districts of China, whence a supply of seeds and plants, and much valuable information was brought. Nurseries were formed in Calcutta, and some ten thousand plants were reared, the greater portion of which were dispatched to Kumaon, though but a small fraction of them reached the Himalayas; whilst a quantity was forwarded to the hill districts of the Madras presidency, but without any good results. The plants dispatched northwards were distributed in several directions, and so well did they thrive, that in the year 1838 many of them had produced seed, which was at once sown, and thus formed fresh nurseries.

In the meantime the existence of the tea-plant in a wild state had been ascertained in the upper districts of Assam, one of the north-eastern provinces of the Bengal presidency; and inquiries having been directed to it, evidence was not long wanting to shew that the plant was growing in not less than a hundred different tracts amongst the dense jungles of that country. In 1837, samples of tea, prepared from the wild plants of the Assam district, were forwarded to Calcutta, and favourably reported on.

Observations and researches instituted in the Assam country went to shew that the district really possessed most of the requisites of soil, position, altitude, and climate. Some valuable reports upon the peculiarities of this district, and the results of a number of experiments in the culture of the indigenous plant, were published at intervals between 1837 and 1840; and from these it appears that the best seasons for the manipulation of the tea-crop are in March, May, and July. Every inquiry goes to prove that the greatest success has been attained whenever the culture has been attempted on hilly slopes, or in the vicinity of rivers, with a temperature ranging from 27° to 80°; indeed, it appears certain that the latter consideration is of far more importance than that of soil.

The China tea-plants introduced into Upper Assam by the instrumentality of the Company's servants have not only thriven remarkably well, but attained a size and vigour unknown to them in their native soil. The first parcels of tea from these districts were highly approved of on their arrival in England, and realised enormous prices, partly owing, in all probability, to their novelty. The result of these sales, however, placed it beyond a doubt that the cultivation of tea could be profitably carried on in that part of India; and, in consequence, a public company, entitled the "Assam Company," was formed for the purpose of carrying on the culture and manufacture of British Indian tea on an extensive scale. The East India Company having thus acted the part of pioneers, handed over their experimental plantations and establishments to the new company, who have since greatly enlarged the plantations and works, and have succeeded in producing a tea superior to any imported into this country from China, and equalled only by the fewer samples which, under the old company's system, used to be occasionally obtained.

During the first years of their operations, the Assam Company encountered many obstacles, arising from the difficulty of procuring labour in sufficient quantity, from the want of skill of their first managers, and, above all, from the extreme remoteness of their property from all supervision. The formation of a Calcutta committee had obviated the latter evil, whilst the remaining difficulties have been successively overcome by patient perseverance; and the company is now on a most solid foundation, having increased their extent of plantation to twelve hundred acres, with a crop in 1853 calculated at 300,000 lbs., which has hitherto realised fully a third above the China teas.

The produce of the company's tea-crop of 1847 realised 9,728*l.* nett; that of 1848, 12,552*l.*; that of 1849, 16,628*l.*; that of 1850, 18,153*l.*; and that of 1851, as above stated, 22,151*l.* The nett average price per pound in the those years was, for 1847, 1*s.* 4*d.*; 1848, 1*s.* $5\frac{1}{16}$*d.*; 1849, 1*s.* $6\frac{13}{16}$*d.*; 1850, 1*s.* $6\frac{2}{16}$*d.*; and 1851, 1*s.* $8\frac{1}{2}$*d.*

In the Himalayan districts the labours of the tea-experimentalists have been equally successful with those carried on in the more easterly province of Assam. About the year 1842, the aid of some of the Chinese cultivators, who had been introduced in the Assamese plantations, was obtained for the tea-farmers in the Kumaon district of the Himalayan country; and by their instrumentality a quantity of black tea was produced and dispatched to Calcutta, whence it was shipped to this country, and pronounced superior in strength and flavour to the generality of Souchongs. By the end of the year 1844 these experimental plantations contained upwards of a hundred thousand plants; and two years later they covered nearly two hundred acres, at various altitudes, varying from 2500 to 6500 feet above the sea-level.

In the year 1848 this cultivation was still further extended, reaching to an extent of 1000 acres, not in one immediate neighbourhood, but stretching through many miles of country, and in some parts reaching the recently acquired Sikh territories on the north-west frontiers.

The quantity of tea produced from these plantations must now be of some importance, and although the great distance of these districts from a port of shipment will always be a barrier to any successful competition with more favoured tea-producing countries, the supply of the local demand, already largely on the increase since this culture has commenced, will of itself prove a trade of no small value. So deeply impressed was the local government with the importance of this new branch of industry, that a grant of ten thousand sterling a year was voted to carry out the experiment until it should, as in Assam, be taken up by private enterprise.

In 1850 the East India Company, determined to lose no opportunity of fully testing the value of this cultivation, dispatched an agent to China to glean all possible information regarding the tea-plant, its natural history, and the manipulation of its leaves; and, if possible, to bring away from the Chinese dominions a fresh supply of plants and seed of the best varieties, as also some experienced cultivators and work-people.

In all these objects their agent was singularly fortunate, having but recently returned to India with a supply of all that was desired, in plants, seed, work-people, and, better still, in accurate data regarding the various processes of the cultivation and manufacture of this article.

The cultivation of coffee in the Indian continent, although frequently and successfully attempted at various periods since 1820, has not until very recently been carried out on any extended scale. In the government botanic gardens in Bengal, and, further south, at Sahrumpore, the berry has been produced in abundance and of good quality; but, from a variety of causes, no European capitalists appear to have undertaken the cultivation of the plant until the complete success of coffee-planting in the neighbouring island of Ceylon tempted several persons possessing the means, to carry out an enlarged experiment on some of the elevated land of the south-western ghauts of the peninsula. Favoured with a rich and deep soil, abundance of cheap labour, and a suitable climate, the operations of the planters of the ghauts have to this date been eminently successful. Several thousand acres of land have been thus brought under cultivation; and the few samples already grown have been considered equal to much of the ordinary plantation sorts imported into this country.

Coffee is grown by the natives in many parts of India, in Bengal, Arracan, Mysore, Malabar, &c.; but in nearly all instances the article is as inferior to the plantation-grown as are the other native-reared productions of the East, and approaches little nearer to it in quality than does the wild crab approximate to the English garden apple.

The culture of opium is still monopolised by the Company, and, together with the manufacture and sale of salt, forms a striking exception to the unrestricted liberty accorded to private enterprise in India on the renewal of the charter in 1833. Both these monopolies are retained on the plea of revenue; and certainly, as regards the former little can be said, as it does not belong to the same list of necessaries as salt.

This drug—the produce of the poppy plant, from which it freely exudes under the great heat of the sun when an incision is made in the capsule—is chiefly in demand amongst the Chinese and the inhabitants of Penang and other eastern settlements, where it is used for purposes of intoxication. Indeed, the trade almost entirely depends upon these places; for nearly nine-tenths of the opium exported from Bengal is shipped to the eastern ports. It has been in vain that the Chinese authorities interdicted the introduction and use of the article under severe penalties; it was in vain that large quantities of the drug were seized on board British vessels some years since, and destroyed, leading, as this act did, to subsequent hostilities between the two nations;—the trade flourishes as of old, in all its wonted vigour.

The opium of Patna is more highly esteemed in Europe than that produced at Benares, although both kinds are made up under similar European inspection. The cultivation of the poppy is now restricted to the above two districts, under a system of license from the government, who alone can purchase the produce from the native growers, and have the power of fixing the price at which it is to be sold to them. The interest of the Company is, however, limited to the sale of the opium in Calcutta, where regular periodical auctions are held, and the drug is disposed of to the highest bidders, who ship it on their own account and risk. The difference realised by the government between their fixed purchasing rate from the native growers and the sale-price in Calcutta forms a considerable item in aid of the revenue. Between the years 1792-3 and 1809-10 the amount of revenue from this source varied from 179,950*l.* to 801,467*l.*[6] How vastly the consumption of this drug must have increased in the East may be judged from the fact, that the amount of opium-revenue was, in 1835-6, 1,399,009*l.*; in 1845-6, it was 2,628,140*l.*; and in 1849-50, the latest year for which any official returns exist, it was not less than 3,309,637*l.*

The continuance of this monopoly is chiefly defended on the ground that the revenue arising from it does not come out of the pockets of the Company's subjects, but from those of foreigners; and so far as this goes,

[6] Milburn's Oriental Commerce, vol. ii. p. 220.

it would appear to be a just ground of defence; but exposed as the trade ever must be to the interference of the Chinese and other authorities, and so entirely dependent as it is on the fancy and caprice of a people whose rulers prohibit its sale, it must be confessed that the Indian government has placed itself in a critical position by depending for a seventh part of its revenues upon such a hazardous traffic; and the more so since there is not only no surplus to fall back upon, but a constantly recurring deficiency in the Indian exchequer. Taking this view then of the opium monopoly, it certainly does appear, that the sooner the Company can relieve this portion of its income from such a position, the better will it consult its true interests. A recent mail from China informs us that the emperor, in order to replenish his exhausted treasury, and enable him to prosecute the war against the Chinese rebels, had consented to admit opium through his customs on payment of a certain tax. This, then, legalises its sale within his dominions; and should he continue the relaxation, there can be very little doubt but that the Chinese cultivators will shortly undertake the growth of the poppy in some of the many districts suited to its development: when this shall be the case, the East India Company may bid adieu to fully two millions of their opium-revenue. Indeed the monopoly will not then be worth the up-keep of the establishment necessary for its preservation.

The opium-revenue is under the supervision of two opium-agents stationed at Patna and Ghazepore, having assistant-agents under them to take cognisance of the culture of the plant and the manufacture of the drug by the ryots, to whom advances have been made, as also to watch that there be no smuggling or illicit production carried on. Extensives stores at both the above places are kept for the reception of the drug, where, previous to its being dispatched to Calcutta for sale, it undergoes a purifying process and careful packing to fit it for the China and European markets.

During the opium-war in China the price of the drug fell so low in Calcutta that the revenue arising from its sale declined from nearly two millions sterling to about three hundred thousand pounds, and there were not wanting those who predicted that, as a matter of income to the government, the cultivation of the poppy would not for the future be worth attending to. Experience has, however, shewn that this was a hastily formed opinion; for at no period of the history of this article has the trade in it to China been carried on so successfully and so extensively as during the few last years.

Equal in antiquity, though not in extent, to the growth of cotton, was the production of silk in the countries of the East. Its limited extent, however, and the monopoly of this valuable traffic in the hands of the Phœnicians, and afterwards by the Persians, restricted its employment within the most confined limits. Until the time of the Roman empire, its very existence appears to have been unknown in the West; and when Dionysius, the imperial geographer, who visited the East in the first years of the Christian era, wrote an account of this new and beautiful product, he speaks of it as a precious web, finer than that of the spider, combed by the natives from flowers, and spun into rich garments of great price.

Of the precise period when silk was first introduced into the West we are not informed; but that it must have been excessively dear, and limited in use to but a few persons of great wealth, may be judged from the fact of the Emperor Aurelian refusing to purchase a single dress of purple silk for his empress on the plea of its great cost, as it could not be bought at the price of gold. The very jealousy with which the silk-trade of the East was guarded, proved in the end fatal to its prosperity. Its extreme scarcity and dearness induced two travelling monks, despite the danger of the act, to bring away from the country of their production, a quantity of the eggs of the silkworm, which they contrived to conceal within a hollow cane; and from this first supply were at length produced the vast broods of those valuable worms, whose labours have enriched not only Italy and France, but the manufacturers of many other countries.

Previous to the middle of the eighteenth century, Indian raw silk formed a very inconsiderable portion of the trade from the East. Its great inferiority to the Italian and French article was for a long period a great barrier to the profitable extension of this branch of Indian trade. The factors of the Company did no more than purchase the silk as it reached their hands from the three filatures, whence alone it came in those days. At Cossimbazar, Rungpore, and Commercolly, the natives grew large tracts of the common mulberry-plant, reared their worms, and reeled the produce of the cocoons; but with so small regard to the exigencies of the worms, and so little care bestowed upon the preparation of the silk, as to render it a most unprofitable and troublesome article in the hands of the European manufacturer; so much was this felt, that until the latter part of the last century, Indian silk was employed but for the manufacture of certain inferior minor articles of haberdashery, and never entered into the composition of satins, or silk piece-goods of any kind. One great cause of this inferiority was to be found in the careless method of winding the silk from the cocoons, which produced such inequality in the thread as to render it all but unserviceable. Besides this, it was loaded with gummy and other extraneous substances, and reeled without the least attention to colour or quality; so that it reached the buyer's hands in hanks comprising all sorts of shades.

This part of their trade proved so annoying, and was attended with such fruitless results, that the Company were at one time on the point of issuing orders to cease all purchases of the article. Instead of acting on this first impulse, the Directors wisely made an effort to remedy the evil complained of, by sending to Bengal one or two persons acquainted with the Italian mode of reeling and assorting silk; these instructors were placed in the heart of the silk-districts, and appear, from after results, not to have laboured in vain. Inducements were at the same time held out to the ryots to extend the cultivation of the mulberry-plant, by allowing them all lands so used free of rent for two years, and afterwards assessing them very moderately. In this manner the silk-trade received an impulse hitherto unknown to it, and the exports of the raw article rose from 80,000 lbs. in 1750, to 320,000 lbs. in 1770.

The partial success which had attended the introduction of a better mode of reeling silk induced the Company to attempt still further reforms; and we accordingly find that in the year 1771 a second supply of practical silk-reelers and mulberry-cultivators from Italy were dispatched to Bengal; proper filatures were established; a better mode of rearing the insects and growing the plants was introduced; and, in addition to these measures, steps were taken to secure a supply of eggs from China, with the view of improving the breed of the Indian worms. Several years elapsed before these improvements were beneficially felt in the quality of the silks imported from Bengal; but that such was the case may easily be seen by the steady increase in the quantity taken by the manufacturers of England, which in 1785 amounted to 576,175 lbs.

The greatest improvement effected by the Company at this period was the total abolition of the contract system, and the substitution for it of agencies throughout the silk-districts, by means of which supplies of the cocoons were constantly obtained from sub-agents called pykars, who received advances in money, and who, in their turn, engaged by similar means for the supply of silkworms from the rearers in the different villages.

The vast improvements effected in England towards the end of the last century in the manufacture of cotton goods tended in a great measure to check the consumption of the more costly article of silk; and we find that from 500,000 lbs. weight of raw silk sold in 1785, the Company did not dispose of more, on the average, than 300,000 lbs. weight in the years 1800 to 1805.

So much better were the silk transactions of the Company managed at this time, that in spite of this decline in the demand for their goods, their yearly profits gradually increased from a few thousands to the enormous amount of 132,982*l.* in 1801. The gradual decline to a certain date, in the imports of Bengal raw silk, from the cause already assigned, may be seen by the following list of exports to Great Britain, taken at intervals of ten years; and in the same may be observed the effect of the gradual relaxation of the Company's trading monopoly in favour of private merchants. In 1782 there were shipped to England from Bengal, 611,071 lbs.; in 1792, 401,445 lbs.; in 1802, 114,744 lbs.; in 1812, 982,427 lbs.; in 1822, 1,042,617 lbs.; and in 1832, 956,453 lbs.

Some idea of the commercial value of this branch of Indian trade may be formed from the fact, that between the years 1776 and 1785, the raw silk imported by the Company, and in the privileged tonnage by private traders, was worth 3,446,757*l.*; from 1786 to 1803, it amounted to 5,221,596*l.*; and from 1804 to 1810, to 3,115,044*l.*; being during these thirty-five years almost equal to 12,000,000*l.* sterling.

Upon the last renewal of the East India charter in 1833, which provided that the Company should no longer engage in mercantile operations, their extensive and well-organised filatures were put up for sale, and after some delay disposed of to private parties.

These establishments were eleven in number, of which the following gave their names to the particular kinds of silk produced by each of them, and by which those varieties are to this day known in commercial circles; they are Bauleah, Commercolly, Cossimbazar, Hurripaul, Jungypoor, Radnagore, Rungpore, Santipore, and Surdah. Besides the above, the Company possessed a number of hired filatures of less note.

The exportations of Bengal raw silk in 1814-15 amounted in value to 231,271*l.*; in 1827-8 to 855,398*l.*; and in 1837-8 to only 465,451*l.* Bringing down these figures to a more recent date, we find that the silk exports of Calcutta were, during the years 1848-9 and 1849-50, to the value of 714,000*l.* and 655,000*l.* respectively.

Besides the China, or mulberry silkworm, there are several varieties of silk-spinning worms indigenous to India, of which mention is made in some of the earliest records of that country. These have been described by several scientific writers, and are known amongst the natives as the mooga, the armidy, the tussah, and the joree worms, all producing fibres, which, if not equal in commercial value to those of the mulberry-worm, are nevertheless esteemed and largely employed amongst the inhabitants of the districts in which they are found. These insects inhabit vast tracts of forest in Upper Assam, in the Madras Presidency, and in that of Bombay; and the cloths made from the raw material are in extensive use amongst not only natives but Europeans, who find them most economical and durable for many purposes.

Some idea may be formed of the extent to which these kinds of indigenous silk are produced, when it is stated that in 1837 there were in one district alone not less than 318,772 pieces of tussah silk manufactured. The food of the wild silkworm is obtained from the trees of the forests inhabited by them, and amongst those known as affording them nourishment are the leaves of the jujube, the castor-oil plant, the peepul, or banyan-tree, some of the laurels, and a few other plants.

So early as 1795, some attempt appears to have been made at Bombay to introduce the silk-worm, but evidently without effect; for until 1823 we hear nothing more of the matter, and then it seems to have been attempted at one of the public jails by the labour of the prisoners, the result of which appears to have been the preparation of a few bales of silk for local consumption. Later still, the zeal and industry of an Italian gentleman were brought to bear upon the subject, and under his directions a better cultivation of the mulberry plant, and an improved method of feeding and reeling was introduced, with slow but perfect success.

In Madras this branch of industry met with great encouragement so long since as 1791. No efforts were spared to induce the natives to enter fully into the rearing of the worm and the growth of the plant; and, as the result shews, the success was, if not so great as in Bengal, still sufficiently encouraging.

CHAPTER IV.

THE COTTON INDUSTRY OF INDIA, ITS HISTORY, EXTENT, AND PROSPECTS.

Few subjects have occupied so much of public attention of late years,—have been so frequently discussed in books, in newspapers, and in parliamentary debates, as that of the production of cotton within the territories of the East India Company. None will be disposed to question the great importance of the subject. Whether we regard cotton in its broadest aspect, as affording ample employment to vast numbers of persons in its growth, transport, and shipment; whether we look at it as furnishing food for gigantic manufacturing establishments in the parent country, scattering wealth and happiness in its path; or whether we view it as an article of social moment, ministering to the health and comfort of the entire human race; whether we consider it as a source of revenue, as a staple of trade and manufacture, or as a great help to civilisation and progress,—we cannot but feel that we have to deal with a most important subject.

India was unquestionably the birth-place of cotton cultivation and cotton manufacture. It is mentioned in the institutes of *Menu*, a work composed eight centuries before the Christian era, with many details relative to its manufacture and uses; and although not named in the *Rig Veda*, of still higher antiquity, there is no doubt that in more than one place the thread alluded to was composed of cotton.

Possessing, therefore, so much antiquity, we need not feel astonished that, until the last half century, the culture, trade, and manufacture of cotton in India should have occupied a most important position in the commercial annals of the world. That the production of cotton goods in India would still have stood forward pre-eminently as a branch of industry, had not the modern improvements of machinery in Europe snatched from it all its ancient prestige, there can be but little doubt; although, as regards the cultivation of the raw material, other causes have been at work to spread it elsewhere, to an extent unprecedented in the history of the world's industry.

It was a remarkable coincidence that at the precise time when Arkwright and Watt were elaborating and perfecting their magnificent improvements of the spinning-machine and steam-engine, the British arms were subjecting vast empires in the East to our dominion, countries which possessed within themselves the germs of an almost boundless production; lands which, from their suitability and fertile nature, might well be expected to furnish illimitable food for the new leviathans of steam and iron which they of Lancashire were creating.

The varieties of cotton known in the commercial world may be referred to three distinct species, each having several varieties. The *Gossypium Barbadosæ* is the species cultivated in the West Indies, North America, and in one or two parts of the peninsula of India.

COTTON PLANT.

Gossypium Peruvianum yields the cotton of Brazil, Pernambuco, Peru, &c. This also has been introduced into some districts of India.

Gossypium Indicum is the species which, in a number of varieties, produces the great bulk of the cotton of India and China.

There is a fourth species, the *Gossypium arborum*, or Tree-cotton of India, unknown to commerce, though yielding a beautifully soft and silky fibre admirably adapted for padding cushions, pillows, &c.

The Indian species is that which now calls for our remarks. Of this there are many varieties, each possessing some distinguishing character of its own, arising from mode of treatment, soil, climate, &c.

It usually attains a height of four to six feet, is bi-triennial, but may be equally cultivated as an annual, germinating and ripening its seed within a period of from four to eight months. The leaves are five-lobed; the flowers are usually found blossoming singly at the extremity of the branches; the petals being of a lively yellow colour, with a small purple spot near the claw. The seeds are five in number, and are clothed with a firmly-adhering greyish down, beneath the short white wool of the capsule.[1]

The qualities by which the value of cottons are determined may be confined to three; viz. length of staple, strength of fibre, and cleanness of sample. Colour, which was at one time thought much of, is no longer looked upon as a matter of moment. Inferior as the cotton of India is allowed to be, as regards its staple and purity, there is every reason to believe that in durability it at least equals the produce of any part of America; and of this fact the Hindoos are themselves perfectly aware.

The accompanying illustration will convey to the reader a tolerably correct idea of the relative length of fibre of the leading qualities of cotton entering the markets of the world.

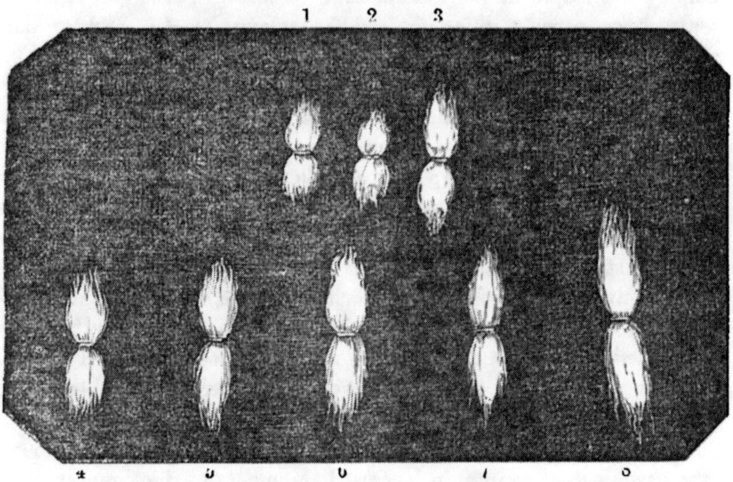

1. Surats.	2. Tinnevelly.	3. Egyptian.	4. Bourbon.
5. Uplands.	6. Pernambuco.	7. Georgian.	8. Sea-Island.

COTTON FIBRE.

In spite of its comparative inferiority, the Chinese have become large consumers of the cotton of India; and from taking a few hundred bales in the early part of the present century, they now consume as much as 50,000,000 lbs. annually. Some quantity is also exported

[1] Roylo's Indian Cotton, p. 140.

into the neighbouring countries on the north-west of India; and if we add to these outlets the home-demand for the manufacture of a variety of dresses, furniture-trappings, &c. in daily use amongst all classes of the natives, it will be seen that the yearly production of cotton within the Indian territories must be on an enormous scale.

It has been stated by one allowed to be a competent authority on all matters connected with the natives of India,[2] that the average consumption of cotton by the inhabitants of Hindostan amounts to not less than twenty pounds for each person. This will give a local annual consumption of 3,000,000,000 lbs.; and, with the quantities taken by Great Britain and China, a total yearly crop of 3,110,000,000 lbs.

High as the average of twenty pounds for each individual may appear at first sight, it is not in reality a large quantity, when we remember that, except amongst the highest classes, cotton dresses form their only wardrobe; and that, in addition to this source of demand, they employ this staple in the manufacture of curtains, cushions, hangings, tents, ropes, carpets, lining for saddles, palanquins, &c., and for many other purposes utterly unknown to Europeans.

From the figures above given, it is evident that, so far as the mere growth of cotton is concerned, India does at this moment produce annually a quantity five times as great as is worked up by the united machinery of Great Britain; in order, therefore, to obtain her supply from India in place of America, England has but to induce the natives of the former country to cultivate one-fifth more of the article, to obtain what she so much desires.

The anxiety manifested by the manufacturers, merchants, and political economists of England, that a large portion of our supply of this raw material should be derived from a country under our own government, in preference to seeing ourselves at the mercy of another nation for eight-tenths of our requirements, is no new feeling. It has been dominant during the greater part of the last sixty years; and although, as regards actual results, in increased shipments to this country, there would appear to be little, if any thing, achieved, it will be as well that we take a rapid survey of the measures adopted at different periods by the East India Company for the furtherance of this object.

As early as the year 1788, the Court of Directors urged the Indian authorities to give every possible encouragement to the growth and improvement of Indian cotton, at the same time ordering a shipment of 500,000 lbs. to be made. Shortly afterwards, screws for the embalement of the article were erected, and a variety of imported seed was

[2] Dr. Wighte.

distributed throughout the peninsula. From this time until the beginning of the present century the shipments of Indian cotton to England fluctuated between 700,000 lbs. and 3,300 lbs., the price of Surat kinds at Liverpool varying from *2s. 5d.* to *8d.* per lb.

In 1801, samples of the produce of Mauritius and Nankin seeds were received in England; and between that period and 1812 bounties were offered for improved samples, reports were received on the cotton resources of the various districts from the collectors, and quantities of West Indian and American seeds were sent out and distributed through various cotton districts, with copies of instructions carefully compiled. The shipments of cotton to England during this period varied from 27,783,000 lbs. to 694,000 lbs., with prices ranging between *3s.* and *8d.*

In 1813 and 1814 the war with America broke out; and strange to say, that although our supplies from the United States entirely ceased while hostilities lasted, the receipts of cotton from British India only amounted in those two years to 5,200,000 lbs., or 2,600,000 lbs. per annum. It was at this time that the first American planter was dispatched to India, with the view of aiding in the improved culture and preparation of cotton, taking with him a number of New Orleans sawgins.

A further encouragement of the efforts of private parties in this important matter was the allowance of the drawback of the whole of the internal and sea duties on cotton exported to Great Britain. This took place in 1816; and the effect of this and other measures was evidenced in the increase of the shipments to England from ten million pounds weight to forty millions in 1817, and eighty-six millions in the following year.

This increase was, however, not of a permanent character; for in the four following years the exports to Liverpool gradually declined to 6,742,000 lbs., prices in England having during that period declined from the war-figure of 1*s.* 6*d.* and 2*s.* to 5¼*d.* and 8½*d.*

From this period until the year 1840 the efforts of the government and of public bodies in India, as well as in this country, were confined to obtaining fresh supplies of seed from various parts of the world, endeavouring to improve the native mode of cleaning the cotton, and the more questionable procedure of offering large bounties for certain quantities and qualities of the article grown in India. The shipments of the article to England had during all this time fluctuated to nearly as great a degree as in any previous times, the extremes being 75,746,000 lbs. and 12,324,000 lbs.; the highest price realised by Surats in the Liverpool market for this period having been 1*s.* 4*d.*, and the lowest 2⅞*d.*

In 1840, Captain Bayles of the Madras army, having returned from a secret mission to the southern states of America, brought with him ten planters skilled in the growth and preparation of cotton, a great quantity of the best cotton-seed, as well as a large assortment of agricultural and mechanical implements employed in the States. Experimental culture on a liberal scale was now commenced in the districts of Broach, within the Bombay presidency; in Coimbatore and Tinnevelly, to the south of Madras; and in the Doab and Bundelcund, within the Bengal presidency. These were followed up by similar attempts at various other points within the three presidencies; the American planters were shifted from one locality to another, with a view of testing the comparative qualities of soil; in some instances model plantations were established and worked under the immediate supervision of these planters; in others, efforts were made to induce the native growers to cultivate some of the American varieties, with the seed of which they were supplied. In all these efforts little expense was spared; yet in spite of the lavish and continued outlay, nothing appears to have been arrived at beyond the conviction that, with but one or two exceptions, much time, labour, and money had been expended without any encouraging results.

Baffled in their attempts at the introduction of new varieties of the plant, the experimenters bent their efforts in another direction, and endeavoured to effect improvements in the culture and preparation of the indigenous species of the country. For several years, indeed up to a very recent period, this appears to have been the main object in view; the latest demonstration made by the Indian authorities has been the importation from England of two hundred cottage saw-gins, which were distributed equally through the three presidencies, and the offer made, through the Agricultural Society of India, of a premium of 500*l.* for an improved cotton-dressing machine adapted to native use.

How far these continued efforts, which have, on the whole, been spread over a period of nearly seventy years, have been attended with success, may be judged from the facts, that in 1848 the shipments of Indian cotton to Great Britain amounted to 84,101,000 lbs., being 4,500,000 lbs. less than in 1844, 13,200,000 lbs. less than in 1841, and 2,400,000 lbs. below the exports of 1818.

Taking the average of a number of years, the export of Indian cotton to England shews a sensible increase since the pacification of Europe. Thus the average shipments to Liverpool from the Indian ports during the five years immediately following the peace were 44,000,000 lbs.; whilst in the five years ending 1848 they amounted to 69,000,000 lbs.; in other words, they have averaged an increase of rather more than fifty per cent in thirty-three years. This augmentation, however, sinks into utter insignificance when compared with the progress of the cotton shipments from the United States to England during the same period, which was, in round numbers, from 45,000,000 lbs. to 600,000,000 lbs., shewing an increase of more than thirteen hundred per cent.

The argument that this increase of Indian cotton is highly satisfactory, seeing that it has taken place in the teeth of constantly falling prices in Europe, goes for very little, inasmuch as America has had the same disadvantage to contend against; for the relative values of the two articles remain much as they were thirty years since.

In the case of America the depression of the European markets has been met by improved and more economical methods of culture and preparation, the result of scientific skill and untiring energy. In India these elements have never been brought to bear beyond the model farms, for reasons which will be presently shewn. Other causes have, however, been at work, and enabled the export to be carried on in spite of the continually depressed markets. These have been a fall in the rate of freights from 14*l.* to 4*l.* 5*s.* and 2*l.* 15*s.* per ton, in other words, from 2½*d.* to ¾*d.* and ½*d.* per lb.; a decline in the exchange between the two countries of quite 8*d.* in the rupee, equal to nearly 2¼*d.* per lb. on the cost of the cotton; the diminution of the cost of inland carriage and insurance, owing to the complete pacification of India: this item gives a saving of 8*d.* per ton per mile on the land-carriage from Berar to Mirzapore, and of 3½*d.* per ton per mile on the water-conveyance thence to Calcutta, equal together to nearly 2½*d.* per lb. on the entire journey; and lastly, the change of route of Berar cotton, to Bombay in place of Calcutta, has effected a saving of ⅓*d.* per lb.; making a total economy of about 7*d.* per lb. on the charges attaching to the bulk of the Indian cottons shipped to England, and which has thus enabled the article to be so exported in the face of lower prices.[3]

By far the greater portion of the English supplies of Indian cotton are shipped from the port of Bombay, as may be seen by reference to the following figures:—

From Bombay	55,201,231	representing an average of 13 years ending 1846.
,, Calcutta	1,293,982	
,, Madras	3,973,074	
,, Tinnevelly	1,110,084	

Having thus seen that, at the end of labours spread over seventy years, after a large outlay of money and labour, after the importation

[3] Chapman's Cotton and Commerce of India, pp. 68-77.

of seed, tools, and superintendence, the quantity of Indian cotton obtained for England amounts to but one-sixteenth in value of her total requirements; that in but few respects does the bulk of this excel in quality that which was exported fifty years since; and that the culture of the plant has been very partially extended or improved in the chief cotton-growing districts, scarcely at all in provinces to which that cultivation is less known,—it behoves us to examine into the causes of this wholesale failure.

It must be borne in mind that the question of improvement of Indian cotton should be considered under three distinct heads: the introduction of better varieties, the amelioration of the quality and condition of the indigenous produce already grown, and the increased culture of the plant.

The opinions of the American planters who were engaged by the East India Company appear to have been that the soils selected for trial of new seed were adverse to the chances of success. That this has been so in several instances, and with some shew of reasoning, there can be little doubt; the black cotton soil has been, in not a few cases, supplanted by the red soil, especially of southern India, where some success has attended the trials thus made. There does not seem, however, to have been much, if any, attention paid to the peculiarities of climate, the degree of moisture, the temperature, nor of these points taken in connexion with varieties of soil.

It will require no argument to shew that conditions affecting the vegetable economy of sugar, coffee, or rice, must be not altogether without their value in regard to the development of the cotton-plant, whether in India or elsewhere. Yet it does not appear that this consideration has entered into the calculations of the many practical men engaged in the long labours of the cotton experiments of India.

It cannot be that, as has been said, any portion of these failures is attributable to the supineness of the agency employed. If the bulk of the experimentalists have been in the employ of government, and therefore not so likely to have taken a lively interest in the matter, what is to be said of the want of success attending private enterprise? All appear to have shared in the common disappointment; and it is clear that we must look elsewhere for causes of failure.

Whilst climate and soil, separately or together, have been at work in retardment of new culture or the introduction of new varieties, there are antagonisms to be found in other quarters, affecting not only these, but the improvement of the indigenous cotton by culture, and by care in picking, equally with the increase in the amount of crop produced.

Foremost amongst these are undoubtedly the almost total absence of roads and canals through the heart of India; absence of interest in the experiment on the part of the ryots, owing to causes I shall presently notice; and lastly, want of all security for the investment of European capital in the cotton-trade of the interior.

The first of these, although it might be supposed not to affect the produce of some of the cotton districts which are situated along the sea-board, has, nevertheless, a very material influence on the crops of these countries; but still more so in those more distant and extensive districts which furnish large quantities of exportable and locally consumed cotton. In the countries of Central India, not less than in those to the north and north-west, owing to the absence of all roads for vehicles, the ordinary means of conveyance is by pack-bullocks, who in vast droves track their slow and weary way across sandy, sterile tracts, through wild jungle-paths, and over steep ghauts, for hundreds of miles. To bring the cotton of Berar alone to Bombay, it is computed that the services of 180,000 head of cattle are required;[4] and when we remember that their journey is for a great distance performed through districts in which both water and fodder are always scarce, it will not be surprising that the utmost uncertainty prevails as to the receipt of crops at the port of shipment. This primitive mode of conveyance is not only the most tedious, but the most costly of any in existence; yet by far the greater part of British India possesses no roads which will allow of the employment of carts.

It is in vain that British enterprise and capital are brought to bear upon the great experiment of cotton, so long as the universal cry for roads is disregarded. British merchants have been found with energy sufficient to brave the difficulties attending the establishment of agencies in the interior; but their ardour is damped, their efforts thwarted, and their capital jeopardised, by the one great crying evil, the utter absence of roads available for carriages. The old mode of transport is of necessity resorted to—that of pack-bullocks; and so slow and costly is this, that long before one crop of cotton be dispatched from the place of growth, the following harvest will have commenced;[5] ships which have been provided in anticipation for the conveyance of this cotton to Europe are meanwhile awaiting its arrival in the harbour of Bombay until the shipping season shall have passed; and the interest on the capital thus indefinitely locked up accumulates, until it forms a heavy and grievous item amongst the charges of the operation.

4 The Cotton and Commerce of India, p. 79.

5 India under a Bureaucracy, p. 105.

It is not, however, in the disregard to the want of proper means of conveying produce from one province to the other that the authorities evince their apathy, and from which the development of the cotton re-

LOADED COTTON-HACKERY.

sources of India languishes. There are many other ways in which the industry of the country suffers; and, perhaps, in none other more surely and severely than in the surrendering of some of the finest and most promising districts, as regards cotton capabilities, into the hands of young and inexperienced civilians.

Facts speak more plainly than theories or arguments; and the following, which bears upon one of the most hopeful tracts of western India, is a case quite to the purpose. "The province of Candeish contains 12,078 square miles, of which it is estimated that the arable portion is 9772. Of this arable area, 1413 square miles are cultivated, and 8359 are lying waste. The population of the whole province was 785,991, according to a census taken in 1851. The number of villages in the whole province is 3837, of which 1079 are now uninhabited. The soil of Candeish is stated to be superior in quality to, and yields heavier crops than that of the Deccan and southern Mahratta country. Although so much of the country now lies in waste, the traces of a former country are to be seen in the mango and tamarind trees, and the many ruined wells which are still to be met with in the neighbourhood of almost every village. Of the five-sixths of the arable land, the five millions of square acres now lying waste, Captain Wingate remarks, *nearly the whole is comparatively fertile*, and suitable to the growth of exportable products, such as cotton, oil-seeds, &c."[6] Here then is a vast tract of most promising country with but one-sixth of its surface brought under cultivation, and having one-third of its once thriving villages entirely deserted! Can any thing speak more plainly than this does, of the neglectful state in which promising districts are left by the rulers of the country? It would be useless to inquire from what cause has arisen the desertion of those 1079 villages; although it is probable that the same indifference which looks calmly on, and provides no amelioration, had something to do with bringing about that melancholy state of things.

Of the immediate prospects held out to this district, which it must be remembered is equal in area to nearly half of Scotland, the reader may form some opinion from the quality of the functionaries placed in charge of it. At the end of July 1850, the Bombay government placed the province in the hands of a young gentleman, no doubt of exceedingly good family, and possibly possessing a first-rate classical education, but who, having only entered the Honourable Company's service in 1847, could not be expected to know any thing of the details of administration, or of the people and the country. This gentleman's assistant was still more juvenile in years and Indian experience, having had about fourteen months' acquaintance with the country. It is needless to speculate upon the amount of public mischief which the administrative experiments of these budding functionaries may bring about, or upon the number of ruined villages, or neglected fields, they may successively try their "'prentice hands" upon.

With regard to the reputed indifference of the ryots to make any attempts at improved modes of culture, or the introduction of new varieties, some grave doubts may well arise. From all available data it would appear, that it is the opposition of the native capitalists, and not the cultivators, that has to be encountered. These men are opposed to change of every kind, dreading the possible loss of any portion of their influence and gains; they are particularly averse to the introduction of any new varieties of the plant, as likely to interfere with the indige-

[6] "Cotton Circular" of Messrs. Ritchie, Stuart, and Co., Bombay, 1852.

nous kind, and which they pretend would bring down upon the country the "evil eye." So determined was the opposition of these bigoted men, that in many places they employed people to go out at night and root up the young American seedlings from the experimental fields.

The ryots indeed are entirely in the hands of this unscrupulous race of men, who alone profit by any improvement in their means, and who by a careful scrutiny of the proceedings of the former, generally contrive to leave them at the end of crop-time as poor as they began.[7] If there is any real indifference on the part of the poor cultivator to improvements, it is the result of the smallness of his wants, added to the utter hopelessness of any attempt at bettering his condition. There is, however, another and stronger cause at work than these; and that is, the want of a certain and sufficient price to compensate for any departure from old-established practices. It has been shewn that the proportion of cotton taken annually for export to Europe does not exceed one twenty-fourth part of the gross produce of the article; and that, for all local purposes, the fibre is as well adapted, or realises as much, when dirty and discoloured as when carefully prepared. As nearly all cultivation is carried on under loans from mahajuns, and other monied men, who purchase the crops at their own price, it follows that the ryot has

[7] "The cotton is produced by the ryot. He is always in his banker's books as deep in proportion to his means as his European master, and can do nothing without aid. The brokers, or cotton-cleaners, or gin-house men, are the middlemen between the chetty and the ryot. The chetties being monied men, make an advance to the broker. The broker is particular in classifying the seed-cotton, and pays for it according to cleanliness, and then he has much of the trash and rotten locks picked out, not to make the cotton better, but because the rubbish chokes the churka, and prevents it from working. The good cotton is then separated from the seed, and the bad stuff which had been taken away from the good is beaten with a stone to loosen up the rotten fibre from the seed, and then it is passed through the churka. The good cotton and this bad stuff are both taken into a little room, six feet by six, which is entered by a low door, about eighteen inches by two feet, and a little hole as a ventilator is made through the outer wall. Two men then go in with a bundle of long smooth rods in each hand, and a cloth is tied over the mouth and nose; one man places his back so as to stop this little door completely to prevent waste, and they both set to work to whip the cotton with their rods, to mix the good and bad together so thoroughly that a very tolerable article is turned out; even after all this bedevilling, if the people get a living price for it, they let it go as it is. But, as is usually the case, they are shaved so close, that they are driven to resort to another means of realising profit. They add a handful or two of seed to every bundle, and this is delivered to the chetties, and the chetties deliver it to their European agents, and the European agents save their exchange, and their object is gained. The cotton is taken by the manufacturer at a low price, because he knows not what he is buying."—*Letter from an American Planter to the Madras Government on Culture of Cotton in India*, p. 37.

little prospect indeed of releasing himself from the thraldom of these harpies, and coming in contact with buyers for the English markets.

To suppose that the agriculturists of India are incapable of being stimulated to any effort at improvement, to believe that they would not strive to better their condition if it were in their power to do so, is to consider them as differing from all other men in every part of the world. It is not found to be so with the Hindoo worker in cities; and unless it can be shewn that a rural life has the power of subverting the natural feelings of mankind, this hollowest of all hollow pretences must fall to the ground.

The want of roads, which has so long operated against the introduction of European agency and capital into the interior, is scarcely of such serious moment as the insecurity attaching to all advances made by the English dealers. It has been the profession of the government to desire that British merchants should open up the country by the establishment of agencies for the purchase of cotton in various districts; yet when the uncertainties and procrastination of the local courts of justice were pointed out, and a request made that private capitalists should be allowed to avail themselves of the summary and only effectual process for recovery of advances which was pursued by the government collectors under similar circumstances, the authorities consistently with the red-tapism which pervades the whole system, declined to accede to so reasonable a request.[8] Nevertheless we are told that the government is most anxious to aid in developing the resources of India!

Looking at all the facts that have been thrown together in this chapter, and summing them up, we find the great cotton question to stand thus. British India, although admitted to be capable of supplying England with the whole of her cotton, furnishes but one-eighth of her imports of that article, the shipments of India cotton to this country in 1847 and 1848 being actually less than they had been at four previous dates; whilst those of 1845 and 1846 were considerably below the exports of the five previous years. The quality of the article, with a few solitary exceptions, varies in no respect from that of fifty years since. English capital and skill have been in vain introduced into the interior, where government, whilst professing a desire to assist, has in reality refused all aid. The Honourable Company have, during a period of about seventy years, introduced a dozen American planters, a score of ploughs, a few hundred bushels of seed, opened a model-farm or two, offered some paltry premiums, and lately dispatched two hundred cotton-gins for distribution amongst two millions of cultiva-

[8] India under a Bureaucracy, p. 108.

tors; and when all these gigantic efforts, paraded through whole hecatombs of dispatches, that would supply ample fuel for a hundred suttees,—when these have all failed, the red-tapists protest that all has been done that can be done! It does not appear to have occurred to the rulers of India, that the same means which have so completely changed the aspect and destiny of other countries might not have been without influence in this tax-devoured land; that what saw-gins, and ploughs, and model-farms, failed to achieve, might peradventure have been accomplished by purifying the courts of law and making a few roads.

The utter neglect of this branch of public works, despite the reports and complaints on the subject from all parts of the vast continent of India, needs a separate chapter, where it will be seen that information upon this vital necessity of the state has long since been furnished to the hands of those whose duty it should have been to have apportioned some honest fraction of the millions wrung from the industry of the people to the satisfying their wants. The remedy was within their grasp; but they preferred the quackery of theoretical experiments, the parade of official dispatches, the mockery and mystification of parliamentary blue-books. One brief emphatic order, meant for obedience, which said, "Let there be roads," would have changed the face of the country, ameliorated the condition of the people, and made the cotton-trade of India with Europe a splendid fact, instead of, as at present, a disgraceful failure.

CHAPTER V.

ROADS, RIVERS, AND RAILWAYS.

To dilate upon the advantages arising from facility of communication through a country so extensive, and in many parts so densely peopled, as India, in a book intended for the millions of Great Britain, would be a task so totally unneeded, that I may at once proceed to that which will most fully illustrate the present subject, and examine to what extent and in what manner the former rulers of India undertook such works of public utility as roads, canals, &c., before proceeding to notice their present condition.

In regions so exposed to seasons of great drought, or, on the contrary, to destructive floods, it might naturally be expected that wherever agriculture was followed, wherever the hand of man sowed the seed that was to minister to his daily wants, there some provision, however rude, however ineffective, would be resorted to in order to guard the husbandman against the consequences of either of the above casualties. The earliest records of Hindoo history tell how works of embankment and irrigation were executed, and how careful were the inhabitants, even in those remote ages, of the fructifying showers, which but for some provision of industry would to a great extent have been lost to the country.

It requires no stretch of the imagination to paint the feelings of a people chiefly occupied by agriculture, who, situated in the vast plains of central and northern India, saw the genial showers of each monsoon falling upon the elevated table-lands, and rushing past them to the great rivers, lost to all useful purposes, and serving but to cause a temporary burst of vegetation in their immediate vicinity, flooding the lands along the river-banks, and then rolling onwards in their downward course over rocks and precipices, until at last they were lost in the mighty ocean far in the south.

Many, though simple, were the early earthworks of the Hindoo husbandmen: huge dams of stone, timber, and soil were flung across the mouths of mountain-gorges; and in the artificial tanks thus formed vast bodies of water would be gathered, for use during the dry seasons by means of channels cut along the slopes of the rocky heights, and led down to the required spots by earthen aqueducts. In other cases the waters of some of the principal rivers were carried by similar channels to spots which were otherwise out of the reach of the fertilising powers of those streams.

The traffic in that more remote period, carried on, as it was, by the rudest vehicles near the largest towns, and by coolies in remote

THE SUGGAR, OR VILLAGE-CART.

districts, does not appear to have called for any extensive roads, nor were bridges in much use; but as time rolled on, as the human race increased with tropical fruitfulness in that teeming land, the wants of man became multiplied and enlarged, and his industrial powers were called forth to satisfy them.

The Mahomedan conquerors of India were ever alive to the necessities of the country; and we find that even those monarchs who were most occupied by war were never unmindful of their subjects, but found

INDIAN CARAVANSERAI AND TRAVELLERS.

time, amidst all their conquests, for works of public utility. Of Feroze Shah we read, that among other undertakings for promoting the prosperity and happiness of his people, he constructed 50 dams across rivers, 30 reservoirs for purposes of irrigation, 40 mosques, 30 colleges, 100 caravanserais for travellers, 100 public baths, and 150 bridges. Besides which, he formed a canal of considerable magnitude—the largest, indeed, at that time in existence—stretching from the Chetang Nala, a tributary of the Sub-Himalayas, from which it derived its supply, into the country west of the Jumna.

To the enterprise of the emperor Akbar, India is indebted for a series of canal-works of greater extent and utility than any previously in existence; he appears to have placed these public works under regularly appointed superintendents called "Chiefs of the Waters," in whose hands were the regulation of the supply, the levying of the rates on the districts irrigated, the maintenance of the embankments, the protection and repairs of sluices and bridges, and all police details in connection with them. Nor was the useful only attended to: the pleasure and comfort of the traveller who might wend his weary way along these works were not forgotten, and the careful monarch ordered by special edict, in reference to the great Jumna canal, that on both sides, as far as the city of Hissar, "trees of every description, both for shade and blossom, be planted, so as to make it like the canal under the trees in paradise; and that the sweet flavour of the fruits may reach the mouth of every one; and that from these luxuries a voice may go forth to travellers, calling them to rest in the cities, where their every want will be supplied."

Not less extensive, and of far greater solidity and finish, was the famous Delhi canal constructed by the emperor Shah Jehan, under the superintendence of his architect, Ali Murdan Khan. This truly noble work took its course from the Feroze canal, southerly, until it reached the base of the Aravilli Mountains, through a shoulder of which a channel sixty feet deep was cut; and thence masonry-work carried the great body of waters through the very heart of the capital, Delhi, at that period in the height of its imperial splendour. Here, after having ministered to the necessities of the husbandmen during a course of several hundred miles, this magnificent aqueduct was made subservient to luxury and taste. A thousand streams flowed from its solid bed on either side, and spreading themselves through masonry channels into every quarter of the royal city, disported, in varied shapes, through marble jets, or cooled the fevered limbs in sculptured baths, or trickled over the gorgeous flowers in harems, lawns, and terraces, or anon flowed to the humble homes of labourers, and slaked the poor man's thirst, and bathed the poor man's brow.

To this day there remains abundant evidence of the multiplicity, the extent, and the fertilising powers of the water-courses fed by the great Delhi canal; traditionary reports amongst the people in the neighbourhood tell that the revenues derived from the villages skirting its banks sufficed for the maintenance of 12,000 horse-soldiers. Some idea of the magnitude of these works, and of the efficiency of the system by which they were regulated may be formed, when it is stated, that on this one canal there were placed a working and protective force of 1000 armed peons, 500 horsemen, a proper staff of officers, and a large body of excavators and masons.[1]

The Eastern Jumna or Doab Canal was another work of the same monarch, though not equal in extent or value to those previously described. The lands of the Punjab were not neglected amidst all these vast undertakings; for although we have no records relating to the works of irrigation in the country of the Five Rivers, there are abundant proofs of the public spirit of the Mahomedan rulers of the country.[2]

It might not be altogether uninstructive to compare the noble and enduring works of these Eastern despots with the progress made in a like direction in our own country, or, indeed, in any western kingdom, at that period. The two pictures, it is greatly to be feared, would not bear comparison. In this country, we know, at any rate, that at the epoch alluded to we possessed not a single canal; that our roads were, with few exceptions, mere cattle-tracks; that our largest cities could not boast of the supply of water, or of the police protection accorded to the humblest towns within the empire of Delhi; nor had an English traveller, in journeying from London to Highgate in those early days, so great a certainty of reaching his destination in safety as had any of Shah Jehan's meanest subjects in travelling from the Punjab frontier to Delhi, or from the latter city to Allahabad.

Each of these barbarous sovereigns expended as much money in works of public utility as would have supported any of the standing armies of Europe in those days.

Throughout many other parts of Hindostan, in the peninsula of India, as well as in the western portions of the country, exist the remains of extensive canals, of massive bunds or dams, and artificial tanks. At no time, until the last convulsions of the Tartar empire, ushering in its approaching decadence, were those works lost sight of by the successive emperors of Delhi. Their public spirit would be well

[1] Calcutta Review, vol. xii. p. 83. [2] Ibid. vol. xii. p. 142.

imitated by the present rulers of the Indian empire, who, with the narrow views which prompt them to look no further than "to-day," frequently undertake canal work, which furnishes them with a large surplus revenue from water-rates, but dare not venture to copy the liberality of their Tartar teachers, and give back to their subjects some portion of the fees in useful roads or wells. In no instance does the petty shop-keeping genius of Leadenhall-street stand forth in such deformity as in this; that whilst large sums have been disbursed for purposes of irrigation, whence an income is at once derived far more than sufficient to cover the whole of the outlay, and yield a steadily-increasing annual revenue, the votes for roads and bridges have been on the most paltry scale.

It is by no means an easy task to ascertain the precise sums which have been spent upon public works in India, seeing that in three different official statements, all emanating from the Court of Directors, we find as many different totals of their annual cost during the fourteen years ending 1850-1, varying from 346,092*l.*[3] down to 197,936*l.* Deducting from the largest sum one-third, which is the usual cost of superintendence, we have 230,667*l.* spent throughout India, about equal to the upkeep of the streets of a large English town.

A reference to official documents shews that in the Bengal and north-west provinces, during the ten years ending 1848-9, the expenditure on roads and bridges was at an average rate of 94,485*l.* per annum; which, as compared with the taxation of these provinces, amounted to something less than three-quarters per cent of the gross revenue; the works of irrigation, by a like calculation, had cost on the average 51,922*l.*; being below the rate of one-half per cent on the gross revenue.

From evidence given recently before the Commons' Committee on Indian affairs, by civil servants of the government, we were told that Bengal, a tract of country far larger than England, possesses but *one* road worthy of the name; and that road chiefly kept up for military purposes. What its real value is to the community may be gathered from the fact, that during certain seasons of the year this military road is for many miles quite impassable for vehicles.[4] Instances are not

[3] Public Works in India, p. 208.

[4] "There is only one metalled road in the Lower Provinces, the grand trunk road, and it is the only road supported at the expense of government. The other roads are made by the landholders on the requisition of the magistrate, or with local funds. It is a striking proof of the little regard paid to the public convenience so far as this

wanting of gentlemen being compelled to leave their carriages deeply imbedded in the slough of this great military trunk-road, and tramp it on foot for a distance of sixty miles towards Benares.[5] This is in a province of Hindostan which has been in our possession for nearly a century, and yields a yearly gross revenue of 14,695,870*l.*, equal to the income of Great Britain, not many years since.

What would have been thought of the imperial executive, had they limited this country to one road between London and York, whilst absorbing fourteen millions in taxation! Can it be matter for astonishment that India has been sinking, year by year, in real prosperity; that her industrial classes have become gradually impoverished and fewer in numbers; that the resources of the country have become stagnant, and that whilst the revenues shew an annual decline, there appears no way for remedying this alarming state of things, but by stopping the greater part of the public works!

As to cross-roads, there are literally *none.* It is stipulated that the zemindars shall maintain the village-roads of their districts from the proceeds of the farmed revenue of land; but it is notorious in India that the fulfilment of this is never attempted; and no steps are taken by the authorities to enforce the regulation. Some of the statistical returns relative to Indian roads are very voluminous, and go into many imposing details, with a view of bewildering the reader with the immensity of the great Indian highways. Some of the roads therein are stated to be 1200 to 1400 miles in length,—very formidable distances doubtless to English minds; but inquiry shews that but little more than half of those roads have ever been constructed; whilst the occasional condition of the completed portions may be judged from what has been previously stated.

With regard to the mail-lines, of which a good deal is made in Blue Books and elsewhere, they are simply bullock-tracks, available only for the camel-couriers employed by government, and the Dâk-

great highway is concerned, that of two small bridges which were carried away by floods in 1847, neither is yet rebuilt, though the situation is in one of the most populous and highly cultivated districts, where the traffic is great, and within thirty-five miles from Calcutta; but in the place of one, only a ferry was for some years established, though both these bridges appeared in the report published by the House of Commons as public works which had been sanctioned; and to the present day they are replaced only with temporary erections, insufficient for the traffic; and on one of them tolls are established where there were none before."—*Petition from Inhabitants of Bengal and Agra*, 1853.

[5] Delhi Gazette, July 1852.

runners (letter-carriers), who convey the mail-bags on their heads or shoulders, from town to town, or between one district and another.[6]

In no instance has the universal want of roads been felt so cruelly as during the famines which unfortunately occur in many parts of India

CAMEL-COURIER.

every ten or dozen years. At such times, although food may be plentiful to wastefulness in one district, in another not more remote than Middlesex and Lancashire, gaunt famine may be sweeping the land by thousands and tens of thousands of human beings; and no price that can be given, not even the ransom of kingdoms, will suffice to bring from all that abundance one single bushel of grain. The roads are im-

[6] "The Calcutta and Bombay mail-road was 1,170 miles in length, of which 168 miles had been previously constructed, and how much completed was not stated. In 1845 the Court were said to have directed that the expenditure on this line should be restricted to the formation of a road adapted to the transit of the mails. Their lordships would perhaps associate the idea of mails with macadamized roads, a mail-coach, a smart coachman, and a guard behind with a blunderbuss to fire at the Thugs and robbers. But the fact was, that a conveyor of mails in India was a pedestrian very lightly clad, carrying a pair of baskets balanced on his shoulders by a bamboo, and a mail-road was but another word for a footpath."—*Speech of the Earl of Albemarle on Indian affairs in the House of Lords, May 2d*, 1853.

passable, the cattle are alike starving, and cities and provinces are depopulated almost within sight of plenty.[7] In 1823 rice sold in Candeish at the rate of 50 lbs. for a shilling; whilst at Poonah, not 200 miles distant, owing to the want of roads, the supply of grain failed them, a famine ensued, and rice sold at 4 lbs. for a shilling.[8] In connection with this very country of Candeish may be mentioned another fact illustrative of the effects of neglecting roads. In the year 1847 the collector of the district was compelled to grant the cultivators remissions of the land-tax; not from any successive failure of crops, but the very reverse. The yield of the province had become augmented so far beyond the local requirements, and the state, or rather the total want of roads, was such a barrier to the disposal of their produce elsewhere, that their crops lay useless on their hands, and they found themselves without the means of meeting the assessment.[9]

In the presidency of which this district forms a portion the cost of superintendence of public works amounted to fifty per cent on the work performed, and yet we learn from the report of Sir George Clerk that a great portion of the outlay had been lost by the bad quality of the work.

Examining the state of roads in the Madras presidency, we find that an outlay of about a half per cent of the revenue is all that is accorded the people, although in many parts the land is fertile to a degree, producing the finest indigo and cotton, and an abundance of good sugar. As a consequence, the roads here are in a most disgraceful state, impassable during the rainy season:[10] and what renders this the more

7 "Famines occur decennially, some of which, within our time, have swept their millions away. In 1833, 50,000 persons perished in the month of September in Lucknow; at Khanpore 1,200 died of want, and half a million sterling was subscribed by the bountiful to relieve the destitute; in Guntoor 250,000 human beings, 74,000 bullocks, 159,000 milch cattle, and 300,000 sheep and goats died of starvation; 50,000 people perished in Marwa; and in the north-west provinces half a million of human lives are supposed to have been lost. The living preyed upon the dead; mothers devoured their children; and the human imagination could scarcely picture the scenes of horror that pervaded the land. In twenty months' time a million and a half of people must have died of hunger, or of its immediate consequences. The direct pecuniary loss occasioned to government by this single visitation exceeded 5,000,000*l.* sterling,—a sum which would have gone far to avert the calamity from which it arose, had it been expended in constructing thoroughfares to connect the interior with the sea-coast, or districts where scarcity prevailed with those where human food was to be had in abundance."—*East Indian Petition presented to the House of Lords*, 1853.

8 Cotton and Commerce of India, p. 114.

9 Ibid.

10 "The road from this extensive district (Cuddapah) to the presidency is in no better state. It is, in short, proverbially bad, even among Madras roads; and there is one part of it which is literally used by the Military Board as a trial-ground to test

cruel is, that the Mysore country possesses some most excellent roads, but which are rendered useless as regards communication with the maritime and trading districts, seeing that in the country contiguous to it there are no roads to meet its own, and therefore they are unavailable beyond its own territories.

AN INDIAN ROAD.

Having thus shewn how cruelly the executive have neglected to carry out the most ordinary construction, or upkeep of roads and bridges, which however essential to the welfare of a people, do not realise any immediate and direct return to the coffers of government, it shall be my task to shew how much more has been done in works producing an early and certain return.

Upwards of forty years have elapsed since the attention of the British government was first seriously directed towards the restoration of the canals and tanks of their Mahomedan predecessors. Surveys were ordered, reports and estimates were sent in, a few experimental

the powers of new gun-carriages, which are pronounced safe if they pass this severe ordeal !"—*Calcutta Review,* December 1851.

canal-pieces were opened, and it was soon made apparent, that however slow a road might be in replenishing the treasury of the Company, there was no question as to the profit attaching to water-works for purposes of irrigation, and that the executive might look to them for results as brilliant as those of any mining operations. Whatever doubts may have existed in the minds of the authorities, in the first instance, as to the propriety of undertaking these truly national works, must have long since vanished; and although much false economy was then practised, to the detriment of these operations, they have, in nearly every case, yielded an annual income equal to the whole sum expended upon them.

At the present time the generality of these canals are in admirable order, and no doubt quite equal to their condition under the Tartar emperors. Some idea may be formed of the extent of these works, and the general efficiency of the arrangements, when it is stated, that on one line, that to the west of the Jumna, there are not less than 214 masonry and timber bridges, 672 stone outlets for irrigation, 11 mills, and 23 mill-bridges, besides an infinity of small cuts and outlets for various purposes.

The extent of land receiving irrigation from this one source was, according to official returns, 1015 square miles; the population benefiting by it nearly 300,000; and the amount of revenue drawn by government from the land so watered was 93,791*l.* annually, nearly all of which was attributable to the use of the stream.

The chief source of direct revenue from these canals is, of course, the water-rent from the villages partaking of the irrigation; and this rent is levied either on the extent irrigated, according to the nature of the cultivation, or by the area of the aperture for feeding the cross channels; these rates vary from two to four shillings per annum per square inch of the opening, and one to ten shillings per acre per annum. Revenue is also derived from the watering of cattle, for the supply of tanks, from mills erected on the canal worked by the stream, from fines and from transit-dues of goods conveyed on them. In 1826-7 the total revenue from all these sources on this one canal amounted to 4215*l.* In 1846-7 the income was 30,288*l.*, leaving a net revenue of 12,027*l.*[11]

To this income, however, must be added the known addition to the land-tax, arising from the increased culture by irrigation; and this in the districts now treated of amounted, a few years since, to not less than 29,691*l.*, which, added to the water-rents, &c. 30,288*l.*, bring up

[11] Calcutta Review, vol. xii. p. 99.

the total to nearly 60,000*l.*; being at the rate of thirty-six per cent on the capital originally sunk in the work, after deducting the yearly working expenses.

The entire length of this canal and its branches is 445 miles, exclusive of the main water-courses, for feeding the village sluices. This extensive line is under the control of a superintendent, five deputies, and seven overseers, all Europeans; besides about 113 native clerks, overseers, and artificers, who are divided into separate districts or zillahs; and have their regular functions of police, revenue, or labour to perform. In addition to their canal duties, they have also charge of extensive plantations of building-trees planted along the banks; and from the sale of the timber thus grown a yearly revenue of fifty per cent on the outlay is derived.[12]

This sketch of the Western Jumna canal will serve for a description of the remainder in Central and Western India and the southern peninsula. Looking at the successful results of these undertakings, and the large amounts of revenue derived from them, it does appear criminal indeed that a more liberal provision for the formation and up-keep of roads is not made in those districts whose necessities cry so loudly for relief.

The same remarks may be applied with equal justice to the revenues derived from the tolls on navigable rivers, which are levied for the ostensible purpose of keeping open the navigation, and originally with the understanding that the tolls were to be devoted to such purposes alone. That this appropriation of tolls is no longer observed may be seen by a statement[13] shewing that in the case of the Nuddea rivers, small tributaries of the Ganges in the lower provinces of Bengal, not one-fourth of the income is applied legitimately, the large balance being paid in to the general treasury, to swell the ways and means of the government, who conveniently looses sight of all stipulations on this head. The effect of this state of things may be inferred from the fact of these rivers being under the superintendence of an Englishman at a monthly salary of 100*l.*; whilst the whole labour establishment under him is kept down to 28*l.* The consequence of this is, that for four months in the year those rivers are quite impassable, although 80,000 boats depend on their waters for navigation, and actually pay tolls for the purpose of keeping open the channels, to the yearly amount of 23,873*l.*; government expends out of this sum but 5848*l.*; of which 1200*l.* is for European superintendence.[14]

[12] Calcutta Review, vol. xii. p. 97.

[13] Calcutta Englishman, Jan. 5, 1853.

[14] "The first superintendent ever appointed was a *protégé* of the Marquis of Hast-

That a system so vicious, so opposed to all sound and enlightened views, should prove ruinous to every branch of industry cannot be matter for wonder; we accordingly find many cities once famed for their arts and manufactures left without trade, half depopulated, and bereft of every vestige of their once happy condition. It is related by a writer of the present century, that in one city alone he was acquainted with the failure of between fifty and sixty bankers and wholesale merchants, and that similar disasters were occurring in other places.

Closely allied to the reconstruction and enlargement of canals of irrigation, and not one whit of less value to an agricultural country, is the embankment of rivers, by means of what are termed *bunds* (masonry work). These bunds, by confining the waters of the river within their proper channel, not only preserve the growing crops of large tracts of low-lying country from destruction during the wet months, but at the same time economise the contents of the rivers against the dry season, when they are turned to account by means of sluices and aqueducts similar to, and under the like arrangements, as those of canals.

Many of the larger rivers of Bengal, and some of those in the Madras presidency, have been thus embanked, and with the happiest results. The protection which has been thus afforded the native landowners and ryots has induced them to undertake culture on a scale and system which, under the insecurity of the old régime, could not have been attempted. In the Tanjore country the fruits of this policy have been most abundant. During a period of forty-five years the local government has expended on embankments and the attendant works not less than 390,000*l*., or at the rate of 8600*l*. per annum. The result has been an increase in the revenues of the district from 314,000*l*. to 493,000*l*., or 179,000*l*. per annum; whilst the population has swollen from 800,000 to 1,300,000.[15] A portion of this increase of revenue and

ings, and the present one was aid-de-camp of Lord Hardinge; an able man, as his report testifies, and a gallant one, by his antecedents, and therefore, we must be permitted to say, out of his proper position. If European superintendence is required, the office is fit for a respectable English workman; and in England a pound or thirty shillings a week would be his remuneration. In connexion with this view of the office, it may be mentioned, that the superintendent is subordinate to the superintending engineer of the lower provinces, to whom the report above alluded to is made, and who reports to the governor of Bengal, who reports to the government of India, which reports to the Court of Directors, which sends the dispatch to the Board of Control, which of course understands and cares nothing or little about the matter; and so this system of taxation on trade and commerce and of jobbery continues, and we fear will continue, unless Parliament institutes searching local inquiries."—*Calcutta Englishman*, January 5, 1853.

[15] Calcutta Review.

population may no doubt be attributable to other and ordinary causes; but there can be no question that by far the greater share is due to the politic outlay upon the river works.

In view of the present wretched state of internal communication in India, the prospect of a system of railroads being carried out in that neglected country appeared as something almost too good for realisation. And so thought the authorities in Leadenhall-street; for in every instance in which a railway company has been started, they seem to have treated the matter as a very playful joke, not at all likely to result in any thing serious. All sorts of difficulties and delays were heaped around these projects; and references out and home again were made with a most determined spirit: but their surest game was contemptuous neglect; for a letter to be noticed at all at the end of many months was rather an unusual thing; and more than one instance is on record when the twenty-four directors took two whole years to concoct a reply to a letter from a railway company!

Procrastination is not confined to the initiatory stages in railway operations; it assails these disturbers of official lassitude in their every stage. It spreads a net-work of red-tape across their path, from which the unfortunates rarely escape. It professes, in high-sounding dispatches meant for the public eye, the utmost desire to forward the views of the railway officials, and at the same moment pens "private and confidential" instructions to local authorities, echoing one emphatic and well-understood command—to delay. The delay, of course, is provided; and often, where least anticipated, difficulties start up which, at first of small apparent moment, give rise eventually to whole reams of official correspondence; whilst the public wonder that, with so many professions of co-operation from the government, such small progress is made with Indian railways.

Madras, which appears likely to be the last to possess a railway, was first in the field; and so long since as 1832 we find a railroad proposed to be made from Madras westwards in the direction of Bangalore. Four years later a survey was made, and a detailed report sent in to the authorities; and in 1845 a company for establishing railway communications in the presidency was formed in London by a number of influential men. In 1847 the company was dissolved, not for want of funds, or from any doubts of the success of the plan, but because the India House officials would not condescend a reply to any of their letters! A portion of the direction, however, persevered, and the result has been that the government agreed to a guarantee of $4\frac{1}{2}$ per cent on 500,000*l.* for ninety-nine years.

The works of the Madras Railway Company have been much retarded. Several lines have been surveyed, but that from Madras to Arcot, and eventually to Bangalore, running almost due west, has been selected as the precursor of the operations, inasmuch as it extends through a district fertile in the extreme. The first section is already partly in progress, and there is no doubt but that the line will be finally extended so as to meet the Great Indian Peninsula Line.

This latter project, originally termed the Great Eastern Railway, was undertaken chiefly in London, in 1842, with a proposed capital of six millions sterling, and an intended line of operations 1300 miles in extent.

In 1848 negotiations had so far progressed with the various authorities of Leadenhall Street, Cannon Row, and Bombay, that a guarantee of 5 per cent was granted the company upon a preliminary outlay of 500,000*l.* for the purpose of opening one section of the line as far as Callian, about thirty-five miles in extent. Operations were eventually commenced, and it was here that the first railway-ground was broken in India. At the present moment fifteen miles of this line, viz. from Bombay to Tannah, are open for traffic, consisting of a single rail, with masonry-work for a double line, and the remainder is expected to be so during the current year. At Callian it is proposed to extend the railway in two directions—one line running in a north-easterly direction to Allahabad on the Ganges, by way of Candeish and other cotton-producing districts; the second extending south-easterly, through Tannah and Poonah, and across a portion of the Nizam's dominions, until it reaches the Madras railway. In addition to the portion now in progress, contracts are in hand for a further extent of 200 miles.

The estimated cost of construction on this line is 15,000*l.* per mile of double rail, the expense of working at 600*l.* per mile; and from the extreme costliness of the present wretched mode of conveyance, there would appear to be no doubt of a handsome dividend being realised on the amount invested. Much of the expense of these works will arise from the difficulty of crossing the ghauts or elevated lands by which Bombay is surrounded; the lowest points admitting of passage, being between one and two thousand feet above the sea-level.

The first indications of a railway movement in the Bengal presidency was early in 1843. Two years later, the formation of two distinct railway companies was announced. One of these, the Great Western of Bengal, with a proposed capital of 4,000,000*l.*, was to open a line from Calcutta to Rajmahal on the Ganges, a distance of about 200 miles. The East India Railway Company proposed, with an equal capital, to construct a line of railroad between Calcutta and Mirzapore, avoiding the valley of the Ganges, and making for its destination by a more direct, and at the same time a more difficult line; this distance was 450 miles.

Eventually these two companies became amalgamated, their capital was reduced to 1,000,000*l.*, and in 1848, under the title of the East Indian Railway Company, they obtained a government guarantee of 5 per cent on their capital, for the purpose of a line, 42 miles in length, to Pandooah, on the road to Rajmahal, and thence, by a branch-rail 79 miles long, to the Burdwan collieries. These works were commenced in September 1850, and are expected to be opened by the end of the present year.

A further capital of a million, for carrying the line to Rajmahal has been raised under a guarantee of $4\frac{1}{2}$ per cent; and for this section surveys are in progress. In both instances the local governments undertake to provide the land.

The Great North of India Railway Company, projected some years since, has at length given place to the Agra, or Upper India Railway Company, which, with a capital of four millions sterling, proposes to connect the northern waters of the Indus with the navigable portion of the Ganges. Starting from Allahabad, where the deep water of the latter river ceases, the railway will in the first section reach Cawnpore, a distance of 130 miles; thence to Furruckabad, another division will extend for 80 miles. Ninety miles further, the ancient city of Agra will be reached; whence, by a fourth stage of 100 miles, Delhi, the famed capital of the Tartar empire, will be gained.

From Delhi to Lahore and the Indus, future lines are looked to as offering a tempting investment for capital. It is thought that most of this line may be completed for 7000*l.* a mile, as the country through which it will extend offers no obstacles to engineering operations, and indeed appears as though specially adapted for such works.

The Upper India Railway would certainly appear to offer peculiar advantages, inasmuch as it will commence at the precise spot where deep water ceases, and where the river steamers are compelled to halt in their upward course. From Allahabad northwards the navigation of the Ganges is so difficult and tedious, that insurance on goods so conveyed is as high as from Calcutta to England; whilst the cost of land-carriage is at the rate of from 4*d.* to 8*d.* per mile. The government sanction to this undertaking, and the consequent guarantee, have at length been received; and steps will therefore be taken towards commencing operations.

It would be difficult to over-estimate the value of railroads to British India, situated, as that vast country is, without the means of conveying its produce from one district to another, unless at a cost and with a delay which in too many instances act as a complete barrier to industrial progress. Considering the immense advantages the inhabitants of Europe have derived from railway communication, although previously in possession of first-rate roads in all directions, and of numerous rivers and canals, it is not too much to say, that to bestow the same powers of locomotion upon people entirely cut off from inter-traffic, except in the immediate vicinity of a few great rivers, is to endow them with another existence, to give them a status and a future of which they could before have had but little idea.

ESCORT OF TREASURE TO UPPER PROVINCES.

CHAPTER VI.

THE COMMERCIAL HISTORY OF THE THREE PRESIDENCIES; WITH A SKETCH OF THE MORALITY OF ANGLO-INDIAN COMMERCE AND BANKING IN THE NINETEENTH CENTURY.

ALTHOUGH in the records of nations, wars and politics occupy the greater share of the historian's attention; although the exploits of the warrior and the subtleties of the diplomatist eclipse the more humble works of the merchant,—it must not be forgotten that it is to commerce the world owes all that is worth fighting and diplomatising for. It was to snatch from the proud Venetian Republic some share of their vast wealth, flowing from the monopoly of Eastern trade, that the ships of Portugal braved the dangers of the Cape of Storms, and tracked unknown and distant seas. It was trade which drew after those brave adventurers the wary Hollander, the jealous Frenchman, the hardy Dane; and it was this commerce which captivated the timid and heavy faculties of the English nation, and drew our ships slowly but surely to engross a share of the marvellous riches of the fabled East.

It was commerce which first attracted our ancestors thither; it is commerce which keeps us there; and it was the pretended exigencies of this same commerce which, during the last half century, brought about the absorption of native states, of independent territories, and of friendly powers. Commerce carried the British arms to the farthest banks of the Indus, and planted our flag at the foot of the lofty Himalayas; commerce gave us unlimited dominion through the Eastern Archipelago, and commerce swept those treacherous seas of pirates. The ruling-power in Indian affairs is balanced after an awkward and unfortunate fashion between Leadenhall Street and Cannon Row; but there is another lever brought to bear, unseen but not unfelt, whose fulcrum rests between the Liverpool Exchange and the Manchester Chamber of Commerce.

A chapter devoted to the rise and progress of the commerce of India would be incomplete without some notice of the trade opened by the nations of continental Europe with the East. As pioneers in this commerce we find the Portuguese, who were first attracted to those remote countries by the great value of the traffic carried on by the Venetians, by way of Egypt, with various regions eastward of the Red Sea; and we learn that their first efforts, after having reached India by the Cape of Good Hope, were directed to the establishment of factories and opening trading communications with such of the ports on the Indian seaboard as they were then acquainted with. The Malabar Coast and the Islands of Malacca and Sumatra were early settled upon on account of the spice-trade, always one of value, and said at that time to have realised two hundred thousand ducats yearly to these enterprising traders.

Along the coast of Guzerat, at Aden, and at the mouths of some rivers in Cambodia and Cochin China, this adventurous people succeeded in establishing themselves, sometimes by diplomacy, anon by force of arms, but always to the prejudice of the natives, who were no match for the strategy and duplicity of the merchants of Portugal.

In the middle of the sixteenth century the Portuguese commerce with India and the eastern islands was at its height, and extended from Japan to the coast of Africa. Scarcely a country or island but had a factory over which waved the flag of their most Christian majesties. The whole of this long string of possessions were placed under the control and guidance of the viceroy of Goa, who alone corresponded with the court of Lisbon. So lucrative was this high post, that it was an ordinary occurrence for an Indian viceroy to return to Portugal with a fortune of more than a quarter of a million sterling; whilst the generals, governors, admirals, and other officials, were proportionately successful.

Without any exact records to guide us in our estimate of the value of this trade, it may yet be fairly assumed to have yielded an annual profit of from 150,000*l.* to 200,000*l.*; and it is recorded by an English traveller of that period that a fleet of Portuguese merchantmen, to the number of 240 sail, was observed on their way to Surat and Cambay.[1]

The annexation of the Portuguese crown to that of Spain, coupled with the general corruption of the country and the Indian officials, the advent of the English in the East, and the successful rivalry of the Dutch, —all these paved the way to the decadence of the once flourishing trade of Portugal with the Indies, until one by one the possessions of that nation were wrested from them, much as they had been gained, by force, by treaty, or by mere commercial rivalry,—until at the present time

[1] Milburn's Oriental Commerce, vol. i. p. 307.

there remain but one or two obscure spots in the East where their authority retains a shadow of existence; and the sole testimony to their once proud and prosperous rule is to be found in the presence of a few thousands of their hybrid descendants scattered through the suburbs of some of the large cities on the coasts and islands of the eastern seas.

If the Dutch cannot lay claim to the honour of acting as pioneers to the direct trade of Europe with the East, they may at any rate boast of having extended their commerce beyond the limits of any other nation of continental Europe, and of having brought their traffic with the people of the many lands eastwards of the Cape to a prosperity it had never previously known. Shrewd, calculating, patient, and industrious, the Dutch were peculiarly fitted to shine as traders; whilst their rivals, the Portuguese, were more engrossed by politics, by ambition, and by religious bigotry.

For some time after the opening of the Cape route and the establishment of a trade between Portugal and the East Indies, the Dutch were content to act as carriers for the rest of Europe, and plied annually between Lisbon and other European ports. Whilst thus engaged they could not fail to learn much concerning the marvellous wealth of India; and prompted by the glowing accounts related of those distant but wonderful places, a number of Dutch merchants united, and dispatched several vessels in succeeding years to endeavour to discover a passage to the China seas by way of the north. It is needless to relate how these attempts failed; but the indirect result was, that the Dutch succeeded in navigating the southern seas, and availed themselves of the new highway by the Cape to open a trading communication with the many islands and countries of the East, where they not only met with no opposition from the natives, but found every where a marked friendliness and disposition to barter with them.

It was early in the year 1596 that the first Dutch fleet of four ships, well freighted with coin and European commodities, sailed from the Texel, under the command of Cornelius Houtman.[2] This was followed by other adventurers from Rotterdam and Zealand; and on the return of the first ships in the following year, laden with the most costly and profitable cargoes, many other fleets sought the same good fortune, and the Dutch commerce with India, sealed as it was by the formation of two distinct trading companies, became henceforth a great fact.

In 1602 the different bodies of merchants interested in these undertakings, uniting in one body, made common cause, and under the title of the "Dutch East India Company," received a charter of incorpora-

[2] Milburn's Oriental Commerce, vol. ii. p. 367.

tion from the States-General, to continue in force for twenty-one years. This gave them the complete monopoly of the eastern trade; whilst the government stipulated in return for a duty of three per cent on all their exports, and a moderate share in their capital, which at that time amounted to 600,000*l.*

Acting in common concert, and pursuing the most vigorous and prompt measures, the new corporation established themselves in many parts of the Indian seas. Before the expiration of a dozen years, the Dutch, in spite of the secret and open opposition of the Portuguese, had succeeded in forming settlements in Persia, Arabia, Western and Eastern India, Pegu, Burmah, Cambodia, Siam, Cochin-China, Japan, and many other islands.

The acquisition of Java, and the expulsion of the Portuguese from all the spice-islands; the establishment of the supreme government of India at the newly-erected city of Batavia in Java; and lastly, the subjugation of the European possessions in Ceylon, followed in rapid succession; and though these successes were clouded with the cruel and unjustifiable massacre of the English at Amboyna, their prosperity received no check; and for the time it appeared that Holland was to enjoy the supreme monopoly of by far the most valuable portion of oriental commerce.

So prosperous were the affairs of the Dutch in the East, that at this time (1653) the declared value of the homeward cargoes had risen from one million to four millions of florins. Their merchantmen numbered thirty sail; whilst fleets of many armed vessels, mounting from sixteen to thirty guns, served to protect their trade, and at the same time to harass that of the English, who were now their only formidable rivals. Their military establishment consisted of six thousand European troops, well disciplined and officered, besides a large body of native militia commanded by Hollanders.

The jealous and cautious policy of the Dutch made them view with the utmost alarm every step taken by the British. No pains were spared to imbue the natives with feelings inimical to the English factors; and whenever the opportunity occurred, they seized upon it to expel the latter from any participation in the commerce of those seas. For a time it seems this policy succeeded to the utmost: the affairs of the Dutch East India Company wore a most prosperous appearance, though hampered by very heavy payments to the government upon each renewal of their charter, and the cost of large armaments dispatched against the English in those seas. At the conclusion of the war with Great Britain their shipments home were valued annually at about

85,000*l.*, consisting chiefly of tea, coffee, spices, sugar, saltpetre, cloths, and silk. The sale of these generally realised 1,700,000*l.*, or one hundred per cent on the invoice or declared value, and probably two hundred per cent on the prime cost.

The expense of their various establishments in the East at this time amounted to about 630,000*l.*, to meet which local revenues gave them nearly 500,000*l.*, the balance having to be provided from the profits of the company, and which it was believed, after paying all foreign and home charges, left a clear million sterling annually.

The war which broke out between England and the States-General in 1795 heralded the downfall of that supremacy which the Dutch East India Company had so long and so successfully maintained. The British had since the previous hostilities greatly strengthened themselves in India; and now that war was again declared, the most active steps were taken to expel their old antagonists from their many strongholds. Ceylon, Amboyna, Banda, Malacca, and other places fell into the hands of the English; and although by the treaty of Amiens many of these were given up to their former masters, it was but for a brief period. On the re-commencement of hostilities in 1804 they were again taken possession of; and finally, in 1811, the last and most important of all, Batavia, fell into the hands of the British, to be, however, again given up by treaty to Holland; and this now remains the sole remnant of the once proud and valuable Dutch East Indies.

The attention of the French was directed to the trade with India by Francis I., and subsequently by Henry III.; but no attempt to take any part in that commerce appears to have been made until early in the seventeenth century; and then so badly managed were the various companies which were formed for the purpose, so ill-equipped were their ships, and so unfortunate the results of most of the voyages, that it was not until 1665 any decided footing was obtained in the East. The company then formed under a royal charter from Louis XIV. succeeded in establishing themselves in the Islands of Madagascar and the Mauritius. Thence expeditions were dispatched to Surat, Masulipatam, St. Thomé, and Pondicherry. At the latter place a permanent establishment was made, a fort erected, factories built, and eventually the seat of the French government in India was firmly established there.

A trade was also opened with China, whence the French carried home some valuable cargoes of teas and silks. The latter goods, however, appear to have alarmed the French manufacturers, who protested so loudly against this branch of the India trade, that the goods were prohibited, and thus a very prolific source of profit was lost to them.

Up to 1730 the affairs of the French company wore an uncertain aspect: during several years they had failed to dispatch a single ship to the East; their finances were in a desperate condition, and despite their privileges and immunities, they found it extremely difficult, and at times quite impossible, to meet all their monetary engagements. About this time, however, more energy appears to have been infused into their proceedings; their fleets became more regular in their departure and return, and from three or four, they gradually extended to a dozen, all of which returned home most profitably laden.

The growth of the French power in the Indian peninsula; the close alliance of their commander with the Great Mogul and the Nabob of Arcot, and the subsequent hostilities with the British forces in India, are all matters which relate to history, and will be found detailed in their proper place. The result of the various struggles in which the forces of the English and French companies were engaged between the years 1740 and 1779, was the all but total loss of the French possessions in continental India.

In 1780 the French trade to the eastern seas was thrown open to private enterprise, which seems to have given a stimulus to the mercantile interest of that country; for we find that from six or seven vessels annually, as many as thirty-eight were in the year 1783 dispatched to India, bringing home large cargoes from the Mauritius, Bengal, Pondicherry, Mozambique, Batavia, and China. This freedom was, however, cancelled in 1785, under the pretext that the goods brought home were ill-selected and not adapted to the wants of the country. The new company, though prosperous in its affairs, did not long enjoy the new privileges; for in 1790 the National Assembly declared, that in two years from that date the Indian trade should again be thrown open to the private merchants of the country, and thus it has remained to the present day.

Pondicherry, Carrical, and other possessions in the peninsula, fell into the hands of the English during the war which followed. In 1810 the islands of Bourbon and Mauritius were captured; the former has since been restored to them by treaty, and this, and the inconsiderable settlement of Mahé, are now the only French possessions to the eastward of the Cape of Good Hope.

Denmark as early as the year 1615 entered upon the trade to India; a few vessels were equipped by an association at Copenhagen, and dispatched to the Coromandel coast, where they succeeded in obtaining a valuable freight. Four years after this the Danish settlement of Tranquebar was formed, and a regular trade opened with many places on that coast and with the Moluccas. The Danish Company had their charter renewed on several occasions with increased powers and privileges; among others, the right of making treaties, and raising troops for the defence of their factories.

Between the years 1732 and 1753 they dispatched sixty ships to India and China, of which not less than thirteen were wrecked or burnt, the remainder returning with valuable cargoes.[3]

At this time the Danish trade to India and China appears to have amounted to about 82,000*l.* a year, leaving the company a clear annual gain of 21,000*l.* During the eleven years ending 1806, the value of the entire trade between Denmark and the Indian ports was, of European goods shipped outwards 57,000*l.* per annum, and that of merchandise imported 104,000*l.* a year. The hostilities which took place in Europe in 1807, ending in the battle of Copenhagen, and the capture of the Danish fleet by Lord Nelson, were followed in the succeeding year by the fall of Tranquebar and Serampore, which from that time have remained in the possession of the English, the trade of the Danes with India having declined to the freighting of one or two ships annually.

When India first became known to the inhabitants of Britain does not clearly appear from any historical records: some writers have alleged that it was not unknown to western Europe even in the time of the ancient Britons; and if we are to believe that the Phœnicians traded with Spain, Cornwall, and the south of Ireland, the account seems to be plausible enough. William of Malmesbury relates, that in the year 883 of the Christian era, Sighelmus, Bishop of Sherborne, in Dorsetshire, was sent by King Alfred to Rome with presents to the Pope, and thence to the East Indies, to visit the tomb of St. Thomas at Meliapour, and that by his means the English people obtained their first impression of the riches of Hindostan.

For many years all intercourse with the East Indies was carried on by an overland route, identically the same as that which has recently been so profitably opened through Egypt; and during that time England was chiefly supplied with oriental produce by a ship which went once a year to Venice, and brought thence a cargo which her owners sold at an enormous profit.[4]

Thus the trade continued until the discovery of the Cape passage, when the English merchants drew their supplies from Lisbon, and where doubtless their impressions of the magnitude of this commerce

[3] Milburn's Oriental Commerce, vol. ii. p. 372.

[4] Ditto, vol. i. introduction.

became greatly wrought upon by the vast stores of precious commodities which met their view.

It was nearly the end of the fifteenth century before the English, under the auspices of Henry VII., attempted to take any part in this valuable trade; but endeavours both in his time and that of his son Henry VIII. proved abortive; and Sir Francis Drake, who fitted out an expedition at his own expense in 1577, was destined to be the first to open any direct communication with the East Indies. Having sailed through the Straits of Magellan, he touched at Ternate, one of the Moluccas, to whose king he rendered valuable assistance in his war with the sovereign of Tidore. In return for this favour the monarch of Ternate agreed to supply the English with all the cloves exported from his country. Sir Francis accordingly took a considerable cargo of that spice on board, and in February 1580 sailed for England, where he arrived on the 3d of November following, by the way of the Cape of Good Hope; having thus not only established his reputation as being the first person who had sailed round the world, but also having gained the credit of opening a direct commercial communication between England and the East.

The enterprise of Captain Cavendish, who made a voyage round the world in concert with Drake, though undertaken more for the purpose of harassing the Spanish and Portuguese, with whom England was then at war, than for any other purpose, afforded such an insight into the trade of India, that a company of British merchants determined to attempt a voyage direct to India by way of the Cape of Good Hope, in defiance of the Portuguese, who claimed the exclusive right of trading by that route. They accordingly dispatched four ships, but with unfortunate results. The design, however, was not abandoned, and some private ships of war having captured a large Portuguese carrack called the *Madre di Dios* of 1600 tons burden, they brought her into Dartmouth. Her cargo, which consisted of spices, calicoes, silks, gold, pearls, China-ware, and other valuables, by a moderate computation was said to be worth upwards of 150,000*l.* sterling; and the possession of this prize encouraged the English to renew their attempts to the East Indies.

In September 1599 the merchants of London resolved to form a company for the purpose of trading with India direct, and the sum of 30,133*l.* was raised for that purpose. The queen was petitioned for a charter, which at the end of the following year was granted, and they were accordingly incorporated under the title of "the Governor and Company of Merchants of London trading to the East Indies." They were permitted to use a common seal, and obtained the exclusive right of trading with India by sea for the term of fifteen years. They were empowered to make bye-laws, and inflict punishment both corporal and pecuniary. They were also allowed to export goods duty free, and were beside endowed with many other important privileges.

In consequence of this charter the merchants began to raise a joint stock for the execution of their design, which became so popular, that in a very short time as much as 72,000*l.* was paid into the treasurer's hands. A fleet of five ships was dispatched under the command of Captain James Lancaster, who was furnished with letters and presents from the queen to the kings of Acheen and Bantam. The fleet sailed from England in February 1601, and arrived at Acheen in June of the following year, where Lancaster was received with marked distinction. They formed a treaty, and having left factors both there and at Bantam, sailed for England, and arrived in the Downs, after a prosperous voyage, on the 11th of September 1603, having taken possession of the island of St. Helena on their way home.

In 1606 Captain Hawkins was dispatched with the *Dragon* and *Hector* to Bantam and the Moluccas; but having experienced much opposition from the Dutch, Spaniards, and Portuguese, all of whom held settlements in those parts, the *Hector* proceeded to Surat; and Hawkins, having succeeded in reaching Agra, presented the letters which he carried from King James I. to the Great Mogul, by whom he was favourably received, and who granted him permission to establish a factory at Surat.

Several other voyages were undertaken, which were eminently successful; and the profits divided were so considerable, that the Company were able to increase their capital by 25 per cent. In 1609, having been much interfered with by private traders, although the fifteen years of their charter had not expired, they petitioned the king for its renewal, which the monarch readily acceded to. Further to prevent any apprehensions that might be entertained of private traders superseding their powers by licenses obtained from the crown, it was expressly stated, that none should be given without the consent of the Company. It was, however, stated, that notwithstanding these privileges, if the trade should not be found profitable to the realm, such exclusive privileges were to cease and determine after three years' warning.

At this period, when their trade had become extensive, the East India Company began to feel the want of one great advantage which the other nations who traded to the East enjoyed; for the Spaniards and Portuguese had harbours of which they were the absolute masters, and which were defended by fortifications well garrisoned; and the

Dutch had also begun to fortify themselves in different places. The ships of the English had hitherto been necessarily exposed to many annoyances, and were often excluded from the eastern ports by the hostility of the other powers, who, in consequence of the possession of their forts, could exclude them from the harbours at their pleasure. The East India Company soon became convinced by experience, that in the distant regions to which their vessels were sent, there was an absolute necessity to support their rights by the exhibition of power, and they determined, accordingly, to have a fleet of their own.

In 1615, the king, upon an application from the Company, sent Sir Thomas Roe as his ambassador to the Great Mogul, by whom he was very favourably received, and who ratified with him a commercial treaty, by which the English gained many important advantages.

Captain Keeling, who commanded one of the ships that sailed with Sir Thomas Roe, arrived at Cranganore in 1616, and obtained permission to trade and erect a factory there.

The Dutch saw with dismay the rapid advance of the English in the trade to India, and took every opportunity to harass and distress them, breaking out at last into open hostilities, seizing the English factors at Jacatra, and destroying their factory. King James, with a view to repress these outrages, granted a commission to sail to the Indian seas with several armed vessels to Sir Thomas Dale, who, on his arrival at Bantam, being joined by the Company's ships, had thirteen sail under his command, and with these he defeated the Dutch fleet. Another engagement ensued, in which the Dutch were again worsted; and though they were afterwards favoured with partial successes, they never after this time appear to have been able to arrest the onward progress of the British in those seas.

The period to which the Company's stock had been limited expired in 1617, when a fresh subscription was opened; and so eager were persons of all ranks to participate in the large profits that had resulted from the Company's operations, that no less a sum than 1,629,040*l.* was underwritten by dukes, earls, knights, judges, countesses, doctors of divinity and physic, merchants, and others, to the number of several thousands.

Surat and Bantam were selected by the Directors as the principal seats of their trade, and all the out-stations in the possession of the Company were placed under the control of their governors.

Thus was laid the foundation of that colossal trade which was afterwards to absorb every other in the East, but which none at that time could foresee, and which few even now can rightly comprehend.

On the 2d of February, 1634, permission was obtained from the Mogul for the Company to trade in the province of Bengal; a license of which advantage was at once taken, and which eventually proved of great national importance.

This permission was soon followed by the acquisition of the town of Madras, where factories and fortifications were erected under the name of Fort St. George; on every side fresh connexions were formed, new branches of commerce were opened. At this period the ships of the Company ceased to make their accustomed circuitous voyages of barter from port to port, which had entailed great delay and heavy expense. They now made their course direct to Calcutta or Madras, between which ports and the minor places of resort, the traffic, or country trade, was henceforth carried on by small native craft.

MADRAS ROADS.

From accounts which were made public in 1676, it appeared that the Company's affairs were in a most flourishing state. They employed from 30 to 35 ships of between 300 and 600 tons burden, which carried out annually bullion to the value of 320,000*l.*, and woollen and other goods worth 100,000*l.* Their returns consisted of pepper, indigo, silks, raw and manufactured, calicoes, &c., which produced 860,000*l.* The cost of their factories, garrisons, &c. in India was 60,000*l.* The value of the various kinds of eastern produce consumed annually in

England at this period was, calicoes, 160,000*l.*; silks, 30,000*l.*; pepper, 6,000*l.*; indigo and drugs, 15,000*l.*; saltpetre, 30,000*l.*

In 1686, a fresh charter, being the sixth, was granted on a far more extended basis, rights being conceded to them which had before been denied; such as the privilege of making war, coining money, &c. The accounts of the association shew that their profits then amounted to a clear 100,000*l.* a year.

The importations of Indian silks and calicoes had now so greatly increased, that the English weavers grew alarmed lest their occupation should be taken from them; and so great was the clamour, and so general the wear of such goods, that it was deemed necessary to prohibit for the future, all importations of these goods.

The incorporation of a new trading company, their disputes with the old body, and their final amalgamation under one general constitution and charter, were the events of the next few years. At the union of these two corporations, it appeared that the old company was possessed of factories and forts in Arabia, Persia, at twenty-four places on the west coast of India, at twelve places along the eastern coast, at twelve places in Bengal, on the Malay peninsula at eight places; also at many spots in the islands of Sumatra, Java, Borneo, and other eastern islands.

In 1753 the Company obtained a fresh charter for thirty-three years, comprising all the previous privileges, political and commercial. Their trade at this time appears to have occupied thirteen to fifteen ships, annually carrying out merchandise and treasure to the value of 500,000*l.*, and bringing back goods worth 1,500,000*l.*

From this period until the close of the eighteenth century, the commercial operations of the East India Company advanced with rapid and gigantic strides. By what means and in what manner is related elsewhere. The expense of long and dangerous wars with native powers, the confusion and neglect into which their affairs appear to have been plunged during this period, entailed upon the Company many heavy liabilities, which required all their commercial resources to enable them to meet. From mere factors and shipping clerks, their servants had become collectors of revenue, councillors, and judges; and surrounded on all sides by temptations of every kind, the common impulse appeared to be a wide-spread scramble for wealth, regardless of the Company's interests. Fortunes were realised in a few years by all who could brave the climate and the mode of life; the lowest appointments in the service were regarded as a certain road to wealth; and thus, whilst its servants of all grades reaped an abundant harvest of rupees, the Company found itself badly served; its enormous revenues and valuable consignments suffering from the neglect and cupidity of those whose time was devoted to their own private ends, instead of the service of the directors. The Company's dividend was reduced from 12½ per cent to 6 per cent per annum; and owing to this state of things, a commission of inquiry into abuses was sent out to India, though with very sorry results.

Despite the annoyances and losses to which their trade was subjected from the French privateers, and the misconduct of so many of their officials, the mercantile operations of the Company had sensibly increased during this period. Their exports to India, including bullion, now amounting to a million and a half sterling; and their shipments homewards to five millions; giving employment to between thirty and forty ships of large tonnage.

The Island of Ceylon was at this time taken possession of by the Company's troops, and retained by them until made over to the crown a few years afterwards; during the time of this occupancy, the trade in cinnamon formed an important item in the Company's transactions, leaving, as it did in those days, an ample margin for profit.

The progress of the Indian trade up to the date of the general peace was not of a very marked character. The unsettled state of political affairs throughout the world, the difficulties always existing during a time of war in the way of commercial intercourse with remote countries, added to the jealous restrictions placed upon private enterprise in all that related to British India, tended to retard the natural growth of this lucrative trade, and for a long period confined it within a comparatively narrow compass.

From the year 1800 to 1810, the value of the goods imported into and exported from Great Britain, from and to India, actually decreased by two millions sterling; as may be seen by the following table:

Years.	Exports to England.			Imports into India.		
	Goods.	Bullion.	Total.	Company's trade.	Private trade.	Total.
	£	£	£	£	£	£
1800—1	1,869,862	583,471	2,453,333	7,595,181	2,721,411	10,316,592
1802—3	2,288,578	1,722,085	4,010,663	6,069,636	3,580,103	9,649,739
1804—5	2,005,171	1,952,651	3,957,822	5,260,521	2,776,814	8,037,335
1806—7	2,550,271	. .	2,550,271	5,181,120	1,745,285	6,926,405
1808—9	2,124,046	. .	2,194,046	5,746,021	2,278,339	8,024,360
1809—10	1,894,045	. .	1,894,045	5,977,280	2,247,760	8,225,040

Taking a period of fifty years up to this date, we gather from official documents that the value of the Company's import trade from India and China amounted in that time to 221,964,498*l.*, having cost 106,324,066*l.*; and that, after deducting all commercial charges belonging to the above, a clear profit was left of 37,980,337*l.* The principal articles on which this gain arose were teas, raw silk, Bengal and Corah piece-goods, or cloths, sugar, pepper, saltpetre, and indigo.

The ships in the service of the Company prior to the general peace numbered 104, their capacity amounting to 90,272 tons, and manned by 7000 seamen; their size ranged from 1200 tons to 500.

The Company's factories at this time numbered twenty-four in the Bengal presidency; twelve within the limits of the Madras government; sixteen within that of Bombay; and about a dozen others in the Eastern seas, in China, and in Persia.[5]

From the date of the earliest establishment of the Company in India, some few private individuals had at various times settled within their territories for purposes of local traffic. Fortunes were realised by them with but few exceptions; although the Company's privileges enabled them to forbid private merchants from participating in the trade with the mother-country.

The only exception to this rigid exclusiveness arose through the commanders and officers of the Company's ships, who were, by an old custom, permitted the free use of about sixty tons of room in each ship homeward-bound, and ninety-six tons outward; and which privilege they usually sold to the private merchants on very favourable terms. The unprivileged traders, unable to remit their gains to England, with the limited exception just noticed, by any other means than Company's bills, found this channel of remittance far too limited for them, as the dominion and intercourse of the British in India extended on every side; and by degrees fell back upon such means of trade or remittance as existed with continental Europe.

The renewed charter of 1793 provided for this anomalous state of things, by allowing private merchants to ship goods to England in Company's vessels, to the extent of 3000 tons a year, at the fixed rates of 5*l.* per ton outwards, and 15*l.* homewards, in time of peace. This new regulation enabled the growing commercial interest of the presidencies to enlarge their transactions; and ultimately, when members of the civil and military services were induced to join in commercial undertakings, the stipulated amount of tonnage was greatly exceeded long

[5] Milburne's Oriental Commerce, vol. i. part 1, introduction.

previously to the relaxation which took place in the restrictions upon private commercial enterprise.

The relaxation of the East India Company's charter in 1814 formed a new and important era in the history of Indian commerce. Up to this date European settlers in the three presidencies were looked upon with the utmost jealousy, and only permitted to locate themselves by special license, obtained with considerable difficulty. A few merchants had settled at Calcutta and Bombay, chiefly, if not entirely, in connection with members of the Company's service. At that period commerce and banking were combined operations, concentrated under one management; for there were then no banking establishments; and the civil and military servants of the company made use of the mercantile firms as depositaries for their savings. In this way the old houses had always an enormous amount of capital at their command, and but seldom needed to apply for financial aid to their banians (native capitalists), whom they treated with exceeding hauteur; and these men, millionaires though they were, regarded the European merchants with feelings of the deepest respect; never entering their offices without putting off their shoes at the door. Even the junior clerks, all of whom were Englishmen, were looked up to with veneration, as they were known to be expectant partners in the houses. From the fact of the intimate connection between the civil servants and the then merchants, the latter were necessarily admitted as equals into the first society.

A BANIAN.

The ameliorations in the old commercial restrictions at this period were not long in producing results. The enormous fortunes realised by the few great houses were not matters of secrecy; and the report of these princely results, achieved, in most cases, within a few years, induced many to leave England and endeavour to obtain a share of their good fortune. By the year 1820 a number of new firms were established, some with a considerable amount of capital, others backed by large consignments of manufactured goods; and these, although treated by the old houses as interlopers, and jealously excluded by themselves and the services from society, soon became connected with the rich banians, who readily advanced whatever sums were needed for carrying out their commercial plans. In some cases the native millionaires were admitted as partners in these new firms; but in all instances treated on terms of equality and friendship.

From this period onwards we find the trade between India and Great Britain rapidly advancing under the influence of this partial freedom of commerce. The larger quantities of produce which the private traders brought to Europe induced an increased demand in Hindostan for goods of British manufacture; and though the shipments from England at that period did not keep pace with the greatly-augmented imports from India, they nevertheless reached a considerable amount.[6]

The impetus which the Indian trade received on the opening of the ports of the East to all classes was not without its evils; the prospect of rapid fortunes which opened out to the many new-comers paved the way to a reckless system of trading, and an improvident style of living, hitherto unknown. Merchants invested in enormous purchases, not only the funds of their native capitalists, but those of persons who had placed their savings in their hands, as in the safe custody of bankers. Crowds of new men flocked out from Liverpool, Manchester, and Glasgow; men whose amount of capital was on a like scale with their principle, and who, having literally nothing to lose, indulged in the illusive hope of finding something to gain.

In 1830 and the following year commercial affairs reached a crisis

6 As the annexed table will shew:

	1818-19.	1822-23.	1826-27.
IMPORTS.	£	£	£
Company's trade	2,211,038	2,520,193	1,964,492
Private ditto	5,701,847	5,677,337	5,186,983
Total imports . . .	7,912,885	8,197,530	7,151,475
EXPORTS.			
Company's trade	2,383,104	1,944,672	1,591,081
Private ditto	8,685,344	8,441,458	7,331,169
Total exports	11,068,448	10,386,130	8,922,250

in Calcutta. The hollowness of the fabric reared by rash speculators, demonstrated itself with a convulsion that will not easily be forgotten by those who witnessed its effects. Indigo, silk, cotton, sugar, all had been dealt, or rather gambled in, to an extent that was only limited by the impossibility of obtaining any further means for carrying on the game. It mattered little whose funds were jeopardised. The savings of the veteran officer, that were to have purchased promotion for his son; the widow's store; the orphan's sole fortune; the private soldier's pittance, scraped from his pay and prize-money; all these were converted into sugars, shipped home in the shape of dyes, or, perchance, sunk in the alluvial soil of an indigo factory.

The bubble burst, scattering ruin and desolation amidst the homes of thousands of helpless victims. None were prepared for the catastrophe, and least of all the heartless men who had caused the mischief. They were not moved; few of them had lost much. The storm overtook them steeped in princely luxuries, deep in selfish physical enjoyment. Bankruptcy stared them and their victims in the face; but how different the result! A month or two without their race-horses, their dinner-parties, and their ducal establishments, and the Insolvent Court kindly enabled them to make a fresh start, as bold, as unabashed as ever; whilst their *constituents* (*i. e.* their victims) became pauperised, and dependent upon charity for a subsistence.

Honour to whom honour is due. Unwilling to snatch a single laurel, however faded, however stained, from the brows of the wearers, I will do what in me lies to render tribute to the fame of those commercial Philistines, the "great houses," as they were called, of Calcutta.

Foremost among these stood the respectable firm of Alexander and Company, who, scorning to "pull-up" for any insignificant amount, earned for themselves the title of Alexanders the Great, by failing for a round sum of four millions sterling. The most fitting commentary upon the career of this truly princely house is the fact of its dividend amounting to precisely six per cent of its liabilities! In other words, the whole amount saved out of this gigantic wreck was 240,000*l.*; the sum irrevocably lost, and the greater part of which was the property of other and innocent parties, was therefore 3,760,000*l.*!

Ferguson and Company's liabilities were 3,600,000*l.*; Palmer and Company failed for something under 3,000,000*l.* sterling; and Mackintosh and Company were involved to the extent of 2,500,000*l.*; but these three firms rather astonished the mercantile world of those days, by paying 36½ per cent, 30 per cent, and 14 per cent, respectively. Altogether, the six "great houses" of Calcutta failed for an aggregate amount of nearly 15,000,000*l.* sterling; paying among them an average of five shillings in the pound; and consequently entailing on their creditors losses to the extent of 11,250,000*l.* sterling![7]

What, it may be asked, was the immediate result of this state of things? I have said that, personally, the great defaulters passed comfortably through the wide and friendly portals of the Calcutta Insolvent Court. Their social position remained as good as ever; the world termed them *unfortunate;* from the governor-general downwards, they were greeted with all the sympathy which men usually shew to martyrs. Commercially, however, they had lost ground. The native banians drew tight their purse-strings; Hindoo baboos began to shew caution ere they "took up" a new house; and even the high civilians and military officials of the government who fraternised so blandly with, who dined and champaigned, the men of fifteen-million celebrity, were not again to be caught, by using the merchants as their bankers.

A BENGAL SIRCAR.

The immediate consequence of these disasters was the establishment of the Agra Bank, chiefly by military men and civil servants, with branches at other stations. The success of this one establishment was followed by the formation of the Bank of Bengal, with a capital of half a million; one-fifth of the shares and the direction being in the hands of the local government. The Union Bank, the North-western Bank of India, and others, quickly followed, opening up a new phase in the history of Indian commerce. It may be well to notice here, as tending to explain the final results of most of these new undertakings, that these institutions could scarcely deserve the name of banks, and might with far greater propriety have been denominated "loan societies," their business having been almost exclusively confined to the granting of loans on the personal security of the negotiators, with some collateral

[7] Calcutta Review, vol. ix. p. 318.

security of no very tangible nature, the loans being mostly repayable by instalments covering a period of several years. These institutions, of course, found no lack of customers; their transactions grew far beyond the expectations of their projectors. More capital was added by issuing fresh shares, which were divided at par amongst the original proprietors; many of whom, not possessing the means of paying the "calls" on them, were kindly allowed to remain indebted to the bank for the amount until they could dispose of the paper to a profit, which was not then a difficult matter, seeing they had been worked up to a considerable premium.

Whilst this was the course of the banking establishments, let us see how fared the many new houses which rose from the ashes of the old firms—the fifteen-million-men of 1830-1. Mercantile credit was no longer on the old basis; it had been shaken too deeply to be again replaced as it stood before. Many of the most wealthy banians had suffered very severely by the above failures; and most of them withdrew their remaining capital from such hazardous risks. The game was, however, taken up by an inferior class of natives; men of far less means, but possessed of ability, and some amount of credit among their countrymen. These new banians had the game pretty much in their own hands, for the new houses were mostly in their power. Although many of these had been mere sircars, or accountants, they assumed airs which their more wealthy predecessors had never taken on themselves; they treated their European connections not only with contemptuous disregard, but often with much insolence. The Hindoo star was in the ascendant, and these men made the most of it.

So little Calcutta credit was there at that time left to the English merchants, with a few solid exceptions, that they would have found it impossible to have made a purchase of produce without the intervention of their banians, had they desired to make the experiment. But this is never attempted; no one buys or sells save through their banian, who is broker, banker, manager, and every thing else, to these new firms. The profit of the agent comes, to a very limited extent, out of his brokerage, interest, and commissions. There are means, far more ample than such for realising handsome returns. To wit: the firm are desirous of shipping 100 tons of sugar, and apply to their banian, who at once takes the matter in hand, and produces a sample from the bazaar which can be had for nine rupees the maund.[8] The partner sees at once that the quality is equal to but eight rupees and a fraction; but he is largely in the banian's books, and

[8] A Bengal weight equal to 82 lbs. English.

dares offer no remonstrance; so the sugar is bought and shipped. If the banian contented himself with putting on board at nine rupees the article worth but eight, the affair might be bad enough; but not so. The grasping broker ships a miserable article not worth more than five or six rupees; which goes home drawn against, through the banks, at the higher rate, and of course entails a heavy loss. The news of this comes out to Calcutta; the merchant storms; but can do nothing, for he is in the power of the banian, who calls all the Hindoo deities to bear testimony to his purity and uprightness, and vows that the London banian must be at the bottom of the mischief.

This, however, is but one trifling incident in an Indian commercial career, as carried on in the present day. It is right that the non-professional reader, who may perchance be ignorant of the mode in which large concerns are worked in the East without capital, or, at any rate, with an amount utterly disproportioned to the business done, should be made acquainted with the modern course of operations in such matters, since the knowledge may serve to explain how it so frequently happens that firms suspend payment for enormous amounts, and yield dividends of but a shilling or two in the pound.

Formerly all the London houses acting as agents for Calcutta and Bombay firms were possessed of ample means, and to a limited extent this is still the case. It was then the practice for these agents or correspondents to purchase or make advances against consignments of manufactured goods, either on their own account, or jointly with their Indian friends, who sold the invoice on arrival, and remitted home the proceeds in bills of exchange or in some article of produce. Under the new régime this is no longer the case. The London firm have a little credit and less money; but they can accept bills drawn against goods to be shipped either on the manufacturers' or their Indian friends' account. This done, the bills are discounted, and so the manufacturer is reimbursed. The goods—grey cloths from Manchester perhaps—are shipped; and then the London merchant, who has not paid a farthing for them, is enabled to draw against them on his India correspondent, through a bank, who takes the bill of lading for security; and in this way the shipper obtains hard cash, with which he buys another parcel of goods—metals, possibly—ships these, draws against them, and with these fresh means repeats the operation, which, it is clear, may be thus carried on to a large extent. Before the first parcel of goods can be sold at Bombay or Calcutta, the manufacturer's bill upon the shipper falls due, and is met by a renewal; that is, by another bill drawn in a similar manner, and understood to be for the purpose of being discounted, to enable the accepter of the first bill to take it up, in other words, to pay it when presented.

Meanwhile the goods arrive at their destination. The agent of the London bank who advanced money upon them holds the bills of lading; and to get these, and consequently the goods, the "Calcutta correspondent" applies to his banian, who at once does the needful, redeems the grey-goods from their bondage, and sells them for his principal. The proceeds are now remitted home in sugar, or silk, or indigo, the bills of lading for which are forwarded to the London house, which at once draws against it, in order to meet the "renewals" of the Manchester bills then falling due; finally, the produce-broker in Mincing Lane makes an advance to the importer on the arrival of the sugar or indigo, which enables him to redeem the bills of lading from the strong-box of the bank, and the goods are sold.

So long as the selling prices at both ends leave a shadow of profit over and above the amount of commissions and other charges, all goes on well. The shipper, the banker, the correspondent, the banian, the London broker, the Manchester manufacturer, all are content. The operations are extended considerably, the commercial wheel is kept moving, money is made, the houses at both ends obtain the reputation of doing a large stroke of business, the partners are looked upon as sharp, shrewd men, and although there may be a few bad debts, a few losses, and now and then a heavy year, the books shew a large amount of commissions earned. Still the banian is a large creditor, though by interest, per centage, &c. he has cleared off more than the amount of their liabilities to him. One or two bad seasons follow rather rapidly; the house has invested largely in estates, an operation popularly termed developing the resources of the country; the banian becomes rather more troublesome and overbearing than of wont; the senior partner takes alarm, withdraws with a hundred thousand pounds, and twelvemonths afterwards the firm suspend payment for a million and a half sterling, at which nobody is in the least degree surprised, except the banian, who wonders how they managed to keep up so long. This, reader, is a faint, and no doubt an imperfect sketch of the course of operations of an Indian commercial house of the present time; and it deserves a place in these pages, as illustrative of that Saxon energy of character, that fine spirit of enterprise which so distinguishes the men of Liverpool and Glasgow, and by means of which they rear gigantic fabrics out of literally nothing. Here we have seen how a fortune of a hundred thousand, and an insolvency of a million and a half, had their first origin in nothing more than a few bales of Manchester "grey-goods."

In the above sketch no mention has been made of the Calcutta banks, although their timely aid would more than probably have been invoked, and with success. What part these huge and iniquitous "loan societies" played in the deep game of hazard that ran riot through the presidencies between 1840 and 1849, it will be now my task to describe, from such data as the chicanery of presidents, vice-presidents, secretaries, and directors, have not been able effectually to suppress.

The years 1847 and 1848 will long be memorable in the annals of Indian joint-stockery; and even now as we are writing, not only are the effects of those years still felt, but the nefarious transactions of that period form the subject of grave deliberation and legal inquiry. The storm that was approaching was ushered in by several minor failures, which to prudent men served as beacons of danger. The *public* were first made aware of the extent to which mutual accommodation was accorded amongst the directors and proprietors of a bank, by the failure, in 1842, of a firm of some *Indian* respectability, when it appeared that the house had received not much less than half a million sterling from the coffers of the Union Bank. That this was no individual or exceptional case is clear from the fact, that on the failure of this very same bank, it was ascertained that some half a dozen firms were at the time liable to it for a trifle within a million sterling.

The year 1847 dragged its slow length along, big with the fate of banks and merchants. In the middle of this year, the directors of the two most notorious banks in Calcutta found themselves in difficulties from the huge accommodations accorded their customers, *i.e.* their own proprietors. The half-yearly meeting of the Union Bank was held in the second week in July; but so pressed were the directors, that money had first to be raised to enable them to jog on and meet their most immediate liabilities. In spite of this, however, the accounts laid before the shareholders at the July meeting were of the most glowing description: enormous profits were announced; the amount of bad or doubtful debts was set down as quite insignificant; and a dividend of three and a half per cent on the half-year was declared. Of course, good-natured, easy gentlemen had been found to audit the accounts, and pass them as all right; the immediate result was, that the unsuspecting shareholders felt quite satisfied, and the public at large were assured, of the integrity of the bank.

Suspicion, however, was but lulled for a time. A fictitious dividend, a fancy balance-sheet failed to give stability to this institution, and towards the end of the year a run on its treasury became evident. The most desperate and unprincipled means were resorted to in the vain hope of averting the impending crisis. Bills sent them for sale and remittance, on account of others, were disposed of, and the proceeds applied to stop a momentary gap, although the directors must have known that they were insolvent, and that a month or two at most would witness the termination of their fictitious existence, and which actually took place in January 1848.

To attempt a mere outline of the winding-up disclosures of the Union Bank would occupy many chapters; and yet how little of the truth was really disclosed! Whatever was gleaned was the result of accident. How planters and merchants had been befriended until the entire capital of the bank was absorbed; how indigo-factories were jobbed on private account with the bank funds; how bank post-bills, at a heavy discount, were received from directors as cash; how paper of all descriptions was floated; how liabilities of presidents and secretaries were transferred to the bank in the Company's books; how young, half-fledged civilians were accommodated with loans at a heavy interest; how, in short, every thing was done that ought not to have been done, and how all ordinary precaution, all proper management, was flung overboard. All this may some day be chronicled in full; I can now but advert to it.

The last and crowning act of the executive of this notable banking institution deserves a few lines, as illustrating the men and the time. By a deed of arrangement the creditors of this bank agreed to compromise their claims for a certain dividend, to be levied by an assessment on the proprietary body. The assessment was paid to the executive committee, and the work of appropriation went on. After a considerable delay, however, some parties not feeling that confidence in the committee which they could have wished, expressed a desire to have their proceedings scrutinised, and the accounts of their trust audited. This, after some grave opposition, was permitted; and the result was, that although every obstacle was thrown in the way of the appointed committee of inquiry, such a report was drawn up and laid before a meeting of shareholders, as in any other part of the world but Calcutta would have caused legal proceedings to have been instituted against the executive. Yet, what was the actual result? Although that meeting was attended by two hundred persons, not *one* was found to move that the damning report be received! On the contrary, a vote of "*confidence*" in the executive was proposed, seconded, and carried; precisely eleven of the two hundred present voted, the remaining one hundred and eighty-nine slunk away abashed at the cool effrontery of their friends. This, reader, occurred not *years* but months since—in the middle of 1852, and that chairman, and his executive assistants, thus publicly "damned with faint praise," are, to this day, the favoured of Calcutta society, moving amongst the *élite* of the "City of Palaces."

Before closing this chapter, it will be well to examine the position of the trade of the three presidencies, and see how far this has kept pace with the onward spirit of the age, and what influence, for good or evil, the commercial gambling I have touched upon, has exercised on the mercantile statistics of British India.

By comparing the imports and exports of India in 1844-5 with those of 1849-50, the latest date for which there are official returns, the result appears most encouraging. In the former year the value of imported merchandise into the three presidencies was 4,261,106*l.*, that of the goods exported 7,993,420*l.*; whilst in the latter year they stood at 10,299,888*l.* and 17,812,299*l.* respectively. This would appear to be a satisfactory result; yet an analysis of these returns[9] presents us with some rather startling anomalies, which require examination and elucidation. It is evident from a glance at the tables alluded to, that not only has the great bulk of the increase been in the trade with other countries than England, but during the past six or seven years the Indian trade has made no onward move; it appears to have reached a point beyond which it is impossible, under existing circumstances, to go.

It has been a practice of late, with certain political writers, to make frequent reference to the vast aggrandisement of our trade to India, as illustrating the expansibility of our commerce under an improved system of commercial legislation. Without in any way questioning the soundness of that legislation, I may, at least, express a wish, that instead of turning back to a particular period for a convenient amount of figures, those writers would examine a little more closely the last six years of the returns in the blue books. It would in that case be seen, that the imports of British goods into the three presidencies were actually less in 1849-50 than in 1844-5, by about half a million sterling; and that in 1847-8 and 1848-9 they were less by upwards of two millions. Comparing the shipments of produce to this country during a period of ten years, similar results are obtained, the amounts having fluctuated between seven and five millions sterling. That there have been seasons of commercial disaster during these periods is true; but it bespeaks a most vicious and deplorable state of things in our Eastern possessions, when we see that during a series of

[9] Appendix E.

years in which the Company added to their territories one hundred and sixty-seven thousand square miles, with eight millions and a half of new population,[10] the imports of British goods shewed an actual annual decrease.

Calculations made in reference to the consumption of British manufactures in different countries[11] shew, that whilst Chili and the States of Rio de la Plata take of our goods to the yearly value of 13*s.* 7*d.* for each inhabitant; and Cuba, Hayti, Brazil, and other countries, consume for each inhabitant 7*s.* 3*d.* annually, British India takes but 1*s.* for every inhabitant. Small as this sum appears, it is in reality much above the actual amount taken by the population generally, which, throughout by far the widest range of the Company's territories, will be represented by no other symbol than a unit. Millions upon millions of Hindoos live and die unpossessed of the smallest fragment, the veriest shred of any British manufactures. What can the miserable ryot spare for Manchester prints, Glasgow cloths, or Birmingham ware, out of the pittance of 6*d.* a week, the proceeds of his heavy toil? Yet were the inhabitants of our Indian territories to take but half as much per head of our goods as the foreigners of Chili and La Plata, British merchants would export to the East merchandise to the yearly value of upwards of thirty-three millions sterling. And no one acquainted with this magnificent country can doubt that, with justice to India, this and much more might be accomplished.

[10] Report on Indian Territories, Appendix, p. 330.

[11] Chapman's Cotton and Commerce of India.

PART IV.

MORAL.

CHAPTER I.

LANGUAGE AND LITERATURE.

THERE is no valid reason for doubting the high antiquity of the Sanscrit language, from which the Hindoo had its origin; indeed we may attribute to it a descent from the earliest dialects, if not even coeval with the confusion of tongues at Babel. It is difficult for western nations to appreciate the beauties of a language so opposed in its construction and tone to that of European tongues; hence many of the peculiarities which, in the original, impart so much of grace and charm to the Sanscrit, are entirely lost in a translation, however perfect. The figures, the associations, the colouring imparted by the Hindoo poets to their works, fail to create sympathy or admiration in the mind of an English reader, even if perused in the original tongue, wanting, as that reader necessarily must be, in the perception of ideas taking their rise from oriental life and eastern thought.

The current languages of India are thirty-one in number, and may be arranged under two distinct heads: those derivable entirely from the Sanscrit; and those, chiefly of the south, based upon a Tamil foundation, though in several instances still blended to a certain extent with Sanscrit words.

When this language ceased to be the vernacular tongue of India, it is in vain to attempt to divine; but it appears certain that at a remote period it gave way to the Prakrit, a corruption of itself; and from this latter have sprung directly the many tongues I am about to mention.

The Prakrit is no longer spoken, though it is still preserved in numerous writings. The languages of the Hindoos which are to this day in common use are derivable from the Sanscrit, though its corrupted offspring appears to be comprised within the country lying to the north of a line drawn from Chicacole, in the Bay of Bengal, to Goa, on the western coast.[1]

[1] Lassen: Institutiones Linguæ Pracriticæ, p. 12.

They are twenty-five in number, viz. Bengâli, Assamese, Orissan, and Tirhutîya, spoken in the eastern provinces; Nepâlese, Câshmiri, and Doguri, prevailing in the north; Panjabî, Multani, Sindi, Kutchi, Guzerati, and Kunkuna, found on the western side; Bikanera, Marwara, Jayapura, Udayapura, Haruli, Braja Bhaka, Malavi, Bundelakhandi, Maghada, and Mahratta, all spoken in the south.

Hindostani, equally derivable from the common source, is not confined to any particular people or locality, but is found in general use by nearly all the natives of Hindostan, in addition to their own individual dialect.

The languages not derivable from the Sanscrit, although admitting many of its words into frequent use, are the Tamil, Telugu, Carnataca, Tuluva, Malayalma, and the Codugu. The Malayalma is known to Europeans as the Malabar tongue, and is found throughout the coasts of the Indian peninsula.

Sanscrit and Pali are the Greek and Latin languages of India. The latter is that in which the Bhuddistical writings are written; the former is the Brahminical language, as well as that in which all learned works and scientific books are penned. It has been pronounced by one well fitted to form an opinion,[2] the most finished of all the dead languages, "of a wonderful structure, more perfect than the Greek, more copious than the Latin, and more exquisitely refined than either."

In this language is to be found an infinity of works upon almost every branch of learning known amongst the orientals; beyond this, however, it is no longer a dialect. There is very little doubt that, in the time of Alexander, this was the language of the upper classes, if not of the great masses of the people; for nearly all the Indian names handed down to us by the writers of that period are Sanscrit. When this ceased to be a living tongue, when it was swept from the highway to the temple and the college, is a question which has not yet been determined.

The Sindhi language is not, as has been sometimes stated, a corruption of Hindostani, but a distinct tongue, based, like many others, upon Sanscrit, and evidently of great antiquity;[3] although so little appears to have been known regarding it, that not long since an oriental scholar declared that no such language existed, it is found spoken with many varieties, according to the different localities of the many tribes.

Besides the language of Sindh proper, the following dialects are

[2] Sir W. Jones's Asiatic Researches, vol. i. p. 422.

[3] Burton's Scinde, chap. iii. p. 69.

spoken: the Siraiki, or language of Siro, in Upper Sindh; the Kachi, spoken in Cutch; the Thaleri, or Jasalmeri, the dialect of Omercoti Jesulmere, and of outcast tribes; and the Takkarana Jiboli, spoken by the hill-tribes to the west of Sindh.

The Hindoo drama, which is the part of their literature with which we are best acquainted, possesses great and varied excellences. Their chief piece, Sacoutalá, has long been known to the European public by the classical version of Sir William Jones; and we have been made acquainted with the principal of the other dramatists by the admirable translations of Professor Wilson.

The drama of India has a wide range in its existence, but there are comparatively few instances of its genius; for though we possess plays that are as old in their composition as the Christian era, and one that was written in Bengal as late as within these fifty years, the whole of the collection which are worthy of notice does not number more than sixty.

That many have been lost there is no doubt, and partly through the way in which they were performed, being only represented once on some great festival, in the hall or inner court of a palace, and consequently losing that popularity and traditional existence which plays in our time derive from repeated performances in different cities and in public theatres. Many must also have been lost from the neglect of the learned, for the taste for this species of poetry seems to be corrupted, and almost entirely extinct among the Brahmins; and though some of the least meritorious specimens are still favourites among the people, Professor Wilson assures us that he never met with more than one Brahmin who could be said to be at all conversant with dramatic literature.

The most voluminous as well as the most ancient portion of Hindoo poetry consists of the sacred, the epic, and the heroic pieces. Upon these Mr. Colebrooke, a very competent authority, has pronounced, in his *Asiatic Researches*, the condemnation that "their general style is flat, diffuse, and no less deficient in ornament than abundant in repetitions;" and, judging from the specimens that have been translated, there appears to be no reason to find fault with this judgment.

Next to the *Vedas* comes the great heroic poem of the *Ramayana*, giving an account of the conquest of Ceylon by Rama. Oriental scholars are energetic in their praises of the simplicity and originality of this composition, of the sublimity, grace, and pathos of many passages, the natural dignity of the actors, and the inexhaustible imagination of the authors: but judging from the specimens which they have rendered into English, and which are mostly from the *Ramayana*, it is difficult to discover the many beauties alluded to; we must there-

RAMA.

fore content ourselves with attributing our disappointment to the impossibility of rendering the peculiarities of the Sanscrit into modern European language.

That these works possess a more than ordinary merit is clear from the fact of their popularity to this day among the great mass of the Hindoo population. Not in the towns alone, but throughout the whole extent of the many provinces of Hindostan, the wondrous deeds of Rama, the conqueror of Ceylon, his miraculous passage to that island, accompanied by more than human aid, and the marvellous incidents of that desperate war, are committed to memory by ryot and artificer, not less by the unlettered and the rude than by the educated. What our *Robin Hood* and *The Knights of the Round Table* were to a large portion of English rural and town population thirty years since, these mystic legends of an all-but fabulous period are to the Hindoo races of the present time.

Of the descriptive powers of the Indian writers an exceedingly favourable specimen is given in the *Méghadúta;* a poem, the hero of which is a spirit banished from heaven, who charges a cloud with a message to his celestial mate, and describes the countries and cities over which it will have to pass, interspersing allusions to the tales which are associated with the different scenes. Blended with the whole are the lamentations of the exile himself, and his recollections of all the beauties and enjoyments from which he is excluded.

The *Gita Govinda, or Songs of Jaya Deeva,* are the best specimens of purely pastoral poetry, and exhibit in perfection the luxuriant imagery, the voluptuous softness, and the want of vigour which uniformly constitute the beauties and defects of Hindoo poetry. There are many other poems, but none that impress us with a very high idea of their value.

For satire the Hindoos have little either of disposition or capacity; but in their tales and fables they are exceedingly rich, and in both species of composition appear to have been the instructors of mankind.

There are, besides, some very respectable writers in the English language amongst the Hindoo people; and not the least creditable portion of their labours are their poetical contributions to periodical literature. One family, that of the Dutts, numbers no fewer than five writers of English poetry amongst its members, all of whom are natives of Bengal, and were educated at the Hindoo college at Calcutta. They may be looked upon as forming a fraction of "Young Bengal;" and in addition to the ephemeral mode of their appearance in public, one or two of them have published small volumes of poetry, which, considering that their authors were composing in a foreign language, must be regarded as very creditable performances.

CHAPTER II.

RELIGION AND CASTE.

THE Brahminical religion, which is the form of worship almost universally prevalent throughout British India, is set forth in the sacred books known as the *Vedas.* They are three in number, though some add a fourth to them. They are written in an ancient form of the Sanscrit language, so antiquated in its character and structure as to be intelligible to none but the most highly-educated Brahmins. Some portions of these religious writings have been rendered into English by one of our most learned oriental scholars;[1] but these translations form so small a part of the whole, that in speaking of the contents of the whole we must be considered as being guided rather by the testimony of Brahmins themselves than by these fragmentary documents.

Each of the sacred Vedas is divided into two parts: the first is called Moutra, and consists entirely of hymns and prayers; the second portion, named Brahmaná, contains rules and precepts relative to a religious life, and an abundance of argumentative matter bearing upon their theological doctrines. In some of the books the theological disquisitions are comprised within a separate and third part, called the Upanishad.

The religion inculcated by the Vedas is of a loftier and purer kind than is perhaps generally supposed. The obscenities and superstition practised in many parts of India must not be taken as representing the Hindoo faith embodied in their scriptures. The leading doctrine of the Brahminical worship is the "unity of God." Their books teach that there is but one deity, the Supreme Spirit, the Lord of the Universe, whose work is the Universe.

The following sketch of the attributes of the Divinity, as rendered by a learned Brahmin, will shew how little polytheism had to do with the original faith of Hindostan.

[1] Mr. Colebrooke.

"Perfect truth; perfect happiness; without equal; immortal; absolute unity; whom neither speech can describe nor mind comprehend; all-pervading; all-transcending; delighted with his own boundless intelligence; not limited by space or time; without feet, moving swiftly; without hands, grasping all worlds; without eyes, all-surveying; without ears, all-hearing; without an intelligent guide, understanding all; without cause, the first of all causes; all-ruling; all-powerful; the creator, preserver, transformer of all things: such is the Great One."[2]

Of the process by which Brahm, the Supreme Being, created the world, Hindoo mythologists are far from being agreed. The most generally received creed, however, is, that Vishnu, the preserving spirit of God, as he slept on the face of the waters after the annihilation of a former world, produced a lotus from his body, from which sprang

BRAHMA.

Brahma, the creator, who produced the elements, formed the present world, and gave birth to the god Siva, the destroyer. After this he

[2] Sir W. Jones, vol. vi. p. 418.

produced the human race. From his head he formed the Brahmins; from his arms the Cshetries, or warriors; from his thighs the Veysias, or merchants; and from his feet, the Sudras, or husbandmen.[3]

Brahma, the creator, is now but a secondary deity amongst the Hindoos, his worship being almost superseded by that of Vishnu and Siva. There are but few temples to him, and still fewer figures. In those which are yet to be seen, we find him represented as a red or golden-coloured figure, with four heads. He has also four arms, in one of which he holds a spoon, in another a string of beads, in the third a water-jug, and in the fourth the sacred Vedas.

Unlike the other personages of the triad, Brahma appears to have had very few *avatars* or manifestations. His descendants were, however, numerous, and many of them were subsequently raised to the rank of deities.

Vishnu, the second person of the triad, is represented of a black or blue colour. He is generally seen placed on a throne of his favourite lotus flower; but sometimes he is to be found reclining on a leaf of that flower, or on the many-headed serpent Ananta, or eternity.

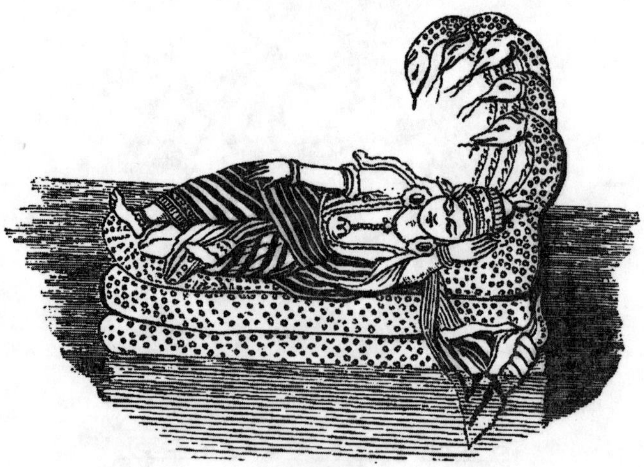

VISHNU.[3]

This deity has had nine *avatars*, and at the tenth it is said the destruction of the world will take place. The ninth of these was his incarnation as Buddha, the reformer of the Hindoo faith, or rather the

[3] Coleman's Mythology of the Hindoos, p. iv.

founder of the Buddhist religion. The heaven of Vishnu is described as being rich and beautiful beyond imagination. Eighty thousand miles in circumference, it is composed entirely of gold, with huge edifices of precious stones; and every luxurious adjunct which the warm and fertile invention of oriental minds could picture.

Siva, the destroyer, the supreme lord of all, vanquished only by Maha Kali, or Eternity, is usually represented of a white or silver colour. Sometimes he has five heads, at other times but one, with a third eye in his forehead; the three eyes being supposed to denote time past, present, and to come. He is often found seated on a throne, and sometimes riding on the bull Nandi. In his hands are represented a small drum, a cup to receive the blood of the slain, two human heads, and a club.[4]

His consort, Parvali, is also frequently represented with him. He has various names, and has had numerous incarnations. Many are

KURMAWATARA.

the temples erected to his worship, and at certain seasons of the year great festivals are held, at which thousands congregate to celebrate some one of his exploits by means of games, offerings, and acts of devotion.

The religion of Brahma, like most other forms of worship, may be

[4] Coleman, p. 62.

divided into two parts, the ritual and the moral, or practical. Numberless are the ceremonials to be observed by the followers of Brahma,

MATSYAVATARA.

Vishnu, and Siva. Ablution and prayer are the chief duties of all devout Hindoos. Of the class of Brahmins five sacraments are daily demanded, viz. studying the Vedas; making oblations to the manes, and to fire in honour of the deity; giving alms, and receiving guests with honour.

The Brahminical code forcibly dwells upon the evil results of a vicious life, both during a present state and hereafter. The upright man, it is expressly declared, need not be cast down even though oppressed with penury, while the unjust man attains no felicity, nor he whose wealth proceeds from false evidence.[5] It is also emphatically declared in the learned and sacred books of the Hindoos, that paramount to all ceremonial observances and rites are the moral duties of man. Those duties, however, appear on closer examination to be rather of a passive than an active character; and although strongly imbued with a generous and elevated spirit, the morality of the Brahmins is at the best little more than a guide to innocent tranquillity.

[5] Menu, chap. iv. p. 76.

The principal changes which have taken place in the religion of India, are the passing from the worship of one true God to the adoration of a crowd of deities more numerous than those of any other known faith, equally with the adoration of deified mortals; the great increase of sects of religion; the employment of a new and more plastic set of Vedas; the great ascendency of the monastic orders over all others; and the inculcation of the doctrine that faith in a particular god is far more efficacious than contemplation, ceremonial observance, and even good works.[6]

We find the fruits of innovation and change in the multiplicity of strange temples to new deities and saints; in the constantly recurring festivals; in the innumerable processions and shows, accompanied as they are with glaring, tinsel pomp; in the penances, the offerings, and oblations, and the multiplicity of devotees and monks revelling in idle, useless sanctity. Indeed, the Hindoo religion as at present existing, may be said to be the Roman Catholicism of the East.

The text-books of the new creed are the *Puranas*, of which there are eighteen, believed by their readers to have been composed by the inspired writer of the *Vedas*, though there is scarcely any doubt of their having been the production of many different pens, and of so late date as from the eighth to the sixteenth century of the Christian era.

Besides the host of gods whose existence is taught in the *Puranas*, there are countless hosts of angels ministering to the spirits of the just in the allotted heavens. There are also evil spirits, such as the Rakshasas and Pisachas, whilst the Bhats correspond with the nursery goblins of the western world.

There is besides an almost innumerable crowd of local gods, worshipped in villages and certain districts, and which in many respects bear a striking resemblance to the Lares of the Romans.

Hindooism, in contradistinction to Buddhism, believes in a future of good or evil. The transmigration of the soul is a leading feature of this doctrine; they still believe that between the different stages of existence they will, according to their merit or demerit, enjoy thousands of years of happiness in heaven, or suffer as long the racks of the infernal regions, of which they have a vast number.

The religious service of the Hindoos is far from being of an elevated or interesting character. For the Brahmin, if he be a strict observer of the ritual, it will prove a task of some hours daily; but the great mass of the people ordinarily content themselves with repeating the name of their patron deity whilst taking their morning bath.

[6] Elphinstone, vo. i. p. 161.

The religious festivals of the Hindoos form no inconsiderable portion of their devotion. Amongst the chief of these may be instanced the festival of Juggernath, a deity before whose shrine more victims have been immolated than have fallen beside the standard of Alexander or the eagle of Napoleon. There are many shrines to this god, but the principal one is at Orissa, whence, at the due season, the colossal image, sixty feet high, is brought forth on its huge, unwieldy car, drawn by thousands of men, women, and children, who consider it a high and holy privilege to be thus employed.

As the ponderous wheels of the vast machine roll lazily onwards, devotees and pilgrims from distant places rush forward and fling themselves beneath the moving mass, and scatter the road with their blood. At the principal feast, the Rath-jattra, as many as sixty thousand persons will be assembled from almost all parts of India. It is believed that several thousands annually lost their lives in this shocking manner, though of late years the practice has considerably fallen off.

Scarcely of less importance than the preceding is the *Dûrga Pûrja*, a festival which takes place early in October in honour of Parvati, the wife of Vishnu, under her second name of Dûrga, which this Eastern Bellona is said to have received in consequence of her victory over a redoubtable giant named Dûrgu. Feasting to excess is carried on during the ten days of this universal holiday; all business is suspended, and none can think of any thing but merrymaking. Some of the wealthy Hindoo gentlemen expend as much as 10,000*l.* in entertaining both Europeans and natives during the Pûrja, and vast numbers of cattle are slaughtered for the poorer classes.

For few things are the Hindoos so remarkable as for their rigorous performance of self-inflicted punishments and austerities during religious festivals. These are either done to propitiate favour for the future, or to efface some misdeed or offence committed, or perhaps in fulfilment of a vow made during sickness. In the latter case, no consideration can induce the person to forego the penance; and though sometimes years may elapse before it can be accomplished, it will still be carried out.

Amongst these severities, we find swinging in the air suspended by cords on hooks forced through the muscles of the back; thrusting a spear through the foot, and walking with the weapon projecting deep into the ground; standing on one foot for many days with the hands held clasped above the head, and the eyes intently fixed upon the burning sun; and lastly, knives, swords, or arrows thrust through the tongue in a great variety of ways.

Fakeers are men who have achieved a degree of sanctity through penances of this sort, and by which they are generally maimed for life. They are looked upon as beings of a sacred character, and are kept liberally supplied with alms wherever they wander. These men are usually very repulsive objects, being filthy in the extreme, and crippled in many hideous ways.

A FAKEER.

The performance of suttee, or self-sacrifice, by the widows of Hindoos, has obtained from very early dates. The mode of death was by a funeral-pile, which the victim ascended, often with much firmness, sometimes with apparent satisfaction, but not unfrequently with terror and reluctance, though aided by plentiful potions of drugs and stimulants.

The East India Company have for many years past laboured to put down both this and the equally barbarous practice of infanticide; for a long period the task appeared a hopeless one, but success has at length crowned their praiseworthy efforts, and within their own territories, as well as those of their allies, these practices may now be said to be almost extinct.

Although the Bhuddhist religion is at the present moment an unknown faith in Hindostan proper, it must not be passed by without notice, seeing that it had its original stronghold in India, and thence spread over a large portion of the eastern world, including as its votaries not fewer than one-third of the human race.

Sakya, or Gotama Buddha, the last of the Buddhas, was born at Pataliputra,[7] or Patna, B.C. 623, attained his Buddhaship, through a long course of meditation and penance, about B.C. 588; and after propagating his faith through the greater part of India and in the island of Ceylon, died at the age of eighty.

The two religions were too antagonistic in their nature to grow and thrive side by side. A long and bitter struggle between these faiths

[7] Palibothra of the Greeks.

resulted in the ascendency of Brahminism, and the final expulsion of Bhuddhism from Hindostan, between the seventh and twelfth centuries of the Christian era.[8] Driven from this part of Asia, the new, or reformed faith made its way northwards to Thibet and Tartary; eastwards to Burmah, Siam, China, and Japan, and southwards to Ceylon and other eastern islands, until it became diffused over a wider range of country, and was acknowledged by a greater number of votaries, than has been the case with any other religion since the creation of mankind.[9]

The creed of the Bhuddhists is essentially one of atheism, although in some parts of northern Asia it assumes a theistical character; yet even amongst such the belief in a God is coupled with the rejection of Him as the creator or ruler of the universe.[10] The true Bhuddhist believes in the eternal existence of nothing but matter, which bears within itself the power of reproduction of beings without the aid of any external agent.

Transmigration under a peculiar aspect forms a part of this belief, and the existence of a superior order of beings, called Buddhas, who have, by a long career of austerities and praiseworthy deeds in various worlds, attained to that rank. The Buddhas are believed to be many in number; and it is the last of them, Gotama, who revealed, or constructed the reformed religion.

This present Buddha, however, although the admitted head of the church, is not worshipped as a deity, or as a being presiding and watching over the destinies of this lower world. He is simply considered as a beacon of intelligence, goodness, and beauty, worthy the imitation of mankind. Having attained the sublime excellency of *Nirwana*, or cessation of existence, he is no longer capable of being worshipped. He is, in fact, but a deification of human intellect, a state of approximation to which every member of the race may attain without reference to position.

Nirwana is not the *destruction* or *annihilation* of an existent being, but the *cessation of his existence.* It is not an absorption into a superior being, as the Brahmins teach; it is not a retreat into a place of eternal repose, free from further transmigration; nor is it a violent destruction of being; but a complete and final *cessation of existence.*

The morality of Buddhism is of a high and pure character; and although the incentive to virtue, the final attainment of *Nirwana,* is so

[8] Asiatic Journal, vol. iv. p. 334.
[9] Christianity in Ceylon, by Sir J. Emerson Tennent, p. 200.
[10] Elphinstone's India, vol. i. p. 303.

widely different from that which influences the Christian, it may easily be seen that its standard is scarcely second to any other code. The Buddhist is forbidden to take the life of even the meanest creature; he is prohibited intemperance, incontinence, dishonesty, and falsehood, all vices that are but too common in the East; whilst the smaller failings of anger, pride, covetousness, hypocrisy, &c. are not forgotten. On the other hand, he is encouraged to the practice of all virtues, the forgiveness of injuries, charity, respect to age and character, contentment, gratitude, moderation in all things, patience, cheerfulness,—all these he is taught to follow as the sure guides to the ultimatum of his desires. "Those," said Buddha, "who practise all these virtues, and are not overcome by evil, will enjoy the perfection of happiness, and attain to supreme renown."

One striking peculiarity of the Buddhist religion is to be found in the garb and lives of the priesthood. They are dressed in robes of yellow cloth, have their heads shaven, go barefooted and bareheaded, live in monasteries, and perform regular daily services in their temples. They are also sworn to poverty and celibacy; and subsist, or are supposed to do so, upon alms. At one time nunneries for women appear to have existed; but none are to be met with at the present time.

A third sect of religionists, though not of very great extent, is that of the Jains, holding a place about midway between the Brahmins and Buddhists. They are, to a certain extent, atheistical, believing in the eternity of matter alone; and whilst they reverence the whole of the Hindoo deities, they add to their Pantheon a long list of saints, who pretty nearly assume with them the rank and attributes of Buddha.

The division of castes in India forms a prominent feature of the Brahminical religion. In early times these classes were four in number, though in the present day several of them are lost, whilst many other subdivisions have sprung up. The first class is that of the Brahmins, who, according to the code of Menu, were held as superior to all other created beings, and possessed considerable immunities. They took rank before kings; their property was considered most sacred; and although their offences were treated with admirable clemency, no leniency awaited the culprit who offended or injured one of their sacred body.

Endowed, however, as they were with so many immunities, their life could scarcely be pronounced an enviable one. Nearly three-fourths of their life were spent in the practice of severe mortifications and austerities, or immersed in the deepest contemplation; and even during the later period of their earthly career, when their penances had ceased, they were enjoined the practice of a devotional meditation upon the delights of a future state, free from all sources of evil and suffering.

The Cshetryas, or military class, speaks for itself. Ranking next to the Brahmins, they were always treated with honour, and enjoyed many advantages over the lower classes. Their duties, as laid down in Menu, appear to have been to defend the people, to give alms, to sacrifice, to read the *Vedas*, and to shun the allurements of sensual pleasures.[11]

Next in rank to the preceding is the Veisyas, or mercantile class, who are enjoined by Menu to practise the rites of religion; not forgetting, of course, donations to the Brahmins, trading, banking, cultivation, and cattle-rearing.

A SUDRA MENDICANT.

The Sudras were the lowest in the scale of society; and every enactment made in reference to them and their position possesses the same

[11] Chap. i. p. 89.

severity of tone. It is declared to be their especial duty to serve the other classes, but in no way to interfere in their callings. Even in the exercise of religious duties, they must perform them in a maimed and imperfect manner. The *Veda* is not allowed to be read even in their presence; nor must any one of them presume to offer their advice.

Should a Sudra be killed, the religious penance for the act is similar to that for killing a cat or a dog. A Sudra is to be fed by the leavings of his master, and to be clad in his rejected garments; and as to worldly possessions, he is not permitted to accumulate the most trifling amount.

Such was the status of the Sudras in the early days of Indian empire; but in modern times, not only have great radical changes and innovations crept into the upper classes, but the two latter may be said no longer to exist; whilst in their places we find scores of other castes, less of a religious nature than of a social character.

There is no longer a servile caste; they have merged quietly but surely in the hundreds of classes now met with on every side in India. Not at all unfrequently these castes coincide with the various trades; such, for instance, as the goldsmiths, the washermen, and the carpenters. These, if more numerous than of old, are certainly far more particular in regard to preserving the integrity of their respective castes which in olden times was seldom done.

CHAPTER III.

MANNERS AND CUSTOMS.

In a region equal in extent to the whole of Europe, with the exception of Russia, which has been the theatre of so many revolutions, numbering within its limits a population of a hundred and twenty millions, and counting not less than a dozen distinct nations, and at least four separate religions, we might reasonably look for a considerable dissimilarity of customs, manners, and character; and undoubtedly such is to be found in very many instances, drawing a line through the country, almost as broad and as marked as that of their dialects.

Not only do the inhabitants of the Deccan and the entire peninsula of India differ from those of Hindostan Proper in most particulars, but the latter, again, have little in common with the dwellers in the north-west; and even within the boundaries of Hindostan we may perceive a marked dissimilarity between the Bengalees and the inhabitants of Gangetic Hindostan. In personal appearance the natives of the northern countries are fairer, better formed, and more robust and energetic than those to the south, who, with the exception of some of the Malabar tribes, are of small stature, darker, effeminate, cunning, and timid to a degree. The communities of most of the towns are composed of bankers, traders, government officials, bazaar-keepers, and domestics. In the rural districts there are few beyond the agriculturists and the village headmen and officers of the government.

The mode of life of the Indian ryot is one of extreme simplicity, amounting but too often to misery, the result of an outward continual pressure kept on him by the zemindar and others of that class. The members of a family dwell with each other from grandfather to grandchild with patriarchal contentedness—one leafy roof, one bamboo-wall, sheltering old and young, the toiler and the tarryer; happy if the simple meal of roots and grain comes at the appointed time,—happy now and then to snatch a mouthful of forbidden rice from the fields their hands cultivate for the tax-farmer,—happy if at harvest-time *all* that crop be not wrung from them in rent and usury.

Poor as is the exterior of the Hindoo hut, with its patch of garden-stuff, its broken wall and its bamboo hedge, its interior wears not a more cheering aspect. A handful of rushes for a carpet covers a part of the mud floor; a few earthen vessels for water or purposes of cookery; a bamboo stool, a rush mat rolled up in one corner, which at night performs the office of a bed,—these make up the household inventory, so poor, so mean, so small in value, that were the insatiate tax-farmer to distrain for his rent, no coin would be found sufficiently minute to purchase them. Glass and crockery are mystic articles to the Hindoo villager: he may have heard of such things at the next town on festival-days, but his own supply of dinner-ware is provided by more bountiful hands than those of Spode and Copeland,—the willow-pattern is supplanted by the Banana leaf. An earthern chattie and rice-dish are articles of luxury. In dress they have as little to boast of. One strip of cotton-cloth, bleached white with constant washings, or perhaps stained yellow or pink, is wound round the loins. On occasions of village or religious festivities a second strip will be flung loosely across the shoulders, to be afterwards carefully laid aside for the next occasion. The women wear a longer piece of white cloth wrapt round them in apparent negligence, and yet so gracefully as to set off the figure to the utmost advantage. Children are seldom clad until they attain the age of eight or nine.[1] The reader has here a picture of that class of Indian cultivators, who, spread over a vast and fertile tract of country, may truly be called the flesh and bone of our Indian empire: from such as these springs the large export-trade of the presidencies, amounting to seventeen millions sterling annually; from such as these is wrung the greater portion of the twenty-two millions sterling of taxation: it is these, whose only knowledge of their English rulers is derived through the medium of the revenue-farmer, whose education is cared for at the annual rate of three farthings per family.

There are, of course, classes superior to the above, scattered over the land: heads of villages, district functionaries, and dwellers in small towns, who pretend to somewhat of Hindoo gentility, whose wives and daughters dwell in distinct apartments, whose sleeping cotton-mat is a little more showy, whose waist-cloth is whiter and more copious, whose earthen drinking-vessels are transformed to utensils of brass, who dine off real plates of clay, and do not tremble at the names of "zemindar" and "Burrah Sahib."[2]

Uncared for, low in the scale of humanity, removed from all soften-

[1] Milbrecht's Protestant Missions in Bengal.

[2] Anglice, great (or English) master.

ing or ennobling influences, the height of their enjoyment, all that they value, is a carouse at the festival of some repulsive deity, or their mid-day gossip and hookah with the heads of their village under the cool shade of a banyan-tree. Home duties and domestic happiness are words without meaning in their ears; their wives and daughters have no social status, no education; they are simply necessary pieces of human furniture for the physical uses of man, and whose sole destiny is to raise families, to boil rice, and finally to die.

There is perhaps less difference in the food of the various classes than in any other respect. With all castes vegetables form the basis of their cookery, though some of the lower orders in large towns are not careful to abstain from eating flesh. Amongst the rural population there is little to be met with beyond a coarse unleavened bread made from various fine grains, with a few boiled vegetables, roots, a little oil or ghee made from buffaloes' milk, and perhaps a dash of some sort of

A HINDOO MEAL.

spice and a little salt. In the southern states of the peninsula rice forms a more prominent feature in their cookery; whilst to the north and north-west, flesh, whether of animals or birds, is more commonly employed in various ways.

In the towns a far greater variety of food is eaten, and generally with more regard to taste and indulgence. In the vicinity of the rivers fish abounds, and forms a staple article of daily food. The use of intoxicating drinks is chiefly confined to large communities, though amongst the Rajpoot tribes opium is used to a large extent. The most common indulgence of nearly all classes is a mixture of betel and areca, aromatic pungent articles, combined with a sort of lime, and occasionally tobacco and spices.

In none of their daily observances does the prejudice of caste so strongly appear as in eating their meals. It is reckoned extreme defilement to eat from a plate or seated on the same mat as used by one of an inferior caste; and this leads to many strange customs, especially amongst the Brahmins, the highest in the social scale. It is not at all unusual for these people to eat from plates formed of the leaves of trees just gathered, in order to prevent pollution. In the same way, and for the same reason, members of the military or mercantile classes, when going a journey, are frequently compelled to dress their own victuals, wanting a cook of their own caste.

The dwellings of the Indian peasantry are generally miserable in the extreme, consisting of seldom more than two small rooms formed of stones and mud rudely thrown together, protected from the heat of the sun and the deluge of tropical showers by a simple roof of jungle-sticks and wild leaves; and usually without any garden-fence about them, they present a striking contrast to the tastily finished mansions of their wealthy countrymen.

The more substantial men of the villages can seldom boast of much more; the chief distinction being that the latter indulge in a fenced garden, and often a second story to their hovels.

On the other hand, the Hindoos of rank indulge in much lavish outlay upon their mansions and pleasure-gardens, many of which vie with the extent and costliness of the Mahometan edifices in the time of the empire.

In the southern part of the peninsula a far greater degree of taste and neatness is displayed in the village dwellings, where not only are they frequently more prettily situated, but a marked regard is paid to the cleanliness and appearance of the cottages.

Every village, no less than each of the towns throughout India, boasts of its bazaar for the sale of the simple necessaries of Oriental life. In the hamlets of the rural districts, the bazaar will consist of a single small shop, whose whole stock consists of grain, some coarse cloths, a few sweetmeats, a collection of earthen vessels, and a bundle or two of tobacco, with occasionally some brass ornaments for the women. In the towns, a group of shops, of various kinds, containing far more miscellaneous stores, may be met with; and in the larger cities whole streets and squares are comprised within the bazaar.

There are besides these bazaars, markets held at short intervals, and fairs generally once or twice in each year upon any particular festival or holiday. An Indian town or city presents a busy, animated scene on market-days. Villagers pour in with their burdens of grain or fruit upon their heads, or with loaded bullock-carts; the narrow streets and lanes become thronged to suffocation. The cries of the carriage drivers, the shouts of the loaded water-carriers, the moaning, heavy song of the palanquin-bearers, the screaming of children, the lowing of cattle; these, with the dust, and heat, and glare of pent-up, badly paved carriage-ways, make up a scene any thing but pleasing to a European traveller.

A WATER-CARRIER.

The amusements, festivals, and religious ceremonies of the Hindoos are all alike distinguished by a great degree of pomp, ostentation, and form. There is much that is pleasing in the manners of the higher classes towards their inferiors, to whom they shew, on all occasions, the utmost affability and courtesy. Presents have from the earliest times formed a leading feature of all holidays, festivals, and family or public ceremonies. These vary according to the means of the donor; from some thousands of pounds sterling down to a bouquet of flowers, or a little rice and fruit.

In many districts this custom has become a most oppressive one, being distorted by the native headmen and officials into a means of wringing from those of the poorer and most helpless classes all such of their substance as may be left them by the zemindars. Each birthday or wedding-day of any of the chiefs or middlemen of a district or village is made the pretext for mulcting the ryot in donations known by the name of *abwabs,* generally in kind. Thus the milkman furnishes a supply of milk, the oil-maker supplies oil for the lamps, the cultivator contributes his quota of grain; and so on through the whole population. The *naibs, gomastas,* and *paiks,* all subordinates attached to the collectors of revenue, levy their own peculiar abwabs upon the prostrate ryots, who are without the power of refusal. So long as the poor cultivators possesses the veriest trifle of produce, so long are they made especial objects of extortion by the human vultures that throng the revenue and judicial establishments of British India.

A NAUTCH OR NATIVE ENTERTAINMENT.

The fairs held throughout India are for the joint purposes of pleasure and trade. They are widely different from such scenes in England, partaking far more of theatrical pomp and show, with more noise, and a greater admixture of foreigners clad in many varied dresses. There is always a certain blending of religious ceremonial with these periodical assemblages, though generally forming but a small feature in the day's proceedings.

The upper classes of the natives of India are much given to entertainments of dancing and music, to which large numbers of their friends are invited. These take place upon any occasion which may offer a pretext for conviviality or sociability; they, indeed, answer to the European evening-parties. Natives of high birth and rank are proud to have their English acquaintances present on these occasions, and often make great preparations for their reception, especially if, as is sometimes the case, the European be an official of note.

It is at these parties that the "Nautch Girls" display the gracefulness, and something more, of their figures, with a studied affectation of ease and grace, which, to a European, carries little beyond repulsion. In some parts of India, especially in the southern states of the peninsula, every temple has a troop of these "Dancing Girls," whose questionable earnings help out the sacred finances of the shrine. Some of them dress with great magnificence, hiring their jewelled robes for the occasion, and which are said occasionally to be worth, with their ornaments, as much as 20,000*l*.

The position of Hindoo women is much changed since the time of Menu; and even from the period when the British rule was established, many important modifications in the position of the females have taken place. During the olden Hindoo time, the women were retired and secluded almost as strictly as amongst the Mahomedans; and there is little doubt but that during the Tartar dynasty this became still more the case.

The code of Menu lays down with considerable minuteness the actual position and duties of the wife as regards her husband; and these are such as can scarcely be termed unfair towards the weaker sex. The strictest obedience of the wife is enjoined; but at the same time the husband is told to leave her at her own disposal in innocent and lawful recreations.[3] He is, moreover, to keep her "constantly supplied with ornaments, apparel, and food at festivals and jubilees."

The code is equally precise in detailing the various duties of the woman, who is to give her undivided care and study to the preparation of daily food, and the superintendence of household utensils.

[3] Menu, chap. ix. p. 2.

As a rule, Hindoo women are totally without education. Parents do not see the advantage that may arise from placing their daughters on an equal footing in this respect with their sons. The smallest expense attending the education of a girl would be, by the father, considered as a foolish waste of money, productive of good to no one.

There are, however, exceptions to even this very general rule amongst the families of the superior classes of Bengalees, where it not very unfrequently happens that the daughter has been taught, not only to read, but to write.

The form of marriage is simple in the extreme, the rite consisting in the bride taking seven steps, repeating a particular verse at each separate step. When the seventh is taken, the marriage is considered

A RIDING ELEPHANT.

indissoluble.[4] Other forms were observed in earlier times; but they have gradually become obsolete. The bride and bridegroom are usually not more than ten years of age when marriage takes place, and seldom more than twelve. At these ceremonies a lavish outlay is often in-

[4] Colebrook: Asiatic Researches, vol. vii. pp. 303-9.

HINDOO FUNERAL PILE.

curred, sometimes beyond the means of the parties. In large cities it is said that from 10,000*l.* to 20,000*l.* sterling will be squandered upon the feastings, illuminations, dancing, processions of elephants, &c. inseparable from a Hindoo wedding in high life.

The custom of burning the dead has obtained in India from time immemorial.

Before burning the body, great care is taken to have it well washed, perfumed, and arrayed with flowers and clean cloths. In some parts

INDIAN KITE.

of India music accompanies the funeral procession to the pyre; but elsewhere the only sounds which disturb the stillness of the scene are the sorrowing exclamations of the soldiers and attendants, and the screams of the many kites and other birds of prey, hovering about.

Of the first institution of Suttee nothing certain is known; though it is undoubtedly of high antiquity, being alluded to by Diodorus Siculus, who wrote before the Christian era, and it appears to have been in practice for a long period previously.

The belief that the widow is subject to any degradation should she survive her husband's death cannot be correct, seeing that it is by no means an uncommon occurrence for the relatives and friends of the family to endeavour, by all the means in their power, to dissuade the woman from the contemplated act: it is notorious that this is not only attempted, but often successfully; and amongst other expedients employed, is so to occupy the time and attention of the widow, that the body of her deceased husband may be removed and burned before she is aware of the fact.[5]

The ceremony of Suttee varies with the local customs of different parts of India; though not perhaps in any essential particulars. In Bengal the widow prepares for the act with many ceremonies, and invariably bathes before mounting the pyre, if possible in the sacred waters of the Ganges. Before firing the funeral altar, the dead and the living are bound together to the pile, so as to preclude the possibility of the latter effecting an escape. In the south of India the women would appear to need no such precautions. A widow will there coolly seat herself on the pyre, and placing the head of the departed husband in her lap, awaits with Roman firmness the moment when the flames of the burning mass shall envelope her in their embraces. In other parts of India the Suttee leaps into the burning mass from an eminence, or the funeral pyre may be below the surface of the ground.

Sometimes the courage of the woman will fail her at the critical time, and she will make a desperate attempt to escape from the cruel death which awaits her; but in this case the attendants invariably thrust her back into the flames. An instance of this kind is on record wherein an English gentleman being present, succeeded in rescuing the widow from the flames, much against the wishes of those present. His conduct was, however, but ill requited by the woman whose life he had thus saved; for on the following day he was not a little surprised at being upbraided by her for having thus shut her out from the companionship of her husband in Paradise.[6]

This practice is far more frequent within the limits of Hindostan Proper than in any other part of India. Indeed, in the western districts it is but seldom that it occurs; whilst south of the Deccan it is almost unknown.

[5] Elphinstone, vol. i. p. 359.

[6] Ibid. vol. i. p. 361.

Amongst other customs prevalent in India, is one, which if it be not universal throughout that vast country, at any rate prevails to an extent which seems scarcely credible, and which was for a long period disbelieved, such is its revolting character.

There are certain Rajpoot tribes of the western and central provinces of British India, who have, almost from time immemorial, sacrificed the lives of a great portion of their female children as soon as born. In a part of the province of Benares, in Kach, and in the neighbouring district of Kalliawar, is to be found this degrading custom in its full vigour. In Kach and Kalliawar alone it is computed, on the lowest calculation, that 2000 female infants are thus annually put to death; whilst in the province of Benares as many more are yearly sacrificed.

The existence of this shocking custom is proved in other localities; though perhaps not to such a great extent as amongst the Rajpoots. The Sikhs of Bhopal, the Minas of Gahazpoor and Toukra, the inhabitants of Rewar and Jholawar, and the Chouans of Marwar, are all known to practise this method of ridding themselves of their daughters.

Not the least revolting feature of the custom is, that most of these infants die by the hands of their *mothers* shortly after their birth; and that none are preserved but such as the father requests may be saved.

This child-murder appears to have had its origin in the difficulty which the heads of families meet with in disposing of their daughters in marriage. By them it is considered incestuous to intermarry with members of the same tribe; their daughters must seek husbands among the tribes at a distance; and as this is often not practicable, and moreover as the poverty of many of the Rajpoots prevents them from providing for the marriage expenses, which custom renders absolutely necessary, they dread the disgrace which inevitably follows the single life of females in India; and with the view of averting this, resort to the barbarous practice of sacrificing their offspring.

The servants of the East India Company were no sooner made aware of the great prevalence of this crime within their own districts and those of friendly states, than they used every effort in their power to put an end to the enormity. So long since as 1819 the attempt was made by attaching heavy penalties to the perpetrators of the crime within the British territory; and in the case of friendly states, their chiefs were bound by treaties to do their utmost to put a stop to the practice. More than thirty years have elapsed since these praiseworthy attempts were first made; and although during that period no effort has been spared, no energy relaxed, it is to be feared that the revolting custom has become too deeply rooted in the habits and feelings of the people to be eradicated by edicts or treaties.

Not less revolting to a humane and civilised mind than the barbarities of Suttee and infanticide, is the long-prevalent and general custom amongst the Hindoos of exposing their sick on the banks of the Ganges to breathe their last within the influence of its holy waters. This they call giving them to Ganga.

No sooner is a patient believed to be beyond the reach of medicine, than, if within a possible distance, he is carried to the banks of the Ganges, and either left to die in one of the small mud huts with which its shores abound, or he will be placed in the stream itself in such a manner that, as its waters rise, death must ensue from drowning. Sometimes the relatives lay the patient on the sandy banks, and commence pouring a quantity of the thick muddy water of the river down his throat, until suffocation ensues, when they believe most firmly that the water has winged the soul to Paradise.

The scenes upon the river-banks are oftentimes most harrowing; the invalid beseeching his friends to save him; the half-drowning man strong enough in his delirious fever to struggle, but in vain, to escape his cruel fate; the mother beseeching her children to save her; the tender infant left upon the beach stretching its tiny hands to one who, in any other country, would be the last to desert it in its helpless agony, but who here, under the baleful influence of a withering superstition, stands coldly by and watches the little struggler sob out its infant life.

There is perhaps no country in which thieves are such adepts in their profession as in India. For how long a period this may have been the case, or whence their proficiency originally came, does not appear; but of the fact there is little doubt. The ordinary fastenings of houses, nay, the very walls themselves, are small protection against the depredations of these daring and practised marauders, who with the greatest facility possess themselves of the most valuable property, without the least chance of prevention or detection. So skilled are they in their art, that they have been known to remove the bed-clothes from under a sleeper, without having been detected.

One of the most formidable enemies of the public in India was the associated band of robbers and murderers called Thugs, who for a series of years committed the most daring enormities against life and property, without any effectual attempts being made to put them down. These

HINDOO LEAVING HER SICK CHILD ON THE BANKS OF THE GANGES.

Thugs were banded together, and generally worked in concert by bodies of three or more. In order to effect their purpose with the greater facility and security, they travelled the least frequented parts of the country in various disguises, and when they found a traveller who appeared to possess sufficient to render him an object worth their trouble, they waylaid him on his journey and dispatched him by strangulation, burying the body or sinking it in a well, so as to escape detection. In some cases they have been known to join company with their victim, and whilst seated together, resting beneath the shade of some wide-spreading tree and listening to a tale of adventure, one of their number approached from the rear, and slipping the fatal noose over the head of the unwary traveller, quickly dispatched him without the chance of escape.

A THUG.

It has been calculated that many thousands of persons have fallen victims to the Thugs, and it is impossible to say how many more they might have immolated, had not their ill-luck tempted them to sacrifice one or two Englishmen. This aggravated wickedness at once aroused the ire and activity of the authorities, who, regardless as they had so long been of the wholesale sacrifice of Hindoo life, could not tolerate the idea of one of their own order being included in the list of victims. The mandate went forth for their suppression; and although many of them contrived to elude the vigilance of the parties placed on their track, their final extinction as a body has at length become a fact, and *Thuggee* is now a matter of past history.

If India has produced its gangs of desperate thieves and murderers, it also furnishes society with sects of an opposite character. The Charans and Bhats are peculiar races regarded by all ranks in a sacred light. These people devote themselves to the protection of property and often of life through dangerous tracts of country where mere physical demonstration would avail but little.[7]

[7] Malcolm's Central India, vol. ii. p. 130.

The many sections into which native Indian society is split by the institution of "caste," are sensibly felt by the European, who finds himself obliged, however moderate his wants may be, to maintain from a dozen to twenty domestics. The "kidmutgar" who waits at table, and has charge of the plate, glass, &c., does not meddle with the food or drinkables, which are in the custody of a higher domestic, a sort of butler.

A KIDMUTGAR.

Gentlemen are attended in their dressing-rooms by a "bearer," who enacts the part of a Hindoo valet; whilst lower still in the grade of domestics is the "mater," who sweeps out the rooms, cleans the dinner-service, &c.

The large cities in India have no water laid on in their houses, the supply of which is brought from neighbouring tanks or wells by a class of men known as "bheesties," who carry the liquid in hogs' skins slung across their backs.

A BEARER.

Another very necessary class of servants are the "dhobies" or washermen, who are constantly employed along the banks of rivers and tanks, beating on large stones the white garments of both sexes with a violence and disregard of stitches and buttons, which, to a new-comer, appears dangerous in the extreme. By this rude process, however, they manage to preserve the cotton and linen clothes of a delicately white colour, not attainable in European countries.

The Sindhi as a people bear a closer resemblance to their Arab ancestors than any other people of the East. In some few respects they resemble the Beloochis; but though muscular, full-proportioned men, they are much fairer than their neighbours, especially the women, some of whose countenances bear a close affinity with the Spanish features and tint. Their habits and moral bearing scarcely warrant the opinion which one would form of these people from their well-developed organism.

Illiterate to a degree, especially the females, their amusements appear to be of a gross and debasing kind. Gambling, cockfighting, hunting, and wrestling make up the excitements of a Sindhi's life; whilst the women pass their time between the frivolities of dress, cards, and the less innocent occupation of intrigue, for which they are notorious.

A MATER.

A BHEESTIE.

The ceremonials of marriage do not differ very materially from those of Hindostan. Equally abounding in forms and observances, they are not one whit less costly; and it is by no means uncommon for the nuptials to be delayed many months through the inability of the parties to incur all the needed expense.

The birth of a child of either sex is welcomed by rejoicings and festivities, limited only by the means of the parents. At four years and four months the boy is sent to school, where he remains until the age of twelve and sometimes fifteen, during which time he goes through a regular course of the Koran, the Sindhi language, and Persian. The female sex are all most miserably uneducated, the men appearing to think they are mischievous and wicked enough without the aid of books and pens.

Betrothal usually takes place when the girl is about twelve and the boy verging on fifteen, though sometimes much earlier. Marriage follows at once, if the means of the parties will allow.

A PEGUAN.

In their manners and general habits the Peguans and Talains, of the Tenasserim and neighbouring provinces, are decidedly superior to the Hindoo, though perhaps less industriously disposed. In all that relates to education, in their freedom from the ban of caste and the slavery of baneful superstition, in the superiority of their social system, these people form a remarkable exception to the state of debasement in which most of the Asiatic nations are plunged.

Perhaps their most remarkable departure from Oriental customs is the social position in which they have placed their women. Although generally without even the education afforded by the Kioungs or village schools, the mothers and wives of these countries occupy a prominent position in society, and take a share in the daily business of life rarely to be met with eastward of the Cape.

A Burman or Peguan will never journey by land so long as he can go by water; and so addicted are they from their earliest infancy to boat travelling, that the canoe enters into almost all their arrangements. Their cattle are fed out of canoes, their children sleep in them, their vessels of domestic use are canoe-shaped, they travel by land in canoe-shaped carriages, and it may be almost said that their earliest and their latest moments are passed in canoes.

Having thus sketched the leading manners and customs of the nations comprised within the limits of British India, I will endeavour to complete the picture by adding a few lines relative to their character.

HINDOO WASHERMEN.

Were an opinion upon this subject formed from the majority of books published on Indian topics, or from the oral evidence of travellers and others, we should indeed arrive at a most unfavourable conclusion, and feel inclined to place our Indian fellow-subjects the very lowest in the scale of humanity. But, unwilling to do this, we consult some of those few who have passed a long life amongst those dwellers in the provinces, who have been beyond the contaminating influence of the larger towns and cities, free from the inoculation of Indo-European morality; and we there learn other and far better things of the bulk of the people.

That falsehood, deception, perjury, timidity, if not actual cowardice, form the leading characteristics of most Hindoos, in all their intercourse with Europeans, there can be but little doubt. Equally true is it that the same race of people can be attached, faithful, honest, and, on emergencies, brave even to the death. If we turn to the oldest records of this people left us by Greek writers, we find such accounts of them as might well induce us to believe that they were detailing the characteristics of a totally different portion of the human family. The pictures drawn by Arrian and Strabo of the character of the Hindoo nations bear no nearer resemblance to their portraiture in modern works, than do the habits and customs of the English of the nineteenth century to those of the ancient Britons.

In the *Indica* of Arrian, as well as in other works of that date, the inhabitants of India are described as sober, moderate, and upright in all their dealings; so honest, as to require no fastenings for their dwellings, nor locks for their treasures. Litigation was unknown amongst them, and truthfulness was ever a most marked characteristic of their nature. Allowing for the impediments which in those remote times must have been in the way of arriving at a complete knowledge of the character of the Hindoos, we cannot but admit that this highly-drawn picture must have had some ground of justification.

In seeking for an explanation of the wide discrepancies between the ancient and the most favourable modern accounts of these people, we must not lose sight of the continued enervating influence of climate upon character, added to the indolence engendered by a wonderfully prolific soil, which, out of its marvellous abundance, produces all that living beings stand in most need of.

These are, however, not all the causes which have been at work upon the character of the Hindoos. Long ages of cruel despotism; generation upon generation ground to the dust by oppression and injustice; each foreign race of masters more exacting than the last. The Tartar vying with the Arab, the Mahomedan with the Afghan, and lastly, the British conquerors of the East, the boasted pioneers of Christianity and civilisation, refining upon Tartar barbarity and cupidity, snatch from the prostrate, helpless nations the last sorry remnants of their once proud nationality; and while they wring from the wretched people their uttermost farthing by a high-pressure taxation, deny them the cheap and ready justice, the abundant irrigation, and the admirable roads, which the bigoted followers of the Prophet, in their darkest ages of despotism, had never withheld.

Before we pass a sweeping condemnation upon so large a body of our fellow-creatures, we should ask, if the policy we have pursued towards them during the last half-century has been such as to bring forth any dormant good qualities. Have we, by our laws, our precepts, and, above all, by our own example, sought to elevate the standard of their morality, to chide and check their vices and their failings? Have our officials been to them bright patterns of integrity and zeal? Have our merchant-princes been worthy examples of honour and upright dealings? Has the enlightened son of Britain held up the mirror of truth to the benighted Indian; or has the dark-skinned, dark-souled gentile shamed the pale-faced Christian with virtues, not of Bible-growth, which, living on in that rank, baneful soil, have still outstripped the blighted offshoots of the gospel-land?

These questions it will be my duty to examine and answer in another place.

PARADISE FLYCATCHER (*Muscipita Paradisi.* See Appendix F.).

CHAPTER IV.

EDUCATION AND CHRISTIANITY.

THE destiny of the Hindoo and other races of the East, under the rule of Great Britain, depends for its good or evil, less upon the form of government, the quality of legislation, or the physical welfare of the community, than upon a proper development of the intelligence, and the morals of the people,—upon the elevation of their national character. As in the more progressive countries of the western world, their future must be shaped by their schools. The safety and integrity of the state hinges upon education, as surely within the tropics as in more temperate zones. The national mind of India will advance, whatever the efforts of government. The Canutes of conservatism will in vain bid the tide of intelligence to recede—thus far shalt thou come, but no farther. The onward current of mind cannot be thus swept back. The printing-press, the steam-engine, and the railroad, are all busy at their work; the sound of their labours reaches already from Cape Comorin to the foot of the Himalayas. The spirit is abroad, and none, not even the mighty men of Leadenhall Street, can quench it. They may, however, do much more—they may *direct* it; and as the winged lightning is guided and made the minister of good, so may the subtle thought of man, the intellect of millions upon millions of the human race, be bent, controlled, and moulded unto good for us and them.

Important though this subject be, it yet forms but an unsatisfactory chapter in the history of British Indian rule. It shews that whilst the most active and intelligent minds, the most carefully weighed schemes have been bent towards the one great bureaucratic object of wringing as much as possible from the great mass of the people, the most ordinary capacities, the smallest monetary grants have, with but a few exceptions, been deemed sufficient for ministering to the mental and social well-being of the community.

It shews, moreover, that if the official work has been scanty as compared with the field, the quality has been equally indifferent. The task appears to have been one of destruction rather than of reformation; to pull down rather than to build up. Heathenism has been replaced by infidelity. Brahma has been dethroned to make way for Tom Paine; the *Vedas* cast aside for the *Age of Reason*. Dagon has indeed been hewn asunder, but the Ark has found no resting-place there. And this too by a Christian government!

Before I proceed to notice the present state of education in India, it will be well to take a survey, however rapid, of the work that has already been performed by governmental and missionary means, thus placing before my readers an epitome of the rise and progress of educational establishments within the three presidencies; and if in doing so I dwell more particularly upon the scholastic institutions of Bengal, it is that data regarding the other presidencies are most meagre and incomplete.

The nature and extent of the work yet to be done may be imagined from the substance of an official report on the state of native education, which tells us that in the most highly cultured districts only sixteen per cent of the teachable population receive any kind of instruction; in the least-cultured district, the proportion receiving teaching of any sort is about two and a quarter per cent; whilst the average of all the districts visited gave but seven and three-fourths per cent of children receiving any tuition whatever. In the same way it has been shewn, that of the adult population not more than five and a half per cent of the aggregate of the visited districts, had received any sort of instruction.[1]

The first attempts made by Europeans to impart education in India were the results of private benevolence and enterprise, and that not to natives, but to Christian children. Rather more than a century has elapsed since a fund was formed by a few philanthropic persons of the Indian metropolis to provide board and education for indigent Christian children, the origin of the existing free school of Calcutta. It was some years later when the local government took the first step in the same direction, and strangely though it may read, that first step was made, not in behalf of the great mass of the people—the Hindoo race, but of their Mahomedan conquerors.

It was in the year 1781 that Mr. Hastings founded the Madrissa, or Mahomedan College, of Calcutta, and fourteen years later a Sanscrit College was established at Benares, for the encouragement of native

[1] Calcutta Review, art. Government Education in Bengal, vol. iii. p. 212.

learning. By the act, the 53d Geo. III., a lac of rupees (10,000*l.*) was ordered to be appropriated "for the revival and improvement of literature, and the encouragement of the learned natives of India, and for the introduction and promotion of a knowledge of the sciences amongst the inhabitants of the British territories in India."

In 1816 the Hindoo college was projected, and five years later established in Calcutta, where as yet, the chief efforts in the cause of education appear to have been made. This was, and still is, by far the most important educational institution in Bengal. The celebrated Rammohun Roy was one of its most active promoters, and threw into the undertaking his entire energy. For the erection of the building 12,000*l.* were voted by the government, and an annual donation of 2,500*l.*, subsequently increased to 3,000*l.*, was granted for the maintenance of the professors, servants, &c. attached to it. Eventually larger sums were voted towards the support of this college, yet, for a long period, without having enlisted on its behalf any proportionate sympathy for the classes intended to be benefited by it, and who continued to regard it and its progress with true Asiatic indifference, so that the good resulting from its establishment has been very far from bearing a proportion to the amount of funds expended on it.

In 1830 Dr. Duff opened the General Assembly's School in Calcutta on Christian principles; and with so much ability and earnest zeal was this establishment conducted, that it very shortly rivalled the Hindoo College in the number and qualifications of its students.

It was not long after the above date, that, in order to direct and systematise the labours of the professors, and superintend the disbursements of the college and other educational grants for the presidency of Bengal, a General Committee of Public Instruction was organised, from the principal departments of the local government. In 1842 this committee was superseded by the present Council of Education, consisting of civil servants of Calcutta of high grade, two natives of little influence, a Judge of the Supreme Court, all unpaid, and a salaried secretary, who is *de facto* the council itself. This secretary is a striking illustration of the manner and the extent to which offices are heaped upon favourites by an Indian government. Besides being a member and the secretary of the Council of Education, and having in consequence to conduct the correspondence of all the colleges and schools under the government of Bengal, he is a professor in the Medical College, the secretary of that college, Government Book Agent, Inspector of Schools, and First Physician to the new Fever Hospital.

In this way should any professor of one of the colleges feel aggrieved at the conduct of the school-inspector, or hampered by any of his regulations, he must forward his complaints to the man who, being both secretary and inspector, has to decide upon all complaints thus brought against himself. In the same manner the sale of books by the secretary becomes a source of great evil, for this functionary not only reaps a large personal profit by the unrestricted price he places upon all books supplied to the various educational establishments, but keeps them furnished with such books as pay him best, and which are precisely those least desired by the professors. Yet to complain is out of the question, for any such matter must be submitted to the book-agent in his capacity of secretary, who would not only decide in his own favour, but in his third capacity of inspector of schools, manage to shew any such rebellious professor the exceeding impolicy, not less than the utter inutility, of raising any such complaints.

The administration of Lord William Bentinck ushered in a revolution in the tactics of government, which, although modified by Lord Auckland, paved the way for important results. Lord Bentinck's minute of March 1835 expressly declared, that inasmuch as it was the great object of the government to promote European literature and science amongst the natives of India, all the funds appropriated for educational purposes would be best employed on English education alone. The minute was acted upon, and the final result has been, that in place of the exclusive orientalism of government education, a combined instruction in the native tongue and in English has found favour in the greater part of central and eastern India; whilst in the north-west provinces, in Assam and Arracan, English has made but few friends, and the popular feeling is exclusively in favour of the vernacular.[2] English is, however, but little valued within the Sanscrit colleges of Calcutta and Benares, and the Madrassa colleges of Hugli and Calcutta, where the teaching continues of a purely oriental character.

The Hindoo College of Calcutta is conducted by six professors, of whom one is principal, and another head-master of the school department. A very inferior education is given in its upper classes to about a hundred and fifty youths, comprising English literature, history, mental and moral philosophy, mathematics, and natural philosophy, surveying, and music. In its school department nearly a thousand pupils are taught by a host of native and a few European professors.

In the lower portion of the building are carried on the Sanscrit

[2] Kerr's Review of Public Instruction in Bengal, part i. p. 90.

College (an institution intended to promote, amongst the natives, the study and use of their sacred language), and the upper and lower school departments of the Hindoo College itself. Connected with the Sanscrit College, there is no European officer who holds any appointment involving supervision and arrangement. On field-days, when some notability is expected—a *burra-sahib*, or influential personage—an imposing appearance is presented by this strange institution. The "Professors" of "Vyakarana," of "Sahitya," of "Alankar," of "Jyotish," and sundry other things equally euphonious and intelligible, muster in great numbers; and, what with robes, turbans, and ornaments, make a great display, looking solid, learned, and profound, as Sanscrit professors ought to look. The students repeat amazing quantities of unintelligible lines and sentences, answer unintelligible questions with equally unintelligible answers; and the *burra-sahib*, profoundly ignorant of the language used, is quite satisfied with their proficiency, bows to the "professors," who bow in return, and then departs, delighted to be able to speak and listen once more to his familiar English.

On any ordinary day the visitor will see, on a table in the midst of a small room, one of the "professors" sitting in oriental fashion, after the manner of tailors; his head is bare, his shoulders are bare; the day is hot, and the roll of muslin which envelopes his body out of doors has been removed; the ample rotundity of the stomach heaves regularly above the muslin folds which encircle the loins and thighs. The shaven crown of the worthy "professor," and his broad quivering back, glow with the heat; whilst a disciple, standing behind him, plies the fan vigorously to and fro, and produces a current of wind that keeps the huge mass partially cool. Around the table are squatted numbers of dirty-looking youths, carefully enveloped in their muslin dresses, as prescribed by the rules, and droning, one by one, over a manuscript page, which is handed from one to another in succession. The majority are dozing, and well they may, for it is sleepy work—the same verses nasally intoned by one after another with unvarying monotony, and doubtless with similar errors. The "professor" seldom speaks, for he too is dozing heavily on the table, anxiously awaiting the bell that is to release him to liberty and dinner. The same scene is being repeated in other similar rooms, where other "professors" are similarly dozing and teaching, and other youths similarly shut up from the light of God's sun, which shines without; and of his soul, which should shine within them.

In the upper and lower school departments of the Hindoo College, which stretch upon either side of the central building, an immense number of classes of native youths, varying in age from ten to twenty, are better taught by European and Hindoo instructors; but in a very different way from that in which they should be taught—a total want of order and system pervading the arrangements, and calling loudly for a thorough reform. It is amazing, that whilst education has progressed at home with such wonderful rapidity during the past few years, every thing in India should still bear the impress of systems long since antiquated and exploded in Europe. A want of simultaneous teaching, and the improved *methodic*, by which large masses are individualised in the modern systems, pervades the class-teaching of the Hindoo College, and renders it comparatively fruitless. The same may be said of education generally in Bengal; nor is the fact to be wondered at, when we remember that there is no one to superintend the various institutions practically acquainted with the subject. What the schools of England would be, were all inspection removed, and were all attention to the subject suddenly to cease amongst the clergy and superintending bodies of the community generally, those of India are. Just enough is taught the youths in these school departments to make them perceive that Brahminism, the religion of their forefathers, is false; just enough to enable them to read English with tolerable fluency, to write it more imperfectly, and to speak it most imperfectly of all. Unless they enter the college department, they learn nothing well; nothing save the conviction that the religion of their fathers is a gross superstition. Very few of them *do* make their way into the college department, not perhaps one in twelve—the eleven leave the walls of their *alma mater* convinced that they have received an excellent education, that virtue and truth, and honour and piety, are all high-sounding words without meaning; that the truest virtue is but the clever concealment of vice; the sublimest truth a decent cloak for ingenious falsehood; honour, the boast of fools and the mockery of wise men; and piety, the failing of enthusiasts or bigots, but the scorn and derision of the talented.

Ascending to the upper story of the building, we arrive at the college department, properly so called.

A large hall at the bend of a wide staircase contains the library and a few portraits; a library containing books enough, were they well-selected, but over-stocked, unfortunately, with inferior works, which the government book-agent found it advisable or profitable to get off his hands. A corridor leads from this hall to the various class-rooms, where men of eminence in their various walks of study give a sound and complete knowledge to the students, of history, mental philosophy, English literature, and mathematics. Here, however, as in the school department, and indeed generally in all the educational institutions of the country, Brahminism is uprooted, and selfishness enthroned in its place in the hearts of the students. They leave the Hindoo, as they do the other colleges, with a profound contempt for religion generally, and a high veneration and esteem for rupees. Brahma and Siva and Vishnu no longer reign in their souls as the gods of their idolatry; for rupees, anas, and pice have taken their place; and before them they are disposed to bow down with infinitely more reverence and faith than their fathers ever did to the former. Enjoyment is, for the future, the rule of their lives—present enjoyment of every kind—much sensual, and a little intellectual.

The Medical College of Calcutta is another most important institution, which, from small beginnings, has gradually grown to the largest dimensions. Its museum, its hospital, its lecture-rooms, and its motley array of students, comprising Hindoos of Bengal, Mahomedans, and Buddhists of Burmah and Ceylon, all render it one of the most interesting of the educational establishments of the City of Palaces; whilst the unbounded liberality of the Council of Education has enabled it far to outstrip all its older competitors, the other colleges, in every material advantage.

Thirty miles from the capital, pleasantly situated on the banks of the Ganges, stands the College of Hadji Mohammed Mohsin, founded and endowed by him for the advancement of Mahomedan learning; but the government of which has, in consequence of litigation and accidents, come into the hands of the Council of Education, and its classes been assimilated to those of the Hindoo College. It is now in its seventeenth year, and numbers, in its school and college department, 400 pupils, taught by six European officers, professors, and masters, and a considerable number of native assistants.

Far away to the east, in the centre of a low wooded district, long noted for its manufacture of muslins, is situated the Dacca College, an institution similar in organisation and government to Mohammed Mohsin's and the Hindoo Colleges. It has now reached its seventeenth year, but is by no means equal to the other two in the numbers of its students. Other similar colleges have been established at Kishnagur, Agra, and Delhi, on the same uniform plan, and with considerable success.

Besides these, the most prominent of the educational institutions of Bengal, schools have been established, some by government, others by native enterprise, assisted by the Council of Education, in the various zillahs, or districts, of the country, but to an extent miserably inadequate to the wants of the population, and with too exclusive an aim at affording instruction in English, to render them what the country requires.

The total of the governmental educational establishments in the Bengal presidency, including those of the north-west provinces, is, for English and mixed instruction, forty-four, and for the native schools one hundred and twelve, maintained at an annual charge of 51,000*l.*, and giving instruction to 11,700 pupils.

The Madras presidency boasts of but few institutions of this description; indeed the only establishment in which teaching in the English tongue takes place is at the University High School in Madras, where thirteen teachers instruct one hundred and eighty pupils. The vernacular schools are at Tanjore, Ramnad, and one or two other places; the total disbursements on account of all which amounts to the yearly sum of 4,350*l.*

The Bombay division fares better than do the benighted of the Coromandel coast; for we find not less than 233 village and district vernacular schools within this presidency, with upwards of 11,000 pupils; in addition to which there are the Elphinstone institutions, consisting of a college containing 42 pupils, instructed by professors of European celebrity, with high and low schools attached, numbering between them upwards of 900 scholars; the Grant Medical College, and the Poonah Sanscrit College; besides schools at Broach, Darwar, Poonah, Ahmednugger, and other places, for instruction in the English and oriental languages. The whole cost of the educational establishments of the Bombay government amounts to something under 15,000*l.* a year.

It may thus be seen that, as far as the government is concerned, the natives of British India, numbering within the limits of the three Presidencies 100,000,000, and paying 22,000,000*l.* sterling in taxes, receive in return something under 70,000*l.* a year in education; which, at the ordinary calculation of five members to every family, gives rather more than three farthings per annum to each household. Carrying our examination and comparison of these melancholy educational statistics still further, we find that the amount of educational grants for the Bengal presidency for one year, viz. 51,000*l.*, is just 2000*l.* less than the cost of a late Governor-general's visit to the Upper Provinces for a few months. We may observe also that the amount of the Bombay educational disbursements is a trifle above the yearly cost of the governor's office and establishment, and his tour to the Deccan; whilst the sum doled out for education in the Madras presidency, with its

17,000,000 of inhabitants, amounts precisely to the allowance for the governor's house-rent; just equals the various emoluments of the pluralist-secretary of the India House; and is neither more nor less than the yearly cost of the dinners and refreshments at the large stone-house in Leadenhall Street.[3]

Finally, we see in the annual financial sheets of the Indian government not less than 2,000,000*l.* sterling set down for the administration of justice, *i. e.* for police to catch, for judges to sentence, and for jailers to imprison offenders against the laws; whilst for that which is the best preventive of crime—education—not more than 70,000*l.* is granted! Well may the reader echo Prince Harry's exclamation to Falstaff, and give vent to his feelings upon the disproportion between the "halfpenny worth" of educational "bread," and the "intolerable deal" of judicial "sack." Indian political economists have yet to learn that, with crime, as in other matters, prevention is better than cure, —schoolmasters cheaper than judges; and that with a more liberal, wholesome allowance of the moral "bread," there need be far less of the costly, ermined "sack."

Turning from this notice of governmental education, I will pass under review the operations of the various missionary bodies in the three presidencies of India. The societies whose servants labour within the territories of the Company number 22, both English and foreign. These bodies number amongst them not less than 1,100 day-schools, with 94,000 pupils, who are instructed in their native language and literature, as well as in a knowledge of the Scriptures, through the vernacular medium. They have also 67 boarding-schools and 91 English establishments, with 14,800 pupils. The above are all for boys; the vernacular institutions are scattered throughout all parts of India, and seldom afford more than an elementary education in addition to instruction in Christian belief. The boarding-schools are chiefly intended for the education of orphans, or the children of native Christians, and are mostly at mission stations. The English schools are confined almost exclusively to large towns, or other populous districts, where a desire to acquire the language is found more strongly implanted. Madras takes the lead by far in the number of establishments, which amounts to 920, with 66,300 pupils; Bengal can shew but 71 schools, with 13,000 scholars; and Bombay numbers but 78 establishments and 5000 scholars.

Whilst all this has been done for the male portion of the heathen population, the females have not been forgotten by the missionaries;

[3] Report of Select Committee on India, 1852, pp. 329-481.

and if, in looking at immediate results, we find that less appears to have been accomplished amongst these, it arises from the far greater amount of prejudice to be overcome in permitting Hindoo women to partake of the blessings of education. The chief success of the missionaries, as yet, has been in the education of the daughters of native converts, or of female orphans saved from some desolating famine or from human sacrifice. In the establishment of female day-schools but little real progress has been made. Here again we find the Madras presidency far outstepping Bombay and the larger presidency of Bengal, having upwards of 200 day-schools, and 41 boarding-schools for females, against 62 day-schools and 45 boarding-schools in the whole remainder of the Company's territories.

One of the most important elements that must enter into our plans for ameliorating the condition of the people of India will be the education of the mothers, from whom the children imbibe their first principles. It has been argued, and with some shew of truth, that whilst it is the custom of the middling and upper classes of the natives of India to exclude their women from public society, the effect of education upon them would be but to give them a desire to enjoy that which is forbidden them, to render them discontented with their lot, and to embitter their lives and the domestic happiness of the father and husband. Though this may be true to a certain extent, there can be no doubt but that education, whatever its trials, whatever its early drawbacks, would strongly enlist the influence of the women, and through them the sympathies of their husbands in the emancipation of the sex from the degraded seclusion in which they now pass their lives, and from which no practical advantage can possibly arise.

That it would require some degree of enlightenment, some amount of public spirit, to induce a Hindoo of good station in life to break through their old-world prejudices, and overturn the barrier of custom, in this matter, there can be no doubt; equally certain is it that were some substantial countenance held out by those high in authority to such amongst the natives as shewed themselves superior to time-worn habits, a resolution would soon be commenced, noble in its aim and mighty in its results. Let education amongst the women of India be preached and taught by the women of England,—let the English lady in India mix freely with her dark sisters,—let the latter feel that there is something to care for beyond the walls of the zenana; and little by little the dark fabric of prejudice will crumble to the ground, and that which would now be an innovation, will, ten years hence, become the fashion.

The people of the Tenasserim provinces have for ages past been highly favoured in regard to education; scarcely a village but contains a kioung, or school-house, in which one or more poonjies, or native priests, reside, and devote several hours of each day to the instruction of the young in the useful acquirement of reading, writing, and arithmetic. In this way there are few indeed of the rural population who are unable to read the native books, or communicate their ideas by writing. In return for this instruction the scholars are expected to

BURMAN POONJIE AND KIOUNG.

render such domestic and personal services to their poonjies as may be needed; and in this way the dry details of caligraphy and chronology are pleasantly relieved by an hour's moist amusement in the priestly rice-field, or an attendance upon the pumpkin-beds and the palm-trees which skirt the domain of the kioung.

In addition to the elementary education thus imparted, the authorities and missions have established a number of schools of a superior description for instruction in English and the vernacular. Two government schools were opened in 1804 at Moulmein and Mergui; and since that period the American Baptist Mission have opened eight native and English boarding and day-schools at Moulmein, with an average attendance of between four and five hundred scholars; in the other provinces the mission have established eighteen normal, boarding, and day-schools, besides a number of district schools under native assistants.

The labours of these missionaries appear to have been already productive of no small amount of good amongst the Talains of Pegu and Tenasserim, who shew an anxiety and aptitude for the acquirement of European accomplishments scarcely to be expected. The study of the Scriptures is also making rapid strides amongst this interesting people, and the mission have already a number of native converts actively engaged in propagating the truths of Christianity throughout the rural districts, to by no means indifferent hearers.

The history of Christianity in India forms perhaps one of the most extraordinary and sorrowful chapters in the records of European aggression upon the East. The supineness and atheistical indifference of our own government in all that relates to the introduction of Christianity within its dominions, whilst standing in strong contrast to the active and bloody propagandism of their Catholic predecessors, by a strange fatality, is working out a like result—the uprooting of all vestiges of the indigenous faith of the land, but implanting nothing better in its place.

The early Portuguese missionaries went amongst the heathen armed with the sword and the firebrand, in place of the Bible and the cross, and accomplished with those weapons what the East India Company of the present day are doing with their "Godless colleges."

Still labouring in the same path of violence and destruction, but adding to it fraud and hypocrisy, came the Jesuits of Spain and France. To pave the way for their progress, these impostors pretended to be Brahmins of the highest caste, denied that they were Europeans, dressed, ate, and preached as the apostles of a Christian Brahma; and to aid their unblushing frauds, forged a *Veda*, which they exhibited to their numerous converts.[4] Wherever fraud failed, violence was resorted to; and with what impunity and what barbarity, the records of the Inquisition of Goa amply and sadly testify. To read the bloody tales of that horrible institution, to peruse the accounts of Mesquita's enormi-

[4] Calcutta Review, vol. xvi. p. 236.

ties, one might well imagine that another miracle had been permitted in that unhappy, heathen land, and that the unclean spirits driven out of man had betaken themselves to a herd of swine in priestly garb. The Moslem saluted his fellow-man with words of gentleness—"In the name of the Prophet, Peace!" The benediction of the holy men of God was, practically, "In the name of Jesus, Murder!"

Following after these pious propagandists were the Dutch, who, whilst they shunned all acts of open violence, not less energetically employed coercion in attaining their object. They bribed heathens to Christianity, or rather to its profession, by the offer of places, and forbad any but such as had been baptised to hold even the meanest appointment under them. In this way thousands enrolled themselves nominally as converts, but who at the same time openly maintained their connection with heathenism, and were universally known amongst their more sincere brethren, who refused to join in the show, as "Government Christians." The descendants of the Jesuits and Presbyterian converts have long since disappeared from the land, and are only remembered in musty ecclesiastical records.

The Dutch, however, were not the only Protestant missionaries in those early days. Others were at work before them, and on much better principles.

To the king of Denmark belongs the honour of having dispatched the first Protestant mission to India in the year 1705. At Tranquebar, then a Danish settlement, this pioneer in the good cause established himself, working against many difficulties and discouragements, until he had fairly established himself and his school, and won from the natives their respect, if not their imitation.

Forty-five years later, we find Kiernander, a zealous servant of the Society for Promoting Christian Knowledge, established at Cuddalore, in the Madras presidency, where he commenced a school; and during eight years strove to make known amongst the natives the truths of Christianity. In 1758 Kiernander moved up to Calcutta, leaving his first charge in the hands of assistants; and in the following year had so far succeeded in his first efforts as to have had nearly two hundred Hindoo and Mahomedan children in his school. In 1770 a church was erected, in which this zealous missionary preached the gospel to the heathens around him. If little progress were achieved by him, or by the other few missionaries who at this early period made any effort at Christianising the Hindoo, it can scarcely be matter of surprise, for the government were at the same moment, not only founding and endowing with a lavish hand colleges for the "preservation and cultivation of the laws, literature, and *religion* of the Hindoos," but actually throwing every possible discouragement in the way of preaching the gospel, which was looked upon by them as perilling the rule of the Company in India!

In the year 1793, when the renewal of the East India charter came before the Houses of Parliament, strenuous attempts were made at home by a philanthropist whose name is imperishably connected with more than one noble crusade against wrong. Wilberforce spared no effort or argument to induce the government of the day to introduce into the new charter clauses directing that Christian education be provided for the natives of British India by schoolmasters and missionaries; and he so far succeeded as to place a series of resolutions to that effect on the journals of the House of Commons, with the sanction of the then president of the India board. Subsequently, however, other and adverse interests were brought to bear upon the executive, and the agitation fell to the ground without at that time producing any good results. In adopting this course the parliament of 1793 were evincing less enlightenment, less regard for religion, than did the legislature of 1698, who, in the reign of William III., provided that a minister be appointed by the Company to every garrison, settlement, &c. within their territories, who should make it their duty to learn within one year of their arrival the Portuguese and native languages, "the better to enable them to instruct the Gentoos, &c., that shall be the servants or slaves of the Company, or of their agents, in the Protestant religion."

The charter having been thus renewed, unconditionally as regards religion, no pains were spared by the local authorities to act up to the spirit of the home legislation, and to hinder any agitation upon points of Christian doctrine which might unsettle and alarm the native mind! With this feeling amongst them, some religious tracts printed and circulated in the native tongue, by the Protestant Danes of Serampore, were called in and destroyed, and the missionaries at that settlement given to understand that no such steps could be permitted; they were, moreover, requested to state where, and to what extent, their Christian publications had been circulated, in order that the Governor-general and his council "might be enabled to counteract their dangerous effects." Not content with this step, the Governor-general prohibited the printing of books of any kind at Serampore; and subsequently becoming alarmed at the labours of the few Britith missionaries in Calcutta, issued instructions that public preaching to natives should at once cease, as well as all works having any tendency to promote conversion to the Christian religion. It is but justice that the name of the Governor-general who thus distinguished himself in antagonism to the gospel should be placed on record with the deed. To the Earl of Minto belongs all the credit, all the honour, of crushing the mission-work of India in the commencement of the nineteenth century, and the equal honour and glory of encouraging and promoting, by all means in his power, the study of Hindoo literature, laws, and *religion*.

A better time was, however, at hand. Hope for the gospel dawned once more in the further renewal of the Company's charter in 1815, when the question was again mooted with the most perfect success. The ban was removed from the missionaries; the lock was struck off the church doors; the Scriptures were permitted to be circulated through the length and breadth of the land, with any comments or arguments that were deemed necessary, and for the first time our Christian government ceased to oppose the diffusion of Christianity in the East.

In strange yet pleasing contrast with the heathenish spirit which ruled the councils of British India in those days, appears the list of ecclesiastics of 1850-1 supported by the government, most of whom are actively engaged in disseminating the light of the gospel amongst the Hindoo and Mussulman population of the country, ably seconded by large numbers of missionaries not less zealous or earnest in the work. What may be the number of workers of the latter class does not appear in any obtainable record; the official documents shew, that at the present time there are three bishops and archdeacons, six senior chaplains, thirty-three chaplains, and eighty-four assistants of the Established Church within the three presidencies, receiving stipends and allowances to the yearly amount of 101,114*l.*; besides six chaplains of the Scotch kirk, receiving with their establishment 6,168*l.* per annum; and some Roman Catholic priests, who are paid 5,150*l.* a year.

One of the earliest fruits of the new spirit, which was now abroad in Hindostan, was the establishment of Bishop's College in the metropolis of India. The first Bishop of the See of Calcutta, Dr. Middleton, laid the foundation-stone of this building in 1820; and though he did not live to see it completed and tenanted, he had at least the satisfaction of knowing that the work was begun. It was the original intention of Bishop Middleton that this institution should be a vast missionary school for the training of preachers to work amongst the heathen; and had he lived to put the mechanism in motion, beyond a doubt he would have fully carried out his plan. Good men and true have followed him in the work; but, imbued with other ideas, they have permitted the mission-school to be absorbed in the University; and thus, although large sums have been annually granted towards this institution, although it possesses an abundant and able staff of professors, and is on the whole well attended, it is difficult to trace the good results of its teachings amongst those for whose especial benefit it was originally planned.

That the missionaries of the many religious societies who have made India their field have not been less active in preaching the Gospel than in imparting education amongst the heathen, there is abundant proof.

At the present moment, fifty-three years from the first commencement of missionary labour in the East, there are distributed over various parts of the Company's territories 360 missionaries actively engaged in preaching the Gospel to the heathen, assisted by upwards of 500 native preachers. They are attached to twenty-two missionary societies, and have founded 270 churches, which are attended by upwards of 15,000 members. Of these members, by far the largest proportion is found in the Madras presidency; whilst within the limits of the Bombay government there are the fewest.

Although it is stated that these labours are being carried on in various districts in almost every part of India, it must be borne in mind that the missionary-stations are for the most part collected in the vicinity of populous towns and cities; whence it is hoped that the spirit of truth, once having taken hold of the people, will be disseminated throughout the surrounding districts. In this manner Calcutta possesses twenty-nine missionaries, established at twelve stations in different parts of the city. Madras is as liberally supplied; Bombay has thirteen missionaries; Agra eight; and Benares eleven.[5]

Comparing this extensive machinery with the actual visible results of its labours, a casual examiner might reasonably feel disappointed. But looking below the upper surface of things, viewing all circumstances together, the number of converts, small though they are, and doubtful in sincerity, as many must be, should rather be a matter of congratulation and pleasant surprise than otherwise.

In no heathen country in the world has superstition become so firmly rooted in the national mind as in India. Aided by caste, by the impress of antiquity, by the powerful arm of a numerous and influential priesthood, and, above all, by the sanction, the openly-avowed countenance and encouragement of the British authorities, it may well be matter for astonishment that even the smallest success has been accomplished. As regards all the educational establishments connected

[5] Calcutta Review, vol. xvi. p. 245.

with the government of India, it is positively forbidden to introduce the subject of Christianity in any way. Not a volume that makes any allusion to the Gospel is permitted within those "godless" walls; not even the name of the Saviour, not the merest idea of the Creator, is allowed to pass the lips, or enter the thoughts, of any within those institutions of a Christian government! Professors who dare to infringe these stringent laws are dismissed; native pupils, who openly become converts to Christianity through missionary efforts, are not permitted to remain as students; and even for an officer of a government college to pen an article advocating Christian views for a local periodical, is visited with the heavy displeasure of the higher powers.[6]

It is not difficult to picture the sad results of this state of things. Year by year the evil grows. Thousands upon thousands of young men are turned loose upon the world infidels in heart and practice. Profligate and unprincipled in their lives, and becoming the heads of families, they propagate the vice and atheism engendered by the British College, to future generations. It has been stated on authority too good to be doubted, that of between fifty and sixty pupils of the Government Hindoo College at Calcutta, who were privately questioned by their principal as to their belief in any creed, *four* only expressed their belief in the religion of the Vedas; a few were undecided; and the remainder openly avowed their utter disbelief in Brahminism, and in all other creeds.[7] This fact is too well known in India to need confirmation; though it may cause some astonishment in England to learn that the only results of the much-vaunted educational grants of the East India Company is the raising up of a race of licentious infidels.

How great the unchristian antagonism of the government is to the labours of the missionary may be partly estimated by the preceding facts; but it is only those who have lived in the East, and who, knowing well the peculiarities of the native character, understand to the full the deep hold which all governmental measures take on the Hindoo mind. They are so accustomed to look up to the government as the parent of all authority, the dispenser of all patronage, the only motive power in a vast society, which owns literally no other public than that of the services, that any thing emanating from it receives at once the impress of popular currency; whilst all opposed to it is regarded with, to say the least, suspicion. It is thus that whilst the missionaries, full of devoted zeal and untiring energy, have with difficulty converted their

[6] Government Education in India, by W. Knighton, M.A. &c. p. 19.
[7] Ibid. p. 18.

hundreds, the government, by the aid of their "Godless colleges," have converted their hundreds of thousands.

The missionaries, however, do not despair; they know that their work progresses, that the good seed is deep in the soil; and that if some of their converts are not so sincere and steadfast as they could desire, there are hundreds who have listened to the Word, and drunk deep of its truths, but who have not yet the courage to avow themselves openly. During the ten years ending 1812, but 161 Hindoos had been converted to Christianity. Within the next ten years the number of converts amounted to 403. The following decade witnessed the conversion of 647; and the period ending 1842, as many as 1055. The ten years just past it is estimated have seen not less than 2000 heathens embracing Christianity.

Not less encouraging than the above, is the fact of more than one native rajah having become converted to the Christian faith. The rajah of Coorj has recently brought his daughter to this country, to be educated in the English tongue, and brought up in the Protestant religion. And still more recently the young Maharajah of the Punjab, Dulup Sing, has been formally admitted into the Christian Church by public baptism, in the presence of a large number of the officials of that government which forbids the mention of the Christian name within its schools.

LOPHOPHORUS IMPEYANUS. See Appendix G.

CHAPTER V.

THE ADMINISTRATION OF JUSTICE.

IN the early periods of Hindoo history the administration of justice was conducted in the most primitive mode, and with the happiest results. The law, like most other institutions, was derived from the celebrated code of Menu, which, if in some particulars savouring of superstition, and occasionally of puerilities, was nevertheless based on a just appreciation of the social rights and duties of man.

The sovereign was declared to be the prime administrator of justice, aided by learned and upright Brahmins. In criminal cases the king was enjoined to see to the proper carrying out of the law; but in civil cases, especially such as were instituted in remote districts, his representatives in the various provinces were expected to act conjointly with such Brahmins as were deputed for the purpose. Their remuneration appears to have been derived from a levy of five per cent on all debts admitted by the defendants, and of ten per cent upon all such as, having been denied, were afterwards proved against them.

It was enjoined upon the administrators of justice that they should carefully observe the countenances, the gestures, and mode of speech of the principal parties concerned in a suit, as well as of their witnesses. They were also to bear in mind the local usages of the district in which a case was tried, the peculiar laws and rules of classes, as well as the customs of traders and others; bearing in mind, under certain reservations, the principles established by former judges. The king, or his representative, was strictly forbidden from deciding causes upon his own opinion, without obtaining the advice and assistance of persons learned in the laws of the country. He was cautioned against encouraging litigation; and counselled to bear with patience and equanimity the irritability of suitors, or the infirmities of old and sick persons, who may have to appear before him. Finally, it was laid down with much solemnity, that the sovereign who received the taxes levied upon the people, without affording them in return a strict measure of justice, was not only guilty of a crime, but one of the worst of criminals; an injunction which it would be well if the present rulers of India would take to themselves and ponder over.

Punishments were sometimes so indistinctly declared as to leave the fate of an offender quite uncertain, and although not always in themselves severe, were frequently very disproportioned to the offence. Thus the slaying a priest, drinking spirits, or stealing gold from a priest, were all crimes classed under one head, and punished alike. Still more inconsistent were the punishments for adultery.

There does not appear to be any express punishment for murder, though, from the general text, it may be gathered that that crime, with arson and robbery attended with violence, was visited capitally. Theft was punished, if small, with a fine; if of greater amount, with cutting off of the hand; but if the thief were taken with the stolen goods upon him, the offence was capital. Receivers of stolen goods, and those who harboured thieves, were punished with the same severity as the thieves themselves. It is remarkable that, in cases of small theft, the fine of a Brahmin offender was at least eight times as great as that of a Sudra; and the scale varies in a similar manner and proportion with regard to all the classes: a king committing an offence was to pay a thousand times as great a fine as would be exacted from an ordinary person. Robbery incurred the amputation of the limb employed in perpetrating the offence; and if the robbery was accompanied by violence, the crime was made capital: all who sheltered robbers, or supplied them with food or implements, were to be punished with death.

The civil code of the Hindoos was far more perfect and reconcilable with our own ideas of strict justice than was their criminal statutes. Indeed, there is a spirit of enlightened impartiality about it, which not only speaks highly for the social condition of the Hindoos of those days, but throws the practice of the Anglo-Indian judicature far into the shade. For this reason, it is proposed to go somewhat more into detail than would otherwise have been the case; and it would be well if our own civil and sessional judges throughout India perused the clauses of this code, and endeavoured to act somewhat in accordance with them. By doing so, they would consult their own reputation, and the happiness and welfare of those over whose rights and liberties they sit in judgment.

That the native system under their former governments worked well, there does not appear to be any reasonable ground for doubting; indeed we have the testimony of men who have studied the subject thoroughly, in evidence of the happy results of the old Hindoo mode of administering the laws. Amongst others, Mr. Elphinstone records his opinion, that in some instances the prosperity of native states, possessing any thing but good government, can only be accounted for by the admirable working of the judicial portion of their institutions.

Various as are the modifications which have crept into the body of the laws, as well as into the rules of practice, the old code of Menu is in native states still looked up to as the source of all judicial administration; indeed very many of the changes effected are only such as have been rendered necessary by the altered circumstances of the times, and the change in native society.

From the consideration of the state of ancient Hindoo law, it becomes a natural transition to pass to a notice of the changes introduced by the English, commencing with their first territorial possessions in India under the imperial grant, by which they were entitled to collect the revenues of Bengal, Behar, and Orissa. With this assumption of the responsibility of government began their connection with the administration of justice, which naturally followed the receipt of revenue.

Between the years 1769 and 1793, various attempts were made to supervise and regulate the administration of justice as it then existed in the hands of the zemindars of the rural districts, whose sole accountability was to the Nizam. With this view separate courts of civil and criminal judicature were appointed in each district, under the superior control of the higher courts of Moorshedabad, which was under the immediate direction of the committee of finance. At a subsequent period these higher courts were removed to Calcutta, much to the inconvenience of suitors. The great evil which pervaded the system at this time was the blending of the judicial and financial offices, the same individual being both collector and judge.

In 1793 Lord Cornwallis introduced some extensive changes into the system, many of them very excellent, and based upon a sound appreciation of the necessity for the reform. As these changes, with slight exceptions, form the groundwork of the present judicial system, it will be as well to describe them.

A civil court was established in each district, presided over by a judge attached to the Company's covenanted service, in no way connected with the collectorate, and aided by an European registrar, whose duty it was to attend to suits of small amount. Besides these, there were native judges, called moonsiffs, appointed to hear cases involving property below fifty rupees in value. Appeals from the decisions of these subordinate officials lay to the civil judge, who was assisted in such cases by the advice of a native law-officer, whose duty it was to expound the Hindoo or Mahomedan law.

Provincial Courts of Appeal were established in Calcutta, Dacca, Patna, and Moorshedabad, presided over by three judges, with a registrar and assistants, all of the covenanted service. To these lay appeals in cases involving property below 1000 rupees in value; whilst such as extended to sums above that amount were referrible to the Supreme Court of Appeal at Calcutta.

For the administration of criminal justice, the judges and officials of the provincial Courts of Appeal were formed into Courts of Circuit, for holding assize. These assizes were held monthly in places where provincial courts were established, four times a year in the Calcutta district, and twice a year in all other districts. These courts took cognisance of all matters above the jurisdiction of the magistrate of the district. Their decision was final in all cases of acquittal, or of punishment less than death or imprisonment for life, if agreeing with the native law-officer appointed to act with them; otherwise the proceedings might be carried before a superior court appointed to hear all such appeals, and stationed at Calcutta.

Modification of these duties, of the rights of appeal, and in some instances of the constitution of the courts, have since the time of Lord Cornwallis taken place; but in all essentials the above represents the constitution of the present judicial system of India. In one particular, however, the spirit of these reforms has been widely departed from by the continued blending of the duties of magistrate and collector in one individual, an error pointed out at that time and wisely guarded against; but which has since been allowed to pervade the whole system, much to the detriment of the bench and the injury of suitors. Of the evils arising from this course every one seems to be aware: not a voice is raised in its favour, and yet from year to year the system continues the same. We find the opinion of this impropriety expressed in every Blue Book, and yet each succeeding publication notes its continuance. In the very last volume may be found the opinion of the lieutenant-governor of the north-western provinces, who does not hesitate to record his idea of the gross incompatibility of the revenue and magisterial functions blended in one individual; and yet this high functionary is averse to effecting any reform, because of "*the inexpediency* of disturbing the present system in any material degree:" whether it be not still more *inexpedient* to leave the large body of native suitors at the mercy of men whose chief attention must ever be devoted to the revenue department of their duties in preference to the judicial, his honour the lieutenant-governor does not state.

This, however, would be comparatively a matter of trifling importance, were the persons acting in this double capacity to make themselves tolerably acquainted with their duties, and to evince a respectable knowledge of judicial matters, but which unfortunately is rarely the case.

In all other parts of the world but India the judicial office is looked upon as the reward of a long service at the bar or in subordinate magisterial capacities; but in that favoured country it is far otherwise. Not only are judges too often inexperienced young men recently from their mother's side, but they are a compound of impracticable collectors and thickheaded magistrates.[1] The feeling there appears to be that any body will do well enough for a judge; and so strongly is this impressed on the minds of English residents, that the bench in India is playfully termed "*the refuge for the destitute.*"

That the case is not being overstated, I will venture to quote from the recently published work[2] of one who must be competent to give a good opinion on these matters, and not likely to paint the system in too dark colours, being a member of the Civil Service upon which he comments. This writer, speaking of promotion as a matter of course, without reference to qualification, and not in any one presidency, but throughout all of them, says: "It seems to be considered that if at this time of life a man is fit for any thing at all, he is fit for a judge; and *if he is fit for nothing, better make him a judge and get rid of him;* for once in that office, he has no claim to further promotion by mere seniority alone."

Here then we see men appointed to fulfil duties of the highest importance, who have not only had no real training in that branch of the service, but who are unfit for any other post. They are sent to the judicial "refuge for the destitute!" And when a few years of training as magistrate have been passed, is it to be supposed that a slight knowledge of criminal procedure can qualify a man for sitting as judge in the civil courts; and that, too, to receive cases in appeal from inferior

[1] "I start with these two simple propositions: first, that throughout the length and breadth of the whole of this presidency those who occupy the judicial bench are totally incompetent to the decent fulfilment of their duties; and secondly, that so long as the present system continues, there is not only no hope of any amelioration, but, on the contrary, things must go on ever from bad to worse, until in the lowest depth there is at last no lower bottom still."—*The Administration of Justice in Southern India*, by J. B. Norton, Esq. 1853.

[2] Campbell's Modern India.

courts presided over by uncovenanted servants and natives of considerable experience? Ignorant of the law of evidence, the rules of practice and of jurisprudence, these judges are expected to arrive at sound conclusions by the aid of the government regulations and the exercise of a little *common sense*—a quality doubtless exceedingly useful in the ordinary avocations of life, but not promising to aid in the solution of legal difficulties, any more than it would enable a man to navigate a ship through dangerous waters, or to conduct a chemical analysis.

It has been argued by some men of the highest standing in the service, that the magisterial experience which every civilian in the revenue department must of necessity acquire, is sufficient, in a great degree, to qualify him for the discharge of judicial functions. Perhaps the best testimony against this reasoning is to be found in the opinion of the Court of Directors, who, in an official communication addressed to the Madras Board of Revenue, "lament the unfitness so frequently displayed by revenue officers in dealing with evidence, or conducting any inquiry in the nature of a judicial proceeding." Fortunately this accidental testimony is not the only evidence we possess of the incapacity of collectors for the exercise of judicial duties; similar opinions, and far stronger in their expression, are to be found amongst the published reports of the local government.[3]

The necessary consequences of this absence of all training are a most lamentable ignorance of the law of evidence or of the value of testimony, a wandering from the point actually at issue to other and immaterial matter, a misapplication of the law whenever attempted to be applied, the admission of the most improper documents or evidence, the oversight of what should be most important evidence, strange and irregular proceedings, incoherent or puerile lines of argument, and decrees often utterly opposed to the testimony on record.[4]

With the above results, can it be wondered at that the labours of the higher appellate judges are greatly enhanced, or that the duties of the really experienced uncovenanted functionaries are greatly multiplied by the extraordinary appeal-decisions given by these incompetent men? The length to which matter, which is really not evidence, is admitted by such judges, is extraordinary; whilst the most important facts, and

[3] "Defective as the system unquestionably was, under which young men, almost immediately on their quitting college, were intrusted with the decision of civil suits, though small in amount, the present system, under which the judge will take his seat on the bench, utterly ignorant of the forms of pleading, of the rules of appeal, and of the constitution and powers of the courts below, which he is expected to control, is a hundred times worse."—*Report of the Honourable Mr. Shakespeare.*

[4] The Administration of Justice in Southern India, by J. B. Norton, Esq. 1853.

perhaps the only facts, bearing upon the case in suit, will be entirely overlooked; and most frequently it happens that a case is tried, appealed, remanded, retried some four or five times, and at last disposed of on a point which, in the hands of a competent man, would have settled it at the very outset.

In the year 1843 an act was passed by the Governor-General in Council, requiring judges to place their decisions on record, with the reasons on which they were founded; thus affording some sort of guarantee, however feeble, for the judge evincing some interest in, and acquaintance with, the decisions to which his name is affixed. The only value of these documents, which have been published from time to time, is in the testimony they bear to the utter inefficiency of the functionaries.[5]

The above was followed up in 1849 by the determination of the High Court of Civil and Criminal Appeal at Madras, to publish monthly reports of their decisions. This has been acted upon; and the contents of these monthly legal miscellanies are indeed of a startling nature. They read far more like fiction than reality; so utterly at variance with all ordinary appreciation of right and wrong, that the reader naturally asks himself if it be possible that these are the fruits of the labours of gentlemen composing the boasted civil service of India, of the relatives of directors, East India proprietors and parliamentary partisans.

Deeply indeed is it to be regretted that these published proofs of the incompetency of Indian judges were not in existence, as no doubt there was ample occasion for them, when "the greatest man of the age" passed a glowing eulogium upon the East India Company's servants, and their mode of administering the affairs of those vast territories, by stating his belief that "the government of India was one of the best and most purely administered governments that ever existed, and one which provided most effectually for the happiness of the people over which it was placed."[6] Had that great commander been in possession of the facts detailed below, there can be no doubt he would have considerably modified his speech, however much to the disappointment of the Court of Directors.

Amongst other extraordinary judgments disclosed by the reports alluded to, is one in a case which involved the large amount of 16*l*., and which had been tried eight times by almost as many functionaries; the last of these Solons declared that he found the evidence so nicely balanced on both sides, and that it was so very likely that none of the

[5] Calcutta Review.

[6] Speech of the Duke of Wellington on the East India Charter Debate, 1833.

witnesses knew any thing about the matter in dispute, that he decided the fairest way would be to divide the property amongst the several claimants. The only case on record which at all approaches this is one related by Knickerbocker in his facetious History of New York, wherein we are told how an upright but whimsical Dutch governor, after carefully weighing the ledgers of the plaintiff and defendant, and finding them equal in weight, decided that they should exchange mutual acquittances for the amount in dispute, and ordered the constable to pay the costs. At any rate, whatever difference there may be in the reality of the two cases, they approach nearly enough in their whimsicality.

Perhaps one of the raciest of these very amusing and luminous decisions, is that of a gentleman holding the office of civil judge of Rajahmundry, who was called upon to adjudicate in a case in which a plaintiff sued for a sum of fifty-five thousand and odd rupees due upon a bond. The judge nonsuited the plaintiff; and not being content with that, actually fined him for bringing the suit, in precisely the amount of his claim, that is to say, fifty-five thousand and odd rupees! Whether this gentleman carried out the joke by ordering the constable to pay the costs, does not appear on record.

Another of these Anglo-Indian Solomons decided upon a case, the merits of which, as he expressly states in his decree, rested entirely upon the authenticity or otherwise of a certain deed. He assumed the deed produced to be genuine, refused to call witnesses to attest to the signatures, or to hear evidence as to its being forged, which was alleged, and gave judgment accordingly; when, on the case being heard in appeal, it appeared that the document was not only not the original it was stated to be, nor even the copy of the original, but the copy of a copy!

The cases in which decisions were given in direct opposition to the facts admitted on both sides appear to be of almost daily occurrence; whilst many suits have been tried, remanded, and retried five or six times before making the discovery that they were barred by the statute of limitations. Again, it is no uncommon event for this singular race of judges to decide upon bonds and instruments in writing, when neither one nor the other had been produced in evidence.

If the specimens of adjudication in civil suits already given are prolific sources for grave reprehension, not less so are the records of the criminal courts recently made public. Were it not that these documents are of a character far too serious to cause any but the most painful feelings, the absurd reasoning, the odd mixture of childish puerility with legal affectation, the groping in the dark, the contradictions, the ignorance displayed, might well raise a smile at the expense of the judicial gentlemen who are placed in a position to exercise control over the lives of their fellow-creatures.

From the published reports of the Suddar criminal appeal-courts, we gather the most extraordinary disclosures relative to the decisions of the lower judges; and, in perusing them, the feeling but too naturally arises, that if these be a fair specimen of the few cases appealed against, how is it with those wherein no appeal is made? Amongst these criminal curiosities may be instanced a case of murder, which a judge recently arrived at his station, found had been heard by his predecessor; the principal witnesses having left previous to his arrival, he proceeded to finish off the trial by re-examining a few witnesses *who happened to be present* on a most trivial point, and took the defence of one of the prisoners. Upon this proceeding, and the evidence previously taken by another party, he convicted the prisoner of murder, and the man was hung!

Further on occurs a case of murder in which the prisoner is convicted, although the body of the alleged murdered man was not found; whilst a third is condemned by a judge who forgot to put the prisoner on his defence. Another functionary trying a prisoner for homicide, declared that he ought to have been indicted for murder; and notwithstanding that the man was on the list for homicide only, convicted him of the graver crime, and sentenced him to death accordingly. The propriety of this proceeding appears to have been doubted by the judge subsequently; for he represents the case to a higher tribunal, with a view of ascertaining if a lighter punishment than death might not be inflicted; because, as he gravely states, "the parties were near relatives, and had been previously on good terms!"

Perhaps one of the most extraordinary of these cases is one in which two prisoners were indicted for the murder of a man at Tellicherry, whilst sleeping quietly in his cot with his son. The wounded man, with his intestines protruding, had been taken to the surgeon of the station, who, seeing that he was only a native, passed him on without examination to the dresser of the hospital, who was not skilful enough to afford him any relief. The surgeon visited the man on the following morning, saw that nothing could be done to save his life, but nevertheless forwarded him to the hospital at Cannonore, many miles distant; where, after all this delay, the apothecary replaced his intestines, but too late, for the man died shortly afterwards. Of this murder one of the prisoners was found guilty, but recommended to mercy by the judge, because of "the darkness of the night, which rendered his identity very doubtful;" and because "the deceased might possibly have survived had his wound been dressed in time."[7]

In another instance two men were sentenced to death for murder, when it appears no evidence had been taken to identify the corpse. The superior judge, in confirming the sentence, notices this neglect, but contents himself with remarking, that the omission "should not have been permitted to occur;" and so the men were hung!

In some of the cases to be met with in these reports the judicial freaks incline to the side of mercy, and are therefore less serious. A woman is sentenced to be hung for the admitted murder of her two children in a fit of passion. The sessions judge changes this award to transportation for life, on the ground that "the females of the lower orders have no control whatever over their tempers."

A second sessions judge convicted a man of a murder committed nineteen years previously, and suggested transportation in place of hanging, because he had behaved well ever since. The supreme judge agrees in the plea for mercy, but on a different ground, viz. on account of the great lapse of time since the murder was committed!

Such are a few, a very few, of the judicial freaks played off in one of the three presidencies of India. They are but a portion of some four thousand and odd cases which came up in appeal to the supreme court, during a period in which more than one hundred and seven thousand cases had been decided and never appealed against. What amount of injustice, blundering, procrastination, and absurdity, was perpetrated in those one hundred and seven thousand unheard-of cases, the reader may perhaps form a tolerably shrewd guess.

Turning to the Bengal presidency, it will not be found that the judges of the north are composed of better stuff than those of the south. In 1849 ninety-six special appeals were admitted to a hearing: in seventy-seven the decision of the judge was reversed, or the case was remanded for some error; in nineteen the appeal was dismissed as groundless: it thus appears that in four out of every five appealed, the judge was wrong.

In the same year there were fifty-eight appeals from the principal Sudder Ameens, or native judges: in thirty-two the inferior court was held to be wrong; in twenty-six the appeal was dismissed as groundless. It appears, therefore, that a fair degree of competence exists in

[7] Criminal Reports of Madras Presidency, quoted by J. B. Norton, in The Administration of Justice in Southern India.

this unjustly depressed class; while the other result exhibits the civil-service judges in one dead level of incompetence.[8]

One or two instances will suffice to prove that the Bengal branch of the service is every way worthy to be ranked with their Madras brethren. The judge of Tirhoot reversed the decision of the native judge below him; but had his own reversed on appeal with the following caustic observation: "The decision of the judge is positively and absolutely unintelligible;" the case is remanded, and he is directed to try it again, and "to write an intelligible judgment upon it." Another case is sent back to the judge on several grounds of error, and besides other remarks, with the following facetious direction: "The judge will likewise be pleased to cite his authority for the opinion, that houses and dwellings appertaining to Europeans in this country are considered personal property."

One of these covenanted luminaries is found deciding a case under a regulation which had been repealed since 1824; whilst another treated as documents of the plaintiff, documents filed by the defendants, and decided against the plaintiff accordingly, stating their case as resting upon those documents; and this too was in reversal of the decision of the native judge below him.[9]

Some few years back there was an attempt made in Calcutta to introduce what were termed the "Black Acts," by rendering all Europeans amenable to the "Company's Courts," instead of, as at present, to the jurisdiction of her Majesty's judges only. Great was the outcry raised against this attempted innovation. For the first time India beheld something approaching to a public demonstration on the part of Europeans. Merchants left their ledgers and their bill-books, civilians forgot their duties, lawyers deserted their clients, shopkeepers their customers, planters neglected their indigo,—all were absorbed in the discussion of that enormous iniquity which contemplated the placing of them on a level with their Hindoo fellow-subjects. It appeared too monstrous to be for a moment tolerated, that English gentlemen should be subjected to the control of a bench notorious for its imbecility and worthlessness; that they should have no better safeguards for their lives and their property than were accorded to the natives of the country. The few Europeans who favoured the innovation declared that they hailed it as the most certain, and indeed the only means of ensuring a thorough reform of the Company's courts. "Once," said they, "bring the English community within their jurisdiction, and the iniquities of the system will be felt too keenly to be tolerated for a week;

[8] Calcutta Englishman, 1853.

[9] Ibid.

their fate will be sealed from that day." But it was easier to keep away from those courts than to reform them; and the Black Acts were accordingly thrown out. It was decided that a system of administering justice which would not be tolerated for Englishmen was quite good enough for natives; that what was very passable sauce for the black goose, could not by any possibility be considered fitting sauce for the white gander.

In looking at the mechanism of the administration of Indian justice, it is not the bench alone that presents such humiliating pictures; from the judge and the magistrate downwards we find but one system prevailing. The whole fabric, from high to low, seems a mass of incompetency and villany; the former pertaining to the European officials, the latter to the native subordinates. Ability may occasionally form a solitary exception amongst the former; but in no instance can it be said that any degree of integrity or honesty is to be met with amidst the low grades of creatures attached to the judge's or the magistrate's offices, whose name is legion; and whose sole occupation consists in distorting the view of justice, and preying upon the native communities about them.

A PEON.

To such enormous magnitude, to such universality has this corruption grown, that the only wonder is that it has not eaten itself out; that it has not died from its own offensiveness. There is no secret about the thing in India. The abomination is in every body's mouth; but then Englishmen do not suffer from it; and hence the reason for all non-interference, hence its barefaced immunity.

Chapters have been written, if not here, in India, holding up to execration the doings of native officials attached to the country courts; and nowhere more completely than in the pages of the *Calcutta Review*.[10] The various grades of subordinates, from sheristader, or interpreter, down to the peon, or constable, seem to have but one object in view, and that the repletion of their pockets at the expense of the suitors.

[10] Vide vol. vi. for 1845; also Mr. Norton's pamphlet.

That it must be so is evident from the great anxiety shewn to obtain even the most humble of these posts, in which perhaps the daily exactions are wrung from the people in single coins. It may be, and no doubt is, that the character of the people who can submit to be so fleeced, must be degraded to a degree; but how can it well be otherwise? What has brought them to that debased level, but long years of hopeless endurance; a century of subjection to rulers, with whom they have nothing in common; who are aliens to them in feeling and in language; with whom they can hold no communion save through the vitiated channel of an interpreter, who sells every word he utters at its market value in silver, or copper, as the case may be.

To what extent the helpless natives are placed at the mercy of these many subordinates may be gathered from a brief statement of the mode in which magisterial business is conducted. A criminal case is reported by the darogah or police superintendent, who sends in lists of the witnesses, and of the parties supposed to be implicated, with a statement of the facts. And here bribery first commences; the darogah draws up the case to suit any party concerned who will submit to his exactions; and if the guilty bribe sufficiently high, they are omitted from the charge altogether, and other innocent parties placed upon the roll instead. Instances—though very rare ones—have occurred in which the officer has inadvertently forwarded two reports on the same case, one representing a certain part as guilty of the charge, the second making it appear that another was guilty. These were, of course, intended for sale; one to either of the parties, according as they would have paid.

These reports are not often read critically, and are merely the basis of further proceedings. The magistrate being also collector, and as such compelled to attend to revenue matters, which to him are of far greater moment than criminals, cannot find time to take down depositions. This duty is accordingly handed over to the mohurrir, or clerk of the court, whose salary amounts perhaps to ten or twelve rupees a month. The examinations are not even made in the presence of the collector-magistrate, who may be miles away at his revenue-office, or in the fields, looking to some collection of land-tax; they will be carried on in the most rapid and loose manner imaginable. Squatting cross-legged in one corner of the court, the mohurrir busily occupies himself in taking down the evidence of the prosecutor or the witnesses, each in their turn; and this is performed strictly in accordance with the wonted practice, guided entirely by the amount of bribery from either side. It is but fair to say that these writers shew no favouritism in the matter; the highest bidder, whoever he may happen to be, obtains their powerful aid. If the prosecutor has secured him, he draws up the plaint in the most eloquent and masterly style, throwing in a variety of points, which, from long experience, he knows will tell with the magistrate; and finally arranges the evidence and the defence in the same telling way. Should the defendant have purchased his cooperation, he makes the plaint in a confused style, throwing in all sorts of contradictions; and writes down "no" when the witnesses say "yes," and *vice versâ*.

At length all is ready for the magistrate to attest these depositions, and forward them to the court above. The plaint is read over by the sheristadar in a loud, hurried voice, and then the evidence, before each witness, who, confused and terrified by the awful presence they find themselves in, pay but small attention to the matter; and on being asked if that is all they have to say, mechanically answer "yes," and are marched out of court. Sometimes the scene is varied by a little rebellion on the part of some witness who has brains enough to detect the forgery introduced into his written evidence. But it is seldom that he is successful. The magistrate is pressed for time, his revenue-books await him, and he usually silences the witness by accusing him of lying, and threatening him with imprisonment. The depositions are attested and sent up to the higher court; and if the witnesses there deny any of the statements contained in them, they are at once set down as perjurers, and run a chance of being punished as such; besides, more weight is always given to evidence *taken by the magistrate on the spot*, and at the time, than to any offered subsequently.

How strongly and how unfavourably does this system contrast with the mode of investigation enjoined by the old Hindoo code, and actually practised at a period when the name of England was unknown, when the Christian religion had no existence! That may have been in some respects a barbarous age, and the old Hindoos may possibly have been, in modern estimation, mere barbarians; yet we are told that it was the then practice for all witnesses to be heard by the judge *in person*, and in presence of both plaintiff and defendant; and that so little was it the custom for magistrates to use unbecoming language to suitors, that even the king was enjoined to bear patiently with the irritability of litigants of all classes.

The extortions, aided frequently by violence or imprisonment, which the petty police of India practise upon the native community, are matters of notoriety in the East; though, it would appear, not so to those whose duty it should be to check such malpractices. One of their ordinary modes of extorting money is, when meeting a party of respectable Hindoos travelling in any remote part of the country, to seize them and lock them up in the nearest chokey, or watch-house, or, failing that, in any cottage at hand. It is vain for the captives to expostulate or threaten. Nothing but a bribe releases them; and the police scoundrels feel pretty safe, for the magistrate is away a hundred miles looking after the land-tax, and the travellers have neither time nor means of reaching him, even if a complaint would avail, which it would not. Should, once in a hundred times, such an occurrence reach the ears of the magistrate, the bribe is of course denied, and as to the imprisonment, the police had warrants for the apprehension of certain parties, for whom they mistook the complainants; it was therefore clearly not *their* fault. Thus the parties aggrieved get no redress, but leave their oppressors triumphant; a result too well expected to be often hazarded.

There are other ways, however, in which the darogah, or police-officer, reaps a harvest. A crime having been committed in some part of his district, he is dispatched to collect facts and evidence, and secure the guilty. The party implicated, if able, of course bribes the willing darogah, who has therefore to search for some victim wherewith to propitiate justice; for he would lose credit if he failed in his task. Some innocent person from an adjoining village is seized, taken into a solitary hut, and there, by the ready peons, beaten with cudgels, until, smarting with the blows, he consents to confess to the crime of which he is not guilty; and at the same time implicates others as being concerned, all of whom are arrested and treated to a similar cudgelling. Their depositions are taken down whilst the smart of the beating is still fresh in their memory; and should they, on reflection, alter their mind, and deny their admissions when before the superior court, they are utterly disbelieved. How far these atrocities are carried out may be judged, when it is known that seventy per cent of the convictions in India are upon confessions by the prisoners!

It is not in the criminal courts alone that all this shocking depravity is exhibited. Civil suitors are equally exposed to the rapacity of darogahs and mohurrirs. These men are notoriously the instruments of great oppression amongst the ryots, who in the event of their becoming involved with their zemindars, have no chance in the courts, where money carries all before it, and where, as a consequence, the wealthy landlord has the native officials completely at his command. Chapters might be written on this subject, did space allow; but it must be apparent from what has been stated in reference to the corrupt practices in the criminal courts, that in the civil administration of justice as great impunity is enjoyed by those who are clothed in "a little brief authority," and who, armed with a despot's power, fail not to use it as such.

Not the least obnoxious part of the legal system of India is that of the tax levied upon all suits in the shape of stamps. Political economists are agreed as to the inexpediency of legal taxation under any shape and to any extent; but the amount levied in India is so enormous, and falls so unfairly on the just and unjust litigant, that no sort of apology can be imagined that shall justify its exaction. The old Hindoo code levied 5 per cent upon all undefended suits, and double that amount on such as, being defended, were cast; amounts moderate enough, and in no case falling on the plaintiff. But under our system, a suitor, however just his claim, cannot prefer it unless it be drawn up on paper stamped according to the amount of the suit. The lowest of these stamps, for claims under 16 rupees in value, cost one rupee, or two shillings, being the amount of an Indian ryot's earnings for one month; and so on up to the value of 64 rupees. The proportion then diminishes in favour of the suitor, but is nevertheless heavy as a mere stamp; and few will dispute that a tax of 35*l.*, levied as a privilege for commencing a suit to recover a debt of 1000*l.*, savours strongly of exaction. In addition, however, to this preliminary tax, each summons for a witness, each answer, reply, rejoinder, &c., in a suit, must be on stamped paper, varying from sixpence to eight shillings; and all petitions for appeal in cases already taxed as above, must in like manner be written on stamped paper. Indian law is therefore labouring under the double disadvantage of being both costly in price, and poor in quality.

The above is an impartial outline of the administration of justice in India, as existing at the present moment, gathered from most trustworthy sources, and garnished with no ornaments of the imagination. What may be the opinions of the natives upon the matter, if, indeed, they have sufficient heart left to think at all, it may not be very difficult to guess. It is to be doubted if they do not feel that, in shaking off the Afghan and Tartar yoke for that of England, they have but exchanged King Stork for King Log; and that twenty-seven millions a year taken from them in taxation might deserve some better, some more efficient protection for their lives and liberty, than is to be found in the present legion of judicial and magisterial locusts, who, under the names of judges, magistrates, amlahs, mohurrirs, darogahs, &c., absorb amongst them an annual sum of two millions sterling.

What the English reader will think of it, there can be still less doubt. He may possibly hesitate ere giving full credence to the possibility of such a state of things existing at the present time, and under the sway of a nation whose proudest boast it is, that where its flag is unfurled, there open-handed justice is meted to high and low. He may for a time imagine that he has been reading of transactions carried on in some back-wood settlements, or in some Siberian provinces, rather than in what is popularly termed the noblest portion of the British empire. He may wonder how it is possible to reconcile such events with the glowing pictures drawn by political orators, or the pretty, touching, farewell exhortations about justice, and honour, and glory, and the natives of India, which fall from the turtle-fed mouths of deputy-chairmen at Haileybury examinations. He may also think, that if all written in this chapter be true, to look for happiness for its people, prosperity for the state, or security and permanency for its government, would be indeed seeking a phantom,—that he might as soon " seek roses in December, snow in June."

CHAPTER VI.

THE PUBLIC OF INDIA, ITS CONSTITUTION AND ITS MORALITY.

In the good old days when George III. was king at home, and when the governor-general was something more than king throughout a territory a hundred times as vast as that of his royal master,—when Indian monarchs were dethroned by a stroke of the pen, or a nod of the vice-regal head,—when rajahs were made and unmade as unceremoniously as children at home dress and undress their dolls,—when British subjects were publicly deported beyond the Company's territories for the most trivial offence to men in high places,—in those good old days it cannot be said that there existed an "Indian Public," in any sense of the word.

Nineteen-twentieths of the British residents of the three presidencies were at that period in government employ, whilst the small fraction remaining did not find it suit their interest to meddle with any thing immediately beyond the circle of their own calling, much less to raise a voice upon any political topic of the day. Indeed it was an almost universal practice for the few trading members of society to purchase the aid and influence of government servants by secretly making them partners in commercial undertakings; and in this way we find that all the earliest mercantile firms in India were more or less connected with the services.

Another fraction of society, that of the Indo-Britains, or, as they are usually termed, the "country born," or Eurasians, were equally regardless of matters political: their entire energies were then, as until very recently, absorbed in the one great struggle of obtaining official employment. Beyond this they appear to have had no ambition. Their aspirations were of red-tape, their dreams of Company's rupees; and provided they could be admitted but to the threshold of the government sanctuary, they were content to stand at the gate and receive of the official crumbs which from time to time fell from the "covenanted" table.

In the same category may be placed a still smaller and far more obscure portion of the social body, the Portuguese descendants, or, as they are termed in some parts of the East, burghers. As for the great mass of the community, the people of India, they, and their fathers before them, had been too long accustomed to the iron despotism of former foreign masters, to contemplate the act of criticising the government of their Christian successors.

Before noticing the *morale* of Indian society at the particular period under review, it may be well to offer a few remarks upon the character and composition of the earlier European community of India, the men who laid the foundation of our empire in the East. The tone and temper of British morality in those early days, that is during the first aggrandisement of the Company's power in India, in the middle of the seventeenth century, may be gathered from a tolerably impartial witness, one of the suite of Sir Thomas Roe, the English ambassador to the Great Mogul. From him we learn how low was the character of the Company's first servants; how their grasping, over-reaching, tyrannical, and immoral conduct made them "a bye-word amongst the heathen;" how the characters of the natives stood out in bright and glowing relief from this sad picture; and how all that was base and degrading was significantly termed "Christian" by the Hindoos. To quote the words of the natives themselves, when speaking of the English and their doings, will perhaps be most to the point. These simple people, according to the writer just alluded to, were wont to exclaim—"Christian religion, devil religion; Christian much drink; Christian much do wrong; much beat, much abuse others."

That this should have been so, will yet scarcely be matter for astonishment, when it is remembered that by far the greater portion of the early adventurers to the East were chiefly the younger sons of the higher and middle classes, young men too troublesome and dangerous from their vices to be retained at home, and whose relatives procured them employment under the Company, in the hope that if spared by the sea and the climate, they might return, though not reformed, at any rate in affluence. Removed from all wholesome restraint, from all healthy influences, invested with vast powers, raised suddenly to great importance, it would have been perhaps too much to expect that such men should have been other than we find them to have been,—that they should have done aught but bring our name and our faith into utter contempt, and so to justify the emphatic charge of the heathen native —"Christian much do wrong!"

Nor was it only in the subordinate officials of those days that these vices existed to such a degree. The picture will stand good for the highest in authority. Governors of presidencies did not hesitate to sacrifice the interest of the Company to their own private ends, with the most unblushing effrontery. It was in vain that one governor was superseded by another; it was but a change in the name, and not unfrequently the disgraced man was outdone in his offences by his successor. We read of one instance of this passing from bad to worse in the case of Sir Nicholas Waite, the Governor of Bombay, whose crimes, immoralities, and cruelties so far shocked and outraged the not over-sensitive feelings of the civil and military functionaries of the presidency, that they took the law into their own hands, rose against their tyrant, hurried him on board ship, and packed him off to England, to render an account of his misdeeds to the Directors.

Evils of such gravity and magnitude as these would of course work a partial cure in the course of time; accordingly we find, from the few records extant of the social condition of the English in India at that period, that as the Company's power and authority became more fixed and matured, and as the communication with those distant possessions became more rapid and certain, a better tone was assumed amongst all grades of European officials, so that at least some few of the outward decencies of morality were observed.

During the eighteenth century the worst features which had so long utterly disgraced the British name in India began to be less prominent in society. Open fraud, mid-day violence, heartless tyranny gave way in due course to bribery, peculation, gambling, horse-racing, drinking, and duelling. Later in the day, the exciting period of Warren Hastings' government, when victory and aggrandisement were the watchwords of the time, did not accomplish much for the better tone of Anglo-Indian morals. On the contrary, the characters of most of the leading officials, from the governor-general and his council downwards, were such as would have proved a hurtful example to a far more elevated society. Whatever *éclat* attaches to the name of Hastings in his military capacity, there can be little doubt that it was purchased at the cost of his individual character. Of the infamous morals of the greater number of those who formed the leading members of Indian society at that day, there are but too many proofs on record. To be licentious, extravagant, neglectful of duty, was to deserve the name of fashionable; to practise any sort of virtue, to be moderately decent in daily life, was the mark of a low, grovelling mind.

There was not in those days any public print, whose warning voice might be raised against the evil practices of the time. Not a single newspaper had then an existence throughout the length and breadth of British India; and although we find that in the year 1780 a publication, called *Hickey's Gazette*, made its appearance in Calcutta, purporting to lay before the community of that city the occurrences of the day, so far from proving a censor of public morals, it but poured oil on the flames; and by its reckless scandal, its coarse ribaldry, and its vituperation of all who possessed a share of respectability, fed the very passions it should have rooted out.

Luxurious living was at this period the rule with all; and although, in much later times, the English in India were far too indulgent in their habits for their health's sake, the license of the two periods cannot be compared. The pay of the junior members of the service did not then amount to a tithe of their present salaries; yet by the kindly aid of the banian, or native money-lender, the youngest of them were enabled to indulge in the most expensive habits, and enthral themselves in debt to an extent which only the most lucrative appointments in after-life, aided by the wholesale peculations of those days, could have enabled them to escape from.

Towards the close of the last century other men came on the scene. Warren Hastings and the unprincipled men of that time were replaced by Lord Cornwallis and his staff, a very different race, in whose breasts honour, and integrity, and gentlemanly feeling were not altogether strange emotions. In the newspapers of these after-times, in the few books then published on India, in all that is handed down to us, we cannot fail to perceive that the grossness, the sensuality, the drunken ruffianism of the previous fifty years had given way to a tone of society, which, if not as moral as we are taught to look for at the present day, was at least an improvement on the previous state of things.

At this period too we find a change of another kind coming over the European dwellers in the East; they were becoming civilised in their daily life; they were altogether better housed and better cared for. The small, slightly built dwellings of 1750 were giving way to those spacious, commodious edifices which have since been considered so necessary at all the presidencies for the comfort and health of the European, and which have justly earned for Calcutta the title of the "City of Palaces."

The native palanquin and bearers were no longer the ordinary mode of conveyance. Hitherto European carriages had been considered the exclusive privilege of a few of the highest functionaries; but at the period of which I am treating, every member of the service enjoyed his evening ride in the carriage which best pleased him. On the esplanade might be seen, at the accustomed hour, every conceivable variety of vehicle, from the civilian's stately carriage and pair down to the indigenous and rapid Ekka.

AN EKKA.

The uncovenanted branch of the Company's service is, at the present time, filled by Englishmen of undoubted energy and ability, in place of the country-born, who formerly monopolised the greater part of its posts; and we thus gain another not unimportant element in Indian society. The planting community is mostly composed of Europeans; and in numbers these form a considerable body. They are, generally speaking, men of intelligence and activity; but the very fact of their isolated position tells against their figuring prominently in any public questions. Scattered thinly over a wide extent of country, they have few opportunities of discussing any topics together, of ascertaining each other's opinions, or of attempting to act in concert upon any given question. Indeed it is most rare that they have an opportunity of taking any part in public matters; and if we except the late agitation respecting what were termed the "Black Acts," we do not find them making any such attempt.

No class of European society has received so large an addition to its ranks, since the opening of the trade, and the establishment of the overland communication, as that of the merchants. Would that I could say as much for the moral tone of this body, as for its extent! Glad indeed should I be if I could point to the traders of the East as bright and worthy offshoots of the parent stock,—as honoured types of that commercial fraternity in the old country whose word is their bond,—whose good name is their noblest capital. It is not that there are no worthy commercial names to be found in Calcutta, Madras, or Bombay. On the contrary, those places boast of merchants whose character stands, in every respect, second to none in our own country; but these are the few bright lights which shine amidst a midnight gloom. A perusal of the chapter which glances at the history of commercial speculation in India during the last twenty years, and contains a passing notice of Calcutta insolvencies from 1830 onwards, will, I think, bear out the sorrowful truth, that in the British Indian possessions the calling of a merchant has been, but too often, the hollow pretext for vast, unmitigated, and heartless swindling.

The practised professional men of fraud, who in the cities of Europe beguile unwary tradesmen, and obtain supplies of goods under false pretences, are comparatively harmless and inoffensive, when placed in juxta-position with the notorious "great houses" of Calcutta.

In Europe these things are little discussed, and still less understood. A crisis at one of the presidencies is spoken of as a mere matter of course; and that which unpityingly scatters to the winds the substance of the widow and the orphan is calmly alluded to in the self-same tone and spirit in which farmers would speak of their smutty wheat or their blighted gooseberries.

Such wide-spread ruin as I have attempted to describe, it might be thought, could not occur again through similar agency. The suffering community would be on their guard, and the same great scheme of gambling could not at any rate be carried on at the expense of a public already such severe sufferers. The contrary, however, has unfortunately been the case; for we have beheld, in 1848, disasters even more calamitous, defalcations more extensive, conduct more reckless and unprincipled, than existed in the hitherto unparalleled years of 1830 and 1832. It is true that in the later period the banks, not the mercantile firms, were the ostensible culprits; but a little inquiry into facts shew, that in the mismanagement and misdeeds of the banking establishments the merchants took a leading part; that they were not only accessories before the fact to the reckless accommodation accorded to the customers of their banks, but that they themselves were the recipients of the loans made but too often without a shadow of justification, and seldom with any further security than bills on insolvent firms, or liens on estates, the cultivation of which was something worse than unprofitable.

When it is remembered, that during the crisis of 1830, and the following years, half a dozen of the "great houses" of Calcutta failed for an aggregate sum of *fifteen millions sterling*, and that their assets yielded but from six to thirty per cent of dividend, or on an average about twenty-five per cent, shewing a loss to their creditors of upwards of eleven millions sterling; and that these merchant-princes were, up to the day of their bankruptcy, living in a style of ducal splendour, I cannot surely be charged with too emphatically denouncing the system which permitted such results as these. Soft and gentle language applied to these cases would be indeed to share in the infamy of the men and the time.

And did society reject these unprincipled leviathans of insolvency from amongst them? Did they close their doors against them? Did they teach their wives and their children to hold in its proper estimation the conduct of men who had heartlessly carried ruin and havoc amongst thousands of dependent families? By no means. They were considered at the worst as having been rather *imprudent*, and were more generally termed unfortunate. There was still no public opinion to the bar of which such men could be brought for judgment. The press of that time faintly recorded their deeds, but deemed it no portion of their duty to pass censure on these mighty sons of Mammon.

Although the social morality of India cannot boast of any healthier tone at the present moment than prevailed thirty years since, I am free to admit that an element of good, hitherto unfelt in the East, is at work—a fraction of the Indian editors are awaking to a right sense of their duty; and some few amongst them have already begun to speak out boldly and truthfully.

If the press of India cannot be said to rank either in talent or tone with that of the parent country, it must be confessed by impartial witnesses, that it is as good as it can afford to be; and looking at all the circumstances of the case, as good and as moral as could be expected. If it is not quite so intellectual, nor nearly so high-minded, nor yet so independent as journalism in England, let the Anglo-Indian public ask who they have to thank but themselves. The Indian press is as worthy a reflex of the state of society in that part of the world, as is the condition of English society mirrored in the journals of this country.[1]

The *Times*, or *Daily News*, published in the presidencies, would be as much out of place as would the *Quarterly* among the Esquimaux. Papers are not usually established for any higher motive than profit; and in such a question of pounds, shillings, and pence, no man having any knowledge of India, would attempt to print such a paper as the London *Examiner* or *Spectator*, even had he the ability at his command to enable him to do so. Editors in India know their readers pretty well, they generally understand the sort of writing which is acceptable to them, and minister accordingly.

One of the most successful journals throughout India is the *Mofussilite*, a bi-weekly journal published at Meerut in Bengal. It was established some dozen years since, and by a judicious catering to the reading wants of the community, it has reached the highest position amongst Indian papers, both as regards circulation and income. Few topics escape its notice; yet these are all handled in such a light and pleasant manner, that even the most uninteresting matters rivet the attention of the Anglo-Indian, whilst in England its columns would possibly be voted "frivolous."

There are other papers of high standing[2] equal in ability to most journals in English provincial towns, and doing well for their proprietors; yet I doubt if, with one or two exceptions, any of these would be read out of India.

The revelations of Indian banking during 1848 and the two following years were monstrous indeed, outstripping in iniquity any thing which had gone before it. The madness of speculation, to call it by its mildest terms, drew within its vortex the merchant, the soldier, and

[1] The following testimony to the tone of the bulk of the Indian press comes from one of their own body, and is therefore not without value:—"We must have a very different class of men conducting our newspapers before the belief in their regard for the public good will, or ought, in the slightest degree to protect them when they meddle with individuals; and their regard for the public very rarely exhibits itself in any other form than virulent attacks on persons. . . . . . It is their privilege for the public good to use what language they please of others; but breathe a syllable against one of them, and the lot is up in arms; they snarl at and bite each other like curs, but hunt their common game like a pack of wild dogs."—*Indian Charter*, Calcutta, 1852.

[2] It is with pleasure that I place on this list of honourable exceptions *The Bombay Times*, *Madras Spectator*, *Calcutta Englishman*, *Friend of India*, and *Indian Charter*.

the official; all alike ran riot with the wildness of the day; all were tainted; and though all did not suffer, although a large portion of the gamblers with other men's means escaped the general wreck, which followed the bursting of the storm of 1847-8, all felt that the ruin might have been theirs, and that what was death to some, was simply a fortune to them.

The moral taint was not, however, confined to the above classes. It spread like a gangrene on all around. The bar of Calcutta, the attorneys of the courts, the very officials of the Supreme Court were infected; and so strong has the feeling with regard to the legal practitioners become amongst the natives and independent Europeans, that few place any degree of confidence in them.

What must be the state of society in India, when we find the majority of the officers of the highest judicial tribunal in the country lending themselves to the most glaring improprieties, and in not a few cases to the most scandalous and heartless transactions? First, in the list of these official defalcators is the late Registrar and Official Administrator and Trustee of the Court, who, after becoming involved in a variety of joint-stock gambling, wound up by resigning his office, leaving his accounts many months in arrears, and his cash-balance deficient to the extent of 70,000*l.* Next comes the Official Assignee and Receiver of the Court, who closely followed in the financial steps of his brother officer: he too resigned, leaving a deficiency of 50,000*l.*, and a corresponding arrears of accounts: this man is still retained in active employment by the court. The Taxing Officer of this tribunal took the benefit of the Insolvent Court in 1847; whilst the Master in Equity, and the Prothonotary of the Court, were both constantly occupied in bank matters and speculations to a great extent, and with ruinous results, in bank shares.

The string of disclosures made before the Chief Justice relative to some of these transactions were so glaringly iniquitous, that, shocked beyond the endurance of even a Calcutta judge, he indignantly expressed a wish that a retrospective law could be passed to insure the punishment of these guilty men. This was, however, but a single opinion; "the voice of one crying in the wilderness" fell not more dead and unheeded on the stones and sands of the desert places, than did this solitary, indignant protest of an upright, conscientious judge, go forth amongst the cold, stony hearts of the European community of Calcutta.

The misdoers stood unabashed before their brethren, for their name was "legion;" they went about, and were greeted with smiles and open houses. They continued to give good dinners, and to receive invitations in return; the *élite* of the Indian world threw wide their portals to do honour to them; and we even find these men seated high up at the table of the governor-general. Far and wide this crying evil has spread; the poison-tree has taken deep root in the social soil, and years must elapse before even the most vigorous and courageous government can hope to eradicate the noxious weed.

All this is not lost upon the native community; they have sense and perception of right and wrong, sufficient to enable them to pass judgment on such things. It has been said recently in high places, that to give the Hindoos a more liberal education would jeopardise the British rule in the East. Alas! can any acts of ours bring greater peril, work deeper mischief in the Hindoo mind, than fraud, embezzlement, and bold mid-day dishonesty, sheltered and patronised by those whose first great duty it should be to punish crime and vice of every grade, and yet have not the heart, the moral strength, to cry out "fie" upon it!

It is but a too common practice to dwell upon the short-comings of the natives of India, to enlarge upon their fraud, falsehood, and extortions. Unfortunately, they cannot be defended. But should we wonder that they are so, when we find them surrounded by men of education and refinement,—gentlemen *par excellence,*—who, if they differ in any way from them, do so only because they stoop not to petty knaveries, but glory in great and daring misdeeds? With the Indian army demoralised to a painful degree, overwhelmed with debt, and shameless of insolvency; civilians charged with the most flagrant delinquencies, yet instead of being punished, removed to other provinces, which, in nine cases out of ten, amounts to promotion; with a bar boasting of a greater amount of delinquency than can be found in any previous time; with attorneys steeped to the eyes in fraud, yet permitted by the judge, who is aware of these facts, to practise in his court;—with all this passing before them, what can we hope for the social improvement of the natives of India? Will they not judge us by our deeds; our faith by its fruits? What can our missionaries say to them that will not bring down upon them the pithy and emphatic retort, which was quoted in the early part of this chapter, "*Christian religion, devil religion; Christian much do wrong?*"

There are two other sections of the European community of India, smaller, and not amenable to the same charges as lie against their more potent brethren, grades which are altogether of recent origin. The English shopkeeping class has sprung into existence in Calcutta, Bombay, and other cities, within the last twenty-five years; they keep magnificent establishments, and are generally well-educated men, and not unfrequently superior in bearing and information to many of their customers. They are mostly sent out on the strength of Birmingham or London houses; and generally contrive to amass fortunes in a very short time. The other section is composed of young men, clerks in government or mercantile employ, equally of modern origin. A quarter of a century since there were very few of either Europeans or natives employed as clerks; the occupation was entirely in the hands of the Eurasians. Of late years, however, numbers of young men have flocked to India from this country, seeking their fortunes, with not much more trading capital than had Richard Whittington of nursery celebrity. Possessed of far more intelligence and energy than the Eurasians, and willing to accept of similar salaries, they soon supplanted the latter, and became a distinct and growing class. Neither of the two above-named sections of society take any part in matters politic, for reasons which will be at once obvious.

At one time the most important class, next to the Europeans, were the Eurasians, or country-born, the offspring of mixed marriages between the Europeans and natives. During the period when a voyage to India occupied six or eight months, and cost far towards 200*l.*, and when none but Company's ships were in the trade, the influx of English females was scanty in the extreme. Not one civilian or officer in ten could provide himself with a wife other than from the ranks of the natives; whilst many were not particular as to the performance of the marriage-ceremony. In this way the supply of Eurasians became large; the sons, especially of those high in the service, were educated for the uncovenanted branch of government employ, whilst their daughters, after receiving an English education, were introduced to society through the position and influence of their fathers, and generally found husbands amongst the covenanted civilians.

With a more rapid and economical communication between England and her eastern dominions, this state of things underwent a marked change. Young English women, from being as rare as black swans, became as plentiful as blackberries in summer. The original source of the Eurasian supply was wanting, and already a diminution of their ranks may be observed.

Absorbed in the all-engrossing topics of daily routine life, eaten up with official importance, the Eurasian uncovenanted servant is too much the creature of red-tapism to form any opinion adverse to those of his immediate superior in office; and accordingly with him, "all that is, is right." It would be, however, most unfair to this class not to admit that they generally perform their duties with diligence and exactness, and usually acquire a far more intimate knowledge of business matters than their British-born superiors.

There is a small section of the Eurasians, of Portuguese descent, possessing no social status, and scarcely known as a class, out of the immediate sphere of their action. They are mostly underlings in offices, some few of them following trades, but seldom in any case doing more than earning a bare livelihood. If there cannot be accorded to these, and their brethren of British descent, any shining qualities, it is fair to confess that, both in their domestic life and general morality, they are free from the disgraceful failings of the bulk of the European community. Rare indeed is it that one of this class makes his appearance as defendant in a court of justice; still more rare is it that any of their race are accused of heavy offences or crimes.

Lastly, I will briefly glance at the constitution of the native society to be met with at the various seats of government. In this list can scarcely be included the Hindoos of high rank who are found in all the large cities of India, as they maintain a position aloof from all ordinary intercourse, mixing only with Europeans on particular occasions. The largest and most influential class of natives of the better ranks are the banians, or capitalists, whose business it is to place out their money at good interest. Their calling necessarily brings them into close and frequent contact with Europeans; and from the earliest days of English commercial enterprise in the East, these men were essential to the conduct of all mercantile and banking affairs.

It is only of late years, however, that British merchants have had recourse to these men for financial purposes. Many houses are upheld by the aid accorded them in this manner; and in some cases, the native capitalist is not only the friend and equal, but the partner of the Englishman; the relative positions of the two classes are thus greatly changed. The merchant is no longer the haughty man of business—the banian is no longer the retiring obsequious broker he was wont to be.

Many of the wealthiest of these banians have risen from very inferior positions, by dint of practising those arts which they have seen adopted by their English compeers; though, in their case, with more success, because more warily, more perseveringly worked out. One name amongst the crowd of these millionaires will exemplify the process of accumulation. Mutty Lol Seal, now notorious for his vast wealth, was originally a sircar or inferior servant in the Calcutta Custom House, on a salary of ten rupees a month. How the earliest foundation of his riches was laid need scarcely be inquired.

The favourite clients of these money-lenders are collectors of revenue, judges, and magistrates, who, once within their toils, once figuring on the debtor side of their ledger, become their certain, if not easy, tools to work out any schemes that may serve their financial projects. Should the client prove obstinate, or should the official not be on their books, which is seldom the case, these wary and finished masters of diplomacy will work out their ends through the great man's wife. Presents of rich shawls, of valuable jewelry, or costly furniture, are the sure baits by which the advocacy of the "Sahib's lady" is but too often secured, and with it the final bending of the tardy official to the wishes of the monied schemer.

A common method by which these unscrupulous men realise large and certain incomes, is to obtain all the petty appointments in the gift of their debtors, be they judges, collectors, or magistrates, for their own creatures, who, as a consideration for the appointments, gladly make over to them a certain portion of their salaries, in addition to a considerable entrance-fee. One case will suffice to illustrate the manœuvres which are resorted to by this class of persons. A banian in the *confidence* of the chief magistrate of Calcutta, that is, the lender to the latter of considerable sums of money, having learnt the intended establishment of a number of suburban police-stations, immediately bought up houses, at a very low rate, in all the districts indicated; and when orders were issued for inquiry as to the tenements favourable for the purposes of the police, the obliging creditor hinted to his client that *he* possessed property in the very localities named; and at the same time expressed a hope that his "friend" would not seek elsewhere for what was wanted. Of course the banian's houses were bought, and for sums four or five times their real value.

With such methods of realising "interest" for monies advanced to officials by banians, it need not be matter for wonder that by far the majority of the service find ready ministers to their wants in this way; and that the creditors are usually most indulgent in their terms.

The altered demeanour of the upper classes of natives to Englishmen has not been without its effect upon their countrymen in the lower ranks of life. By them the European is no longer held in the veneration he was of old; his word is no longer of value; and it is not too much to say that, with a few honourable exceptions, the British merchant cannot now obtain the smallest credit for purchases, unless through the guarantee of his banian.

The familiarity which has of late sprung up between the eastern and western races, though it may too often be blended with contempt on the part of the Hindoos, has led to a gradual loosening of time-honoured prejudices; which, combined with the spread of education, must, before long, as it has already commenced, work a great social revolution in the feelings, the tastes, the wants, and the very constitution of native society. "Young Bengal" is even now "a fact;" and though, as is sometimes the case, the earliest aspirations of the new-born are not of the loftiest or worthiest nature; though the budding genius of these disciples of the modern school are somewhat beclouded by tobacco-smoke; though their predilections are too much in the direction of brandy-pawnee,—hope bids us have faith in their future, whispering us that when these frivolities have lost their novelty, they will be cast aside in sober earnestness of purpose—exchanged for better, nobler things—that the young Hindoo generation will arise, and, shaking from them the errors and apathy of ages, make for themselves a reputation and a name, as wide, as beautiful, as glorious as their own magnificent and fruitful land.

But what of the rural population of British India?—of fully three-fourths of the hundred millions within the limits of the Company's territories? The leaves of the forest-trees, the stones of the desert, the sands of the sea-shore, have as much to do in forming an Indian public, as have the ryots of that vast country. Ground down to the lowest possible condition, physically and morally debased, the too apt imitators of masters, who have for two thousand years held iron sway over them; they no longer represent the contented, happy race, of whom we read in ancient Indian histories.

With no hope for the future, what does the ryot care for the present? Can the poor wretch, who lives on the breath of his mahajun or zemindar, have a thought or a feeling for public matters? If perchance he ever has the courage to *think*, he may remember that, of his miserable harvest of eighty shillings in the year, forty or fifty go to the government and the tax-renters; and that whilst he is left, after all his toil, to subsist on thirty shillings a year, or one penny a day, an English foreigner rules his district in all the luxury of Eastern splendour. It is not too much to say, that the yearly income of one of these tillers of the soil will be smoked in cheroots by a junior civilian in a week. Broken in spirit, abject in mind, the sole aspiration of the poor ryot is that he may not die of starvation before his next harvest be ripe!

It has been the fashion with a certain set of writers to belaud the present administration of Indian government; to talk of the security, the long peace accorded the population of the presidencies; and to compare their present life as infinitely more tranquil and free from the calamities of war, than during the rule of Mahomedan dynasties! As well might they boast of the safety and security of the poor captive pining away his existence in the dungeons of the Inquisition, because the ordinary risks of life could not reach him! Anarchy and despotism may be scourges in their way, but political and social annihilation are far worse. Man may struggle against the former, but sinks before the latter: oppression calls forth resistance, and in the strife for freedom there is a nobility of feeling engendered, that elevates and sustains even the poor Hindoo. Take away that power of resistance, paralyse his energies, sweep beyond his reach every thing that can make life worthy of a man, prostrate him to the dust,—and though he be told he need fear no external enemy, that the Afghan and the Tartar are no longer to be dreaded, and that he enjoys the immeasurable privilege of being the subject of the most honoured and powerful sovereign in the world, I fear he cannot be made to appreciate the wondrous change: he will feel, if he feels at all, that he is a degraded, abject being,—an Indian ryot! The snow-capped mountains of the East, the mighty rivers, the noble forests, the green hills and valleys, the fertile plains —all these we still behold, the tyranny of man is powerless with *them*—but with his fellow-kind he has done his worst.

A ZEMINDAR.

APPENDIX AND INDEX.

APPENDIX A.

THE FUTURE GOVERNMENT OF INDIA.

On June 3d, 1853, Sir C. Wood introduced in the House of Commons a Bill for the government of India, which, with some slight modifications, has since become law. The principal features of this measure may be thus epitomised:

The relations of the Board of Control and the Court of Directors are to remain as hitherto.

The thirty members of the Court are to be reduced to eighteen: twelve elected in the usual way, and six nominated by the Crown from persons who have resided in India for ten years, either as servants of the Company, or as merchants or barristers. One-third of the whole number to go out every second year, but to be again eligible. The Directors to receive salaries of 500*l*. a year, and the chairman and deputy chairman 1000*l*. a year.

No change is made in the general control which the governor-general exercises over the Indian government; but a lieutenant-governor of Bengal will be appointed; the lieutenant-governor of Agra will be continued; and a new presidency on the Indus will be created.

A commission will be appointed in England to digest and put into shape the draughts and reports of the Indian Law-Commission appointed in 1833. It is also proposed to enlarge the legislative council; giving the governor-general power to select two, the heads of the presidencies one each, and making the chief-justice of the Queen's Court and one other judge members, in all twelve: the governor-general to have a veto on their legislation.

The privilege hitherto exercised by the Court of Directors of nominating all students to Haileybury and Addiscombe is to cease, except in respect to the appointments to the military service, which still remain in their hands.

The admission to the colleges, and consequently to the service, to be thrown open to public competition; properly qualified examiners being appointed by the Board of Control.

The present legislation to continue in force until Parliament shall otherwise determine.

APPENDIX B.

TABLE *of the Revenue-Charges and Debt of British India from* 1804-5 *to* 1849–50.

YEARS.	Revenues.	India and Home charges.	Surplus.	Deficit.	Indian debt.
	£	£	£	£	£
1804–05	15,403,409	17,672,017	..	2,268,608	25,626,631
1809–10	15,525,055	15,551,097	..	26,042	28,897,742
1822–23	19,645,000	19,792,000	..	147,000	29,382,600
1835–36	16,391,000	14,924,152	1,466,848	..	29,832,299
1837–38	16,070,000	15,289,682	780,318	..	30,249,893
1838–39	16,320,000	16,701,000	..	381,000	30,231,162
1839-40	15,512,000	17,650,000	..	2,138,000	30,703,778
1841–42	16,834,000	18,605,000	..	1,771,000	34,378,288
1843–44	18,284,000	19,724,000	..	1,440,000	37,639,829
1845–46	18,998,000	20,493,376	..	1,495,376	38,992,734
1847–48	18,748,000	20,659,791	..	1,911,791	43,085,263
1848–49	19,442,000	20,915,115	..	1,473,115	44,204,080
1849–50	21,686,172	21,621,326	64,846	..	46,908,054

APPENDIX B (*continued*).

COMPARATIVE STATEMENT *of the Revenues and Charges of each Presidency for* 1835–6 *and* 1849–50. (Campbell's *Modern India.*)

PRESIDENCIES.	1835–36.			Per centage charges, 1835-36.
	Gross revenue.	Net revenue.	Charges.	
	£	£	£	
Bengal	8,100,000	6,584,300	5,173,000	79
Agra	5,100,000	4,060,000	674,000	16½
Madras	4,898,213	3,823,400	2,948,400	77
Bombay.	252,033	1,923,300	2,046,300	106½
	20,680,024	16,391,000	10,741,700	66

	1849–50.			Per centage charges, 1849-50.
	Gross revenue.	Net revenue.	Charges.	
	£	£	£	
Bengal	10,907,802	8,724,726	8,333,504	95½
Agra	5,452,700	4,535,400	1,076,500	19¾
Madras	5,005,900	3,779,229	3,294,323	87
Bombay.	3,851,176	2,337,942	2,635,012	106½
New territory, Punjab and Scinde . . .	2,540,275	2,308,875	1,118,242	48
	27,757,853	21,686,172	16,457,581	76

APPENDIX C.

STATEMENT *of the Land-Revenue of British India for* 1849–50.

DIVISIONS.	Area in square miles.	Population.	Gross land-revenue.	Charges.	Net land-revenue.	Gross revenue per square mile.	Per centage of charges on revenue.
			£	£	£		
Bengal . . .	113,702	36,848,981	3,506,070	325,730	3,180,340	31·	9⅓
N.-W. Provinces	89,972	26,199,688	4,422,500	382,000	4,140,500	49·3	8⅗
Punjab . . .	75,000	7,500,000	1,479,700	130,000	1,349,700	19·14	9
Madras . . .	144,829	16,339,426	3,479,437	478,000	3,001,437	24·	13¾
Bombay . .	67,945	9,210,273	2,290,969	1,262,684	1,028,285	33·14	55
Total . .	491,448	96,098,368	15,178,674	2,578,414	12,600,262		

APPENDIX D.

TABLE *of the Imports of Cotton into Great Britain from the United States and India respectively, with the Prices of the two kinds.*

YEARS.	Imports from United States.	Imports from India.	Price of other than East Indian cotton at Liverpool.	Price of Surat cotton at Liverpool.
	lbs.	lbs.	per lb. *d.* *d.*	per lb. *d.* *d.*
1800	16,000,000	6,629,822	16 to 36	10 to 18
1802	23,500,000	2,679,483	12 „ 38	10 „ 18
1804	25,750,000	1,166,355	10 „ 18	8 „ 15
1806	24,250,000	2,725,450	15 „ 21½	12 „ 17
1808	8,000,000	4,729,200	15½ „ 36	14 „ 25½
1810	36,000,000	27,783,700	14½ „ 22½	12½ „ 19
1812	26,000,000	915,950	13 „ 23½	12 „ 16
1814	War with U. S.	4,725,000	23 „ 37	18 „ 25
1816	57,750,000	10,850,000	15 „ 21	14 „ 18½
1818	58,333,000	86,555,000	16½ „ 22	7 „ 20½
1820	89,999,174	20,294,400	8 „ 13¾	6¾ „ 12
1822	101,031,766	6,742,050	5¾ „ 11	5½ „ 8½
1824	92,187,662	17,796,100	7 „ 10½	5½ „ 8
1826	130,858,203	22,644,300	5¼ „ 8¾	4½ „ 7
1828	151,752,289	29,670,200	5 „ 7⅜	3½ „ 5½
1830	210,885,358	12,324,200	5⅜ „ 7⅞	3 „ 6
1832	219,756,753	38,249,750	5 „ 8	3½ „ 5½
1834	269,203,075	32,920,865	8½ „ 10½	5¼ „ 7¾
1836	289,615,692	75,746,926	7⅝ „ 11	5½ „ 8½
1838	431,437,888	40,229,495	6¾ „ 9	5½ „ 6½
1840	487,856,504	77,010,917	5¼ „ 7	4 „ 5
1842	405,325,600	96,555,186	4 „ 6	3¼ „ 4½
1844	517,218,622	88,639,608	3¾ „ 4⅝	4 „ 4¼
1846	382,526,000	33,711,420	4⅛ „ 7	3½ „ 5
1848	600,247,488	84,101,961	3½ „ 5½	2⅝ „ 3¾

APPENDIX E.

STATEMENT *of the Annual Value of Merchandise imported into, and exported from, the three Presidencies of India, from and to all countries, for the ten years ending* 1849–50, *at 2s. the rupee.*

YEARS.	IMPORTS.				
	Bengal.	Madras.	Bombay.	Total.	Of which from England.
	£	£	£	£	£
1840–41	4,590,755	768,932	3,056,252	8,415,940	6,014,339
1841–42	4,262,910	678,326	2,847,328	7,788,565	5,439,564
1842–43	3,915,185	581,180	3,107,236	7,603,602	5,354,901
1843–44	4,474,472	652,263	3,691,061	8,817,797	6,347,349
1844–45	5,933,990	1,046,894	3,773,181	10,754,065	7,952,179
1845–46	5,232,617	849,913	3,004,948	9,087,479	6,477,143
1846–47	5,313,442	881,804	2,701,417	8,896,664	6,420,404
1847–48	4,671,361	976,664	2,949,591	8,597,617	5,790,228
1848–49	4,356,014	948,072	3,040,717	8,344,804	5,512,110
1849–50	5,283,170	906,004	4,110,713	10,299,888	7,578,980
	EXPORTS.				
	Bengal.	Madras.	Bombay.	Total.	Of which to England.
	£	£	£	£	£
1840–41	8,060,565	1,044,165	4,350,853	13,455,584	7,054,388
1841–42	8,066,384	1,242,582	4,516,251	13,825,217	7,120,748
1842–43	7,363,435	1,301,991	4,886,397	13,551,824	5,820,965
1843–44	9,891,109	1,208,655	6,153,712	17,253,477	7,760,128
1844–45	9,822,197	1,641,462	5,126,552	16,590,212	7,240,619
1845–46	9,815,675	1,411,217	5,801,780	17,028,673	6,658,943
1846–47	9,234,393	1,516,146	4,604,897	15,355,437	6,511,686
1847–48	7,961,857	1,277,296	4,073,243	13,312,397	5,683,826
1848–49	9,038,863	1,212,462	5,837,175	16,088,501	6,191,959
1849–50	10,148,038	1,272,884	5,891,376	17,312,299	7,026,470

APPENDIX F.

The Paradise Flycatcher, or Sultana Bulbul of the Hindoos (*Muscipita Paridisi*), is met with in jungles, gardens, and shrubberies, from the warmer parts of the Himalayas to the most southern extremity of Ceylon. It is a peculiarly graceful bird, the body and long sweeping tail of the male being white, with the primaries black, edged with white. The body and tail of the female are of a reddish brown, with the breast-feathers clouded grey.

APPENDIX G.

The Monaul, Golden Fowl, or Impeyan Pheasant (*Lophophorus Impeyanus*, Gould), is met with in great numbers throughout the Himalayan districts. The male bird has a remarkably beautiful plumage, its crest, head, and throat being of a rich bronzy green; the middle of the neck is purple, glossed with a coppery hue; back and wing coverts rich purple, each feather tipped with bronzy-green; the legs and feet are of a greenish ash, whilst across the lower part of the back is a band of pure white. The female is buffy-brown mixed with black and white. A more beautiful object can scarcely be imagined than this gorgeously plumaged bird taking his lofty and sweeping flight through the air, full in the light of the noon-day sun, the rays of which are reflected in surpassing brilliancy from his brightly-tipped feathers.

The above, extracted from Mr. Gould's great work on the Birds of Asia, in course of publication, was too late to find a place in the introductory chapter on Indian Natural History. The acknowledgments of the author are due to Mr. Gould for the permission to copy the birds which illustrate this volume from his splendid collection.

INDEX.

Abwabs, villagers' presents, 283.
Adam's-bridge, sandstones of, 12.
Afghan race, end of the, 66.
Agriculture of the Hindoos, 317.
Ahmed Shah, his wars, 94.
Akbar, submission of Delhi, Agra, and the Punjab to the rule of, 69.
—— death and character of, 72.
—— reform of taxation and policy by, 276.
Albuquerque, bold conduct of, 102.
Ali Moorad, deposition of, 247.
Aliwal, battle of, 231.
Ameers, annihilated power of the, 221.
Amherst, Earl, governor-general, 189.
—— proclamation of war by, 192.
—— leaves India, 206.
Animals and reptiles, 30.
Appah Sahib, seizure and escape of, 183.
Arab rule, declension of, 50.
Arabs, invasion of the, 47.
Architecture, antiquity of Indian, 291.
—— neglect of the study of eastern, 292.
Arcot, negotiations with nabob of, 156.
Army, Mahratta, how composed, 256.
Assam, invasion and conquest of, 81.
Assaye, defeat of Mahrattas at, 159.
Astronomy, Hindoo system of, 301.
Auckland, appointment of Lord, 209.
Aurungzebe, embarrassment of, 85.
—— death and character of, 86.
Baber, reign and death of, 67.
Bajee Rao's treaty with the English, 178.
—— seizure of landholders' estates, 175.
Bandoola, death of, 202.
Banjaras, the tribe of, 257.
Bench, the criminal, 457.
Bentinck, administration of Lord William, 207.
Birds of Asia and their localities, 31.
Black Hole, death of English prisoners in the, 114.
—— Acts, violent opposition to, 458.
Brahma, the priesthood of, 252.
British India, ancient extent of, 1.
—— natural divisions and mountain ranges of, 2.
British India, population and rulers of, 6.
—— climate of, 15.
Brougham, Lord, on "Cornwallis's permanent settlement," 281.
Buddhistical temples, 295.
Burmese defeated, 195.
—— harassing attacks of the, 194.
—— assembling of, at Bassein, 241.
—— night-attack of the, 191.
—— rout of the, 201.
Burnes, massacre of Sir A., 214.
Calcutta, concession to English in, 90.
Candahar, invasion of, by the emperor of Delhi, 75.
Casim, government and disgrace of, 49.
Cave-temples of India, 293.
Centralisation, its perniciousness, 260.
Central India, position and geographical features of, 4.
Chand-u-lal raises an army headed by British officers, 166.
Christianity, early progress of, 441.
—— labours of Danes to promote, 442.
—— opposition of government to the spread of, 443.
Church, present strength of the Established, 444.
Clive, re-appointment of Lord, 124.
—— wholesome reforms effected by, 125.
—— conquests of, in Bengal, 115.
—— complete establishment of British supremacy by, 119.
Coal-deposits of Bengal, 20.
Coffee, cultivation of, 330.
Collectors, the efficiency of, 267.
Commerce, monopoly of, by the Venetians, 99.
Commercial community of India, 470.
—— its morality, 470.
Company's dominions, 269.
Conquest, laws of, 255.
Coote, victories of Sir Eyre, 116.
Cotton, India, varieties of soil adapted to, and cultivation of, 26.
—— manufacture, improvements in, and effects, 307.

Covenanted and uncovenanted servants compared, 262.
Crisis, the commercial of 1848, 473.

Daher, defeat of, 48.
Dalhousie, Earl of, appointed governor-general, 233.
Dara and Shuja, revolt of, 80.
Dead, ceremonies at burning of, 419.
Deccan, extent and population of the, 3.
—— aborigines and dialects of the, 42.
—— kingdoms and states of the, 43.
—— conquests of Akbar in the, 71.
—— competition for the throne of the, 88.
—— interference of Europeans in the wars in the, 112.
—— prolonged hostilities in the, 117.
—— fresh troubles in the, 126.
Delhi, the rajah of, attacks the Mahomedans, 57.
—— the slave kings of, 61.
—— revolution and war in, 120.
Diamond-cutting, 316.
Diseases of India, native and foreign, 19.
Domestics, classes of, in India, 424.
Dost Mohammed made prisoner, 213.
—— war with, 210.
Durgoon, Sal, capture of, 205.
Dutch possessions in the East taken by the English, 148.
—— annihilation of fleet of the, 118.
Dyes, many varieties of, 27.

East India Company, early career of, 87.
—— first established, 108.
—— early progress of, 110.
Education, missionary labours in, 438.
—— absence of, in Hindoo females, 429.
—— in the Tenesserim provinces, 440.
—— Lord W. Bentinck's minute on, 433.
—— governmental system of, 435.
—— collegiate establishments for, 436.
—— government disbursements on, 437.
—— great importance of, in India, 430.
—— early steps for the diffusion of, 431.
—— Bengal Council of, 432.
Ellenborough, appointment of, 216.
—— regretted departure of, 223.
English, first appearance in India of, 107.
—— retreat and defeat of the, 215.
Eurasians, or country-born, the, 475.

Farokhsad and his successors, 58.
Farokhsir, reign and deposition of, 89.
Ferozepore, battle of, 228.
—— British retire upon, 219.
—— encampment at, 227.
Fibrous materials, value of, exported in 1849-50, 312.
Firuz, state of the kingdom during the reign of, 64.
Flax fibre, relative strength of, 24.
Flora, the Indian, 29.
Fossil remains and Kunker, 13.
French fleet defeated on the Madras coast, 137.
—— settlements attacked by the English, 111.

Gama, extension of Portuguese trade by Vasco de, 101.
—— second expedition to India of Vasco de, 103.
Gandaboo, treaty signed at, 204.
Ganges, delta of the, 5.
—— navigated by steamers, 208.
Gems of India, 20.
Geography, slight knowledge of, by Hindoos, 303.
Ghaznie, the Ghorian sultan of, 59.
Ghoorkas, defeat of, 173.
Ghuznee, capture of, 212.
Gold-working, 315.
Goojerat, battle of, 236.
Government, existing, 259.
Grains, pulse, and fruits, 28.
Granitic formation and alluvium, 14.
Grasses and fibrous plants, 23.
Gwalior, condition of, 222.

Haileybury, nature of education at, 263.
Hardinge, Sir H., governor-general, 224.
Harvest-time and its anxieties, 319.
Hastings, Warren, governor-general, 128.
—— charges of corruption against, 129.
—— quarrel between Francis and, 130.
—— judicial changes effected by, 142.
—— large sums of money raised by, 143.
—— retirement from the government, 144.
—— Marquis of, governor-general, 169.
Hindoo Rajah defeated at Canouj, 60.
Hindoos, the early dynasties of the, 37.
—— ancient account of the, 427.
—— various influences on the character of the, 428.
—— example afforded by the British to the, 429.
Hindostan, early government of, 251.
Holkar and Lake, action between, 162.
———— peace concluded between, 163.
—— insanity of, and consequent division of the regency, 165.
—— defeat of, 185.
Humayun, deposition and restoration of, 68.
Hyder Ali, first war of English with, 127.
—— league of the French with, 132.
—— invasion of English territories by, 133.
—— massacre of English troops by, 134.

Hyder Ali, defeat of, at Vellore, 135.
—— death of, 138.
Imports, average from India between 1771 and 1793, 308.
India, early kingdoms of, 41.
—— geological features of, 9, 10.
—— Greek accounts of, 45.
—— rivers, bays, and fishes of, 33.
—— manufactures of, 305.
Indigo, its prohibition in the Austrian dominions, 321.
—— planters, and their treatment, 323.
—— source of, and how produced, 322.
Infanticide, custom of female, 421.
Inquisition established at Goa, 106.
Insects, great abundance of, 32.
Insurrections in reign of Akbar, 70.
Invulnerables, the Burmese, 198.
Irrigation, Hindoo mode of, 318.
Jehan Ghir, accession of, 72.
—— death of, in Cashmere, 74.
Jeipal and Sibektegin, war between, 51.
Jesuits, first establishment of the, in India, 105.
Judges, incapacity of, in India, 453.
—— published judgments of, 454.
—— model decisions of, 455.
Judicial establishments, modern, 451.
—— promotion in India, 452.
—— subordinates, native, 459.
Justice, Hindoo administration of, 448.
Jute, the growth of, and trade in, 311.
Kemmendine, hostilities at, 200.
Khoord Cabool pass, victory at, 217.
Lahore reduced by Mahomedans, 54.
—— treaty of, 232.
Lake, Gen., marches against Agra, 161.
Landholders' rights, 274.
Land-tax in the three presidencies, 261.
Laterite rocks, 11.
Lattial system, or club-law, 324.
Laws, Hindoo code of, 449.
—— modification of, 450.
Magada, kings of, 40.
Magistrate's court, scenes in a, 461.
Maha Bandoola, march of, 199.
—— Barat, the, 39.
Mahmoud, his conquests eastward, 53.
—— death and character of, 55.
Mahomedan rule, 258.
Mahratta war, end of the, 188.
Mahrattas, rise of the, 76.
—— wars with the, 83.
—— commencement of hostilities with, 131.
—— war begun with, 157.
—— peace concluded with, 187.
Marriage, form and cost of, 418.
Martaban, attack of, 242.
Massaud, military operations of, 56.
Medical treatment and peculiarities, 300.
Medicinal plants, gums, and starches, 27.
Medicine, the practice of, 299.
Menu, the code of, 254.
Metallurgy of India, 313.
Missionaries, extent of labours of, 445.
—— progress of conversion by, 447.
Mohammed Toghlak, despotism of, 63.
Momunds, incursions of the, 246.
Monsoons, winds and rains of the, 16.
Moodkee, the battle of, 229.
Morad and Aurungzebe, rising of, 77.
Morality of the early Indo-British, 467.
Mubarik, murder of the last of the Khilji race, 62.
Munro, Sir T., system of assessment, 284.
Music, Hindoo, 298.
Mutiny among the British troops, 123.
Nadir Shah, conquests of, 91.
Napier, Sir Charles and the Ameers, encounter between, 220.
Native officials, 266.
—— states, annexation of, 270.
—— community affected by English example, 474.
—— millionaires, proceedings of, 479.
Natives, justice to them, 268.
Navigation scarcely known, 304.
Nepaul, war in, 171.
—— disastrous operations in, 172.
Nepaulese outrage upon officers and police, 170.
Opium, culture and monopoly, 331.
—— its sale legalised in China, 332.
Oude, honourable employment of British officers in, 271.
—— unsettled state of affairs in, 154.
Pagham, Mew, encounter at, 203.
Palaces of native princes, 296.
Patna, disturbances at, 122.
Pegu, second engagement at, 245.
Peguans, habits, manners, &c. of the, 426.
Peishwa, misunderstanding with the, 176.
—— plans of, against the English, 180.
—— engagement with the English, 181.
—— defeated near Poonah, 184.
—— deposition of the, 184.
Permanent settlement by Lord Cornwallis, 280.
Persia, British embassy to court of, 168.
Persians, massacre at Delhi by the, 92.
Pindarries, attack upon the, 179.
—— predatory incursions of the, 167.
—— dispersion of, 186.
Police, roguery of the Indian, 462.

Population, the Indian rural, 478.
Portuguese, hostilities with the, 84.
—— early progress of the, 100.
—— Emperor of Delhi wages war against the, 104.
—— decline of the rule of, 109.
Press, the Indian, 472.
Professor, sketch of an Indian, 434.
Prome, march towards, 243.
—— and Pegu taken by the English, 244.
Punjab and Scinde, extent of, 7.
—— the five rivers of the, 46.
RAILWAYS and electric telegraphs, 239.
Rajpootana, early rajahs of, 44.
Rama, exploits of, 38.
Rangoon, evacuation of, 193.
Revenue, 278.
—— early mode of collecting the, 272.
Rice, cultivation of, 320.
Rock and cave temples, 294.
Ryots, their average incomes, 279.
—— their condition and prospects, 479.
Ryotwari system, its evils, 285.
SALE, General, arrival of, 218.
Salt-tax, 286; evils of, 287.
Sanitaria, elevations, &c. of, 18.
Saracenic conquests in the East, 98.
Scindia, renewal of intrigues by, 174.
Seringapatam, English march on, 150.
—— capture of, and death of Tippoo, 151.
Sevaji assumes the title of rajah, but is compelled to resign, 82.
Shah Jehan, captivity, death, and character of, 78, 79.
Sibektegin, the victory of, 52.
Sick, exposure of, by the Ganges, 422.
Sikh leaders, surrender of the, 237.
Sikhs, recrossing of the Sutlej by the, 230.
—— second war with the, 234.
Silk, manufacture of, in India, 309.
—— antiquity of, 333.
—— endeavours of the Company to improve its mode of production, 334.
—— worms, different species of, 336.
Sindhi, appearance, character, and customs of the, 425.
Slave-trade agitation favourable to East-India sugars, 326.
Smelting, difference between Indian and Welsh, 314.
Society of India, the early English, 466.
—— changes in, 468, 469.
Sovereign, the duties of, 253.
Stamps, cost of Indian law, 463.
Sugar-cane, the, 325.
Suttee, prevalence of, 420.

TAMERLANE, Hindostan devastated by, 65.
Tartar empire, decline of the, 95.
—— and English, rule of, compared, 277.
Tea, cultivation of, in Assam, 328.
—— crops, produce of the Company's, 329.
—— plant, report by Dr. Royle on, 327.
Temperature of Calcutta, Madras, and Bombay, 17.
Temples of Cashmere, 297.
Tenant-holdings, 275.
Tenasserim and Peguan provinces, natural history of, 34.
—— inhabitants of, 8.
—— cession of the province of, 197.
Textile products, 306.
Thugs, the great power and final extinction of the, 423.
Tippoo Sahib, defeats English army, 136.
—— renewal of hostilities by, 139.
—— negotiates with the English, 140.
—— treaty of peace concluded with, 141.
—— Cornwallis declares war against, 145.
—— defeat of, near Seringapatam, 146.
—— peace concluded with, 147.
Tobacco, locality and quality of, 28.
Townships, their municipality and independence, 273.
Trade, early routes of the Indian, 97.
Trichinopoly besieged by French, 113.
Trimbukjee, flight of, 177.

VANSITTART, short and disastrous administration of Mr., 121.

WAR, the science of, amongst the Hindoos, 255.
—— improvements in the art of, 256.
Wellesley, Colonel, appointed governor of Seringapatam, 152.
—— expedition against the Mauritius, prepared by, 153.
Women, social position of, 417.
Woods, ornamental and useful, 22.
Woollen products, 310.
"Writer," the, in India, 264.

ZEMINDARI system, and its fruit, 282.
Zodiacal and planetary systems, 302.

THE END.

THE NATIONAL ILLUSTRATED LIBRARY.

In Monthly Volumes, 2s. 6d. each.

Containing about 320 pages and 50 Engravings. Crown 8vo, handsomely bound in cloth, gilt, price per volume, 2*s.* 6*d.*; or handsomely bound in morocco, 7*s.* 6*d.* per volume; or two volumes in one, morocco, 10*s.* 6*d.*; or 2 vols. in one, calf, marbled edges, 9*s.*

VOLS. 1 TO 4.

BOSWELL'S LIFE of DR. JOHNSON. Complete in four volumes. With numerous Portraits, Views, and characteristic Designs, engraved from authentic sources. Third Edition.

VOL. 5.

The ILLUSTRATED BOOK of ENGLISH SONGS, from the Sixteenth to the Nineteenth Century. With Fifty Engravings from original designs. Third Edition.

VOL. 6.

The MORMONS, or LATTER-DAY SAINTS. An Account of the Rise and Progress of this new Religious Sect. Illustrated with Forty Engravings from original sources. Third Edition.

VOL. 7.

The ORBS of HEAVEN; or, the Planetary and Stellar Worlds. A popular Exposition of the great Discoveries and Theories of Modern Astronomy. Illustrated with Nebulæ, Portraits, Views, Diagrams, &c. Fourth Edition.

VOL. 8.

PICTURES of TRAVELS in the SOUTH of FRANCE. From the French of ALEXANDRE DUMAS. With Fifty spirited Engravings on Wood. Second Edition.

VOLS. 9 & 13.

HUC'S TRAVELS in TARTARY, THIBET, and CHINA, in 1844, 5, and 6. Unabridged Edition. Two vols. With numerous Daguerreotyped Illustrations, and a Map of the Countries, clearly illustrating the Route of MM. HUC and GABET.

VOL. 10.

A WOMAN'S JOURNEY round the WORLD. Unabridged. From the German of MADAME PFEIFFER. In one volume. With Engravings printed in Colours. Third Edition.

NATIONAL ILLUSTRATED LIBRARY.

Vols. 11 & 12.

MEMOIRS of EXTRAORDINARY POPULAR DELUSIONS. By Charles Mackay, LL.D. Illustrated with One Hundred and Twenty Engravings from scarce Prints and other authentic sources. Second Edition.

"These volumes will captivate the attention of readers who, according to their various tempers, feel either inclined to laugh at or sigh over the follies of mankind."—*Times.*

"A popular name for a book exactly of the kind calculated to be popular. . . . . . The subjects are treated with much talent, and the whole forms a very amusing work for readers of every class." —*Literary Gazette.*

Vol. 14.

BOSWELL'S JOURNAL of a TOUR to the HEBRIDES. Companion Volume to "Boswell's Life of Johnson," with the Index to the "Life." By R. Carruthers, Esq., of Inverness. Second Edition.

"This volume, one of the interesting series composing the 'National Illustrated Library,' forms Vol. V. of 'Boswell's Life of Johnson,' already published. The journal of this memorable tour yields to none of the other portions of 'Boswell's Life of Johnson' in varied interest and incident.' —*Morning Advertiser.*

Vol. 15.

NARRATIVE of a RESIDENCE at the CAPITAL of the KINGDOM of SIAM. With a Description of the Manners and Customs of the Modern Siamese. By Frederic Arthur Neale, formerly in the Siamese Service, Author of "Eight Years in Syria," &c.

Vol. 16.

The ILLUSTRATED BOOK of SCOTTISH SONGS, from the Sixteenth to the Nineteenth Century. With numerous Illustrations.

*** The Book of English Songs bound up with the Book of Scottish Songs, 2 vols. in 1, cloth, gilt, 5*s*.

"A very fair selection, or, what the compiler not inappropriately terms it, 'the cream of the cream' of Scottish Song. The volume, like all the other volumes of the 'Illustrated Library,' is handsomely got up, and is well worthy of a place either in the cabinet or on the drawing-room table along with works of ten times its price."—*Fifeshire Journal.*

Vol. 17.

PICTURESQUE SKETCHES of LONDON, PAST and PRESENT. By Thomas Miller, Author of the "History of the Anglo-Saxons," &c. &c.

"This volume of the 'Illustrated Library' will fully sustain the character which that series of elegant publications holds in public estimation. London is an inexhaustible mine, a world in itself, from whence the philosopher and the satirist, the antiquarian and the man of the world, may extract matter suited to their several tastes."—*Glasgow Herald.*

NATIONAL ILLUSTRATED LIBRARY.

Vol. 18.

MADAME PFEIFFER'S VISIT to ICELAND and the SCANDINAVIAN NORTH. Companion Volume to "A Woman's Journey round the World." Second Edition.

"The volume is printed uniformly with 'A Woman's Journey round the World,' and is highly creditable to the translator, the illustrator, and the printer."—*Globe.*

Vol. 19.

The ISRAEL of the ALPS. A History of the Persecution of the Waldenses. By the Rev. Dr. Alexis Muston. Second Edition.

"The History of the Vaudois is one of those striking episodes in the history of mankind which cannot be written too often, nor studied from too many points of view."—*Athenæum.*

Vol. 20.

MADAME PFEIFFER'S VISIT to the HOLY LAND, EGYPT, and ITALY. Uniform with "A Woman's Journey round the World" and "Visit to Iceland." With tinted Engravings. Second Edition.

Vols. 21 & 22.

A NARRATIVE of the UNITED STATES' EXPLORING EXPEDITION. Two Volumes. With numerous Drawings made from the Sketches of the Artist who accompanied the Expedition, illustrative of the Manners, Customs, and Personal Appearance of the Inhabitants, and Views of the Scenery of the Countries visited.

Vols. 23 & 24.

The ILIAD of HOMER. Translated into English Verse by Alexander Pope. A new edition, with Notes, Illustrations, and Introduction, by the Rev. Theodore Alois Buckley, M.A., Chaplain of Christ Church, Oxford. Two Volumes.

. This Edition of Homer's Iliad contains the classical compositions of Flaxman beautifully drawn by T. D. Scott, Esq., and engraved in the most careful manner by J. L. Williams, Esq.

In morocco, extra, for School Prizes, two volumes, 15*s.*

Or two volumes in one, 10*s.* 6*d.*; ditto, calf, marbled edges, 9*s.*

"The most notable new edition is Pope's Homer, with Flaxman's designs, and a variety of other illustrations; explanatory notes, with 'parallel passages,' by the editor, Mr. Buckley; and an introduction which gives a judicious estimate of Pope, and enters sensibly into the question of whether there ever was such a man as Homer."—*Spectator.*

"We are glad to see the projectors of the 'National Illustrated Library' enriching their series with such books as this. It is very nicely printed; the reduced designs from Flaxman are always graceful, even when in their minuteness the expression of the original is occasionally lost; and the editorship is scholarly and sufficient. On the marvellous cheapness of such volumes at half-a-crown a piece, we need not say a word."—*Examiner.*

"It also contains eighty-nine illustrations of the epic action, copied from the celebrated series of designs by Flaxman. The moderate price of this book, combined with its great beauty, renders it one of the most interesting productions of the cheap press recently issued in this country."—*Observer.*

NATIONAL ILLUSTRATED LIBRARY.

Vol. 25.

The ODYSSEY of HOMER, with Flaxman's Illustrations, &c. One vol. Edited by Rev. Theodore Alois Buckley.

Vol. 26.

The COMPLETE ANGLER of IZAAK WALTON and CHARLES COTTON. New Edition, superbly illustrated with Fifty Engravings of Fishes, Fishing-tackle, Flies, and Portraits and Landscapes. Edited by Ephemera of "Bell's Life in London."

*** This Edition of the Complete Angler contains 100 pages of Notes, both explanatory of the text and adapting to modern experience and practice its obsolete instructions.

Vol. 27.

EXTRAORDINARY MEN; their BOYHOOD and EARLY LIFE. Illustrated with 50 Engravings of Portraits, Birthplaces, Incidents, &c. &c.

Vol. 28.

The PILGRIM'S PROGRESS from this World to that which is to come. By John Bunyan. A new Edition, with a Memoir by J. M. Hare. The Allegory illustrated with Thirty Outline Drawings, and the Biographical Sketch with interesting relics and recollections of the Author.

*** To ensure the completeness of the present Edition, it has been carefully reprinted *verbatim*, without abridgment or interpolation, from the genuine old editions of John Bunyan.

Vol. 29.

WANDERINGS in SPAIN. From the French of Gautier. Copiously illustrated by M'Quoid.

Vol. 30.

The LIFE of ALEXANDER POPE, with Extracts from his Correspondence. By R. Carruthers, Esq., of Inverness. Illustrated with Portraits of distinguished Contemporaries of Pope, Scenes connected with the Poet's Life and Works, and Incidents from his Career.

*** Great pains have been taken to render this edition accurate and complete. Several important mistakes of the previous biographers and editors of Pope have been rectified, and new information added. The Poetical Works of Alexander Pope, complete in three volumes, uniform with "The Life," are in preparation, and will shortly be published. Edited by R. Carruthers.

Vol. 31.

The PUBLIC and DOMESTIC LIFE of the RIGHT HON. EDMUND BURKE. By Peter Burke, Esq., of the Inner Temple and the Northern Circuit. Profusely illustrated with Portraits, Scenes of Events, and Landscape Views, relating to the great Orator, and the other noted persons of his time and career.

INGRAM, COOKE, AND CO. 227 STRAND.